LEARNING
Microsoft®
Office 2003

Suzanne Weixel
Jennifer Fulton
Faithe Wempen
Nancy Stevenson

PEARSON

Prentice
Hall
DDC

Vice President and Publisher: Natalie E. Anderson
Executive Acquisitions Editor: Jodi McPherson
Executive Editor: Jennifer Frew
Associate Director IT Product Development: Melonie Salvati
Editorial Assistant: Jasmine Slowik
Manufacturing Buyer: Natacha St. Hill Moore
Production Manager: Gail Steier de Acevedo
Technical Editors: Kathy Berkemeyer and James Reidel
Cover Designer: Amy Capuano
Composition: Shu Chen and Elviro Padro
Associate Director, Multimedia Production: Karen Goldsmith
Manager, Print Production: Christy Mahon
Printer/Binder: Quebecor World Book Services/Dubuque
Cover Printer: Phoenix Color Corporation

PEARSON
Prentice
Hall
DDC

10 9 8 7 6 5 4 3 2 1
ISBN 0-13-036522-X

Table of Contents

Table of Contents

Table of Contents

Introduction

Microsoft Office 2003 is Microsoft's suite of application software. The Standard version includes Word, Excel, Outlook, and PowerPoint. The Professional version includes the above applications plus Access and Publisher. This book covers Word (the word processing tool), Excel (the spreadsheet tool), PowerPoint (the presentation tool), Access (the database tool), and Outlook (the tool used to create and manage e-mail, schedule information, tasks, notes, and contacts). Because Microsoft Office is an integrated suite, the components can all be used separately or together to create professional-looking documents and to manage data.

How We've Organized the Book

Learning Microsoft Office 2003 is made up of eight sections:

- **Basics—Included on CD** ⊘
  This short chapter introduces essential Microsoft Office 2003 skills—including starting Microsoft Office, using the mouse and keyboard, screen elements, and an overview of the applications. If you are completely new to the Office suite, you should start with this lesson. All of the lessons on CD can be printed out or viewed on-screen. See page ix for details on how to access the files.

- **Word 2003**
  With Word you can create letters, memos, Web pages, newsletters, and more.

- **Excel 2003**
  Excel, Microsoft's spreadsheet component, is used to organize and calculate data, track financial data, and create charts and graphs.

- **Access 2003**
  Access is Microsoft's powerful database tool. Using Access you will learn to store, retrieve, and report on information.

- **PowerPoint 2003**
  Create dynamic on-screen presentations with PowerPoint, the presentation graphics tool.

- **Outlook 2003—Included on CD** ⊘
  This brief introduction to Outlook shows how to navigate many of the views and tools in Outlook.

- **Challenge Lesson—Included on CD** ⊘
  This chapter combines critical thinking, application integration, and Internet skills. In each exercise, only basic step directions are given—you need to rely on your own skills to complete the exercise.

- **Advanced Lessons—Included on CD** ⊘
  These lessons cover advanced Word, Excel, and Access skills.

Each chapter in **Learning Microsoft Office 2003** is made up of several lessons. Lessons are comprised of short exercises designed for using Microsoft Office 2003 in real-life business settings. Every application exercise (except for the Critical Thinking Exercises and the Challenge Exercises) is made up of seven key elements:

- **On the Job**. Each exercise starts with a brief description of how you would use the features of that exercise in the workplace.
- **Exercise Scenario**. The Microsoft Office tools are then put into context by setting a scenario.
- **Terms**. Key terms are included and defined at the start of each exercise, so you can quickly refer back to them. The terms are then highlighted in the text.
- **Notes**. Concise notes for learning the computer concepts.
- **Procedures**. Hands-on mouse and keyboard procedures teach all necessary skills.

- **Application Exercise**. Step-by-step instructions put your skills to work.
- **On Your Own**. Each exercise concludes with a critical thinking activity that you can work through on your own. You are challenged to come up with data and then additionally challenged to use the data in a document. The *On Your Own* sections can be used as additional reinforcement, for practice, or to test skill proficiency.
- In addition, each lesson ends with a **Critical Thinking Exercise**. As with the *On Your Owns*, you need to rely on your own skills to complete the task.

Working with Data and Solution Files

As you work through the exercises in this book, you'll be creating, opening, and saving files. You should keep the following instructions in mind:

- For many of the exercises you can use the data files provided on the CD-ROM that comes with this book. The data files are used so that you can focus on the skills being introduced—not on keyboarding lengthy documents. The files are organized by application in the **Datafiles** folders on the CD-ROM.
  - ✓ See *What's on the CD* for more information on the data files.
- When the application exercise includes a file name and a CD icon ☉, you can open the file provided on CD.
- The Directory of Files at the beginning of each section lists the exercise file (from the CD-ROM) you can open to complete each exercise.
- If the exercise includes a CD icon ☉ and a keyboard icon ⌨, you can choose to work off of either the data file or a file that you created in an earlier exercise.

- Unless the book instructs otherwise, use the default settings for text size, margin size, and so on when creating a file. If someone has changed the default software settings for the computer you're using, your exercise files may not look the same as those shown in this book. In addition, the appearance of your files may look different if the system is set to a screen resolution other than 800 x 600.
- All the exercises instruct you to save the files created or to save the exercise files under a new name. You should verify the name of the hard disk or network folder to which files should be saved.

What's on the CD ⊙

We've included on the CD:

- **Microsoft Office 2003 Basics** covers fundamental Office skills. If you are completely new to the Office suite, you should start with this section. The Basics lessons are provided in PDF format. You will need Adobe Reader in order to open the files. If you do not have Adobe Reader on your machine, go to http://www.adobe.com for a free download of the software.

- **Challenge Lesson** combines critical thinking, application integration, and Internet skills.

- **Advanced Lessons** for word processing, spreadsheet, and database. The bonus lessons cover more advanced skills.

- **Data files** for many of the exercises. This way you don't have to type lengthy documents from scratch.

- **Glossary of business and financial terms** used in the workplace, the financial arena, and *Learning Microsoft Office 2003*. Key business terms help you understand the work scenarios and the data that is used to complete the exercises.

- **Touch 'N' Type Keyboarding course** was designed for those who would like to learn to type in the shortest possible time. The keyboarding skill-building drills are also ideal for those who wish to practice and improve their keyboarding. The exercises can be printed out, copied, and distributed.

- **Computer Literacy Basics**. These exercises include information on computer care, computer basics, and a brief history of computers.

To Access the Files Included with This Book ⊙

1. Insert the *Learning Microsoft Office 2003* CD in the CD-ROM drive.

2. Navigate to your CD-ROM drive; right-click ⚐ start and choose Explore from the shortcut menu.

3. Navigate to your CD-ROM drive.

4. Right-click the folder that you wish to copy.

5. Navigate to the location where you wish to place the folder.

6. Right-click and choose Paste from the Shortcut menu.

Support Material

A complete instructor support package is available with all the tools teachers need:

- Annotated Instructor's Guide includes entire student book with teacher notes, course curriculum guide, and lesson plans. Solution files included on CD-ROM.
  (ISBN: 0-13-147170-8)

- Test booklet includes application pretests, posttests, and final exam. Includes customizable test bank on CD-Rom.
  (ISBN: 0-13-147157-0)

- Printout of exercise solutions with solution file CD-ROM.
  (ISBN: 0-13-147156-2)

- 25-slide PowerPoint visual aids correlated to the book.
  (ISBN: 0-13-147169-4)

- Deluxe visual aids with 125-slide PowerPoint presentation correlated to the book.
  (ISBN: 0-13-146586-4)

Word 2003

Lesson 1

Lesson 2

Lesson 3

Lesson 4

Lesson 5

Lesson 6

Lesson 7 (on CD 💿)

Lesson 8 (on CD 💿)

Directory of Data Files on CD

Exercise 1

Skills Covered:

♦ **Start Word** ♦ **The Word Window** ♦ **Change the Word Window**
♦ **Type in a Document** ♦ **Correct Errors**
♦ **Use Undo, Redo, and Repeat**
♦ **Save a New Document** ♦ **Close a Document**
♦ **Types of Business Documents** ♦ **Exit Word**

On the Job

Word is the word processing application included in the Microsoft Office 2003 suite. You use Word to create text-based documents such as letters, memos, reports, flyers, and newsletters. The first step in mastering Word is learning how to start the program and create a document.

You are the office manager at the Michigan Avenue Athletic Club in Chicago, Illinois. A new personal trainer has recently joined the staff, and you must type up a brief biography that will be made available at the club and sent to prospective members. In this exercise, you will start Word, create and save a document, and then exit Word.

Terms

Default A standard setting or mode of operation.

View The way a document is displayed on screen.

Elements Menus, icons, and other items that are part of an on-screen interface.

Word wrap A feature that causes text to move automatically from the end of one line to the beginning of the next line.

Paragraph mark (¶) A **nonprinting** character inserted in a document to indicate where a paragraph ends.

Nonprinting characters Characters such as paragraph marks and tab symbols that are not printed in a document but that can be displayed on the screen.

Undo The command for reversing a previous action.

Redo The command for reversing the Undo command.

Business document A professional document used to communicate information within a company, or between one company and another.

Personal business document A document used to communicate information between an individual and a company.

Notes

Start Word

- To use Word 2003 you must first start it so it is running on your computer.

- You use Windows to start Word.

  ✓ *Different methods of starting Microsoft Office 2003 programs are covered in "Getting Started with Microsoft Office 2003," Exercise 1.*

- When Word is running, it is displayed in a window on your screen.

The Word Window

- Word opens a new, blank document using standard, or **default**, settings. Default settings control features of a new document, such as the margins, the line spacing, the character font, and the font size.

- Word starts with a new blank document open in Print Layout **view** and displays **elements** for accessing tools and menus to create, edit, format, and distribute a document.

- The following illustration identifies elements of the Word window. The numbers following each element correspond to the numbers next to the descriptions that follow.

  ✓ *By default, the Getting Started task pane is displayed when you start Word. For information on using task panes, refer to "Getting Started with Microsoft Office 2003," Exercise 2.*

The Word window

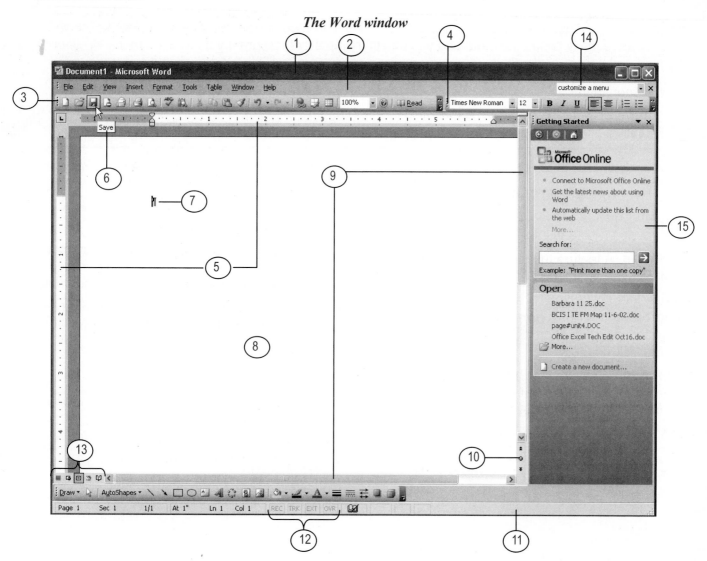

Title bar (1)
- Displays the program and document name.

Menu bar (2)
- Displays the names of the main menus. Select a menu name for a list of commands.

Standard toolbar (3)
- Displays buttons for accessing common features and commands, such as saving, opening, and printing a file.
  - ✓ *Toolbar buttons change according to your most recent selections. To see additional buttons, click the Toolbar Options button.*

Formatting toolbar (4)
- Displays buttons for accessing common formatting features and commands, such as bold, italic, and centering text.

Rulers (5)
- The horizontal ruler measures the width of the document page; it displays information such as margins, tab stops, and indents.
- The vertical ruler measures the height of the document page.
  - ✓ *The vertical ruler is displayed only in Print Layout view and Print Preview.*

ScreenTip (6)
- Displays the name of the element on which the mouse pointer is resting.

Insertion point (7)
- A blinking vertical line that displays to the right of the space where characters are inserted in a document.

Document window (8)
- The area where you type document text or insert graphics, tables, or other content.

Scroll boxes (9)
- Used with a mouse to shift the on-screen display up and down or left and right.

Select Browse Object button (10)
- Used to shift the on-screen display according to a selected object, such as by page, by picture, or by heading.

Status bar (11)
- Displays information, such as the currently displayed page, currently displayed section, how many pages are in the document, where the insertion point is located, and which mode buttons are active.

Mode buttons (12)
- Used to change the way Word operates to make creating and editing documents easier.
  - ✓ *Active mode buttons appear bold.*

View buttons (13)
- Used to change to one of five available document views. These options are also available on the View menu.

Type a question for help box (14)
- Used to access Help information. Type a question to display a list of topics for which help is available.
  - ✓ *For more about using Help, refer to Exercise 4 of "Getting Started with Microsoft Office 2003."*

Task pane (15)
- An area in which you can access commands and options for certain program features.

Change the Word Window

- You can change the default settings to control which Word elements are displayed.
  - You can show or hide toolbars.
  - You can show or hide rulers.
  - You can show or hide task panes.
  - You can change views.

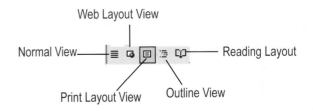

- Normal view is used for most typing, editing, and formatting.
- Print Layout view displays a document on-screen the way it will look when it is printed.
- Web Layout view wraps text to fit the window, the way it would on a Web page document.

- Outline view is used to create and edit outlines.
- Reading Layout view adjusts the display of text to make it easier to read documents on-screen.

Type in a Document

- By default, the insertion point is positioned at the beginning (left end) of the first line of a new document.
- You simply begin typing to insert new text.
- Characters you type are inserted to the left of the insertion point.
- **Word wrap** automatically wraps the text at the end of a line to the beginning of the next line.
- When you press the Enter key, Word inserts a **paragraph mark** and starts a new paragraph.
- After you type enough text to fill a page, Word automatically starts a new page.
  - ✓ *Note that Word includes many features designed to make your work easier, such as a spelling checker. These features are often displayed automatically on-screen as colored underlines or buttons. Simply ignore these features for now; you learn to use them later in this book.*

Correct Errors

- You can delete characters to the left of the insertion point by pressing the Backspace key.
- You can delete characters to the right of the insertion point by pressing the Delete key.
- You can cancel commands before you execute them by pressing the Escape key or clicking a Cancel button if available.

Use Undo, Redo, and Repeat

- Use the **Undo** command to reverse a single action made in error, such as deleting the wrong word.
- The Undo command also lets you change your mind about an entire series of actions used to edit or format a document.
- Use the **Redo** command to reinstate any actions that you reversed with the Undo command.
- If the Undo command and the Undo button are dimmed and entirely gray, there are no actions that can be undone.

- If the Redo button is dimmed, there are no actions that can be redone.
- Sometimes when there are no actions to redo, the Repeat command is available from the Edit menu in place of Redo. Use Repeat to repeat the most recent action.

Save a New Document

- As mentioned, Word starts with a new blank document named *Document1* open on-screen.
  - ✓ *Subsequent new documents are named consecutively: Document2, Document3, etc. You will learn more about creating additional new documents in Exercise 2.*
- If you want to have a file available for future use, you must save it on a removable disk, on an internal fixed disk, or on a network disk.
- When you save a new document, you must give it a name and select the location where you want it stored.
- Word automatically adds a period and a three-character file extension to the end of the file name to identify the file type. By default, the file extension is *.doc*, which identifies a document file.
  - ✓ *By default, file extensions are not displayed in Windows.*
- To specify a disk for storing the document, you select the disk drive letter. Floppy disk drives are usually drives A: and B:. A hard drive is usually drive C:. Additional storage locations are labeled consecutively. For example, a CD-RW drive may be D, and so on.
- You can store documents in a folder called *My Documents*, or you can select a different folder. You can also create a new folder when you save a document.

Close a Document

- A document remains open on-screen until you close it.
- Close a document when you are finished working with it.
- If you try to close a document without saving it, Word prompts you to save it.
- You can close a document without saving it if you do not want to keep it for future use or if you are not happy with changes you have made since you last saved the document.

Types of Business Documents

- Some common **business documents** used by most companies include letters, memos, fax covers, invoices, purchase orders, press releases, agendas, reports, and newsletters.

- Certain businesses—or departments within a larger company—may have specialized documents. For example, a law office or legal department produces legal documents such as wills, contracts, and bills of sale.

- In additional, individuals create **personal business documents** such as letters, research papers, and resumes.

- Most business documents have standard formats, which means each type of document includes similar parts. For example, an agenda should always include the following:

- The meeting start and end time and location
- The topics to be covered
- The duration each topic will be discussed
- The main speakers for each topic

- Throughout this book you learn how to set up and create many types of business documents.

Exit Word

- When you are done using Word, you exit the Word application.
- If you try to exit Word without saving your documents, Word prompts you to do so.
- If you exit Word without closing your saved documents, Word closes them automatically.

Procedures

Start Word

1. Click **Start** [Start] ....Ctrl+Esc
2. Click **All Programs**............P
3. Click **Microsoft Office** on the Programs menu.
4. Select **Microsoft Office Word 2003**.

Change the Word Window

To show or hide toolbars:

1. Click **View**................Alt+V
2. Click **Toolbars**................T
   ✓ Check mark next to toolbar name indicates that toolbar is already displayed.
3. Click the toolbar name.

To show or hide ruler:

1. Click **View**................Alt+V
   ✓ Check mark next to ruler indicates ruler is displayed.
2. Click **Ruler**................L

To change view:

1. Click **View**................Alt+V
2. Click **Normal**................N
   OR
   Click **Web Layout**............W
   OR
   Click **Print Layout**............P

OR
Click **Reading Layout**.........R
OR
Click **Outline**................O

OR
- Click a View button.
  ✓ Also, to switch to Reading Layout mode you may click the Read button [Read] on the Standard toolbar.

Correct Errors

- Press **Backspace** [Backspace] to delete character to *left* of insertion point.
- Press **Delete** [Del] to delete character to *right* of insertion point.
- Press **Escape** [Esc] to cancel command or close dialog box.
- Click **Cancel** [Cancel] to close dialog box.

Undo the Previous Action
(Ctrl+Z)

- Click **Undo** button.
  OR
1. Click **Edit**................Alt+E
2. Click **Undo**................U

Undo a Series of Actions
(Ctrl+Z)

- Click **Undo** button repeatedly.
  OR
1. Click **Undo** drop-down arrow.
   ✓ The most recent action is listed at the top of the Undo drop-down list.
2. Click last action in the series to undo all previous actions.

Redo the Previous Action
(Ctrl+Y)

- Click **Redo** button.
  OR
1. Click **Edit**................Alt+E
2. Click **Redo**................R

Redo a Series of Actions
(Ctrl+Y)

- Click **Redo** button repeatedly.
  OR
1. Click **Redo** drop-down arrow.
2. Click the last action in the series to redo all previous actions.

Repeat the Previous Action
(Ctrl+Y or F4)

1. Click **Edit** .... ⟦Alt⟧+⟦E⟧
2. Click **Repeat** .... ⟦R⟧

Save a New Document
(Ctrl+S)

1. Click **Save** button 🖫.
   OR
   a. Click **File** .... ⟦Alt⟧+⟦F⟧
   b. Click **Save** .... ⟦S⟧
2. Click **Save in** drop-down arrow .... ⟦Alt⟧+⟦I⟧
3. Select **drive** and **folder**.
4. Select **File name** text box .... ⟦Alt⟧+⟦N⟧
5. Type **file name**.
6. Click **Save** .... ⟦Alt⟧+⟦S⟧

To create a new folder for storing files:

1. Click **Save** button 🖫.
   OR
   a. Click **File** .... ⟦Alt⟧+⟦F⟧
   b. Click **Save** .... ⟦S⟧
2. Click **Create New Folder** button 📁.
3. Type **new folder name**.
4. Click **OK** .... ⟦Enter⟧
   ✓ *The new folder automatically becomes the open folder.*

Close a Document *(Ctrl+W)*

- Click **Document Close Window** button ⟦X⟧.
  OR
1. Click **File** .... ⟦Alt⟧+⟦F⟧
2. Click **Close** .... ⟦C⟧

3. Click **Yes** to save document .... ⟦Y⟧
   OR
   Click **No** to close without saving .... ⟦N⟧

Exit Word

- Click **Program Close** button ⟦X⟧.
  OR
- Double-click the **Program Control** icon ⟦W⟧.
  OR
1. Click **File** .... ⟦Alt⟧+⟦F⟧
2. Click **Exit** .... ⟦X⟧
3. Click **Yes** to save open documents......................... ⟦Y⟧
   OR
   Click **No** to close without saving .... ⟦N⟧

Exercise Directions

✓ *Note that the Word documents in the illustrations use the default 12-point Times New Roman font, unless otherwise noted. Fonts are covered in Exercise 7.*

1. Start Word.
2. Type the first paragraph shown in Illustration A.
   ✓ *Remember that you do not have to press **Enter** at the end of each line. Word wrap automatically moves the text to the next line as necessary.*
3. At the end of the paragraph, press **Enter** twice to start a new paragraph and insert a blank line between the paragraphs.
4. Undo the previous action.
   ✓ *When you execute the Undo command, Word reverses the action of pressing Enter twice. Sometimes Word combines actions for the purpose of Undo and Redo. In this case, it considers pressing Enter twice one action (called Typing on the Undo drop-down menu).*
5. Redo the previous action.
   ✓ *Word redoes the action of pressing Enter twice.*
6. Type the second paragraph shown in Illustration A.

7. If you make a typing error, press Backspace to delete it, and then type the correct text.
   ✓ *Word marks spelling errors with a red wavy underline, and grammatical errors with a green wavy underline. If you see these lines in the document, proofread for errors.*
8. Change to Web Layout view.
9. Change to Print Layout view.
10. Change to Normal view.
11. Change to Reading Layout mode.
12. Open the File menu.
13. Close the File menu.
14. Hide the ruler.
15. Show the ruler.
16. Hide the Formatting toolbar.
17. Show the Formatting toolbar.
18. Save the document with the name **TRAINER**.
    ✓ *Your instructor will tell you where to save the documents you create for use with this book.*
19. Close the document, saving all changes if prompted.
20. Exit Word.

Illustration A

Michigan Avenue Athletic Club is pleased to announce that David Fairmont has joined our staff. David is a licensed personal trainer with extensive experience in cardiovascular health. He holds a master's degree in health management from the University of Vermont in Burlington, Vermont. After graduation, he remained at UVM as an instructor. He recently moved to the Chicago area with his family.

We are certain that David will be a valuable addition to our staff. His skills and experience make him highly qualified and his attitude and personality make him a lot of fun to have around. David is available for private, semi-private, and group sessions. Please contact the club office for more information or to schedule an appointment.

On Your Own

1. Create a new document in Word.
2. Save the file as **OWD01**.
3. Type a brief biography about yourself, using at least two paragraphs.
4. Correct errors as necessary.
5. Practice changing from one view to another.
6. Display and hide different toolbars.
7. Close the document, saving all changes, and exit Word when you are finished.

Exercise 2

Skills Covered:

◆ **Create a New Document** ◆ **Work with Show/Hide Marks**
◆ **Move the Insertion Point in a Document** ◆ **Use Click and Type**
◆ **Save Changes** ◆ **Preview an Open Document**
◆ **Print** ◆ **About Press Releases**

On the Job

Mastering insertion point movements in Word is necessary to enter and edit text anywhere in a document. You save changes to keep a document up-to-date as you work. When you want to have a hard copy version of a document, you must print it. Preview a document before you print it to make sure there are no errors and that it looks good on the page.

Michigan Avenue Athletic Club has decided to issue a press release announcing the hiring of a new personal trainer. In this exercise, you will create a new document and type the press release. You will practice moving the insertion point around the document and you will align text with the click and type feature. When you have completed the press release, you will save the changes, preview the document, and then print it.

Terms

Insertion point The flashing vertical line that indicates where the next action will occur in a document on-screen.

Horizontal alignment The position of text on a line in relation to the left and right margins.

Hard copy A document printed on paper.

Press release A short document used to provide information about a company, organization, or event to the media.

Media outlet A means of mass communication, such as a newspaper, magazine, television station, radio station

Notes

Create a New Document

■ As you learned in Exercise 1, when you start Word it opens and displays a new blank document called *Document1*.

■ You can create additional new documents without closing and restarting Word.

■ Each new document is named using consecutive numbers, so the second document is *Document2,* the third is *Document3,* and so on until you exit Word or save a file with a new name.

■ In Word, you can create a new document using the New dialog box, the Getting Started task pane, the New Document task pane, or the New Blank Document button on the Standard toolbar.

Work with Show/Hide Marks

- When you type in Word you insert nonprinting characters like spaces, tabs, and paragraph marks along with printing characters like letters and numbers.

- Displaying nonprinting characters on-screen is helpful because you see where each paragraph ends and if there are extra spaces or unwanted tab characters.

- On-screen, the most common nonprinting characters are displayed as follows:
  - Space: dot (•)
  - Paragraph: paragraph symbol (¶)
  - Tab: right arrow (→)
  - ✓ *Other nonprinting characters include optional hyphens and line breaks.*

Move the Insertion Point in a Document

- The **insertion point** indicates where text will be inserted or deleted.

- You can move the insertion point anywhere in the existing text with keystrokes or mouse clicks.

- Scrolling to shift the document view does not move the insertion point.

Use Click and Type

- Use the Click and Type feature to position the insertion point anywhere in a blank document to begin typing.
  - ✓ *Click and Type cannot be used in Normal view or Outline view.*

- When Click and Type is active, the mouse pointer changes to indicate the **horizontal alignment** of the new text.
  - ✓ *You learn more about horizontal alignment in Exercise 4.*

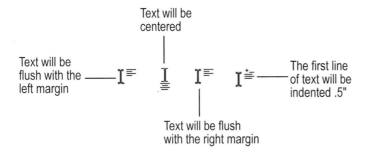

Text will be flush with the left margin

Text will be centered

Text will be flush with the right margin

The first line of text will be indented .5"

Save Changes

- To keep revisions permanently, you must save changes that you make to a document.

- Saving frequently ensures that no work will be lost if there is a power outage or you experience computer problems.
  - ✓ *The Document Recovery feature also helps insure that you won't lose your work in case of a computer failure. Refer to Exercise 4 of "Getting Started with Microsoft Office 2003" for more information.*

- Saving replaces the previously saved version of the document with the most recent changes.

Preview an Open Document

- Use Print Preview to display a document as it will look when printed.

Print

- Printing creates a **hard copy** version of a document.

- Your computer must be connected to a printer in order to print.

About Press Releases

- Use a **press release** to announce information about your company to **media outlets**.

- For example, you can issue a press release about new products, trends, developments, and even to provide tips or hints.

- The media outlet may provide you with publicity by reporting the information.

- A press release should be no more than one page in length. It should provide the basic facts, details that define why the content is newsworthy, and who to contact for more information.

- The basic parts of a press release include the following:
  - Contact information
  - Headline
  - Location
  - Lead paragraph
  - Additional information and details

Procedures

Create a New Document *(Ctrl+N)*

1. Start Word.
2. Click **New Blank Document** button ⬜ on the Standard toolbar.

OR

1. Start Word.
2. Click **View** .... `Alt`+`V`
3. Click **Tas_k Pane**.................. `K`

   ✓ *If the Getting Started or the New Document task pane is not displayed, select it from the Other Task Panes drop-down list.*

4. Click **Blank document** button ⬜.

Show or Hide Marks

- Click **Show/Hide ¶** button ¶ on the Standard toolbar.

OR

1. Click **Tools**.................. `Alt`+`T`
2. Click **Options**.................. `O`
3. Click **View** tab ....`Ctrl`+`Tab`
4. Select **All** checkbox .... `Alt`+`L` in Formatting marks section.
5. Click **OK**...........................`Enter`

Insertion Point Movements

To move with the mouse:

- Click mouse pointer in text where you want to position insertion point.

To move with the keyboard:

- One character left ....`←`
- One character right..............`→`
- One line up ....`↑`
- One line down......................`↓`
- Previous word..............`Ctrl`+`←`
- Next word ....`Ctrl`+`→`
- Up one paragraph........`Ctrl`+`↑`
- Down one paragraph ...`Ctrl`+`↓`
- Beginning of document...............`Ctrl`+`Home`
- End of document ....`Ctrl`+`End`
- Beginning of line.............`Home`
- End of line..........................`End`

Use Click and Type

1. Change to Print Layout view.
2. Click at location where you want to position insertion point.

To enable Click and Type:

1. Click **Tools** .... `Alt`+`T`
2. Click **Options** .... `O`
3. Click **Edit** tab ....`Ctrl`+`Tab`
4. Select **Enable click and type** checkbox.............`Alt`+`C`
5. Click **OK** ....`Enter`

Save Changes *(Ctrl+S)*

1. Click **Save** button 💾.

   OR

   a. Click **File**...............`Alt`+`F`
   b. Click **Save**......................`S`

2. Select the disk and folder where you want to save the file.
3. Enter a file name.
4. Click **Save** button

   [Save] ....`Alt`+`S`

Preview a Document

1. Click **Print Preview** button 🔍.

   OR

   a. Click **File**...............`Alt`+`F`
   b. Click **Print Pre_view** ....`V`

2. Press **Page Down** to see next page.
3. Press **Page Up** to see previous page.
4. Click **Close** button [Close].

Print *(Ctrl+P)*

- Click **Print** button 🖨.

   ✓ *This prints the document with the default settings.*

   OR

1. Click **File** ....`Alt`+`F`
2. Click **Print** ....`P`
3. Click **OK** ....`Enter`

Exercise Directions

1. Start Word, if necessary.

2. Create a new document and save it as **PRESS**.

3. Click the Print Layout View button to change to Print Layout view if necessary.

   ✓ Select View, Print Layout.

4. Display all nonprinting characters.

5. Use Click and Type to center the insertion point on the first line of the document.

6. Type the text shown on the first line of Illustration A.

   ✓ Ignore any automatic features that are displayed as underlines or buttons.

7. Use Click and Type to move the insertion point so it is flush left on the third line of the document. You will be able to see if you have positioned the insertion point on the third line by looking at the paragraph marks on-screen. There should be one paragraph mark at the end of the first line, a second paragraph mark on the second (blank) line, and a third paragraph mark to the left of the insertion point on the third line.

   ✓ If you press Enter twice to start a new paragraph and leave a blank line as you did in Exercise 1, the insertion point will still be centered. That's because Word carries formatting such as horizontal alignment forward from one paragraph to the next. You must use Click and Type to change the alignment to flush left.

8. Type the rest of the document shown in Illustration A.

   ✓ Depending on the default settings on your computer, Word may automatically format the Web address in the last paragraph as a hyperlink by changing the color to blue and applying an underline. If you click the hyperlink, your computer may try to log onto the Internet to locate the site. You can remove the hyperlink by right-clicking on it, then clicking Remove Hyperlink on the context menu.

9. Move the insertion point back to the second sentence in the first paragraph of the press release and delete the text **in Burlington, Vermont**. Do not delete the final period.

10. Move the insertion point between the words **offer** and **spa** in the last sentence of the second paragraph.

11. Type the word **exceptional**.

12. If necessary type a space between the new word **exceptional** and the existing word **spa**.

13. Save the changes you have made to the document.

14. Display the document in Print Preview.

15. Close Print Preview.

16. Print the document.

17. Close the document, saving all changes.

David Fairmont Joins Michigan Avenue Athletic Club

Chicago, IL -- Michigan Avenue Athletic Club is pleased to announce that David Fairmont has joined our staff as a personal trainer. Mr. Fairmont holds a master's degree in health management from the University of Vermont in Burlington, Vermont. He is a licensed personal trainer with extensive experience in cardiovascular health.

Michigan Avenue Athletic Club is a full-service athletic facility conveniently located in downtown Chicago. The facility includes racquetball and tennis courts, an indoor pool, multiple exercise rooms, and a vast array of equipment for individual use and group lessons. We also offer spa services, a pro shop, and a cafe.

For more information about David Fairmont or membership in our club, please call 312-555-3521, or visit us on the Web at www.michaveclub.com.

On Your Own

1. Create a new document.
2. Save the file as **OWD02**.
3. Draft a press release announcing that you are taking a course to learn how to use Microsoft Office 2003.
4. Using Click and Type, center a headline at the top of the document.
5. Using Click and Type, move the pointer back to the flush left or first line indent position to type the rest of the press release. Include information such as your instructor's name, the textbook you are using, and when the course will be completed.
6. Save the changes, and then preview the document to see how it will look when printed.
7. Print the document.
8. Close the document when you are finished, saving all changes.

Exercise 3

Skills Covered:

◆ **Correct Spelling as You Type** ◆ **Correct Grammar as You Type**
◆ **Check Spelling** ◆ **Check Grammar** ◆ **Use the Thesaurus**

On the Job

A professional document should be free of spelling and grammatical errors. Word can check the spelling and grammar in a document and recommend corrections.

The marketing director at Michigan Avenue Athletic Club has asked you to create a mission statement explaining the corporate goals. In this exercise, you will type the statement and then improve it by correcting the spelling and grammar.

Terms

Smart tag A feature of Word 2003 designed to let you perform actions within Word that you would normally have to open another application to accomplish. For example, you can add a person's name and address to an Outlook contact list using a smart tag in Word.

Thesaurus A listing of words with synonyms and antonyms.

Synonyms Words with the same meaning.

Antonyms Words with opposite meanings.

Notes

Correct Spelling as You Type

- By default, Word checks spelling as you type and marks misspelled words with a red, wavy underline.

  This is an example of a missspelled word|

- Any word not in the Word dictionary is marked as misspelled, including proper names, words with unique spellings, and many technical terms. Word will also mark double occurrences of words.

- You can ignore the wavy lines and keep typing, correct the spelling, or add the marked word to the dictionary.

- If the wavy underlines distract you from your work, you can turn off the Check spelling as you type feature.

  ✓ *Word uses a few other underlines to mark text on-screen. For example, blue wavy underlines indicate inconsistent formatting and purple dotted lines indicate **smart tags**. You learn about checking for inconsistent formatting in Exercise 20.*

Correct Grammar as You Type

- Word can also check grammar as you type, identifying errors such as punctuation, matching case or tense, sentence fragments, and run-on sentences.

- Word marks grammatical errors with a green, wavy underline.

  This is an example of a grammatical errors|

- Word picks out grammatical errors based on either the Grammar Only style guide or the Grammar and Style style guide.

- As with the spelling checker, you can ignore the green wavy lines and keep typing, or correct the error.

- If the wavy underlines distract you from your work, you can turn off the Check grammar as you type feature.

Check Spelling

- You can check the spelling in an entire document or in part of a document.

- To check the spelling in part of a document, you must first select the section you want checked.

- The spelling checker identifies any word not in the Word dictionary as misspelled, including proper names, words with unique spellings, and technical terms.

- When Word identifies a misspelled word, you can correct the spelling, ignore the spelling, or add the word to the dictionary.

Correct spelling with Spelling Checker

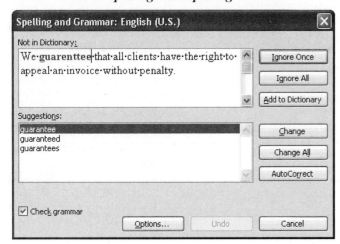

Check Grammar

- By default, Word checks the grammar in a document at the same time that it checks the spelling.

- When Word identifies a grammatical mistake, you can accept the suggestion or ignore it.

Correct grammar with Grammar Checker

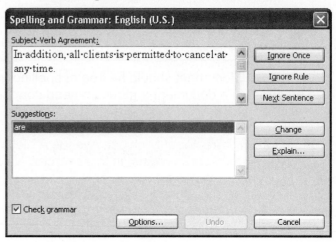

Use the Thesaurus

- Use the **thesaurus** to search for **synonyms**, definitions, and **antonyms** for any word.

- The results of the search are displayed in the Research task pane.

- Click a plus sign to expand the list to show additional words.

- Click a minus sign to collapse the list to hide some words.

- Use the available drop-down list to insert a word from the results list at the current insertion point location, copy it at a different location, or look it up in the thesaurus.

- By default, Word searches an English thesaurus, but you can select to search all available reference books, or a thesaurus in a different language.

- A thesaurus can improve your writing by helping you eliminate repetitive use of common words and to choose more descriptive words.

Procedures

Correct Spelling as You Type

1. Right-click red, wavy underline.
2. Click correctly spelled word on context menu.

   OR

   - Click **Ignore All** .... `I`
   - Click **Add** to add word to dictionary .... `A`

To turn off Automatic Spelling Checker:

1. Click **Tools** .... `Alt`+`T`
2. Click **Options** .... `O`
3. Click the **Spelling & Grammar** tab .... `Ctrl`+`Tab`
4. Deselect **Check spelling as you type** checkbox ...... `Alt`+`P`
5. Click **OK** .... `Enter`

Correct Grammar as You Type

1. Right-click grammatical error marked with green, wavy underline.
2. Click correct grammar option on context menu.

   OR

   Click **Ignore Once** to hide the underline .... `I`

To turn Off Automatic Grammar Checker:

1. Click **Tools** .... `Alt`+`T`
2. Click **Options** .... `O`
3. Click the **Spelling & Grammar** tab .... `Ctrl`+`Tab`
4. Deselect **Check grammar as you type** checkbox ...... `Alt`+`G`
5. Click **OK** .... `Enter`

Select Grammar Style

1. Click **Tools** .... `Alt`+`T`
2. Click **Options** .... `O`
3. Click the **Spelling & Grammar** tab .... `Ctrl`+`Tab`
4. Click **Writing style** drop-down arrow .... `Alt`+`W`
5. Click desired **style** .. `↕`, `Enter`
6. Click **OK** .... `Enter`

Check Spelling (F7)

1. Position insertion point where you want to start checking.

   ✓ *Word checks document from the insertion point forward.*

   OR

   Select text you want to check.
2. Click **Spelling and Grammar** button `ABC✓`.

   OR

   a. Click **Tools** .... `Alt`+`T`

   b. Click **Spelling & Grammar** .... `S`
3. Choose from the following options:

   - Click correctly spelled word in **Suggestions** list .... `Alt`+`N`
   - Click **Change** .... `Alt`+`C`
   - Click **Change All** to change the word everywhere in document .... `Alt`+`L`
   - Change the misspelled word manually in the **Not in Dictionary** text box.
   - Click **Ignore Once** to continue without changing word .... `Alt`+`I`
   - Click **Ignore All** to continue without changing word and without highlighting it anywhere else in document .... `Alt`+`G`
   - Click **Add to Dictionary** to add word to dictionary .... `Alt`+`A`
4. Repeat step 3 options for every misspelled word.
5. Click **OK** when Word completes check .... `Enter`

   ✓ *Word may prompt you to check the formatting in your document. Click Yes to check the formatting, or No to close the prompt without checking the formatting. For more information on checking formatting, refer to Exercise 20.*

Check Grammar (F7)

1. Position insertion point where you want to start checking.

   OR

   Select text you want to check.
2. Click **Spelling and Grammar** button `ABC✓`.

   OR

   a. Click **Tools** .... `Alt`+`T`

   b. Click **Spelling & Grammar** .... `S`
3. Choose from the following options:

   - Click the correct grammar in **Suggestions** list ..... `Alt`+`N`
   - Edit the error manually in the **Not in Dictionary** text box.
   - Click **Change** .... `Alt`+`C`
   - Click **Ignore Once** to continue without changing text .... `Alt`+`I`
   - Click **Ignore Rule** to continue without changing text and without highlighting error if it occurs anywhere else in document .... `Alt`+`G`
   - Click **Next Sentence** to skip highlighted error and continue checking document .... `Alt`+`X`
   - Click **Explain** .... `Alt`+`E` to display information about grammatical error.
4. Repeat step 3 options for every grammatical error.
5. Click **OK** when Word completes check .... `Enter`

   ✓ *Word may prompt you to check the formatting in your document. Click Yes to check the formatting, or No to close the prompt without checking the formatting. For more information on checking formatting, refer to Exercise 20.*

Search the Thesaurus *(Shift+F7)*

1. Click on the word you want to look up.
   - ✓ *The insertion point should be positioned within the word.*
2. Click **Tools** .... `Alt`+`T`
3. Click **Language** .... `L`
4. Click **Thesaurus** .... `T`

OR

1. Display the Research task pane.
2. Enter desired word in **Search for** box.
3. Click **Show results from:** drop-down arrow.
4. Select desired thesaurus.
5. Click **Start searching** button .... `Enter`

Insert a synonym:

1. Position the insertion point where you want to insert the word.

   OR

   Select the word to replace.
2. Move the mouse pointer to touch the synonym in the Results list.
   - ✓ *A drop-down arrow is displayed.*
3. Click the drop-down arrow to the right of the synonym.
4. Click **Insert** .... `I`

Look up a synonym:

- Click the word in the Results list.

OR

1. Move the mouse pointer to touch the word in the Results list.
   - ✓ *A drop down arrow is displayed.*
2. Click the drop-down arrow to the right of the word.
3. Click **Look Up** .... `L`

Copy a synonym:

1. Move the mouse pointer to touch the word in the Results list.
   - ✓ *A drop-down arrow is displayed.*
2. Click the drop-down arrow to the right of the word.
3. Click **Copy** .... `C`
4. Right-click in the document where you want to insert the copied word.
5. Click **Paste** .... `P` on the shortcut menu.

Locate a synonym as you type:

1. Right-click on the word you want to look up.
2. Click **Synonyms** on context menu .... `Y`
3. Click desired **synonym** on submenu .... `⤸`, `Enter`

   OR

   Click **Thesaurus** .... `T` to open the Research Task Pane.

Exercise Directions

1. Start Word, if necessary.
2. Create a new document.
3. Save the file as **MISSION**.
4. Display paragraph marks.
5. Begin at the top of the screen and type the paragraphs shown in Illustration A, including all the circled errors.
6. As you type, correct the spelling of the word **committed**.
   - ✓ *The AutoCorrect feature may automatically correct this word. If it does, continue typing. AutoCorrect is covered in Exercise 4.*
7. As you type, correct the grammar in the first sentence of the second paragraph.

8. Check the spelling and grammar starting at the beginning of the document.
   a. Correct the spelling of the words **committed**, **personal**, and **professional**.
   b. Capitalize the word **Under** at the beginning of the second sentence in the second paragraph.
   c. Ignore all occurrences of the proper name **Chardudutta Saroj**.
   d. Correct the spelling of the word **environment**.
   e. Change the double comma in the middle of the last sentence in the second paragraph to a single comma.
9. Use the Thesaurus to replace the word **hope** in the last sentence.
10. Display the document in Print Preview.
11. Print the document.
12. Close the document, saving all changes.

Illustration A

The Michigan Avenue Athletic Club is comitted to excellence. We encourage our
employees and our members to strive for the highest goals, meet all challenges with
spirit and enthusiasm, and work hard to achieve personel and professionel harmony.

At MAAC, we respects individuality and value diversity under the guidance of
General Manager Ray Peterson and Exercise Director Charudutta Saroj we hope to
provide an enviromnent where people feel comfortable, safe,, and free to pursue their
physical fitness goals.

On Your Own

1. A mission statement is used to define the purpose and goals of a business or organization. Think about your purpose and goals in terms of this class. Consider what you hope to achieve, what you would like to learn, as well as how you want to interact with your instructor and classmates.

2. When you are ready, create a new document in Word.

3. Save the document as **OWD03**.

4. Type your own mission statement for this class in the blank document.

5. Check and correct the spelling and grammar.

6. Use the Thesaurus to improve the wording of your document.

7. Print the document.

8. Ask someone in your class to read the statement and to provide written and oral feedback.

9. Integrate the suggestions into the document.

10. Save your changes, close the document, and exit Word when you are finished.

Exercise 4

◆ Use AutoCorrect ◆ Select Text in a Document
◆ Replace Selected Text ◆ Align Text Horizontally
◆ Align a Document Vertically ◆ About Memos

On the Job

As you type a document, Word's AutoCorrect feature automatically corrects common spelling errors before you even know you've made them. You must select text in a document in order to edit it or format it. For example, changing the horizontal and vertical alignment can improve the appearance of a document and make it easier to read.

You are an assistant in the personnel department at Whole Grains Bread, a manufacturer of specialty breads and pastries based in Larkspur, California. In this exercise, your supervisor has asked you to type a memo to employees about a new automatic deposit payroll option.

Terms

AutoCorrect A Word feature that automatically corrects common spelling errors as you type.

Caps Lock Keyboard key used to **toggle** uppercase letters with lowercase letters.

Toggle A command that turns a particular mode on and off. Also, to switch back and forth between two modes.

Select Mark text for editing.

Contiguous Next to or adjacent.

Noncontiguous Not next to or adjacent.

Highlight To apply a colored background to the text to call attention to it.

Horizontal alignment The position of text in relation to the left and right page margins.

Flush Lined up evenly along an edge.

Vertical alignment The position of text in relation to the top and bottom page margins.

Selection bar A narrow strip along the left margin of a page that automates selection of text. When the mouse pointer is in the selection area, the cursor changes to an arrow pointing up and to the right.

Notes

Use AutoCorrect

AutoCorrect dialog box

- **AutoCorrect** automatically replaces spelling errors with the correct text as soon as you press the spacebar after typing a word.

- Word comes with a built-in list of AutoCorrect entries including common typos like *adn* for *and* and *teh* for *the*.

- AutoCorrect can also replace regular characters with symbols, such as the letters *T* and *M* enclosed in parentheses (TM) with the trademark symbol, ™. It will also insert accent marks in words such as café, cliché, crème, and déjà vu.

- AutoCorrect also corrects capitalization errors as follows:

  - TWo INitial CApital letters are replaced with one initial capital letter.

  - The first word in a sentence is automatically capitalized.

  - The days of the week are automatically capitalized.

- Accidental use of the cAPS LOCK feature is corrected if the **Caps Lock** key is set to ON.

- You can add words to the AutoCorrect list. For example, if you commonly misspell someone's name, you can add it to the list.

- You can also set Word to use the spelling checker dictionary to determine if a word is misspelled and to correct it automatically.

- If AutoCorrect changes text that was not incorrect, you can use Undo or the AutoCorrect Options button to reverse the change.

- If you find AutoCorrect distracting, you can disable it.

Select Text in a Document

- You must **select** text already entered in a document in order to edit it or format it.

- You can select any amount of **contiguous** or **noncontiguous** text.

  ✓ *You can also select nontext characters, such as symbols; nonprinting characters, such as paragraph marks; and graphics, such as pictures.*

- Selected text appears **highlighted** on screen as white characters on a black background.

Selected text in a document

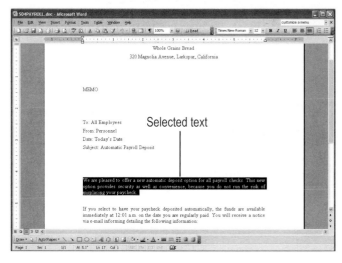

Replace Selected Text

- You can replace selected text simply by typing new text.

- You can delete selected text by pressing the Delete key or the Backspace key.

Align Text Horizontally

- **Horizontal alignment** is used to adjust the position of paragraphs in relation to the left and right margins of a page.

  ✓ *You have already used Click and Type to align text horizontally in a document.*

- There are four horizontal alignments:

  - *Left.* Text is **flush** with left margin. The text along the right side of the page is uneven (or ragged). Left is the default horizontal alignment.

  - *Right.* Text is flush with right margin. The text along the left side of the page is uneven (or ragged).

  - *Center.* Text is centered between margins.

  - *Justify.* Text is spaced so it runs evenly along both the left and right margins.

- You can use different alignments in a document.

Text aligned in a document

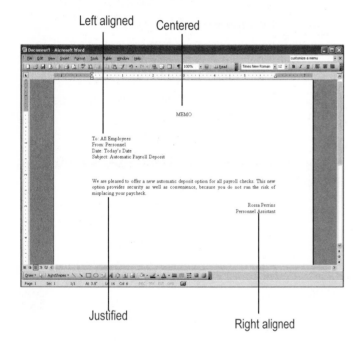

Align a Document Vertically

- **Vertical alignment** is used to adjust the position of all text on a page in relation to the top and bottom margins.

- There are four vertical alignments:

  - *Top:* Text begins below the top margin. Top is the default vertical alignment.

  - *Center:* Text is centered between the top and bottom margins.

  - *Justified:* Paragraphs are spaced to fill the page between the top and bottom margins.

  - *Bottom:* The last line of text begins just above the bottom margin.

- Centering vertically can improve the appearance of some one-page documents, such as flyers or invitations.

- Vertical justification improves the appearance of documents that contain nearly full pages of text.

About Memos

- A memo, or memoranda, is a business document commonly used for communication within a company.

- Unlike a letter, a memo is not usually addressed to a particular individual and does not include a formal closing.

  ✓ *You will learn about business letters in Exercise 5.*

- Usually, a memo includes the company name, the word memo, the headings To:, From:, Date:, and Subject, and the memo text.

- One blank line is used to separate parts of a memo.

- The writer may include his or her name, title, and/or signature at the end of the memo text.

- If someone other than the writer types the memo, that person's initials should be entered below the memo text. In addition, if there is an attachment or an enclosure, the word Attachment or Enclosure should be entered after the text (or the typist's initials).

- Some variations on this memo format include typing headings in all uppercase letters, typing the subject text in all uppercase letters, and leaving additional spacing between memo parts. Also, the word memo may be omitted.

Procedures

Use AutoCorrect

Add words to the AutoCorrect list:

1. Click **Tools** .... `Alt`+`T`
2. Click **AutoCorrect**
   Options .... `A`
3. Click in **Replace**
   text box .... `Alt`+`R`
4. Type misspelled word to add.
5. Click in **With** text box ... `Alt`+`W`
6. Type correct word.
7. Click **Add** button
   `Add`
   .... `Alt`+`A`
8. Click **OK** .... `Enter`

Set AutoCorrect Options:

1. Click **Tools** .... `Alt`+`T`
2. Click **AutoCorrect**
   Options .... `A`
3. Select or deselect checkboxes
   as desired:
   - **Show AutoCorrect**
     options buttons .... `Alt`+`H`
   - **Correct TWO INitial**
     CApitals .... `Alt`+`O`
   - **Capitalize first letter of**
     sentences .... `Alt`+`S`
   - **Capitalize first letter of**
     table cells .... `Alt`+`C`
   - **Capitalize names of**
     days .... `Alt`+`N`
   - **Correct accidental**
     usage of cAPS lOCK
     key .... `Alt`+`L`
   - **Automatically use**
     suggestions from the
     spelling checker ... `Alt`+`G`
4. Click **OK** .... `Enter`

Disable AutoCorrect:

1. Click **Tools** .... `Alt`+`T`
2. Click **AutoCorrect**
   Options .... `A`
3. Deselect **Replace text as you**
   type checkbox. .... `Alt`+`T`
   ✓ *Clicking should remove check*
     mark; if not, click checkbox
     again.

Use AutoCorrect Options button:

1. Click word that was
   automatically corrected.
   ✓ *A small blue box is displayed*
     below the word.
2. Rest mouse pointer on **blue**
   box ⬚.
   ✓ *The AutoCorrect Options*
     button is displayed.
3. Click **AutoCorrect Options**
   button ⚡ ▾.
4. Select one of the following:
   - **Change back** .... `H`
     to reverse the change.
   - **Stop Automatically**
     Correcting .... `A`
     to remove the word from
     the AutoCorrect list.
   - **Control AutoCorrect**
     Options .... `C`
     to open the AutoCorrect
     dialog box.

Select Using the Keyboard

1. Position insertion point to left of
   first character to select.
2. Use following key combinations:
   - One character
     right .... `Shift`+`→`
   - One character left.. `Shift`+`←`
   - One line up .... `Shift`+`↑`
   - One line down .... `Shift`+`↓`
   - To end of line........ `Shift`+`End`
   - To beginning
     of line............... `Shift`+`Home`
   - To end of
     document ..... `Shift`+`Ctrl`+`End`
   - To beginning of
     document ... `Shift`+`Ctrl`+`Home`
   - Entire document ..... `Ctrl`+`A`

Select Using the Mouse

1. Position insertion point to the
   left of first character to select.
2. Hold down left mouse button.
3. Drag to where you want to stop
   selecting.
4. Release mouse button.

Mouse Selection Shortcuts

One word:
   - Double-click word.

One sentence:
1. Press and hold **Ctrl** .... `Ctrl`
2. Click in sentence.

One line:
   - Click in **selection bar** to the
     left of the line.
     ✓ *In the selection bar, the mouse*
       pointer changes to an arrow
       pointing up and to the right ⬀.

One paragraph:
   - Double-click in selection bar to
     the left of the paragraph you
     want to select.

Document:
   - Triple-click in selection bar.

Select noncontiguous blocks

1. Select first block.
2. Press and hold **Ctrl** .... `Ctrl`
3. Select additional block(s).

Cancel a Selection

   - Click anywhere in document.
   OR
   - Press any arrow key .... ⬀

Replace Selected Text

1. Select text to replace.
2. Type new text.
   OR
   Press **Delete** .... `Del`
   to delete selected text.

Align Horizontally

1. Position insertion point in paragraph to align.

   OR

   Select paragraphs to align.

   OR

   Position insertion point where you intend to type text.

2. Click alignment button:

   - **Center** ▤ .... `Ctrl`+`E`
   - **Right** ▤ .... `Ctrl`+`R`
   - **Justify** ▤ .... `Ctrl`+`J`
   - **Left** ▤ .... `Ctrl`+`L`

Align Vertically

1. Click **File**.................... `Alt`+`F`
2. Click **Page Set_up** .... `U`
3. Click **Layout** tab .... `Alt`+`L`
4. Click **Vertical alignment**.................... `Alt`+`V` drop-down arrow.
5. Select **Vertical alignment** option:...................... ↕ , `Enter`
   - **Top**
   - **Center**
   - **Justified**
   - **Bottom**
6. Click **OK** .... `Enter`

Exercise Directions

1. Start Word, if necessary.

2. Create a new document and save it as **PAYROLL**.

3. Display nonprinting characters, if necessary.

4. Open the AutoCorrect dialog box.

   a. Add the misspelled word **Magonlia** to the AutoCorrect list; replace it with the correctly spelled **Magnolia**.

   b. Add the misspelled word **personell** to the AutoCorrect list; replace it with the correctly spelled **personnel**.

   c. Add the two words **pay check** to the AutoCorrect list; replace them with the single word **paycheck**.

   d. Select all AutoCorrect option check and then click OK to close the dialog box.

5. Type the document shown in Illustration A.

   - Type the actual date in place of the text *Today's date*.

   - Type your own name in place of the text *Student's Name*.

   - Type the circled errors exactly as shown in the illustration.

     ✓ *Notice that Word automatically corrects the errors.*

   - Press Enter twice to start new paragraphs and leave blank lines as marked on the illustration.

6. Save the document.

7. Horizontally align the text in the document as marked on the illustration.

   a. Select the lines marked for centering.

   b. Center the selected text.

   c. Select the three paragraphs marked for justification.

   d. Justify the selected paragraphs.

   e. Select the lines marked for right alignment.

   f. Right align the selected text.

8. Select the text **New Option** on the *Subject:* line near the top of the document and replace it with the text **Automatic Payroll Deposit**.

9. Check and correct the spelling and grammar in the document. Ignore all proper names.

10. Display the document in Print Preview.

11. Center the document vertically on the page.

12. Display the document in Print Preview again.

13. Justify the document vertically.

14. Display the document in Print Preview again.

15. Print the document.

16. Close the document, saving all changes.

Illustration A

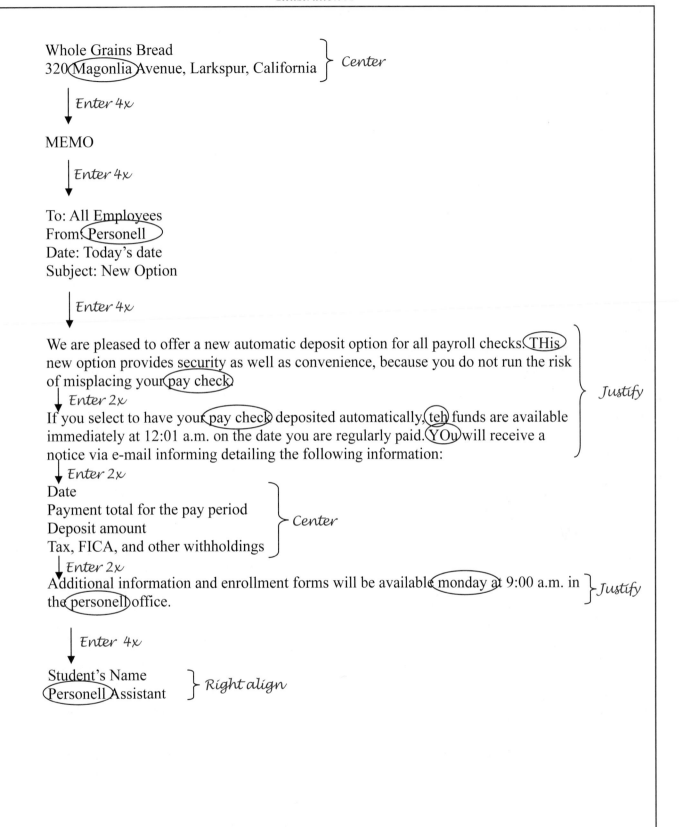

On Your Own

1. Create a new document in Word.
2. Save the file as **OWD04**.
3. Add words that you commonly misspell to the AutoCorrect list.
4. Type a memo to your instructor introducing yourself. Use correct formatting for a memo.
5. In the body of the memo, include your name (try misspelling it to see if AutoCorrect fixes it) and things you think are your strengths and your weaknesses. If you want, include information from the Mission Statement you created in the On Your Own section of Exercise 3.
6. Change the horizontal alignment of some of the text in the memo.
7. Change the vertical alignment of the document.
8. Check the spelling and grammar.
9. Print the document.
10. Ask someone in your class to read the document and offer suggestions.
11. Incorporate the suggestions.
12. Close the document, saving all changes.

Exercise 5

♦ **Format a Business Letter**
♦ **Insert the Date and Time in a Document**
♦ **Use Uppercase Mode** ♦ **Change Case in a Document**

On the Job

Write business letters as a representative of your employer to communicate with other businesses, such as clients or suppliers, or to communicate with individuals, such as prospective employees. For example, you might write a business letter to request a job quote from a supplier, or to inquire about a loan from a bank.

You are the assistant to Mr. Frank Kaplan, the Franchise Manager for Whole Grains Bread. He has asked you to type a letter to a franchisee about opening a new shop outside California. In this exercise, you will compose a full-block business letter.

Terms

Full block A style of letter in which all lines start flush with the left margin—that is, without a first-line indent.

Modified block A style of letter in which some lines start at the center of the page.

Salutation The line at the start of a letter including the greeting and the recipient's name, such as *Dear Mr. Doe*.

Computer's clock The clock/calendar built into your computer's main processor to keep track of the current date and time.

Case The specific use of upper- or lowercase letters.

Notes

Format a Business Letter

■ There are different letter styles of business letters.

   • In a **full-block** business letter, all lines start flush with the left margin.

   • In a **modified-block** business letter, certain lines start at the center of the page.

      ✓ *Modified-block business letters will be covered in Exercise 6.*

■ The parts of a business letter are the same regardless of the style.

■ Vertical spacing is achieved by inserting blank lines between letter parts.

■ Refer to the illustration on page 30 to identify the parts of a business letter.

   • Return address (may be omitted if the letter is printed on letterhead stationery)

   • Date

   • Inside address (to whom and where the letter is going)

   • **Salutation**

   • Body

27

- Signature line
- Title line (the job title of the letter writer)
- Reference initials (the initials of the person who wrote the letter, followed by a slash, followed by the initials of the person who typed the letter)
    - ✓ *Whenever you see "yo" as part of the reference initials in an exercise, type your own initials.*
- Special notations (included only when appropriate):
    - Mail service notation indicates a special delivery method. It is typed in all capital letters, two lines below the date. Typical mail service notations include *CERTIFIED MAIL, REGISTERED MAIL,* or *BY HAND.*
    - Subject notation identifies or summarizes the letter topic. The word *Subject* may be typed in all capital letters or with just an initial capital. It is placed two lines below the salutation.
        - ✓ *The word* Re *(meaning with regard to) is sometimes used in place of the word* Subject.
    - Enclosure or attachment notation indicates whether there are other items in the envelope. It is typed two lines below the reference initials in any of the following styles: *ENC., Enc., Encl., Enclosure, Attachment.*
        - ✓ *If there are multiple items, the number may be typed in parentheses following the notation.*
    - Copy notation indicates if any other people are receiving copies of the same letter. It is typed two lines below either the enclosure notation, or reference initials, whichever is last. It may be typed as Copy to:, cc:, or pc: (photocopy) with the name(s) of the recipient(s) listed after the colon.

Insert the Date and Time in a Document

- Use the Date and Time feature to insert the current date and/or time automatically in a document.

- The inserted date and time are based on your **computer's clock**. A variety of date and time formats are available.

The Date and Time dialog box

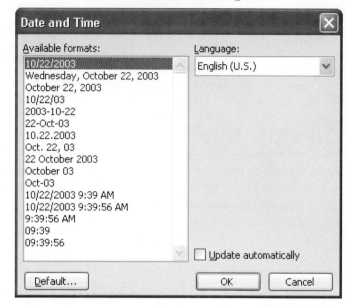

- You can set Word to update the date or time automatically whenever you save or print the document.

Use Uppercase Mode

- Use Uppercase Mode to type all capital letters without pressing the Shift key.
- Uppercase Mode affects only letter characters.
- When Uppercase Mode is on, the Caps Lock indicator on your keyboard is lit.

Change Case in a Document

- You can automatically change the **case** of text in a document.
- There are five case options:
    - Sentence case: First character in sentence is uppercase.
    - lowercase: All characters are lowercase.
    - UPPERCASE: All characters are uppercase.
    - Title Case: First character in each word is uppercase.
    - tOGGLE cASE: Case is reversed for all selected text.

Procedures

Format a Full-Block Business Letter

1. Start 2" from the top of the page............................ Enter **4x**

   ✓ *Press Enter four times to leave 2" of space.*

   ✓ *If you are using stationery with a printed letterhead, you may have to adjust the spacing.*

2. Insert the date.

3. Leave one blank line and type the mail service notation........... Enter **2x**

4. Leave three blank lines and type the inside address .... Enter **4x**

5. Leave a blank line and type the salutation .... Enter **2x**

6. Leave one blank line and type the subject notation..... Enter **2x**

7. Leave a blank line and type the letter body ..... Enter **2x**

8. Leave a blank line and type the closing........... Enter **2x**

9. Leave three blank lines and type the signature line.......... Enter **4x**

10. Press **Enter** .... Enter

11. Type the title line .... Enter

    ✓ *If you are not using letterhead stationery, type the return address information below the title line.*

12. Leave a blank line and type the reference initials. .. Enter **2x**

13. Leave a blank line and type the enclosure notation .... Enter **2x**

14. Leave a blank line and type the copy notation .... Enter **2x**

Insert the Date and/or Time

1. Position the insertion point.

2. Click **Insert**.................. Alt+I

3. Click **Date and Time**........... T

4. Click the desired format.

   ✓ *Select Update automatically checkbox if you want date and/or time to update when you save or print document.*

5. Click **OK** .... Enter

Uppercase Mode

1. Press **Caps Lock** .... Caps Lock

2. Type text.

To turn off Uppercase Mode:

• Press **Caps Lock**.............. Caps Lock

Change Case

1. Select text.
   OR
   Position insertion point where new text will begin.

2. Click **Format** .... Alt+O

3. Click **Change Case** .... E

4. Click the case you want:

   • **Sentence case**............. S

   • **lowercase** L

   • **UPPERCASE** .... U

   • **Title Case**.................... T

   • **tOGGLE cASE** .... G

5. Click **OK**........................... Enter

   ✓ *You can also select text and then press **Shift+F3** to toggle through sentence case, lowercase, and uppercase. Release the keys when the desired case is in effect.*

Exercise Directions

1. Start Word, if necessary.

2. Create a new document and save it as **EXPAND**.

3. Type the letter shown in Illustration A.

   • Press the Enter key between parts of the letter as indicated.

   • Insert the current date using the MONTH DAY, YEAR format found third from the top in the Date and Time dialog box.

   • Set the date so that it does not update automatically.

   • Use Uppercase mode to type the mail notation.

     ✓ *Word may display ScreenTips as you type certain parts of the letter (for example, CERTIFIED MAIL). Simply ignore them and continue typing.*

4. Save changes to the document.

5. Change the text on the Subject line to title case.

6. Change all occurrences of the text **Whole Grains Bread** to uppercase.

7. Check the spelling and grammar in the document.

   • Ignore all proper names.

8. Display the document in Print Preview.

   ✓ *If the document does not fit on one page, you may have inserted too many blank lines. Make sure you have nonprinting characters displayed so you can see the paragraph marks, count the marks, and delete any extras.*

9. Close the document, saving all changes.

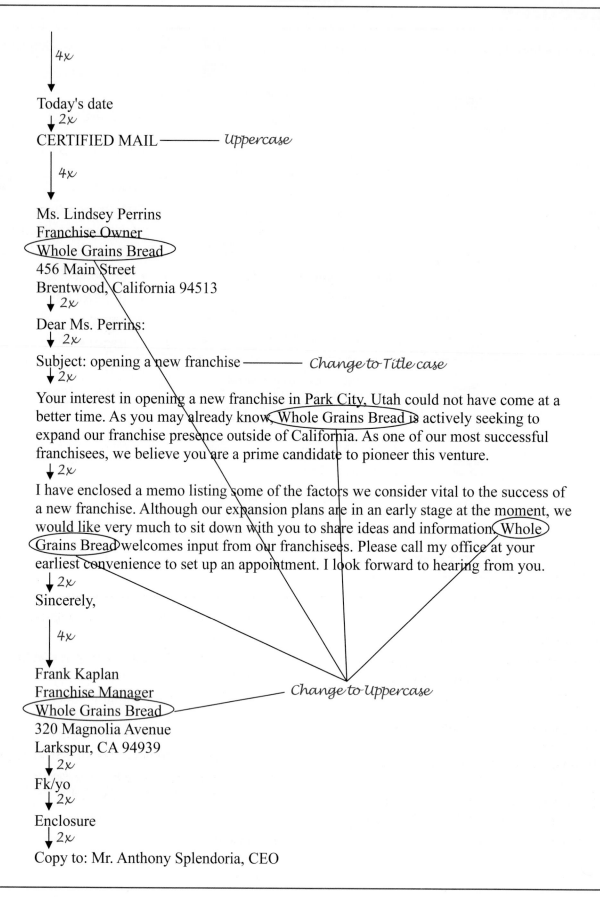

4x

Today's date

↓ 2x

CERTIFIED MAIL ———— *Uppercase*

4x

Ms. Lindsey Perrins
Franchise Owner
Whole Grains Bread
456 Main Street
Brentwood, California 94513

↓ 2x

Dear Ms. Perrins:

↓ 2x

Subject: opening a new franchise ———— *Change to Title case*

↓ 2x

Your interest in opening a new franchise in Park City, Utah could not have come at a better time. As you may already know, Whole Grains Bread is actively seeking to expand our franchise presence outside of California. As one of our most successful franchisees, we believe you are a prime candidate to pioneer this venture.

↓ 2x

I have enclosed a memo listing some of the factors we consider vital to the success of a new franchise. Although our expansion plans are in an early stage at the moment, we would like very much to sit down with you to share ideas and information. Whole Grains Bread welcomes input from our franchisees. Please call my office at your earliest convenience to set up an appointment. I look forward to hearing from you.

↓ 2x

Sincerely,

4x

Frank Kaplan
Franchise Manager
Whole Grains Bread ———— *Change to Uppercase*
320 Magnolia Avenue
Larkspur, CA 94939

↓ 2x

Fk/yo

↓ 2x

Enclosure

↓ 2x

Copy to: Mr. Anthony Splendoria, CEO

On Your Own

1. Create a new document in Word.

2. Save the document as **OWD05**.

3. Representing your school or organization, draft a full-block business letter to a local newspaper asking them to include information about upcoming events in a calendar listing. School events might include athletic contests, such as a homecoming football game, club activities, field trips, band and choir concerts, or vacation days.

4. In the letter, indicate that you have attached the necessary information and that you are sending a copy to your instructor.

5. Test different case options for different parts of the letter.

6. Check the spelling and grammar in the document.

7. Print the document.

8. Ask someone in your class to read the letter and provide comments and suggestions.

9. Incorporate the suggestions into the document.

10. Save your changes, close the document, and exit Word when you are finished.

Exercise 6

On the Job

You use tabs to align text in a document, such as the date in a modified-block business letter. If a letter is just a bit too long to fit on a single page, use *Shrink to Fit* to automatically reduce the printed length of a document so it fits on one page.

The Manager of the pro shop at the Michigan Avenue Athletic Club has asked you to type a letter to a supplier regarding an incomplete order. In this exercise, you compose a modified-block business letter using tabs, Shrink to Fit, and Full Screen view.

Terms

Tab A location (or measurement) you use to align text.

Tab leader A series of characters inserted along the line between the location of the insertion point when you press the Tab key and the tab stop.

Font A set of characters with a specific size and style.

Notes

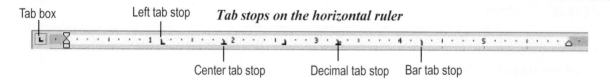

Tab stops on the horizontal ruler

Tab box · Left tab stop · Center tab stop · Decimal tab stop · Bar tab stop

Set Tabs

- **Tabs** are used to indent a single line of text.
- Each time you press the Tab key, the insertion point advances to the next set tab stop.
- There are five types of tab stops:
  - **⌊** Left: Text starts flush left with the tab stop.
  - **⌋** Right: Text ends flush right with the tab stop.
  - **⊥** Center: Text is centered on the tab stop.
  - **⊥** Decimal: Decimal points are aligned with the tab stop.
  - **⌶** Bar: A horizontal bar is displayed at the tab stop position. Text starts 1/10" to the right of the bar.
- By default, left tab stops are set every ½" on the horizontal ruler.
- You can set any type of tab stop at any point along the ruler.
- You can use the Tabs dialog box to set precise tab stops.

- You can also select a **tab leader** in the Tabs dialog box.

- You can set tabs before you type new text, for the current existing paragraph, or for selected multiple paragraphs.

- Once you set tabs, the formatting will be carried forward each time you press the Enter key to start a new paragraph.

Tabs dialog box

Format a Modified-Block Business Letter

- A modified-block style letter is set up with all lines starting flush with the left margin except the date, closing, signature, and title lines, which begin at the center point of the page.

  ✓ *The parts of a modified-block style letter are the same as those of a full-block style letter. The special notations are used when appropriate.*

- A left tab stop set at the center point of the page enables you to position the insertion point quickly where you need it.

  ✓ *Using a center tab stop or centered alignment centers the text; you must use a left tab stop in order to position the text to start at the center point of the page.*

Shrink to Fit

- Shrink to Fit automatically reduces the **font** size and spacing in a document just enough to fit the document on one less page.

- Use Shrink to Fit if the last page of a document contains only a small amount of text.

- The Shrink to Fit feature is available only in Print Preview mode.

Full Screen View

- In any view, including Print Preview, use Full Screen view to display a document without the title bar, toolbars, ruler, scroll bars, status bar, or taskbar.

- Full Screen view lets you see more of your document on-screen at one time.

Procedures

Set Tabs

To set a left tab stop:

1. Position insertion point in paragraph to format.
   OR
   Select paragraphs to format.
2. Click ruler where you want to set tab stop.

To set a different type of tab stop:

1. Position insertion point in paragraph to format.
   OR
   Select paragraphs to format.

2. Click the **Tab** box.

   ✓ *Each time you click, the tab stop icon on the tab box changes. Stop when tab stop you want is displayed.*

3. Click ruler where you want to insert new tab stop.

To set a precise tab stop:

1. Position insertion point in paragraph to format.
   OR
   Select paragraphs to format.

2. Click **Format** .... `Alt`+`O`

3. Click **Tabs** .... `T`
4. Select type of tab:
   - **Left** .... `Alt`+`L`
   - **Center** .... `Alt`+`C`
   - **Right** .... `Alt`+`R`
   - **Decimal** .... `Alt`+`D`
   - **Bar** .... `Alt`+`B`
5. Click in the **Tab stop position** .... `Alt`+`T`
6. Type precise position.
7. Click **OK** .... `Enter`

To select a tab leader:

1. Position insertion point in paragraph to format.
   OR
   Select paragraphs to format.
2. Click **Format** .... `Alt`+`O`
3. Click **Tabs** .... `T`
4. Select existing tab
   OR
   Set new tab
5. Select type of tab leader:
   - **1 None** .... `1`
   - **2** .... `2`
   - **3**------- .... `3`
   - **4** ____ .... `4`
6. Click **OK** .... `Enter`

To clear a tab stop:

1. Position insertion point in paragraph to format.
   OR
   Select paragraphs to format.
2. Drag tab stop marker off ruler.
   OR
1. Click **Format** .... `Alt`+`O`
2. Click **Tabs** .... `T`
3. Click **Clear All** .... `Alt`+`A`
   OR
   a. Select tab stop(s) to clear.
   b. Click **Clear** .... `Alt`+`E`
4. Click **OK** .... `Enter`

Format a Modified-Block Business Letter

1. Start 2" from top of page .... `Enter` **4x**
   - ✓ *Press Enter four times to leave 2" of space.*
   - ✓ *If you are using stationery with a printed letterhead, you may have to adjust the spacing.*
2. Set left tab stop at 3".
3. Press **Tab** .... `Tab`
4. Insert date.
5. Leave three blank lines and type inside address ..... `Enter` **4x**
6. Leave a blank line and type the salutation .... `Enter` **2x**
7. Leave a blank line and type the letter body .... `Enter` **2x**
8. Leave a blank line .... `Enter` **2x**
9. Press **Tab** .... `Tab`
10. Type the closing.
11. Leave three blank lines .... `Enter` **4x**
12. Press **Tab** .... `Tab`
13. Type signature line.
14. Move to next line and press **Tab** .... `Enter`, `Tab`
15. Type title line.
16. Leave a blank line and type reference initials .. `Enter` **2x**

Shrink to Fit

1. Click **Print Preview** button .
   OR
   a. Click **File** .... `Alt`+`F`
   b. Click **Print Preview** .... `V`
2. Click **Shrink to Fit** button .
3. Click **Close** button `Close` .

Full Screen View

1. Click **View** .... `Alt`+`V`
2. Click **Full Screen** .... `U`

To display screen elements again:

- Press **Esc** .... `Esc`
  OR
- Click **Close Full Screen** button 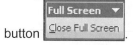 .

Exercise Directions

1. Start Word, if necessary.
2. Create a new document and save it as **ORDER**.
3. Type the letter shown in Illustration A.
   - ✓ *When you type the letter as shown in the illustration, it will not fit on a single page.*
   - Set a left tab stop at 3" on the ruler.
   - Position the date, closing, signature, and title at the tab stop.
   - Press the Enter key between parts of the letter as indicated.
   - Insert the current date using the MONTH DAY, YEAR format found third from the top in the Date and Time dialog box.
   - Set the date so that it does not update automatically.
4. Check the spelling and grammar and make changes as suggested.
   - Ignore all proper names.
5. Display the document in Print Preview.
6. Shrink the document to fit on a single page.
7. Display the document in Full Screen view.
8. Display the screen elements again.
9. Print the document.
10. Close the document, saving all changes.

Illustration A

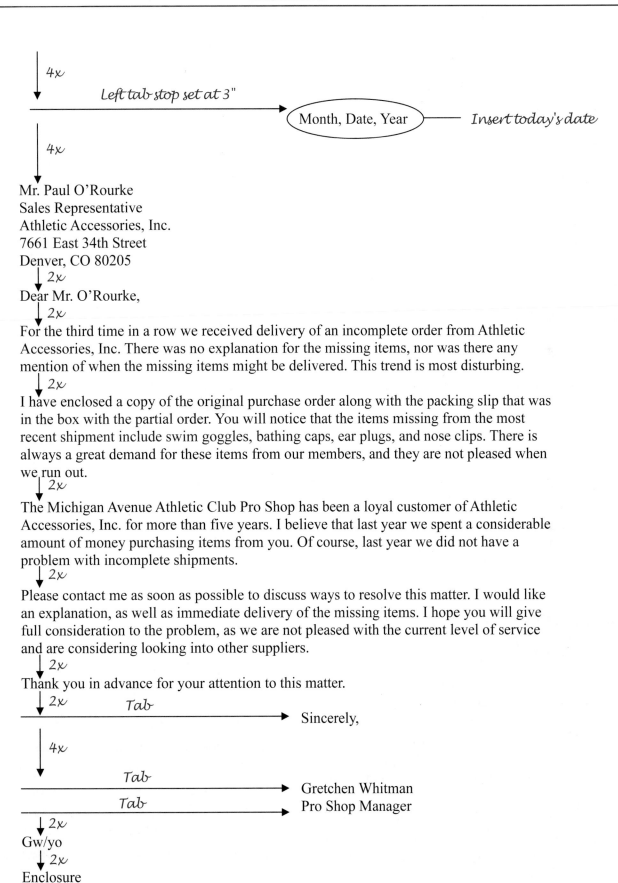

4x

Left tab stop set at 3"

Month, Date, Year — *Insert today's date*

4x

Mr. Paul O'Rourke
Sales Representative
Athletic Accessories, Inc.
7661 East 34th Street
Denver, CO 80205

2x

Dear Mr. O'Rourke,

2x

For the third time in a row we received delivery of an incomplete order from Athletic Accessories, Inc. There was no explanation for the missing items, nor was there any mention of when the missing items might be delivered. This trend is most disturbing.

2x

I have enclosed a copy of the original purchase order along with the packing slip that was in the box with the partial order. You will notice that the items missing from the most recent shipment include swim goggles, bathing caps, ear plugs, and nose clips. There is always a great demand for these items from our members, and they are not pleased when we run out.

2x

The Michigan Avenue Athletic Club Pro Shop has been a loyal customer of Athletic Accessories, Inc. for more than five years. I believe that last year we spent a considerable amount of money purchasing items from you. Of course, last year we did not have a problem with incomplete shipments.

2x

Please contact me as soon as possible to discuss ways to resolve this matter. I would like an explanation, as well as immediate delivery of the missing items. I hope you will give full consideration to the problem, as we are not pleased with the current level of service and are considering looking into other suppliers.

2x

Thank you in advance for your attention to this matter.

2x   *Tab*

Sincerely,

4x

Tab

Gretchen Whitman

Tab

Pro Shop Manager

2x

Gw/yo

2x

Enclosure

On Your Own

1. Create a new document in Word.
2. Save the file as **OWD06**.
3. As a representative of a school organization, draft a modified-block business letter to a company that sells music CDs by mail telling the company that your organization did not receive the complete order in the last shipment.
4. List the music CDs that you ordered and indicate which titles were missing in the shipment.
5. Preview the document. Make sure it fits on one page.
6. Display the document in Full Screen view.
7. Change back to display all screen elements.
8. Print one copy of the document.
9. Ask someone in your class to read the letter and to provide comments and suggestions.
10. Incorporate the suggestions into the document.
11. Close the document, saving all changes.

Exercise 7

Skills Covered:

◆ **Format a Personal Business Letter** ◆ **Select Fonts**
◆ **Change Font Size** ◆ **Apply Font Styles** ◆ **Apply Underlines**
◆ **Create Envelopes** ◆ **Create Labels**

On the Job

Write personal business letters to find a job or communicate with businesses such as your bank or your insurance company. For example, you might write a personal business letter to your insurance company to ask about a claim that needs to be paid. The letter serves as a formal record of your inquiry. To send it, you need to print an accompanying envelope or label. Use fonts, font sizes, underlines, and font styles to dress up the appearance of a document. Fonts are a basic means of applying formatting to text and characters. They can set a mood, command attention, and convey a message.

You are interested in obtaining a position as a tour guide for Voyager Travel Adventures. In this exercise, you will create and format a personal business letter asking about job opportunities. You will also create an envelope you could use to mail the letter and return address labels which you will save in a separate document. Finally, you will create a **resume** to include with the letter.

Terms

Resume A document listing information about a person's education, work experience, and interests.

Return address The author's address, typically appearing at the very top of the letter as well as in the upper-left corner of an envelope.

Letterhead Paper with a company's name and address already printed on it.

Font A complete set of characters in a specific face, style, and size.

Font face The character design of a font set.

Serif A font that has curved or extended edges.

Sans serif A font that has straight edges.

Script A font that looks like handwriting.

Font size The height of an uppercase letter in a font set.

Font style The slant and weight of characters in a font set.

Delivery address The recipient's address printed on the outside of an envelope.

Notes

Format a Personal Business Letter

■ A business letter written on behalf of an individual instead of on behalf of another business is considered a personal business letter.

■ A personal business letter includes the same elements as a business letter, minus the title line and reference initials, and plus a **return address**.

✓ *If the paper has a **letterhead**, omit the return address.*

- A personal business letter can be full block or modified block.
  - In full block, type the return address following the signature.
  - In modified block, type the return address above the date.
    - ✓ *For more information on the parts of a business letter, refer to Exercise 5.*

Select Fonts

- Each **font** set includes upper- and lowercase letters, numbers, and punctuation marks.
- There are three basic categories of **font faces**:
  - **Serif** fonts are easy to read and are often used for document text.

A Serif Font

  - **Sans serif** fonts are often used for headings.

A Sans Serif Font

  - **Script** face fonts are often used to simulate handwriting on invitations or announcements.

A Script Font

- A fourth font category includes decorative fonts which may have embellishments such as curlicues or double lines designed to dress up or enhance the characters.

A Decorative Font

- The default Word font is Times New Roman, a serif font.
- The current font name is displayed in the Font box on the Formatting toolbar.
- Click the Font box drop-down arrow to display a menu of all available fonts. The fonts appear in alphabetical order, but recently used fonts are listed at the top.

Font list

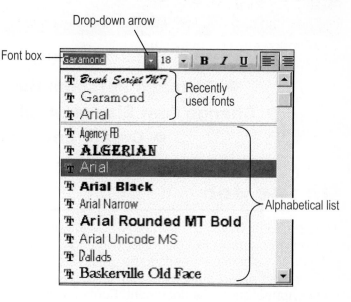

- Both Microsoft Office and Windows come with built-in fonts; you can install additional fonts.
- Fonts can be changed before or after you enter text in a document.
- You can set the tone of a document by putting thought into the fonts you select.
  - ✓ *More than two or three font faces makes a document look disjointed and unprofessional.*

Change Font Size

- **Font size** is measured in points. There are 72 points in an inch.
- The default Word font size is 12 points.
- The current font size is displayed in the Font Size box on the Formatting toolbar.
- Click the Font Size drop-down arrow to display a menu of font sizes.

Font Size list

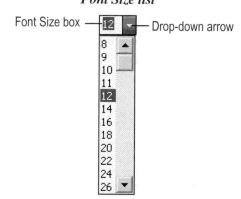

Apply Font Styles

■ The most common **font styles** are **bold** and *italic*.

■ When no style is applied to a font, it is called regular.

  ✓ *Font styles can be combined for different effects, such as bold italic.*

Apply Underlines

■ There are 17 types of underlines available in Word, which include:

  • Single (underlines all characters, including nonprinting characters such as spaces and tabs)

  • Words only

  • Double

  • Dotted

  • Thick

  • Dash

  • Dot dash

  • Dot dot dash

  • Wave

The Font dialog box lets you select a font, font size, font style, and underline at the same time

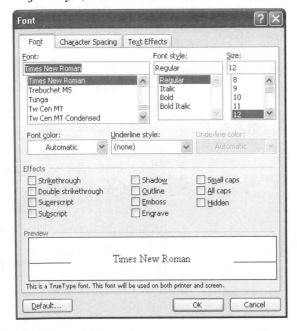

Create Envelopes

■ Word has a feature that automatically sets up an envelope for printing.

■ If a letter document is open on-screen, Word picks up the inside address for the envelope's **delivery address**.

■ You can print the envelope immediately or add it to the beginning of the open document and save it to print later.

The Envelopes tab of the Envelopes and Labels dialog box

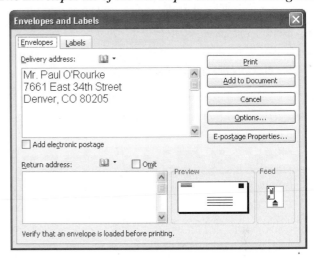

Create Labels

■ Use the Label feature to create mailing labels, file folder labels, or diskette labels.

■ The Label feature automatically sets up a document to print on predefined label types.

■ You select the manufacturer and label type loaded in the printer.

■ By default, Word creates a full page of labels using the inside address from the current document.

■ You can change the default to create labels using the return address or to create a single label.

The Labels tab of the Envelopes and Labels dialog box

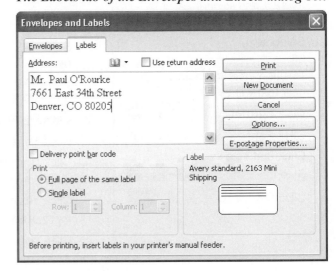

Procedures

Select Font

1. Select text.
   OR
   Position insertion point where new text will be typed.
2. Click **Font** drop-down arrow.
3. Click font name .... `↓`, `Enter`
   - ✓ *The font list is alphabetical; however, recently used fonts are listed at the top of the list.*

OR

1. Select text.
   OR
   Position insertion point where new text will be typed.
2. Click **F**ormat .... `Alt`+`O`
3. Click **F**ont .... `F`
4. Click font name in **F**ont list .... `↓`
5. Click **OK** .... `Enter`

Change Font Size

1. Select text.
   OR
   Position insertion point where new text will be typed.
2. Click **Font Size** drop-down arrow.
3. Click font size .... `↓`, `Enter`
   - ✓ *You can also type desired font size directly into Font Size box, then press Enter. You can even type half sizes, such as 10.5, 12.5, and so on.*

OR

1. Select text.
   OR
   Position insertion point where new text will be typed.
2. Click **F**ormat .... `Alt`+`O`
3. Click **F**ont .... `F`
4. Click font size in **S**ize list .... `Alt`+`S`, `↓`
5. Click **OK** .... `Enter`

Apply Font Styles

1. Select text.
   OR
   Position insertion point where new text will be typed.
2. Click font style button:
   - **Bold** `B` .... `Ctrl`+`B`
   - **Italic** `I` .... `Ctrl`+`I`
   - ✓ *To remove font styles repeat steps 1 and 2.*

OR

1. Select text.
   OR
   Position insertion point where new text will be typed.
2. Click **F**ormat .... `Alt`+`O`
3. Click **F**ont .... `F`
4. Click font style in **F**ont style list .... `Alt`+`Y`, `↓`
   - ✓ *To remove font styles click Regular.*
5. Click **OK** .... `Enter`

Apply Underlines (*Ctrl+U*)

1. Select text.
   OR
   Position insertion point where new text will be typed.
2. Click **U**nderline button `U` .... `Alt`+`U`
   - ✓ *Repeat steps to remove underline.*

OR

1. Select text.
   OR
   Position insertion point where new text will be typed.
2. Click **F**ormat .... `Alt`+`O`
3. Click **F**ont .... `F`
4. Click **U**nderline style drop-down arrow .... `Alt`+`U`
5. Click desired underline type.
   - ✓ *Click (None) to remove underline.*
6. Click **OK** .... `Enter`

Create an Envelope

1. Click **T**ools .... `Alt`+`T`
2. Click **L**etters and Mailings .... `E`
3. Click **E**nvelopes and Labels .... `E`
4. Click **E**nvelopes tab ... `Alt`+`E`
5. Type **D**elivery address .... `Alt`+`D`
   - ✓ *If inside address is already entered, skip to step 6.*
6. Type **R**eturn address .... `Alt`+`R`
   OR
   Select **O**mit checkbox .... `Alt`+`M`
   - ✓ *If Omit checkbox is selected, you cannot type in Return address text box.*
7. Click **P**rint button `Print` .. `Alt`+`P`
   OR
   Select **A**dd to Document .... `Alt`+`A`

Create a Single Label

1. Click **T**ools .... `Alt`+`T`
2. Click **L**etters and Mailings .... `E`
3. Click **E**nvelopes and Labels .... `E`
4. Click **L**abels tab .... `Alt`+`L`
5. Click **Si**ngle label option .... `Alt`+`N`
6. Click **O**ptions .... `O`
7. Select option from **L**abel products list .... `Alt`+`P`
8. Select option from **P**roduct number list .... `Alt`+`U`
   - ✓ *Make sure correct printer and tray information is selected.*
9. Click **OK** .... `Enter`

10. Type **label text**.
    - ✓ *If inside address is already entered, skip to 11.*

11. Make sure labels are loaded in printer.

12. Click **Print** button
    [Print] .. Alt + P

Create Return Address Labels

1. Click **Tools** .... Alt + T

2. Click **Letters and Mailings** .... E

3. Click **Envelopes and Labels** .... E

4. Click **Labels** tab .... Alt + L

5. Select **Use return address** checkbox .... Alt + R

6. Click **Options** .... Alt + O

7. Select option from **Label products** list............... Alt + P

8. Select option from **Product number** list................. Alt + U
    - ✓ *Make sure the correct printer and tray information is selected.*

9. Click **OK** .... Enter
    - ✓ *Make sure labels are loaded in printer.*

10. Click **Print** button
    [Print] . Alt + P
    OR
    a. Click **New Document** .... Alt + D
    b. If prompted to save the return address, click **No** .. N
    c. Click **Save** button 💾 to save labels.

Exercise Directions

Create the Letter

1. Start Word, if necessary.

2. Create a new document and save it as **REQUEST**.

3. Type the letter shown in Illustration A.
   - Use the full-block format for the letter.
   - Insert today's date using the Month Date, Year format. Make sure the date will not update automatically.
   - Use the default font and font size.

4. Check the spelling and grammar.

Create the Envelope

1. Create an envelope for the letter.
   - Use your name and address as the return address.

2. Add the envelope to the document.
   - When prompted to save the new return address as the default, choose No.

3. Preview the document.

4. Print the document.

5. Save the changes to the document.

Create the Labels

1. Create return address labels for the document.
   a. Use the return address in the document.
   b. Create a full page of the same label.
   c. Save the label document as **LABELS**.
   - ✓ *Do not save the return address as the default.*

2. Preview the new label document.

3. Print the label document.
   - ✓ *You can print the labels on standard letter-sized paper if you do not have labels available.*

4. Close the label document, saving all changes.

5. Close the letter document, saving all changes.

Create the Resume

1. Create a new document and save it as **RESUME**.

2. Type the document shown in Illustration B.

3. Apply font formatting, tabs, and alignments as marked.
   - ✓ *Unless otherwise marked, use the default 12-point Times New Roman font.*

4. Leave one blank line between each section as shown.

5. Preview the **RESUME** document. If necessary, shrink the document to fit on a single page.

6. Print the document.

7. Close the **RESUME** document, saving all changes.

41

Your Street Address
Your City, Your State, Your Postal Code

Today's date

Ms. Maria Sanchez
President
Voyager Travel Adventures
1635 Logan Street
Denver, CO 80205

Dear Ms. Sanchez:

I am writing to inquire about tour leader opportunities at Voyager Travel Adventures. I recently graduated from the state university with a degree in recreational management and a minor in business administration. I am looking for a position that will challenge my abilities both physically and mentally, and I believe that Voyager Travel Adventures offers just that.

While studying for my degree, I worked as a trip leader for teen adventure tours during the summer and school vacations. I also worked as a lifeguard for the city and volunteered as a youth counselor at a local outdoor education facility. I believe that my experience and positive outlook on life combined with my knowledge of nature and first aid make me uniquely suited for a job at your company.

I am available to begin work immediately and would love to schedule an appointment for an interview at your earliest convenience. Please refer to my enclosed resume for additional information.

I look forward to hearing from you soon.

Sincerely,

Your Name

Enc.

Illustration B

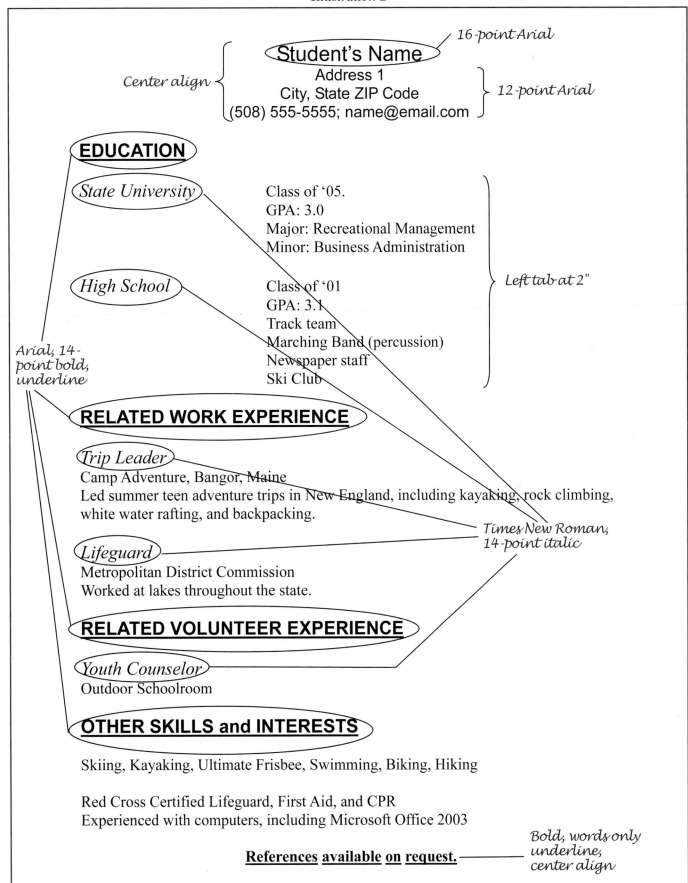

16-point Arial

Student's Name

Center align

Address 1
City, State ZIP Code
(508) 555-5555; name@email.com

12-point Arial

EDUCATION

State University

Class of '05.
GPA: 3.0
Major: Recreational Management
Minor: Business Administration

Left tab at 2"

High School

Class of '01
GPA: 3.1
Track team
Marching Band (percussion)
Newspaper staff
Ski Club

Arial, 14-point bold, underline

RELATED WORK EXPERIENCE

Trip Leader

Camp Adventure, Bangor, Maine
Led summer teen adventure trips in New England, including kayaking, rock climbing, white water rafting, and backpacking.

Lifeguard

Metropolitan District Commission
Worked at lakes throughout the state.

Times New Roman, 14-point italic

RELATED VOLUNTEER EXPERIENCE

Youth Counselor

Outdoor Schoolroom

OTHER SKILLS and INTERESTS

Skiing, Kayaking, Ultimate Frisbee, Swimming, Biking, Hiking

Red Cross Certified Lifeguard, First Aid, and CPR
Experienced with computers, including Microsoft Office 2003

References available on request.

Bold, words only underline, center align

On Your Own

1. Create a new document in Word.

2. Save the file as **OWD07**.

3. Draft a personal business letter. For example, you might write a letter asking about summer job opportunities. If you have a job, you could write to your employer asking to take a vacation day in the coming month. You can also draft a personal letter to a company with whom you do business asking for a credit on returned merchandise or to a college asking about application requirements. Record stores, clothing stores, or sporting goods stores are companies you might use.

   ✓ *If smart tag indicators are displayed, you can ignore them or turn them off. To turn them off, Click Tools, and then click AutoCorrect Options. Click the Smart Tags tab and deselect the Label text with smart tags check box. Click OK to close the dialog box and continue working.*

4. Ask a classmate to review the letter and offer comments and suggestions. Incorporate the comments and suggestions into the document.

5. Create an envelope for your letter and attach it to the document.

6. Create your own mailing labels using the return address from your letter, and save them in a separate document with the name **OWD07-2**.

7. Check the spelling and grammar before printing the documents.

8. Save your changes, close all open documents, and exit Word when you are finished.

Exercise 8

You are the manager of the café at Michigan Avenue Athletic Club. On a recent trip to California you ate at a Whole Grains Bread franchise, and you are interested in offering some of their products at your café. In this exercise, you will start by creating a business letter proposing the idea to the sales manager at Whole Grains Bread. Next, you will create an envelope for the letter along with return address labels. Finally, you will create a flyer about the café that you can attach to the letter. You will use alignments and font formatting to make the flyer visually exciting.

Exercise Directions

Create the Letter

1. Start Word, if necessary.
2. Create a new document and save it as **PROPOSAL**.
3. Display nonprinting characters.
4. Make sure AutoCorrect is on.
5. Type the letter in Illustration A exactly as shown, including all circled errors.
   - ✓ *Notice that AutoCorrect automatically inserts the accent when you type the word* **café**.
6. Insert the date in the Month Date, Year format so that it does not update automatically.
7. Correct spelling and grammatical errors.
   - Add your name to the dictionary, if necessary.
   - Ignore all proper names.
   - If necessary, correct all spelling errors that AutoCorrect does not automatically change.
8. Search the thesaurus to find an appropriate replacement for the word **assortment**.
9. Save the changes you have made to the document.
10. Display the document in Print Preview.
11. Display the document in Full Screen view.
12. Return the document to Normal view.

Create an Envelope and Labels

1. Create an envelope for the letter and add it to the document. Omit the return address.
2. Print the document.

3. Close the document, saving all changes.
4. Create return address mailing labels for yourself using the following information:

   > **Your Name**
   > **Café Manager**
   > **Michigan Avenue Athletic Club**
   > **235 Michigan Avenue**
   > **Chicago, IL 60601**

5. Save the labels document with the name **RETURN**.
6. Display the **RETURN** document in Print Preview, and then print it.
   - ✓ *If you do not have labels available, print it on regular paper.*
7. Close the **RETURN** document, saving all changes.

Create a Flyer

1. Create a new document.
2. Save the document as **FLYER**.
3. Display nonprinting characters.
4. Type the document shown in Illustration B, using the specified alignments, font formatting, and tabs.
5. Check the spelling and grammar in the document.
6. Display the document in Print Preview.
7. If the document is longer than one page, shrink it to fit; if it is shorter than one page, adjust the vertical alignment to improve the appearance, as necessary.

8. Print the document.

9. Share the flyer with a classmate and ask for comments and suggestions.

10. Incorporate the comments and suggestions into the document.

11. Close the document, saving all changes.

Illustration A

Today's date —————— *Insert the date in month, date, year format*

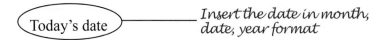

Ms. Carol Chen
Sales Manager
Whole Grains Bread
320 Magnolia Avenue
Larkspur, CA 94939

Dear Ms. Chen:

On a recent trip to California I had the good fortune of eating in a Whole Grains Bread restarant. I was quite impressed with the quality and assortment of the the food, as well as with the atmosphere and the service. The franchise owner gave me your name and address along with the information that you may be interested in expanding outside the california area.

As the managers of an athletic club café that prides itself on ofering healthy yet satisfying food, I is very interested in learning more about the Whole Grains Bread product line. If possible, I would like very much to carry some of your items in our café ALternatively, we may be interested in becoming a frenchise.

I have attached a flyer that we use to advertise specials and events to our members so that you can see some of the items we have now and how we market them. I think the flyer illustrates the spirit and enthusiesm of our club.

I looks forward to hearing from you soon,

Sincerely,

Your Name
Café Manager

Attachment

The MAAC Café
Great Food! Reasonable Price!

Specializing in:

Light Meals
Healthy Snacks
Smoothies
Fat-free Desserts

Friendly

Reliable

Fast

Affordable

Open for breakfast, lunch, and dinner
Menus change often, so check the board daily

Fresh Fruit   Fresh Salad
Frozen Yogurt   Bagels
Muffins   Sandwiches

Hours: 7:30 a.m. until 9:30 p.m. MAAC café is located on the main concourse overlooking the racquetball courts.

Exercise 9

Skills Covered:

◆ **Use Proofreaders' Marks** ◆ **Open a Saved Document**
◆ **Open a Recently Saved Document** ◆ **Insert and Edit Text**
◆ **Use Overtype Mode** ◆ **Save a Document with a New Name**

On the Job

When you are ready to revise or improve a document that you've already created and saved, open it again in Word. Use the Save As command to save a copy of the document with a new name or in a new location. For example, you might need to write a letter that is similar to one you wrote earlier. Instead of starting from scratch, you can open the original letter, save it as a new document, then edit it.

As the Office Manager for Michigan Avenue Athletic Club, you have decided that you need to revise the press release that you wrote earlier regarding the new personal trainer who has joined the staff. In this exercise, you will open the press release document and save it with a new name. You will then revise the document and save the changes. Finally, you will print the document.

Terms

Proofreaders' marks Symbols written on a printed document by a copyeditor or proofreader to indicate where revisions are required.

Places bar A strip of buttons on the left side of certain dialog boxes used to open common folders quickly.

Insert mode The method of operation used for inserting new text within existing text in a document. Insert mode is the default.

Overtype mode The method of operation used to replace existing text in a document with new text.

Notes

Use Proofreaders' Marks

■ Often, you may need to revise a Word document based on a marked-up printed copy of the document. **Proofreaders' marks** on printed documents are written symbols that indicate where to make revisions.

■ Following is a list of common proofreaders' marks:

• 〰〰〰 indicates text to be bold.

• ∧ indicates where new text should be inserted.

• ⟿ indicates text to be deleted.

• ⸗ indicates where a new paragraph should be inserted.

• ≡ indicates that a letter should be capitalized.

• _____ or ⟨ital⟩ indicates text to be italicized.

• ⟨highlight⟩ indicates text to highlight.

•][indicates text to center.

✓ *There are many other common proofreading symbols. You can find a list in Webster's Collegiate Dictionary, or The Chicago Manual of Style.*

Open a Saved Document

■ To revise a Word document that has been saved and closed, open it again in Word.

■ Use the Open dialog box to locate files that you want to open.

Current folder

Open dialog box

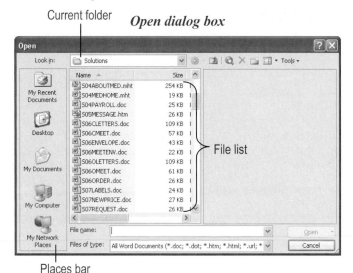

Places bar

File list

Open a Recently Saved Document

■ The four most-recently used Word documents are listed at the bottom of the File menu and in the Open section on the Getting Started task pane.

✓ *The listed file names may also include the complete path to the file, which means the folder and/or disk where the file is stored. Since you can have a file with the same name stored in different locations, be sure you select the one you really want to open.*

Open saved documents from the File menu

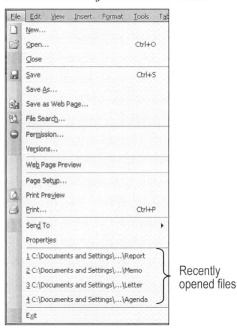

Recently opened files

■ You can also display a list of shortcuts to recently used files and folder in the Open dialog box.

✓ *Recently used documents of all types may be listed on the My Recent Documents menu in Windows. Open the Start menu, click My Recent Documents, then click the document you want to open.*

Insert and Edit Text

■ By default, you insert new text in a document in **Insert mode**. Existing text moves to the right as you type to make room for new text.

■ You can insert text anywhere in a document.

■ You can also insert nonprinting characters, including paragraph marks to start a new paragraph, tabs, and spaces.

Use Overtype Mode

■ To replace text as you type, use **Overtype mode**.

■ In Overtype mode, existing characters do not shift right to make room for new characters. Instead, new characters replace existing characters as you type, deleting existing characters.

■ Most editing should be done in Insert mode, so you do not accidentally type over text that you need.

Save a Document with a New Name

■ The Save As feature lets you save a copy of a document in a different location or with a different file name.

■ Use the Save As command to leave the original document unchanged while you edit the new copy.

Save As dialog box

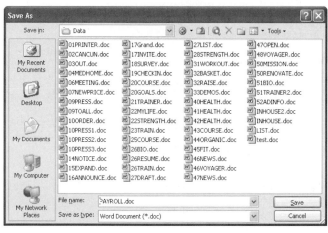

Procedures

Open a Saved Document
(Ctrl+O)

1. Click **Open** button ☐.
   OR
   a. Click **File**............... `Alt`+`F`
   b. Click **Open**..................... `O`
2. Click **Look** in
   drop-down arrow .... `Alt`+`I`
3. Select drive or folder.
   - ✓ *If necessary double-click folder name.*
   OR
   Click folder in Places Bar to open it.
4. Double-click document name.
   OR
   a. Click document name.
   b. Click **Open**..................... `O`

Open a Recently Saved Document

1. Click **File**..................... `Alt`+`F`
2. Click document name at bottom of menu.
   OR
1. Click **View**..................... `Alt`+`V`
2. Click **Task Pane** .... `K`
   - ✓ *If the Getting Started task pane is not displayed, select it from the Other Task Panes drop-down list.*
3. Click document name at top of task pane.

Insert Text

1. Position insertion point to right of character where you want to insert new text.
2. Type new text.

Overtype mode

1. Position insertion point to left of first character you want to replace.
2. Press **Insert** key................. `Ins`
   OR
   Double-click **OVR**
   indicator `OVR`.
   - ✓ *OVR indicator appears in bold when active.*
3. Type new text.

To turn off Overtype mode:

- Press **Insert** key again....... `Ins`
  OR
- Double-click **OVR** indicator
  `OVR` again.
  - ✓ *OVR indicator appears dimmed when inactive.*

Save a Document with a New Name

1. Click **File** .... `Alt`+`F`
2. Click **Save As** .... `A`
3. Type new file name.
4. Select new drive and/or folder.
5. Click **Save**
   button [Save].

Exercise Directions

1. Start Word, if necessary.
2. Open ⌨**PRESS** or open 💿**09PRESS**.
   - ✓ *If necessary, ask your instructor where this file is located.*
3. Save the file as **NEWPRESS**.
4. Make the revisions as indicated by the proofreaders' marks in Illustration A.
   a. Insert new text as marked.
   b. Replace text as marked.
   c. Apply font styles as marked.
   d. Insert your own name in place of the text **Your Name**.
5. Check the spelling and grammar.
6. Print the document.
7. Close the document, saving all changes.

Illustration A

Enter 4X

For Immediate Release *(bold)*

Enter 2X

Contact:——▶Your Name — Left tab at set at 1"

——▶312-555-3521 — *Italics*

Enter 4X

David Fairmont Joins Michigan Avenue Athletic Club

Bold

Chicago, IL-- Michigan Avenue Athletic Club is pleased to announce that David Fairmont has joined our staff as a personal trainer. Mr. Fairmont holds a master's degree in health management from the University of Vermont in Burlington, Vermont. He is a licensed personal trainer with extensive experience in cardiovascular health.

He is also fluent in Spanish, and he enjoys mountain biking in his spare time.

Michigan Avenue Athletic Club is a full-service athletic facility ~~conveniently~~ located in downtown Chicago. The facility includes racquetball and tennis courts, an indoor pool, *five* ~~multiple~~ exercise rooms, and a vast array of equipment for individual use and group lessons. We also offer spa services, a pro shop, and a café.

For more information about David Fairmont or membership in our club, please ~~call~~ *contact Your Name at* 312-555-3521, or visit us on the Web at www.michaveclub.com.

¶In addition to our athletic facilities, the club sponsors social gatherings and supports many local charities.

On Your Own

1. Open **OWD06**, the document you created in the On Your Own section of Exercise 6, or open **09LETTER**.

2. Save the file as **OWD09**.

3. Make revisions to the document using Insert mode and Overtype mode.

4. Check the spelling and grammar in the document.

5. Print the document.

6. If possible, exchange the printed document with a classmate.

7. Use proofreader's marks to indicate at least three changes to the document. For example, apply font styles or replace text.

8. Retrieve your document and make the changes as marked.

9. Close the document, saving all changes.

Exercise 10

◆ **Use Split Screen View**
◆ **Open Multiple Documents at the Same Time**
◆ **Arrange Documents On-screen** ◆ **Compare Documents Side by Side**

On the Job

Use Split Screen view to see different sections of the same document on-screen at the same time. For example, you may want to see a table of contents at the beginning of a document while you work in a section at the end of the document. Open multiple documents when you need to work with more than one document at a time. For example, if you are planning a meeting, you may need to work with an agenda and a list of attendees at the same time.

As an assistant at the Michigan Avenue Athletic Club, you often have many different tasks to attend to at the same time. Today, the Pro Shop Manager has asked you to modify a letter to a supplier regarding an incomplete order, and the General Manager has asked you to make sure the correct version of a press release about a new personal trainer is sent out. Both managers want the tasks completed as soon as possible, but the letter to the supplier must go out today, while the press release will not be issued until tomorrow. In order to be successful, you must demonstrate productive work habits and attitudes such as dependability and punctuality. You must also stay organized and learn to prioritize your tasks.

In this exercise, you will first open the letter to the supplier and use Split Screen view to make the necessary changes. You will save the changes and print the letter along with an envelope. When the letter is complete, you will move on to the press release. You will arrange all versions of the press release on-screen and select the two you believe are the most accurate. You will then compare the two side by side to determine which is correct. You will then print the correct press release.

Terms

Active document The document in which the insertion point is currently located. Commands and actions occur in the active document.

Tile Arrange windows so they do not overlap on-screen.

Synchronous scrolling A feature that links the scroll bars in two windows so that when you scroll in one window the other window scrolls as well.

Independent scrolling The ability to scroll a window without affecting the display in other open windows.

Notes

Use Split Screen View

- Split the screen into two panes so you can see and work in different sections of a single document.

- Word tiles the panes one above the other within the program window.

- Each pane has its own scroll bars so you can scroll each section independently from the other.

- Each pane also has its own rulers.

- There is only one menu bar, one title bar, and one set of toolbars.

- Commands affect the active pane. For example, you can change the zoom in the top pane without affecting the bottom pane.

- You can make edits and formatting changes in either pane.

- Use the mouse to move the insertion point from one pane to the other.

One document in Split Screen view

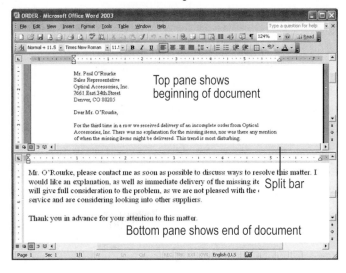

Open Multiple Document at the Same Time

- You can open multiple Word documents at the same time.

- By default, each open document is represented by a button on the Windows taskbar.

- However, if there is not enough room on the taskbar to show all buttons, they are grouped into one Word button.

- By default, the **active document** is displayed on-screen while other open documents are hidden.

- Only one document can be active at a time. You can identify the active document window by the following:

  - The active document contains the insertion point.

  - The active document window has a brighter colored title bar than other open document windows.

  - The active document window is represented by the "pressed in" taskbar button.

Arrange Documents On-screen

- You can arrange all open documents on-screen at the same time.

- Word **tiles** up to three open documents one above the other.

- If there are more than three open documents, Word fits them on-screen by tiling some of them side by side as well.

- The more open documents there are, the smaller each document window is on-screen. Therefore, editing with more than two documents arranged on-screen may be difficult.

  ✓ *To keep a document from being arranged on-screen with other open documents, minimize it.*

Active title bar

Multiple documents tiled on-screen

Compare Documents Side by Side

- You can select to compare the active document with another open document by arranging them side by side.

- By default, both windows are set to use **synchronous scrolling**, but you can use **independent scrolling** of you want.

- Changes you make to the view in one window affect the other window as well.

- If the windows move or are resized on the desktop, you can reset their position to side by side.

Compare documents side by side

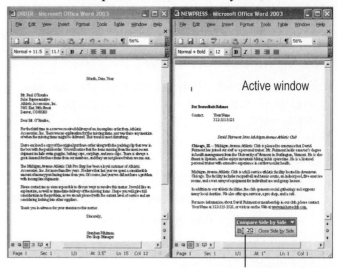

Compare Side by Side toolbar

Procedures

Open Split Screen View

- Double-click **Split box** at top of vertical scroll bar.

OR

1. Click **Window** .... Alt + W
2. Click **Split** .... S

   ✓ *Mouse pointer changes to a resizing pointer and a dark gray bar extends horizontally across the screen.*

3. Click at location where you want to split the screen.

Remove Split Screen View:

- Double-click **Split bar** that divides window.

OR

1. Click **Window** .... Alt + W
2. Click **Remove Split** .... S

Resize Split Screen Panes:

1. Position mouse pointer so it touches **Split bar**.

   ✓ *Pointer changes to a resizing pointer.*

2. Press and hold **left mouse button**.

3. Drag **Split bar** up or down to desired position.

Open Multiple Documents
(Ctrl+O)

1. Open first document.
2. Open second document.
3. Continue opening documents as desired.

Arrange Documents on Screen

1. Open all documents.
2. Click **Window** .... Alt + W
3. Click **Arrange All** .... A

Display active document only:

- Click active document's **Maximize** button 🔲.

Switch among open documents:

1. Click **Window** .... Alt + W
2. Click desired document name.

OR

- Click in desired document window.

OR

- Press Ctrl + F6 until desired document is active.

OR

- Click taskbar button representing desired document.

   ✓ *If there is a group taskbar button, click the button, then click desired document.*

Compare Documents Side by Side

1. Open both documents.
2. Click **Window** .... Alt + W
3. Click **Compare Side by Side with** *documentname* .... B

If more than two documents are open:

1. Click **Window** .... Alt + W
2. Click **Compare Side by Side with** .... B
3. Click name of file to compare .... ↓
4. Click **OK** .... Enter

Toggle Synchronous Scrolling:

- Click **Synchronous Scrolling** button 🔛 on Compare Side by Side toolbar.

   ✓ *If button is highlighted, synchronous scrolling is set. Click it again to allow independent scrolling.*

Reset Windows:

- Click **Resets Window Position** button 🔛 on Compare Side by Side toolbar.

Remove side by side arrangement:

1. Click **Window** .... Alt + W
2. Click **Close Side by Side** ... B

OR

- Click **Close Side by Side** [Close Side by Side] on Compare Side by Side toolbar.

Exercise Directions

Letter

1. Start Word, if necessary.
2. Open ☺ **10ORDER**.
3. Save the file as **ORDER2**.
4. Change the date to today's date.
5. Display the document in Split Screen view.
6. Adjust the zoom in the top pane to Page Width.
7. Adjust the contents of the top pane to display from the inside address through the first paragraph of the letter.
8. Click in the bottom pane and adjust the zoom to Text Width.
9. Scroll down in the bottom pane until you see the paragraph beginning **Please contact me as soon as possible...**
10. Insert the recipient's name at the beginning of the sentence. Refer to the information in the top pane to make sure you use the correct name and spelling.
11. Use correct grammar and punctuation. For example, make sure to include a comma after the name and to change the uppercase **P** at the beginning of the sentence to lowercase. When you have made the changes, your screen should look similar to Illustration A.
12. Remove the split screen.
13. Check the spelling and grammar in the document.
14. Preview the document.
15. Create an envelope for the document and add it to the letter. Omit the return address.
16. Print the document.
17. Close the document, saving all changes.

Press Release

1. In Word, open the file ☺ **10PRESS1**.
2. Open the file ☺ **10PRESS2**.
3. Open the file ☺ **10PRESS3**.
4. Arrange all three documents on the screen.
5. Make **10PRESS1** active. This is clearly the oldest of the three. It does not have as much information or detail as the others.
6. Close **10PRESS1** without saving any changes.
7. Arrange the remaining two documents on the screen.
8. Make **10PRESS2** active.
9. Select to compare it side by side with **10PRESS3**.
10. Set the zoom of **10PRESS3** to Text Width. Your screen should look similar to Illustration B.
11. The press releases look similar, but are not exactly the same. Read one and then the other to determine which is more complete.
12. If necessary, adjust the zoom to increase the size of the text on-screen.
13. Close the side by side display.
14. Close **10PRESS3** without saving any changes.
15. Save **10PRESS2** as **FINALPRESS**.
16. Maximize the document. Replace the text Your Name with your name in both locations.
17. Check the spelling and grammar in the document.
18. Preview the document.
19. Print the document.
20. Close the document, saving all changes.

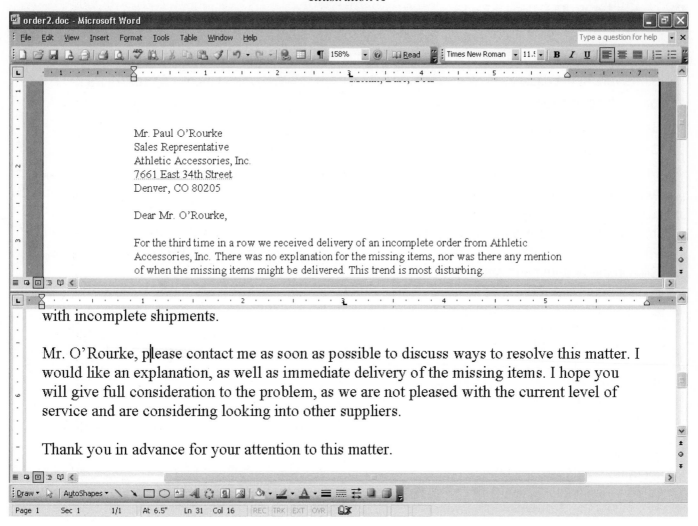

Mr. Paul O'Rourke
Sales Representative
Athletic Accessories, Inc.
7661 East 34th Street
Denver, CO 80205

Dear Mr. O'Rourke,

For the third time in a row we received delivery of an incomplete order from Athletic Accessories, Inc. There was no explanation for the missing items, nor was there any mention of when the missing items might be delivered. This trend is most disturbing.

with incomplete shipments.

Mr. O'Rourke, please contact me as soon as possible to discuss ways to resolve this matter. I would like an explanation, as well as immediate delivery of the missing items. I hope you will give full consideration to the problem, as we are not pleased with the current level of service and are considering looking into other suppliers.

Thank you in advance for your attention to this matter.

Illustration B

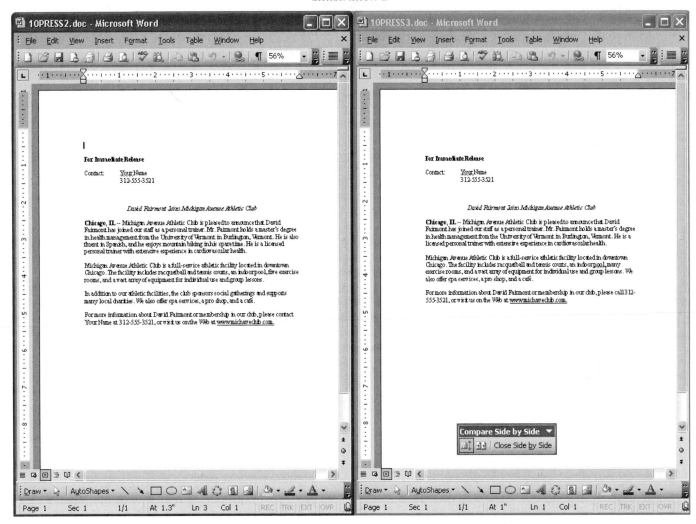

On Your Own

1. Look around your classroom and note the types of technology that you have available. For example, the hardware may include desktop computers, printers, networks drives, CD-ROM drives, monitors, keyboards, and so on. The software may include the Microsoft Office 2003 programs as well as other programs.

2. In addition, consider how each item is used for a different purpose or to accomplish specific tasks.

3. Create a new document in Word.

4. Save the document as **OWD10**.

5. Create a document listing the available hardware and software and the appropriate use for each item.

   ✓ *For example, you might use an inkjet printer for printing color documents. You might have a floppy disk drive for storing small files that you need to take to a different computer. You use Word to create text-based documents and PowerPoint to create presentations.*

6. Include a heading for the entire document, such as Available Technology, and headings for each category: hardware and software.

7. Use tabs to separate the items on the left from the appropriate tasks on the right.

8. As your list gets longer, use Split Screen View to make sure you don't duplicate items that you have already entered.

9. When you believe the list is complete, check the spelling and grammar and then print the document.

10. Close the document, saving all changes.

11. Get together with a classmate who also completed the assignment.

12. Open both your document and his or her document in Word.

13. Working together, compare the two documents side by side to see if you have missing items, or have incorrect information about appropriate usage.

14. Using a different font or font style, make changes to the documents as necessary.

   ✓ *With the different font, you'll be able to see the information you had originally, and the information you added based on your collaboration with a classmate.*

15. Close all open documents, saving all changes.

Exercise 11

Skills Covered:

◆ **Move Text** ◆ **Use Cut and Paste**
◆ **Use the Clipboard** ◆ **Use Drag-and-Drop Editing**
◆ **Move a Paragraph**

On the Job

Move text to rearrange a document quickly without retyping existing information. You can move any amount of text, from a single character to an entire page.

The Manager of the café at the Michigan Avenue Athletic Club has asked you to revise an advertising flyer. In this exercise, you will open the existing document and use different methods to rearrange the text.

Terms

Cut To delete a selection from its original location and move it to the Clipboard.

Paste To insert a selection from the Clipboard into a document.

Clipboard A temporary storage area that can hold up to 24 selections at a time.

Drag-and-drop editing The action of using a *mouse* to drag a selection from its original location and drop it in a new location.

Notes

Move Text

- While editing, you may decide you need to move text that is already typed in a document to a new location.

- You can move text within a document or from one document to another.

- Word's move commands can save you from deleting and retyping text.

- Be sure to consider nonprinting characters when you select text to move:
  - Select the space following a word or sentence to move along with text.
  - Select the paragraph mark following a paragraph or line to move paragraph formatting and blank lines with text.

- Use Undo to reverse a move that you made unintentionally.

Use Cut and Paste

- Use the **Cut** and **Paste** commands to move text in a document.

- The Cut command deletes selected text from its original location and moves it to the **Clipboard**.

- The Paste command copies the selection from the Clipboard to the insertion point location.

- Up to 24 selections can remain in the Clipboard at one time.

- You can access the Cut and Paste commands from the Edit menu, from the Standard toolbar, from a shortcut menu, or with keyboard shortcuts.

Use the Clipboard

- Use the Clipboard task pane to access selections for pasting.

- The last 24 items cut or copied are displayed in the Clipboard.

- You can paste or delete one or all of the items.

- You can turn the following Clipboard options off or on:

  - Show Office Clipboard Automatically. Sets the Clipboard task pane to open automatically when you cut or copy a selection.

  - Show Office Clipboard when Ctrl+C pressed twice. Sets Word to display the Clipboard task pane when you press and hold the Ctrl key and then press C on the keyboard twice.

  - Collect Without Showing Office Clipboard. Sets the Clipboard task pane so it does not open automatically when you cut or copy data.

  - Show Office Clipboard Icon on Taskbar. Displays a Clipboard icon at the right end of the taskbar if there are selections on the Clipboard. Double-click the icon to open the Task Pane.

  - Show Status Near Taskbar When Copying. Displays a ScreenTip with the number of items on the Clipboard when you cut or copy a selection.

Use Drag-and-Drop Editing

- Use **drag-and-drop editing** to move text with the mouse.

- Drag-and-drop editing is convenient when you can see the text to move and the new location on the screen at the same time.

Select Paste Formatting Options

- When you paste text into a new location Word automatically displays the Paste Options button.

- Click the Paste Options button to display a list of options for formatting the text in the new location.

The Paste Options button

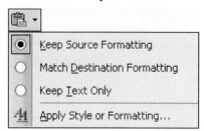

Move a Paragraph

- You can quickly move an entire paragraph up or down in a document.

Clipboard task pane

Selections to paste

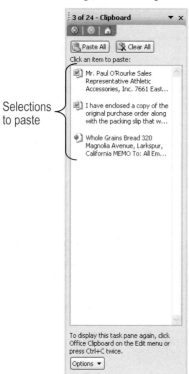

Procedures

Move Text

1. Select text to move.
2. Press **F2** key .... [F2]
3. Position insertion point at new location.
4. Press **Enter** .... [Enter]

Use Cut and Paste to Move Text *(Ctrl+X, Cltr+V)*

1. Select text to move.
2. Click **Cut** button [✂].
   OR
   a. Click **E**dit .... [Alt]+[E]
   b. Click **Cu**t .... [T]
   OR
   a. Right-click selection.
   b. Click **Cu**t .... [T]
3. Position insertion point in new location.
4. Click **Paste** button [📋].
   OR
   a. Click **E**dit .... [Alt]+[E]
   b. Click **P**aste .... [P]
   OR
   a. Right-click new location.
   b. Click **P**aste .... [P]

Display the Clipboard Task Pane

1. Press and hold **Ctrl** .... [Ctrl]
2. Press **C** .... [C]
3. Press **C** .... [C]
   OR
1. Click **E**dit .... [E]
2. Click **Office Clip**board .... [B]
   OR
1. Click **V**iew .... [Alt]+[V]
2. Click **Tas**k Pane .... [K]
3. Click **Other Task Panes** drop-down arrow.
4. Click **Clipboard**.

Paste an Item from the Clipboard

1. Display Office Clipboard
2. Position insertion point in new location.
3. Click item to paste.
   OR
   Click **Paste All** button
   [📋 Paste All] to paste all selections from the Clipboard.

Set Clipboard Options

1. Display Clipboard task pane.
2. Click **Options** drop-down button [Options ▼].
3. Select desired option:
   - **Show Office Clipboard A**utomatically .... [A]
   - **Show Office Clipboard when Ctrl+C P**ressed **Twice** .... [P]
   - **C**ollect Without Showing Office Clipboard .... [C]
   - **Show Office Clipboard Icon on T**askbar .... [T]
   - **Show S**tatus Near Taskbar When Copying .... [S]

   ✓ *A check mark indicates the option is selected.*

Delete Selections from the Clipboard

1. Right-click selection to delete.
2. Click **D**elete .... [D]
   on context menu.
   OR
   Click **Clear All** button
   [✗ Clear All] to delete all selections from the Clipboard.

Use Drag-and-Drop Editing to Move Text

1. Select text to move.
2. Move mouse pointer anywhere over selected text.
3. Press and hold left mouse button.
4. Drag mouse to position mouse pointer/insertion point at new location.

   ✓ *As you drag, the mouse pointer changes to a box with a dotted shadow attached to an arrow* 🖫.
5. Release mouse button to move selection.

Move a Paragraph

1. Position insertion point anywhere within paragraph to move.
   OR
   Select the paragraphs to move.
2. Press .... [Alt]+[Shift]+[↑]
   OR
   Press .... [Alt]+[Shift]+[↓]
3. Repeat step 2 until paragraph is in desired location.

Select Paste Formatting Options

1. Paste text at new location.
2. Click **Paste Options** button [📋].
3. Select one of the following:
   - **Keep Source Formatting** .... [K]
     to maintain formatting from original location.
   - **Match D**estination **Formatting** .... [D]
     to apply existing formatting to new text.
   - **Keep T**ext Only .... [T]
     to remove all applied formatting.
   - **Apply Styles or Formatting** .... [A]
     to open Styles and Formatting task pane.

     ✓ *The Styles and Formatting Task Pane is covered in Exercise 20.*

Exercise Directions

1. Start Word, if necessary.

2. Open 🖭 **11FLYER**.

3. Save the file as **CAFE**.

4. Revise the document so it resembles the document shown in Illustration A.

   a. Select the line **Great Food! Reasonable Price!**, including the paragraph mark at the end of the line.

   b. Cut the selection to the Clipboard.

   c. Position the insertion point on the blank line following the text **Menus change often so check the board daily**.

   d. Paste the selection in the new location.

   e. Click the Paste Options button and then click Match Destination Formatting.

   f. Select the four lines beginning with the line on which the text **Fresh Fruit** and **Fresh Salad** are entered. Include the blank line after the list of items.

   g. Press and hold Shift+Alt and then press Up arrow eight times to move the selected paragraphs up on the page.

   h. Select the text **Hours: 7:30 a.m. until 9:30 p.m.**

   i. Drag the selected text and drop it on the blank line below the headline: **The MAAC Café**.

   j. Insert a new blank line after the line with the hours on it that you just moved. The document should look similar to the one in Illustration A.

5. Check the spelling and grammar in the document.

6. Display the document in Print Preview.

7. Print the document.

8. Close the document, saving all changes.

The MAAC Café
Hours: 7:30 a.m. until 9:30 p.m.

Specializing in:

Light Meals
Healthy Snacks
Smoothies
Fat-free Desserts

Fresh Fruit   Fresh Salad
Frozen Yogurt   Bagels
Muffins   Sandwiches

Friendly

                                              Reliable

Fast

                                             Affordable

Open for breakfast, lunch, and dinner
Menus change often, so check the board daily
Great Food! Reasonable Price!

MAAC café is located on the main concourse overlooking the racquetball courts.

On Your Own

1. Think about how you would create a resume for yourself.

2. Look up information about how to format a resume. You might find the information in a career guidance center, in the library, or on the Internet. You can also ask your instructor or refer to the resume that you typed in Exercise 7.

3. Once you have selected a format, gather the information you would like to include on the resume. For example, you should include the schools you have attended, as well as any volunteer or paid work experience. Be sure to include the dates and locations.

4. You can also include clubs, teams and organizations to which you belong, awards that you have won, certifications that you have received, and any other interests that you have.

5. When you have all of the information you need, create a new document in Word.

6. Save the file as **OWD11**.

7. Based on the format you selected, enter the text to create the resume.

8. Save the changes as you work.

9. Apply formatting to enhance the appearance of the text.

10. Move text as necessary so that the information in is the correct order and so that it looks good on the page.

11. When you have completed the document, check the spelling and grammar.

12. Print the document.

13. Ask a classmate to review the document and make comments and suggestions.

14. Incorporate the suggestions into the document.

15. Close the document, saving all changes.

Exercise 12

◆ Use Copy and Paste
◆ Use the Drag-and-Drop Feature to Copy

On the Job

Copy or move text from one location to another to speed up your work and avoid repetitive typing. You can copy or move any amount of text, from a single character to an entire document.

In this exercise, you will copy text to complete the flyer for the Michigan Avenue Athletic Club café.

Terms

Copy To create a duplicate of a selection and move it to the Clipboard.

Notes

Use Copy and Paste

- Use the Copy and Paste feature to copy existing text from one location in a document and paste it to another location.

- The **Copy** command stores a duplicate of selected text on the Clipboard, leaving the original selection unchanged.

- The Paste command pastes the selection from the Clipboard to the insertion point location.

- You can access the Copy and Paste commands from the Edit menu, the Standard toolbar, a shortcut menu, or with keyboard shortcuts.

- Use the Clipboard task pane to choose which selection to paste into the document.
  - ✓ *The same Clipboard used for moving is used for copying. For more information, refer to Exercise 11.*

- Use the Paste Options button to control formatting when copying text just as you use it when moving text.
  - ✓ *For more information about the Paste Options button, refer to Exercise 11.*

- You can also use the Clipboard to copy and paste a selection from one document into a different document.

Use the Drag-and-Drop Feature to Copy

- Use drag-and-drop editing to copy text with the mouse.

- The Drag-and-Drop feature is convenient when you can see the text to copy and the new location on the screen at the same time.

Procedures

Use Copy and Paste
(Ctrl+C, Ctrl+V)

1. Select the text to copy.
2. Click **Copy** button 📋.
   OR
   a. Click **Edit** .... `Alt`+`E`
   b. Click **Copy** .... `C`
   OR
   a. Right-click selection.
   b. Click **Copy** .... `C`
3. Position insertion point in new location.
4. Click **Paste** button 📋.
   OR
   a. Click **Edit** .... `Alt`+`E`
   b. Click **Paste** .... `P`
   OR
   a. Right-click new location.
   b. Click **Paste** .... `P`

Display the Clipboard Task Pane

1. Press and hold **Ctrl** .... `Ctrl`
2. Press **C** .... `C`
3. Press **C** .... `C`
   OR
1. Click **Edit** .... `E`
2. Click **Office Clipboard** .... `B`
   OR
1. Click **View** .... `Alt`+`V`
2. Click **Task Pane** .... `K`
3. Click **Other Task Panes** drop-down arrow.
4. Click **Clipboard**.

Paste an Item from the Clipboard

1. Display Clipboard task pane.
2. Position insertion point at new location.
3. Click item to paste.
   OR
   Click **Paste All** button
   📋 Paste All to paste all selections from the Clipboard.

Delete Selections from the Clipboard

1. Right-click selection to delete.
2. Click **Delete** .... `D`
   on context menu.
   OR
   Click **Clear All** button
   ❎ Clear All to delete all selections from the Clipboard.

Use Drag-and-Drop to Copy Text

1. Select text to copy.
2. Move mouse pointer anywhere over selected text.
3. Press and hold left mouse button.
4. Press and hold the **Ctrl** key...................................... `Ctrl`
5. Drag mouse to position mouse pointer/insertion point at new location.
   ✓ *As you drag, the mouse pointer changes to a box with a dotted shadow and a plus sign attached to an arrow* 📦.
6. Release mouse button to copy selection.
7. Release the **Ctrl** key .... `Ctrl`

Exercise Directions

1. Start Word, if necessary.

2. Open 🔘 **12CAFE**.

3. Save the file as **CAFE2**.

4. Use the following steps to revise the document so it looks like the one in Illustration A.

5. Select the word **Friendly** and copy it to the Clipboard. Do not select the paragraph mark.

   ✓ *It may take a few tries to select the word without the paragraph mark. Press and hold the Shift key, then use the arrow keys to select each character.*

6. Position the insertion point on the last line in the document and paste the selection.

7. Type a period after the word, and press the Spacebar to insert a blank space. Don't worry if the document extends to more than one page.

8. Select the word **Reliable** and copy it to the Clipboard. Again, do not select the paragraph mark.

9. Position the insertion point at the end of the document and paste the selection.

10. Type a period after the word, and press the Spacebar to insert a blank space.

11. Select the word **Fast** and drag it to the end of the last line. Type a period, and press the spacebar.

12. Select the word **Affordable** and drag it to the end of the last line. Type a period.

13. Center the text on the last line.

14. Check the spelling and grammar in the document.

15. Display the document in Print Preview. It should look similar to the one in the Illustration.

16. If necessary, use Shrink to Fit to fit the document on a single page.

17. Print the document.

18. Close the document, saving all changes.

On Your Own

1. Create a new document in Word.

2. Save the file as **OWD12**.

3. Create a letter in which you apply for an officer's position of a group or organization to which you might belong. For example, the group could be a school club. The officer's position could be secretary, treasurer, or president.

4. Consider whether you can use any of the information you entered in your resume in the letter. For example, you might want to include information about other clubs to which you belong.

5. Open the document 🖮**OWD11**, your resume which you created in the On Your Own section of Exercise 11, or open 🔘 **12RESUME**.

6. Save the file as **OWD12-2**.

7. Copy at least two items from **OWD12-2** to the **OWD12** document.

   • First, copy an item from **OWD12-2** to the Clipboard. Next position the insertion point in the **OWD12** document. Finally, paste the item from the Clipboard into the **OWD12** document.

8. Complete the letter.

9. Display the document in Print Preview. Make editing or formatting changes as necessary.

10. Check the spelling and the grammar.

11. Print the document.

12. Ask a classmate to review the document and make comments or suggestions.

13. Incorporate the suggestions into the document.

14. Close the document, saving all changes.

The MAAC Café
Hours: 7:30 a.m. until 9:30 p.m.

Specializing in:

Light Meals
Healthy Snacks
Smoothies
Fat-free Desserts

Fresh Fruit	Fresh Salad
Frozen Yogurt	Bagels
Muffins	Sandwiches

Friendly

Reliable

Fast

Affordable

Open for breakfast, lunch, and dinner
Menus change often, so check the board daily
Great Food! Reasonable Price!

MAAC café is located on the main concourse overlooking the racquetball courts.

Friendly. Reliable. Fast. Affordable.

Exercise 13

Skills Covered:

◆ **Open a Document as Read-Only** ◆ **Open a Document from Windows**
◆ **Document Properties** ◆ **File Types**
◆ **Use Basic Search to Find a File**

On the Job

Word offers many options for opening a document. For example, open a document as read-only when you do not want to allow changes made to the original file. (You must save the file with a new name in order to save changes.) You can use Windows features to open a document and start Word at the same time, and you can use Word to open files created with different word processing programs. You can even locate and open a file when you don't know the file name. And you can use Document Properties to identify important information about a file, such as the name of the author and the main topic.

Voyager Travel Adventures is organizing a trip to Alaska. The Public Relations Director stored a file with some information you need to create a press release on your computer without telling you the folder location. In this exercise, you will search for the file and then open it as read-only. You will make changes to the file, including entering document properties, and you will save it in plain text format.

Terms

Read-only A mode of operation in which revisions cannot be saved in the original document.

Document Properties Categories of information about a document.

Keywords Important words found in a document. Keywords can be used to classify a document.

File type The format in which the file is stored. Usually, the file type corresponds to the program used to create the file.

File extension A dot followed by three or four characters at the end of a file name, used to indicate the file type. For example, a *.doc* file extension indicates a Word document file.

File icon The icon used to represent a file in a file list, such as Windows Explorer or Word's Open dialog box.

Compatible file type A file type that Word can open, even though it was created and saved using a different program.

XML An abbreviation for Extensible Markup Language, which is an industry standard file format.

Wildcard character A text character used as a placeholder for one or more characters.

Notes

Open a Document as Read-Only

- Opening a document as **read-only** is a safeguard against accidentally making changes.

- Word prompts you to use Save As to save revisions made to a document opened as read-only in a new document with a different file name.

- The words *Read-Only* appear in the title bar of a document opened as read-only.

Open a Document from Windows

- Use the Windows Start Menu to open a document and start Word at the same time.
    - Click My Recent Documents on the Start menu to select from a menu of recently used files.
    - Locate and open any document using Windows Explorer.
    - You can also open a Word document using the Open Office Document dialog box accessed from the Windows All Programs menu.

Document Properties

- With the **Document Properties** feature you can save information that is unique to a particular document.

- Document Properties lets you enter information in five categories.

- Three of the more useful categories are:
    - General properties: Include the type of document, its size, its location, when it was created, last accessed, and last modified.
        - Use General properties to check file storage and access information.
    - Summary properties: Include a document title, subject, author, **keywords**, and comments.
        - Use Summary properties to save summary information with a document.
    - Statistics properties: Include the number of pages, paragraphs, lines, words, characters, and bytes in the document.
        - Use Statistics properties to create documents of a specific length or word count.

- You can set Word to display the Properties dialog box automatically each time you save a document.

The Summary page of the Properties dialog box

File Types

- Files are saved in different **file types**, depending on the application used to create, save, and open the file.

- In Windows and Windows applications, file types can be identified by the **file extension** and by the **file icon**.

- Word 2003 can open documents saved in **compatible file types**. For example, Word can open text files, Web page files, **XML** files, and files created with other versions of Word.

- You can save a compatible file in its original file type or as a Word document file.

■ Some common file types include the following:

- Word document files   .doc
- Word template files   .dot
- Text files   .txt
- Web pages   .htm
- Excel workbooks   .xls
- Access databases   .mdb
- PowerPoint presentations   .ppt

Use Basic Search to Find a File

■ Word has a Search feature that can help you find a file stored anywhere on your computer system, even if you can't remember the file name.

■ Use a basic search to locate a file that contains specified text in its title, contents, or properties.

■ Enter text in the Search text box to locate files containing that text. The text may be in the body of the file, or in the document properties.

- Word finds files containing various forms of the search text. For example, if you enter *run*, Word finds documents containing *run*, *running*, or *ran*.

- You can use **wildcard characters** in the search text.

  ◆ * represents one or more characters.
  ◆ ? represents any single character.

■ Before starting a search, select the disks or folders to search, as well as the types of files to search for.

- If you know the folder to search, type it in the *Search in* box.

- Alternatively, select the checkbox beside the folder(s) to search.

■ In the *Results should be* box, select the types of files to find:

- Anything. Finds all file types.

- Office Files. Finds all files created with Office programs. You can select the specific program type.

- Outlook Items. Finds only files created with Microsoft Outlook.

- Web Pages. Finds only Web page files.

■ You can search using the Search task pane, or by opening the Search dialog box from the Open dialog box. Both methods offer you the same options in slightly different formats.

Search task pane

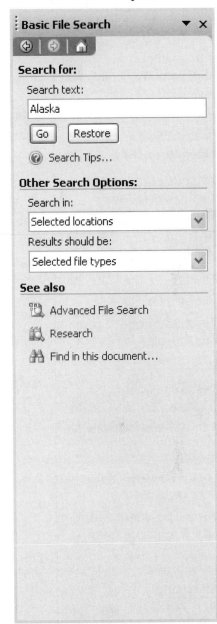

■ Word displays files matching your criteria in the Search Results list.

Procedures

Open a Document as Read-Only *(Ctrl+O)*

1. Click **Open** button ⬚.
   OR
   a. Click **File** .... `Alt`+`F`
   b. Click **Open** .... `O`
2. Click document name.
3. Click **Open** drop-down arrow ⬚ `Open ▼`.
4. Click **Open Read-Only** .... `R`

Open a Word Document from the Windows Start Menu

1. Click **Start** button
    .... `Ctrl`+`Esc`
2. Select **My Recent Documents** .... `D`
3. Click document name.

Open a Word Document From Windows Explorer

1. Right-click **Start** button `start`.
2. Click **Explore** .... `X`
3. Select drive where folder/file is located.
4. Open folder.
5. Double-click document name that you want to open.

Open a Word Document From Windows All Programs Menu

   ✓ *This procedure does not work in Windows 2000.*
1. Click **Start** button
   `start` .... `Ctrl`+`Esc`
2. Click **All Programs** .... `P`
3. Click **Open Office Document**.
4. Click **Look in** drop-down arrow .... `Alt`+`I`
5. Select drive or folder where document is stored.
   ✓ *If necessary double-click folder name.*
   OR

Click folder in Places bar to open it.
   ✓ *This procedure does not work in Windows 2000.*
6. Double-click document name.
   OR
   a. Click document name.
   b. Click **Open** .... `O`

Use Document Properties

1. Click **File** .... `Alt`+`F`
2. Click **Properties** .... `I`
3. Select desired tab .... `Ctrl`+`Tab`
   For example:
   • Click **Summary** tab and type summary information.
   • Click **Statistics** tab to see statistical information.
   • Click **General** tab to see file storage and access information.
4. Enter data as desired.
5. Click **OK** .... `Enter`

Automatically Display Properties Dialog Box

1. Click **Tools** .... `Alt`+`T`
2. Click **Options** .... `O`
3. Click **Save** tab .... `Ctrl`+`Tab`
4. Select **Prompt for document properties** checkbox .... `Alt`+`I`
5. Click **OK** .... `Enter`

Open a Compatible File Type *(Ctrl+O)*

1. Click **File** .... `Alt`+`F`
2. Click **Open** .... `O`
3. Click the **Look in** drop-down arrow .... `Alt`+`I`
4. Select the disk or folder.
   ✓ *Alternatively, click the folder you want to open in the Places bar.*
5. Click the **Files of type** drop-down arrow .... `Alt`+`T`
6. Click the file type.
7. Click the desired file name.

8. Click **Open** .... `Alt`+`O`
   ✓ *If the File Conversion dialog box is displayed, click OK.*

Save a Compatible File *(Ctrl+S)*

1. Open the compatible file.
2. Click **File** .... `Alt`+`F`
3. Click **Save** .... `S`
4. Click **Yes** .... `Y`
   to save the file in its original format.
   OR
   Click **No** .... `N`
   to save the file as a Word document.

Save a Compatible File as a New File in Word Format

1. Open the compatible file.
2. Click **File** .... `Alt`+`F`
3. Click **Save As** .... `A`
4. Click the **Save as type** drop-down arrow .... `Alt`+`T`
5. Click **Word document (*.doc)**.
6. Click the **File name** text box .... `Alt`+`N`
7. Type the new file name.
8. Click **Save** .... `Alt`+`S`

Search for Files from the Search Task Pane

1. Click **File** .... `Alt`+`F`
2. Click **File Search** .... `H`
3. Type search text in **Search text** box.
   ✓ *If necessary, delete existing text first.*
4. Click **Search in:** drop-down arrow.
5. Select folders as follows:
   • Click **plus sign** to expand list .... `+`
   • Click checkbox to select folder .... `Space`
6. Click **Results should be:** drop-down arrow .... `Tab`, `Space`

7. Click **plus sign** to expand list .... [+]

8. Click desired file type(s)............. [↑], [↓], [Space]

9. Click **Go** button [Go].

10. Click file to open.
    OR
    Click **Modify** button [Modify] to display Basic Search task pane again.

    ✓ *To interrupt a search before it is complete, click the Stop button* [Stop]*.*

Search for Files from the Open Dialog Box

1. Click **File**.................... [Alt]+[F]

2. Click **Open**........................... [O]

---

3. Click the **Look in** drop-down arrow .... [Alt]+[I]

4. Select the disk or folder.

    ✓ *Alternatively, click the folder you want to open in the Places Look in bar.*

5. Click **Tools** drop-down arrow [Tools ▾] .... [Alt]+[L]

6. Click **Search**....................... [S]

7. Click **Basic** tab, if necessary .... [Ctrl]+[Tab]

8. Type search text in **Search text** box.

    ✓ *If necessary, delete existing text first.*

9. Click **Search in**: drop-down arrow .... [Alt]+[I]

10. Select folders as follows:

• Click **plus sign** to expand list.................... [+]

• Click check box to select folder.............. [Space], [Enter]

11. Click **Results should be**: drop-down arrow .... [Alt]+[B]

12. Click **plus sign** to expand list....................................... [+]

13. Click desired file type(s)....[↑], [↓], [Space], [Enter]

14. Click **Go** .... [Alt]+[G]

15. Double-click file to open.
    OR
    Click file to open.

16. Click **OK**......................... [Enter]

17. Word displays Open dialog box.

18. Click **Open** .... [Alt]+[O]

Exercise Directions

✓ *Before beginning this exercise, make sure that the* ☉ **13ALASKA** *file is stored somewhere on your computer or computer network. Ask your instructor for more information.*

1. Start Word, if necessary.

2. Search your computer for the file about the tour using the following steps:

    a. Open the Search task pane or the Search dialog box.

    b. Enter the Search text **Tour to Alaska**.

    c. Select the folder(s) to search. For example, if the file is stored locally, choose to search drive C or My Computer. If the file is stored on a network, choose the network drive. The more you can narrow down the location, the faster the search will be.

    d. Select Word Files in the Files Should be list.

    e. Start the search.

3. Open the document from the Search Results list.

4. Save the file as **ALASKA**.

5. Using the Document Properties dialog box, check the number of words in the document.

6. Enter the following summary information:
    Title: **Alaska Press Release**
    Subject: **Tour to Southeast Alaska**
    Author: **Your name**
    Manager: **Peter Lane**
    Company: **Voyager Travel Adventures**

Category: **Press Release**
Keywords: **Alaska, Tour, Adventure**
Comments: **Text supplied by Lane. Revised for distribution**.

7. Check the spelling and grammar in the document.

8. Display the document in Print Preview.

9. Print the document.

10. Close the document.

11. Open the document as read-only.

12. Change the headline to **Tour Southeast Alaska with Voyager Travel**.

13. Save the changes.

    ✓ *Word will display the Save As dialog box.*

14. Save the document in plain text format, with the name **ALASKA2**.

15. In the File Conversion dialog box, make sure the Insert line breaks checkbox is selected, and then click OK.

16. Close the document, saving all changes. If prompted, save the file in text format, not Word format.

17. Open the **ALASKA2.TXT** file in Word. The text file should look similar to the one in the illustration.

18. Close the file, saving all changes.

For Immediate Release

Contact: Your Name
                303-555-8397

Tour Southeast Alaska with Voyager Travel

Denver, CO -- Voyager Travel is offering a 10-day tour of Southeast Alaska. This
remarkable part of the state is home to bald eagles, grizzly bears, humpback
whales and
orcas, as well as many other species of animals. Join Voyager Travel to
experience this
exciting area.

Summer in Alaska offers nearly 14 hours of daylight, leaving loads of time for
exploration and adventure. Some of the scheduled activities include kayaking,
white-
water rafting, hiking, and biking. Opportunities for other activities will be
available. A
registered guide will accompany you on your travels. Some of the destinations
include
Sitka, Juneau, Skagway, Haines, and Gustavus. Travel from destination to
destination
may be by ferry, train, floatplane or automobile. Lodging is at hotels, inns,
and bed and
breakfasts.

Departure dates are set for July 13 and August 14. The tour is limited to 12
participants,
so reserve your space early. The tour is all-inclusive. For complete pricing and
other
information call 303-555-8397, or visit our website: www.vtadventures.com.

On Your Own

1. Search for **OWD12**, the file you created in the On Your Own section of Exercise 12, or search for ⊙ **13LETTER**.

2. Open the file as read-only.

3. Use the Properties dialog box to check the number of words in the document.

4. Note the file size, date created, and date last modified.

5. Enter document properties, including Title, Subject, Manager, Company, Category, Keywords, and Comments.

6. Try saving the document.

7. Save the file as **OWD13**.

8. Save the file in text format as **OWD13-2**.

9. Print the file.

10. Close the document, saving all changes.

Exercise 14

Skills Covered:

◆ **Preview a Closed Document**
◆ **Print Files without Opening Them**

On the Job

Preview a document before opening it or printing it to make sure it is the correct file. Print files without opening them to save time or to print more than one document at once.

As a travel agent for Voyager Travel Adventures, you have been asked to find out if any employees are interested in going on the first Alaska tour. In this exercise, you will preview, open, and revise the press release about the tour. Then you will create a memo to employees. Finally, you will print both documents.

Notes

Preview a Closed Document

- By default, Word displays a list of files in the Open dialog box.

- You can change the display in the dialog box to show a preview of the document selected in the file list.

- Previewing is useful for making sure a document is the one you want before you open it or print it.

- Most documents are too large to be displayed completely in the dialog box; use the scroll arrows in the preview area to scroll up and down.

- If you don't want to display a preview, you can set the Open dialog box to display large or small file icons, the default file list, file details, such as size, type, and date last saved, or document properties.

- Files are sorted in the files list based on when they were created or modified.

Preview a document in the Open dialog box

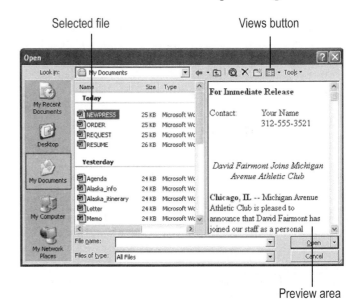

Selected file   Views button

Preview area

Print Files without Opening Them

■ To save time, you can print a document from the Open dialog box without opening it.

■ Print without opening when you are certain the document is ready for printing.

✓ *You can also print a document without opening it from the Open Office dialog box or from Windows Explorer.*

■ You can select more than one file at a time for printing in the Open dialog box.

■ Selecting multiple files for printing sends them all to the printer, where they will be printed one after the other.

■ All selected files must be in the same folder.

Procedures

Preview a Closed Document

1. Click **File** .... Alt + F
2. Click **Open** .... O
3. Click **Views** button drop-down arrow [▦ ▾].
4. Click **Preview** [▤] V
5. Click document name to preview.

✓ *If necessary, select drive and/or folder to locate document.*

To turn Preview off:

1. Click **File** .... Alt + F
2. Click **Open** .... O
3. Click **Views** button drop-down arrow [▦ ▾].
4. Select another view:

  • Click **Thumbnails** [▦] ... T
  • Click **Tiles** [▤] .... S
  • Click **Icons** [▥] .... N
  • Click **List** [▤] L
  • Click **Details** [▦] .... D
  • Click **Properties** [▤] ..... R

  ✓ *Or click the Views button repeatedly to cycle through the Views options.*

Print a File without Opening It

1. Click **File** .... Alt + F
2. Click **Open** .... O

✓ *If necessary, select drive and/or folder to locate document.*

3. Click **Tools** button [Tools ▾] .... Alt + L
4. Click **Print** .... P

Print Multiple Files

1. Click **File** .... Alt + F
2. Click **Open** .... O
3. Click the first document name.
4. Press and hold **Ctrl** .... Ctrl
5. Click each additional document name.
6. Click **Tools** button [Tools ▾] .... Alt + L
7. Click **Print** .... P

Exercise Directions

1. Start Word, if necessary.

2. In the Open dialog box, preview 🖮**ALASKA**, the document you created in Exercise 13, or preview 💿 **14ALASKA**.

3. Change the Open dialog box to display document properties instead of the preview.

4. Open the document and save it as **TOUR**.

5. Make revisions as indicated in Illustration A.

6. Check the spelling and grammar in the document.

7. Close the document, saving all changes.

8. Create a new document and type the memo shown in Illustration B, or open 💿 **14MEMO**.

9. Save the document as **NOTICE**, and then close it.

10. Preview the **NOTICE** document in the Open dialog box.

11. Print both the **TOUR** and **NOTICE** documents without opening them.

Illustration A

For Immediate Release

Contact: Your Name
                303-555-8397

Voyager Travel Adventures Announces a New Tour to Alaska

Denver, CO -- Voyager Travel is offering a 10-day tour of Southeast Alaska. This remarkable part of the state is home to bald eagles, grizzly bears, humpback whales and orcas, as well as many other species of animals. Join Voyager Travel *Adventures* to experience this exciting *unique and* area. *part of our country.*

Summer in Alaska offers nearly 14 hours of daylight, leaving ~~loads~~ *plenty* of time for exploration and adventure. Some of the scheduled activities include kayaking, white-water rafting, hiking, and biking. Opportunities for other activities will be available. A registered guide will accompany you on your travels. Some of the destinations include Sitka, Juneau, Skagway, Haines, and Gustavus. Travel from destination to destination may be by ferry, train, floatplane or automobile. Lodging is at hotels, inns, and bed and breakfasts.

Departure dates are set for July 13 and August 14. The tour is limited to 12 participants, so reserve your space early. The tour is all-inclusive. For complete pricing and other information call 303-555-8397, or visit our website: www.vtadventures.com.

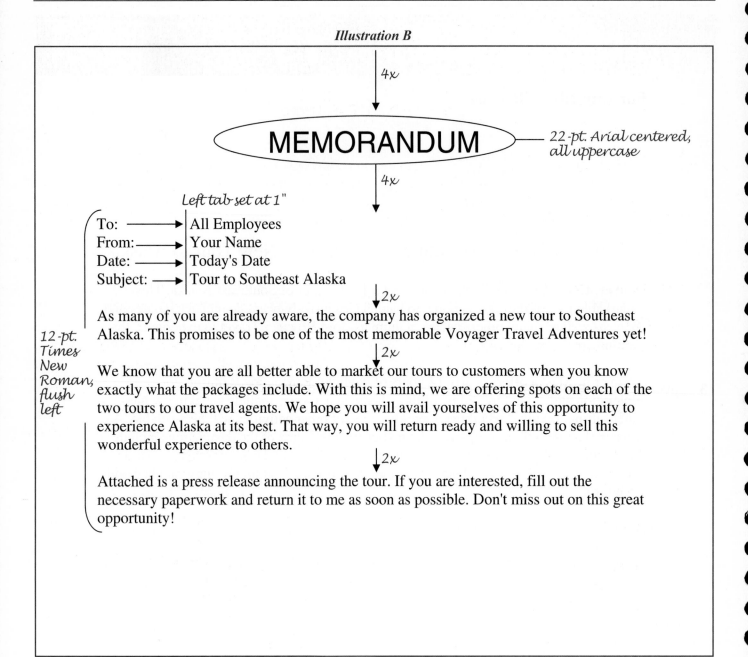

Illustration B

MEMORANDUM — 22-pt. Arial centered, all uppercase

4x

4x

Left tab set at 1"

To: → All Employees
From: → Your Name
Date: → Today's Date
Subject: → Tour to Southeast Alaska

12-pt. Times New Roman, flush left

↓2x

As many of you are already aware, the company has organized a new tour to Southeast Alaska. This promises to be one of the most memorable Voyager Travel Adventures yet!

↓2x

We know that you are all better able to market our tours to customers when you know exactly what the packages include. With this is mind, we are offering spots on each of the two tours to our travel agents. We hope you will avail yourselves of this opportunity to experience Alaska at its best. That way, you will return ready and willing to sell this wonderful experience to others.

↓2x

Attached is a press release announcing the tour. If you are interested, fill out the necessary paperwork and return it to me as soon as possible. Don't miss out on this great opportunity!

On Your Own

1. Start Word.
2. Preview some of the documents that you have created for the On Your Own sections of previous exercises, or preview ⊘**14LETTER**, ⊘**14TECH**, and ⊘**14RESUME**.
3. Display file properties instead of the preview.
4. Display the preview again.
5. Print at least two of the documents without opening them.
6. When you are finished, exit Word.

Exercise 15

The Franchise Manager wants to contact another potential franchisee outside of California. In this exercise, you will open an existing letter, save it with a new name, revise it using the techniques you have learned so far, and add Document Properties. You will then search for and open a document listing factors for franchise success, which you will save in a compatible file format. Finally, you will preview and print both documents.

Exercise Directions

1. Start Word, if necessary.

2. Open ⌨**EXPAND** or 💿**15EXPAND** as read-only.

3. Save the file as **EXPAND2**.

4. Insert, delete, and replace text as marked on Illustration A.

5. Enter Document Properties summary information as follows:

    Title: **Letter to Martin Hamilton**
    Subject: **Potential Franchisee**
    Author: **Your Name**
    Manager: **Frank Kaplan**
    Company: **Whole Grains Bread**
    Category: **Letter**
    Keywords: **Franchise, Expansion, Phoenix, Arizona**.
    Comments: **Letter regarding expanding franchises outside California**.

6. Check the spelling and grammar.

7. Save the changes.

8. Close the document.

9. Use a basic search to locate 💿**15SUCCESS** using the search text **Success Factors**.

10. Open the document.

    ✓ You may close the task pane, if you want.

11. Save the document in Rich Text Format with the file name **SUCCESS**.

    ✓ Rich Text Format preserves some of the font formatting that Plain Text format does not preserve. It adds an .rtf file extension to the file name.

12. Copy and move text as marked on Illustration B.

13. Close the document, saving all changes.

14. Preview the **EXPAND2** and **SUCCESS** documents without opening them.

    ✓ Remember, to display the SUCCESS document in the Open dialog box you will have to select All Files to display all file types.

15. Print both the **EXPAND2** and **SUCCESS** documents without opening them.

16. Exit Word.

Today's date ———————— *Replace with today's date*

~~CERTIFIED MAIL~~

~~Ms. Lindsey Perrins~~
~~Franchise Owner~~
~~WHOLE GRAINS BREAD~~
~~456 Main Street~~
~~Brentwood, California 94513~~

Mr. Martin Hamilton
Manager
Osborne Bistro
772 Osborne Street
Phoenix, AZ 85013

Dear ~~Ms. Perrins:~~ Mr. Hamilton:

Subject: Opening A New Franchise

Your interest in opening a new franchise in ~~Park City, Utah~~ *Phoenix, Arizona* could not have come at a better time. As you may already know, WHOLE GRAINS BREAD is actively seeking to expand our franchise presence outside of California. As ~~one of our most successful franchisees,~~ *a successful bistro manager* we believe you are a prime candidate to pioneer this venture.

I have enclosed a ~~memo~~ *document* listing some of the factors we consider vital to the success of a new franchise. Although our expansion plans are in an early stage at the moment, we would like very much to sit down with you to share ideas and information. WHOLE GRAINS BREAD welcomes input from our franchisees. Please call my office at your earliest convenience to set up an appointment. I look forward to hearing from you.

Sincerely,

Frank Kaplan
Franchise Manager
WHOLE GRAINS BREAD
320 Magnolia Avenue
Larkspur, CA 94939

Fk/yo

Enclosure

Copy to: Mr. Anthony Splendoria, CEO

Illustration B

Copy the word
Five and paste
it in the title,
matching the
destination
formatting

Whole Grains Bread
Franchise Success Factors

*Paste word
Five here*

Whole Grains Bread offers fresh breads and pastries to specialty shops up and down the West Coast. In addition, Whole Grains Bread franchises bring a unique dining experience to customers at many locations.

At **Whole Grains Bread**, we believe there are certain standard factors that contribute to the success of any franchise. After careful study, we have found that our most successful operators share some significant values and methods of operation. If a franchisee or manager takes these factors into consideration for day-to-day operations, the success of his or her store is virtually guaranteed.

Five Factors for Success

*Move this sentence so it
is a new paragraph
between the list and
the last paragraph*

Cleanliness counts
The customer comes first
Be courteous to all
Treat employees with respect
Listen and respond to compliments, criticism, and complaints

At this time, **Whole Grains Bread** is looking to expand outside of the West Coast. We are actively seeking men and women who are willing to incorporate these factors into their daily business lives in order to build and maintain a successful **Whole Grains Bread** franchise. For more information call 415-555-3200.

Exercise 16

Skills Covered:
◆ Apply Font and Text Effects ◆ Font Color
◆ Highlight Text ◆ Format Painter

On the Job

You can enhance text using font effects, text effects, and colors. You can highlight text to change the color around the text without changing the font color. Highlighting is useful for calling attention to text and for making text stand out on the page. Use the Format Painter to quickly copy formatting from one location to another. The Format Painter saves you time and makes it easy to duplicate formatting throughout a document.

You have been asked to design a document advertising the Alaska tour for Adventure Travel, Inc. If the company approves of the document, it will be made available in the office and posted as a Web page on the company Web site. In this exercise, you will create the document using font effects, text effects, and color. You will also highlight text and use the Format Painter to copy formatting.

Terms

Text effects Effects used to animate text on-screen.

Font effects Formatting features used to enhance or emphasize text.

Highlight formatting Applying a color background to selected text.

Notes

Apply Font and Text Effects

- Font and **text effects** are used to enhance and emphasize text in a document.

- Word includes numerous **font effects** for enhancing and emphasizing text, including the ones available in the Font dialog box:

  - Strikethrough
  - Double strikethrough
  - Superscript
  - Subscript
  - Shadow
  - Outline
  - Emboss
  - Engrave
  - Sᴍᴀʟʟ ᴄᴀᴘs
  - ALL CAPS

- ✓ *Hidden is also an option in the Effects area of the font dialog box. Hidden text is not displayed on-screen or printed unless you select to display it.*

- Text effects are animations used in documents that will be viewed on-screen. They cannot be printed.

- Select font and text effects in the Font dialog box.

The Font dialog box

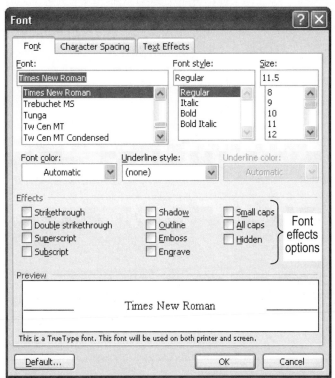

Font Color

- Use color to enhance text in documents that will be viewed on-screen or printed on a color printer.
- You can change the color of an underline independently from the color of the font.

Highlight Text

- Highlighting calls attention to text by placing a color background on the text.
- You can highlight text as a decorative or visual effect, but Word's Highlighter feature is commonly used like a highlighter pen on paper to mark text that requires attention.
- Yellow is the default highlight color, but you can change the color of **highlight formatting**.
  - ✓ *Color highlighting will print in color when printed on a color printer and print in gray when printed on a black and white printer.*

Format Painter

- Use the Format Painter to copy formatting from existing formatted text to existing unformatted text.

Procedures

Apply Font Effects

1. Select text.
   OR
   Position insertion point where new text will be typed.
2. Click **Format** .... Alt + O
3. Click **Font** .... F
4. Select checkbox for desired effect(s).
   - ✓ *Clear check mark to remove effect.*
5. Click **OK** .... Enter
   - ✓ *Select text and press Ctrl+Spacebar to remove all character formatting.*

Apply Text Effects

1. Select text.
   OR
   Position insertion point where new text will be typed.
2. Click **Format** .... Alt + O

3. Click **Font** .... F
4. Click **Text Effects** page tab .... Alt + X
5. Click desired **Animation** ...... Alt + A, ↑/↓
   - ✓ *View a sample of the effect in the Preview area.*
6. Click **OK** .... Enter

Apply Font Color

1. Select text.
   OR
   Position insertion point where new text will be typed.
2. Click **Format** .... Alt + O
3. Click **Font** .... F
4. Click **Font color** drop-down arrow .... Alt + C
5. Click desired color ... 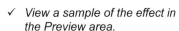, Enter
   - ✓ *Click Auto to select default color.*
6. Click **OK** .... Enter

OR
1. Select text.
   OR
   Position insertion point where new text will be typed.
2. Click **Font Color** button drop-down arrow ![A].
3. Click desired color.

Apply Color to Underlines

1. Select underlined text.
   OR
   Position insertion point where new underlined text will be typed.
2. Click **Format** .... Alt + O
3. Click **Font** .... F
4. Click **Underline** color drop-down arrow .... Alt + I
5. Click desired **color**.
   - ✓ *Click Auto to select default color.*
6. Click **OK** .... Enter

Apply Highlights

Highlight existing text:

1. Select text.
2. Click **Highlight** button [icon].
   - ✓ *Repeat steps to remove highlight.*

OR

1. Click **Highlight** button [icon].
   - ✓ *Mouse pointer changes to look like an I-beam with a pen attached to it.*
2. Drag across text to highlight.
3. Click **Highlight** button [icon] again to turn off Highlight feature.

Change highlight color:

1. Click **Highlight** button drop-down arrow [icon].
2. Click new color.
   - ✓ *Click None to select the automatic background color.*

Copy Formatting

Copy formatting once:

1. Select formatted text.
2. Click **Format Painter** button [icon].
   - ✓ *The mouse pointer looks like an I-beam with a paintbrush:* [icon]
3. Select text to format.
   - ✓ *Click a word to quickly copy the formatting to that word.*

Copy formatting repeatedly:

1. Select formatted text.
2. Double-click **Format Painter** button [icon].
3. Select text to format.
4. Repeat step 3 until all text is formatted.
5. Click **Format Painter** button [icon] to turn off Format Painter.

Exercise Directions

1. Start Word, if necessary.
2. Open ⊚ **16ANNOUNCE**.
3. Save the document as **ANNOUNCE**.
4. Apply the formatting shown in the Illustration A.
   a. Change the font and font size as marked.
   - ✓ *If the specified font is not available on your computer, select a different font.*
   b. Set horizontal alignments as marked.
   c. Apply font and text effects as marked.
   d. Change font color as marked.
   e. Apply highlighting as marked.
   - ✓ *Use the Format Painter to copy formatting whenever possible.*

5. Check the spelling and grammar.
6. Display the document in Print Preview. It should look similar to the illustration.
   - ✓ *The animated effects do not appear in Print Preview or in a printed document.*
   - ✓ *If the document is longer or shorter than the one shown, check to see if you inadvertently formatted the blank lines between paragraphs. In the illustration, all blank lines have the default 12-point Times New Roman formatting.*
7. Save the changes.
8. Print the document.
9. Close the document, saving all changes.

On Your Own

1. Create an invitation to an event such as a birthday party, graduation, or meeting.
2. Save the document as **OWD16**.
3. Format the document using the techniques you have learned so far, including fonts, alignment options, and font effects.
4. Change the font color for some text.
5. Try some text effects.
6. Try different underline styles.
7. Copy the formatting from one location to another.
8. Preview the document and print it.
9. Ask a classmate to review the document and make comments or suggestions.
10. Incorporate the suggestions into the document.
11. Save your changes, close the document, and exit Word.

Illustration A

28-pt. Broadway, centered, blue —— **Voyager Travel Adventures**

TRAVEL BEYOND YOUR WILDEST DREAMS ——

16-pt. Broadway, centered, blue, and small caps, with a sea green wavy underline

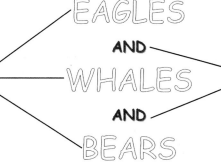

28-pt. Comic Sans MS, centered, blue, outline, and all caps

EAGLES

AND

WHALES

AND

BEARS

18-pt. Comic Sans MS, centered, sea green, shadow, and small caps

OH, MY! ——

72-pt. Broadway, centered, red, shadow, small caps, with Las Vegas Lights

14-pt. Comic Sans MS, justified

Join Voyage Travel Adventures for a guided tour of Southeast Alaska. Spend glorious 14-hour days exploring one of the greatest wilderness areas in the U.S. Enjoy kayaking, rafting, hiking, fishing, and biking through magnificent scenery. Spend relaxing, comfortable evenings in well-equipped lodges and inns. Itinerary includes stops in Sitka, Juneau, Haines, Gustavus, and Skagway.

Bright Green highlight

20-pt. Comic Sans MS, red, outline, small caps

DEPARTURE DATES: JULY 13

Left tab at 2.5"   AUGUST 14

14-pt. Comic Sans MS, justified

For complete itinerary, availability, pricing, and other information call 303-555-8397, or visit our website: www.vtadventures.com.

Exercise 17

◆ Use Symbols

On the Job

Use symbols to supplement the standard characters available on the keyboard and to add visual interest to documents. For example, you can insert symbols such as hearts and stars into documents as borders or separators.

The Marketing Directory of Whole Grains Bread has asked you to create a flyer announcing the grand opening of a new cafe. In this exercise, you will create the flyer using the formatting techniques you have learned so far. You will also insert symbols to enhance the flyer.

Terms

Symbol Shapes, mathematical and scientific notations, currency signs, and other visual elements you can insert in documents by using the Symbol dialog box.

Notes

Use Symbols

- **Symbols** are characters that cannot be typed from the keyboard, such as hearts, stars, and other shapes, as well as foreign alphabet characters.

- Symbols can be selected, edited, and formatted in a document just like regular text characters.

- Several symbol fonts come with Microsoft Office 2003 and others are available through vendors and shareware.

- Many regular character fonts also include some symbol characters.

- To insert a symbol, you first select a font, then select the desired symbol in the Symbol dialog box.

- You can also insert special characters such as paragraph marks and ellipses from the Special Characters tab of the Symbol dialog box.

- You can also select from a list of recently used symbols.

- Some symbols have number codes you can use for identification, and some have shortcut keys you can use to insert the symbol into a document.

- When you insert symbols, the default font formatting is applied to the character. You can change the font size, style, and effects just as you can for regular text characters.

Symbol dialog box

Current font · Selected symbol · Recently used symbols · Code · Shortcut key combination

Procedures

Insert Symbols

1. Position insertion point where you want to insert a symbol.
2. Click **Insert**.................. `Alt`+`I`
3. Click **Symbol**..................... `S`
4. Click **Font** drop-down arrow................. `Alt`+`F`
5. Select any symbol **font** .... `↓`, `Enter`
6. Click desired **symbol**....................... `Tab`, `→`
7. Click **Insert**................. `Alt`+`I`

   ✓ *Repeat the steps to insert additional symbols without closing the Symbol dialog box.*

8. Click **Close**........................ `Esc`

Exercise Directions

1. Start Word, if necessary.
2. Open 🖸 **17GRAND**.
3. Save the document as **GRAND**.
4. Format the text as marked in the Illustration A.
   a. Use a serif font for the entire document. (Times New Roman is used in Illustration A.)
   b. Apply font sizes, colors, and effects as shown.
      ✓ *Be careful not to change the font size and formatting of the blank lines in the document. They should remain at 12-point Times New Roman.*
   c. Apply alignments as shown.

5. Use the Wingdings font to insert symbols as marked in the illustration.
   ✓ *Adjust the font size and formatting of symbol characters the same way you adjust the font size and formatting of text characters.*
   ✓ *Hint: Use Copy and Paste to copy a symbol from one location to another, or use the Repeat command (Ctrl+Y) to repeat the insertion. Use the Format Painter to copy formatting.*
6. Display the document in Print Preview. It should look similar to the illustration.
7. Print the document.
8. Close the document, saving the changes.

On Your Own

1. Open the document **OWD16**, the document you created in exercise 16, or open 🖸 **17INVITE**.
2. Save the document as **OWD17**.
3. Use symbols to enhance the document. For example, use symbols as separators between words or paragraphs, or use them to decorate or emphasize the document.
4. Try different symbol fonts.

5. Try changing the font size for a symbol inserted in a document.
6. Try repeating a symbol to create a line across the page.
7. Preview and print the document.
8. Ask a classmate to review the document and offer comments and suggestions.
9. Incorporate the comments and suggestions into the document.
10. Close the document, saving all changes.

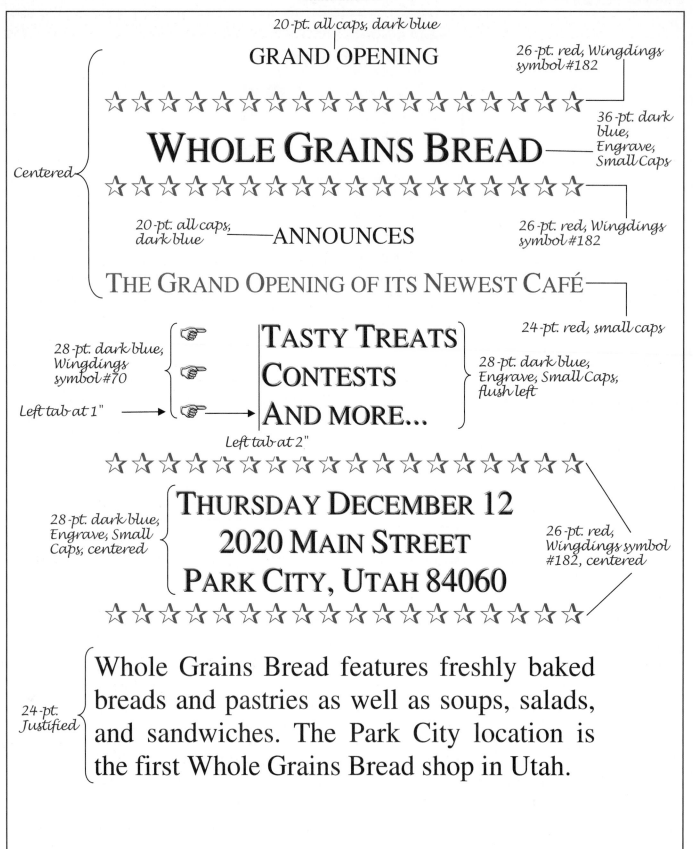

20-pt. all caps, dark blue

GRAND OPENING

26-pt. red, Wingdings symbol #182

Centered

36-pt. dark blue, Engrave, Small Caps

WHOLE GRAINS BREAD

20-pt. all caps, dark blue

ANNOUNCES

26-pt. red, Wingdings symbol #182

THE GRAND OPENING OF ITS NEWEST CAFÉ

24-pt. red, small caps

28-pt. dark blue, Wingdings symbol #70

TASTY TREATS
CONTESTS
AND MORE...

28-pt. dark blue, Engrave, Small Caps, flush left

Left tab at 1"

Left tab at 2"

28-pt. dark blue, Engrave, Small Caps, centered

THURSDAY DECEMBER 12
2020 MAIN STREET
PARK CITY, UTAH 84060

26-pt. red, Wingdings symbol #182, centered

24-pt. Justified

Whole Grains Bread features freshly baked breads and pastries as well as soups, salads, and sandwiches. The Park City location is the first Whole Grains Bread shop in Utah.

88

Exercise 18

Skills Covered:

◆ Line Spacing ◆ Paragraph Spacing ◆ Indent Text

On the Job

Format documents using the right amount of space between lines, paragraphs, and words to make the pages look better and the text easier to read. Use indents to call attention to a paragraph, to achieve a particular visual effect, or to leave white space along the margins for notes or illustrations.

In response to a member survey, the Michigan Avenue Athletic Club is instituting a few new policies and programs. In this exercise, you will use line and paragraph spacing and indents to format a document explaining the new programs. You will also apply font formatting, alignments, and tabs to the document.

Terms

Line spacing The amount of white space between lines of text in a paragraph.

Leading Line spacing measured in points.

Paragraph spacing The amount of white space between paragraphs.

Indent A temporary left and/or right margin for lines or paragraphs.

Notes

Line Spacing

- **Line spacing** sets the amount of vertical space between lines. By default, line spacing in Word is set to single space. Line spacing can be measured in either lines (single, double, etc.) or in points.

- When line spacing is measured in points, it is called **leading** (pronounced *ledding*).

> By default, Word uses leading that is 120% of the current font size. For a 10-point font, that means 12-point leading. This paragraph is formatted with the default leading for a 12-point font (14.4 pts.).

> Increase leading to make text easier to read. In this paragraph, the font is still 12 points, but the leading has been increased to exactly 16 points.

> Decrease leading to fit more lines on a page. In this paragraph, the leading has been set to exactly 10 points, while the font size is still 12 points. Keep in mind that decreasing leading makes text harder to read.

✓ *You should never decrease leading so much that the text is difficult to read. The above sample should be considered an example of poor formatting.*

- Line spacing measured in lines can be set to single spaced, 1.5 spaced, or double spaced.

Paragraph Spacing

- **Paragraph spacing** affects space before and after paragraphs.

- Amount of space can be specified in lines or in points. The default is points.

- Use increased paragraph spacing in place of extra returns or blank lines.

Indent Text

- There are five types of **indents**:
  - *Left* indents text from the left margin.
  - *Right* indents text from the right margin.
  - *Double* indents text from both the left and right margins.
  - *First line* indents just the first line of a paragraph from the left margin.
  - *Hanging* indents all lines but the first line from the left margin.

- Indent markers on the horizontal ruler show where current indents are set.

Indents in a document

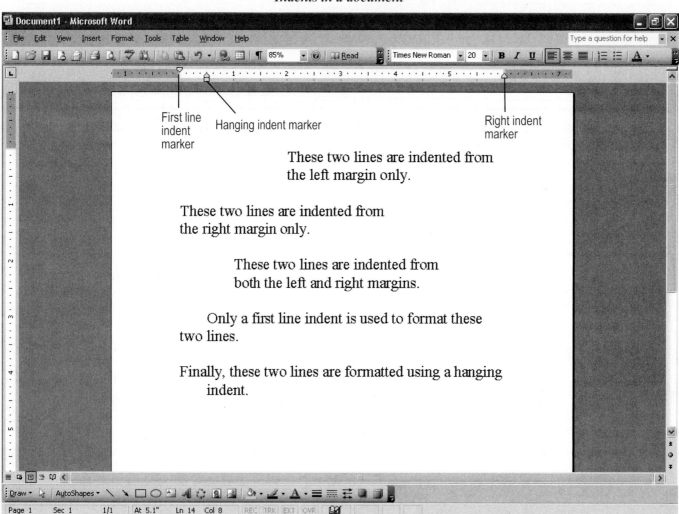

Procedures

Set Line Spacing
(Ctrl+1, Ctrl+2, Ctrl+5)

1. Position insertion point where text will be typed.
   OR
   Position insertion point in paragraph to change.
   OR
   Select paragraphs to change.
2. Click **Line Spacing** button  drop-down arrow on Formatting toolbar.
3. Click desired spacing option.
   - ✓ *Click More to open the Paragraph dialog box.*

OR

1. Position insertion point where text will be typed.
   OR
   Position insertion point in paragraph to change.
   OR
   Select paragraphs to change.
2. Click **Format**.............. Alt + O
3. Click **Paragraph** .... P
   - ✓ *To open the Paragraph dialog box quickly, right-click paragraph to format, then click Paragraph.*
4. Click **Indents and Spacing** page tab .... Alt + I
5. Click **Line spacing** ...... Alt + N
6. Select a **line spacing option:**.................... ↓ , Enter
   - Single
   - 1.5 lines
   - Double
   OR
   a. Select **leading option:** .... ↓ , Enter
      - **At least** to set a minimum leading.
      - **Exactly** to set an exact leading.
      - **Multiple** to specify a percentage by which to increase leading.

---

   b. Click **At** box............ Alt + A
   c. Type value in points.
7. Click **OK** .... Enter

Set Paragraph Spacing

1. Position insertion point where text will be typed.
   OR
   Position insertion point in paragraph to change.
   OR
   Select paragraphs to change.
2. Click **Format** .... Alt + O
3. Click **Paragraph** .... P
   - ✓ *To open the Paragraph dialog box quickly, right-click paragraph to format, then click Paragraph.*
4. Click **Indents and Spacing** page tab........ Alt + I
5. Click **Before** text box... Alt + B
   OR
   Click **After** text box ..... Alt + E
6. Type amount of space to leave.
   - ✓ *By default, spacing is in points. Type li after value to specify lines.*
7. Click **OK** .... Enter

Indent Text

Quickly indent from the left:

1. Position insertion point where text will be typed.
   OR
   Position insertion point in paragraph to change.
   OR
   Select paragraphs to change.
2. Click **Increase Indent** button ⧉ .
   OR
   Click **Decrease Indent** button ⧉ .
   OR
   Drag **Left-indent** marker ⧗ on ruler.

Indent from the left and/or right:

1. Position insertion point where text will be typed.
   OR

   Position insertion point in paragraph to change.
   OR
   Select paragraphs to change.
2. Drag **Left-indent** marker ⧗ on ruler.
3. Drag **Right-indent** marker ⧉ on ruler.

Set precise left and/or right indents:

1. Click **Format** .... Alt + O
2. Click **Paragraph** .... P
3. Click **Indents and Spacing** page tab .... Alt + I
4. Click **Left** text box .... Alt + L
5. Type distance from left margin.
6. Click **Right** text box .... Alt + R
7. Type distance from right margin.
8. Click **OK**........................... Enter

Indent first line only *(Tab)*:

1. Position insertion point where text will be typed.
   OR
   Position insertion point in paragraph to change.
   OR
   Select paragraphs to change.
2. Drag **First Line indent** marker ⧉ .
   OR
   a. Click **Format** .... Alt + O
   b. Click **Paragraph** .... P
   c. Click **Indents and Spacing** page tab .... Alt + I
   d. Click **Special** drop-down arrow .... Alt + S
   e. Click **First line** ..... ↓ , Enter
   f. Click **By** text box .... Alt + Y
   g. Type amount to indent.
   h. Click **OK**..................... Enter

Set hanging indent *(Ctrl+T):*

1. Position insertion point where text will be typed.
   OR
   Position insertion point in paragraph to change.
   OR
   Select paragraphs to change.

2. Drag **Hanging indent** marker
   OR
   a. Click **Format** .... `Alt`+`O`
   b. Click **Paragraph** .... `P`
   c. Click **Indents and Spacing** page tab .... `Alt`+`I`

   d. Click **Special** drop-down arrow .... `Alt`+`S`
   e. Click **Hanging** ...... `↓`, `Enter`
   f. Click **By** text box .... `Alt`+`Y`
   g. Type amount to indent.
   h. Click **OK** .... `Enter`

Exercise Directions

1. Start Word, if necessary.
2. Open ☺ **18SURVEY**.
3. Save the document as **SURVEY**.
4. Follow steps 5 through 9 to achieve the results shown in Illustration A.
5. Apply font formatting as shown.
   ✓ *Unless otherwise noted, 12-point Arial is used in the illustration.*
6. Insert symbols as marked in the illustration.

7. Set alignments and tabs as marked in the illustration.
   ✓ *Unless otherwise noted, paragraphs are justified.*
8. Set line spacing, paragraph spacing, and indents as shown in the illustration.
9. Check spelling and grammar.
10. Display the document in Print Preview. It should look similar to the illustration.
11. Print the document.
12. Close the document, saving all changes.

On Your Own

1. Think of some documents that could benefit from line spacing, paragraph spacing, and indent formatting. For example, many instructors require reports and papers to be double spaced. First drafts of documents that will be read by others should be double spaced so reviewers can jot notes or make corrections. A resume can be set up neatly using spacing and indent features, as can a reference list.
2. Plan a document that will contain brief (one paragraph each) descriptions of three types of technology used in business.
   a. Start by selecting three items, such as software programs, hardware devices, or the Internet.
   b. If necessary, research the items using a library or the Internet so that you have the information you need to write the descriptions.
3. Create a new document in Word.

4. Save the file as **OWD18**.
5. Type a title or headline at the top of the document and a brief introduction.
6. Type the paragraphs describing each of the three items. Include a definition of each item, and explain its function or purpose. Include information about what tasks the item should be used for. Use proper grammar and punctuation.
7. Format the document using line and paragraph spacing and indents, as well as font formatting, tabs, and alignments.
8. Save the changes and print the document.
9. Ask a classmate to review the document and offer comments and suggestions.
10. Incorporate the suggestions into the document.
11. Save your changes, close the document, and exit Word.

Illustration A

28-pt. Arial

Center

Michigan Avenue Athletic Club

235 Michigan Avenue ❖ Chicago, Illinois 60601 — *16-pt. Arial*

Phone: (312) 555-3521 ❖ Fax: 312-555-4521 ❖ E-mail: mail@michiganaveclub.com

Wingdings symbol 118

9-pt. Arial, leave 24 pts. of space after

Contact: Your name
          Extension 344

Flush left, left tab set at 1", leave 24 pts. of space after second line

10-pt. Arial Indent 3" from left, leave 18 pts. of space after

Michigan Avenue Athletic Club is dedicated to providing a safe and friendly environment for all members. We support a policy of inclusion and diversity, of understanding and cooperation. Our goal is to challenge members physically, mentally, and intellectually, and to encourage success in all endeavors.

— MAAC Mission Statement

10-pt. Arial. leave 6 pts. of space before, set leading to at least 14 pts. and indent 1.25" from both the left and the right

Double-spaced, first line indent .5", leave 6 pts. of space before and after.

The results of a recent member survey have turned up three areas where members would like to see improvements. The primary areas of concern are security, access to equipment at peak usage times, and social activities for singles. In response, Michigan Avenue Athletic Club plans to institute the following policies and procedures:

Bold

Hanging indent to 1", leave 12 pts. of space before and after, set leading to exactly 14 points

Security The Club will install security cameras in the lobby, outside all entrances and exits, and outside the locker rooms. In addition, a new member check-in policy will be established to insure that only members and their guests have access to the facilities.

Wait times The Club will establish a sign-up procedure for equipment to reduce waiting times. It will also monitor usage to determine the most popular equipment and then purchase new items.

Singles The Club will plan and sponsor a minimum of four events each month for singles only. Activities may include parties, tournaments, and classes at the club as well as excursions such as ski trips, river cruises, or bike rides.

Exercise 19

On the Job

Lists are an effective way to present items of information. Use a bulleted list when the items do not have to be in any particular order, like a grocery list or a list of objectives. Use a numbered list when the order of the items is important, such as directions or instructions. Use Sort to organize a list into alphabetical or numerical order.

As the Customer Service Manager at the Michigan Avenue Athletic Club, you have recently received a number of complaints about the club's check-in policy. In this exercise, you will edit and format a memo to employees about the proper check-in procedure. You will use a bulleted list and a numbered list, and you will sort the bulleted list into alphabetical order.

Terms

Bullet A dot or symbol that marks an important line of information or designates items in a list.

Sort To organize items into a specified order.

Notes

Bulleted Lists

- Use **bullets** to mark lists when the order of items does not matter.

- Word has seven built-in bullet styles.

- The default bullet symbol is a simple black dot, indented .25" from the left margin. The symbol is followed by a .5" left tab, and the text on subsequent lines is indented to .5".

- You can create a customized bullet by changing the font and/or paragraph formatting of one of the built-in bullet styles, or by selecting a different bullet symbol.

- Once you apply a bullet style, that style becomes the default until you apply a different one.

- Word automatically carries bullet formatting forward to new paragraphs in a list.

Select a bullet style in the Bullets and Numbering dialog box

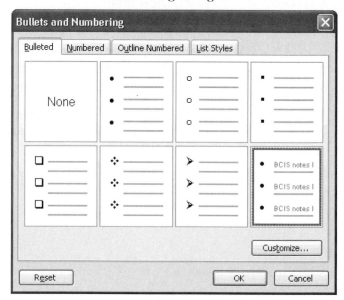

94

Numbered Lists

- Use numbers to mark lists when the order of items matters, such as for directions or how-to steps.

- Word automatically renumbers a list when you add or delete items.

- Word comes with seven numbering styles, but the default numbering style is an Arabic numeral followed by a period.

- You can select a different number style in the Bullets and Numbering dialog box, or customize the formatting to create a new style.

- Word automatically carries number formatting forward to new paragraphs in a list.

- You can restart numbering in the middle of a list.

Select a number style in the Bullets and Numbering dialog box

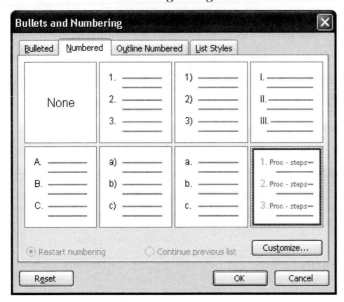

Sort

- Word can automatically **sort** items into alphabetical, numerical, or chronological order.

- A sort can be ascending (A to Z or 0 to 9) or descending (Z to A or 9 to 0).

- The default sort order is alphabetical ascending.

- Although the Sort command is on the Table menu, sorting is available for arranging lists, paragraphs, or rows in regular text as well as a table.

Options for a default sort

Procedures

Create Bulleted List

Use the default bullet:

1. Position insertion point where you want to start list.
   OR
   Select paragraphs you want in the list.
2. Click **Bullets** button `[☰]`.

Select a different bullet style:

1. Position insertion point where you want to start list.
   OR
   Select paragraphs you want in the list.
2. Click **Format** .... `Alt`+`O`
3. Click **Bullets and Numbering** .... `N`
4. Click **Bulleted** page tab .... `Alt`+`B`
5. Click desired Bullet style .... `↓` `↑` `→` `←`
6. Click **OK** .... `Enter`

Customize bullet symbol:

1. Position insertion point where you want to start list.
   OR
   Select paragraphs you want in list.
2. Click **Format** .... `Alt`+`O`
3. Click **Bullets and Numbering** .... `N`
4. Click **Bulleted** page tab .... `Alt`+`B`
5. Click desired Bullet style .... `↓` `↑` `→` `←`
6. Click **Customize** .... `Alt`+`T`
7. Click **Character** .... `C`
8. Click desired symbol .... `Tab`, `↓` `↑` `→` `←`
   ✓ *You can select a different font if you want.*
9. Click **OK** .... `Enter`
10. Click **OK** .... `Enter`

Customize bullet formatting:

1. Position insertion point where you want to start list.
   OR
   Select paragraphs you want in list.
2. Click **Format** .... `Alt`+`O`
3. Click **Bullets and Numbering** .... `N`
4. Click **Bulleted** page tab .... `Alt`+`B`
5. Click desired Bullet style .... `↓` `↑` `→` `←`
6. Click **Customize** .... `Alt`+`T`
7. Click **Indent at** .... `A`
8. Type value to set bullet indent.
9. Click **Tab space after** .... `B`
10. Type value to set left tab following bullet.
11. Click **Indent at** .... `I`
12. Type value to set text indent.
13. Click **Font** .... `F`
14. Select font formatting options.
15. Click **OK** .... `Enter`
16. Click **OK** .... `Enter`

Turn off bullets:

- Click **Bullets** button `[☰]`.
  ✓ *To remove existing bullets, select bulleted list then click Bullets button.*

Create Numbered List

Use default number style:

1. Position insertion point where you want to start list.
   OR
   Select paragraphs you want in list.
2. Click **Numbering** button `[☰]`.

Select different number style:

1. Position insertion point where you want to start list.
   OR
   Select paragraphs you want in list.
2. Click **Format** .... `Alt`+`O`
3. Click **Bullets and Numbering** .... `N`
4. Click **Numbered** page tab .... `Alt`+`N`
5. Click Number style .... `↓` `↑` `→` `←`
6. Click **OK** .... `Enter`

Customize number style:

1. Position insertion point where you want to start list.
   OR
   Select paragraphs you want in list.
2. Click **Format** .... `Alt`+`O`
3. Click **Bullets and Numbering** .... `N`
4. Click **Numbered** page tab .... `Alt`+`N`
5. Click Number style .... `↓` `↑` `→` `←`
6. Click **Customize** .... `T`
7. Click **Font** .... `F`
8. Select font formatting options.
9. Click **OK** .... `Enter`
10. Click **Number style** .... `N`
11. Select desired style.
12. Click **Start at** .... `S`
13. Type starting number.
14. Click **Number position** .... `U`
15. Select desired alignment.
    ✓ *This positions the number in relation to the indent setting.*
16. Click **Aligned at** .... `A`
17. Type value to set number indent.
18. Click **Tab space after** .... `B`
19. Type value to set left tab following number.
20. Click **Indent at** .... `I`
21. Type value to set text indent.
22. Click **OK** .... `Enter`
23. Click **OK** .... `Enter`

Turn off numbering:

- Click **Numbering** button ▤.
  - ✓ *To remove numbers, select numbered list, then click Numbering button.*

Restart numbering in the middle of a list:

1. Position insertion point in paragraph where you want to restart numbering.
2. Click **Format**............... `Alt`+`O`
3. Click **Bullets and Numbering**......................`N`
4. Click **Numbered** page tab.................`Alt`+`N`
5. Click **Restart Numbering**....`R`
6. Click **OK**......................`Enter`

OR

1. Right-click number where you want to restart numbering.
2. Click **Restart Numbering**....`R`

Reset customized bullets or numbers:

1. Position insertion point in formatting list.
   OR
   Select paragraphs in list.
2. Click **Format** ....`Alt`+`O`
3. Click **Bullets and Numbering** ....`N`
4. Click **Numbered** page tab ....`Alt`+`N`
   OR
   Click **Bulleted** page tab ....`Alt`+`B`
5. Click style to reset ....`↓``↑``→``←`
6. Click **Reset** ....`Alt`+`E`
7. Click **Yes** ....`Y`
8. Click **OK** ....`Enter`

Sort a List

Use default sort order:

1. Select the paragraphs you want sorted.
2. Click **Table** ....`Alt`+`A`
3. Click **Sort** ....`S`
4. Click **OK** ....`Enter`

Use a numerical or chronological sort:

1. Select the paragraphs you want sorted.
2. Click **Table**.................`Alt`+`A`
3. Click **Sort** ....`S`
4. Click **Type** drop-down arrow ....`Alt`+`Y`
5. Click **Number**...........`↓`, `Enter`
   OR
   Click **Date** ....`↓`, `Enter`
6. Click **OK**......................`Enter`

Reverse the sort order:

1. Select the paragraphs you want sorted.
2. Click **Table**.................`Alt`+`A`
3. Click **Sort** ....`S`
4. Click **Descending**.......`Alt`+`D`
5. Click **OK**.........................`Enter`

Exercise Directions

1. Start Word, if necessary.
2. Open 💿**19CHECKIN**.
3. Save the document as **CHECKIN**.
4. Edit and format the document as shown in Illustration A.
   a. Set fonts, font sizes, and alignments as shown.
      - ✓ *Unless otherwise noted, use 12-point Arial, flush left.*
   b. Set tabs and set paragraph spacing as shown.
   c. Insert symbols as shown.
   d. Use the default bullet style to turn the five guidelines into a bulleted list.
   e. Select the bullet style shown in the illustration.
   f. Use the default number style to turn the four steps for evacuation into a numbered list.
   g. Select a different number style.
   h. Change back to the default number style.
   i. Sort the bulleted list into ascending alphabetical order.
5. Check the spelling and grammar.
6. Display the document in Print Preview. It should look similar to the one in the Illustration.
7. Print the document.
8. Close the document, saving all changes.

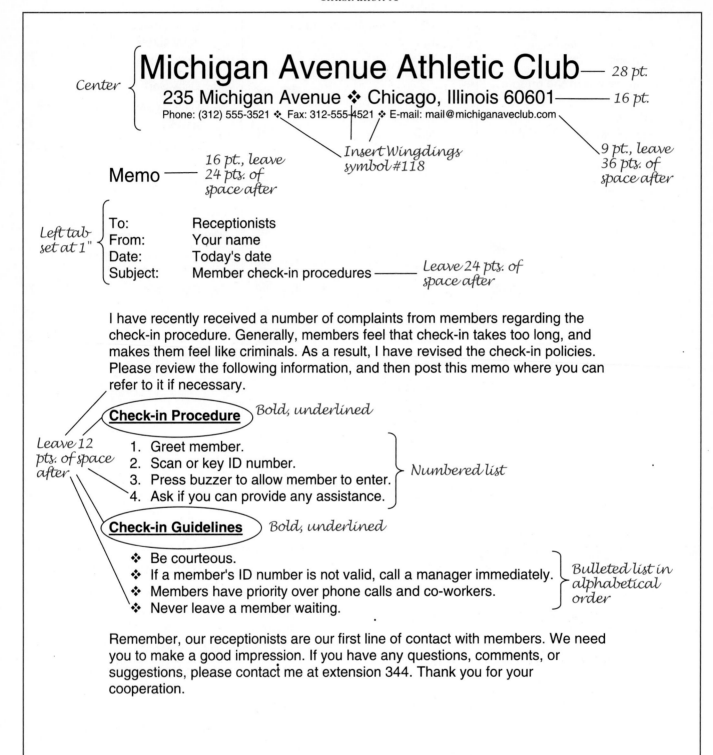

Center {

Michigan Avenue Athletic Club — *28 pt.*
235 Michigan Avenue ❖ Chicago, Illinois 60601 — *16 pt.*
Phone: (312) 555-3521 ❖ Fax: 312-555-4521 ❖ E-mail: mail@michiganaveclub.com

Insert Wingdings symbol #118

9 pt., leave 36 pts. of space after

Memo — *16 pt., leave 24 pts. of space after*

Left tab set at 1" {
To: Receptionists
From: Your name
Date: Today's date
Subject: Member check-in procedures — *Leave 24 pts. of space after*

I have recently received a number of complaints from members regarding the check-in procedure. Generally, members feel that check-in takes too long, and makes them feel like criminals. As a result, I have revised the check-in policies. Please review the following information, and then post this memo where you can refer to it if necessary.

<u>Check-in Procedure</u> *Bold, underlined*

Leave 12 pts. of space after

1. Greet member.
2. Scan or key ID number.
3. Press buzzer to allow member to enter.
4. Ask if you can provide any assistance.

Numbered list

<u>Check-in Guidelines</u> *Bold, underlined*

❖ Be courteous.
❖ If a member's ID number is not valid, call a manager immediately.
❖ Members have priority over phone calls and co-workers.
❖ Never leave a member waiting.

Bulleted list in alphabetical order

Remember, our receptionists are our first line of contact with members. We need you to make a good impression. If you have any questions, comments, or suggestions, please contact me at extension 344. Thank you for your cooperation.

On Your Own

1. Create a new document in Word.

2. Save the file as **OWD19**.

3. Type a bulleted list of five things you'd like to accomplish in the next year. These can be goals for school, work, or personal development. Examples might include earning a better grade in math, completing a project on the job, or getting in better shape by exercising and eating right.

4. Sort the list in alphabetical order.

5. Using a different font, type a numbered list that includes at least five steps describing how you expect to accomplish one of the items in the bulleted list.

6. Change the sort order of the bulleted list to descending order.

7. Save the changes and then print the document.

8. Ask a classmate to review the document and make suggestions and comments.

9. Incorporate the suggestions and comments into the document.

10. Save your changes, close the document, and exit Word.

Exercise 20

Skills Covered:

◆ **Apply Styles** ◆ **Create a Style** ◆ **Edit a Style**
◆ **Reapply Direct Formatting** ◆ **Check Formatting**
◆ **Clear Formatting**

On the Job

Word provides many ways to apply and remove formatting in documents. Use styles to apply a collection of formatting settings to characters or paragraphs. Styles help ensure continuity in formatting throughout a document. You can also set Word to check for formatting inconsistencies in much the same way it checks for spelling and grammatical errors.

Restoration Architecture has contracted with a training company to provide computer training for employees. You have been asked to prepare a document listing the courses that will be available for the first three months of the year. In this exercise, you will use styles and direct formatting to apply consistent formatting to the document.

Terms

Style A collection of formatting settings that can be applied to characters or paragraphs.

Style sheet A list of available styles.

Direct formatting Individual font or paragraph formatting settings applied directly to text, as opposed to a collection of settings applied with a style.

Notes

Apply Styles

- **Styles** make it easy to apply a collection of formatting settings to characters or paragraphs all at once.
- Word includes built-in styles for formatting body text, headings, lists, and other parts of documents.
- Different Word templates have different **style sheets** depending on formatting required for the document. For example, the default Normal template uses only five styles, while the Resume template includes 25 styles.

The Style list for the Normal template style sheet

100

- You can apply a style to existing text, or select a style before you type new text.
- You can select a style from the drop-down style list or from the Styles and Formatting task pane.

Styles and Formatting task pane

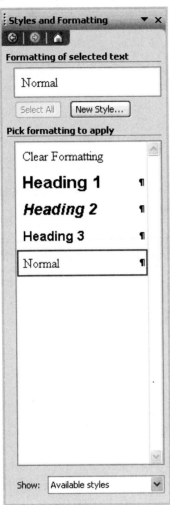

Create a Style

- You can create new styles for formatting your documents.
- Styles can contain font and/or paragraph formatting.
- Style names should be short and descriptive.
- The style will be added to the style sheet for the current document.

Edit a Style

- You can modify an existing style.
- When you modify a style that has already been applied to text in the document, the formatted text automatically changes to the new style.

- If you modify a style and give it a new name, it becomes a new style; the original style remains unchanged.

Reapply Direct Formatting

- When you apply **direct formatting** to text in a document, Word automatically adds information about the direct formatting to the name of current style in the Style box on the Formatting toolbar.
- The direct formatting is also added to the Style drop-down list and to the list of available formatting in the Styles and Formatting task pane.
- This makes it easy to reapply direct formatting that you have already used to selected text.
- This feature is similar to the Format Painter, but you do not have to scroll through the document from the formatted text to the text you want to format.

Check Formatting

- Use Word's Format Checker to insure consistent formatting throughout a document.
- Word underlines formatting inconsistencies with a wavy blue underline.
- You can ignore the blue lines and keep typing, or correct the error.
- The automatic format checker is off by default; you must turn it on to use it.
- If the wavy underlines distract you from your work, you can turn off the automatic formatting checker.

Clear Formatting

- You can quickly remove all formatting from selected text.
- Clearing the formatting from text removes both direct formatting and styles.
- After you clear the formatting, text is displayed in the default normal style for the current document. For the default document, that means single spaced 12-point Times New Roman, flush left.
- You can clear formatting using the Style list, or the Styles and Formatting task pane.
- To quickly remove direct character formatting only from selected text, press Ctrl+Spacebar; to remove direct paragraph formatting, press Ctrl+Q.

Procedures

Apply a Style

1. Click in the paragraph.
   OR
   Select the text.
2. Click the **Style** drop-down arrow `Normal` on the Formatting toolbar.
3. Select style to apply .... ↑, ↓, Enter

Apply a Style Using the Task Pane

1. Click in the paragraph.
   OR
   Select the text.
2. Click the **Styles and Formatting** button  on the Formatting toolbar.
   OR
   a. Click **Format**.......... Alt + O
   b. Click **Styles and Formatting** .... S
3. Click style to apply in **Pick formatting to apply** list.
   ✓ If necessary, scroll through the list to find the desired formatting.

Create a Style

1. Format text or paragraph.
2. Click in the **Style** box `Normal` on the Formatting toolbar.
3. Type style name.
4. Press **Enter**...................... Enter

Edit a Style

1. Change formatting of text or paragraph formatted with the style.
2. Click in **Style** box `Normal` on the Formatting toolbar.
3. Press **Enter**...................... Enter
4. Click **Update the style to reflect recent changes?** .... Alt + U
5. Click **OK**........................... Enter

Reapply Direct Formatting

1. Select text to format.
2. Click the **Style** drop-down arrow `Normal` on the Formatting toolbar.
3. Select direct formatting to apply .... ↑, ↓, Enter
   OR
1. Select text to format.
2. Click the **Styles and Formatting** button 🗛 on the Formatting toolbar.
   OR
   a. Click **Format** .... Alt + O
   b. Click **Styles and Formatting**.................... S
3. Click direct formatting to apply in **Pick formatting to apply** list.
   ✓ If necessary, scroll through the list to find the desired formatting.

Turn on Automatic Format Checking

1. Click **Tools** .... Alt + T
2. Click **Options** .... O
3. Click the **Edit** tab .... Ctrl + Tab
4. Select **Mark formatting inconsistencies** checkbox .... Alt + F
5. Click **OK** .... Enter

Check Formatting as You Type

1. Right-click formatting inconsistency marked with blue, wavy underline.
2. Click desired correct formatting option on context menu.
   OR
   Click **Ignore Once** to hide this occurrence I
   OR
   Click **Ignore Rule** to hide all occurrences .... U

Clear Formatting

1. Select text.
2. Click the **Style** drop-down arrow `Normal` on the Formatting toolbar.
   OR
   Click the **Styles and Formatting** button `Normal` on the Formatting toolbar.
   OR
   a. Click **Format** .... Alt + O
   b. Click **Styles and Formatting** .... S
3. Select **Clear Formatting** .... ↑, ↓, Enter
   ✓ Clear Formatting is usually found at the top of the drop-down style list or at the top of the Formatting to Apply list.

Exercise Directions

1. Start Word, if necessary.

2. Open ⊙ **20COURSE**.

3. Save the document as **COURSE**.

4. Follow the steps to apply styles and formatting as marked in Illustration A.

5. Apply the Heading 1 style to the company name.

6. Apply the Heading 3 style to the names of the months.

7. Increase the font size of the company name to 26 points, center it, and increase the amount of space after it to 12 points.

8. Create a new style based on the modified Heading 1, named **New Heading 1**.

9. Apply the New Heading 1 style to the text **Training Schedule**.

10. Format the company address line as follows:

    a. Increase the font size to 14 points.

    b. Center the line horizontally.

    c. Apply italics.

11. Reapply the formatting you have just applied to the company address to the names of the three courses.

12. Format the paragraph describing the Word 1 course as follows:

    a. Change the font to 14-point Arial.

    b. Justify the alignment.

    c. Indent the paragraph 1" from both the left and the right.

    d. Leave 12 points of space before and after the paragraph.

13. Create a style named **Course Description** based on the formatting of the course description.

14. Apply the **Course Description** style to the paragraphs describing the Word 2 and Word 3 courses.

15. Add a new line to the end of the document.

16. Clear all formatting from the new line, then type: **Enrollment forms are available in the HR office or on the company Intranet.**

17. Center align the text entered in step 16.

18. Select the options to keep track of formatting and mark formatting inconsistencies.

    ✓ *Notice that Word displays a blue wavy underline under the company name and the description of the Word 1 course.*

19. Right-click the wavy blue underline under the company name to see what Word suggests.

20. Select to replace the direct formatting with the style.

21. Right-click the description of the Word 1 course and then select to replace the direct formatting with the style.

22. Modify the Course Description style to leave only 6 points of space before the paragraph.

    ✓ *Notice that when you apply the change, all paragraphs formatted with the style are changed.*

23. Check the spelling, grammar, and formatting in the document.

24. Display the document in Print Preview. It should look similar to the one in Illustration A.

25. Print the document.

26. Close the file saving all changes.

New Heading 1 ——— # Restoration Architecture

Normal, plus 14-pt. italics, centered.

8921 Thunderbird Road ✧ Phoenix, Arizona 85022 ✧ 602-555-6325

New Heading 1 ——— ## Training Schedule

January

Heading 3

Course Description

Microsoft Word 1 ———

This introductory course will cover the basics of using Microsoft Word 2003 to create common business documents. By the end of the course you will know how to create, format, edit, and print text-based documents such as letters, memos, and reports.

February

Course Description

Microsoft Word 2 ———

A continuation of the Word 1 course, this intermediate level class will delve into some of the more intriguing features of Microsoft Word 2003. By the end of the course you will know how to use mail merge to generate form letters, labels, and envelopes, set up a document in columns, include headers and footers, and insert pictures.

Same as address

March

Course Description

Microsoft Word 3 ———

This final course in the Microsoft Word series covers advanced features. By the end of this course you will know how to use tables, create and modify outlines, use e-mail and Internet features in Word, and share documents with other users.

Normal, centered ——— Enrollment forms are available in the HR office or on the company Intranet.

On Your Own

1. Start Word and open **OWD19**, the document you created in the On Your Own section of Exercise 19, or open ⊙**20GOALS**.

2. Save the document as **OWD20**.

3. Clear all formatting from the document.

4. Use styles to format the document. You can use existing styles, modify existing styles, or create new styles.

5. Apply some direct formatting for emphasis, then reapply the formatting to other text in the document.

6. Check the spelling, grammar, and formatting in the document.

7. Save changes and then print the document.

8. Ask a classmate to review the document and offer comments and suggestions.

9. Incorporate the suggestions into the document.

10. Close the document, saving all changes.

Exercise 21

On the Job

Format a one-page report so that it is attractive and professional. Set margins to meet expected requirements and to improve the document's appearance and readability. For example, leave a wider margin in a report if you expect a reader to make notes or comments; leave a narrower margin to fit more text on a page.

The Michigan Avenue Athletic Club has realized that many members are not sure what a personal trainer can offer. In this exercise, you are responsible for formatting a one-page report explaining what a personal trainer is and how to select one. The report will be distributed to all members and will be included in marketing packets given to prospective members.

Terms

Margins The amount of white space between the text and the edge of the page on all four sides.

Gutter Space added to the margin to leave room for binding.

Section In Word, a segment of a document defined by a section break. A section may have different page formatting from the rest of the document.

Portrait orientation The default position for displaying and printing text horizontally across the shorter side of a page.

Landscape orientation Rotating document text so it displays and prints horizontally across the longer side of a page.

Notes

About Document Production

- There are three basic steps to producing any business document: planning, creating, and publishing.

- The planning stage requires you to think about such questions as the type of document you want to create, who will receive the document, and whether there are any special publishing requirements.

- For example, you might consider what paper to print on, if color ink should be used, how many copies to print, or whether you will need to print on both sides of a page.

- If the project seems too complex, you may decide to use a desktop publishing package, such as Microsoft Office Publisher, instead of using a word processing package, such as Microsoft Office Word.

106

- During the planning stage you should create a schedule that includes milestones, such as how long it will take to gather the information you need, when the first draft will be complete, how long it will take for a review process, and when the final document will be complete.

- The creation stage involves selecting page and document settings, such as margins and page size, and entering and formatting the text and graphics

- The publishing stage involves outputting the document using either your desktop printer or a commercial printer. In some cases, the document may be published electronically on a Web site.

Set Margins

- **Margins** are measured in inches.

- Default margins in Word are 1.25" on the left and right and 1" on the top and bottom.

- You can also set a **gutter** width to leave room for binding multiple pages.

- Margin settings can affect an entire document, or the current **section**.

  ✓ *To set margins for a single paragraph, use indents as described in Exercise 18.*

- On the rulers, areas outside the margins are shaded gray, while areas inside the margins are white.

  ✓ *To see both vertical and horizontal rulers, use Print Layout view.*

- Light gray bars mark the margins on the rulers.

Set Page Orientation

- There are two page orientations:
  - **Portrait**
  - **Landscape**

- Portrait is the default orientation and is used for most documents, including letters, memos, and reports.

- Use landscape orientation to display a document across the wider length of the page. For example, if a document contains a table that is wider than the standard 8.5" page, Word will split it across two pages. When you change to landscape orientation, the table may fit on the 11" page.

Format a One-Page Report

- Traditionally, a one-page report is set up as follows:
  - Left and right margins are 1".
  - The title is positioned 2" from the top of the page.

  ✓ *If you need to fit more text on the page the title may be positioned 1" from the top.*

  - The report title is centered and in either all uppercase or title case.
  - Spacing following the title ranges from ¾" (54 pts.) to 1" (72 pts.).
  - Text is justified.
  - Lines are double spaced.
  - First-line indents are between .5" and 1".

Procedures

Set Margins in Print Layout View

1. Move the mouse pointer over the margin marker on the ruler.
   - ✓ *The mouse pointer changes to a double-headed arrow, and the ScreenTip identifies the margin.*
2. Drag the margin marker to a new location.
   - ✓ *Press and hold the Alt key while you drag to see the margin width.*

Set Margins in any View

1. Click **File**..................... `Alt`+`F`
2. Click **Page Setup** .... `U`
3. Click **Margins** tab .... `Ctrl`+`Tab`
4. Click **Top** text box........ `Alt`+`T`
5. Type top margin width.
6. Click **Bottom** text box.................... `Alt`+`B`
7. Type bottom margin width.
8. Click **Left** text box........ `Alt`+`F`
9. Type left margin width.
10. Click **Right** text box ..... `Alt`+`H`
11. Type right margin width.
12. Click **Gutter** text box ... `Alt`+`G`
13. Type gutter width.
14. Click **Gutter position** drop-down arrow .... `Alt`+`U`
15. Select desired gutter location.
16. Click the **Apply to** drop-down arrow........................... `Alt`+`Y`
17. Select **This point forward**.
    OR
    Select **Whole document**.
18. Click **OK** .... `Enter`

Set Page Orientation

1. Click **File** .... `Alt`+`F`
2. Click **Page Setup**.............. `U`
3. Click **Margins** tab.
4. Click **Portrait**.............. `Alt`+`P`
   OR
   Click **Landscape** .... `Alt`+`S`
5. Click **OK** .... `Enter`

Exercise Directions

1. Start Word, if necessary.
2. Open 📀 **21TRAINER**.
3. Save the document as **TRAINER**.
4. Change the margins to 1" on all sides of the page.
5. Format the report as shown in Illustration A.
6. Apply the Heading 1 style to the title, then apply direct formatting as follows:
   a. All uppercase.
   b. Centered
   c. 72 points of space before and 54-points of space after.
7. Format the body text as follows:
   a. Use a 12-point serif font for the body text. (Times New Roman is used in the illustration.)
   b. Justify and double-space all body text paragraphs.
   c. Leave 6 points of space before and after each paragraph.
   d. Indent the first line of each body text paragraph by .5".
8. If the document extends onto a second page, change the top and bottom margins to .75".
9. Check the spelling and grammar.
10. Change the page orientation to Landscape.
11. Display the document in Print Preview.
12. Print the document.
13. Change the page orientation back to Portrait.
14. Print the document.
15. Close the document, saving all changes.

Illustration A

2" from top of page: 1" margin
plus 72 pts. of space before title

Heading 1, centered ——— **IS A PERSONAL TRAINER RIGHT FOR YOU?**

54 pts. of space after title

Almost everyone could benefit from the services of a personal trainer. In addition to designing a personalized workout program, a good trainer provides motivation and encouragement. He or she helps you understand how to fit exercise into your life and teaches you how to make the most out of your exercise time. The lessons you learn from a trainer help insure a safe, effective workout, even when you are exercising on your own. ——— *All body text is justified, double-spaced, .5" first line indent, 6 pts. of space before and 6 pts. of space after*

Working with a trainer should be a satisfying and rewarding experience. There are many different reasons for hiring a personal trainer. Some people want the motivation of a workout partner, others require specialized services for rehabilitation, and still others are interested in achieving weight loss goals. Before hiring a trainer, make sure he or she has experience helping people with goals similar to your own. Ask for references, and then contact at least three. You should also interview the trainer to find out if you are compatible. You should feel comfortable talking and working together, and you should trust the trainer to respect your time and efforts.

Verify that the trainer is certified by a nationally recognized organization such as the

1" margin   *1" margin*

American Council on Exercise, the American College of Sports Medicine, or the National Strength and Conditioning Association. Many trainers have degrees in subjects such as sports medicine, physical education, exercise physiology, or anatomy and physiology.

For more information about personal trainers, contact Candace at extension 765.

1" margin

On Your Own

1. Create a new document in Word.

2. Save the file as **OWD21**.

3. In the third person, draft a one-page report about yourself. For example, draft a document that you could include in a directory for an organization of which you are a member. Think of the *About the Author* paragraphs found in books and magazines, or the *About the Performers* paragraphs found in a theater program.

4. Double space the report.

5. Use correct document formatting for a one-page report.

6. Use other formatting effects, if appropriate, such as fonts, lists, and symbols.

7. Check the spelling and grammar, then save and print the document.

8. Ask a classmate to review the document and offer comments and suggestions.

9. Incorporate the suggestions into the document.

10. Save your changes and close the document.

Exercise 22

Skills Covered:

◆ Use AutoFormat ◆ AutoFormat as You Type

On the Job

Use the AutoFormat feature to automatically apply styles and other common formatting options to a document. AutoFormat can save you time and help insure consistent formatting throughout a document.

A personal trainer at Michigan Avenue Athletic Club has given you a report on strength training that she would like to hand out to her clients. In this exercise, you will use AutoFormat to format the report.

Terms

Em dash A symbol that is approximately the width of the typed letter M.

Straight Quotes Quotation marks that drop straight down instead of curving to the left or right.

Smart Quotes Quotation marks that curve left or right toward enclosed text.

Notes

Use AutoFormat

- The AutoFormat feature automatically applies styles such as headings and lists to an entire document.

- In addition, it replaces typed characters with symbols. For example, it replaces a double hyphen (--) with an **em dash** (—) and **straight quotes** (") with **smart quotes** (").

- By default, Word applies formatting for a general document, such as a report, but you can specify formatting for a letter or e-mail message.

- You can also select to mark each change so that you can review them individually using Word's Track Changes feature.
  - ✓ *You learn about tracking changes in Exercise 43.*

- Select AutoFormat options on the AutoFormat page of the AutoCorrect dialog box.
  - ✓ *Note that if AutoFormat is turned on, it has been automatically applying formatting to your text all along. For example, it may be replacing straight quotation marks with smart—or curved—quotes.*

The AutoFormat page of the AutoCorrect dialog box

- When AutoFormat as you type is active, Word applies the selected styles and replaces typed characters with symbols as soon as you enter the text in the document.
- For example, if you type two hyphens and then press the spacebar, Word automatically replaces the hyphens with a dash.

The AutoFormat As You Type page of the AutoCorrect dialog box

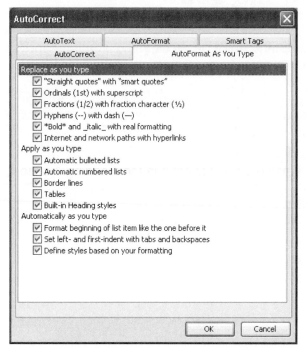

AutoFormat As You Type

- You can set Word to automatically format a document as you type.

Procedures

Set AutoFormat Options

1. Click **Format** .... `Alt`+`O`
2. Click **AutoFormat** .... `A`
3. Click **Options** .... `O`
4. Click options as desired.
   - ✓ *A check mark in a checkbox indicates option is selected. Click it to remove the check mark and deselect the option.*
5. Click **OK** .... `Enter`
6. Click **Cancel** .... `Esc`

Use AutoFormat

1. Click **Format** .... `Alt`+`O`
2. Click **AutoFormat** .... `A`
3. Make sure **AutoFormat now** .... `A`
   option button is selected
   - ✓ *For information on reviewing changes, refer to Exercise 43.*
4. Click **Please select a document type to improve the formatting process** drop-down arrow .... `P`
5. Click desired document type .... `↓`, `↑`, `Enter`
6. **OK** .... `Enter`

Turn On AutoFormat as You Type

1. Click **Format** .... `Alt`+`O`
2. Click **AutoFormat** .... `A`
3. Click **Options** .... `O`
4. Click **AutoFormat as You Type** page tab .... `Ctrl`+`Tab`
5. Click options as desired.
   - ✓ *A check mark in a checkbox indicates option is selected. Click it to remove the check mark and deselect the option.*
6. Click **OK** .... `Enter`
7. Click **Cancel** .... `Esc`

Exercise Directions

1. Start Word, if necessary.

2. Open ⊙ **22STRENGTH**.

3. Save the document as **STRENGTH**.

4. Open the AutoFormat page of the AutoCorrect dialog box.

5. Select all available options in the Apply section and the Replace section.

6. Switch to the AutoFormat as you type page.

7. Select to replace ordinals with superscript and hyphens with dashes.

8. Use AutoFormat to format the document.

9. Insert a new line at the end of the document.

10. Type the subhead **Strength Training at MAAC** and format it in the Heading 1 style.

11. Start a new line and type the following paragraph:

    At Michigan Avenue Athletic Club, we offer strength training equipment for all levels and abilities. Orientation classes are conducted on the 1st Tuesday of every month -- no reservation is required. Other classes may be available. Feel free to schedule a complementary session with one of our personal trainers. They are all certified for strength training and conditioning instruction.

12. Notice as you type that Word replaces the ordinal (1st) with superscript (1st) and the double hyphen (--) with a dash (–).

13. Check the spelling and grammar in the document.

14. Display the document in Print Preview. It should look similar to Illustration A.

15. Print the document.

16. Close the document, saving all changes.

On Your Own

1. Start Word and open **OWD21**, the document you created in the On Your Own section of Exercise 21, or open ⊙ **22MYLIFE**.

2. Save the document as **OWD22**.

3. Clear all formatting from the document.

4. Select all AutoFormat options.

5. Use AutoFormat to format the document.

6. Compare the document to the **OWD21**, the version you created in Exercise 21.

7. Save your changes and close the document.

About Strength Training

Use strength training to increase your metabolism, burn fat, build muscle, and keep your bones and connective tissue strong. Strength training is sometimes called weight training—or weight lifting. It involves using resistance to exercise muscles. The resistance is usually provided by free weights or machines. Machines are generally easier to use, while free weights require a bit more coordination. Most health clubs offer both.

What to Know Before You Start

A good strength training regimen works all muscle groups 1 or 2 days a week. It is important not to work the same muscle two days in a row. Therefore, you should know which muscles are in each group. If you're a beginner, hire a personal trainer to help you get started. The trainer will help you identify your goals, set the number of repetitions and amount of resistance, and teach you the proper way to use machines or free weights. Using weights or machines incorrectly can result in serious injury.

The Workout

A key to successful strength training is developing a routine. Always start with a warm up to prevent injury. Move slowly and deliberately. Strength training is not a race. Continue a routine for at least six weeks before increasing the difficulty level. Always stretch between sets and after the workout.

The number of reps and sets you complete depend on your goals as well as your abilities. For example, if you want to lose body fat, you need to use enough weight that you can only complete 10 to 12 reps and 1 -3 sets, resting no more than 1 minute between sets. For muscle gain you should use enough weight that you can only complete 6 to 8 reps, but you should do at least 3 sets. You should also rest at least three days between sets.

Conclusion

Strength Training is an excellent way to tone your body. Use it in combination with cardiovascular exercise to maintain a healthy body.

Strength Training at MAAC

At Michigan Avenue Athletic Club, we offer strength training equipment for all levels and abilities. Orientation classes are conducted on the 1st Tuesday of every month—no reservation is required. Other classes may be available. Feel free to schedule a complementary session with one of our personal trainers. They are all certified for strength training and conditioning instruction.

Exercise 23

◆ **Critical Thinking**

You are responsible for preparing a document for Restoration Architecture employees who are participating in the in-house training program. In this exercise, you will format the document using font formatting, symbols, lists, line and paragraph spacing, indents, styles, and margins.

Directions

1. Start Word, if necessary.

2. Open ✍ **23TRAIN**.

3. Save the file as **TRAIN**.

4. Set the margins to 1" on the top, left and right, and to .75" on the bottom.

5. Format the title with a 20-point blue, sans serif font (Arial is used in Illustration A) in all uppercase letters, centered, with 36 points of space after.

6. Create a new style named **New Heading 3** based on the Heading 3 style. The new style should use a 16-point plum colored, sans serif font, small caps, and a solid underline. It should have 12 points of space before and after.

7. Apply the New Heading 3 style to the headings **Introduction**, **Come Prepared**, and **Behavior in Class**.

8. Insert an appropriate Wingding symbol at the beginning of each heading.

9. Apply direct formatting to the remaining Normal text as follows:
   a. 14-point serif font
   b. Leading of exactly 17 points
   c. Justify the alignment.

10. Format the three items in the list under the heading **Introduction** as a numbered list, using letters instead of numbers.

11. Set paragraph spacing to leave 6 points of space before the first item in the list and after the last item in the list.

12. Apply a different color highlight to each item in the list.

13. Change the indents of the list so the left indent is .5" and the hanging indent is .5" (set at 1" on the horizontal ruler).

14. Create two bulleted lists under the heading **Come Prepared** (refer to the illustration) using an appropriate Wingding symbol as a bullet.

15. Set paragraph spacing to leave 6 points of space before the first item in each list and after the last item in each list.

16. Sort all three lists into descending alphabetical order.

17. Emphasize the text **come prepared** at the end of first sentence under the heading **Come Prepared** by applying bold italics font formatting and red color.

18. Reapply the formatting you applied in step 17 to the text **maintain a professional attitude** in the last paragraph.

19. Check the spelling, grammar, and formatting in the document.

20. Display the document in Print Preview. It should look similar to the one in the illustration. If necessary use Shrink to Fit to fit it on a single page.

21. Print the document.

22. Close the document, saving all changes.

WHAT TO EXPECT FROM IN-HOUSE TRAINING

📖 INTRODUCTION

In-house training course are offered to insure that employees have the opportunity to stay current in their selected fields, or to provide instruction that the employer requires. In general, you can expect the following from most in-house training courses:

    A.   Experienced teachers
    B.   Focused content
    C.   Hand-on training

📖 COME PREPARED

One of the most important things you can do to insure your success in any in-house training course is to *come prepared*. If there is any homework or outside reading to complete, be sure it is done on time. Also, there are a few basic items you should always bring to class:

- ☑ Pencil
- ☑ Pen
- ☑ Notebook

In addition, there may be items that are specific to the course as well as optional items. For example:

- ☑ Water bottle
- ☑ Pencil sharpener
- ☑ Calculator

📖 BEHAVIOR IN CLASS

Keep in mind that although in-house training classes may feel like a day off, you are still at work. You should *maintain a professional attitude* at all times. The other members of the class are your co-workers, who you will see every day. The information you are learning is designed to enhance your job performance. With that said, you should make every effort to be relaxed, to have fun, and to get as much as possible out of the course. If you pay attention, ask questions, and complete the assignments, you will find that in-house training is a positive, enjoyable experience.

Exercise 24

On the Job

Log on to the Internet to access information on any subject and to communicate with other people. Use Word's Internet features to make using the Internet easy and familiar.

Your supervisor at Restoration Architecture is going to a meeting in San Diego, California. She is interested in visiting the zoo while she is there and has asked you to locate some basic information, such as the hours, the admission fees, and whether there are any special exhibits. In this exercise, you will use the Internet to locate the San Diego Zoo site. You will add the site to your Favorites folder and save the page that has the information you need locally so you can read it offline in Word.

Terms

Internet A worldwide network of computers.

World Wide Web A system for finding information on the Internet through the use of linked documents.

Internet Service Provider (ISP) A company that provides access to the Internet for a fee.

Web browser Software that makes it easy to locate and view information stored on the Internet. Common browsers include Internet Explorer and Netscape Navigator.

Shareware Software that can be downloaded from the Internet for free or for a nominal fee.

Web site A set of linked Web pages.

Web page A document stored on the World Wide Web.

Uniform Resource Locator (URL) A Web site's address on the Internet.

Hyperlinks or links Text or graphics in a document set up to provide a direct connection with a destination location or document. When you click a hyperlink, the destination displays.

Notes

Internet Basics

- Anyone with a computer, an **Internet** connection, and communications software can access the Internet and the **World Wide Web**.

- For a fee, **Internet Service Providers (ISP)** provide you with an e-mail account, **Web browser** software, and Internet access.

- Microsoft Office 2003 comes with the Internet Explorer Web browser, although your computer may be set up to use a different browser.

  ✓ *This exercise assumes you are using Internet Explorer. If your computer is set up to use a different browser, ask your instructor for directions.*

- Some things available via the Internet and the World Wide Web include e-mail communication, product information and support, reference material, shopping, stock quotes, travel arrangements, real estate information, **shareware,** and games.

Use Internet Features in Word

- If you have a connection to the Internet and Web browser software, you can use Word's Web toolbar to access the Internet.

Web toolbar

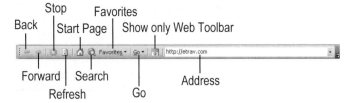

- Word remains running while you use the Internet, so you can go back and forth from Word to the Internet sites that you have opened on your browser.

- To locate a **Web site**, **Web page**, or document, you enter its Internet address, or **Uniform Resource Locator (URL)**, in the Address field on the Web toolbar.

- If you don't know the URL of a site, you can search the Web for the site you want using an Internet search engine.

- Most sites provide **hyperlinks**, also called **links**, to related pages or sites. Text links are usually a different color and underlined to stand out from the surrounding text. Graphics may also be links.

- When the mouse pointer rests on a link, the pointer changes to a hand with a pointing finger, and a ScreenTip shows the destination.

Save a Web Page Locally

- You use your browser's Save As command to save a Web page on your computer.

- Once you save a Web page, you can access it while you are working offline.

- When you save a Web page you can select from four file types:
  - Web page, complete. This saves all of the associated files needed to display the Web page, including graphics, in a separate folder in the same location as the HTML file.

- Web Archive. Saves a snapshot of the current Web page in a single file.

- Web Page, HTML only. Saves the information on the Web page but does not save the associated files.

- Text Only. Saves the information in plain text format.

- If you don't need to save an entire Web page, you can paste selected information into a Word document.

- You can also use your browser to print a Web page.
  - ✓ *Be aware that most Web pages print on more than one sheet of paper. To save time and resources, print only the information you really need.*

The Favorites Folder

- Use the Favorites folder on your computer to store the URLs of Web sites you like to access frequently.

- You can also add locally stored files and folders to your Favorites folder.

- The easiest way to add a URL to the Favorites folder is by using your Web browser, but you can use Word as well.

- Access the Favorites folder from Word or from Windows when you want to go directly to one of your favorite sites.

The Favorites Folder

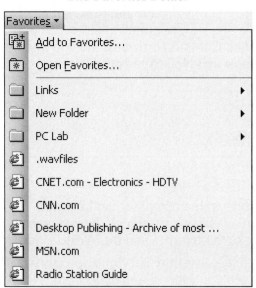

Procedures

Use Internet Features in Word

To display the Web toolbar:

1. Click **View**................. Alt + V
2. Select **Toolbars**................. T
3. Click **Web** .... ↑ , ↓ Enter

OR

1. Right-click on any toolbar.
2. Click **Web** .... ↑ , ↓ Enter

   ✓ *Be sure to select the Web toolbar, and not the Web Tools toolbar.*

To search the Web:

   ✓ *You must have an Internet connection and an account with an ISP in order to search the Web.*

1. Click **Search the Web** button 🔍 .

   OR

   a. Click **Go** Go ▾ .... Alt + G
   b. Click **Search the Web** .... W

      ✓ *The default search site will vary depending on ISP. Common Search sites include Yahoo!, AltaVista, and Excite.*

2. Type search topic in **Search** text box.
3. Click **Search** button.

   ✓ *The name on the search button (Find It, Go Get It, etc.) will vary depending on the search site.*

4. Click a hyperlink on the Search Results page to go to that site.

To go to a specific URL:

1. Type URL in Address drop-down list box on Web toolbar.
2. Press **Enter** .... Enter

OR

1. Click **Go** Go ▾ .... Alt + G
2. Click **Open Hyperlink** 📇 ... O
3. Type the URL in the Address list box.
4. Click **OK** .... Enter

To go to a previously visited URL:

1. Click **Address** list drop-down arrow on Web toolbar.
2. Click URL.

To use a hyperlink:

1. Move mouse pointer to touch link.
2. Click left mouse button.

To display the previously displayed page or document:

- Click **Back** button ⏴ Back on the Browser's toolbar.

To display the next Web page:

- Click **Forward** button ⏵ on the Browser's toolbar.

   ✓ *If the Back or Forward button is dimmed on the toolbar, there is no page to go to.*

Save a Web page locally:

1. Open Web page in browser.
2. Click **File** .... Alt + F
3. Click **Save As** .... Alt + A
4. Type file name.
5. Select storage location.
6. Click **Save as type** .... Alt + T + ↓ drop-down arrow.
7. Click desired file type.
8. Click **Save** .... Alt + S

The Favorites Folder

To use Internet Explorer to add a site to your Favorites folder:

1. Open Internet site to add to Favorites.
2. Click **Favorites** .... Alt + A
3. Click **Add to Favorites** .... A
4. Type site name if necessary.................. Alt + N

   ✓ *Your browser automatically enters a site name; you can edit it if you want.*

5. Click **OK**.......................... Enter

To use Word to add a file to your Favorites folder:

1. Open file to add to Favorites.
2. Click **Favorites** button  .... Alt + S on Web toolbar.
3. Click **Add to Favorites** .... A

   ✓ *The Add to Favorites dialog box is similar to the Save As dialog box.*

4. Type a name.
5. Click **Add** .... Alt + A

To go to a site from your Favorites folder:

1. Click **Favorites** button Favorites ▾ .... Alt + S
2. Click site name.

   ✓ *If necessary, Word starts your Web browser to connect to the Internet and display the site.*

Exercise Directions

1. Start Word, if necessary.
2. Display the Web toolbar.
3. On the Address line, type the following and press Enter:
   www.google.com
4. In the Search text box type **San Diego Zoo**.
5. Click the **Search** button.
6. Scroll down the search results page, and click the link that says Welcome to SanDiegoZoo.org!

   ✓ *The results may vary. If you do not see this link, locate any other link that will lead to the zoo.*

7. The Visitor Information page for the zoo opens in your browser.
8. Click the **Back** button to return to the search results page.
9. Click the **Forward** button.
10. Scroll up and down the page to read the information.
11. Use your Web browser to add the page to your Favorites folder.
12. Click the Calendar link at the top of the page.
13. Scroll through the page to see what events are scheduled in the upcoming months.
14. Click the Back button to return to the previous page.
15. Rest your mouse pointer on the word Visit in the menu bar across the top of the page to display a menu of links.
16. Click the Zoo Visitor Info link.
17. Save the Visitor Information page in Web archive format with the name **VISITOR**.
18. Close the browser and disconnect from the Internet if necessary.
19. Open the **VISITOR** document in Word. It opens in Web Layout view, and should look similar to the Illustration.

    ✓ *If the document is not listed in the Open dialog box, change the list to display all file types.*

    ✓ *The Web site may have changed since the writing of this book.*

20. Use Word to add the **VISITOR** document to your Favorites folder.
21. Close the document, saving all changes.

Illustration A

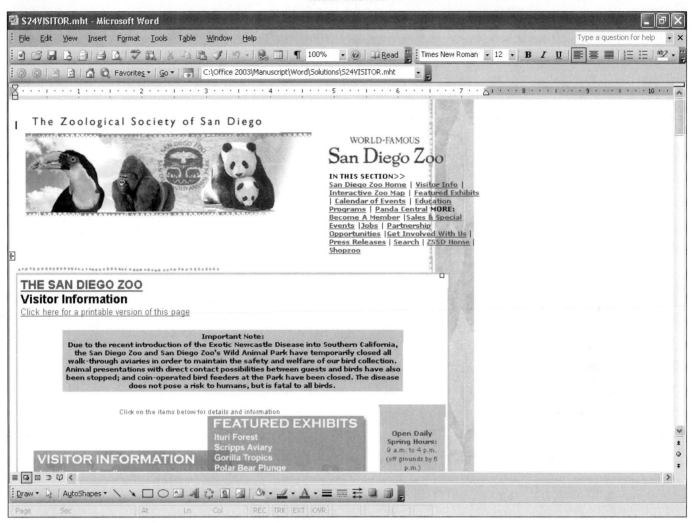

On Your Own

1. If you have access to the Internet, use it to locate a Web site about something that interests you. For example, search for information about your hometown, a sports team that you follow, or a writer, musician, or artist you admire.

2. When you find a site you like, add it to your Favorites folder.

3. Save one of the pages you find as a Web archive document so you can spend more time reading it offline. Save it as **OWD24**.

   ✓ *If you want, try saving the page in one or more of the other available formats so you can see the difference when you open the saved file in Word.*

4. Disconnect from the Internet.

5. In Word, open **OWD24** or open ☺ **24WEB**.

6. Read the document in Word.

7. Close the document and exit Word.

Exercise 25

◆ **Create a Web Page Document in Word** ◆ **Use Web Layout View**
◆ **Use Web Page Titles** ◆ **Apply a Background** ◆ **Apply a Theme**
◆ **Preview a Web Page**

On the Job

Save Word documents in HTML, XML, or MHTML format so that you can display them on the World Wide Web or on a company intranet. You can use Word features and tools to edit and format the documents.

You have been asked to post the in-house training course schedule for Restoration Architecture on the company's intranet. In this exercise, you will open the existing training course document and save it as a Web page. You will then format it with color, a theme, and a background. You will also view it in your browser.

Terms

Web server A computer connected to the Internet used to store Web page documents.

MHTML A format used for storing Web pages as single files so they can be easily transmitted over the Internet.

HTML (Hypertext Markup Language) A file format used for storing Web pages.

XML (Extensible Markup Language) A file format used for displaying and exchanging data via the World Wide Web.

Microsoft Office tags Codes embedded in a Web Page document created with a Microsoft Office program. The codes enable you to edit the document using the original program.

Background The color, pattern, or fill displayed on the page behind data in a document.

Fill effect A texture, shading, picture, or pattern used as a background.

Theme A unified set of design elements and colors that can be applied to a document.

Web bullets Graphics files inserted as bullet markers.

Graphics lines Graphics files inserted as horizontal rules or dividers.

Notes

Create a Web Page Document in Word

- You can save an existing Word document as a Web page so it can be stored on a **Web server** and viewed online.
- You can also create a new blank Web page document.

- By default, when you create a new Web page in Word the file is saved as a single file in **MHTML** format.
- When you save an existing document as a Web page you can choose from four Web page formats:

- Single File Web Page. Saves a Web page and all associated text and graphics in a single file in MHTML format. This is the default option.

- Web Page. Saves the document in **HTML** format. Associated graphics files such as bullets, lines, and pictures are stored in a separate folder that is linked to the HTML file.

  ✓ *The folder has the same name as the HTML file, followed by an underscore and the word files, like this: Filename_files. Use caution when moving or renaming the graphics files or the folder they are stored in. If Word cannot identify the files, the page will display without graphics elements.*

- **XML** Document. Saves a file in XML format.

- Web Page, Filtered. Saves a file in HTML format without **Microsoft Office tags**. This reduces the file size, but limits some functionality for editing the file.

  ✓ *This option is recommended for advanced users only.*

The Save As Web Page dialog box

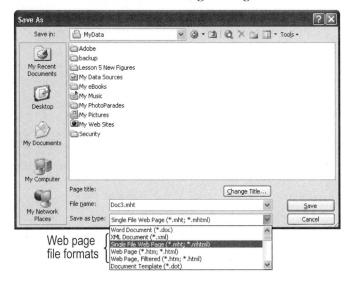

Web page file formats

Use Web Layout View

- Web Layout view displays documents in Word as they will look on the Web.

- Word automatically switches to Web Layout view when you save a document as a Web page, when you create a new Web page document, or when you open an existing Web page document.

- You can also switch to Web Layout view using the View menu or the View buttons.

- Web Layout view lets you edit a document for viewing on-screen, instead of for printing on a page.

- Features of Web Layout view include:
  - Wordwrapping to fit the window, not a page.
  - Graphics positioned as they would be in a Web browser.
  - Backgrounds (if there are any) displayed as they would be in a browser.

Use Web Page Titles

- Web page titles are displayed in the Web browser title bar.

- By default, Word uses the file name or the first line of document text as the Web page title.

- You can set or change the page title name from the Save As dialog box.

Apply a Background

- By default, Word documents—including Web pages—have a plain white **background**.

- Add visual interest or create an effect by applying a color, pattern, **fill effect**, or picture to a document background.

- You should coordinate backgrounds for pages in a Web site to establish continuity.

Apply a Theme

- Word comes with built-in **themes** you can use to format any Word document.

- Each theme includes a background, font formatting, and graphics elements such as **Web bullets** and **graphics lines**.

- You can select a theme to apply consistent formatting to a document.

- Themes can be used with any Word document, but they are particularly useful for formatting Web pages.

Preview a Web Page

- Use Web Page Preview to see how a Word document will look in a Web browser.

- You can display regular Word documents or Web page documents in Web Page Preview.

- When you preview a Web page document, Word opens the document in your default browser.

- You cannot edit a document in Web Page Preview.

Procedures

Save a Document as a Single File Web Page

1. Open the document.
2. Click **File** .... `Alt`+`F`
3. Click **Save as Web Page**.... `G`
4. Type file name.
   - ✓ *If necessary, open the folder, disk, or server where the file will be stored.*
5. Click **Save** button

   `Save` .... `Alt`+`S`

Save a Document in a Different Web Page Format

1. Open the document.
2. Click **File** .... `Alt`+`F`
3. Click **Save as Web Page**.... `G`
4. Type file name.
   - ✓ *If necessary, open the folder, disk, or server where the file will be stored.*
5. Click **Save as type** drop-down arrow .... `Alt`+`T`
6. Click desired file format .... `↑`, `↓`, `Enter`
7. Click **Save** button

   `Save` .... `Alt`+`S`

Create a New Blank Web Page Document

1. Click **File** .... `Alt`+`F`
2. Click **New** .... `N`
3. Click **Web Page** in New Document task pane.

4. Click **File** .... `Alt`+`F`
5. Click **Save as** .... `A`
6. Type file name.
   - ✓ *If necessary, open the folder, disk, or server where the file will be stored.*
7. Click **Save as type** drop-down arrow .... `Alt`+`T`
8. Click desired file format .... `↑`, `↓`, `Enter`
9. Click **Save** button

   `Save` .... `Alt`+`S`

Change to Web Layout View

- Open Web page document in Word.

  OR

- Click **Web Layout View** button 🔲.

  OR

1. Click **View** .... `Alt`+`V`
2. Click **Web Layout** .... `W`

Set a Web Page Title to a Saved Web Page

1. Click **File** .... `Alt`+`F`
2. Click **Save As** .... `A`
3. Click **Change Title** button

   `Change Title...` .... `Alt`+`C`
4. Type new title.
5. Click **OK**
6. Click **Save** button

   `Save` .... `Alt`+`S`

Apply a Background

1. Open file to format.
2. Click **Format** .... `Alt`+`O`
3. Click **Background** .... `K`
4. Click desired color.

   OR

   a. Click **Fill Effects** .... `F`
   b. Click desired page tab .... `Ctrl`+`Tab`
   c. Select desired effect.
   d. Click **OK** .... `Enter`

Apply a Theme

1. Open file to format.
2. Click **Format** .... `Alt`+`O`
3. Click **Theme** .... `H`
4. Select desired Theme .... `Alt`+`T`, `↑`, `↓`
5. Click **OK** .... `Enter`
   - ✓ *Not all themes are installed automatically; if a theme you select is not installed, use the Setup disk to install it, or select a different theme.*

Use Web Page Preview

1. Click **File** .... `Alt`+`F`
2. Click **Web Page Preview**.... `B`

Close Web Page Preview

1. Click **File** .... `Alt`+`F`
2. Click **Close** .... `C`

124

Exercise Directions

1. Start Word, if necessary.

2. Open ⌨COURSE or open ⊙25COURSE.

3. Save the file as **COURSE2**.

4. Use the following steps to format the document as shown in the illustration.

5. Apply the Layers Theme to the document.

   ✓ *This theme uses the Georgia font. If Georgia is not installed on your system, Word automatically substitutes a different font.*

6. Highlight each of the three months/course/course descriptions by using a different font color. Change the **January** information to Blue, the **February** information to Red, and the **March** information to Green.

7. Change the month names to bullet items.

8. Change the background of the document to the Newsprint Texture fill effect.

9. Save the document as a Single File Web page with the name **COURSE2** and the Web page title Restoration Training Schedule.

10. Change the color of the font for the first three lines to Plum.

11. Change the color of the font for the last line in the document to Plum.

12. Check the spelling and grammar in the document.

13. Display the document in Web Page Preview. It should look similar to the one in Illustration A.

    ✓ *The illustration is shown in Full Screen View. You may have to scroll to view the entire page.*

14. Close Web Page Preview.

15. Print the document.

16. Close the file, saving all changes.

On Your Own

1. Plan a personal Web page. Decide the information you would like to include and how you want the page to look. For example, you should include your name what you like to do, who your favorite musicians and sports teams are, where you go to school, or where you work. You might include favorite sayings, upcoming events in your life, or fun things your family or friends plan to do. If you have a connection to the Internet, you might browse other pages to get some ideas.

2. When you are ready, create a new document in Word.

3. Save the file as **OWD25**.

4. Use this document to design a Web page and enter the text.

5. Save the changes, and then save the document as a Single File Web page with the name **OWD25-2**.

6. Apply formatting to improve the appearance of your Web page. For example, change the font formatting, apply a theme or background, create lists, and so on.

7. View the document in Web Layout view.

8. Use Web Page Preview to look at your new Web page in your browser software.

9. Ask a classmate to view the Web page and to offer comments or suggestions.

10. Close Web Page Preview.

11. Incorporate the suggestions into the document.

12. Close the document, saving all changes, and exit Word.

Illustration A

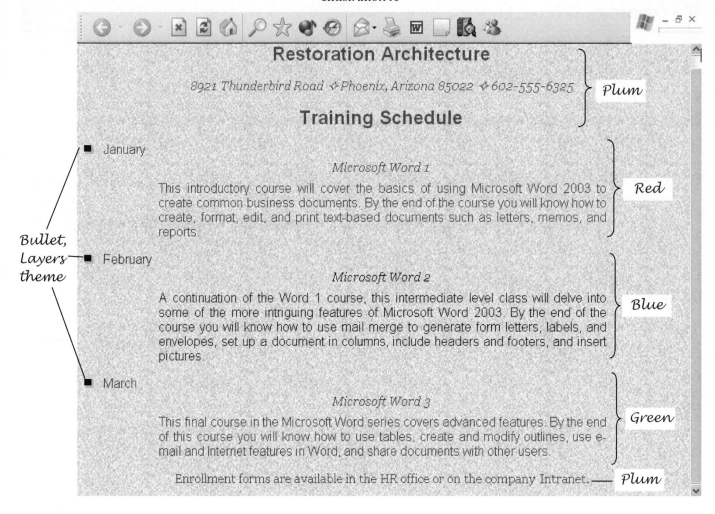

Plum

Restoration Architecture

8921 Thunderbird Road ✧ Phoenix, Arizona 85022 ✧ 602-555-6325

Training Schedule

■ January

Red

Microsoft Word 1

This introductory course will cover the basics of using Microsoft Word 2003 to create common business documents. By the end of the course you will know how to create, format, edit, and print text-based documents such as letters, memos, and reports.

Bullet, Layers theme

■ February

Blue

Microsoft Word 2

A continuation of the Word 1 course, this intermediate level class will delve into some of the more intriguing features of Microsoft Word 2003. By the end of the course you will know how to use mail merge to generate form letters, labels, and envelopes, set up a document in columns, include headers and footers, and insert pictures.

■ March

Green

Microsoft Word 3

This final course in the Microsoft Word series covers advanced features. By the end of this course you will know how to use tables, create and modify outlines, use e-mail and Internet features in Word, and share documents with other users.

Enrollment forms are available in the HR office or on the company Intranet. **Plum**

Exercise 26

◆ Open a Web Page Document in Word ◆ Create Hyperlinks

On the Job

Open an existing Web page document in Word so you can edit it or format it. Create a hyperlink to connect related documents to each other, to connect a Word document to a Web site, or to connect one location in a document to another location in the same document. For example, create hyperlinks from a report topic to an Internet site where more information can be found. Hyperlinks let you expand the boundaries among documents and among computers because, in effect, you can link to information stored anywhere on the Internet.

You have created a Web page document listing training courses for Restoration Architecture. In this exercise, you will open the Web page in Word and insert hyperlinks to help readers navigate through the Web page. You will also link the Web page to a Word document describing what employees should expect from in-house training and to a Web site that provides more information about Microsoft Office products.

Terms

Hyperlink Text or graphics linked to a destination file or location. Click the link to jump to the destination.

Hyperlink destination The location displayed when the hyperlink is clicked.

Hyperlink source The document where the hyperlink is inserted.

Bookmark A nonprinting character that you insert and name so that you can quickly find a particular location in a document.

Notes

Open a Web Page Document in Word

- Use the Open dialog box to open a Web page document in Word the same way you open a regular Word document.
- The document displays in Web Layout view.
- When you save the document, it remains in its original Web page format.
- By default, if you try to open a Web page document from Windows, the document displays in your Web browser, not in Word.

Create Hyperlinks

- **Hyperlinks** can be used to link locations within a single document, to link two documents, or to link a document to an e-mail address.
- Hyperlinks can be created in any Word document, including HTML files.
- When you format text as a hyperlink, Word automatically applies the Hyperlink style, which usually uses a blue font and a solid underline.
- Once you click the hyperlink, the font color changes.

- A **hyperlink destination** does not have to be in the same file format as the **hyperlink source** document. For example, you can link a Word document file to a Web page file or to an Excel file, and the like.

- The hyperlink destination can be a file stored on your computer, on your company intranet, or a site on the Internet.

- When you click a hyperlink to an e-mail address, Word starts your e-mail program and displays a new e-mail message. The address and subject are filled in with the hyperlink information.

- You can create a hyperlink within a document for moving to the top of the document, to a specific heading, or to a **bookmark**.

  ✓ *You learn about bookmarks in Exercise 41.*

- By default, in Word documents you must press Ctrl and click the hyperlink in order to go to the hyperlink destination. This helps avoid accidental access.

- If you want, you can change the setting so that you don't have to press Ctrl.

- You can edit and format hyperlink text the same way you edit and format regular text.

- If you change the setting so that you don't have to press Ctrl to follow a hyperlink, you must select the hyperlink before you can edit it or format it.

- You can change a hyperlink destination.

- You can remove a hyperlink completely.

The Insert Hyperlink dialog box

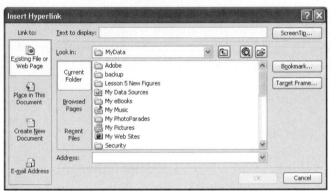

Procedures

Open a Web Page Document in Word

1. Click **File** .... Alt + F
2. Click **Open** .... O
3. Click **file name**.
   ✓ *If necessary, open the folder or disk where the file is stored.*
4. Click **Open** .... Alt + O

Insert a Hyperlink within a Document *(Ctrl + K)*

1. Position insertion point where you want to insert hyperlink.
   OR
   Select text to change to a hyperlink.

2. Click **Insert Hyperlink** button.
   OR
   a. Click **Insert** .... Alt + I
   b. Click **Hyperlink** I
3. Click **Place in this document** in Link to bar .... Alt + A
4. In the **Select a place in this document list**, click hyperlink destination .... Alt + C, ↓
   ✓ *If necessary click the expand symbol (+) to expand the list to show additional headings and/or bookmarks.*

5. Click **OK** .... 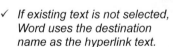Enter
   ✓ *If existing text is not selected, Word uses the destination name as the hyperlink text.*

Insert a Hyperlink to a Different Document

1. Position insertion point where you want to insert hyperlink.
   OR
   Select text to change to a hyperlink.
2. Click **Insert Hyperlink** button.
   OR
   a. Click **Insert** .... Alt + I
   b. Click **Hyperlink** I

3. Click **Existing File or Web Page** in the Link to bar .... Alt + X

4. In the **Address** text box, type the hyperlink destination file name... Alt + E, *type file name*

   ✓ *Word automatically completes the file name as you type based on recently used file names; stop typing to accept the entry or keep typing to enter the name you want.*

   OR

   a. Click **Current Folder** in the Look in bar .... Alt + U
      to display a list of files stored in the current folder

   b. Click the file name in the list of files.

   OR

   a. Click **Browsed Pages** to display a list of recently viewed Web pages .... Alt + B

   b. Locate and click file name.

   c. Click **OK** .... Enter

   OR

   a. Click **Recent Files**.. Alt + C
      to display a list of recently used files.

   b. Click the file name in the list of files.

5. Edit **Text to display** .... Alt + T

   ✓ *Word displays this text as the hyperlink in the document.*

6. Click **OK** .... Enter

Insert a Hyperlink to a Web Page

1. Position insertion point where you want to insert the hyperlink.
   OR
   Select text to change to a hyperlink.

2. Click **Insert Hyperlink** button 🔗.
   OR

   a. Click **Insert** .... Alt + I

   b. Click **Hyperlink** I

3. Click **Existing File or Web Page** in Link to bar ...... Alt + X

4. In the **Address** text box, type the hyperlink destination URL .... Alt + E, *type URL*

   ✓ *Word automatically completes the URL as you type based on other URLs you have typed in the past. Stop typing to accept the entry, or keep typing to enter the URL you want.*

   OR

   a. Click **Browsed Pages** .... Alt + B
      to display a list of Web pages you have recently accessed.

   b. Click the URL or site name you want in the list of files.

5. Edit **Text to display** .... Alt + T

   ✓ *Type the text you want displayed for the hyperlink. Word displays this text as the hyperlink.*

6. Click **OK** .... Enter

Insert a Hyperlink to an E-Mail Address

1. Position insertion point where you want to insert the hyperlink.
   OR
   Select text to change to a hyperlink.

2. Click **Insert Hyperlink** button 🔗.
   OR

   a. Click **Insert** .... Alt + I

   b. Click **Hyperlink** I

3. Click **E-mail Address** in Link to in bar .... Alt + M

4. In the **E-mail address** text box, type the e-mail address .... Alt + E, *type address*

   ✓ *This address will be inserted in the to line of the e-mail message.*

   OR

   Click the address in the **Recently** used e-mail addresses list.............. Alt + C, ↓, Enter

5. In the **Subject** text box, type the text you want displayed in the e-mail Subject text box. .... Alt + U, *type text*

6. Click **OK** .... Enter

Remove a Hyperlink

1. Right-click hyperlink text.

2. Click **Remove Hyperlink** .... R

   ✓ *This removes hyperlink, not the text.*

Change a Hyperlink Destination

1. Right-click hyperlink text.

2. Click **Edit Hyperlink** .... H

3. Select new destination.

4. Click **OK** .... Enter

Set Word to Follow Hyperlink On Click

1. Click **Tools** .... Alt + T

2. Click **Options** .... O

3. Click **Edit** tab .... Ctrl + Tab

4. Deselect **Use CTRL+Click to follow hyperlink** checkbox .... H

5. Click **OK** .... Enter

Select a Hyperlink

1. Right-click hyperlink text.

2. Click **Select Hyperlink** .... S

Exercise Directions

1. Start Word, if necessary.
2. Open ⌨TRAIN or open 💿26TRAIN.
3. Save the file as **TRAIN2**.
4. Insert a new line at the top of the document and clear all formatting from it.
5. Type the text **RETURN**, and then press **Enter**.
6. Display the document in Print Preview.
7. If the document extends on to two pages, use the Shrink to Fit command to fit it on one page.
8. Close Print Preview, and then close the document, saving all changes.
9. In Word, open the file ⌨COURSE2 or open 💿26COURSE.

    ✓ *Remember, this is a Web page document. If you try to open it from Windows, it will open in your browser, not in Word.*

10. Save the file as **COURSE3**.
11. Edit and format the document using the following steps.

    ✓ *Refer to Illustration A to see the completed document.*

12. Position the insertion point at the end of the heading **Training Schedule** and press **Enter**.
13. Apply the Normal style to the new blank line.
14. Type **January** and press **Enter**.
15. Type **February** and press **Enter**.
16. Type **March** and press **Enter** twice.
17. Type the following: **Questions?** and press **Enter** twice.
18. Type **Click here to read about in-house training** and press **Enter** twice.
19. Type **Click here to learn more about Microsoft Office**.
20. Insert a hyperlink from the text **January** that you typed in step 14 to the heading **January**.
21. Insert a hyperlink from the text **February** that you typed in step 15 to the heading **February**.
22. Insert a hyperlink from the text **March** that you typed in step 16 to the heading **March**.
23. At the end of each course description paragraph, press **Enter** and type **Back to Top**.
24. Insert hyperlinks from each occurrence of **Back to Top** to the top of the document.
25. Insert a hyperlink from the text you typed in step 18 to the **TRAIN2** document.
26. Insert a hyperlink from the text you typed in step 19 to the URL www.microsoft.com/office/
27. Increase the font size of all hyperlink text to 16 points.
28. Test the hyperlinks to navigate through the **COURSE3** document.

    ✓ *Use the hyperlinks to go to each month heading, then to return to the top of the document.*

29. Test the hyperlink to go to the **TRAIN2** document.
30. In the **TRAIN2** document, insert a hyperlink from the text **RETURN** back to the **COURSE3** document.
31. Test the hyperlink to return to the **COURSE3** document.
32. Test the hyperlink to go to the Microsoft Office Web site.

    ✓ *You may be prompted to sign on to your ISP.*

33. Click the Back button on your browser's toolbar to return to the **COURSE3** document.
34. Close the simulation or disconnect from the Internet, if necessary.
35. Close all open documents, saving all changes.

Illustration A (Page 1 of 2)

Restoration Architecture

8921 Thunderbird Road ✧ Phoenix, Arizona 85022 ✧ 602-555-6325

Training Schedule

<u>January</u> ——— *Hyperlink to heading January*
<u>February</u> ——— *Hyperlink to heading February*
<u>March</u> ——— *Hyperlink to heading March*

Questions?

Hyperlink to
TRAIN2.DOC

<u>Click here to read about in-house training.</u>

<u>Click here to learn more about Microsoft Office.</u>

Hyperlink to
www.microsoft.com/office/

■ January

Microsoft Word 1

This introductory course will cover the basics of using Microsoft Word 2003 to create common business documents. By the end of the course you will know how to create, format, edit, and print text-based documents such as letters, memos, and reports.

<u>Back to Top</u> ——— *Hyperlink to top of document*

■ February

Microsoft Word 2

A continuation of the Word 1 course, this intermediate level class will delve into some of the more intriguing features of Microsoft Word 2003. By the end of the course you will know how to use mail merge to generate form letters, labels, and envelopes, set up a document in columns, include headers and footers, and insert pictures.

<u>Back to Top</u> ——— *Hyperlink to top of document*

■ March

Microsoft Word 3

This final course in the Microsoft Word series covers advanced features. By the end of this course you will know how to use tables, create and modify outlines, use e-mail and Internet features in Word, and share documents with other users.

<u>Back to Top</u> ——— *Hyperlink to top of document*

Enrollment forms are available in the HR office or on the company Intranet.

On Your Own

1. Think about the documents you have created in the On Your Own sections of previous exercises and identify the ones you might link together into a Web site. For example, you could link the Web page to the list of things you'd like to accomplish, to your resume, or to the announcement of the upcoming event.

2. Open the document **OWD25**, your personal Web page, or open ⊙ **26WEB**.

3. Save the file as **OWD26**.

4. Open the document **OWD12-2**, your resume, or open ⊙ **26RESUME**.

5. Save the file as **OWD26-2**.

6. Create a hyperlink from **OWD26** to **OWD26-2**. You can create new hyperlink text, or use text that is already entered in the document.

7. Create a link back to the Web page from the resume.

8. Open the document **OWD21**, the one-page biography, or open ⊙ **26BIO**.

9. Save the file as **OWD26-3**.

10. Create a hyperlink from **OWD26** to **OWD26-3**. Again, you can create new hyperlink text, or use text that is already entered in the document.

11. Create a link back to the Web page from the biography.

12. If you have access to the Internet, try linking your Web page to a Web site that you like.

13. Test the links.

14. Save the changes to all documents, then close the documents.

Exercise 27

Skills Covered:

◆ **Create E-Mail in Word**
◆ **Attach a Word Document to an E-Mail Message**
◆ **Send a Word Document as E-Mail**

On the Job

E-mail is suitable for jotting quick notes such as an appointment confirmation. You can create and format e-mail messages in Word and then send the messages via Outlook or Outlook Express. When you need to communicate in more depth, you can attach a Word document to the message, or simply send a document as the message itself. You can exchange e-mail messages via the Internet or an intranet with anyone who has an e-mail account, including coworkers located down the hall, in a different state, or halfway around the world.

As the Assistant to the Franchise Manager at Whole Grains Food, you have been compiling a list of potential locations for expanding the business outside of California. In this exercise, you will use e-mail to communicate with the Franchise Manager. First, you will create and send a brief e-mail message about the expansion. Then, you will follow up with a second message to which you will attach the list or potential locations. You will then send a copy of a memo you plan to distribute about the expansion.

Terms

E-mail (electronic mail) A method of sending information from one computer to another across the Internet or intranet.

Internet A global network of computers.

Intranet A network of computers within a business or organization.

Mail service provider A company that maintains and controls e-mail accounts.

Outlook A personal information management program that includes e-mail features that comes with the Microsoft Office suite.

Outlook Express An e-mail program that is included as part of the Microsoft Internet Explorer Web browser.

E-mail address The string of characters that identifies the name and location of an e-mail user.

To Mail notation that indicates to whom an e-mail message is addressed.

Cc (carbon copy) Mail notation that indicates to whom you are sending a copy of the message.

Subject The title of an e-mail message.

Message window The area in an e-mail message where the message body is typed.

Attachment A document attached to an e-mail message and sent in its original file format.

Notes

Create E-mail in Word

- You can use Word to create **e-mail** messages.

- You can edit and format the messages with Word's editing and formatting features, including the spelling and grammar checkers and AutoCorrect.

- To send e-mail messages you must have the following:

  - A connection to the **Internet** or to an **intranet**.

  - An account with a **mail service provider**.

  - An e-mail program such as **Outlook** or **Outlook Express**.

- In addition, your e-mail program must be correctly configured with your e-mail account information.

  ✓ *For more information about sending and receiving e-mail refer to the Outlook section in this book.*

- To send an e-mail message you must know the recipient's **e-mail address**.

- E-mail messages have four basic parts:

  - The recipient's address is entered in the **To**: text box.

  - The addresses of other people receiving copies of the message are entered in the **Cc**: text box.

  - A title for the message is entered in the **Subject** text box.

  - The body of the message is typed in the **message window**.

- The message is sent using your e-mail program.

E-mail in Word

Attach a Word Document to an E-mail Message

- You can attach a Word document to an e-mail message.

- The original document remains stored on your computer, and a copy is transmitted as the **attachment**.

- An attached message is sent in its original format.

- The message recipient can open the attached Word document on his or her computer in Word, or in another application that is compatible with Word.

Send a Word Document as E-mail

- You can send an entire Word document as an e-mail message without attaching it to another message.

- Word adds an Introduction text box to the message header when you send a Word document as e-mail. This text box gives you more room to enter information about the document.

- The original document remains stored on your computer, and a copy is transmitted as e-mail.
- The transmitted document is sent in HTML format so it retains its original formatting when opened in the recipient's e-mail application.
  - ✓ *If you don't want to send or attach an entire document, you can paste a selection from the document into the e-mail message. Simply copy the text from the Word document, make the message window active, and then paste the text into the message.*

Send a Word document as e-mail

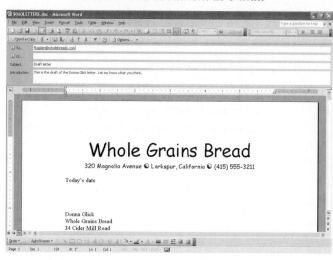

Procedures

Create an E-mail Message in Word

1. Click **File** .... `Alt`+`F`
2. Click **New** .... `N`
3. Click **E-mail message**  in the New Document task pane.
4. Fill in **To**: information .... *type recipient's address*
5. Press **Tab** .... `Tab`
6. Fill in **Cc**: information .... *type additional recipients' addresses*
7. Press **Tab** .... `Tab`
8. Fill in **Subject** information .. *type subject title*
9. Press **Tab** .... `Tab`
10. Type and format message text.
11. Click **Send** button

    `Send` .... `Alt`+`S`

    - ✓ *Log on to transmit message as necessary.*

Attach a Word Document to an E-mail Message

1. Compose an e-mail message.
2. Click **Insert File** button 📎 ▾
3. Select file to attach.
   - ✓ *Select disk or folder from Look in drop-down list, then double-click folder name to locate file.*
4. Click **Insert** .... `Alt`+`S`
   - ✓ *Word adds a new text box to the message heading called Attach: and enters the document name.*
5. Click **Send** button

     .... `Alt`+`S`

OR

1. Open or create the document to attach.
2. Click **File** .... `Alt`+`F`
3. Click **Send To** .... `D`
4. Click **Mail Recipient (as Attachment)** .... `A`
5. Compose e-mail message.
   - ✓ *By default, Word enters the document name in the Attach text box.*
6. Click **Send** button

    `Send` .... `Alt`+`S`

Send an Existing Word Document as E-mail

1. Open document to send.
2. Click **E-Mail** button 📧.
3. Fill in **To**: information .... *type recipient's address*
4. Press **Tab** .... `Tab`
5. Fill in **Cc**: information .... *type additional recipients' addresses*
6. Press **Tab** .... `Tab`
7. Fill in **Subject** information . *type subject title*
   - ✓ *By default, Word enters the document name in the Subject text box. You can edit it if necessary.*
8. Press **Tab** .... `Tab`
9. Fill in **Introduction** information *type introductory text.*
10. Click **Send a Copy** ...... `Alt`+`S`
    - ✓ *If you change your mind about sending the document as e-mail, simply click the E-Mail button 📧 again. Word removes the message heading from the document.*

Exercise Directions

✓ *This exercise uses a fictitious e-mail address. If you try to send the messages, they will be returned as undeliverable.*

1. Start Word, if necessary.

2. Compose an e-mail message as follows:

    a. Enter the address:
       fkaplan@wholegrainsbread.com

    b. Skip the Cc box.

    c. Enter the subject: **Expansion**

    d. Enter the message

       Mr. Kaplan,

       Per your request I have compiled a list of potential sites outside of California that may be suitable for Whole Grains Bread franchises. I can send it via e-mail if you want to take a look.

       Thanks.

3. Check the spelling and grammar in the message.

4. Format the text in a 14-point serif font, such as Times New Roman.

5. Change the color of the company name—Whole Grains Bread—to blue, and then apply bold, italics and a solid underline. The message should look similar to the one in Illustration A.

6. Save the message and then close it. If prompted, name the file **MESSAGE**.

7. Open the document ☉ **27LIST**.

8. Save the document as **LIST**.

9. Sort the items in the list alphabetically in ascending order.

10. Apply a numbered list format to the items.

11. Change paragraph formatting to leave 6 pts. of space before and after each item in the list.

12. Check the spelling and grammar in the document.

13. Save the file and close it.

14. Compose another e-mail message as follows:

    a. Enter the address:
       fkaplan@wholegrainsbread.com

    b. Skip the Cc box.

    c. Enter the subject: **List of Sites**

    d. Enter the message:

       Mr. Kaplan,

       As promised, here is the list of potential sites. Let me know what I should do next.

       Thanks.

15. Format the message text in a 14-pt. serif font.

16. Attach the document **LIST** to the e-mail message. The message should look similar to the one in Illustration B.

17. Save and close the message. If prompted, name the file **ATTACH**.

18. Open the document ☉ **27DRAFT**.

19. Save the document as **DRAFT**.

20. Prepare to send **DRAFT** as e-mail by creating an e-mail document and entering the following message heading information:

    a. Enter the address:
       fkaplan@wholegrainsbread.com

    b. Enter the subject: **Memo About Expansion**

    c. Enter the introduction: **Here's a copy of the memo I plan to send to franchisees. Let me know what you think.**

21. Save and close the message. If prompted, save it as **EMAIL**.

22. Close all open documents, saving all changes.

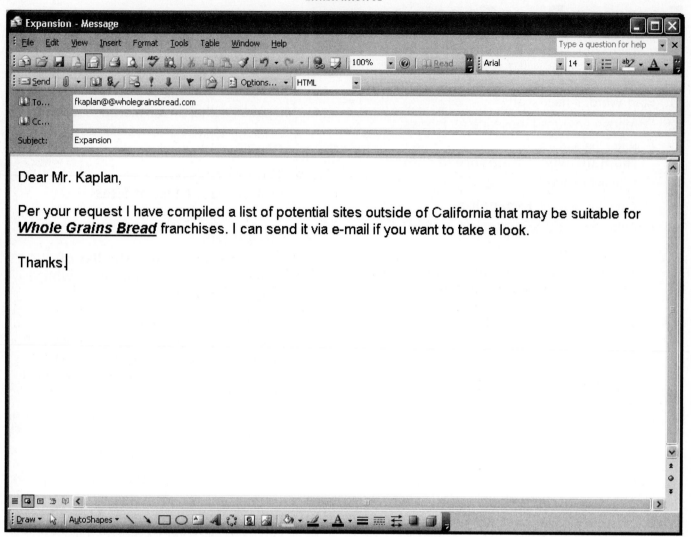

Illustration B

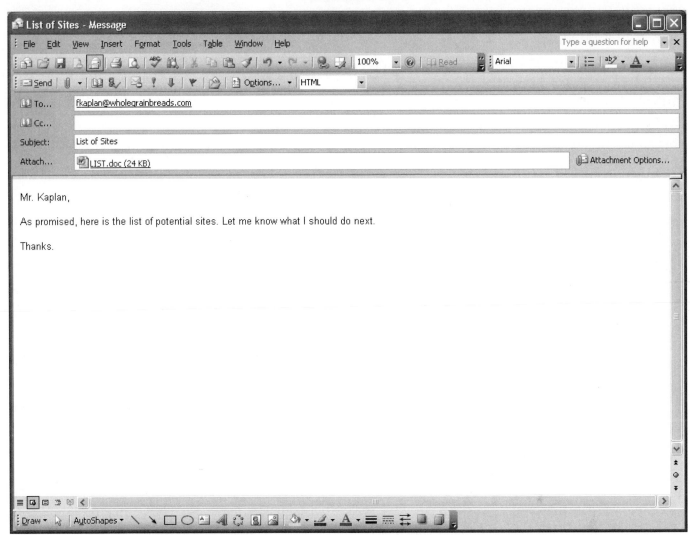

On Your Own

1. Look up and record e-mail addresses for friends, coworkers, and companies.

2. Send an e-mail message to a friend or coworker and ask him or her to send one back to you.

3. Create a new document and save it as **OWD27**.

4. Type a letter to someone else whose e-mail address you have. For example, type a letter to a teacher requesting a missed homework assignment, or to your employer.

5. Attach the document to an e-mail message and send it.

6. Check your e-mail to see if you received a reply.

7. When you are finished, close all open documents, and exit all open applications.

Exercise 28

You have been hired to develop a Web site for Michigan Avenue Athletic Club. In this exercise, you will browse the Internet looking at other health club sites and save a Web page that you like. You will create and format a Web page document, and you will insert hyperlinks linking the Web page to a regular Word document.

Exercise Directions

1. Start Word, if necessary.
2. Display the Web toolbar.
3. On the Address line, type the following and press Enter:

   www.ballyfitness.com
4. Go back to Word.
5. On the Address line, type the following and press Enter:

   www.goldsgym.com
6. Go back to Word.
7. On the Address line, type the following and press Enter:

   www.metfitclub.com
8. Save the Web page in Web Archive format with the name METFIT.
9. Close your Web browser.
10. Create a new blank single file Web page document in Word.
11. Save the file as MAACPAGE, with the page title **Michigan Avenue Athletic Club Home Page**.
12. Apply the Edge theme to the document.
13. Using the default font, type and format the document shown in Illustration A.
14. Check the spelling and grammar in the document.
15. Open the file ⊙ 28STRENGTH.
16. Save the file as STRENGTH2.
17. Apply the Canvas texture background to the document.
18. Insert a new blank line at the beginning of the document and clear all formatting from it.
19. On the new line, type **Return to Home Page**.
20. Insert a hyperlink from the text **Return to Home Page** to the MAACWEB document.
21. Insert a new blank line at the end of the document and type: **Click here to request information via e-mail**.
22. Select the text **e-mail** and insert a hyperlink to **mail@michaveclub.com**, with the subject **Strength Training Info**.
23. Test the *Return to Home Page* hyperlink.
24. In the MAACPAGE document, insert a hyperlink from the text **Weekly Spotlight** to the STRENGTH2 document.
25. Display the file in Web Page Preview. It should look similar to the one in the illustration.
26. Test the hyperlink.
27. Close all open documents, saving all changes.

Illustration A

26 pts., plum, centered

MICHIGAN AVENUE ALTHETIC CLUB

18 pts. plum, centered, leave 24 pts. of space before

WHERE EVERYONE IS A WINNER

16 pts., black, justified, leave 24 pts. of space before

Welcome to the wonderful world of the Michigan Avenue Athletic Club. We're a full-service health and fitness club dedicated to providing a friendly and supportive atmosphere for people of all ages and abilities. We offer a vast array of equipment and classes including aerobics, spinning, yoga, kickboxing, and strength training. We have racquetball and tennis, an indoor pool, spa services, a pro shop, and a café.

Use the links below to learn more about membership, special events, and to access our weekly spotlight on physical fitness.

- Membership rates
- About the staff
- Calendar of events
- Weekly spotlight

Bullet list, 16 pts., black, justified, leave 6 pts. of space before. Last item links to STRENGTH2 document

16 pts., black, justified, leave 6 pts. of space before

Exercise 29

◆ **Create a Table** ◆ **Enter Data in a Table** ◆ **Select in a Table**
◆ **Change Table Structure** ◆ **Format a Table**

On the Job

Create tables to organize data into columns and rows. Any information that needs to be presented in side-by-side columns can be set up in a table. For example, a price list, an invoice, and a resume are all types of documents for which you should use a table. The table format lets you align information side by side and across the page so the information is easy to read.

Restoration Architecture is offering the staff training courses. In this exercise, you will create a memo that includes a list of courses being offered. You will set up the course list in a table.

Terms

Table A grid comprised of horizontal rows and vertical columns into which you can enter data.

Column A vertical series of cells in a table.

Row A horizontal series of cells in a table.

Column markers Markers on the horizontal ruler that indicate column dividers.

Dividers The lines that indicate the edges of cells in a table. Dividers do not print, although they are indicated on-screen by either gridlines or borders.

Border A line drawn around the edges of an element, such as a table or a table cell. Borders can also be drawn around paragraphs and pages.

Cell The rectangular area at the intersection of a column and a row in a table, into which you enter data or graphics.

Gridlines Nonprinting lines that can be displayed around cells in a table.

End of row/cell marks Nonprinting characters used to mark the end of a cell or a row in a table.

Notes

Create a Table

- **Tables** are easier to use than tabbed columns when setting up and organizing data in **columns** and **rows**.

- You can create a table in any Word document; they are frequently used to align data on Web page documents.

- You select the number of columns and rows you want in the table.

- Word creates the table at the insertion point location.

- By default, Word sizes the columns equally across the width of the page.

- **Column markers** on the horizontal ruler show the location of the right **divider** of each column.

- By default, Word places a ½-pt. **border** around all **cells** in a table.

A table with four columns and four rows

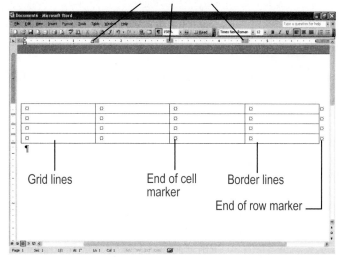

■ Tables have three unique nonprinting elements:
  - **Gridlines**
    - ✓ *Gridlines are only displayed if there are no table borders and if you select the Show Gridlines commands on the Table menu.*
  - **End of cell markers**
  - **End of row markers**

Enter Data in a Table

■ You enter data in the cells of a table.

■ Row height increases automatically to accommodate as much data as you type.

■ Column width does not change automatically. Text wraps at the right margin of a cell the same way it wraps at the right margin of a page.

■ To move from cell to cell you press Tab, or click in another cell with the mouse.

■ When you press Enter in a cell, Word starts a new paragraph within the cell.

■ You can edit and format text within a cell the same way you do outside a table.

Select in a Table

■ As with other Word features, you must select table components before you can affect them with commands.

■ You select text within a cell using the standard selection commands.

■ You can select one or more columns, one or more rows, one or more cells, or the entire table.

■ Selected table components appear highlighted.

Change Table Structure

■ Change a table's structure by inserting and deleting columns, rows, or cells.

■ You can insert components anywhere in a table.

■ You can delete any component.

■ Data entered in a deleted column or row is deleted as well.

■ You choose which way to shift existing cells when cells are inserted or deleted.

Format a Table

■ You can format text within a table using standard Word formatting techniques. For example, use font formatting, alignments, spacing, indents, and tabs to enhance text in a table.

■ You can apply formatting to selected text, or to selected cells, columns, or rows.

■ Use Table AutoFormat to quickly apply formatting effects to an entire table.

■ AutoFormat styles include border lines, shading, color, fonts, and other formatting.

Table AutoFormat dialog box

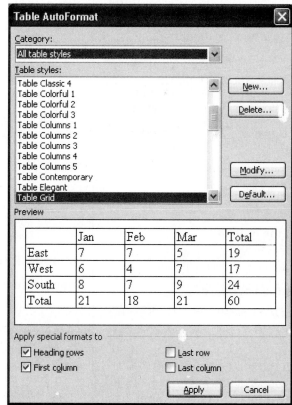

■ AutoFormat overrides existing formatting. Therefore, you should apply AutoFormat first, then apply additional formatting as needed.

Procedures

Create a Table

To use the toolbar button:

1. Position insertion point.
2. Click **Insert Table** button ▦.
3. Drag the mouse pointer across the grid to select desired number of columns and rows.
4. Release the mouse button.

To use menu commands:

1. Position insertion point.
2. Click **Table**.................`Alt`+`A`
3. Select **Insert**.....................`I`
4. Click **Table**.......................`T`
5. Type **number of columns**....................`Alt`+`C`
6. Press **Tab**..........................`Tab`
7. Type **number of rows**........................`Alt`+`R`
8. Click **OK**...........................`Enter`

To show/hide gridlines:

1. Click **Table**..................`Alt`+`A`
2. Click **Show Gridlines**.........`G`
   OR
   Click **Hide Gridlines**..........`G`

   ✓ *The default border is not hidden when you select to hide gridlines.*

To move the insertion point in a table:

With the mouse

- Click mouse pointer where you want to position insertion point.

With the keyboard

- One cell left................`Shift`+`Tab`
- One cell right......................`Tab`
- One cell up...........................`↑`
- One cell down.....................`↓`
- First cell in column.....`Alt`+`Page Up`

- Last cell in column......`Alt`+`Page Down`
- First cell in row........`Alt`+`Home`
- Last cell in row..........`Alt`+`End`

Enter Data in a Table

1. Click in desired cell.
2. Type data.
3. Press **Tab**..........................`Tab`
4. Type data in next cell.
5. Repeat until all data is entered.

Select in a Table

1. Position insertion point within table component to select.

   ✓ *For example, click in cell if selecting cell; click anywhere in row if selecting row, etc.*

2. Click **Table**.................`Alt`+`A`
3. Click **Select**.........................`C`
4. Click one of the following:
   - **Table**...........................`T`
   - **Column**.........................`C`
   - **Row**............................`R`
   - **Cell**............................`E`

Select Adjacent Components

1. Select first component.
2. Press and hold **Shift**..........`Shift`
3. Click in last component to select.

   ✓ *This method enables you to select adjacent columns, adjacent rows, or adjacent cells.*

Change Table Structure

Insert columns or rows:

1. Position insertion point within table.

   ✓ *To insert more than one component, select as many as you want to insert. For example, to insert two columns, select two columns.*

2. Click **Table**.................`Alt`+`A`

3. Click **Insert**........................`I`
4. Click one of the following:
   - **Columns to the Left**.....`L`
   - **Columns to the Right**...`R`
   - **Rows Above**...............`A`
   - **Rows Below**................`B`
   - **Cells**............................`E`

   ✓ *Select option for shifting existing cells to make room for new cells, then click OK.*

Delete entire table, columns, rows, or cells:

1. Select or click in the row or column to delete.
2. Click **Table**.................`Alt`+`A`
3. Select **Delete**.....................`D`
4. Click one of the following:
   - **Table**...........................`T`
   - **Columns**.......................`C`
   - **Rows**...........................`R`
   - **Cells**............................`E`

   ✓ *Select option for shifting existing cells to fill in deleted cell area, then click OK.*

Apply AutoFormat

1. Click **Table**.................`Alt`+`A`
2. Click **Table AutoFormat**.....`F`
3. Select table style..`Alt`+`T`, `↓`
4. Click **Apply**...`Alt`+`A` or `Enter`

Format Text in a Table

1. Select text or cell(s) to format.
2. Apply formatting as with regular document text.

Exercise Directions

1. Start Word, if necessary.
2. Create a new document.
3. Save the file as **SCHEDULE**.
4. Type the document shown in Illustration A.
   a. Type the text and leave blank lines as shown.
      - ✓ *Remember to replace the text Your name and Today's date with the appropriate information.*
   b. Insert a table with three columns and four rows.
   c. Enter the data in the table as shown.
      - ✓ *To enter an en dash between the times, simply type a space, a hyphen, and a space. By default, AutoFormat automatically replaces the hyphen and spaces with an en dash after the second number is typed.*
5. Select the last two rows in the table.
6. Insert two new rows above the selected rows.
7. Enter the following data in the new rows:
   Advanced Word Conference
   Room A   8:30 – 11:45

   Excel for Beginners Conference
   Room B   1:30 – 3:30
8. Insert a new column to the left of the Time column.

9. Enter the following data in the new column:
   Days
   Tuesday, Thursday
   Monday, Wednesday
   Tuesday, Wednesday
   Monday, Thursday
   Friday
10. Delete the row for the Word for Beginners course.
11. Apply the Table Contemporary AutoFormat to the table.
12. Apply italics to all of the course names.
    - ✓ *Select the text, then apply the formatting.*
13. Check the spelling and grammar in the document.
14. Preview the document. It should look similar to the one in Illustration B.
15. Save the changes and print the document
16. Close the document and exit Word.

On Your Own

1. Think of documents that would benefit from table formatting. Some examples include a weekly schedule, meeting agenda, travel itinerary, sales report, telephone/address list, and roster.
2. Create a new document in Word.
3. Save the file as **OWD29**.
4. Use a table to set up the document as a telephone list. The list could include friends, family members, or members of a club or organization to which you belong.
5. Use at least three columns—one for the first name, one for the last name, and one for the telephone number. You may use more columns if you want to include mailing addresses, e-mail addresses, cell phone numbers, or other information.

6. Include at least eight names in the list.
7. Apply an AutoFormat to the table. If you are not satisfied with the results, try a different AutoFormat.
8. Check the spelling and grammar in the document, then print it.
9. Ask a classmate to review the document and offer comments or suggestions.
10. Incorporate the suggestions into the document.
11. Close the document, saving all changes.

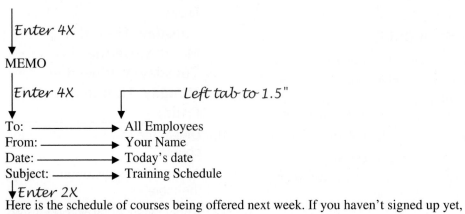

Enter 4X

MEMO

Enter 4X   *Left tab to 1.5"*

To: ⟶ All Employees
From: ⟶ Your Name
Date: ⟶ Today's date
Subject: ⟶ Training Schedule

Enter 2X
Here is the schedule of courses being offered next week. If you haven't signed up yet, please see me immediately.

Enter 2X

Course Name	Location	Time
Word for Beginners	Conference Room A	8:30 – 11:45
Advanced Excel	Conference Room B	8:30 – 11:45
Introduction to the Internet	Media Lab	1:30 – 3:30

Illustration B

MEMO

To: All Employees
From: Your Name
Date: Today's date
Subject: Training Schedule

Here is the schedule of courses being offered next week. If you haven't signed up yet, please see me immediately.

Course Name	Location	Days	Time
Advanced Word	Conference Room A	Monday, Wednesday	8:30 – 11:45
Excel for Beginners	Conference Room B	Tuesday, Wednesday	1:30 – 3:30
Advanced Excel	Conference Room B	Monday, Thursday	8:30 – 11:45
Introduction to the Internet	Media Lab	Friday	1:30 – 3:30

Exercise 30

Skills Covered:

◆ **Set Alignments within Table Cells** ◆ **Align Table on the Page**
◆ **Column Width and Row Height**

On the Job

Use alignment options and tabs to make tables easy to read. Numbers are usually aligned flush right in a cell, while text can be flush left, centered, justified, or rotated to appear vertical. You can vertically align data in a cell as well. Decimal tabs are especially useful in tables for aligning dollar values. Other ways to improve the appearance of a table include aligning the table horizontally on the page and adjusting column width and row height.

Michigan Avenue Athletic Club is planning a major renovation. In preparation, it has surveyed members to find whether they want more tennis courts, more racquetball courts, more equipment rooms, or a lap pool. In this exercise, you will create a memo to the general manager that includes the results of the survey. You will use alignment options to set up the data in the table. You will also set row heights and column widths, and you will align the table horizontally on the page.

Terms

Column width The width of a column in a table, measured in inches.

Row height The height of a row in a table, measured in inches.

Notes

Set Alignments within Table Cells

- You can set horizontal alignment within a cell the same way you set alignment in a document by using paragraph formatting and tabs.

- In a table, numbers are usually right aligned, and text is either left aligned or centered.

- All tab stops can be used within a table cell, but the most useful is the decimal tab stop.

- Decimal tab stops automatically align numbers such as dollar values within a cell or a column.

- You can vertically align data at the top of the cell, centered in the cell, or at the bottom of the cell. The default is at the top.

Text aligned in a table

Centered Vertically		Top Align
	Bottom Align	
Centered Horizontally	Flush Left	Flush Right
Tex can be justified within a table cell; however, there should be at least three lines of text.		
		$2,500.00
		$425,000.00
		$325.00
		$46,870.00

Aligned on decimal tab

Align Table on the Page

■ You can left align, right align, or center a table on the page.

Table tab of the Table Properties dialog box

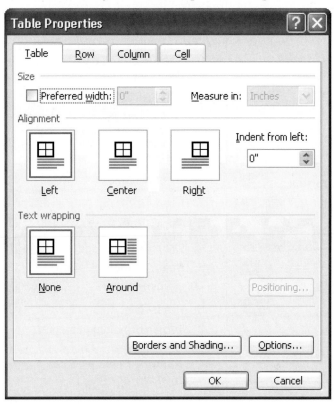

Column Width and Row Height

■ By default, Word creates columns of equal **column width**, sized so the table extends from the left margin to the right margin.

■ Rows are sized according to the line spacing on the line where the table is inserted.

■ By default, **row height** automatically increases to accommodate lines of text typed in a cell.

■ You can drag column dividers to increase or decrease column width.

   ✓ *Press and hold the Alt key as you drag to see the column width measurements displayed on the ruler.*

■ In Print Layout view, you can drag row dividers to increase or decrease row height.

   ✓ *You cannot drag row dividers in Normal view.*

■ You can set precise measurements for columns, rows, cells, and entire tables in the Table Properties dialog box.

Procedures

Set Alignments in Table Cells

To change horizontal alignment:

1. Position insertion point in cell.
   OR
   Select component to format.
2. Click desired alignment button on Formatting toolbar:
   - **Align Left** 📄.
   - **Center** 📄.
   - **Align Right** 📄.
   - **Justify** 📄.

To set tabs in a cell:

1. Position insertion point in cell.
   OR
   Select component(s) to format.
2. Click Tab box at left end of horizontal ruler to select tab stop type.
3. Click desired position on horizontal ruler.

   ✓ *For more information on tabs, refer to Exercise 6.*

To advance insertion point one tab stop within a cell:

- Press .... `Ctrl`+`Tab`

To change vertical alignment:

1. Position insertion point in cell.
   OR
   Select component to format.
2. Click **Table** .... `Alt`+`A`
3. Click **Table Properties** .... `R`
4. Click the **Cell** tab .... `Alt`+`E`
5. Click desired Vertical Alignment option:
   - **Top** .... `Alt`+`P`
   - **Center** .... `Alt`+`C`
   - **Bottom** .... `Alt`+`B`
6. Click **OK** .... `Enter`

Align Table Horizontally in Document

1. Select table.
2. Click desired alignment button on Formatting toolbar:
   - **Center** 🖹.
   - **Align Right** 🖹.
   - **Align Left** 🖹.

OR

1. Click anywhere in table.
2. Click **Table**................. `Alt`+`A`
3. Click **Table Properties** .... `R`
4. Click the **Table** tab...... `Alt`+`T`
5. Click desired Alignment option:
   - **Left** 🔲 .... `Alt`+`L`
   - **Center** 🔲 .... `Alt`+`C`
   - **Right** 🔲 .... `Alt`+`H`
6. Click **OK**........................... `Enter`

Change Column Width

1. Position mouse pointer on column divider.
   - ✓ *Pointer changes to a double-vertical line with arrows pointing left and right.*
2. Click and drag divider left or right.
   - ✓ *Press* `Alt` *at the same time that you drag the divider to see the width displayed on the horizontal ruler.*

OR

1. Click in column.
2. Click **Table** .... `Alt`+`A`
3. Click **Table Properties** .... `R`
4. Click **Column** tab .... `Alt`+`U`
5. Select **Preferred Width** checkbox .... `Alt`+`W`
6. Press **Tab** .... `Tab`
7. Type column width.
8. Click **OK** .... `Enter`

   OR

   a. Click **Next Column** button `Alt`+`N`

   OR

   Click **Previous Column** button `◀◀ Previous Column` `Alt`+`P`

   b. Repeat steps 5-8 to set additional column widths.
   c. Click **OK** .... `Enter`

Change Row Height

1. Click **Print Layout View** button 🔲 .
2. Position mouse pointer on row divider.
   - ✓ *Pointer changes to a double-horizontal line with arrows pointing up and down.*
3. Click and drag divider up or down.
   - ✓ *Press* `Alt` *at the same time that you drag the divider to see the height displayed on the vertical ruler.*

OR

1. Click in row.
2. Click **Table** .... `Alt`+`A`
3. Click **Table Properties**........ `R`
4. Click **Row** tab .... `Alt`+`R`
5. Select **Specify Height** checkbox .... `Alt`+`S`
6. Press **Tab** .... `Tab`
7. Type row height in inches.
   - ✓ *Select Exactly in Row height is box to fix row height at specified size.*
8. Click **OK** .... `Enter`

   OR

   a. Click **Next Row** button `Alt`+`N`

   OR

   Click **Previous Row** button `↥ Previous Row` `Alt`+`P`

   b. Repeat steps 5-8 to set additional row heights.
   c. Click **OK** .... `Enter`

Exercise Directions

1. Start Word, if necessary.
2. Create a new document.
3. Save the file as **DATA**.
4. Use the following steps to create the document shown in Illustration A.
5. Type the memo text.
6. Create a table with five columns and five rows and enter the data as shown.
   - ✓ *You can enter the data before setting alignments in step 7, or after.*
7. Set alignment as follows:
   a. Align the data in the first column centered horizontally and vertically.
   b. Align the data in columns 2, 3, and 4 flush right horizontally and on the bottom vertically.
   c. Align the data in column 5 flush left horizontally and on the bottom vertically.
   d. Center the data in the first row horizontally and on the top vertically.
   e. Use a decimal tab to align the prices in the fifth column, approximately .5" from the left edge of the column.
      - ✓ *Notice that the numbers align automatically as soon as you set the tab.*

8. Make the text in the first column and the first row 14 pts. and bold.
9. Set preferred column widths as follows:
   - Column 1: 1.5"
   - Column 2: .75"
   - Column 3: .75"
   - Column 4: .75"
   - Column 5: 1.5"
10. Set all rows to be at least .5" high.
11. Center the entire table horizontally on the page.
12. Check the spelling and grammar.
13. Display the document in Print Preview. It should look similar to the one in Illustration A.
    - ✓ *If necessary, adjust the column widths so your document looks like the illustration.*
14. Print the document.
15. Close the document, saving all changes.

On Your Own

1. Plan and conduct a survey in class. You might survey your classmates about a current issue such as school dress codes or how much they are willing to pay for lunch or you might just ask classmates to name their favorite color, favorite food, or favorite animal.
2. When you have completed the survey and have the results handy, create a new document in Word.
3. Save the file as **OWD30**.
4. Type a title for the document.
5. Create a table in the document so you can enter the results of the survey. Use as many as columns and rows as necessary.
6. Apply an AutoFormat if you want, or manually format the text in the table.

7. Set column width and row height as necessary.
8. Align the data so it looks good and is easy to read. Remember, numbers are usually aligned right and text is usually aligned left.
9. Center the table on the page.
10. Type a brief summary or conclusion paragraph based on the data.
11. Check the spelling and grammar in the document.
12. Save the changes and print the document.
13. Ask a classmate to review the document and offer comments and suggestions.
14. Incorporate the suggestions in the document.
15. Save all changes, close the document, and exit Word.

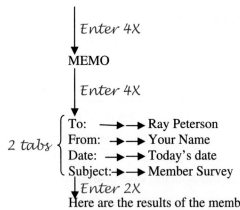

Enter 4X

MEMO

Enter 4X

2 tabs {
To: ⟶▶⟶ Ray Peterson
From: ▶⟶ Your Name
Date: ▶⟶ Today's date
Subject:▶⟶ Member Survey
}

Enter 2X

Here are the results of the member survey. I have also included information about the potential costs associated with each item. We can use this data to help decide where we want to focus our efforts during the renovation.

Enter 4X

	Want	Do not Care	Do not Want	Potential Cost
Tennis court	19	10	5	$50,000.00
Racquetball court	25	15	7	$50,000.00
Equipment room	45	22	2	$75,000.00
Lap pool	8	5	12	$115,000.00

Exercise 31

◆ **Tables and Borders Toolbar**
◆ **Draw a Table** ◆ **Move and Resize Tables**
◆ **Merge and Split Cells** ◆ **Rotate Text** ◆ **Wrap Text**

On the Job

Word's Draw Table tool gives you great flexibility to organize tables the way you want them, not necessarily in rigid columns and rows. You can layout the table cells exactly as you want them in order to organize text and data. You can then move and resize the table, if necessary, merge and split cells, and rotate the text to achieve the exact effect you need.

The Exercise Director at Michigan Avenue Athletic Club has asked you to design a flyer announcing a series of new classes. In this exercise, you will open and format a document describing the classes. You will then create a table listing the schedule of classes, and integrate it into the flyer.

Terms

Merge Combine multiple adjacent cells together to create one large cell.

Header row A row across the top of a table in which heading information is entered.

Split Divide one cell into multiple cells, either vertically to create columns or horizontally to create rows.

Notes

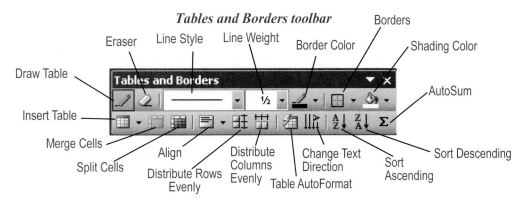

Tables and Borders toolbar

Tables and Borders Toolbar

- Use the buttons on the Tables and Borders toolbar to create and format tables.

  ✓ *If the toolbar is in your way while working, move it or dock it across the top of the document window.*

Draw a Table

- Word's Draw Table feature lets you create tables with uneven or irregular columns and rows.
- You must use Print Layout view to draw a table.

- When you draw a table, the mouse pointer functions as a pencil.

- You drag the pointer to draw lines vertically or horizontally to create cell dividers.
- Word creates straight lines at 90 degree angles to existing cell dividers, even if you do not drag in a straight line.
- You can draw a diagonal line across a cell as a visual element or border, not to split the cell diagonally.
- New cells can be drawn anywhere. Rows and columns do not have to extend across the entire table.
- You can combine the Insert Table command with the Draw Table command to customize any table.

Move and Resize Tables

- You can drag the table anchor to move the table anywhere on the page.
- You can drag the sizing handle to change the table size.

Table anchor and sizing handle

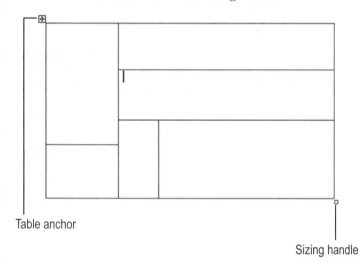

Table anchor

Sizing handle

Merge and Split Cells

- You can **merge** horizontally adjacent cells or vertically adjacent cells.
- You can use the eraser tool to erase dividers between cells, thus merging the cells.
- If you erase a divider on the outer edge of the table, you simply erase the border line, not the divider itself.
- Merging is useful for creating a **header row** across a table.
- **Split** a cell to insert dividers to create additional columns or rows.

Rotate Text

- Rotate text direction within a cell so text runs from left to right, from top to bottom, or from bottom to top.

Rotate text in a table

Text direction is vertical bottom to top.	Text direction is the default left to right.	Text direction is vertical top to bottom.

Wrap Text

- By default, tables are inserted on a blank line above or below existing text.
- You can set Word to wrap text around the table.
- Wrapping text around a table integrates the table object into the text so text appears above, below, and on either side of the table.

Procedures

Display Tables and Borders Toolbar

- Click **Tables and Borders** button ⊞ on the Standard toolbar.

OR

1. Click **View**.....................Alt+V
2. Click **Toolbars**.....................T
3. Click **Tables and Borders**.

OR

1. Right-click any toolbar.
2. Click **Tables and Borders**.

Draw a Table

1. Click **Table**..................Alt+A
2. Click **Draw Table**.................W

OR

Click **Draw Table** button ✏ on Tables and Borders toolbar.

✓ *The mouse pointer resembles a pencil.*

3. Click where you want to position upper-left corner of the table.
4. Drag diagonally down and to the right.
5. Release mouse button where you want to position lower-right corner of the table.

✓ *This draws one cell.*

6. Click and drag mouse pointer to draw horizontal borders and vertical borders.

✓ *As you drag, Word displays a dotted line where the border will be. Once you drag far enough, Word completes the line when you release the mouse button.*

7. Press **Esc**...........................Esc
to turn off Draw Table.

OR

Click **Draw Table** button ✏.

Move a Table

1. Rest mouse pointer on table so anchor is displayed.
2. Click and drag table anchor to new location.

✓ *A dotted outline moves with the mouse pointer to show new location.*

3. Release mouse button to drop table in new location

Resize a Table

1. Rest mouse pointer on table so sizing handle is displayed.
2. Click and drag sizing handle to increase or decrease table size.

✓ *A dotted outline moves with the mouse pointer to show new size.*

3. Release mouse button to resize table.

Merge Cells

1. Select cells to merge.
2. Click **Merge Cells** button ⊞ on Tables and Borders toolbar.

OR

a. Click **Table** ....Alt+A
b. Click **Merge Cells** ....M

Merge Cells and Erase Table Dividers

1. Click **Eraser** button ✎ on Tables and Borders toolbar.
2. Click on border to erase.

Split a Cell

1. Select cell to split.
2. Click **Split Cells** button ⊞ on Tables and Borders toolbar.

OR

a. Click **Table**.............Alt+A
b. Click **Split Cells**.............P

3. Enter **Number of columns** to create ....Alt+C, *number*
4. Enter **Number of rows** to create ....Alt+R, *number*
5. Click **OK**.........................Enter

Rotate Text

1. Click in cell to format.

OR

Select components to format.

2. Click **Change Text Direction** button ⊞ on Tables and Borders toolbar.
3. Click button repeatedly to toggle through the three available directions.

Wrap Text Around a Table

1. Click in table.
2. Click **Table**.................Alt+A
3. Click **Table Properties** ....R
4. Click **Table**........................T
5. Click **Around** ....Alt+A
6. Click **OK**.........................Enter

Exercise Directions

1. Start Word, if necessary.

2. Open 💿 **31WORKOUT**.

3. Save the file as **WORKOUT**.

4. On the first line of the document, use the Draw Table tool to draw a cell approximately 4" wide and 4" high.

   ✓ *Use the rulers as guides to measure the height and width of cells as you draw, but don't worry if the table components are not sized exactly.*

5. Create three columns by drawing vertical lines through the cell. Try to size the columns as follows:

   Column 1: 1" wide
   Columns 2 and 3: 1.5" wide

6. Leave the first column intact, and create five rows across the second and third columns as follows:

   Row 1: .5" high
   Rows 2, 3, and 4: 1" high
   Row 5: .5" high

7. Merge the cells in the top row of the right two columns, and then merge the corresponding cells in the bottom row.

8. Leaving the top and bottom rows intact, use the Split Cells tool to create two rows within each of the cells in the third column (refer to Illustration A to see the desired result).

9. Enter the text in the table as shown in Illustration A, using the following formatting and alignments to achieve the desired result:

   a. Column 1 (program name): 28-pt. serif, rotated so it runs from bottom to top, centered horizontally and vertically.

   b. Row 1 (table title): 28-pt. serif, bold, centered horizontally and vertically.

   c. Dates: 16-pt. serif, aligned left, and centered vertically.

   d. Exercise types: 16-pt. serif, aligned left horizontally, and aligned with the cell bottom vertically.

   e. Bottom row: 10-pt. serif, center aligned.

   ✓ *Adjust the column widths as necessary.*

10. Format the text that is not in the table in a 14-point sans serif font (Comic Sans MS is used in the illustration). Bold the title.

11. Center the first three lines of text below the table.

12. Leave 30 points of space after the third line.

13. Underline the first 4 words of the first paragraph.

14. Leave 6 points of space after the first three paragraphs of text in the document.

15. Set text to wrap around the table.

16. Position the table flush right on the page, with its top at about 2" on the vertical ruler.

17. Resize the table to decrease its height to about 3.5".

18. Check the spelling and grammar in the document.

19. Display the document in Print Preview. It should look similar to the one in the illustration.

20. Print the document.

21. Close the document, saving all changes.

Illustration A

Work Out with David
A series of introductory exercise classes with
Personal Trainer David Fairmont

Work Out with David is a series of three classes designed to introduce members to some of the exercise opportunities here at Michigan Avenue Athletic Club.

Each hour-long session focuses on two complementary types of exercise. The first 15 minutes will be spent learning about the exercises, including the equipment that

Work Out with David	Schedule	
	January 8	Step Aerobics
		Pilates
	January 15	Spinning
		Yoga
	January 22	Kickboxing
		Free Weights
	Space is limited. Please sign up as soon as possible.	

may be involved. The rest of the class includes a warm up, active participation and a cool down.

David Fairmont is our newest personal trainer. He holds a master's degree in health management from the University of Vermont in Burlington, Vermont, and he is certified in cardiovascular exercise and strength training.

Work Out with David is geared toward those with limited exercise class experience, but all members are welcome to join. There is no fee for participation, but class size is limited. Please see Katie at the front desk to enroll.

On Your Own

1. Create a new document in Word.
2. Save the file as **OWD31**.
3. Type a personal business letter to an employer or to your parents explaining why you need a raise. Write at least two paragraphs about why you deserve the raise and what you plan to do with the additional funds. Include information about how you spend the money you receive now.
4. To illustrate your point, draw a table in the letter and list items that you have purchased in the past two weeks. For example, include CDs, books, meals, movie tickets, and other expenses. The table should have at least three columns—for the date, the item, and the cost. List at least four items.
5. Merge a row across the top of the table and type in a title.
6. Try rotating text in some of the cells.
7. Use different alignments in the table cells.
8. Set the text in the letter to wrap around the table.
9. Try moving and resizing the table to improve the appearance of the letter.
10. When you are satisfied with the appearance of the table and the letter, check the spelling and grammar and print the document.
11. Ask a classmate to review the document and offer comments and suggestions.
12. Incorporate the suggestions into the document.
13. Close the document, saving all changes.

Exercise 32

◆ **Calculations in a Table** ◆ **Number Formats**
◆ **Cell Borders and Shading** ◆ **Sort Rows**

On the Job

Perform basic calculations in tables to total values in a column or row. If the values change, you can update the result without redoing the math. At the same time, you can format the calculation results with one of Word's built-in number formats. Sorting rows helps you keep your tables in order, while cell borders and shading let you dress up your tables to make them look good as well as to highlight important information.

A Whole Grains Bread franchise is offering a special gift basket for Earth Day. In this exercise, you will create a document to advertise the gift basket. You will use a table to organize the information and to calculate costs. You will format the table using cell borders and shading.

Terms

Spreadsheet An application, such as Microsoft Office's Excel 2003, used for setting up mathematical calculations.

Function A built-in **formula** for performing calculations, such as addition, in a table.

Formula A mathematical equation.

Field A placeholder used to insert information that changes, such as the date, the time, a page number, or the results of a calculation.

Line style The appearance of a line.

Line weight The thickness of a line.

Shading A color or pattern used to fill the background of a cell.

Notes

Calculations in a Table

- Word tables include basic **spreadsheet functions** so you can perform calculations on data entered in tables.
- By default, Word assumes you want to add the values entered in the column above the current cell or in the row beside the current cell.
- Word enters the calculation result in a **field**, so it can be updated if the values in the table change.
- For anything other than basic calculations, use an Excel worksheet, not a Word table.

The Formula dialog box set up to total the column

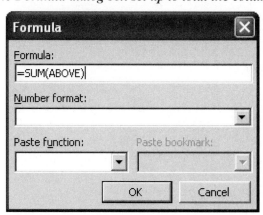

159

Number Formats

- When you set up a calculation in a table, you can select a number format to use for the result.

- Number formats include dollar signs, commas, percent signs, and decimal points.

Number formats

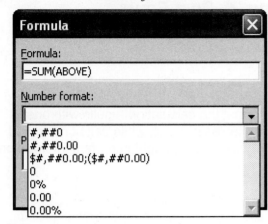

Cell Borders and Shading

- By default, Word applies a ½-pt. black solid line border around all table cells.

- Use the Tables and Borders toolbar buttons to change the borders and shading of table cells.

- You can select borders and shading before you draw new cells, or apply them to selected cells.

  - Select a different **line style**.

  - Select a different **line weight**.

  - Change the border color.

  - Erase or add border lines.

  - Add color or **shading**.

- Selected border and shading formatting remain in effect until new formatting is selected.

  ✓ When table borders are removed, you can see table cells on-screen by displaying gridlines.

Sort Rows

- Sort rows in a table the same way you sort lists or paragraphs.

  ✓ See Word, Exercise 19.

- Rows can be sorted according to the data in any column.

- For example, in a table of names and addresses, rows can be sorted alphabetically by name or by city, or numerically by ZIP Code.

- Word rearranges the rows in the table but does not rearrange the columns.

Procedures

Total Values in a Column or Row

1. Click in cell where you want the total to be displayed.
2. Click **Table**................... `Alt`+`A`
3. Click **Formula**..................... `O`

   ✓ By default, Word enters the formula for totaling the values in the cells in the column above or the row to the left.

4. Click **Number format** .. `Alt`+`N`
5. Click desired format ...... `↑`, `↓`
6. Click **OK**.......................... `Enter`

Update the Total

1. Select the field in the cell where the total is displayed.
2. Press **F9** .... `F9`

OR

1. Right-click selection.
2. Click **Update Field**............... `U`

   ✓ You must update the total each time one of the values used in the formula is changed. The total is not updated automatically.

Sort Rows

1. Select the data in the column by which you want to sort.
2. Click **Sort Ascending** button `A/Z↓` to sort from A to Z or from 0 to 9.

   OR

   Sort **Descending** button `Z/A↓` to sort from Z to A or from 9 to 0.

   ✓ If the sort should not include the first row, click Table, Sort and select the My list has Header row option button, then click OK.

OR

1. Click **Table**.................. `Alt`+`A`
2. Click **Sort**........................... `S`
3. Click **Sort by**............... `Alt`+`S`
4. Click desired column.
5. Click **Type**................... `Alt`+`Y`

6. Click either:
   - **Text**
   - **Number**
   - **Date**
7. Click either:
   - **Ascending**............. `Alt`+`A`
   - **Descending**........... `Alt`+`D`

   ✓ If the sort should not include the first row, make sure the My list has Header row option button is selected.

8. Click **OK** .... `Enter`

Sort by Multiple Columns

1. Click **Table** .... `Alt`+`A`
2. Click **Sort** .... `S`
3. Click **Sort by** .... `Alt`+`S`
4. Click desired column.
5. Click **Type** .... `Alt`+`Y`
6. Click either:
   - **Text**
   - **Number**
   - **Date**
7. Click either:
   - **Ascending**............. `Alt`+`A`
   - **Descending**........... `Alt`+`D`
8. Click **Then by**.............. `Alt`+`T`
9. Click desired column.
10. Click **Type** .... `Alt`+`P`
11. Click either:
    - **Text**
    - **Number**
    - **Date**
12. Click either:
    - **Ascending**............. `Alt`+`C`
    - **Descending**........... `Alt`+`N`
13. Click **Then by**.............. `Alt`+`B`
14. Click desired column.
15. Click **Type** .... `Alt`+`E`
16. Click either:
    - **Text**
    - **Number**
    - **Date**

17. Click either:
    - **Ascending** .... `Alt`+`I`
    - **Descending** .... `Alt`+`G`

    ✓ If the sort should not include the first row, make sure the My list has Header row option button is selected.

18. Click **OK**........................... `Enter`

Apply Cell Borders

1. Select cell(s) to format.
2. Click **Borders** drop-down arrow.
3. Click Border style.

   ✓ Border buttons are toggles—click on to display border; click off to hide border.

Select Line Style

1. Click **Line Style** drop-down arrow.
2. Click desired line style.

   ✓ Click No Border to remove border lines.

3. Click on a border line to apply the style.

Select Line Weight

1. Click **Line Weight** drop-down arrow.
2. Click desired line weight.
3. Click on a border line to apply the style.

Select Line Color

1. Click **Border Color** button.
2. Click desired color.
3. Click on a border line to apply the style.

Select Cell Shading

1. Click in cell to shade.
2. Click **Shading Color** drop-down arrow.
3. Click desired color.
4. Click **No Fill** to remove shading or color.

Exercise Directions

1. Start Word, if necessary.
2. Open 📀 **32BASKET**.
3. Save the file as **BASKET**.
4. Move the insertion point to the last line of the document.
5. Use either the Draw Table tool or the Insert Table command to create a table with two columns and five rows.
6. Enter the data shown in Illustration A.
7. Align all dollar values with a decimal tab set at approximately 4" on the Horizontal ruler.
8. Preview the document. It should look similar to the one in Illustration A.
9. Sort the rows in descending order according to the values in the price column.
   - ✓ *Remember not to sort the header row.*
10. Insert a new row at the end of the table.
11. In the first cell in the new row, type **Total**.
12. In the last cell of the new row, insert a formula to calculate the total cost.
    - ✓ *Select the currency format showing two decimal places.*
13. Insert a row above the total.
14. In the left column, type **1 bottle all natural sparkling white grape juice**.
15. In the right column type **$6.59**.
16. Update the calculation result.
17. Apply the Table Grid 8 AutoFormat to the table.
18. Apply a dark blue double-line border around all of the cells in the bottom row.
    - ✓ *If you have trouble seeing the change on-screen, try zooming in to a higher magnification.*
19. Remove the borders between columns in the bottom row.
    - ✓ *Do not merge the cells. Just remove the printing border lines.*
20. Apply a 12.5% gray shading to all of the cells in the bottom row.
    - ✓ *ScreenTips display the % Gray Shading.*
21. Resize the table so it is approximately 4" wide by 3½" high.
22. Set column 1 to be approximately 2.5" wide and column 2 to be approximately 1.5" wide
23. Vertically align the text with the cell bottom in the top and bottom rows.
24. Vertically center the text in rows 2, 3, 4, 5, and 6.
25. Center the table horizontally on the page.
26. Check the spelling and grammar.
27. Preview the document. It should look similar to the one in Illustration B.
28. Print the document.
29. Close the document, saving all changes.

On Your Own

1. Open the document **OWD31**, the letter asking for a raise that you wrote in the On Your Own section of Exercise 31, or open 📀 **32RAISE**.
2. Save the file as **OWD32**.
3. Sort the rows in the table into descending numerical order, according to the amount of the expenses.
4. Add a row to the bottom of the table.
5. Label the row **Total**.
6. Calculate the total amount of expenses in the table. Make sure the result is displayed in dollar format.
7. Change one or more of the values in the table.
8. Update the calculation.
9. Format the table using cell borders and shading. For example, use borders and shading to highlight the cell in which the total is displayed.
10. Check the spelling and grammar, then print the document.
11. Ask a classmate to review the document and offer comments and suggestions.
12. Incorporate the suggestions into the document.
13. Close the document, saving all changes.

Whole Grains Bread
Earth Day Gift Basket
Specially Priced at $39.99

Celebrate Earth Day by sending someone you love a beautiful gift basket filled with all natural treats. The basket includes all of the items listed below, as well as an Earth Day surprise. The basket is beautifully arranged and wrapped using recycled materials. Local delivery is included in the special price.

Basket includes:	Regularly priced:
1 tin granola	$10.99
5 organic pears	$5.99
1 dozen specialty muffins	$15.99
2 - 8 oz. all natural fruit preserves	$12.99

Whole Grains Bread
Earth Day Gift Basket
Specially Priced at $39.99

Celebrate Earth Day by sending someone you love a beautiful gift basket filled with all natural treats. The basket includes all of the items listed below, as well as an Earth Day surprise. The basket is beautifully arranged and wrapped using recycled materials. Local delivery is included in the special price.

Basket includes:	Regularly priced:
1 dozen specialty muffins	$15.99
2 - 8 oz. all natural fruit preserves	$12.99
1 tin granola	$10.99
5 organic pears	$5.99
1 bottle all natural sparkling grape juice	$6.59
Total	**$52.55**

Exercise 33

◆ Critical Thinking

Voyager Travel Adventures has been collecting demographic information about clients who participate in adventure travel vacations. In this exercise, you will create a memo to the vice president of marketing listing some of the interesting demographics in table form.

Exercise Directions

1. Start Word, if necessary.
2. Open 💿 **33DEMOS**.
3. Save the document as **DEMOS**.
4. In the memo heading, replace the sample text **Your Name** and **Today's date** with the appropriate information.
5. Between the first two paragraphs of the memo, insert a table with three columns and eight rows.
6. Set all columns to be 1" wide and all rows to be .25" high.
7. Enter the following data:

Age	0 – 18	3%
	19 – 25	17%
	26 – 35	20%
	36 – 45	30%
	46 – 55	20%
	55 +	10%
Gender	Male	54%
	Female	46%

8. Vertically align all data on the bottom of the cells.
9. Left align the data in columns 1 and 2.
10. Right align the data in column 3.
11. Insert a new row at the top of the table.
12. Merge the cells in the new row.
13. In the new row, type the table title: **CLIENT DEMOGRAPHICS**.
14. Center the table title horizontally and vertically.
15. Insert another blank row above the row labeled **Gender**.

16. Apply the Table Contemporary AutoFormat to the table.
17. Apply a single line ¾-pt. outside border to the entire table.
18. Between the second and third paragraphs of the memo, insert a table with two columns and five rows.
19. Enter the following data:

River Rafting	77
Backpacking	25
Kayaking	84
Biking	43
Skiing	21

20. Align the data in column 2 flush right.
21. Sort the rows in ascending alphabetical order by the data in column 1.
22. Delete the label and data for Skiing.
23. In the blank cell at the bottom of column 1, type **Total** and right align it.
24. In the blank cell at the bottom of column 2, insert a formula to calculate the total number of respondents.
25. Right-align all data in column 2.
26. Insert a new column at the left side of the table.
27. Set the new column to be 1" wide, column 2 to be 1.5" wide and column 3 to be .5" wide.
28. Set all rows to be .25" high.
29. Merge the cells in the first column.
30. Using 14-pt. bold, type **Favorite Activity per Respondent** in column 1.

31. Rotate the text in column 1 so it reads from the bottom of the table to the top, and center align the text.

32. Apply a 1-pt. Indigo border around the inside and outside of all cells in the table.

33. Apply a 10% gray shading to column 1.

34. Apply a 20% gray shading to rows 1, 3, and 5.

35. Center the table on the page.

36. Change the number of respondents who prefer kayaking to **95**.

37. Update the result of the calculation.

38. Check the spelling and grammar in the document.

39. Display the document in Print Preview. It should look similar to the illustration.

40. Print the document.

41. Close the document, saving all changes.

Illustration A

MEMO

To: Dan Euell, V.P. Marketing
From: Your name
Date: Today's date
Subject: Client Demographics

I thought you might like a preview of the client demographic data we have been collecting. I find the age breakdowns quite interesting. We might want to consider targeting some tours to families with teenagers.

CLIENT DEMOGRAPHICS		
Age	0 – 18	3%
	19 – 25	17%
	26 – 35	20%
	36 – 45	30%
	46 – 55	20%
	56+	10%
Gender	Male	54%
	Female	46%

Also of note: based on the data you see in the table below, our clients would most like to experience tours that involve water.

Favorite Activity per Respondent	Backpacking	25
	Biking	43
	Kayaking	95
	River Rafting	77
	Total	240

We should have the complete report by the end of next week. We'll meet then to go over the results.

Exercise 34

Skills Covered:

♦ **Mail Merge Basics** ♦ **Use Mail Merge**
♦ **Create a New Address List** ♦ **Use Merge Fields**

On the Job

Use Mail Merge to customize mass mailings. For example, with Mail Merge you can store a document with standard text, such as a form letter, and then insert personalized names and addresses on each copy that you generate or print. You can also use Mail Merge to generate envelopes, labels, e-mail messages, and directories, such as a telephone list.

A letter inviting Michigan Avenue Athletic Club members to join a volleyball team becomes a simple task using the Mail Merge feature. The form letter will be personalized with each person's name and address. In this exercise, you will create the letter document and the data source address list, and you will merge them to generate the letters.

Terms

Mail Merge A process that inserts variable information into a standardized document to produce a personalized or customized document.

Main document The document containing the standardized text that will be printed on all documents.

Merge field A placeholder in the main document that marks where and what will be inserted from the data source document.

Merge block A set of merge fields stored as one unit. For example, the Address block contains all of the name and address information.

Data source The document containing the variable data that will be inserted during the merge.

Office address list A simple data source file stored in Access file format, which includes the information needed for an address list, such as first name, last name, street, city, state, and so on.

Outlook contact list The names, addresses, and other information stored as contacts for use in the Microsoft Office Outlook personal information manager program.

Microsoft Office Access database A file created with the Access program, used for storing information.

Merge document The customized document resulting from a merge.

Field One item of variable data, such as a first name, a last name, or a ZIP Code.

Record A collection of variable data about one person or thing. In a form letter merge, for example, each record contains variable data for each person receiving the letter: first name, last name, address, city, state, and ZIP Code.

Address list form A dialog box used to enter mailing list information for a data source file.

Notes

Mail Merge Basics

- Use **Mail Merge** to create mass mailings, envelopes, e-mail messages or labels.

- To create a mail merge, you must have two files:
  - A **main document**, which contains information that won't change, as well as **merge fields** and **merge blocks**, which act as placeholders for variable information. For example, you might have a form letter that has merge fields where the address and greeting should be.

- A **data source** file, which contains variable information such as names and addresses. Word lets you use many types of data source files for a merge, including an **Office address list**, an **Outlook contact list**, or a **Microsoft Office Access database**.

- During the merge, Word generates a series of **merge documents** in which the variable information from the data source replaces the merge fields entered in the main document.

- You can print the merge documents or save them in a file for future use.

- You can use the Mail Merge task pane or the buttons on the Mail Merge toolbar to access Mail Merge features and command.

A main document

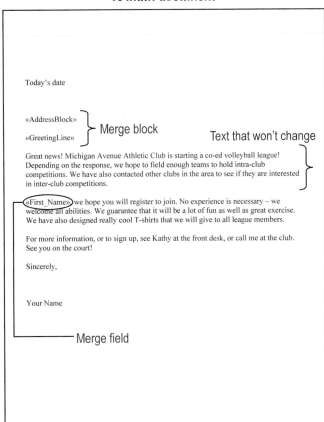

A series of merge documents

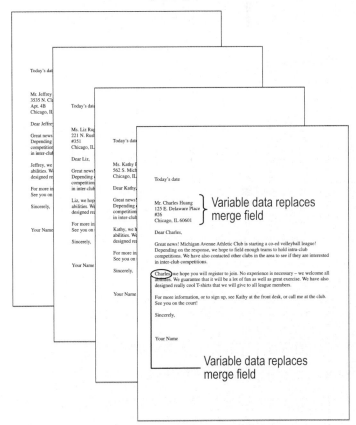

Use Mail Merge

- The Mail Merge task pane prompts you through the process of conducting a merge.
- There are six steps to complete the merge:
  - The first step is to select the type of main document you want to create:

Letters	used for letters or other regular Word documents such as reports, flyers, or memos.
E-mail messages	used to create messages to send via e-mail.
Envelopes	used to create personalized envelopes.
Labels	used to create personalized labels.
Directory	used for lists such as rosters, catalogs or telephone lists.

  - The second step is to select a starting document. You may select to start from the current document, an existing document, or a new document based on a template.
  - The third step is to select recipients. In this step, you locate or create the data source file, and then select the individual recipients to include in the merge.
  - If you select to create a new list, Word prompts you through the steps for creating the data source file by entering the variable data for each recipient.
  - The fourth step is to create the main document. In this step, you type and format the data you want included in each merge document, and you insert the merge fields or merge blocks where Word will insert the variable data.

    ✓ *If the text is already typed in the document, you simply insert the merge fields and merge blocks in step 4.*

  - The fifth step is to preview the merge documents. In this step, you have the opportunity to see the merge documents before you print them. This lets you check for spelling, punctuation, and grammatical errors and make corrections.
  - The final step is to complete the merge. You have the option of printing the merge documents, or saving them in a new file for later use.

Create a New Address List

- An Office address list is a simple data source file used to store all of the variable information required to complete a mail merge.
- The data is stored in a table format, with each column containing one **field** of information and each row containing the **record** for one recipient.

The list of recipients stored in an address list

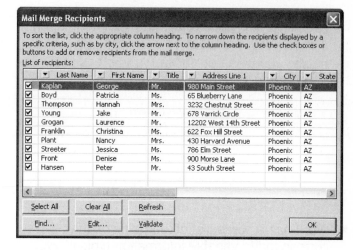

- You enter the data in an **address list form** that has already been set up to include the necessary fields.
- You save the file the same way you save any Office file—by giving it a name and selecting a storage location.
- By default, Word stores the file in the My Data Sources folder, which is a subfolder of My Documents. You can store the file in any location you choose.
- If a field in the data source is blank, the information is left out of the merge document for that record.
- You can use an address list file many times, with different main documents.
- You can sort the list, and you can select the specific recipients you want to include in the merge.

An address list form

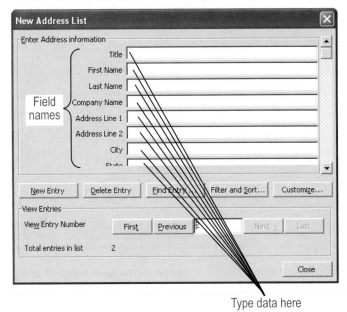

Field names

Type data here

Use Merge Fields

- Word has a preset list of merge fields that correspond to variable information typically used in a mail merge, such as First Name, Last Name, and ZIP Code.

- It also creates merge blocks for certain common sets of fields, such as a complete Address, so that you can insert one merge block instead of inserting numerous merge fields.

- You insert the merge fields or blocks in the main document at the location where you want the corresponding variable data to print.

- You must type all spaces and punctuation between merge fields. Merge blocks, however, include standard punctuation and spacing, such as a comma following the city.

- By default, when you insert a merge field, you see the field name enclosed in merge field characters (<< >>). The field may be shaded, depending on your system's field code option settings.

  ✓ *The field code option settings are found on the View tab in the Options dialog box. Select Options from the Tools menu, and then click the View tab.*

- You may insert merge fields more than once in a document. For example, you can insert a name merge field in multiple locations in order to personalize a letter.

Procedures

Use Mail Merge to Generate a Form Letter Using a New Address List Data Source File

Select the main document:

1. Open a new blank document.
2. Click **Tools** .... Alt + T
3. Select **Letters and Mailings** .... E
4. Click **Mail Merge** .... M
   ✓ *The Mail Merge task pane opens.*
5. Click the **Letters** options button in the Mail Merge task pane.
6. Click **Next: Starting document** in the Mail Merge task pane.

7. Click the **Use the current document** option button in the Mail Merge task pane.
8. Click **Next: Select recipients** in the Mail Merge task pane.

Create an address list data source file:

1. Click the **Type a new list** option button in the Mail Merge task pane.
2. Click **Create** in the Mail Merge task pane.
   ✓ *The New Address List form is displayed.*
3. In the Title text box, type the title for the first person you want to add to the address list.
4. Press **Enter** .... Enter
   or **Tab** .... Tab
   ✓ *Press Shift+Tab to move to previous field.*

5. Type the person's first name.
6. Press **Enter**.................... Enter
   or **Tab**.............................. Tab
7. Continue typing variable data until record is complete.
   ✓ *You may leave blank any fields for which information is not available or necessary.*
8. Click **New Entry** .... Alt + N
   ✓ *Word displays next blank address form.*
9. Repeat steps 3–8 until you have entered the information for all recipients.
   ✓ *You can edit the data source file in the future. For example, you can add and delete records. For more information, refer to Exercise 35.*

10. Click **Close** .... Esc
  - ✓ *Word displays the Save Address List dialog box.*
11. Type file name.
12. Click **Save** button

 .... Alt + S

  - ✓ *Word displays the Mail Merge Recipients dialog box. By default, all recipients are selected. For information on selecting specific recipients, refer to Exercise 36.*
13. Click **OK** .... Enter
14. Click **Next: Write your letter** in the Mail Merge task pane.
  - ✓ *Word displays the starting document, and a list of available merge blocks.*

Create a form letter document:

1. In the main document, begin typing the letter, including all text and formatting as you want it to appear on each merge document. For example, type the date and move the insertion point down four lines.
2. Position the insertion point at the location where you want the recipient's address displayed, and then click

   Address block 🖹 in the Mail Merge task pane.
   OR
   Click **Insert Address Block**

   button 🖹 on Mail Merge toolbar.
  - ✓ *Word displays the Insert Address Block dialog box.*

3. Select desired options.
4. Click **OK** .... Enter
   OR
   a. Click **More items** 🖻 in the task pane.
      OR
      Click **Insert Merge Fields**

      button 🖻 on Mail Merge toolbar.
     - ✓ *Word displays the Insert Merge Field dialog box.*
   b. Click field to insert ... ⬆, ⬇
   c. Click **Insert** .... Alt + I
   d. Click **Close** .... Esc
5. Continue typing and formatting letter, repeating steps to insert merge fields or merge blocks at desired location(s).
6. Save the document.
7. Click **Next: Preview your letters** in the Mail Merge task pane.
  - ✓ *Word displays the first merge document.*

Preview merge documents:

1. Click the **Next recipient** button

   ⟩⟩ in the Mail Merge task pane.
   OR
   Click the **Next record** button

   ▶ on the Mail Merge toolbar.
   OR
   Click the **Previous recipient**

   button ⟨⟨ in the Mail Merge task pane.
   OR
   Click the **Previous record**

   button ◀ on the Mail Merge toolbar.
2. Click **Next: Complete the Merge** in the Mail Merge task pane.

Complete the merge:

- Click **Print** button 🖨 to open the Print dialog box to print the merged documents.

OR

1. Click **Edit individual letters**

   button 🖹 to create a new file containing all merged letters.
  - ✓ *Word displays the Merge to File dialog box.*
2. Click **OK** .... Enter
   to merge all letters to a new file.
  - ✓ *You can make changes to individual letters, and/or save the document to print later.*

Exercise Directions

1. Start Word, if necessary.
2. Create a new blank document.
3. Save the file as **FORM**.
4. Open the Mail Merge task pane.
5. Select to create a letter, using the current document.
6. Create a new address list to use as a data source document.
7. Enter the recipients from the table below into the data source file.
8. Save the data source file as **SOURCE**.
9. Select to use all recipients in the merge, then close the Mail Merge Recipients dialog box.

10. Type the document shown in Illustration A, inserting the merge fields and merge blocks as marked.
    a. Set address options to exclude the company address and only include the country if it is not the United States.
    b. Select the Greeting line option to use the recipient's first name only.
    c. Remember, merge blocks include punctuation and spacing, but merge fields do not.
11. Check the spelling and grammar in the document.
12. Preview the merged documents.
13. Complete the merge by generating a file containing all of the individual records.
14. Save the file as **LETTERS**.
15. Print the file.
16. Close all open documents, saving all changes.

Title	First Name	Last Name	Address Line 1	Address Line 2	City	State	ZIP Code
Mr.	Jeffrey	Halloran	3535 N. Clark Street	Apt. 4B	Chicago	IL	60601
Ms.	Liz	Rupert	221 N. Rush Street	#351	Chicago	IL	60601
Ms.	Kathy	Figit	562 S. Michigan Avenue		Chicago	IL	60601
Mr.	Charles	Huang	125 E. Delaware Place	#26	Chicago	IL	60601
Mr.	Keith	Newmann	882 W. Polk		Chicago	IL	60601

On Your Own

1. Think of ways Mail Merge would be useful to you. For example, are you involved in any clubs or organizations that send out mass mailings? Do you send out "Holiday Letters" every year? Are you responsible for regular reports that contain variable data, such as sales reports or forecasts?
2. Use Mail Merge to create a form letter.
3. Save the main document as **OWD34-1**.
4. Create an address list data source file that includes at least five records.

5. Save the data source file as **OWD34-2**.
6. Type the letter, inserting merge fields and merge blocks as necessary.
7. Check the spelling and grammar in the document.
8. Merge the documents into a new file.
9. Save the merge document file as **OWD34-3**.
10. Print the letters.
11. Close all open documents, saving all changes.

Today's date

«AddressBlock»

} *Insert merge blocks*

«GreetingLine»

Great news! Michigan Avenue Athletic Club is starting a co-ed volleyball league!
Depending on the response, we hope to field enough teams to hold intra-club
competitions. We have also contacted other clubs in the area to see if they are interested
in inter-club competitions.

Insert merge field — «First_Name» we hope you will register to join. No experience is necessary – we
welcome all abilities. We guarantee that it will be a lot of fun as well as great exercise.
We have also designed really cool T-shirts that we will give to all league members.

For more information, or to sign up, see Kathy at the front desk, or call me at the club.
See you on the court!

Sincerely,

Your Name

Exercise 35

Skills Covered:

◆ Merge with an Existing Address List ◆ Edit an Address List
◆ Customize Merge Fields ◆ Merge Envelopes and Labels

On the Job

If you have an existing data source document, you can merge it with any main document to create new merge documents. This saves you from retyping repetitive data. For example, using an existing Address List data source makes it easy to create envelopes and labels to accompany a form letter merge that you created previously. You can edit the data source to add or remove records, or to customize merge fields to include specialized information not included in the default Address List data source file.

To mail out the form letters for Michigan Avenue Athletic Club, you need to print envelopes. In this exercise, you will create an envelope main document and merge it with the same Address List file you used in Exercise 34. You will then edit the Address List and customize the merge fields. Finally, you will use the Address List to print labels to use on the packages containing the T-shirts promised to every person who joins the league.

Terms

There is no new vocabulary in this exercise.

Notes

Merge with an Existing Address List

- Once you create and save an Office Address List data source file, you can use it with different main documents.

- In Step 3 of the Mail Merge task pane you can locate and open the data source file you want to use.

  ✓ *You can also click the Open Data Source button*
  on the Mail Merge toolbar to display the
  Select Data Source dialog box.

The Select Data Source dialog box

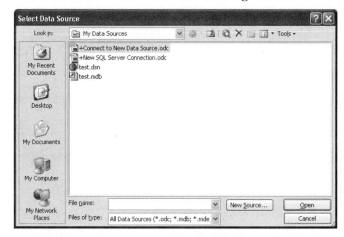

- You can also use existing data source files created with other applications, including Microsoft Office Access.

✓ *If you select a data source created with Access, you must specify which table or query to use, and the merge fields inserted in the Word document must match the fields used in the Access file.*

- Using an existing data source saves you the time and trouble of retyping existing data.

Edit an Address List

- You can easily edit an existing Address List.
- You can change information that is already entered.
- You can add or delete information, including entire records.

Customize Merge Fields

- Customize merge fields to change field names, delete unused fields, or add fields specific to your needs. For example, you might want to add a field for entering a job title.
- You can also move fields up or down in the field list.

The Customize Address List dialog box

Merge Envelopes and Labels

- To create envelopes using Mail Merge, select Envelopes as the main document type.
- To create labels using Mail Merge, select Labels as the main document type.
- When you create an envelopes main document, Word prompts you to select envelope options so that the main document is laid out just like the actual paper envelopes on which you will print.

The Envelope Options dialog box

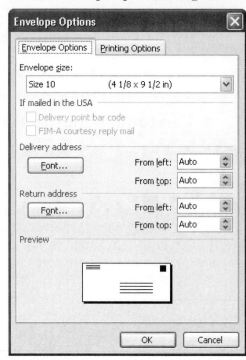

- Likewise, when you create a labels main document, you must select label options so that the label layout on-screen is the same as the actual labels.
- When you select the size and format of the envelopes or labels, Word changes the layout of the current document to match. Any existing data in the document is deleted.

The Label Options dialog box

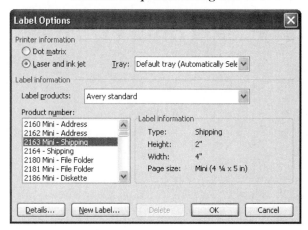

- To merge with envelopes or labels, you can create a new data source file as covered in Exercise 34, or use an existing data source file.
- You can merge the envelopes or labels to a printer or to a new document to save, edit, or use at a later time.

Procedures

Use Mail Merge to Generate Envelopes or Labels Using an Existing Address List Data Source File

Select the main document:

1. Open a new blank document.
2. Click **Tools** .... Alt + T
3. Select **Letters and Mailings** .... E
4. Click **Mail Merge** .... M
5. Click the **Envelopes** option button in the Mail Merge task pane to create envelopes.

   OR

   Click the **Labels** option button in the Mail Merge task pane to create labels.
6. Click **Next: Starting document** in the Mail Merge task pane.

   ✓ *The next step depends on whether you are merging envelopes or labels. To merge envelopes, continue with the procedures for selecting envelope options. To merge labels, continue with the procedures for selecting label options. Once the options are selected, continue with the procedures for selecting recipients.*

To select envelope options:

1. Click the **Change Document Layout** option button in the Mail Merge task pane.
2. Click **Envelope Options** in the Mail Merge task pane.

   ✓ *Word displays the Envelope Options dialog box.*
3. Click **Envelope size** .... Alt + S
4. Click desired size .... ↑, ↓, Enter
5. Click **OK** .... Enter

   ✓ *Word changes the layout of the current document. If a warning is displayed, click OK to continue or Cancel to cancel the change.*
6. Click **Next: Select recipients** in the Mail Merge task pane.

To select label options:

1. Click the **Change Document Layout** option button in the Mail Merge task pane.
2. Click **Label Options** in the Mail Merge task pane.

   ✓ *Word displays the Label Options dialog box.*
3. Select label options.
4. Click **OK** .... Enter

   ✓ *Word changes the layout of the current document. If a warning is displayed, click OK to continue or Cancel to cancel the change.*
5. Click **Next: Select recipients** in the Mail Merge task pane.

Select an existing Address List data source file:

1. Click the **Use an existing list** option button in the Mail Merge task pane.
2. Click **Browse** in the Mail Merge task pane.

   ✓ *Word opens the Select Data Source dialog box.*
3. Locate and select the desired data source file.
4. Click **Open** button

    .
5. Word displays the Mail Merge Recipients dialog box.

   ✓ *By default, all recipients are selected. For information on selecting specific recipients, refer to Exercise 36.*
6. Click **OK** .... Enter
7. Click **Next: Arrange your envelope/labels** in the Mail Merge task pane.

   ✓ *Word displays the starting document, and a list of available merge blocks.*

Arrange the envelope:

1. In the main document, type any text you want to appear on each printed envelope. For example, type a return address in the upper-left corner.
2. Position the insertion point at the location where you want the recipient's address displayed.

   ✓ *By default, Word creates a text box on the envelope document where the address should print.*
3. Click **Address block** in the Mail Merge task pane.

   OR

   Click **Insert Address Block** button on Mail Merge toolbar.

   ✓ *Word displays the Insert Address Block dialog box.*
4. Select desired options.
5. Click **OK** .... Enter

   OR

   a. Click **More items** in the task pane.

   OR

   Click **Insert Merge Fields** button on Mail Merge toolbar.

   ✓ *Word displays the Insert Merge Field dialog box.*

   b. Click field to insert... ↑, ↓
   c. Click **Insert** .... Alt + I
   d. Click **Close** .... Esc
6. Type any other standard text required on the envelope.
7. Insert additional fields or blocks as necessary.
8. Click **Next: Preview your envelopes** in the Mail Merge task pane.

   ✓ *Word displays the first merge document.*

Arrange the labels:

1. In the first label, position the insertion point at the location where you want the recipient's address displayed.

2. Click **Address block** 🗋 in the Mail Merge task pane.
   OR
   Click **Insert Address Block** button 🗋 on Mail Merge toolbar.
   - ✓ *Word displays the Insert Address Block dialog box.*

3. Select desired options.

4. Click **OK**..........................`Enter`
   OR
   Click **More items** 📄 in the Task Pane.
   OR
   Click **Insert Merge Fields** button 🖹 on Mail Merge toolbar.
   - ✓ *Word displays the Insert Merge Field dialog box.*
   a. Click field to insert... `↑`, `↓`
   b. Click **Insert** .... `Alt`+`I`
   c. Click **Close** .... `Esc`

5. Type any other standard text and/or punctuation required on the label.

6. Insert additional fields or blocks as necessary.

7. Click **Update all labels**
   `Update all labels` in the task pane to copy the layout from the first label to all other labels.
   - ✓ *Alternatively, click **Propagate Labels** 🗘 on the Mail Merge toolbar.*
   - ✓ *Notice that Word automatically inserts a Next Record field on each label.*

8. Click **Next: Preview your labels** in the Mail Merge task pane.
   - ✓ *Word displays the first merge document.*

Preview merge documents:

1. Click the **Next recipient** button `>>` in the Mail Merge task pane.
   OR
   Click the **Next record** button `▶` on the Mail Merge toolbar.
   OR
   Click the **Previous recipient** button `<<` in the Mail Merge task pane.
   OR
   Click the **Previous record** button `◀` on the Mail Merge toolbar.

2. Click **Next: Complete the merge** in the Mail Merge task pane.

Complete the merge:

- Click **Print** 🖨 to open the Print dialog box and print the merged documents.
   OR
1. Click **Edit individual envelopes** 🗐 to create a new file containing all merged envelopes.
2. Click **OK** .... `Enter` to complete the merge.
   - ✓ *You can make changes to individual envelopes or labels, and/or save the document to print later.*

Edit an Existing Address List

1. Click **Mail Merge Recipients** button 🗗 on Mail Merge toolbar.
   OR
   In Step 3 or Step 5 in Mail Merge task pane, click **Edit recipient list** 🗗.

2. Click **Edit** .... `Alt`+`E`
   - ✓ *Word displays the Address List dialog box, with the record for the first recipient displayed.*

3. Do any the following:
   To add a new record:
   a. Click **New Entry** ..... `Alt`+`N`
   b. Enter variable information as covered in Exercise 34.

To delete a record:

a. Click **Delete Entry** . `Alt`+`D` to delete the entry currently displayed.

b. Click **Yes**................ `Alt`+`Y` to delete the entry.
   OR
   - Click **No** .... `Alt`+`N` to cancel the deletion.
   - ✓ *You cannot undo an entry deletion.*

To edit a record:

a. Display record to edit.
   - ✓ *Use the Next `Next`, Previous `Previous`, First `First`, and Last `Last` buttons to scroll through the records.*

b. Edit variable data as desired.

4. Click **Close**....................... `Enter`
5. Click **OK** .... `Enter`

Customize Merge Fields

1. Click **Mail Merge Recipients** button 🗗 on Mail Merge toolbar.
   OR
   In Step 3 or Step 5 of Mail Merge task pane, click **Edit recipient list** 🗗.

2. Click **Edit**.................... `Alt`+`E`
   - ✓ *Word displays the Address List dialog box, with the record for the first recipient displayed.*

3. Click **Customize** .... `Alt`+`Z`
   - ✓ *Word displays the Customize Address List dialog box.*

4. Do any of the following:
   To add a field:
   a. Click **Add** .... `Alt`+`A`
   b. Type field name.
   c. Click **OK**..................... `Enter`

To delete a field:

a. Click field to
   delete............ ⬆, ⬇, Enter

b. Click **Delete**............ Alt+D

c. Click **Yes** .... Alt+Y
   to delete the field and all
   data entered in the field.
   OR

   • Click **No**............ Alt+N
     to cancel the deletion.

**To change the order of fields
in the field list:**

a. Click field to
   move .... ⬆, ⬇, Enter

b. Click **Move Up** .... Alt+U
   to move the field up one
   line in list.

OR

• Click **Move
  Down**............... Alt+N
  to move field down one
  line in list.

5. Click **OK**.......................... Enter

6. Click **Close** .... Enter

7. Click **OK**.......................... Enter

Exercise Directions

✓ In this exercise you will use ⌨**SOURCE** the Office
Address List file you created in Exercise 34. If that file
is not available on your system, prior to starting the
exercise copy the file 💿 **35SOURCE** and save the
copy as **SOURCE**.

✓ To copy the file, right-click the file name and select
Copy. Right-click the destination folder and select
Paste. Right-click the copied file name and select
Rename. Type the new file name and press Enter.

Create Envelopes

1. Start Word, if necessary.
2. Create a new blank document.
3. Save the document as **MAINENV**.
4. Open the Mail Merge task pane
5. Select to create envelopes.
6. Select Envelope options.
7. Select envelope size 10.
8. Select to use an existing address list file as a
   data source document.
9. Locate and open **SOURCE**.
10. Close the Mail Merge Recipients dialog box.
11. Set up the envelope main document as shown
    in Illustration A.
    a. Type the return address.
    b. Insert the Address merge block.
12. Check the spelling and grammar in the
    document.
13. Preview the merged documents.
14. Complete the merge by generating a file
    containing all of the individual envelopes.
15. Save the file as **ENVELOPES**.

16. If requested by your instructor, print the merge
    documents.

    ✓ If you do not have actual envelopes, you can print the
    merge documents on regular paper.

17. Close all open files, saving all changes.

Create Labels

1. Create a new blank document.
2. Save the file as **MAINLAB**.
3. Start the Mail Merge Wizard.
4. Select to create labels.
5. Select Label Options.
6. Select Avery standard number 2163
   Mini-Shipping labels.
7. Select to use an existing address list file as a
   data source document.
8. Locate and open **SOURCE**.
9. Customize the merge fields as follows:
   a. Delete the Company Name field.
   b. Delete the Work Phone field.
   c. Add a T-Shirt Size field.
   d. Move the new field down after the E-mail
      Address field.
   e. Add a Membership Type field.
   f. Move the new field down after the T-shirt
      size field.
10. Add a new record to the address list using the
    following information:
    **Ms. Janine Flaherty
    391 S. Wabash Avenue
    Chicago, IL 60601
    T-Shirt Size: M
    Membership Type: Full**

11. Fill in the new fields for all existing records using the information in the following table:

	Size	Membership Type
Jeffrey Halloran	XL	Full
Liz Rupert	S	Student
Kathy Figit	M	Junior
Charles Huang	L	Full
Keith Newmann	XL	Full

12. Close the Mail Merge Recipients dialog box.

13. Set up the labels main document as shown in Illustration B.

    a. Insert the individual merge fields as shown.
       ✓ *Don't worry if the field names wrap onto multiple lines.*

    b. Type text, punctuation, and spacing as shown.

    c. Once you set up the first label, use Update all labels to automatically set up the other labels.

14. Check the spelling and grammar in the document.

15. Preview the merged documents.

16. Complete the merge by generating a file containing all of the individual labels.

17. Save the file as **LABELS**.

18. Close all open files, saving all changes.

Illustration A

Michigan Avenue Athletic Club
235 Michigan Avenue
Chicago, IL 60601

«AddressBlock»

Illustration B

«Title» «First_Name» «Last_Name»
«Membership_Type» Member
«Address_Line_1»
«Address_Line_2»
«City», «State» «ZIP_Code»

Enclosed shirt size: «TShirt_Size»

On Your Own

1. Create a new document in Word.

2. Save it as **OWD35-1**.

3. Use the Mail Merge Wizard to create envelopes, using **OWD34-2** as the data source.

   ✓ *If* **OWD34-2** *is not available, make a copy of* 💿 **35DATA** *and save it as* **OWD35-2**.

4. Add at least one new record to the data source.

5. Delete at least one field.

6. Add at least one field.

7. Fill in all missing information for the existing records.

8. Merge the envelopes to a new document.

9. Save the merge document as **OWD35-3**.

10. Close all open documents, saving all changes.

Exercise 36

Skills Covered:

◆ **Sort Recipients in an Address List** ◆ **Select Specific Recipients**
◆ **Create a Directory with Merge**

On the Job

You can use Mail Merge to create a directory, such as a telephone directory, an address list, or a customer directory. Mail Merge makes it easy to select records in your data source file so you can include only specific recipients in a merge. You can also sort the data source file so that the merge documents are generated in alphabetical or numerical order.

Michigan Avenue Athletic Club has asked you to create a directory of its personal trainers to give out to members. You have an existing Office Address List file that lists all trainers and exercise instructors. In this exercise, you will use the existing Address List data source file, from which you will select the records you need. You will also sort the list before generating the directory.

Terms

Column heading The label displayed at the top of a column.

Directory A single document listing data source file entries.

Notes

Sort Recipients in an Address List

- You can quickly change the order of records in an address list based on the data entered in any column in the list.

- Simply click any **column heading** in the Mail Merge Recipients dialog box to sort the records into ascending order.

- Click the column heading again to sort the records into descending order.

Select Specific Recipients

- By default, all recipients in an Address List are selected to be included in a merge.

- You can select the specific recipients you want to include. For example, you might want to send letters only to the people who live in a specific town.

- To indicate that a recipient is selected, Word displays a check in the checkbox at the left end of the recipient's row in the Mail Merge Recipients dialog box.

- You click the checkbox to clear the check, or click the empty box to select the recipient again.

An Address List with only some recipients selected

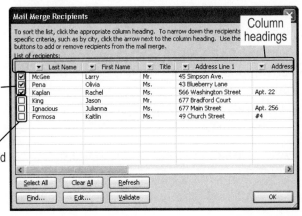

Create a Directory with Mail Merge

- Use Mail Merge to create a **directory**, such as a catalog, an inventory list, or a membership address list.

- When you merge to a directory, Word creates a single document that includes the variable data for all selected recipients.

- You arrange the layout for the first entry in the directory; Mail Merge uses that layout for all entries.

- You may type text, spacing, and punctuation, and you can include formatting. For example, you might want to include labels such as *Name:*, *Home Phone:*, and *E-Mail:*.

The layout for a directory

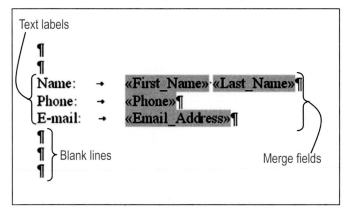

Text labels

¶
¶
Name: → «First_Name» «Last_Name»¶
Phone: → «Phone»¶
E-mail: → «Email_Address»¶
¶
¶ } Blank lines
¶

Merge fields

The merged directory

Name: Jackie Loring
Phone: 312-555-3522
E-mail: jloring@michaveclub.com

Name: Trisha Chung
Phone: 312-555-3523
E-mail: trish@michaveclub.com

Name: Tom Dybreski
Phone: 312-555-3524
E-mail: tomd@michaveclub.com

Procedures

Use Mail Merge to Generate a Directory Using an Existing Address List Data Source File

Select the main document:

1. Open a new blank document.
2. Click **Tools**.................
3. Select **Letters and Mailings**............................ Ⓔ
4. Click **Mail Merge**................ Ⓜ
5. Click the **Directory** option button in the Mail Merge task pane.
6. Click **Next: Starting document** in the Mail Merge task pane.
7. Click the **Use the current document** option button in the Mail Merge task pane.
8. Click **Next: Select recipients** in the Mail Merge task pane.

Select an existing Address List data source file:

1. Click the **Use an existing list** option button in the Mail Merge task pane.
2. Click **Browse** button 🔲 in the Mail Merge task pane.
   - ✓ *Word opens the Select Data Source dialog box.*
3. Locate and select the desired data source file.
4. Click **Open** 🔲.
   - ✓ *Word displays the Mail Merge Recipients dialog box.*
5. Click **OK**.......................... Enter
6. Click **Next: Arrange your directory** in the Mail Merge task pane.
   - ✓ *Word displays the starting document, and a list of available merge blocks.*

Arrange the directory:

1. In the current document, position the insertion point at the location where you want the first entry in the directory displayed.
2. Insert the merge fields or merge blocks as necessary to set up the first entry.
3. Type any additional text, spacing, or punctuation you want in the first entry.
   - ✓ *Typed data will be repeated as part of each entry in the directory.*
4. Save the document.
5. Click **Next: Preview your directory** in the Mail Merge task pane.
   - ✓ *Word displays the first entry in the document.*

Preview merge documents:

1. Click the **Next recipient** button  in the Mail Merge task pane.
   OR
   Click the **Next record** button ▶ on the Mail Merge toolbar.
   OR
   Click the **Previous recipient** button << in the Mail Merge task pane.
   OR
   Click the **Previous record** button ◀ on the Mail Merge toolbar.
2. Click **Next: Complete the merge** in the Mail Merge task pane.

Complete the merge:

1. Click **To New Document** button 🔲 to create the directory document.
   - ✓ *Word displays the Merge to New Document dialog box.*
2. Click **OK**.......................... Enter
   - ✓ *You can make changes to the document and/or save the document to print later.*

Sort Recipients in an Address List

1. Click **Mail Merge Recipients** button on Mail Merge toolbar.
   OR
   In Step 3 or Step 5 of Mail Merge task pane, click **Edit recipient list** 🔲.
2. Click **column heading** by which you want to sort.
   - ✓ *To sort in descending order, click column heading again.*
3. Click **OK**.......................... Enter
   - ✓ *Records will be merged in current sort order.*

Select Specific Recipients

1. Click **Mail Merge Recipients** button 🔲 on Mail Merge toolbar.
   OR
   In Step 3 or Step 5 of Mail Merge task pane, click **Edit recipient list** button .
2. Do one of the following:
   - Click **checkbox** at left of row to deselect recipient.
   - Click **blank checkbox** to select recipient.
   - Click **Clear All**........ Alt+Ⓐ to deselect all recipients.
   - Click **Select All** ...... Alt+Ⓢ to select all recipients.
3. Click **OK**.......................... Enter

Exercise Directions

1. Make a copy of the Office Address List file ⊙ **36MAACDATA**, and name the copy **MAACDATA**.

   ✓ *To copy the file, right-click the file name and select Copy. Right-click the destination folder and select Paste. Right-click the copied file name and select Rename. Type the new file name and press Enter.*

2. Start Word, if necessary.

3. Create a new blank document.

4. Save the document as **MAINDIR**.

5. Start Mail Merge.

6. Select to create a directory, using the current document.

7. Select to use an existing address list file as a data source document.

8. Locate and open **MAACDATA**.

9. Deselect all records for exercise instructors.

10. Sort the list in ascending order by Last Name.

11. Close the Mail Merge Recipients dialog box.

12. Set up the directory main document as shown in Illustration A.

    a. Type the labels using a 14 point serif font such as Times New Roman, in bold.

    b. Leave a 1.5" tab space between the labels and the merge fields.

    c. Enter two blank lines at the end of the document.

13. Complete the merge by generating a new directory document.

14. Save the directory document in a new file, named **DIRECTORY**.

15. Edit the file as shown in Illustration B.

    a. Insert five new lines at the beginning of the document.

    b. Centered on line 1, type **Michigan Avenue Athletic Club**. in a 26-point serif font.

    c. Centered on line 2, type the address as shown in a 12-point serif font.

    d. Leave line 3 blank.

    e. Centered on line 4, type **Directory of Personal Trainers** in a 20-point serif font.

    f. Leave remaining lines blank.

16. Check the spelling and grammar in the document.

17. Display the document in Print Preview. It should look similar to the one shown in Illustration B.

18. Print the directory.

19. Close all open files, saving all changes.

Illustration A

Name:	→	«First_Name»·«Last_Name»¶
Phone:	→	«Phone»¶
E-Mail:	→	«Email_Address»¶
Specialty:	→	«Specialty»¶
¶		
¶		

Michigan Avenue Athletic Club

235 Michigan Avenue, Chicago, Illinois 60601

Directory of Personal Trainers

Name: Trisha Chung
Phone: 312-555-3523
E-Mail: trish@michaveclub.com
Specialty: Strength Training

Name: Tom Dybreski
Phone: 312-555-3524
E-Mail: tomd@michaveclub.com
Specialty: Cardio Health

Name: David Fairmont
Phone: 312-555-3525
E-Mail: dfairmont@michaveclub.com
Specialty: All

Name: Abby MacLeish
Phone: 312-555-3528
E-Mail: abbymac@michaveclub.com
Specialty: Rehabilitation

Name: Sam Ruhail
Phone: 312-555-3529
E-Mail: sruhail@michaveclub.com
Specialty: Weight Loss

On Your Own

1. Create a new document in Word.
2. Save it as **OWD36-1**.
3. Use the Mail Merge Wizard to create a directory, using **OWD34-2** as the data source.
   - ✓ If **OWD34-2** is not available, make a copy of 💿 **36DATA** and save it as **OWD36-2**
4. Select to include only certain entries.
5. Sort the list.
6. Merge the directory to a new document.
7. Save the directory as **OWD36-3**.
8. Edit the directory document to include a title.
9. Check the spelling and grammar.
10. Complete the merge by generating a new document.
11. Print the directory.
12. Close all open documents, saving all changes.

Exercise 37

◆ Filter Recipients
◆ Merge to an E-mail Message

On the Job

You can use Mail Merge to generate mass e-mailings in much the same way you can generate form letters. You type the message text you want each recipient to read, and insert merge fields to customize or personalize the message. Word automatically uses your e-mail program to send the messages. Filter the recipient list to quickly select the records you want to use.

You must notify all Michigan Avenue Athletic Club exercise instructors that there is an important meeting tomorrow. In this exercise, you will use Mail Merge to create an e-mail message about the meeting, and you will filter an existing data source file to select only exercise instructors as recipients.

Terms

Filter To display records based on whether or not they match specified criteria.

Criteria Specific data used to match a record or entry in a data source file or list.

MAPI A Microsoft standard that allows messaging programs to work together.

Notes

Filter Recipients

- You can **filter** the records in an Address List in order to display records that match specific **criteria**.

- The records that match the criteria are displayed, while those that don't match are hidden.

- Only the displayed records are used in the merge.

Merge to an E-mail Message

- Use Mail Merge to set up and complete a merge using e-mail messages as the main document.

- You type the message text, and then insert merge fields as desired.

- You must be sure your data source includes a field for an e-mail address; the information entered in the e-mail address field will be inserted as the recipient's address in the message header.

- You select options for merging to e-mail in the Merge to E-mail dialog box. For example, you may enter the text that will be displayed in the Subject field of the message header, and select the format to use for the message—either HTML, plain text, or as an attachment.

Merge to E-mail Dialog Box

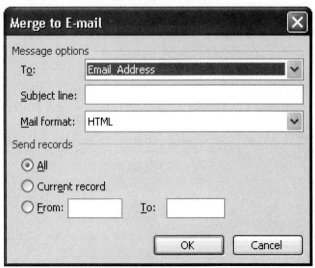

- When you merge to e-mail, Word does not create a merge document as it does when you merge letters, envelopes, or labels. Instead, the messages are created and sent to your Outbox.

- To successfully complete a merge to e-mail, you must have a **MAPI**-compatible e-mail program, such as Microsoft Office Outlook, installed and set up for use with Microsoft Office Word.

Procedures

Use Mail Merge to Merge to E-Mail

Select the main document:

1. Open a new blank document.
2. Click **Tools** .... Alt +T
3. Select **Letters and Mailings** .... E
4. Click **Mail Merge** .... M
5. Click the **E-mail messages** option button in the Mail Merge task pane.
6. Click **Next: Starting document** in the Mail Merge task pane.
7. Click the **Use the current document** option button in the Mail Merge task pane.
8. Click **Next: Select recipients** in the Mail Merge task pane.

Select an existing Address List data source file:

1. Click the **Use an existing list** option button in the Mail Merge task pane.
2. Click **Browse** button 🔲 in the Mail Merge task pane.
   - ✓ *Word opens the Select Data Source dialog box.*

3. Locate and select the desired data source file.
4. Click **Open** button

   [Open]

   - ✓ *Word displays the Mail Merge Recipients dialog box.*
5. Click **OK** .... Enter
6. Click **Next: Write your e-mail message** in the Mail Merge task pane.
   - ✓ *Word displays the starting document in Web Layout view, and a list of available merge blocks.*

Arrange the message:

1. In the current document, type the message text as you want it to appear on each e-mail message.
2. Insert the merge fields or merge blocks as necessary to complete the message.
3. Click **Next: Preview your e-mail message** in the Mail Merge task pane.
   - ✓ *Word displays the first entry in the document.*

Preview e-mail messages:

1. Click the **Next recipient** button

   [>>] in the Mail Merge task pane.

   OR

   Click the **Next record** button

   [▶] on the Mail Merge toolbar.

   OR

   Click the **Previous recipient** button [◀] in the Mail Merge task pane.

   OR

   Click the **Previous record** button [◀] on the Mail Merge toolbar.
2. Click **Next: Complete the merge** in the Mail Merge task pane.

Complete the merge:

1. Click **Electronic Mail** button.
   - ✓ *Word displays the Merge to E-mail dialog box.*
2. Click **To**: drop-down arrow .... `Alt`+`O`
3. Select field that specified recipient's e-mail address.
4. Click **Subject line** box .... `Alt`+`S`
5. Type text you want displayed in message header subject line.
6. Click **Mail format** drop-down arrow .... `Alt`+`M`
7. Select desired format.
8. Select other options as desired.
9. Click **OK** .... `Enter`

   - ✓ *Messages are sent to your Outbox. If necessary, start your e-mail program, sign on to the Interent, and send the messages.*

Filter Recipients

1. Click **Mail Merge Recipients** button 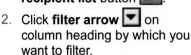 on Mail Merge toolbar.
   OR
   In Step 3 or Step 5 of Mail Merge task pane, click **Edit recipient list** button.
2. Click **filter arrow** ▼ on column heading by which you want to filter.
   - ✓ *Word displays a list of data.*

3. Select data to filter by.
   - ✓ *Word displays only those entries that match the selected data.*
   OR
   Select one of the following:
   - **[All]** to display all entries.
     - ✓ *Use this option to remove an existing filter.*
   - **[Blanks]** to display entries in which the current field is blank.
   - **[Nonblanks]** to display entries in which the current field is not blank.
     - ✓ *The filter arrow on the column heading changes to blue so you know which column is used for the filter.*
4. Click **OK** .... `Enter`

Exercise Directions

1. Make a copy of the Office Address List file ⊙ **37MAACDATA**, and name the copy **MAACDAT2**.
   - ✓ *To copy the file, right-click the file name and select Copy. Right-click the destination folder and select Paste. Right-click the copied file name and select Rename. Type the new file name and press Enter.*
2. Start Word, if necessary.
3. Create a new blank document.
4. Save the document as **MAINMAIL**.
5. Start the Mail Merge Wizard.
6. Select to create an e-mail message, using the current document.
7. Select to use an existing address list file as a data source document.
8. Locate and open **MAACDAT2**.
9. Filter the list to display only exercise instructors.
   a. Click the filter arrow on the Position column heading.
   b. Click Exercise Instructor.
10. Close the Mail Merge Recipients dialog box.

11. Set up the e-mail message main document as shown in Illustration A.
    - Use a 14-point sans serif font, such as Arial.
12. Check the spelling and grammar in the document.
13. Preview the messages.
14. Select to complete the merge as follows:
    a. Select to merge Electronic Mail.
    b. In the Merge to E-mail dialog box, leave Email_Address as the option in the To: box.
    c. Type **Instructor Info Session** in the Subject line box.
    d. Leave HTML as the option in the Mail format box.
    e. Select to send All records.
    f. Click OK.
15. If necessary, start your e-mail program, log on to Internet, and send all messages.
16. Close all open files, disconnect if necessary, and save all changes.

Illustration A

«First_Name»¶
¶
Please·note·that·the·meeting·for·all·exercise·instructors·has·been·rescheduled·to·3:30·p.m.·
tomorrow·(Wednesday)·in·aerobics·studio·1.¶

On Your Own

1. Create a new document in Word.

2. Save it as **OWD37-1**.

3. Use the Mail Merge Wizard to create e-mail messages using **OWD34-2** (the data source document you first used in Exercise 34) as the data source.

   ✓ If **OWD34-2** is not available, create a copy of ⊙ **37DATA** to use, saving the copy as **OWD37-2**.

4. If necessary, edit the list to fill in the e-mail address information for all records.

5. Filter the list to only the records you want to include in the merge.

6. Type the e-mail message, inserting merge fields as necessary.

7. Check the spelling and grammar.

8. Complete the merge and send the e-mail messages.

9. Close all open documents, saving all changes.

Exercise 38

◆ Critical Thinking

Voyager Travel Adventures wants you to create participant directories for three upcoming tours so the leaders know the experience level of each person in the group. In addition, you need to send out letters to all participants confirming tour selections. In this exercise, you will use Mail Merge to create the letters and the directories. You will create a new data source file that you can use for all merges. The file will need to be customized to include fields specific to your needs. It will also need to be filtered and sorted to complete each merge.

Exercise Directions

Create Form Letters

1. Start Word, if necessary.
2. Create a new blank document.
3. Save the file as **TOURS**.
4. Start Mail Merge.
5. Select to create a letter, using the current document.
6. Create a new address list to use as a data source document.
7. Customize the address list as follows:
   a. Rename the Company field to **Level**.
   b. Add a field named **Tour**.
   c. Delete the Work Phone field.
   d. Delete the Home Phone field.
   e. Delete the E-Mail Address field.
   f. Move the Level and the Tour fields down to the bottom of the list.
8. Enter the recipients from the table in Illustration A on the following page into the data source file.
9. Save the data source file as **NAMES**.
10. Sort the data source file alphabetically by Level.
11. Select to use all recipients in the merge, then close the Mail Merge Recipients dialog box.
12. Type the document shown in Illustration B, inserting the merge fields as marked.
13. Check the spelling and grammar in the document.

14. Preview the merged documents.
15. Complete the merge by generating a new file containing all merged records.
16. Save the file as **CONFIRM**.
17. Print the file.
18. Close all open documents, saving all changes.

Create a Directory

1. Create a new blank document.
2. Save the file as **ENROLLED**.
3. Start Mail Merge.
4. Select to create a directory, using the current document.
5. Use the **NAMES** address list as the data source file.
6. Sort the list alphabetically by last name.
7. Filter the list to display only the people signed up for the Alaska tour.
8. Set up the directory as shown in Illustration C, using a 12-point serif font.
9. Preview the directory.
10. Generate the directory and save it in a new file named **ASTOUR**.
11. Add the title **Alaska Tour Participant List** in a 24-point sans serif font at the top of the directory.
12. Check the spelling and grammar in the document.
13. Print the document.

14. Close the document, saving all changes.

   ✓ *The Enrolled document should still be open on-screen, with the Mail Merge task pane displaying Step 6.*

15. Go back through Mail Merge to step 5.

16. Edit the Recipient list to change the filter from Alaska to Costa Rica.

17. Preview the directory.

18. Generate the directory and save it in a new file named **CRTOUR**.

19. Add the title **Cost Rica Tour Participant List** in a 24-point sans serif font at the top of the directory.

20. Check the spelling and grammar in the document.

21. Print the document.

22. Close the document, saving all changes.

23. Repeat steps 15–22 to create a directory for the Kenya tour, names **KENTOUR**.

24. Close the **ENROLLED** document, saving all changes.

Illustration A

Mr.	Gary	Doone	10 Quail Drive	Largo	FL	33771	Beginner	Alaska
Ms.	Elizabeth	Dubin	1001 Starkey Road	Northborough	MA	01532	Beginner	Alaska
Ms.	Janice	Loring	17 Cherlyn Drive	Westford	MA	01886	Advanced	Kenya
Mr.o	Antonio	DiBuono	2 Parkview Circle	Chelmsford	MA	01824	Intermediate	Costa Rica
Ms.	Katharine	Peterson	27 Concord Road	Bethesda	MD	20814	Intermediate	Alaska
Ms.	Marianne	Flagg	314 Green Street	Washington	DC	20015	Advanced	Costa Rica
Mr.	Howard	Jefferson	41 Marvel Court	Marlboro	MA	01752	Intermediate	Alaska
Mr.	Julian	Lovett	4526 Amherst Lane	Sudbury	MA	01776	Advanced	Kenya
Ms.	Christina	Bottecelli	49 Weatherly Place	Etna	NH	03750	Intermediate	Kenya
Ms.	Rose	Mekalian	6409 33rd Street N.W.	Auburn	ME	04210	Beginner	Costa Rica
Mr.	Dana	Teng	7 Ranch Road	San Francisco	CA	94121	Intermediate	Kenya
Mr.	Luis	Martinez	98 Sudbury Street	Northborough	MA	01532	Beginner	Costa Rica

Today's date

«AddressBlock»

«GreetingLine»

This letter confirms that you have registered for our «Tour» tour. This tour is one of our most popular, and we know you will have a wonderful time.

On your registration form you specified that your level of experience is «Level». If this is not accurate, please let us know as soon as possible. Your tour guide customizes some parts of the tour based on the participant's experience.

We will send you more information two weeks prior to your departure date, including a participant list, a packing list and a detailed itinerary. In the meantime, if you have any questions, please feel free to call.

Thank you for choosing Voyager.

Sincerely,

Your name

Illustration C

¶
¶
¶
«Title»·«First_Name»·«Last_Name»¶
«City»,·«State»¶
Level:→«Level»¶
¶
¶
¶
¶

Excel 2003

Lesson 1

Getting Started with Excel 2003
Exercises 1-6

Lesson 2

Working with Formulas and Formatting
Exercises 7-12

Lesson 3

Working with Functions, Formulas, and Charts
Exercises 13-19

Lesson 4

Advanced Printing, Formatting, and Editing
Exercises 20-27

Lesson 5 (on CD 💿)

Advanced Chart Techniques
Exercises 28-31

Lesson 6 (on CD 💿)

Advanced Functions, PivotCharts, and PivotTables
Exercises 32-36

Lesson 7 (on CD 💿)

Internet and Integration with Excel
Exercises 37-40

Directory of Data Files on CD

Exercise #	File Name	Page #
1	None	202
2	None	209
3	03BAKEY SCHEDULE 7-21, 03BAKEY SCHEDULE 7-20	216
4	04MAAC INVOICE 2	223
5	05BALANCE SHEET	227
6	06INVOICEWS	229
7	07INVENTORY	233
8	08INVENTORY	237
9	09TRIPBUDGET	242
10	10PAYROLL	246
11	11SPASERVICES 2	250
12	12BREADSALES	252
13	13BIDANALYSIS	257
14	14RHSALES	262
15	15BIDANALYSIS	266
16	16DAILYBREADSALES	271
17	17DAILYBREADSALES	277
18	18DAILYBREADSALES 2, Bread.jpg	282
19	19RHSales 2, restoration architecture logo 2.jpg	285
20	20TRIPBUDGET2	291
21	21BALANCE SHEET 2	297
22	22RHSALES 2	301
23	23INVENTORY 3, 23VTAMonthlySales	304
24	24PAYROLL 2	308
25	25INCOMETAX, 25TAXWS	312
26	26BREADSALES 2	317
27	27WGBP&L, 27BREADSALES 2, 27WGBINVENTORY	319

Exercise 1

Skills Covered:

◆ **Start Excel 2003** ◆ **The Excel Window** ◆ **Excel Menu and Toolbars**
◆ **Explore the Worksheet Using the Mouse and Keyboard**
◆ **Change Between Worksheets** ◆ **The View Menu** ◆ **Exit Excel**

On the Job

When you want to analyze business, personal, or financial data and create reports in a table format consisting of rows and columns, use the Microsoft Office Excel spreadsheet application in the Microsoft Office suite.

You've recently been hired as a marketing specialist for Voyager Travel Adventures, and you've enrolled yourself in a class to learn to use Excel. In this exercise, you will start Excel, familiarize yourself with the Excel window, change your view of the worksheet, and practice moving around the worksheet using the mouse and the keyboard.

Terms

Workbook An Excel file with one or more worksheets.

Worksheet The work area for entering and calculating data made up of columns and rows separated by gridlines (light gray lines). Also called a *spreadsheet*.

Cell A cell is the intersection of a column and a row on a worksheet. You enter data into cells to create a worksheet.

Active cell The active cell contains the cell pointer. There is a dark outline around the active cell.

Task pane A vertical window that provides quick access to common commands such as opening and creating workbooks, searching for workbooks, getting help, and so on.

Formula bar As you enter data into a cell, it simultaneously appears in the Formula bar, which is located above the worksheet frame.

Cell reference The location of a cell in a worksheet as identified by its column letter and row number. This is also known as the cell's *address*.

Scroll A way to view locations on the worksheet without changing the active cell.

Sheet tabs Tabs that appear at the bottom of the workbook window, which display the name of each worksheet.

Tab scrolling buttons Buttons that appear just to the left of the sheet tabs, which allow you to scroll hidden tabs into view.

Notes

Start Excel 2003

- Start Excel using the Start menu.

The Excel Window

- When Excel starts, it displays an empty **workbook** with three worksheets.
  - A **worksheet** contains rows and columns that intersect to form **cells**.
- A black border appears around the **active cell**.
- You can change the active cell using the mouse or the keyboard.
- The Getting Started **task pane** appears on the right. You can use the commands displayed there to open a workbook you've worked on recently, or to start a new workbook.
  - ✓ *You'll learn more about using the Getting Started task pane in Exercise 2.*
- The name box, located on the left side of the **Formula bar**, displays the cell reference of the active cell (its column letter and row number).
- A **cell reference** is the known as the *address* of a cell.

Name box

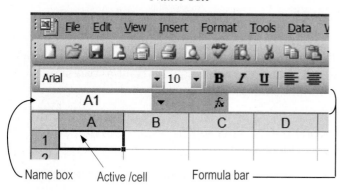

Name box   Active /cell   Formula bar ————

- To help you identify the cell reference for the active cell, Excel highlights its column label (above the worksheet) and row number (to the left of the worksheet).
  - ✓ *Notice, for example, that the active cell shown in the Name box figure is surrounded by a dark outline. The active cell's address or cell reference, A1, appears in the Name box just to the left of the Formula bar. Notice also that the column label A and the row label 1 are highlighted in order to make it easier for you to identify the address of the current cell.*

Excel Menu and Toolbars

- The menu bar, Standard toolbar, Formatting toolbar, formula bar, and Ask a Question box appear at the top of the workbook window while the status bar appears at the bottom.
- The Standard and Formatting toolbars share one row but you can use the View, Toolbars, Customize command, Options tab to change this option.
- If your Standard and Formatting toolbars continue to share one row, not all of the toolbar buttons will be displayed—only the ones you use the most will be displayed.
  - To display hidden buttons, click the Toolbar Options button at the right end of the toolbar and click the button you want to use.
- The menu bar, toolbars (except for the Formula bar), and the Ask a Question box are similar to those used in Word and are covered in Exercise 1 of the Word section of this text.

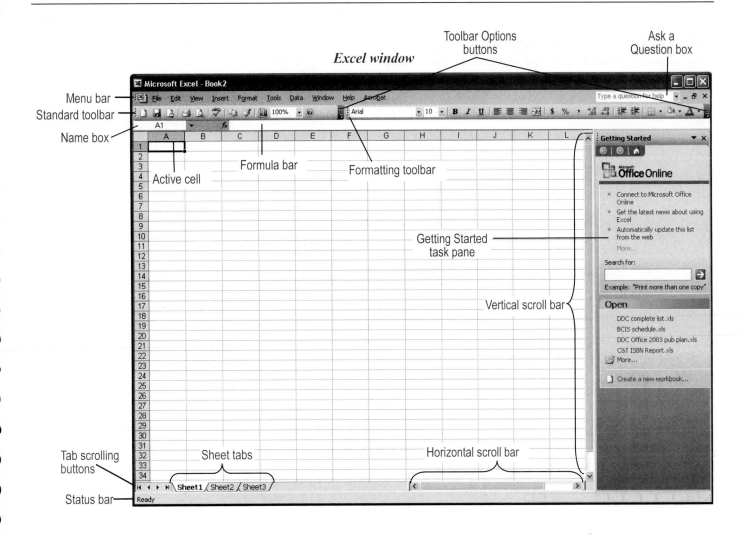

Excel window

Menu bar

Standard toolbar

Name box

Active cell

Formula bar

Formatting toolbar

Toolbar Options buttons

Ask a Question box

Getting Started task pane

Vertical scroll bar

Tab scrolling buttons

Sheet tabs

Horizontal scroll bar

Status bar

Explore the Worksheet Using the Mouse and Keyboard

- Since the workbook window displays only a part of a worksheet, you **scroll** through the worksheet to view another location.

- Use the mouse or keyboard to scroll to different locations in a worksheet.

- With the mouse, you can scroll using the horizontal or vertical scroll bars.

  ✓ *Using the mouse to scroll does not change the active cell.*

- With the keyboard, you can scroll by pressing specific keys or key combinations.

  ✓ *Scrolling with the keyboard changes the active cell.*

- There are 256 columns and 65,536 rows available in a worksheet, but you don't need to fill the entire worksheet in order to use it—just type data into the cells you need.

Active cell in bottom-left corner of worksheet

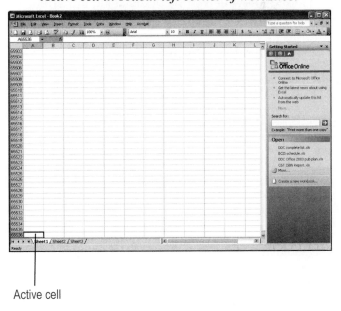

Active cell

Active cell in bottom-right corner of worksheet

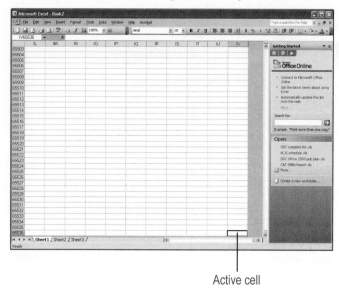

Active cell

Available toolbars

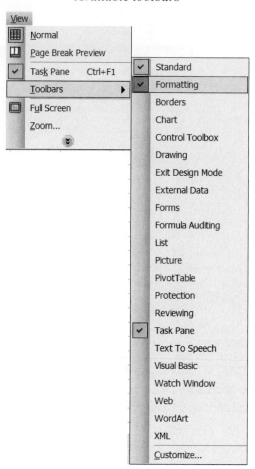

Change Between Worksheets

- By default, each workbook comes with three worksheets. You can add or delete worksheets as needed.

    ✓ *You'll learn how to add and remove worksheets in Exercise 11.*

- You enter related data on different worksheets within the same workbook.

    ✓ *For example, you can enter January, February, and March sales data on different worksheets within the same workbook.*

- Change between worksheets using the **sheet tabs** located at the bottom of the Excel window.

    ✓ *If a particular worksheet tab is not visible, use the **tab scrolling buttons** to display it.*

The View Menu

- To view or hide the Formula bar, Status bar, or task pane, select or deselect them from the View menu.

    ✓ *When you click the View menu several options are hidden. Wait a few seconds for the menu to expand automatically, or click the arrows at the bottom of the menu.*

- The Toolbar command on the View menu displays a submenu with a list of available toolbars.

    • Choose a toolbar from this list to display it.

    • Choose the toolbar again to hide it.

- If you need to expand the worksheet to fill the screen, choose Full Screen. The menu bar is still displayed for commands and a Close Full Screen dialog box appears in order to return to the default view.

- The Zoom command magnifies cells in a worksheet by the amount you choose.

    ✓ *You can also change the Zoom by selecting the Zoom level you want from the Zoom button located on the Standard toolbar.*

Zoom dialog box

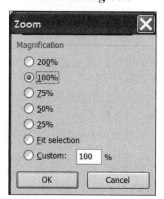

Zoom button on the Standard toolbar

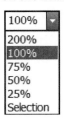

Exit Excel

■ When your worksheet is complete and you want to close the Excel application, use the Exit command from the File menu.

Procedures

Start Excel

1. Click **Start**

    .... `Ctrl` + `Esc`

   ✓ *If your keyboard has a Windows key (a key with the Windows logo on it) you can press that key at any time to display the Start menu.*

2. Select **All Programs** .... `P`
3. Click **Microsoft Office** .... `↓`, `Enter`
4. Click **Microsoft Office Excel 2003** .... `↓`, `Enter`

Change Active Cell Using Keyboard

- One cell right .... `→`
- One cell left........................... `←`
- One cell down...................... `↓`
- One cell up .... `↑`
- One screen up .... `Page Up`
- One screen down .... `Page Down`
- One screen right........ `Alt` + `Page Down`
- One screen left .... `Alt` + `Page Up`
- First cell in current row ... `Home`
- First cell in worksheet .... `Ctrl` + `Home`
- Last used cell in worksheet .... `Ctrl` + `End`

Change Active Cell Using Mouse

- Click desired cell.

Change Active Cell Using Go To (Ctrl+G)

1. Press **F5** .... `F5`

   OR

   a. Click **Edit**............... `Alt` + `E`
   b. Click **Go To** .... `G`

   ✓ *Go To list box displays last four references that you accessed.*

2. Type cell reference in **Reference** text box.
3. Click **OK** .... `Enter`

Change Active Cell Using Name Box

1. Click in Name box.
2. Type cell reference.
3. Press **Enter** .... `Enter`

Scroll Using Mouse

To scroll one row up or down:

- Click up or down scroll arrow, located at the top or bottom of the vertical scroll bar.

To scroll one column left or right:

- Click left or right scroll arrow, located at either end of the horizontal scroll bar.

To scroll one screen right or left:

- Click horizontal scroll bar to right or left of scroll box.

To scroll one screen up or down:

- Click vertical scroll bar above or below scroll box.

To scroll to beginning rows:

- Drag vertical scroll box to top of scroll bar.

To scroll to beginning columns:

- Drag horizontal scroll box to extreme left of scroll bar.

To scroll to last row containing data:

- Press **Ctrl** and drag vertical scroll box to bottom of scroll bar.

Change to a Different Worksheet

- Click the tab of the worksheet you want to display.

  ✓ *If the worksheet tab you need is not displayed, click the appropriate tab scrolling button. The first or last buttons display the first or last worksheet tab. The middle tab scrolling buttons move the sheet tabs one sheet in the direction of the arrow.*

Display Standard and Formatting Toolbars in Two Rows

1. Click **View** .... `Alt` + `V`
2. Click **Toolbars** .... `T`

   OR
   Right-click on toolbar.

3. Click **Customize** .... `C`
4. Click **Options** tab........ `Ctrl` + `Tab`

   ✓ *Press Ctrl+Tab until Options page displays.*

5. Select **Show Standard and Formatting toolbars on two rows** checkbox. .... `Alt` + `S`

   ✓ *Removes check mark from option.*

6. Click **Close** button

    .... `Enter`

Display or Hide Task pane

1. Click **View** .... `Alt`+`V`
2. Click **Task pane** .... `K`

   ✓ *The Getting Started task pane appears by default. You can change to a different task pane by clicking the down arrow and selecting one from the list.*

   ✓ *Return to the Getting Started task pane by clicking the Home button* 🏠 *.*

   ✓ *View hidden options on a task pane by clicking the arrow at the bottom or top of the pane.*

Display or Hide Formula Bar

1. Click **View** .... `Alt`+`V`
2. Click **Formula Bar** .... `F`

Display or Hide Status Bar

1. Click **View** .... `Alt`+`V`
2. Click **Status Bar** .... `S`

Display or Hide Toolbar

1. Click **View** .... `Alt`+`V`
2. Click **Toolbars** .... `T`
3. Select toolbar name .... `↓`
4. Click toolbar name .... `Enter`

Set Zoom Percentage

1. Click **View** .... `Alt`+`V`
2. Click **Zoom** .... `Z`
3. Set percentage .... `↓`|`↑`
4. Click **OK** .... `Enter`

Set Zoom Percentage with Zoom Button

1. Click arrow on **Zoom** button `10 ▼` .
2. Select zoom level.

   ✓ *You can also type the zoom percentage you want to use in the box on the Zoom button, and press Enter.*

Exit Excel

1. Click **File** .... `Alt`+`F`
2. Click **Exit** .... `X`

   OR

   Click **Application Close** button ⊠ .

Exercise Directions

1. Follow these steps to start Excel from the taskbar.
   a. Click Start.
   b. Select All Programs, Microsoft Office, and then Microsoft Office Excel 2003.

2. Move the active cell pointer using the keyboard:
   a. Press the right arrow key four times until cell E1 is highlighted.
   b. Press the down arrow key four times until cell E5 is highlighted.

   ✓ *View the cell references in the name box.*

3. Click cell H9 to make it the active cell.

   ✓ *View the cell reference in the name box.*

4. Press F5 to activate the Go To command.

5. In the Reference text box, type **T98**.

6. Click OK.

   ✓ *The active cell changes to T98.*

7. Click in the name box to change the active cell to the following, pressing Enter after each new cell address:
   - B1492 (Row 1492, column B)
   - A65536 (Bottom left of worksheet)
   - IV65536 (Bottom right of worksheet)
   - A1 (Home)

8. Click the tab for Sheet 2 to display it.

9. Click cell D4.

10. Point to the horizontal scroll bar and click the right scroll arrow.

    ✓ *The worksheet moves right by one column but the active cell does not change.*

11. Point to the horizontal scroll bar and click to the left of the scroll box.

    ✓ *The worksheet moves left by one screen but the active cell does not change.*

12. Point to the horizontal scroll bar, and then drag the scroll box all the way to the right.

    ✓ *The view of the worksheet has changed again but the active cell does not change.*

13. Click the down scroll arrow on the vertical scroll bar three times.

    ✓ *The worksheet moves down three rows but the active cell does not change.*

14. Click the tab for Sheet 1 to redisplay it.

    ✓ *The active cell for Sheet 1 remains the same (A1). It did not change even as you changed the active cell on Sheet 2.*

15. Rest the mouse pointer on each visible button on the Standard and Formatting toolbars until the ScreenTip appears.

    ✓ *A ScreenTip appears under the button with the name of the button.*

16. Click the Toolbar Options button next to the Microsoft Office Excel Help button, located on the Standard toolbar.
    - ✓ *A menu appears, displaying the hidden buttons from both toolbars.*

17. Click Show Buttons on Two Rows.
    - ✓ *If the buttons are already displayed on two rows, select to have them displayed on one row and skip to step 20.*
    - ✓ *The Standard and Formatting toolbars are displayed on two separate rows. This allows all the buttons to be visible.*

18. Click the Toolbar Options button.

19. Select Show Buttons on One Row.
    - ✓ *Drag the left edge of the Formatting toolbar to the right until the display is the way you prefer.*

20. Select View, Zoom to display the Zoom dialog box.

21. Click in the Custom box and type **150** then click OK.
    - ✓ *The Zoom changes to 150%, so cells appear much larger.*

22. Point to the Zoom button and click its down arrow.
    - ✓ *The Zoom menu appears.*

23. Select 100% from the Zoom menu.
    - ✓ *Cells are restored to their normal size as you return to 100% magnification.*

24. Click View, Toolbars, Borders to display the Borders toolbar.
    - ✓ *The Borders toolbar appears, floating in the middle of the worksheet.*

25. Click View, Toolbars, Borders to hide the Borders toolbar.
    - ✓ *You can also click the Close button on a floating toolbar to hide it.*

26. Click the Close button ☒ to exit Excel.

On Your Own

1. Create a new workbook document.

2. Click cell G7.
   - ✓ *View the cell reference in the name box.*

3. Move the active cell pointer to cell D21 using the keyboard.

4. Click below the scroll box in the vertical scroll bar.
   - ✓ *The worksheet moves down one screen but the active cell does not change.*

5. Drag the scroll box all the way to the top of the vertical scroll bar.
   - ✓ *The view of the worksheet changes but the active cell does not change.*

6. Use the horizontal scroll bar to scroll one screen to the right.

7. Use the horizontal scroll bar to scroll one screen to the left.

8. Change to Sheet 3.

9. Use the Go To command to make V20 the active cell.

10. Use the Name box to make AA1000 the active cell.

11. Make A1 the active cell.

12. Return to Sheet 1.

13. Display the Standard and Formatting toolbars in two rows.

14. Hide the Formula bar.

15. Redisplay the Formula bar.

16. Change the View, Toolbar, Customize options so that the Standard and Formatting toolbars will once again appear on the same row.

17. Change the Zoom percentage to 155%.

18. Return the Zoom percentage to 100%.

19. Exit Excel without saving the current workbook document.

Exercise 2

Skills Covered:

◆ **Create a New (Blank) Workbook**
◆ **Create a Workbook from a Template**
◆ **Enter Labels** ◆ **Make Simple Corrections** ◆ **Undo and Redo**
◆ **Delete (Clear) Cell Contents** ◆ **Save a Workbook**
◆ **Recover a Workbook After a Crash** ◆ **Close a Workbook**

On the Job

To create your first worksheet, you begin by entering the column and row titles (the labels that appear to the right of each row of data and above each data column). Next, you enter the numeric data, using the row and column labels to help you enter each amount into the correct cell. As you enter data, you may make a few mistakes and then find out how easy it is to correct them. Finally, you save your workbook before exiting Excel so that the entries are not lost.

You are the Accounts Receivable Supervisor at the Michigan Avenue Athletic Club, and a member has charged several services and has not paid them. You need to create an invoice detailing the charges, with a special reminder that the balance must be paid soon or club privileges will be suspended. You'll begin the invoice and complete it in a later exercise.

Terms

Blank workbook The Excel default workbook contains three worksheets or sheets.

Template A workbook with certain labels, formulas, and formatting preset, saving you time in creating commonly used worksheets, such as sales invoices or balance sheets.

Label Text in the first row or column of a worksheet that identifies the type of data contained there.

Defaults The standard settings Excel uses in its software, such as column width or number of worksheets in a workbook.

Undo The command used to reverse one or a series of editing actions.

Redo The command used to redo an action you have undone.

Notes

Create a New (Blank) Workbook

■ Excel displays a **blank workbook** when you open the Excel application.

■ A blank workbook initially contains three blank worksheets into which you can enter data.

■ When you need to create a new, blank workbook, click the New button on the Standard toolbar, select Create a new workbook from the Getting Started task pane, or select Blank workbook from the New Workbook task pane.

Create new workbooks using the Getting Started task pane

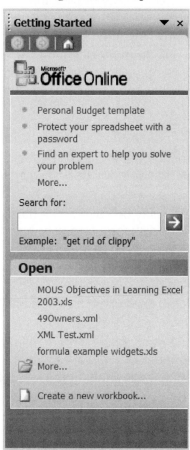

Or the New Workbook task pane

Create a Workbook from a Template

- To save time when creating a new workbook from scratch, select an Excel **template.**

- When you select a template for a new workbook, a lot of the work is already done for you, including most of the formatting, formulas, and layout design.

- After the new workbook is created from the template, simply enter your data.

  ✓ *For example, if you start a new workbook using the Sales Invoice template, simply enter your company's name and address where indicated, then type the individual items you want to appear on the invoice.*

- From the Getting Started or New Workbook task pane, you can search Microsoft's Web site for templates to use.

- From the New Workbook task pane, you can also select a template already stored on your system, on a company Web site, or on Microsoft's Web site.

- On your computer, Excel provides a small number of templates for use in creating common forms, such as balance sheets, sales invoices, expense statements, and time cards. There's even a template for comparing loans.

- You can create additional templates for your own use and store them on your computer as well.

- In addition to using templates to create new workbooks, you can base a new workbook on a copy of an existing workbook by selecting that option from the New Workbook task pane.

Enter Labels

- The first character entered into a cell determines what type of cell it is—a label, number, or formula cell.

- If you enter an alphabetical character or a symbol (` ~ ! # % ^ & *( ) _ \ | { } ; : ' " < > ,?) as the first character in a cell, you are entering a **label**.

- A label generally represents text data, such as the labels: Blue, Sally Smith, Ohio, or Above Average.

- The **default** width of each cell is 8.11 characters wide in the standard font (Arial, 10 point); therefore, a label longer than the cell width will display fully only if the cell to the right is blank, or if the column is made wider to accommodate the long entry.

- Excel supports up to 32,000 characters in a cell entry.

- As you type a label into a cell, it appears in the cell and the Formula bar.

- To enter the label in the cell, type the text and then do any of the following to finalize the entry: press the Enter key, an arrow key, the Tab key, click another cell, or click the Enter button (the green check mark) on the Formula bar.

  ✓ *To enter multiple lines in a cell such as Overtime above and Hours below, type Overtime, press and hold Alt, then press Enter. Type Hours on the second line in the cell and press Enter to finalize the entry.*

- A label automatically aligns to the left of the cell, making it a left-justified entry.

Entry appears in cell and Formula bar

Make Simple Corrections

- As you type data into a cell, if you notice a mistake before you press Enter (or any of the other keys that finalize an entry), you can press the Backspace key to erase characters to the left of the insertion point.

- Before you finalize an entry, you can press the Escape key or click the Cancel button (the red X) on the Formula bar to cancel it.

- After you enter data, you can make the cell active again (by clicking it, pressing an arrow key, etc.) and then type a new entry to replace the old one.

- You can also double-click a cell in which the entry has been finalized to enable cell editing and then make changes to only part of the entry.

Undo and Redo

- Use the **Undo** command from the Edit menu or the Undo button on the Standard toolbar to reverse any editing action.

- With the Undo command, you can reverse up to 16 previous editing actions.

- The Undo command on the Edit menu names the last editing action to be reversed.

- You can also redo (reinstate any action you've undone in error) up to 16 reversed actions using the **Redo** command.

Delete (Clear) Cell Contents

- Press the Escape key or click the Cancel box on the Formula bar to clear a cell's contents before finalizing any cell entry.

- To erase data from a cell after it has been finalized, use the Clear, Contents command from the Edit menu or the Delete key on the keyboard.

Save a Workbook

- After entering data into a workbook, you must save it, or that data will be lost when you exit Excel.

- A workbook may be saved on a hard drive or a removable disk for future use. A saved workbook is referred to as a file.

- You must provide a name for the file when you save it. File names should be descriptive, with a limit of 255 characters for the name, drive, and path.

- A file name may contain letters, numbers, and spaces, but not \ / : * ? " < > or | .

- Excel automatically adds a period and a file type extension (usually .xls) to the end of a file name when you save it.

Save As dialog box

- Workbooks are saved in the My Documents folder by default, although you may select another location if you like. You can also create new folders in which to store your workbooks.

- Data can also be saved in other formats, such as Lotus 1-2-3 or older versions of Excel.

  ✓ *You might want to save data in a different format in order to share that data with someone who uses a different version of Excel, or a different spreadsheet program, such as Lotus 1-2-3.*

- Once you've saved a workbook, you need only click the Save button as you work to resave any changes made since the last save action. You will not need to reenter the file name.

Recover a Workbook After a Crash

- Even after saving your workbook data in a file, you must periodically resave it in order to avoid accidental loss of new data you are entering in an open workbook.

- You can lose changes that you have not yet saved if Excel locks up for some reason (refuses to respond), or you suddenly lose power.

- To avoid accidental loss of data, click the Save button periodically to resave new changes.

- If you forget to resave a workbook, your data may not be lost if Excel has saved it for you using its AutoRecovery feature.

- By default, AutoRecovery automatically saves changes made to a file every 10 minutes. You can have AutoRecovery save changes more often or turn it off completely if you want.

- If AutoRecovery is on and Excel is restarted after a power loss or program crash, the Document Recovery task pane will automatically appear.

- Manually saved workbooks are listed as [Original], while versions created by AutoRecovery are listed as [Recovered].

- Use the Document Recovery task pane to view each version of a workbook and to select the version you want to save.

  ✓ *AutoRecovery is not a perfect process, so don't be tempted to select that version of a workbook after a crash. Review each version listed and select the one that contains the most complete version of your document. To avoid critical data loss, your best bet is to manually save open workbooks as often as you can.*

Document Recovery task pane

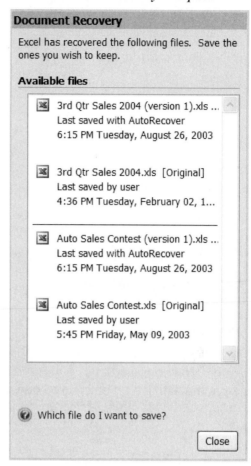

Close a Workbook

- Save a workbook before you close it or you will lose the current data or updated entries that you made.

- If you attempt to close a workbook or close Excel before saving, you will be prompted to save the changes.

- If you have more than one file open, Excel allows you to close and save all of the files before you exit the program.

Procedures

Create a New, Blank Workbook (Ctrl+N)

- Click **New** button .

OR

1. Click **View**.................. Alt + V
2. Click **Task pane**.................. K
3. Click **Home** button 🏠 to display Getting Started task pane.
4. Click **Create a new workbook** link.

OR

1. Click **File**.................... Alt + F
2. Click **New**.......................... N
3. Click **Blank workbook** in the New Workbook task pane.

Create a New Workbook from a Supplied Template

1. Click **File**.................... Alt + F
2. Click **New**.......................... N
3. Click **On my computer**.
4. Click the **Spreadsheet Solutions** tab.............. Ctrl + Tab
5. Double-click the desired template.

   ✓ Some of these templates may not be installed, in which case, you'll need to insert the Office CD-ROM when prompted.

Search Microsoft's Web Site for a Template

1. Click **File**.................... Alt + F
2. Click **New**.......................... N

   ✓ The New Workbook task pane appears. You can skip steps one and two and use the Getting Started task pane if you like to complete the rest of these steps.

3. Click in **Search Online for** box.
4. Type search criteria.

   ✓ For example, type inventory or petty cash.

5. Click **Go**.

6. Click template to preview it.
7. Click **Download**........... Alt + D

   ✓ Instead of searching for templates by name, browse through categories of templates on Microsoft's Web site by clicking the **Templates on Office Online** link.

Enter Labels

1. Click cell for data entry...... ↕
2. Type label text.
3. Press **Enter**..................... Enter

OR

Press any arrow key to enter label and move to next cell.

OR

Click **Enter** button ✔ on Formula bar.

Correct Data while Typing

1. Type character(s) in cell.
2. Press **Backspace** key .. Backspace to erase characters to left of insertion point.

Cancel entry while still typing:

- Press **Escape** key .... Esc

OR

- Click **Cancel** button ✕ on Formula bar.

Replace Cell Contents

1. Click cell with data to be replaced.
2. Type new data.

Edit Cell Data

1. Select cell.
2. Click in Formula bar.

OR

Double-click cell.

3. Make correction.
4. Press **Enter**..................... Enter

   ✓ To replace an entry with something else, simply select the cell and type the new entry.

Undo Last Action (Ctrl+Z)

- Click **Undo** button .

OR

1. Click **Edit**..................... Alt + E
2. Click **Undo** action name...... U

Redo Last Reversed Action (Ctrl+Y)

- Click **Redo** button 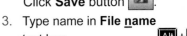.

OR

1. Click **Edit**..................... Alt + E
2. Click **Redo** action name...... R

Undo Multiple Actions

1. Click **Undo** arrow ▾.
2. Drag through actions to undo, and then click.

   ✓ You can only undo consecutive actions, beginning with the action at the top of the list.

Delete (Clear) Cell Contents

1. Select desired cell(s).
2. Press **Delete** key............... Del

OR

   a. Click **Edit** .... Alt + E
   b. Click **Clear** .... A
   c. Click **Contents**............... C

Save Workbook (Ctrl+S)

1. Click **File** .... Alt + F
2. Click **Save** .... S

OR

Click **Save** button 💾.

3. Type name in **File name** text box.......................... Alt + N
4. Click **Save in** drop-down arrow .... Alt + I
5. Select drive and folder in which to save workbook.

   ✓ You can skip steps 4 and 5 and click a folder on the Places bar, such as My Documents.

6. Click **Save**........................ Enter

   ✓ *To save the workbook in a different file format such as Lotus 1-2-3, select that format from the **Save as type** list before you click Save.*

Recover a Workbook

   ✓ *After a program crash, or power outage, the Document Recovery task pane automatically appears.*

1. In the Document Recovery task pane, click the entry for any version of the workbook you're looking to recover.

   ✓ *The contents of that version of the workbook appears.*

2. Select another version of the same workbook to view it.

3. Once you've decided on the version you wish to keep, close all other versions of the workbook (if open).

4. In the Document Recovery list, point to the entry for the workbook version you want to save.

   ✓ *An outline surrounds the entry you point to, and a drop-down list arrow appears to the right.*

5. Click the arrow on the drop-down list and select **Save As**............................. S

6. If needed, change the file name to match the workbook's original file name.

   ✓ *If you selected one of the [Recovered] versions of the workbook, the file name will not be the same as the original file name, so you'll need to edit it slightly to make it match when you save.*

7. Click **Save** .... Enter

8. Click **Yes** to save changes.. Y

Close Workbook

1. Click **File**..................... Alt + F

2. Click **Close** C

3. Click **Yes** to save changes.. Y
   OR
   Click **No** to cancel changes .. N

Exit Excel and Save Files

1. Click **File**..................... Alt + F

2. Click **Exit**............................ X

3. Click **Yes to All** to save all changes........................ A
   OR
   Click **No** to exit without saving changes .... N

Exercise Directions

1. Start Excel, if necessary.

2. Start a new document using the Sales Invoice template.

   ✓ *Look on your computer for the template, on the Spreadsheet Solutions tab.*

   ✓ *If you want, change the zoom to a lower level so you can see the complete invoice.*

3. Save the file as **MAAC INVOICE**.

4. The active cell pointer is already located in cell D13. Type **Hogi Chen** but *do not press Enter*.

5. Instead, press Backspace to erase characters as needed, and change the entry to **Hoji Chen**, then press Enter.

6. In cell D14, type **12 W. 21st Street** and click the Enter button on the Formula bar.

7. Use the arrow keys to move to cell D15, and type the city: **Chicago**. Press Tab to finalize the entry and move to cell F15.

8. Type **IL**, press Tab, and type **60602**. Press Enter.

9. Begin typing the phone number: **881-2127**, but before finalizing, you realize that you do not have the correct number so press Esc to abort the entry.

10. Type the rest of the entries shown in Illustration A. Correct any errors by pressing Backspace, or if the entry has already been finalized, by retying it.

11. Click cell D52 (the farewell statement) and press Delete to erase the contents in the cell.

12. Close the file and exit Excel, saving all changes.

Illustration A

INVOICE

Customer

Name	Hoji Chen
Address	12 W. 21st Street
City	Chicago State IL ZIP 60602
Phone	

Misc

Date	
Order No.	
Rep	
FOB	

Qty	Description	Unit Price	TOTAL
	Massage - per hour		
	Facial		
	Skin wrap		
	Resistance training - per hour		
		SubTotal	
		Shipping	
	Tax Rate(s)		
		TOTAL	

Payment Select One...

Comments	
Name	
CC #	
Expires	

Office Use Only

Invoice is overdue. To retain your club privileges, you must pay the balance in full by 4/5/05.

On Your Own

1. Create a new workbook using the template Weekly Time Sheet by Client and Project.

   ✓ *Search for the template using the keywords time sheet, and select the Weekly Time Sheet by Client and Project template stored on Microsoft's Web site.*

2. Save the file as **OXL02**.

3. Enter the information shown in Illustration B.

   ✓ *The values in the Total column are automatically calculated.*

4. Save the changes, close the file, and exit Excel.

Illustration B

ABC Bus Tours

2152 W. Haveland Ave.
Suite 204
Clarksville, Ohio 54112

Employee: Juan Cordiz
Manager: Benita Williams
Employee phone: -6251
Employee e-mail: jcordiz@abcbustours.com

Week ending: 4/6/2003

Weekly Time Sheet

Day		Client Code	Project Code	Billable Hours	Other Hours	Total
Monday	3/31/2003	CH201	First Baptist Church	5.50	2.50	8.00
Tuesday	4/1/2003	CL767	St. Robert's Boys Club	3.75	4.25	8.00
Wednesday	4/2/2003	CL998	Clarksville Quilt Guild	6.25	1.75	8.00
Thursday	4/3/2003	SC491	Hillcrest Middle Scholl	3.50	5.25	8.75
Friday	4/4/2003	CL998	Clarksville Quilt Guild	2.25	6.00	8.25
Saturday	4/5/2003	CH201	First Baptist Church	1.75		1.75
Sunday	4/6/2003					
			Total hours	23.00	19.75	42.75

Exercise 3

Skills Covered:

◆ **Open Workbooks** ◆ **Change from Workbook to Workbook**
◆ **Compare Workbooks** ◆ **AutoComplete** ◆ **Pick From List**
◆ **AutoCorrect** ◆ **Spell Check**

On the Job

When you've saved and closed a workbook, if you need to view it again or make changes, you must open it first. After opening several workbooks, you may want to arrange them on-screen so you can view their contents at the same time. When entering data, take advantage of the many time-saving features Excel offers: Excel's AutoComplete feature, for example, automatically completes certain entries based on previous entries that you've made. AutoCorrect automatically corrects common spelling errors as you type, while the spelling checker checks your worksheet for any additional errors.

You're the Head Chef at Whole Grains Bread, and you need to complete the baking schedule for today so the other chefs will know what all needs to be done for delivery tomorrow. You want to compare today's schedule with yesterday's, in order to compile a list of any items that were not completed on time. Those items will be given the highest priority.

Terms

AutoComplete A feature used to complete an entry based on previous entries made in the column containing the active cell.

Pick From List A shortcut used to insert repeated information.

AutoCorrect A feature used to automate the correction of common typing errors.

Spelling checker A tool used to assist you in finding and correcting typographical or spelling errors.

Notes

Open Workbooks

- When you have saved and closed a workbook, you can open it from the same drive, folder, and file name you used during the save process.

- In the Open dialog box, click the Look in text box arrow to display a drop-down list with the drives or folders.

- If the location of the workbook is shown on the Places bar, click its icon to display that location's contents.

✓ *The Places bar is located on the left side of the Open dialog box, and it contains icons to common places such as My Recent Document and My Documents folders, the Desktop, Network Places, and the drives in My Computer.*

✓ *You can customize the Places bar with buttons that point to the folders you use often, making it easier to open and save files to them.*

- Click the Views button in the Open dialog box to preview a file, change the list to display file details, or display the properties of a file.

Places bar   *Open dialog box*

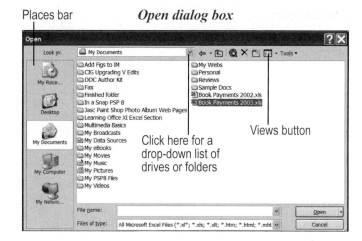

Click here for a
drop-down list of
drives or folders

Views button

■ You can access a recently used file without
opening the Open dialog box, by clicking its file
name from the list displayed in the Open section
of the Getting Started task pane, or at the
bottom of the File menu.

*Workbooks listed in the Open section of the
Getting Started task pane*

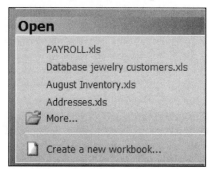

■ A newly opened workbook becomes the active
workbook and hides any other open workbook.

Change from Workbook to Workbook

■ When more than one workbook is open, use the
Window menu to change to a different workbook
by selecting it from the displayed list of names.

Window menu displays list of open files

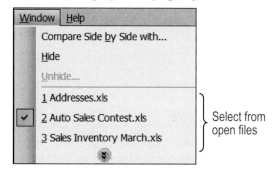

Select from
open files

■ You can also change between workbooks by
clicking a workbook's button on the Windows
taskbar.

Open workbooks on taskbar

■ If you have too many documents from various
programs open, the open Excel workbooks may
appear in a stacked button on the taskbar. Click
the arrow on this stack to display a list of open
workbooks.

Stacked workbooks on taskbar

Compare Workbooks

■ If you want to view the contents of two
workbooks simultaneously, use the Compare
Side by Side command on the Window menu.

- The two workbooks you select are arranged
  one of top of the other, with the screen split
  horizontally.

- With the Synchronous Scrolling button on the
  Compare Side by Side toolbar, you can view
  the exact same cells in each workbook simply
  by scrolling within one workbook.

- To flip the workbooks so that the currently
  active workbook is displayed on top, use the
  Resets Window Position button.

Compare Side by Side toolbar

Synchronous
Scrolling
button

Close Side by Side

Resets Window Position button

■ If you want to view the contents of more than
one workbook, you can arrange all open
workbooks in one of four ways:

- Tiled: arranges windows in small, even
  rectangles to fill the screen.

- Horizontal: arranges windows one on top of
  the other.

- Vertical: arranges windows side by side.

- Cascade: creates a stack of windows with only the title bar in view.

Arrange Windows dialog box

AutoComplete

- When you need to repeat a label that has already been typed in the same column, the **AutoComplete** feature allows you to enter the label automatically.

AutoComplete a label entry

	City	St
t.	Bloomington	IL
nut	Marion	IL
e	Bloomington	IL
ay	Breckenridge	CC
Dr.	Marion	

Pick From List

- If several labels are entered in a list and the next items to be typed are repeated information, click the right-mouse button to display the **Pick From List** command on the shortcut menu.

List of labels for next entry in column

	City	State
d St.	Bloomington	IL
estnut	Marion	IL
Drive	Bloomington	IL
n Way	Breckenridge	CO
Hill Dr.		
	Bloomington	
	Breckenridge	
	Marion	

✓ *The cells in the list and the cell to be typed must be contiguous and in the same column.*

AutoCorrect

- If you type a word incorrectly and it is in the **AutoCorrect** list, Excel automatically changes the word as you type.
- You can add words to the AutoCorrect list that you often type incorrectly.
- AutoCorrect automatically capitalizes the first letter of a sentence and names of days of the week; corrects incorrectly capitalized letters in the first two positions in a word; and undoes accidental use of the Caps Lock key.
- When certain AutoCorrections are made, you're given an option to remove the corrections by clicking the arrow on the AutoCorrect button that appears, and selecting the action you want to take.

AutoCorrect Button

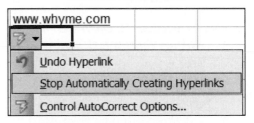

AutoCorrect dialog box

Spell Check

- To check the spelling of text in a worksheet and obtain replacement word suggestions, use the **spelling checker** feature.

Procedures

Open Recent Workbook

1. Click **File** .... `Alt`+`F`
2. Click the workbook you want to open from the list at the bottom of the menu.
   - ✓ *You can also open recently used files by clicking a workbook link displayed in the in the Open section of the Getting Started task pane.*

Open Older Workbook *(Ctrl+O)*

1. Click **Open** button 📂.
   OR
   a. Click **View** .... `Alt`+`V`
   b. Click **Task pane** .... `K`
   c. Click **More**.
2. If the workbook you want to open is not listed in the current folder, perform one of the following:
   a. Click **Look in** .... `Alt`+`I`
   b. Select desired
      drive .... `↕`, `Enter`
   OR
   Double-click folder
   name .... `Tab`, `↕`, `Enter`
   OR
   Click the appropriate button on the Places bar.
3. Click the file you want to open.
4. Click **Open** .... `Enter`

Change to Different Open Workbook

1. Click **Window** .... `Alt`+`W`
2. Click workbook name in list at bottom of menu ...... `↕`, `Enter`
   OR
   - Click anywhere in open workbook window.
   OR
   - Click workbook's button on Window's taskbar.
     - ✓ *If too many workbooks are open, they may be stacked in a single button on the taskbar. If so, click the button and then click the workbook you want to switch to from those listed.*

Compare Side by Side

1. Click **Window** .... `Alt`+`W`
2. Click **Side by Side** .... `B`
3. If more than two workbooks are open:
   a. Select workbook to compare
      to current workbook ...... `↕`
   b. Click **OK** .... `Enter`

End Side by Side Comparison

1. Click **Window** .... `Alt`+`W`
2. Click **Close Side by Side** .... `B`

Arrange Open Workbooks

1. Click **Window** .... `Alt`+`W`
2. Click **Arrange** .... `A`
3. Select from four options:
   - **Tiled** .... `T`
   - **Horizontal** .... `O`
   - **Vertical** .... `V`
   - **Cascade** .... `C`
4. Click **OK** .... `Enter`

AutoComplete

1. Type part of label.
   - ✓ *Repetitive text is highlighted as you type label.*
2. Press **Enter** .... `Enter`
   - ✓ *Just continue typing if you do not want to repeat label.*

Pick From List

1. Right-click cell to receive entry.
2. Click **Pick From Drop-down List** .... `K`
3. Click desired text.

Create AutoCorrect Replacement

1. Click **Tools** .... `Alt`+`T`
2. Click **AutoCorrect Options** .... `A`
3. Click **Replace** .... `Alt`+`R`
4. Type misspelled word.
5. Click **With** .... `Alt`+`W`
6. Type replacement characters.

7. Click **Add** .... `A`
8. Click **OK** .... `Enter`

Check Spelling *(F7)*

1. Select a cell.
   - ✓ *If you don't start the spell check from the beginning of the worksheet, Excel completes the spell check then displays "Do you want to continue checking at the beginning of the sheet?"*
2. Click **Spelling** button .
   OR
   a. Click **Tools** .... `Alt`+`T`
   b. Click **Spelling** .... `S`
3. To change the spelling of a word:
   - Click correctly spelled word in **Suggestions** list. .... `Alt`+`N`
   OR
   - Change the misspelled word manually in the **Not in Dictionary:** text box .... `Alt`+`D`
4. Select an option:
   - Click **Change** .... `Alt`+`C`
   - Click **Change All** to change the word everywhere in document .... `Alt`+`L`
   - Click **Ignore Once** to continue without changing word .... `Alt`+`I`
   - Click **Ignore All** to continue without changing word and without highlighting it anywhere else in document .... `Alt`+`G`
   - Click **Add to Dictionary** to add word to dictionary .... `Alt`+`A`
5. Repeat steps 3 and 4 for every misspelled word.
6. Click **OK** when Excel completes check. .... `Enter`

Exercise Directions

1. Start Excel, if necessary.

2. Open ⊙ 03Bakery Schedule 7-21.

3. Save the file as **Bakery Schedule 7-21**.

4. Open ⊙ 03Bakery Schedule 7-20.

5. Save the file as **Bakery Schedule 7-20**.

6. Using the Window, Arrange command, arrange the two workbooks on-screen in a tiled fashion.

7. Click within the window of the **Bakery Schedule 7-21** workbook to activate it.

   ✓ Notice that the title bar of the active workbook's window is dark blue, while the inactive workbook's title bar is a lIgher blue.

   ✓ Notice that when you scroll, the two windows are not kept in synch.

8. Maximize the **Bakery Schedule 7-21** workbook.

   ✓ The 03Bakery Schedule 7-20 workbook is no longer visible.

9. Change to the **Bakery Schedule 7-20** workbook by clicking its button on the taskbar.

10. Compare using the Windows, Compare Side by Side command.

    ✓ Notice that when you scroll, the two workbooks display the same cells—they are kept in synch with each other.

11. Click in the **Bakery Schedule 7-21** workbook to activate it, then double-click cell A10 to enable cell editing, then type **(r)** after **Whole Grains Bread**.

    ✓ After you press Enter to finalize the entry, notice that AutoCorrect has changed Whole Grains Bread (r) to Whole Grains Bread®.

12. Type the data as shown in Illustration A.

    ✓ Notice that the items left over from the previous day's baking have already been added to the top of the list.

    a. As you type the customer names, use the AutoComplete feature to speed up the process.

    b. Use the Pick From Drop-down List feature to enter the item names.

13. Click cell A10.

14. Use the spelling checker to check your worksheet.

    a. At the first error, select **Bakery** from the Suggestions list, then click Change.

    b. Click Change All to correct all instances of Village.

    c. Click Ignore All to ignore all instances of Gribaldi's.

    d. Click Ignore All to ignore all instances of Ristorante.

       ✓ This is a correct spelling. It is the Italian word for restaurant.

    e. Click OK at the end of the spelling check.

15. Close **Bakery Schedule 7-20**.

16. Close the **Bakery Schedule 7-21** workbook, saving all changes.

Illustration A

Whole Grains Bread ®						
Bakery Schedule						
Date:	7/21/2005					
		Customer	Item	Qty Needed	Qty Shipped	Still Needed
		Café Latte	Bagels, various	25		25
		Café Latte	Muffins, various	50		50
		Village Green	Wheat Rolls	50		50
		Java Café	Pastries, various	25		25
		Village Green	Wheat Bread	20		20
		Village Green	White Bread	12		12
		Mikes Steak House	Wheat Rolls	1875		1875
		Gribaldi's Ristorante	Garlic Bread	100		100
		Gribaldi's Ristorante	Pastries, various	85		85
	Enter this text	Java Café	Croissants	75		75
		Java Café	Muffins, various	75		75
		Green Street Market	Wheat Bread	325		325
		Green Street Market	White Bread	325		325
		Green Street Market	Baguettes	200		200
		Green Street Market	Croissants	150		150
		Green Street Market	Rolls	150		150

On Your Own

1. Start Excel, if necessary.

2. Open ⊙ **03TEACHERS**.

3. Start a new workbook, and save the file as **OXL03**.

    ✓ *Here you'll create a report to track homework assignments. You'll start by entering information about each assignment—in later lessons, you'll add the dates when the assignments are due and make other adjustments.*

4. Type a title for the report in row 2.

5. Label column A: **ASSIGNMENTS**.

6. Label column C: **SUBJECT**.

7. Label column E: **ASSIGNED BY**.

8. In column A, type a list of assignments, such as a book report, term paper, chapters to read, or a topic report (such as a report on China).

9. In column C, type the name of the class in which the assignment was given. If you repeat names, use AutoComplete and Pick From List to complete the entries.

10. Arrange the two open workbooks vertically.

11. Using the list of teachers in **03TEACHERS**, type the name of the teacher who assigned each homework assignment.

12. Close **03TEACHERS** and maximize the **OXL03** window.

13. Type your school's Web address in cell G2, like this: **www.coolschool.org**.

    ✓ *If your school doesn't have a Web site, make up an appropriate Web address.*

    ✓ *Notice that AutoCorrect automatically creates a hyperlink from the entry by underlining it and making it blue. If you click this link, Internet Explorer starts, and displays the Web address. You don't want this to happen, so you'll change the link back into ordinary text.*

14. Revert the Web address back to simple text by moving the active cell pointer to cell F2 (use the arrow keys and do not click the cell). Click the AutoCorrect button that appears in the left-hand corner of the cell when you point to it, and select the Undo Hyperlink option.

15. Spell check the workbook.

16. Close the workbook, saving all changes.

Exercise 4

◆ **Enter Numeric Labels and Values** ◆ **Enter Dates** ◆ **Create a Series**
◆ **Change Data Alignment** ◆ **Change Column Width**

On the Job

Because Excel allows you to work with numbers so easily, numeric values are one of the most common Excel entry types. After typing numbers and labels into a worksheet, you can improve its appearance by changing the alignment of data and the widths of columns. If entering a series of labels (such as Monday, Tuesday, Wednesday) or values (such as 1, 2, 3), use Excel's AutoFill feature to save data-entry time and reduce errors.

You are the Accounts Receivable Supervisor at the Michigan Avenue Athletic Club, and a member has charged several services and has not paid them. You started to create an invoice detailing the charges, but you needed to learn a bit more about Excel before you were ready to continue. In the meantime, your boss has customized the worksheet and asked you to complete it. In this exercise, you'll enter in quantity and price amounts, and on another worksheet you will enter member information for tracking the overdue amount.

Terms

Value A number entered in the worksheet.

Numeric label A number entered in the worksheet as a label, not as a value—such as the year 2005 used as a column label.

Label prefix An apostrophe (') used to indicate that a number is really a label and not a value.

Series A list of sequential numbers, dates, times, or text.

Standard column width The default number of characters that display in a column based on the default font.

Notes

Enter Numeric Labels and Values

- A cell contains a **value** when its first character begins with either a number or one of the following symbols (+, − , =, $).
- Type the value, and then do one of the following to enter it into the cell:
  - Press the Enter key.
  - Press an arrow key.
  - Click the Enter box on the Formula bar.
  - Click another cell.

- If you enter a value that contains more than 11 digits into a cell that uses the default format, Excel will display the number in scientific notation.
  - ✓ *For example, the entry 123,456,789,012 is displayed as 1.234567E+11.*
  - ✓ *To display the number in a different format, apply the number format you want to use, as explained in Exercise 8.*

- If you see pound signs displayed in a cell instead of a number, simply widen the column to display the value.

  ✓ *If a number is displayed in scientific notation, widen the column and apply a different format to the cell as explained in Exercise 8.*

- A **numeric label**, such as a Social Security number, is a number that will not be used in calculation.

- Begin the entry of a numeric label with an apostrophe (') as a **label prefix** to indicate that the number should be treated as a label (text) and not as a value.

- Although the label prefix (') is shown on the Formula bar, it is not displayed on the worksheet or printed.

- When you enter a value with an apostrophe, Excel displays a green triangle in the upper left-hand corner of the cell. Select the cell again, and an error button appears. Click the button and confirm that the number is really a label (Ignore Error), or that the value was entered in error and should be treated as a number (Convert to Number).

Error button appears after you enter a numeric label

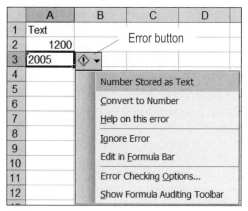

Enter Dates

- You can enter a date using one of these date formats:
  - mm/dd/yy, as in 1/14/05 or 01/14/05
  - mm/dd, as in 3/14
  - dd-mmm-yy, as in 14-Jan-05
  - dd-mmm, as in 14-Jan

    ✓ *The current year is assumed.*

  - mmm-yy, as in Jan-05

    ✓ *The first day of the month is assumed.*

- After entering a date, you can change its display to suit your needs.

  ✓ *For example, you can change the date 1/14/05 to display as January 14, 2005.*

- To enter time, follow a number with **a** or **p** to indicate AM or PM, like this:

  10:43 p

- You can enter a date and time in the same cell, like this:

  10/16/99 2:31 p

Create a Series

- A **series** is a sequence of numbers (such as 1, 2, 3), dates (such as 10/21/05, 10/22/05, 10/23/05), times (such as 2:30, 2:45, 3:00), or text (such as January, February, March).

- To enter a series based on the active cell, drag the fill handle, a small square in the lower-right corner of the active cell that turns into a plus sign (+), over the range of cells you want to fill with the series.

  ✓ *For example, type January into a cell, then drag the fill handle down or to the left to create the series January, February, March, and so on.*

Drag the fill handle of the active cell to create a series

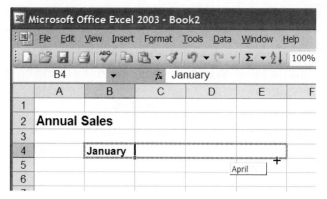

  ✓ *A smart tag appears under the mouse pointer, displaying the values of the series you're creating. The series values appear in the cells after you release the mouse button.*

- To create an incremental series (i.e., 1, 3, 5, 7), enter the data for the first and second cells of a series, select the two cells, then drag the fill handle for the selection over the range of cells to fill.

- You can also use the fill handle to copy formatting (such as bold, italics, and so on) from one cell to adjacent cells, and not its value.

Change Data Alignment

- When a label is typed in a cell, it automatically aligns to the left of the cell. Values are automatically right aligned.

- To improve the appearance of a worksheet, you can change the alignment of column labels, row labels, and other data.

Example of how data is aligned in cells

	A	B	C	D	E	F	G
	Salame Browne		Text data is automatically aligned to the left				
	$129.87		Values are automatically aligned to the right				
	499-0231		Numeric labels entered with an apostrophe are aligned to the left				

- To align data, use the alignment buttons on the Formatting toolbar or choose other alignment options through the Format Cells dialog box.

Format Cells dialog box

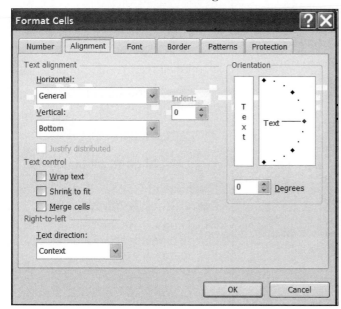

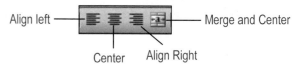

Alignment buttons on Formatting toolbar

Align left ──── ▤ ▤ ▤ ⊞ ──── Merge and Center

Center   Align Right

- To center a label across the columns use the Merge and Center button on the Formatting toolbar.

  ✓ *You most often use this option to center a worksheet title within a range of cells. The Merge and Center button actually merges the selected cells into one large cell and then centers the data in the newly merged cell.*

  ✓ *To get Merge and Center to work properly, enter the data into the first cell in a range, and then select adjacent cells to the right.*

Change Column Width

- The default Excel workbook is set for a **standard column width** (8.11 characters in the standard font of Arial, 10 point).

- You can change (widen or narrow) the column widths individually so that text or values fit the longest entry or be arranged more neatly on the page.

- Changing column width changes the width of an entire column or a group of columns—not the width of a single cell.

- You can quickly adjust a column to fit the longest entry in that column, or you can set the column to any width you like.

- You can also shrink text to fit in a cell (the Shrink to fit option on the Alignment tab of the Format Cells dialog box), regardless of its width. (The text size readjusts automatically if the column width is changed.)

Procedures

Enter Numeric Label

✓ *A number entered as a numeric label is left aligned and cannot be calculated.*

1. Select cell........................... ⬚
2. Type **apostrophe**................ ⬚
3. Type number.
4. Press **Enter**....................... Enter

   ✓ *If a green triangle appears in a the cell, select it again to display the error button, then click its down arrow and select the option **Ignore Error** from its list.*

   ✓ *You can select multiple cells prior to choosing Ignore Error.*

Enter Value

✓ *A number entered as a value is right-aligned and can be calculated.*

1. Select cell........................... ⬚
2. Type number.
   ✓ *Start the entry with a number from zero to nine, a decimal point, or a dollar sign ($). Enclose a negative number in parentheses () or precede it with a minus sign (-).*
3. Press **Enter**....................... Enter
   ✓ *If Excel displays pound signs (######), the column needs to be widened. Double-click the right border of the column heading to display the value.*

Create a Series Using Mouse

1. Enter the value to copy in active cell.
2. Select the cell, and then point to its fill handle.

   ✓ *The mouse changes to* **+** *.*

3. Drag the fill handle down, up, left, or right to copy the value.
4. Click arrow on **AutoFill** **Options** button ⬚ and select an option:

✓ *If you don't select an option from the AutoFill button, then the range is filled with a series as explained below. Also, the button disappears after you enter data into any other cell.*

✓ *You can select multiple cells at once, and choose the same option for all of them.*

- **Copy Cells**
  ✓ *Copies the contents of the first cell into the fill range.*

- **Fill Series**
  ✓ *Increases the value in the first cell by one to fill each cell in the fill range.*

- **Fill Formatting Only**
  ✓ *Copies the formatting of the first cell, but not its value.*

- **Fill Without Formatting**
  ✓ *Same as Fill Series option, but this does not copy the formatting of the first cell to the cells in the fill range.*

- **Fill Days**
  ✓ *Fills cells in the range with dates one day apart.*

- **Fill Weekdays**
  ✓ *Fills cells in the range with dates one day apart, skipping over dates that fall on weekends.*

- **Fill Months**
  ✓ *Fills cells in the range with dates one month apart.*

- **Fill Years**
  ✓ *Fills cells in the range with dates one year apart.*

Create an Incremental Series Using Mouse

1. Enter first and second data in adjacent cells.
   ✓ *The text can be numbers, dates, or times, such as 2:45 and 3:00.*
2. Select the two cells containing series data.

---

3. Point to fill handle.
4. Drag fill handle down, up, left, or right.

   ✓ *Using the two cells as a sample, cells in the range are filled with values that increase or decrease by that same amount.*

   ✓ *If desired, click the arrow on the AutoFill button that appears and select an option as explained in the previous procedure. However, if you select any of the date options, the dates in the fill range will still be incremented based on the two sample cells.*

Align Entry Using Formatting Toolbar

1. Select cell(s) containing label(s) .... ⬚
2. Click **Align Left** button ⬚ .
   OR
   Click **Center** button ⬚ .
   OR
   Click **Align Right** button ⬚ .

Merge and Center Entry Using Formatting Toolbar

1. Drag across the cell with entry and adjacent cells to select them.
2. Click **Merge and Center** button .

   ✓ *Data is centered within the selected range. If you want, you can left or right align data within the merged cell by clicking the Align Left or Align Right buttons on the Formatting toolbar.*

   ✓ *To unmerge the cells (and create separate cells again), click the **Merge and Center** button to turn it off.*

Align Labels Using Format Cells Dialog Box

1. Select cell(s) containing label(s)............................. `↕↔`
2. Click **Format**................. `Alt`+`O`
3. Click C**e**lls .... `E`
4. Click **Alignment** tab.... `Ctrl`+`Tab`
5. Click **Horizontal**.......... `Alt`+`H`
6. Click **Left (Indent)** .... `L`, `Enter`
   OR
   Click **Center** .... `C`, `Enter`
   OR
   Click **Right**.............. `R`, `Enter`

   ✓ *You can also select two lesser used options: **Fill** (repeats data in cell to fill cell completely, regardless of its width) or **Justify** (adds spaces between characters as needed to fill the cell completely).*

7. Click **OK**............................ `Enter`

Change Column Width Using Menu

1. Select any cell in column to change.
2. Click **Format** .... `Alt`+`O`
3. Click **Column** .... `C`
4. Click **Width**......................... `W`
5. Type number (0-255) in Column Width text box.

   ✓ *This value represents the number of characters wide you want the column to be, using the standard font.*

6. Click **OK** .... `Enter`

Change Column Width Using Mouse

1. Point to right border of column heading to be sized.
2. Pointer becomes ╂.
3. Drag ╂ left or right to desired width.

   ✓ *Excel displays column width above and to the right of the mouse pointer as you drag.*

Set Column Width to Fit Longest Entry

- Double-click right border of column heading.
OR
1. Select column to size............ `↕↔`, `Ctrl`+`Space`
2. Click **Format** .... `Alt`+`O`
3. Click **Column**. .... `C`
4. Click **AutoFit Selection**...... `A`

   ✓ *This command will adjust column widths that have not been previously changed in a worksheet.*

Set Standard Column Width

   ✓ *This command will adjust column widths that have not been previously changed.*

1. Click **Format** .... `Alt`+`O`
2. Click **Column**. .... `C`
3. Click **Standard Width** .... `S`
4. Type new number (0–255) in Standard Column Width text box.

   ✓ *This number represents number of characters to be displayed in cell using the standard font.*

5. Click **OK**.......................... `Enter`

Exercise Directions

1. Start Excel, if necessary.
2. Open 💿 **04MAAC Invoice 2**.
3. Save the file as **MAAC Invoice 2**.
4. Click cell D16 and enter the phone number **288-0217**.
5. Complete the Misc section as shown in Illustration A.

   ✓ *Make sure the invoice and the member numbers are entered as a numeric label.*
   ✓ *Use your initials in the Rep field.*

6. Enter the Qty and Unit Price values for the services used by Hoji, as shown in Illustration A.

   ✓ *The total for each item and the total invoice amount is computed automatically.*
   ✓ *If you see a dialog box asking you to confirm that you've entered a number, click Yes.*

7. Change to the Account Tracking worksheet.
8. Enter the date **3/8/05** in cell B10. Enter the date **3/15/05** in cell B11.

9. Select both cells, and then copy the date series to cells B12, B13, and B14 by dragging its fill handle.

   ✓ *Select the option, Fill Series from the AutoFill button menu.*

10. Set the width of columns B, C, and D to fit the longest entry.
11. Adjust the width of column A to 15.44 characters.
12. Enter the amount paid on 3/22/05: **$50.00**.

   ✓ *You need only enter the value, 50, and the cell formatting will display the value as $50.00.*

13. Drag across cells A1, B1, C1, and D1 to select them, then merge and center the worksheet title as shown in Illustration B.
14. Center the **Date**, **Amt. Pd.**, and **Balance** column labels.
15. Spell check the worksheet.
16. Close the workbook, saving all changes.

Michigan Avenue Athletic Club
235 Michigan Ave.
Chicago, Illinois 60601
312-555-4521

Invoice No. 4178

INVOICE

Customer

Name	Hoji Chen
Address	12 W. 21st Street
City	Chicago State IL ZIP 60602
Phone	288-0217

Misc

Date	3/23/2005
Member No.	77894
Rep	JF

Qty	Description	Unit Price	TOTAL
2.5	Massage - per hour	$ 100.00	$ 250.00
1	Facial	$ 75.00	$ 75.00
1	Herbal wrap	$ 65.00	$ 65.00
3.25	Resistance training - per hour	$ 30.00	$ 97.50
		SubTotal	$ 487.50
		Shipping	
		Tax Rate(s)	
		TOTAL	$ 487.50

Payment   Select One...

Comments
Name
CC #

Office Use Only

Illustration B

	A	B	C	D	
1	Account Tracking Data				
2					
3	Member Name:	Hoji Chen			
4	Member #:	77894			
5					
6	Total Charges:	$ 487.50			
7					
8	Payment Tracking:				
9		Date	Amt. Pd.	Balance	
10		3/8/2005	$ 65.00	$ 422.50	
11		3/15/2005	$ -	$ 422.50	
12		3/22/2005	$ 50.00	$ 372.50	
13		3/29/2005		$ 372.50	
14		4/5/2005		$ 372.50	
15					

On Your Own

1. Open a new workbook in Excel and save it as **OXL04**.

2. Create a worksheet to track inventory. For example, you might want to track your CD collection, or your books. For a business, club, or organization, you might want to track office supplies or equipment.

3. In row 1, type a title for your inventory report.

4. Enter the following labels as column headings starting in column A:

   ITEM
   DESCRIPTION
   COST

5. In the rows below each column heading, enter the appropriate data for at least five items.

   ✓ *If you enter numeric labels, be sure to include the label prefix (').*

6. Adjust the column width so you can read all of the data entered in the report.

7. Center the column heading labels.

8. Right align all number values.

9. Left align all text (except the column headings).

10. Merge the cells in row 1 and center the report title over the worksheet.

11. Save the worksheet, close the file, and exit Excel.

Exercise 5

On the Job

One of the benefits of Excel is its ability to create formulas within a worksheet that perform calculations. When you make a change to a cell that is referenced in a formula, Excel performs the recalculation, and the formula result is automatically updated to reflect the change.

HelpNow MedCenter is seeking to expand its operations in nearby cities, and a balance sheet must be prepared for prospective franchisees. Most of the information has already been compiled by accounting, but there are some calculations you need to add to complete it. As the new Franchise Director, you also have some ratio comparisons you want to add to attract potential investors.

Terms

Formula An instruction Excel uses to calculate a number.

Mathematical operators Symbols used in mathematical operations: **+** for addition, **-** for subtraction, ***** for multiplication, **/** for division, and **^** for exponentiation.

Order of mathematical operations The order in which Excel performs the calculations specified in a formula.

Notes

Enter a Formula

- A **formula** is a worksheet instruction that performs a calculation.

- You enter a formula in the cell where the answer should display.

- As you type a formula, it displays in the cell and in the Formula bar.

- After you enter a formula into the cell, the answer displays in the cell while the formula appears in the formula bar.

- When creating formulas, you use cell references, values, and **mathematical operators**.
  - ✓ *A formula can also contain Excel's predefined "functions," which are covered in Exercise 13.*

- The following are standard mathematical operators used in formulas:
  - + Addition
  - - Subtraction
  - * Multiplication
  - / Division
  - ^ Exponentiation

- The equal sign (=) must be typed at the beginning of a formula. For example, the formula =B2+B4+B6 adds the values in these cell locations together.

- When you make a change to a value in a cell that is referenced in a formula, the answer in the formula cell automatically changes.

- The **order of mathematical operations** is important to remember when creating formulas.
  - When calculating a formula, Excel performs operations enclosed in parentheses first.
  - Exponential calculations have the next priority.
  - Moving left to right within the formula, multiplication and division operations are then calculated before the addition and subtraction operations.

- When typing a percentage as a value in a formula, you can enter it with the percent symbol or as a decimal.
- Excel automatically provides assistance in correcting common mistakes in a formula (for example, omitting a parenthesis).

Procedures

Enter Formula Using Mathematical Operators

1. Click cell where answer should display...................
2. Press **Equal** `=` ....
3. Type formula.
   - ✓ *Example: =(C2+C10)/2*
4. Press **Enter** .... Enter

   - ✓ *Instead of typing a cell reference into a formula, you can simply click the appropriate cell.*

Exercise Directions

1. Start Excel, if necessary.
2. Open ☉ **05Balance Sheet**.
3. Save the file as **Balance Sheet**.
4. In cell D31, type a formula to calculate the total fixed assets: **=D28+C29+C30**.

   - ✓ *Click the cells in the formula instead of typing their addresses. For example, type = then click cell D28. Type + then click C29. Type another + and click C30.*

5. In cell E32, calculate the total assets by entering this formula: **=D18+D31**.
6. In cell K37, calculate the total liabilities and net worth by entering this formula: **=J36+J28+J23+J18**.

7. In cell E6, type a formula that calculates the company's current ratio (the ratio of current assets to current liabilities): **=D18/J18**.
8. In cell E7, type a formula that calculates the company's quick ratio (a ratio that's similar to the current ratio, except that it takes inventory into account): **=(D18-C16)/J18**.

   - ✓ *In this formula, you must use parentheses to get the correct answer. If you type D18-C16/J18, then Excel will divide cell C16 by J18, then take that total from cell D18.*

9. Adjust column widths as needed to display data fully.
10. Spell check the workbook.
11. Close the file, saving all changes.

On Your Own

1. Start Excel, if necessary.

2. Start a new workbook in Excel and save it as **OXL05**.

   ✓ *As the treasurer of the Art Club, you'll use Excel to set up a worksheet for tracking the total weekly candy sales for your current fundraiser.*

3. Enter a title for the worksheet in row 2.

4. Label the columns as follows:

   Member Name
   Candy
   Price
   Number Sold
   Total Sales

5. Type sales data for the first member, using multiple rows to list each type of candy sold by that person.

   ✓ *For example, the first row might be: Jane Brown, Milk chocolate candy bars, price 1.50, 10 sold. The next line might be: Jane Brown, Toffee bars, price 2.25, 17 sold.*

   ✓ *Enter at least three people, with each person selling at least two types of candy. In the Member Name column, use the fill handle to copy the person's name to additional rows as needed.*

6. In the Total Sales column for the first item, enter a formula that multiples the value in the Price column by the value in the Number Sold column.

7. Repeat step 6 for each item.

8. Below the last item in the Total Sales column, enter a formula that adds the total sales for each item to compute a grand total for the week.

9. To the left of the cell that contains the grand total, type the label **Weekly Total**.

10. Adjust the width of columns so you can read all of the data.

11. Spell check the worksheet.

12. Close the worksheet, saving all changes.

Exercise 6

As the Manager of Spa Services at the Michigan Avenue Athletic Club, you've decided to create a worksheet to be used to track the clients using the spa so that they can be properly billed. After creating the worksheet, you'll enter the last of today's clients on the Invoice Worksheet you prepare each day for the Accounting Department.

Exercise Directions

1. Start Excel, if necessary.
2. Start a new, blank workbook.
3. Save the file as **SpaServices**.
4. In cell A2, type **Michigan Avenue Athletic Club Spa Services**.
5. In cell A4, type **Date:** and in cell B4, enter today's date.
6. Complete the Massage section, as shown in Illustration A.
   a. To enter the numbers in column A, type **1** in cell A9, and use the fill handle to create a series. Be sure to select **Fill Series** from the AutoFill Options menu.
   b. Enter the cost per hour, **100**, in cell D9, and use the fill handle to copy the value down the column as shown.
   c. In cell F9, type a formula that computes the cost of the massage by taking the cost per hour times the duration. Using the fill handle, copy this formula down the column as shown.

7. Complete the rest of the sections of the worksheet as shown in Illustration A.
8. Adjust the columns widths to fit the data.
9. Enter the client data as well, using Illustration B as your guide. Adjust the column widths again to fit the client names.
10. Open 💿 **06InvoiceWS**.
11. Save the file as **InvoiceWS**.
12. Arrange the two workbooks on-screen in a tiled fashion.
13. In row 13 of the **InvoiceWS** workbook, enter the billable data for Anna Bolea's Herbal Wrap.
    ✓ *The Pick From Drop-down List and the AutoComplete features can help you enter some of this data.*
14. Adjust column widths as needed to display data.
15. Spell check both workbooks.
16. Close both workbooks, saving all changes.

Illustration A

	A	B	C	D	E	F	G	H	I	J
1										
2	Michigan Avenue Athletic Club Spa Services									
3										
4	Date:	11/12/2005								
5										
6		Massage						Herbal Wrap		
7										
8		Client Name	Masseur	Cost per hour	Duration	Cost		Client Name	Clinician	Cost
9	1			100			1	Sharie Otis	CQ	65
10	2			100			2	Anna Bolea	CQ	65
11	3			100			3			65
12	4			100			4			65
13	5			100			5			65
14	6			100			6			65
15	7			100			7			65
16	8			100			8			65
17	9			100			9			65
18	10			100			10			65
19										
20										
21		Facial					Revitalizer: 30 minute massage, mini-facial, and herbal wrap			
22										
23		Client Name	Clinician	Cost			Client Name	Clinician	Cost	
24	1			75	1	Sze Yim Wong	JF	175		
25	2			75	2			175		
26	3			75	3			175		
27	4			75	4			175		
28	5			75	5			175		
29	6			75	6			175		
30	7			75	7			175		
31	8			75	8			175		
32	9			75	9			175		
33	10			75	10			175		

Illustration B

	Client Name	Masseur	Cost per hour	Duration	Cost		Client Name	Clinician	Cost
1	Connor Hiatt	JF	100	1.25	125	1	Sharie Otis	CQ	65
2	Tonya Matthews	BW	100	0.5	50	2	Anna Bolea	CQ	65
3	Anna Bolea	BW	100	0.75	75	3			65
4			100		0	4			65
5			100		0	5			65
6			100		0	6			65
7			100		0	7			65
8			100		0	8			65
9			100		0	9			65
10			100		0	10			65

	Facial				Revitalizer: 30 minute massage, mini-facial, and herbal wrap			
	Client Name	Clinician	Cost		Client Name	Clinician	Cost	
1	Tonya Matthews	CQ	75	1	Sze Yim Wong	JF	175	
2	Giancarlo Sucre		75	2			175	
3			75	3			175	

Exercise 7

◆ Select Ranges ◆ Range Entry Using Collapse Button

On the Job

Select a group of cells (a range) to copy, move, or erase them in one step, or to quickly apply the same formatting throughout the range. You can also perform calculations on cell ranges—creating sums and averages, for example.

You're the Inventory Manager of the Voyager Travel Adventures retail store, and it's time to organize the monthly inventory. To help you and your crew take inventory, you've created a new inventory workbook. You have some adjustments to make before inventory day tomorrow, but they are only minor ones so you should have the workbook ready to go by the end of the day.

Terms

Range A block of cells in an Excel worksheet.

Contiguous range A block of adjacent cells in a worksheet.

Noncontiguous range Cells in a worksheet that act as a block, but are not necessarily adjacent to each other.

Notes

Select Ranges

- A **range** is an area made up of two or more cells.

- When you select cells A1, A2, and A3, for example, the range is indicated as A1:A3.

- The range A1:C5 is defined as a block of cells that includes all the cells in columns A through C in rows one through five.

- A range of cells can be **contiguous** (all cells are adjacent to each other) or **noncontiguous** (not all cells are adjacent to each other).

- When a range is selected, the active cell is displayed normally, but the rest of the cells appear highlighted, as shown.

Selected range of contiguous cells

Last Name	First Name	Address	C
Sechrest	Shawn	1901 Cloud St.	B
Willard	Dave	714 S. Chestnut	M
Loving	Greg	807 Vale Drive	B
Sechrest	Art	988 Aspen Way	B
Willard	Pat	808 Hill Ct	M

Selected range of noncontiguous cells

Last Name	First Name	Address	C
Sechrest	Shawn	1901 Cloud St.	E
Willard	Dave	714 S. Chestnut	N
Loving	Greg	807 Vale Drive	E

Range Entry Using Collapse Button

- When you need to enter cell addresses or ranges in a dialog box, you may click the Collapse button on the right side of the text box to return to the worksheet temporarily and select the range.

- After selecting the range, click the Collapse button to return to the dialog box to finalize your selections.

Example of text box with Collapse button

Collapse button

Procedures

Use Keyboard to Select Range of Cells

To select range of adjacent cells:

1. Press arrow key(s) .... to move to first cell of range.

2. Press **Shift** + **arrow** key .... **Shift** +

To select entire column containing active cell:

- Press **Ctrl** + **Spacebar** ..... **Ctrl** + **Space**

To select entire row containing active cell:

- Press **Shift** + **Spacebar** .. **Shift** + **Space**

To select adjacent rows:

1. Press arrow keys .... to move to cell in first row to select.

2. Press and hold down **Shift** .... **Shift**, then press **spacebar** ..... **Space**, to select first row.

3. While still pressing **Shift**, press up or down arrow key........ to select additional adjacent rows.

To select worksheet from top-left cell to bottom-right cell:

1. Press arrow keys .... to move to first cell in selection.

2. Press and hold down **Ctrl**, then press and hold down **Shift**, then press and release **End** ...... **Ctrl** + **Shift** + **End**

3. Release **Ctrl** and **Shift** keys.

Use Mouse to Select Range of Cells

To select range of adjacent cells:

- Click and drag across cells.

To select noncontiguous cells and ranges:

- Click and drag across first selection of cells.

- Press and hold **Ctrl** as you click additional cells, and/or drag over additional ranges.

To select entire row:

- Click row heading.

To select entire column:

- Click column heading.

To select adjacent rows:

- Click and drag across row headings.

To select adjacent columns:

- Click and drag across column headings.

To select noncontiguous rows:

1. Click row heading.

2. Press and hold down **Ctrl** key and click additional row headings.

To select noncontiguous columns:

1. Click column heading.

2. Press and hold down **Ctrl** key and click additional column headings.

Range Entry Using Collapse Button

1. Click **Collapse** button at right of text box.

   ✓ *The dialog box collapses to provide a better view of the worksheet.*

2. Select desired cell(s) by following either the keyboard or mouse method described here.

3. Press **Enter** .... **Enter**

   OR

   Click **Collapse** button .

   ✓ *The dialog box returns to normal size and the text box displays the cell reference(s). Continue making selections within the dialog box as needed.*

Exercise Directions

1. Start Excel, if necessary.
2. Open 💿 **07Inventory**.
3. Save the file as **Inventory**.
4. On the Snowboarding and Heliskiing worksheet, select columns C-I.
5. Adjust the column width of the selected columns to 8.67 characters.
   - ✓ *The solution file may show a different column width depending on your screen resolution.*
6. Select the noncontiguous range that includes the cells C8, D8, H8, and I8.

7. Click the Center button to center the column labels.
8. Select the contiguous range, E8:G8.
9. Click the Merge and Center button to center the label over the three columns.
10. Spell check the workbook.
    - ✓ *Change Snowski to Snow ski, and change sandwhich to sandwich. Leave freeride and lite as spelled.*
11. Close the workbook, saving all changes.

On Your Own

1. Open the file named **OXL05** that you created in the On Your Own section of Exercise 5, or open the file 💿 **07CANDY**.
2. Save the file as **OXL07**.
3. Select the range of cells containing the column labels (Member Name, etc.), and change the cell alignment to center.
4. Select the range of cells containing the member names and candy names, and change the cell alignment to right.
5. Select the columns that contain the **Price**, **Number Sold**, and **Totals Sales** labels, and set the column widths to exactly 10.5.
   - ✓ *The solution file may show a different column width depending on your screen resolution.*
6. Spell check the workbook.
7. Close the workbook, saving all changes.

Exercise 8

◆ **Format Data** ◆ **Change Font and Font Size**
◆ **Number Formats** ◆ **Apply Percent Format** ◆ **Apply Comma Format**
◆ **Apply Currency Format** ◆ **Add Color to Cells and Cell Data**

On the Job

When you change the appearance of worksheet data by applying various formats, you also make that data more attractive and readable.

The inventory worksheet is almost completed, but as the Inventory Manager of the Voyager Travel Adventures retail store, you expect more from yourself. Since you have the time before inventory day tomorrow, you want to spruce up the worksheet prior to printing by adding some formatting.

Terms

Format To apply attributes to cell data to change the appearance of the worksheet.

Font The typeface or design of the text.

Font size The measurement of the typeface in points ($1/72$ of an inch).

Number format A format that controls how numerical data is displayed, including the use of commas, dollar signs (or other symbols), and the number of decimal places.

Percent format A style that displays decimal numbers as a percentage.

Comma format A style that displays numbers with a thousands separator (,).

Currency format A style that displays dollar signs ($) immediately preceding the number and includes a thousands separator (,).

Accounting format A style that vertically aligns with dollar signs ($), thousands separators (,), and decimal points.

Fill A color that fills a cell, appearing behind the data.

Pattern A secondary color added to the background of a cell in a pattern.

Notes

Format Data

■ **Format** data by selecting it and clicking the appropriate buttons on the Formatting toolbar or by choosing options from the Format Cells dialog box.

Change Font and Font Size

■ A **font** is a set of characters with a specific design and name.

■ The **font size** of a set of characters is based on its average height in points. One point is equal to $1/72$ of an inch.

■ Change the font and font size of your data to improve its appearance and to make it more readable.

■ You can apply special effects—such as bold, italics, or underline—to any font you select.

- You make font, font size, and special effects changes through the Formatting toolbar or the Format Cells dialog box.

Change font and font size with the Formatting toolbar

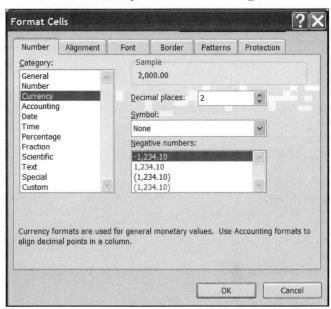

- The way in which your data appears after making font and font size changes is dependent on your monitor and printer.

  ✓ *If your monitor cannot display a particular font, it will choose a similar font to replace it with. However, when you print the data out, the actual font you picked may be used. To avoid this discrepancy between what you see on-screen and what is printed, use Windows TrueType fonts whenever possible.*

- Windows TrueType fonts are "true" to their on-screen appearance—what you see is what you will get when your data is printed.

  ✓ *TrueType fonts are identified with a small TT in front of their name in the Font drop-down list on the Formatting toolbar.*

- When you change the size of a font, Excel automatically adjusts the row height but does not adjust the column width.

- By default, data appears in Arial 10-point font. You can change the standard (default) font and font size if you want, or you can apply different fonts and font sizes to selected data.

Number Formats

- When formatting numerical data, you may want to change more than just the font and font size— you may want to also apply a **number format**.

- The number format determines the number of decimal places and the position of zeros (if any) before/after the decimal point. Number formats also place various symbols such as dollar signs or percentage signs with formatted numbers. You can also add dollar signs and commas with the number format you select.

- Changing the format of a cell does not affect the actual value stored there or used in calculations—it affects only the way in which that value is displayed.

- You can quickly apply Currency, Percent, or Comma format to numerical data using the buttons on the Formatting toolbar.

- You can also increase or decrease the number of decimal places displayed in a number with buttons on the Formatting toolbar.

- To apply other number formats, or to adjust the settings used by default with Currency, Percent, or Comma format, use the Number tab of the Format Cells dialog box.

Number tab of Format Cells dialog box

Apply Percent Format

- To change data entered as decimals (such as .75) into percentages (75%), use the **percent format**.

Apply Comma Format

- If you want to make large numbers easier to read, use the **comma format** to include commas in the number, as in 2,345,945.98.

Apply Currency Format

- The currency and accounting formats may be used for formatting money values.

- **Currency format** displays numbers with currency symbols: dollar signs, commas, and decimals. For example, $21,456.83.

- **Accounting format** displays numbers in a style similar to currency format, but the dollar signs are aligned to the far left of the cell, with additional spaces inserted between the dollar sign and the first digit, depending on the column width. For example, $ 21,456.83.

  ✓ *When you use the Currency button on the Formatting toolbar to apply a number format, you're really applying Accounting format.*

Add Color to Cells and Cell Data

- To focus attention on particular areas of the worksheet, such as the column or row labels or important totals, fill the cell background with color. You can add color to your data as well.

- You can add color (called a **fill**) to a cell with the Fill Color button on the Formatting toolbar. Add color to the text in a cell with the Font Color button.

- With the Format Cells dialog box, you can select from a wider variety of color fills. You can also include a **pattern**.

Color or pattern added to cells

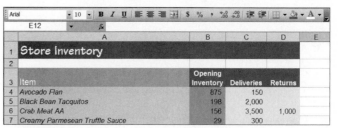

Procedures

Change Font Using Font Box

1. Select cells or characters in cells to format.
2. Click **Font** list box arrow
   .
3. Select font .... ⬆⬇ , Enter

Change Font Size Using Font Size Box

1. Select cells or characters in cells to format.
2. Click **Font Size** list box arrow 10 ⏷.
3. Select number in list...................... ⬆⬇ , Enter

   OR

   a. Click **Font Size** box 10 ⏷.
   b. Type desired number.
   c. Press **Enter** .... Enter

Percentage Number Format

1. Select cell(s) to format.
2. Click **Percent Style** button %.

   OR

   a. Click **Format**.......... Alt + O
   b. Click **Cells** .... E

c. Select **Number** tab........... Ctrl + Tab
d. Click **Percentage** in **Category** list box .... Alt + C , ⬆⬇
e. Click **Decimal places** ..... Alt + D
f. Set number of places.
g. Click **OK** .... Enter

Comma Number Format

1. Select cell(s) to format.
2. Click **Comma Style** button ⸴.

   OR

   a. Click **Format** .... Alt + O
   b. Click **Cells** .... E
   c. Select **Number** tab .. Ctrl + Tab
   d. Click **Number** in **Category** list box .... Alt + C , ⬆⬇
   e. Click **Decimal places** ..... Alt + D
   f. Set number of places.
   g. Click **Use 1000 Separator**...... Alt + U
   h. Click **OK** .... Enter

Currency Number Format

1. Select cells(s) to format.
2. Click **Format** .... Alt + O
3. Click **Cells**......................... E
4. Select **Number** tab..... Ctrl + Tab
5. From the **Category** list box click **Currency** .... Alt + C , ⬆⬇
6. Set decimal places and choose currency symbol.
7. Click **OK** .... Enter

Accounting Number Format

1. Select cell(s) to format.
2. Click **Currency Style** button $.

   OR

   a. Click **Format** .... Alt + O
   b. Click **Cells**..................... E
   c. Select **Number** tab .... Ctrl + Tab
   d. From the **Category** list box click **Accounting** .. Alt + C , ⬆⬇
   e. Click **Decimal places** .... Alt + D

f. Set number of places.

g. You can choose a symbol other than the US dollar and specify how negative numbers display in the cell.

h. Click **OK** .... Enter

Increase or Decrease Decimal Places

1. Select cell(s) to format.

2. Click **Increase Decimal** or

Decrease Decimal buttons on the Formatting toolbar.

Add a Color Fill

1. Select cell(s) to format.

2. Click the arrow on the **Fill Color** button and select a color.

   ✓ You can also add a fill by choosing Format, Cells, clicking the Patterns tab and selecting a color.

   ✓ Add a pattern to a fill by selecting its color from the Pattern list on the Patterns tab of the Format Cells dialog box. Be sure to choose a pattern for the second color from the top of the Pattern list.

Add Color to Data

1. Select cell(s) to format.

2. Click the arrow on the **Font Color** button and select a color.

   ✓ You can also add a color to text by choosing Format, Cells, clicking the Font tab and selecting a color from the Color list.

Exercise Directions

1. Start Excel, if necessary.

2. Open **08Inventory**.

3. Save the file as **Inventory 2**.

4. Select the range D9:H27.

5. Using the Comma Style button, apply comma style to the selection.

6. Click the Decrease Decimal button twice to remove the decimal places.

7. Select the ranges C9:C27 and I9:I27.

8. Click the Currency Style button to apply Accounting format to the selection.

9. Apply these fonts to the following cells or ranges:

   ✓ If you don't have these exact same fonts, choose ones of your own, using Illustration A as an example.

   a. A1: Boulder, 24 point

   b. A6: Boulder, 16 point

   c. A8:I8: Zurich Cn BT, 12 point

10. Apply the following color fills:

    a. A1:I5: Tan

    b. A6:I7: Sea Green

    c. A8:I8: Pale Blue

    d. D9:D27: Tan

    e. H9:H27: Tan

11. Widen any columns, if necessary. See Illustration A.

12. Spell check the workbook.

13. Close the workbook, saving all changes.

Illustration A

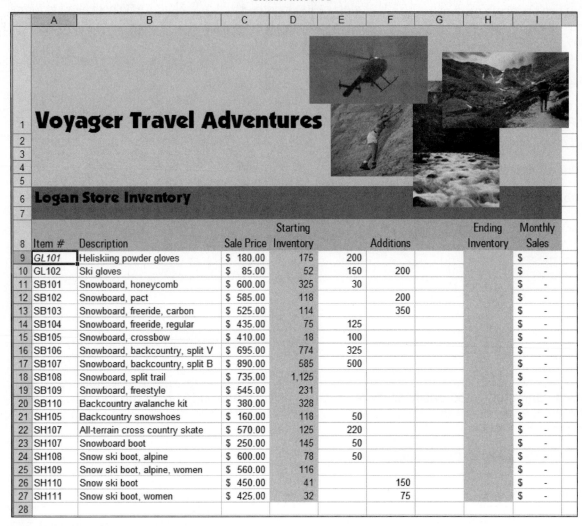

	Item #	Description	Sale Price	Starting Inventory		Additions		Ending Inventory	Monthly Sales
9	GL101	Heliskiing powder gloves	$ 180.00	175	200				$ -
10	GL102	Ski gloves	$ 85.00	52	150	200			$ -
11	SB101	Snowboard, honeycomb	$ 600.00	325	30				$ -
12	SB102	Snowboard, pact	$ 585.00	118		200			$ -
13	SB103	Snowboard, freeride, carbon	$ 525.00	114		350			$ -
14	SB104	Snowboard, freeride, regular	$ 435.00	75	125				$ -
15	SB105	Snowboard, crossbow	$ 410.00	18	100				$ -
16	SB106	Snowboard, backcountry, split V	$ 695.00	774	325				$ -
17	SB107	Snowboard, backcountry, split B	$ 890.00	585	500				$ -
18	SB108	Snowboard, split trail	$ 735.00	1,125					$ -
19	SB109	Snowboard, freestyle	$ 545.00	231					$ -
20	SB110	Backcountry avalanche kit	$ 380.00	328					$ -
21	SH105	Backcountry snowshoes	$ 160.00	118	50				$ -
22	SH107	All-terrain cross country skate	$ 570.00	125	220				$ -
23	SH107	Snowboard boot	$ 250.00	145	50				$ -
24	SH108	Snow ski boot, alpine	$ 600.00	78	50				$ -
25	SH109	Snow ski boot, alpine, women	$ 560.00	116					$ -
26	SH110	Snow ski boot	$ 450.00	41		150			$ -
27	SH111	Snow ski boot, women	$ 425.00	32		75			$ -
28									

On Your Own

1. Open the file 📖OXL07 that you created in the On Your Own section of Exercise 7, or open 💿08CANDY.

2. Save the file as **OXL08**.

3. Apply the Comma format to the data in the Price and Total Sales columns.

4. Apply the Currency format with no decimal places to the data instead.

5. Finally, apply the Accounting format with two decimal places to the same data in the Price and Total Sales columns.

6. Change the font for all the data in B5:F13 to Verdana, and increase the font size to 11 points.

7. Increase the font size of the title to 18 points, and apply bold and italics effects. Select the cells that contain the title and fill them with yellow.

8. Increase the font size of the column labels to 14 points. Apply a light yellow color fill. Change the text color to green. Apply these same changes to cell E13. Change the font for E13 to Arial.

9. Adjust the width of columns as necessary so that you can see all of the data in the worksheet.

10. Spell check the workbook.

11. Close the workbook, saving all changes.

Exercise 9

Skills Covered:
◆ Copy and Paste Data ◆ Copy Formats
◆ Relative Reference ◆ Absolute Reference
◆ Preview and Print a Worksheet

On the Job

Excel provides many shortcuts to save you time as you enter data and write formulas in your worksheets. For example, you can use the copy and paste features to reuse data and formulas in the same worksheet, in another worksheet, or in another workbook. The **AutoFill** handle bypasses the copy and paste features and allows you to copy data to adjacent cells quickly and easily. After copying data and completing a report, you can preview and print a hard copy.

As an Adventure Coordinator for Voyager Travel Adventures, it's your job to make all the arrangements needed to create a unique and thrilling adventure vacation for your clients. Today, the Tell City Thrill Seekers Club has asked for an estimate of expenses per person for a special trip that combines white water rafting, backcountry hiking, rock climbing, and all-terrain skating. You've completed a budget for them which can be adjusted easily as more of their club members sign up for the trip. You've also created a profit analysis for the company, computing the total profit for the booking (upon which your commission is based). To complete the two worksheets, you need to create some formulas and copy them.

Terms

AutoFill A method used to copy data from a cell or range of cells to an adjacent cell or range of cells by dragging the fill handle.

Clipboard A feature of Windows that holds data or graphics that you have cut or copied and are ready to be pasted into any document.

Fill handle Dragging this handle, located in the lower-right corner of the active cell, will copy cell contents, formatting, or a formula to adjacent cells.

Format Painter A button on the Standard toolbar that allows you to copy formatting from a selected object or cell and apply it to another object or cell.

Relative cell reference A cell address expressed in relation to the cell containing the formula. For example, rather than naming a cell such as A3 in a formula, a relative cell reference might identify a cell three columns to the left of the cell containing the formula. When such a formula is copied, the relative cell references are adjusted to reflect the new location of the formula cell.

Absolute cell reference A cell address, such as E14, referenced in a formula that does not change based on the location of the cell that contains the formula.

Print Preview A feature used to display a document as it will appear when printed.

Notes

Copy and Paste Data

- Copying data involves two actions: copying and pasting.
  - When you copy data, the copy is placed on the **Clipboard**.
  - When you paste data, that data is copied from the Clipboard to the new location.

- Worksheet data (labels, values, and formulas) may be copied to another cell, a range of cells, another worksheet, or another workbook. Excel data can also be copied to documents created in other programs, such as Word.

- To copy a range of data to a new location, use the Copy and Paste buttons on the Standard toolbar or the Copy and Paste commands from the Edit menu.

- If the cells to which you want to copy data are adjacent to the original cell, you can use the **fill handle** to copy the data.
  - ✓ *In Exercise 4, you learned how to use the fill handle to create a series. Here, you'll learn to use the fill handle to copy labels, values, and formulas to adjacent cells instead of creating a series.*

- When you copy data, its format is copied as well and overrides any format in the destination cell.
  - ✓ *You can override this and copy just the data without copying its formatting.*

- If data exists in the destination cell, that data will be overwritten.

- You can dynamically link data as you paste it, in order to have that data change automatically whenever the original data changes.

Copy Formats

- You can copy formatting from one cell to another, without copying the value.

- The **Format Painter** button ![icon] on the Standard toolbar allows you to copy all the formats (from one cell to another.
  - You can copy a cell's font, font size, font color, cell border, or cell fill color/pattern.
  - Number formats, column widths, and cell alignment are also copied.

- Conditional formatting (formatting that depends on the current value in a cell) is copied as well.

- With the Format Painter, you paint the format from one cell onto as many other cells as you like.

- You can paint formats from one range to another, although the ranges must be of similar size.

Relative Reference

- When you copy a formula to another cell, Excel uses **relative cell referencing** to change the formula to reflect its new location.
  - ✓ *For example, the formula =B4+B5 written in column B becomes =C4+C5 when copied to column C or =D4+D5 when copied to column D, etc.*

Absolute Reference

- Usually, you want the cell addresses in the original formula to change when you copy it. Sometimes, you don't want it to change, so you need to create an **absolute cell reference**.

- Absolute cell references do not change when a formula is copied.

- To make a cell reference absolute, enter a dollar sign ($) before both the column letter and row number of that cell in the formula.
  - ✓ *For example, the formula =$B$4+$B$5 written in column B remains =$B$4+$B$5 when copied to column C. The cell addresses do not adjust based on the new formula location.*

- You can also create mixed cell references, where the column letter part of a cell address is absolute, and the row number is relative, or vice-versa.
  - ✓ *For example, the formula =B$4+B$5 written in column B changes to =C$4+C$5 when copied to column C. The cell addresses partially adjust based on the new formula location.*

- Sometimes, you may wish to copy a formula's result, and not the actual formula.
  - ✓ *For example, if cell B10 contains the formula =B2-B3 with a result of $1200, and you copy that formula to cell C10, the formula will change to =C2-C3. The result of this copied formula would be based on the contents of cells C2 and C3. However, if all you want to do is to show the result, $1200, in another location of the worksheet, copy the value of cell B10 instead of its formula.*

Preview and Print a Worksheet

- You may print the selected worksheet(s), an entire workbook, or a selected data range.

- Use the Print command from the File menu to access the print options in the Print dialog box.

- To view the output before you print, use the **Print Preview** command, which appears on the File menu, in the Print dialog box, and as a button on the Standard toolbar.

Print dialog box

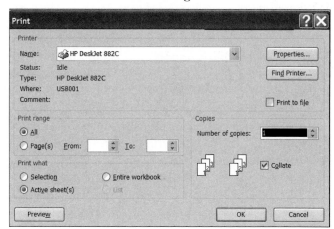

Procedures

Copy Data *(Ctrl+C)*

1. Select cell(s) to copy.
2. Click **Edit** ....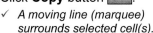
3. Click **Copy** C

   OR

   Click **Copy** button .
   - ✓ A moving line (marquee) surrounds selected cell(s).
4. Select cell(s) to receive data.
   - ✓ Click upper-left cell of destination range or select entire range of cells to receive data on current worksheet, another worksheet, or another workbook.

Paste Data *(Ctrl+V)*

1. Click **Edit** ....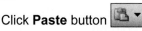
2. Click **Paste** .... P

   OR

   Click **Paste** button .
   - ✓ Press **Escape** key to remove marquee that surrounds original selected cell(s).
   - ✓ If you paste formatting along with data and you don't want to do that, click the Paste Options button that appears and select the desired option.

Paste Formula Result

1. Click arrow on **Paste** button .
2. Select **Values** V

Copy Formula Using AutoFill

1. Select cell(s) to copy.
2. Point to fill handle.
   - ✓ Mouse shape changes to crosshair.
3. Drag fill handle across or down to adjacent cells to fill them.

Copy Formats Using Format Painter

- Select cell(s) containing the formats to copy.

To copy formats only once:

a. Click **Format Painter** button on Standard toolbar.
b. Click cell or drag over range where you want to apply formats.

OR

To copy formats to several cells or ranges:

a. Double-click the **Format Painter** button on the Standard toolbar.
b. Click or drag over destination cells.

c. Repeat step b to copy formats to as many cells or ranges as desired.
d. Click **Format Painter** button to end copying.

Print Worksheet *(Ctrl+P)*

1. Select sheet(s) to print.
   - ✓ To print a range of data instead of an entire sheet, select that range now.
2. Click **File** .... Alt + F
3. Click **Print** .... P
4. Select appropriate print options.

OR

- Click **Print** button .
   - ✓ When you click the Print button on the Standard toolbar, the active worksheet is sent directly to the printer without displaying the Print dialog box.

Print Preview a Worksheet

1. Click **File** .... Alt + F
2. Click **Print Preview** V

   OR

   Click **Print Preview** button on the toolbar.
3. Select options from the Print Preview toolbar.
4. Click **Close** button 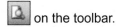 to close Print Preview.

Exercise Directions

1. Start Excel, if necessary.

2. Open 💿 **09TripBudget**.

3. Save the file as **TripBudget**.

4. On the Trip Budget worksheet, in cell E11, type a formula to compute the cost per person for the first item.

   ✓ *You'll need to first calculate the total cost to the club for the first item by taking the item cost times the number of that item required for the trip. Then take this total cost and divide it by the number of people signed up for the trip, which has been entered in cell I14.*

   ✓ *You'll want to use absolute referencing when referring to cell I14, since you'll be copying the formula down the column, and you want all the formulas in column E to refer to this exact cell.*

5. Copy the formula in cell E11 to the range E12:E31.

6. On the Cost Analysis worksheet, in cell E11, type a formula to compute the total cost to the company for the first item.

   ✓ *Take the company's cost for the first item times the number of that item needed.*

7. In cell G11, enter a similar formula to compute the club's cost for the first item.

8. In cell H11, enter a formula to compute the company's profit.

   ✓ *Take the club's cost minus the company's cost to compute the profit.*

9. Copy the formula from cell E11 to the range E12:E31. Copy the formula from cell G11 to the range G12:G31. Copy the formula in cell H11 to the range H12:H31.

10. Widen any columns as necessary.

11. Spell check each worksheet.

12. Preview the Trip Budget worksheet.

13. Print two copies of the completed worksheet.

    ✓ *Each copy of the worksheet will print on two pages; in Exercise 20, you'll learn how to print the worksheet sideways on the paper, so that it prints on only one page.*

14. Close the workbook, saving all changes.

On Your Own

1. Open a new workbook in Excel.

2. Save the file as **OXL09**.

3. Imagine that you are general manager of CD Mania, a chain of music stores. Set up a worksheet showing the monthly sales for three stores in the first three months of the year.

4. In row 1, type a title for the worksheet.

5. Label columns for: **Store**, **Jan**, **Feb**, and **Mar**.

6. List data for three different stores in the rows below the column labels. You can make up names for the stores, and sales totals.

   ✓ *For example, Store 1 might have had sales of $21,548 in January, $27,943 in February, and $25,418 in March.*

7. Apply the Accounting format, 2 decimal places, to the sales data.

8. In the row below the data for the third store, enter the label **Totals**.

9. In the Totals row for the Jan column, enter a formula to add the January sales for all three stores.

10. Copy the formula to the Totals row for Feb and Mar.

11. Add a column for the April sales data. Label the column **Apr**.

12. Copy the data for each store from the Jan column into the April column.

13. Copy the Totals formula from the Mar column to the Apr column.

14. Adjust the width of the columns so you can read all of the data in the worksheet.

15. Apply formatting such as font, font size, fill color, and text color changes to improve the appearance of the worksheet.

16. Spell check the workbook.

17. Preview then print the file.

18. Close the workbook, saving all changes.

Exercise 10

Skills Covered:
◆ Insert and Delete Columns and Rows
◆ Move Data (Cut/Paste) ◆ Drag-and-Drop Editing

On the Job

After you create a worksheet, you may want to rearrange data or add additional information. For example, you may need to insert additional rows to a section of your worksheet because new employees have joined a department. With Excel's editing features, you can easily add, delete, and rearrange entire rows and columns. You can also move or drag and drop sections of the worksheet with ease.

You are the Payroll Manager at Whole Grains Bread. The conversion to an in-house payroll system is next week, and you want to test out a payroll worksheet the staff will use to collect and enter payroll data into the computer system. You're about ready to test out the worksheet using the home office data, but you need to modify it slightly first.

Terms

Cut The command used to remove data from a cell or range of cells and place it on the Clipboard.

Paste The command used to place data from the Clipboard to a location on the worksheet.

Drag-and-drop feature A method used to move or copy the contents of a range of cells by dragging the border of a selection from one location in a worksheet and dropping it in another location.

Notes

Insert and Delete Columns and Rows

■ You can insert or delete columns or rows when necessary to change the arrangement of the data on the worksheet.

■ When you insert column(s) into a worksheet, existing columns shift their position to the right.

   ✓ *For example, if you select column C and then insert two columns, the data that was in column C is shifted to the right, and becomes column E.*

■ Likewise, if you insert row(s) into a worksheet, existing rows are shifted down to accommodate the newly inserted row(s).

   ✓ *For example, if you select row 8 and insert two rows, the data that was in row 8 is shifted down to row 10.*

■ After inserting a column or row, you can use the Insert Options button to choose whether or not formatting from a nearby row or column should be applied to the new rows or columns.

Insert Options button

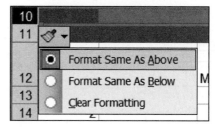

■ When you delete a column or row, existing columns and rows shift their positions to close the gap.

   ✓ *Any data in the rows or columns you select for deletion is erased.*

✓ *Data in existing columns is shifted back to the left to fill the gap left by deleted columns.*

✓ *In a similar manner, data in existing rows is shifted up to fill any gaps.*

■ Instead of deleting columns or rows, you can hide them temporarily and then redisplay them as needed.

✓ *You might do this, for example, to hide data from a coworker who's not authorized to view it.*

Move Data (Cut/Paste)

■ To move data from one place in the worksheet to another, use the **Cut** and **Paste** commands from the Edit menu or the buttons on the Standard toolbar.

■ When you cut data from a location, it is temporarily stored on the Clipboard. That data is then copied from the Clipboard to the new location when you paste.

■ If data already exists in the location you wish to paste to, Excel overwrites it.

• Instead of overwriting data with the Paste command, you can insert the cut cells and have Excel shift cells with existing data down or to the right.

■ When you move data, its format is moved as well.

✓ *You can override this and move just the data.*

Drag-and-Drop Editing

■ The **drag-and-drop feature** allows you to use the mouse to copy or move a range of cells simply by dragging them.

■ The drag-and-drop process works like this: first, you select a range to copy or move, and then you use the border surrounding the range to drag the data to a different location. When you release the mouse button, the data is "dropped" there.

✓ *An outline of the selection appears as you drag it to its new location on the worksheet.*

✓ *Drag and drop normally moves data, but you can copy data instead by simply holding down the Ctrl key as you drag.*

Example of drag-and-drop editing

■ Insert, delete, move, and copy operations may affect formulas, so you should check the formulas after you have made changes to be sure that they are correct.

■ When a drag-and-drop action does not move data correctly, use the Undo feature to undo it.

Procedures

Insert Columns/Rows with Menu

1. Select as many adjacent columns or rows you need to insert.
   - ✓ Drag across column letters or row numbers to select entire column(s) or row(s).
2. Click **Insert** .... `Alt`+`I`
3. Click **C**olumns..................... `C`

   OR

   Click **R**ows .... `R`
   - ✓ New columns are inserted to the left of selected columns. New rows are inserted above selected rows.
   - ✓ To select whether or not to copy nearby formatting, click the Insert Options button and choose an option such as Format Same as Above or Clear Formatting.

Insert Columns/Rows with Mouse

1. Select as many adjacent columns or rows you need to insert.
   - ✓ Drag across column letters or row numbers to select entire column(s) or row(s).
2. Right-click selection.
3. Click **I**nsert .... `I`
   - ✓ To select whether or not to copy nearby formatting, click the Insert Options button and choose an option such as Format Same as Above or Clear Formatting.

Delete Columns/Rows with Menu

1. Select column(s) or row(s) to be removed.
2. Click **E**dit .... `Alt`+`E`
3. Click **D**elete .... `D`

Delete Columns/Rows with Mouse

1. Select column(s) or row(s) to be removed.
2. Right-click selection.
3. Click **D**elete .... `D`

Hide Columns or Rows

1. Select the columns or rows you wish to hide.

2. Click **F**ormat .... `Alt`+`F`
3. Click **C**olumn .... `C`

   OR

   Click **R**ow........................... `R`
4. Click **H**ide........................... `H`

Unhide Columns or Rows

1. Select surrounding columns or rows.
2. Click **F**ormat .... `F`
3. Click **C**olumn .... `C`

   OR

   Click **R**ow........................... `R`
4. Click **U**nhide .... `U`

Cut Data *(Ctrl+X)*

1. Select cell(s) to move.
2. Click **E**dit.................... `Alt`+`E`
3. Click Cu**t**............................. `T`

   OR

   Click **Cut** button 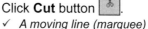.
   - ✓ A moving line (marquee) surrounds selected cell(s).

Paste Data *(Ctrl+V)*

1. Select cell(s) to accept data.
   - ✓ You only need to select the top-left cell of destination range. You can also move data to another worksheet or another workbook.
2. Click **E**dit.................... `Alt`+`E`
3. Click **P**aste.......................... `P`

   OR

   Click **Paste** button .
   - ✓ If you paste formatting along with data and you don't want to do that, click the Paste Options button that appears and select the desired option.

Insert Data between Cells

1. Click **I**nsert.................. `Alt`+`I`
2. Click C**e**lls .... `E`
3. Click **Shift cells right**.......... `I`

   OR

   Shift cells down................. `D`
4. Click **OK** .... `Enter`

Move Selection with Drag-and-Drop Editing

1. Select cell or range of cells to move.
2. Move mouse pointer to border of selection.

   To move selection to destination cells and *overwrite* existing data:
   a. Drag selection outline to new location.
   b. Release mouse button.
   c. Click **OK**...................... `Enter`

   To move selection to destination cells and *insert* between existing data:
   a. Press **Shift** while dragging selection outline to column or row gridline .... `Shift`
   - ✓ If you drag outline to column gridline, existing data shifts right. If you drag outline to a row gridline, existing data shifts down.
   b. Release mouse button and then Shift key.

Copy Selection with Drag-and-Drop Editing

1. Select cell or range of cells to copy.
2. Move mouse pointer to border of selection.

   To copy selection to destination cells and *overwrite* existing data:
   a. Press **Ctrl** while dragging selection outline to column or row gridline .... `Ctrl`
   b. Release **Ctrl** key, then mouse button.

   To copy selection to destination cells and *insert* between existing data:
   a. Press **Ctrl+Shift** and drag selection outline to column or row gridline .... `Ctrl`+`Shift`
   - ✓ If you drag the outline to column gridline, existing cells shift right. If you drag outline to row gridline, existing cells shift down.
   b. Release mouse button, then **Ctrl** and **Shift** keys.

Exercise Directions   *Extra Credit*

1. Start Excel, if necessary.
2. Open 💿 **10Payroll**.
3. Save the file as **Payroll**.
4. Select the range E11:J12 and use drag and drop editing to copy it to the range beginning at cell E23.
5. Delete the values in cells E24:F24.
6. Select the range F23:J24 and use cut and paste to move it to the range beginning in cell G23.
7. In cell F23, type the label **Overtime Hours**.
   a. Enter the label on two lines by pressing Alt+Enter after the word Overtime.
   b. Apply bold format to cell F23.
8. In cell G24, type a formula to compute the gross pay.
   ✓ *Take regular hours times the rate, and add that to overtime hours times 1.5 times the rate.*
   ✓ *Remember that you'll need to use parentheses to tell Excel to calculate each multiple before adding them together.*
9. Copy the formulas to G25:G35.
10. Copy the Fed Tax, SS Tax, State Tax, and Net Pay formulas from the Salaried Employees table.
11. Insert a row above row 23.
12. In cell A23, type **Hourly Employees**.
    a. Apply Arial, 12 point, bold font to cell A23.
13. Insert a new column to the left of column E.
14. Type the label, **Dpt No.** in cells E11 and E24.
15. Widen columns, as necessary.
16. Spell check the worksheet.
17. Print the worksheet.
18. Close the file, saving all changes.

On Your Own

1. Open the file **OXL09**, created in the On Your Own section of Exercise 9, or open 💿 **10CDMANIA**.
2. Save the file as **OXL10**.
3. Insert two new rows above the Totals row, and enter sales data for two new stores.
4. Insert a column between March and April, and label the column **Qtr 1**.
5. In the Qtr 1 column, type formulas to total the first quarter sales (January through March) for each store.
6. Where the Totals row and the Qtr 1 column meet, type a formula that calculates the grand total for Qtr 1.
7. Using drag and drop, copy the store names (and the Store and Totals labels) to an area a few rows below the sales data—but in the same column.
   ✓ *You're creating a duplicate sales area below the current area that will eventually store the sales amounts for the second quarter—April, May, and June.*
8. Using Cut and Paste, move the April column totals to this new sales area, below the data for January.
9. Add labels for **May**, **June**, and **Qtr 2** in the columns to the right of the April column.
10. In the Qtr 2 column, type formulas to total the second quarter sales (May through June) for each store.
11. Widen columns as needed.
12. Spell check the workbook.
13. Print the worksheet.
14. Close the workbook, saving all changes.

Illustration A

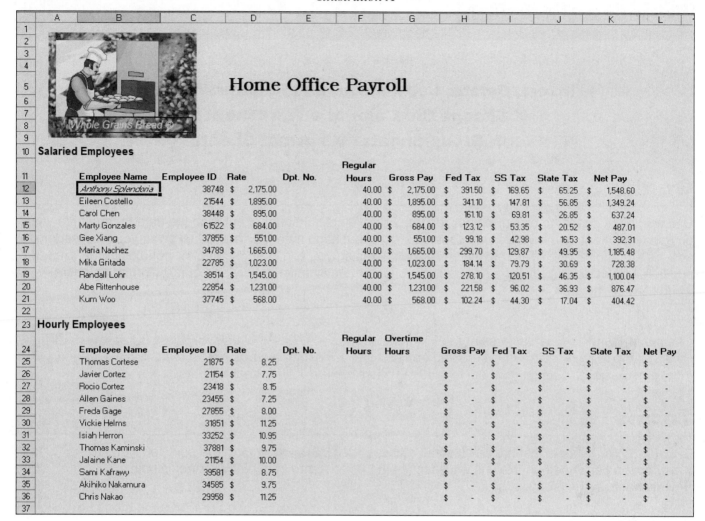

	Employee Name	Employee ID	Rate		Dpt. No.	Regular Hours	Gross Pay		Fed Tax		SS Tax		State Tax		Net Pay
Salaried Employees															
12	Anthony Splendoria	38748	$ 2,175.00			40.00	$ 2,175.00	$	391.50	$	169.65	$	65.25	$	1,548.60
13	Eileen Costello	21544	$ 1,895.00			40.00	$ 1,895.00	$	341.10	$	147.81	$	56.85	$	1,349.24
14	Carol Chen	38448	$ 895.00			40.00	$ 895.00	$	161.10	$	69.81	$	26.85	$	637.24
15	Marty Gonzales	61522	$ 684.00			40.00	$ 684.00	$	123.12	$	53.35	$	20.52	$	487.01
16	Gee Xiang	37855	$ 551.00			40.00	$ 551.00	$	99.18	$	42.98	$	16.53	$	392.31
17	Maria Nachez	34789	$ 1,665.00			40.00	$ 1,665.00	$	299.70	$	129.87	$	49.95	$	1,185.48
18	Mika Gritada	22785	$ 1,023.00			40.00	$ 1,023.00	$	184.14	$	79.79	$	30.69	$	728.38
19	Randall Lohr	38514	$ 1,545.00			40.00	$ 1,545.00	$	278.10	$	120.51	$	46.35	$	1,100.04
20	Abe Rittenhouse	22854	$ 1,231.00			40.00	$ 1,231.00	$	221.58	$	96.02	$	36.93	$	876.47
21	Kum Woo	37745	$ 568.00			40.00	$ 568.00	$	102.24	$	44.30	$	17.04	$	404.42

Hourly Employees

	Employee Name	Employee ID	Rate		Dpt. No.	Regular Hours	Overtime Hours	Gross Pay		Fed Tax		SS Tax		State Tax		Net Pay	
25	Thomas Cortese	21875	$ 8.25					$ -	$	-	$	-	$	-	$	-	
26	Javier Cortez	21154	$ 7.75					$ -	$	-	$	-	$	-	$	-	
27	Rocio Cortez	23418	$ 8.15					$ -	$	-	$	-	$	-	$	-	
28	Allen Gaines	23455	$ 7.25					$ -	$	-	$	-	$	-	$	-	
29	Freda Gage	27855	$ 8.00					$ -	$	-	$	-	$	-	$	-	
30	Vickie Helms	31851	$ 11.25					$ -	$	-	$	-	$	-	$	-	
31	Isiah Herron	33252	$ 10.95					$ -	$	-	$	-	$	-	$	-	
32	Thomas Kaminski	37881	$ 9.75					$ -	$	-	$	-	$	-	$	-	
33	Jalaine Kane	21154	$ 10.00					$ -	$	-	$	-	$	-	$	-	
34	Sami Kafrawy	39581	$ 8.75					$ -	$	-	$	-	$	-	$	-	
35	Akihiko Nakamura	34585	$ 9.75					$ -	$	-	$	-	$	-	$	-	
36	Chris Nakao	29958	$ 11.25					$ -	$	-	$	-	$	-	$	-	

Exercise 11

Skills Covered:

◆ **Insert, Delete, Copy, Move, and Rename Worksheets**
◆ **Change the Color of a Worksheet Tab**
◆ **Group Sheets** ◆ **Format Sheets**

On the Job

Use workbook sheets to organize your reports. For example, instead of entering the data for an entire year on one worksheet, use multiple worksheets to represent each month's data. Excel gives you the freedom to add, delete, move, and even rename your worksheets so you can keep a complex workbook organized. In addition, you can group multiple sheets and work on them simultaneously and quickly format an entire worksheet in one step.

As the Manager of Spa Services at the Michigan Avenue Athletic Club, you were just not satisfied with the spa invoicing worksheet you created earlier. After using it for awhile, you've reworked it a bit and now it seems easier to use, so now you're ready to make copies of it for tracking each day's services.

Terms

Grouping Worksheets that are selected as a unit; any action performed on this unit will affect all the worksheets in the group.

Active sheet tab The selected worksheet; the tab name of an active sheet is bold.

Notes

Insert, Delete, Copy, Move, and Rename Worksheets

- The default workbook window contains three sheets named Sheet1 through Sheet3.

- The sheet tab displays the name of the sheet.

- Right-click a sheet tab to display a shortcut menu that allows you to insert, delete, rename move, and copy worksheets. You can also change the color of a worksheet's tab.

- You do not need to delete unused sheets from a workbook since they do not take up much room in the file; however, if you plan on sharing the file, you may want to remove unused sheets to create a more professional look.

- Renaming sheets and coloring sheet tabs make it easier to keep track of the data on individual sheets.

Sheet tab shortcut menu

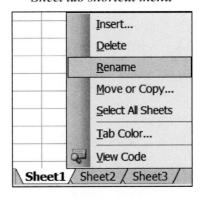

- Moving sheets allows you to place them in a logical order within the workbook.

- When you copy a worksheet, you copy all of its data and formatting. However, changes you later make to the copied sheet do not affect the original sheet.

Change the Color of a Worksheet Tab

- Change tab colors to group worksheets together visually.

- If you change the color of a sheet tab, that color appears when the tab is not selected.

- When a colored sheet tab is clicked, its color changes to white, with a small line of its original color at the bottom of the tab.

  ✓ *For example, an orange sheet tab changes to white with a thin orange line at the bottom when it is selected.*

Group Sheets

- If you want to work on several worksheets simultaneously, select multiple worksheets and create a **grouping**.

- Grouped sheet tabs appear white when selected, and the name of the **active sheet tab** appears in bold.

- When you select a grouping, any editing, formatting, or new entries you make to the active sheet are simultaneously made to all the sheets in the group.

  ✓ *For example, you can select a group of sheets and format, move, copy, or delete them in one step. You can also add, delete, change, or format the same entries into the same cells on every selected worksheet.*

  ✓ *Remember to deselect the grouping when you no longer want to make changes to all the sheets in the group.*

Format Sheets

- One way in which you can quickly give your worksheets a professional look is to format them using AutoFormat.

- Using AutoFormat saves you time, because you won't have to format the column labels, row labels, and data manually.

- After you select an AutoFormat, Excel applies that format throughout the worksheet.

- You can select only part of an AutoFormat's attributes to apply.

  ✓ *For example, you could apply just the number formats and fonts, but not the alignments, patterns, borders, widths, and heights.*

Procedures

Select One Sheet

1. If necessary, click tab scrolling buttons to view hidden sheet tabs.
2. Click sheet tab to select it.

Select All Sheets

1. Right-click any sheet tab.
2. Select **Select All Sheets** .... 🖰, Enter

Select Consecutive Sheets

1. If necessary, click tab scrolling buttons to view hidden sheet tabs.
2. Click first sheet tab in group.
3. If necessary, to view additional hidden sheet tabs click tab scrolling buttons.
4. Press **Shift** and click last sheet tab in group.

  ✓ *The word [Group] appears in the title bar.*

Select Nonconsecutive Sheets

1. If necessary, click tab scrolling buttons to view hidden sheet tabs.
2. Click first sheet tab in group.
3. If necessary, to view additional hidden sheet tabs click tab scrolling buttons.
4. Press **Ctrl** and click each subsequent sheet tab to be included in group.

  ✓ *The word [Group] appears in the title and task bars.*

Ungroup Sheets

1. Right-click any sheet tab in group.
2. Click **Ungroup Sheets** .... 🅄
OR
- Click any sheet tab not in group.

Delete Sheet(s)

1. Select sheet tab(s).
2. Right-click sheet tab.
3. Click **Delete** .... 🄳
4. Click **Delete** to confirm deletion of a sheet with data .... Enter

Rename Sheet

1. Double-click sheet tab.
   OR
   a. Right-click sheet tab.
   b. Select **Rename** .... 🅁
2. Type new name.
3. Press **Enter** .... Enter

Insert Sheet(s)

1. Select number of sheet tabs as sheets to be inserted.
2. Right-click sheet tab.

  ✓ *The new sheets will be inserted before the first sheet in the group.*

3. Click **Insert** .... `I`
4. Select **General tab** of
   Insert dialog box.......... `Ctrl` + `Tab`
5. Select **Worksheet**............ `↹`
6. Click **OK**........................... `Enter`

Move Sheet(s) within Workbook

1. If necessary, click tab scrolling buttons to view hidden sheet tabs.
2. Click and drag selected sheet tab(s) to new sheet tab position.
   - ✓ *Mouse pointer shape changes to ⬚. Black triangle indicates where sheet will be inserted.*

Copy Sheet

1. If necessary, click tab scrolling buttons to view hidden sheet tabs.
2. Select sheet tab.
3. Press and hold **Ctrl**, as you click and drag selected sheet tab to its final position.

- ✓ *Mouse pointer shape changes to ⬚ with a plus sign. Black triangle indicates where sheet will be inserted.*

- ✓ *To copy multiple sheets at once, select them, then choose **Edit, Move,** or **Copy Sheet.** Select a location to place the copies from the Move or Copy dialog box, choose **Create a copy,** and then click **OK.***

Change Tab Color

1. Select the sheet tab(s) you wish to make the same color.
2. Right-click sheet tab in group.
3. Click **Tab Color** .... `T`
4. Select a color.................... `↹`
5. Click **OK** .... `Enter`

- ✓ *You can remove the color on a tab by repeating these steps and choosing **No Color** in step 4.*

Use AutoFormat

- ✓ *Applying an AutoFormat to an extremely large worksheet may cause the system to crash.*

1. Select the data range you want to format, or select multiple ranges if you like.

- ✓ *You can format the exact same range on multiple sheets by positioning the cursor within the data range, and selecting the tabs of the sheets you want to format.*

2. Click **Format** .... `Alt` + `O`
3. Click **AutoFormat** .... `A`
4. Select the format you want to apply. .... `↹`
5. To apply only selected parts of the format, click **Options**............... `Alt` + `O`
6. From the expanded dialog box, select only the formats you want to apply:
   - **Number** .... `N`
   - **Border** .... `B`
   - **Font** .... `F`
   - **Patterns**........................ `P`
   - **Alignment** .... `A`
   - **Width/Height**................. `W`
7. Click **OK**............................. `Enter`

Exercise Directions

1. Start Excel if necessary.
2. Open 💿 **11SpaServices 2**.
3. Save the file as **SpaServices 2**.
4. Copy the Monday worksheet six times.
5. Rename the new worksheets **Tuesday, Wednesday, Thursday, Friday, Saturday,** and **Sunday**.
6. Move the worksheets as needed to arrange them in order from Sunday to Saturday.
7. Select all the worksheets.
8. Apply the Classic 2 AutoFormat to all the sheets.

9. Restore the two-line column labels: Massage Duration, Massage Cost, and Herbal Wrap. (See Illustration A.)
   - ✓ *Press Alt+Enter to get text to wrap to the second line.*
10. Adjust column widths as needed to fully display data.
11. Ungroup the sheets.
12. Delete the Tuesday sheet since the spa is closed on Tuesdays.
13. Color the weekend tabs blue-gray, and the weekday tabs violet to match the colors in the worksheet.
14. Spell check the workbook.
15. Print the entire workbook.
16. Close the file, saving all changes.

Illustration A

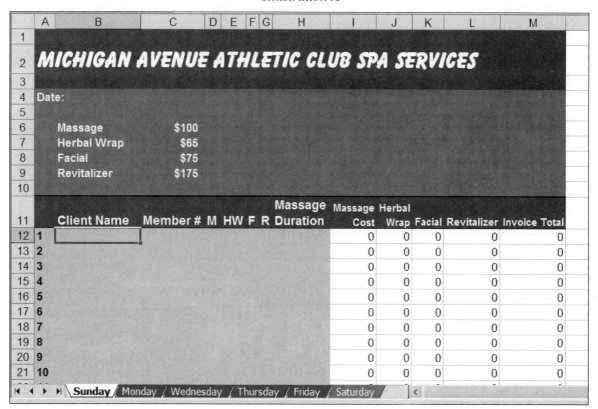

On Your Own

1. Open a new workbook in Excel.

2. Save the file as **OXL11**.

3. Set up a worksheet for tracking weekly income.

   ✓ *For this exercise, assume that you receive income from a part-time job, along with a weekly allowance. Also, you've decided to sell some old CDs, so record the sales from that effort. In addition, your birthday falls during week 3 of this month, and you usually receive money gifts from several relatives.*

4. Delete Sheet 2 and Sheet 3.

5. On Sheet 1, enter a title for the worksheet in row 2.

6. Label columns B through H for the days of the week.

7. In the rows in column A, list your sources of income: **Job**, **Allowance**, **CD sales**, and **Gifts**.

8. Copy Sheet 1 three times, to create four worksheets.

9. Label the four sheets: **Week 1**, **Week 2**, **Week 3**, and **Week 4** respectively. Assign a unique color to each week's tab.

10. Enter data in all three worksheets. You may or may not have income for each day, or for each category (job, allowance, CD sales, or gifts).

11. Group the worksheets and enter formulas to calculate the total income for each category as well as for each day of the week.

    ✓ *Label the column and row where the results are displayed correctly.*

    ✓ *Select the data and totals, and apply the numeric format of your choice.*

12. Select the data range of one sheet, then group the worksheets and apply the AutoFormat of your choice—but do not apply the AutoFormat's Number format.

13. Widen columns as needed to display data.

14. Spell check the workbook.

15. Print the entire workbook.

16. Close the file, saving all changes.

Exercise 12

As Sales Director at the Whole Grains Bread, it's your job to monitor sales throughout the company. Today you're designing a workbook to track three month's worth of sales at each of your various locations.

Exercise Directions

1. Start Excel, if necessary.
2. Open ⊚ **12BreadSales**.
3. Save the file as **BreadSales**.
4. Apply the following formats to the July worksheet:
   a. A11:F11: Architect 18-point white font, dark red color fill.
   ✓ *If the Architect font is not installed on your system, apply a font similar to the one shown in Illustration A.*
   b. A12:B29: Architect 10-point white font, sea green color fill.
   c. C12:E12: Architect 12-point font, light yellow color fill.
   d. C13:E29: Architect 10-point font, light yellow color fill. Currency Style number format, with no decimal places.
   e. F12: Architect 12-point white font, sea green color fill.
   f. F13:F29: Architect 10-point white font, sea green color fill. Currency Style number format with no decimal places.
5. In cell F13, enter a formula to compute the net profit, taking total sales for that city minus costs such as ingredients and labor.
6. Copy the formula to the range F14:F27.
7. Edit cell B18 to read **Portland 1, OR**.
   a. Insert a row beneath row 18.
   b. In cell B19, enter **Portland 2, OR**.
   c. Copy the net profit formula to cell F19.

8. Insert a column to the left of column D.
   a. In cell D12, type **Coupons**.
   b. Adjust the formula in cell G13 to subtract this extra cost from the net profit.
   c. Copy this adjusted formula down column G.
9. Adjust column widths to fit the data.
10. Copy the July worksheet three times.
    a. Name the extra worksheets **August**, **September**, and **Qtr 3** and arrange them in that order.
    b. Color the tabs for July, August, and September light yellow.
    c. Color the tab for Qtr 3 sea green.
11. Change to the Qtr 3 worksheet.
    a. Change cell A11 to read **Qtr 3 Sales Report – Totals by City**.
    b. Select the ranges A11:G12 and A25:G30.
    c. Using Copy and Paste, copy the selection to the range beginning in cell I11.
    d. Change cell I11 to read, **Qtr 3 Sales Report – Totals by Month**.
    e. Change cell J13 to **July**.
    f. Change cell J14 to **August**.
    g. Change cell J15 to **September**.
12. Adjust columns widths as needed to display data fully.
13. Spell check the workbook.
14. Preview each sheet, and print the workbook.
15. Close the file, saving all changes.

Illustration A

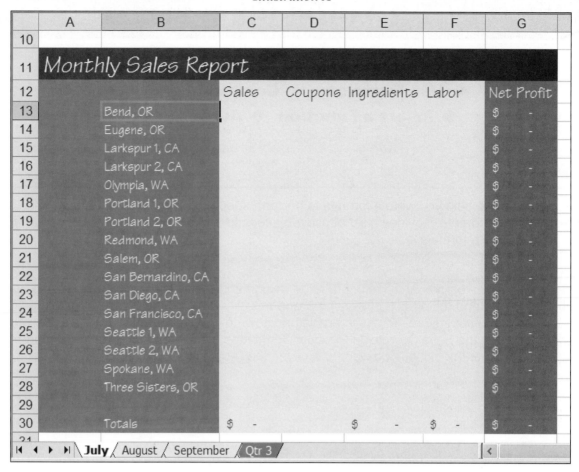

	A	B	C	D	E	F	G
10							
11	Monthly Sales Report						
12			Sales	Coupons	Ingredients	Labor	Net Profit
13		Bend, OR					$ -
14		Eugene, OR					$ -
15		Larkspur 1, CA					$ -
16		Larkspur 2, CA					$ -
17		Olympia, WA					$ -
18		Portland 1, OR					$ -
19		Portland 2, OR					$ -
20		Redmond, WA					$ -
21		Salem, OR					$ -
22		San Bernardino, CA					$ -
23		San Diego, CA					$ -
24		San Francisco, CA					$ -
25		Seattle 1, WA					$ -
26		Seattle 2, WA					$ -
27		Spokane, WA					$ -
28		Three Sisters, OR					$ -
29							
30		Totals	$ -		$ -	$ -	$ -

July / August / September / Qtr 3

Illustration B

Qtr 3 Sales Report - Totals by Month

	Sales	Coupons	Ingredien	Labor	Net Profi
July					$ -
August					$ -
September					$ -
Totals	$ -		$ -	$ -	$ -

Exercise 13

On the Job

Use an Excel function to help you write a formula to perform specific calculations in your worksheets. Excel's Insert Function feature provides a list of available functions with a wizard to assist you in "filling in the blanks" to complete a formula.

You're the owner of Restoration Architecture, a large design and construction firm specializing in the remodeling, redesign, and restoration of existing properties. The bid results are in for a project involving the restoration of several homes in an historic downtown neighborhood. The homes were recently purchased by the Save Downtown Phoenix Committee, who asked for the bids. Unfortunately, your company didn't get the bid, so you want to analyze the results and determine how far off the mark you were.

Terms

Function A predefined formula that uses the values in the cells you select to calculate its answer.

Function name The name given to one of Excel's predefined formulas.

Argument The parts of a formula that are variable. You select the cells or cells for each argument, and Excel calculates the answers based on their values.

Nest To use a function as an argument within another function.

AutoCalculate A feature that temporarily performs the following calculations on a range of cells without making you write a formula: Average, Count, Count Nums, Max, Min, or Sum.

Notes

Use Functions

- Excel provides built-in formulas called **functions** to perform special calculations.
- A function contains these elements in the following order:
  - The equal symbol (=) starts the function.
  - The **function name** is entered in upper- or lowercase letters.
  - An open parenthesis separates the **arguments** from the function name.

- The argument(s) identify the data required to perform the function.
- A closed parenthesis ends the argument.

  Example: =SUM(A1:A40)

  ✓ *This sum function adds the values listed as arguments, which in this case is a single range of cells A1 through A40.*

- Most functions allow multiple arguments, separated by commas.

  ✓ *For example, =SUM(A1:A40,C1:C40) adds the values in the ranges A1:A40 and C1:C40.*

■ A function may be inserted into a formula.

  ✓ *For example, =B2/SUM(C3:C5) takes the value in cell B2 and divides it by the sum of the values in the range C3:C5.*

■ When a function is used as an argument for other functions, it is **nested** within those functions.

  ✓ *For example, =ROUND(SUM(B12:B23),2)) totals the values in the range, B12:B23, then rounds that total to two decimal places.*

Common Functions

■ You'll find these functions to be the ones you use most often:

  ● =SUM( ) adds the values in a range of cells.
  ● =AVERAGE( ) returns the arithmetic mean of the values in a range of cells.
  ● =COUNT( ) counts the cells containing numbers in a range of cells (blank cells or text entries are ignored).
  ● =MAX( ) finds the highest value in a range of cells.
  ● =MIN( ) finds the lowest value in a range of cells.
  ● =ROUND( ) adjusts a value to a specific number of digits.

    ✓ *When a cell is formatted to a specified number of decimal places, only the display of that value is affected. The actual value in the cell is still used in all calculations. For example, if a cell contains the value 13.45687, and you decide to display only the last two decimal places, then the value 13.46 will display in the cell, but the value, 13.45687 will be used in all calculations.*

    ✓ *Let's say you have a long column of numbers such as this:*

      Sales Projections

      2147.8347

      2866.1633

      2593.0049

      Total: 7607.0029

      You're not interested in the extra digits past a penny, so you simply change the formatting, and the numbers appear like this:

      Sales Projections

      2147.83

      2866.16

      2593.00

      Total: 7607.00

  ✓ *As you can see, the column of numbers looks as if it has been added incorrectly, even though the total shown is technically correct. So, if you plan on displaying a limited number of decimal places and not whole numbers, you might want to use the ROUND function to adjust each value so that the displayed value is equal to the actual value used in calculations.*

  ✓ *For example, use the ROUND function to round the value 2147.8347 to 2147.8400, like this:*

    Sales Projections

    2147.8400

    2866.1600

    2593.0000

    Total: 7607.0000

  ✓ *If you then display only two decimal places in each cell, the total will look correct:*

    Sales Projections

    2147.84

    2866.16

    2593.00

    Total: 7607.00

  ✓ *Of course, if you are interested in every digit of the calculated sales projections, then display them fully so that your totals will look correct.*

  ● Use the drop-down arrow on the AutoSum button Σ ▾ on the Standard toolbar to quickly insert a SUM, AVERAGE, COUNT, MIN, or MAX function.

Insert a Function

■ You can enter a function by typing it, or you can use the Insert Function dialog box to help you locate a specific function and enter the correct arguments.

■ To insert a function instead of typing it, click the Insert Function button fx on the Formula bar.

■ In the Insert Function dialog box, you can type a brief description of the function you want to use to display a list of corresponding functions.

  ✓ *For example, you could type the description, "add numbers" to find a function you could use to add a column of numbers.*

  ✓ *You can also display functions by typing the name of the function (if you know it) or by choosing a category from the Or select a category list.*

  ✓ *When you enter a formula using Insert Function, Excel automatically enters the equal sign in the formula.*

Insert Function dialog box

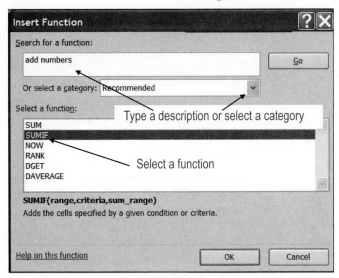

Function Arguments dialog box

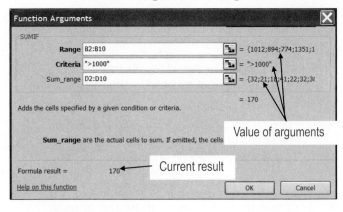

- After selecting a function, you're prompted to enter the appropriate arguments into a second dialog box—Function Arguments.
  - In the Function Arguments dialog box, you can select cells instead of typing them by using the Collapse Dialog button located at the right of each text box.
  - Required arguments are displayed in bold.
  - As you enter the arguments, the value of that argument is displayed to the right of the text box.
  - Excel calculates the current result and displays it at the bottom of the dialog box.
  - If you need help understanding a particular function's arguments, click the Help on this function link, located in the lower right-hand corner of the dialog box.

AutoCalculate

- When you want to quickly calculate the Average, Count, Count Nums, Max, Min, or Sum for a range of cells on your worksheet, without actually entering a formula, use **AutoCalculate**.
- Using the mouse, drag across a range of cells to display the AutoCalculation (default is SUM) on the Status bar.
- To use a different function with AutoCalculate, right-click the AutoCalculate result on the Status bar and pick from the list of functions.

AutoCalculate function list

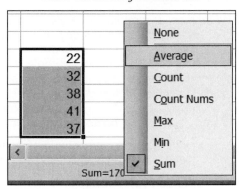

Procedures

Enter a Function Manually

1. Click cell where result should display.....................
2. Press **Equal** ....
3. Type function name.
4. Press **Left Parenthesis** ......
5. Enter arguments, separated by commas.

You can enter:
- Numeric value
- Cell reference
- Range of cells
- Range name
- Function
  - ✓ You can select a range of cells by dragging over them, rather than typing the range address.

6. Press **Right Parenthesis**....
7. Press **Enter**......................

Insert a Function

1. Click cell where result should display ....
2. Click **Insert Function** button
   OR
   a. Click **Insert** .... Alt + I
   b. Click **Function** ....

3. Perform one of the following:

   a. Type the function name or a brief description in the **Search for a function** text box. .... Alt + S

   b. Click **Go** ....
   OR

   Select category from **Or select a category** list ...... Alt + C ,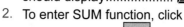

4. Select function from **Select a function** list .... Alt + N ,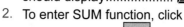

5. Click **OK** .... Enter

   ✓ The Function Arguments dialog box appears.

6. Click argument text box ...... Tab

7. Type data.
   You can enter:
   • Numeric value
   • Cell reference
   • Range of cells
   • Range name
   • Function

   ✓ To enter a cell reference or range of cells from the worksheet, click the Collapse button located to the right of the argument text box, select the cell(s), and then click the Collapse button again to expand the dialog box.

8. Repeat steps 6 and 7 to complete arguments.

9. Click **OK** .... Enter

Enter a Common Function

1. Click cell where result should display ....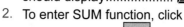

2. To enter SUM function, click **AutoSum** button Σ ▾ .
   OR
   To enter AVERAGE, COUNT, MAX, or MIN function, click the arrow on **AutoSum** button Σ ▾ and select the function you want.

   ✓ Excel guesses the range you want to use with the function you selected.

3. If the selected range is not the one you want to use, select the range you want by dragging over it with the mouse.

   ✓ You can also drag the blue bounding box surrounding the selected cells to some other range. You can resize the bounding box as well, to make it fit the range you want to sum.

4. Press **Enter** .... Enter

   ✓ You can enter any function you want with the AutoSum button by simply selecting **More Functions** from the AutoSum list. This displays the Insert Function dialog box where you can enter the appropriate arguments for the function.

Edit a Function

1. Click result cell ....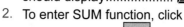
2. Click in Formula bar.

3. Type correction.
   OR

   a. Click **Insert Function** button fx on Formula bar to redisplay Formula Arguments dialog box.

   b. Click argument text box.

   c. Type correction.

4. Click **OK** .... Enter

Enter a Function into a Formula

1. Click formula cell .... 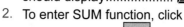 where answer will display.

2. Press **Equal** .... =

3. Type the beginning part of the formula.

4. At the point in the formula where you wish to use a function, type the function name.

5. Press **Left Parenthesis** ...... (

6. Type arguments(s).

7. Press **Right Parenthesis** ...)

8. Press **Enter** .... Enter

Use AutoCalculate

1. Select cells .... Shift + 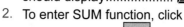 you want to calculate.

2. View result of calculation on Status bar.
   OR

   a. Right-click result displayed on the Status bar.

   b. Click desired function in list .... 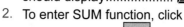 , Enter

Exercise Directions

1. Start Excel, if necessary.

2. Open ◎ **13BidAnalysis**.

3. Save the file as **BidAnalysis**.

4. In cell G10, use the AutoSum button to enter a formula that calculates the total of the values in cells C10:F10.

   ✓ Since cell C10 is blank, AutoSum will initially select the range D10:F10. Resize the bounding box or drag to select the correct range.

   ✓ The Formula Error button appears because Excel thinks you've made an error by not including the value in cell B10 in the SUM range. Ignore it for now.

5. Copy this formula to the range G11:G20.

   a. Select the range G10:G20, click the Formula Error button, and select Ignore Error from the menu.

   b. Use the Format Painter button to copy the format in cell G22 to G17.

6. In cell B37, use the Insert Function button to search for a function to create a formula that calculate the average contractor's bid for the per unit cost.

   ✓ *Hint: Take the average of all the bids in the range B10:B20.*

   a. Copy this formula to C37:G37.

   b. Click the Formula Error button in cell C37 and select Ignore Error to ignore the error caused by trying to divide by zero. The error will be fixed in a later exercise.

7. In cell B38, create a formula to calculate the percentage difference between the average bid and the bid made by Restoration Architecture.

   ✓ *Take Restoration's bid minus the average bid, and divide that by the average to compute a percentage. Be sure to use the necessary parentheses to compute the first total before you divide.*

   a. Nest this formula within the ROUND function, so that the result is rounded to four digits.

   b. Copy this formula to the range C38:G38.

   c. Again, click the Formula Error button in cell C38 and select Ignore Error.

d. Create a similar formula in cell B45 to calculate the percentage difference between the engineer's estimate and Restoration's bid.

e. Copy this formula to C45:G45.

8. In cell B39, enter a formula that displays the lowest contractor bid for the per unit cost.

   ✓ *In other words, display the minimum bid from the range, B10:B20.*

   a. Copy this formula to C39:G39.

   b. In cell B40, enter a similar formula to display the highest contractor bid for the per unit cost.

   c. Copy this formula to C40:G40.

9. Widen any columns as necessary.

10. Use AutoCalculate to check your results.

   ✓ *Remember that to select non-contiguous ranges, press Ctrl and drag over each range. The sum of the selected ranges appears in the Status bar. To view the results using other functions (such as AVERAGE), right-click the word **Sum** on the Status bar and select a different function.*

11. Spell check the worksheet.

12. Print the worksheet. Your results should look similar to Illustrations A and B.

13. Close the file, saving all changes.

Illustration A

	A	B	C	D	E	F	G
4							
5		Bid Results - Canal Street Neighborhood Homes Restoration Project					
6		No. of homes to be restored:		11			
7	Resoration Architecture						
8				Additional Bids on Project			
9		Unit Bid	Base Bid	Alt #1	Alt #2	Alt #3	Base Bid + Alt
10	BJW, Ltd.	$ 97,854.00		$ 6,981.00	$ 9,726.00	$ 12,758.00	$ 29,465.00
11	Craftsman, Inc.	$ 89,475.00		$ 7,051.00	$ 8,974.00	$ 12,332.00	$ 28,357.00
12	Meguro Construction	$ 92,441.00		$ 6,200.00	$ 9,795.00	$ 9,785.00	$ 25,780.00
13	Mendoza Inc.	$ 88,459.00		$ 7,500.00	$ 8,945.00	$ 10,235.00	$ 26,680.00
14	New Mark Designs	$ 99,487.00		$ 5,985.00	$ 9,760.00	$ 9,989.00	$ 25,734.00
15	Ravuru Renovations	$ 92,335.00		$ 6,193.00	$ 8,554.00	$ 11,995.00	$ 26,742.00
16	Renovation Ventures	$ 91,415.00		$ 6,300.00	$ 10,000.00	$ 10,335.00	$ 26,635.00
17	Resoration Architecture	$ 89,445.00		$ 6,115.00	$ 9,784.00	$ 11,578.00	$ 27,477.00
18	TOH Construction	$ 91,225.00		$ 6,451.00	$ 10,800.00	$ 10,100.00	$ 27,351.00
19	Williams Brothers Renovators, Ltd.	$ 96,485.00		$ 5,531.00	$ 9,875.00	$ 10,600.00	$ 26,006.00
20	Woo Home Designs	$ 93,415.00		$ 6,751.00	$ 10,633.00	$ 10,049.00	$ 27,433.00

Illustration B

	A	B	C	D	E	F	G
28							
29							
30							
31		Bid Analysis - Canal Street Neighborhood Homes Restoration Project					
32							
33	Resoration Architecture						
34					Additional Bids on Project		
35		Unit Bid	Base Bid	Alt #1	Alt #2	Alt #3	Base Bid + Alt
36	Resoration Architecture	$ 89,445.00	$ -	$ 6,115.00	$ 9,784.00	$11,578.00	$ 27,477.00
37	Average of All Bids	$ 92,912.36	#DIV/0!	$ 6,459.82	$ 9,713.27	$10,886.91	$ 27,060.00
38	Difference (+/-)	-3.73%	#DIV/0!	-5.34%	0.73%	6.35%	1.54%
39	Lowest Bid	$ 88,459.00	$ -	$ 5,531.00	$ 8,554.00	$ 9,785.00	$ 25,734.00
40	Highest Bid	$ 99,487.00	$ -	$ 7,500.00	$10,800.00	$12,758.00	$ 29,465.00
41							
42							
43	Restoration Architecture	$ 89,445.00	$ -	$ 6,115.00	$ 9,784.00	$11,578.00	$ 27,477.00
44	Engineers Estimate	$ 91,500.00	$ 1,006,500.00	$ 6,500.00	$ 9,500.00	$ 11,250.00	$ 1,125,250.00
45	Difference (+/-)	-2.25%	-100.00%	-5.92%	2.99%	2.92%	-97.56%

On Your Own

1. Open the **OXL10** file you created in the On Your Own section of Exercise 10, or open ☉ **13CDMANIA**.

2. Save the file as **OXL13**.

3. Enter May and June sales data for each store.

4. Use the AutoSum button to enter formulas that calculate sales totals for May and June.

5. Apply Accounting Style, 2 decimal places, to the sales data and totals.

6. Widen any columns as needed.

7. Beginning in row 20, create a summary section that includes the following:

   a. In row 20, type the word **Summary**.

   b. In row 22, beginning in column B, enter the name of the months, January through June.

   c. In column A, beginning in row 23, type the labels **Average Sales**, **Maximum Sales by Any Store**, and **Minimum Sales by Any Store**.

   d. In row 23, enter formulas that calculate the average sales for each month—January through June.

   e. In row 24, enter formulas that display the sales total of the store that sold the most for that month.

   f. In row 25, enter formulas to display the total for the store that sold the least that month.

   g. In cell A27, type the label **Total number of times sales were over $25,000**.

   h. In cell B27, enter a formula that calculates the total number of times any store sold more than $25,000 in any given month.

   ✓ To calculate this, you'll need to use the COUNTIF function. Because COUNTIF only counts the valid cells in one range, you'll need to use two COUNTIF functions in one formula and add their results together.

   ✓ To use COUNTIF, select the range you want to analyze, then type the condition you want to compare against—which in this case, is >25000, which means "greater than 25000."

8. Use the AutoCalculate function to check the formula results.

9. Widen any columns as needed.

10. Spell check the worksheet.

11. Apply formatting as you like, and print the worksheet.

12. Close the file, saving all changes.

Exercise 14

Skills Covered:

◆ **Natural Language Formulas** ◆ **Comments**

On the Job

Write natural language formulas and add comments to your worksheet to help you read the formulas or remember why you included certain information in your worksheet.

You are the CFO (Chief Financial Officer) of Restoration Architecture, and it's time for the quarterly revenue recap. This time, however, you want to make some modifications that will make the formulas easier to follow. This will help you in future quarters, when you use this workbook as a template for new workbooks.

Terms

Natural language formula A formula that refers to column or row heading labels instead of a cell reference or range.

Comment A text note attached to a worksheet cell.

Notes

Natural Language Formulas

- Excel allows you to create **natural language formulas** that refer to column and row labels in place of the cell reference or range.

  ✓ *When "natural language" is used in a formula the column or row label must be spelled exactly as the column or row label appears on the worksheet.*

- For example, =SUM(Jan) totals the range of cells in the Jan column that are located either above or to the left of the formula.

Column label in a natural language formula

- If you've used a label more than once in a worksheet, Excel may ask you to select the label to which you're referring in your natural language formula.

Identify Label dialog box

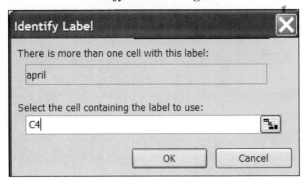

- To use natural language formulas, you must first turn on that option on the Calculations tab of the Options dialog box, as explained in the Procedures.

  ✓ *This option makes natural language available for formulas in the current workbook only. You must repeat the procedure to turn the option on for additional workbooks.*

Comments

- To attach a text note to a cell (maximum of 255 characters), use the Insert Comment command.

- A red triangle appears in the upper-right corner of any cell with an attached **comment**.

- To display the comment, simply rest the mouse pointer on the comment indicator (the red triangle).

- Comments help explain data, formulas, and labels used in a complex worksheet. You can insert comments as reminders to yourself, but they are especially useful for explaining a worksheet shared with others.

Comment displayed on worksheet

April	May	June
$ 25,978.33	$ 26,148.96	$ 25,
$ 19,258.44	$ 23,497.81	$ 22,
$ 19,258.44	$ 18,750.66	$ 21
$ 64,495.21		

Jennifer Fulton:
Sales promotion in April helped to boost sales above average.

- If you want, you can display all the comments on a worksheet with a single command.

Procedures

The following option must be turned on for natural language formulas to work within a particular workbook:

1. Click **Tools** .... Alt + T
2. Click **Options** .... O
3. Click **Calculation** tab.... Ctrl + Tab
4. Select **Accept labels in formulas** option .... Alt + B
5. **Click OK** .... Enter

Create Natural Language Formula

1. Click formula cell .... where answer will display.
2. Press **Equal** .... =
3. Type name of function.
4. Type open parenthesis .... (

5. Type arguments using column or row labels instead of cell reference or range.
6. Type close parenthesis ....)
7. Press **Enter** .... Enter

Create Comment

1. Select cell to attach comment.
2. Click **Insert** .... Alt + I
3. Click **Comment** .... M
4. Type text.
   ✓ *Note that handles appear around the box to resize or move it.*
5. Click outside box.
   ✓ *A red triangle now displays in the upper-right corner of the comment cell.*

Display Comment

- Move mouse pointer over cell that contains a comment.
  ✓ *Comment appears in a small yellow box beside the cell.*
  ✓ *To display all comments in a worksheet, choose **View, Comments**. Select **View, Comments** again to hide them again.*

Edit Comment

1. Right-click cell with comment.
2. Click **Edit Comment** .... E
3. Make correction.
   ✓ *Drag a handle to increase or decrease the size of the box.*
4. Click outside of box.

Delete Comment

1. Right-click cell with comment.
2. Click **Delete Comment** ...... M

Exercise Directions

1. Start Excel, if necessary.
2. Open 🎧 **14RHSales**.
3. Save the file as **RHSales**.
4. Turn on the natural language feature for this workbook.
5. In cell B18, use the SUM function to create a natural language formula that calculates the total sales for July.
6. Copy this formula to cells C18:D18.
   - ✓ *Notice that Excel creates a series from your formula. For example, in cell C18, Excel creates the formula, =SUM(August) and does not simply copy the formula =SUM(July) from cell B18.*
7. In cell B19, use the AVERAGE function to create a natural language formula that calculates the average sales for July.
8. Copy this formula to cells C19:D19.
9. Add a comment to cells D12 and D14 that indicates those projects have been completed.
10. Using the mouse, view the comments one at a time.
11. Using the View, Comments command, display all the comments.
12. Delete the comment in cell D12, then hide the remaining comment.
13. Adjust column widths as needed.
14. Spell check the worksheet.
15. Print the worksheet. Your results should look like Illustration A.
16. Close the file, saving all changes.

Illustration A

	A	B	C	D	E
1					
2					
3					
4					
5		3rd Qtr Revenues by Project			
6					
7	Restoration Architecture				
8					
9		July	August	September	Qtr 3 Totals
10	The Rossen House in Heritage Square	$ 328,118.00	$ 456,221.00	$ 298,485.00	$ 1,082,824.00
11	Carnegie Library	$ 41,325.00	$ 78,945.00	$ 85,664.00	$ 205,934.00
12	512 N. Oak Street	$ 32,995.00	$ 28,445.00	$ 18,445.00	$ 79,885.00
13	18 South Pendleton Ave.	$ 7,855.00	$ 27,958.00	$ 31,225.00	$ 67,038.00
14	Old Barn Quilts	$ 4,522.00	$ 12,889.00	$ 18,645.00	$ 36,056.00
15	Orpheum Theatre	$ 125,995.00	$ 285,941.00	$ 275,884.00	$ 687,820.00
16	Carousel in Litchfield Park	$ 72,145.00	$ 63,145.00	$ 21,778.00	$ 157,068.00
17					
18	Totals by Month	$ 612,955.00	$ 953,544.00	$ 750,126.00	
19	Average Revenue per Job	$ 87,565.00	$ 136,220.57	$ 107,160.86	

On Your Own

1. Open a new workbook in Excel.

2. Save the file as **OXL14**.

3. Create a worksheet to estimate your anticipated college or school expenses for next year.

4. Enter a worksheet title in row 1.

5. Label column B **September** for September's expenses.

6. Use the fill handle to create the column labels for October through May.

7. Enter row labels for each different type of expense.

   ✓ *Examples might include books, school supplies (such as notebooks, pens, and paper), computer supplies, gas and car maintenance, parking, and extras (such as concert tickets and dinners out).*

8. Enter values for the expense items in each month.

   ✓ *If some expenses are the same for every month, copy and paste the data, or use the fill handle.*

9. Label the row below the last expense item **Totals**, and then create a natural language formula to sum September's expenses.

10. Copy the formula to the other columns.

11. Format the worksheet data as currency.

12. Apply other formatting to improve the worksheet's appearance.

13. Adjust column widths as needed.

14. Add comments to several cells explaining your estimates.

15. Spell check the workbook.

16. Print the workbook. Your results should look similar to Illustration B.

17. Close the file, saving all changes.

Illustration B

	A	B	C	D	E	F	G	H	I	J
1	Estimated College Expenses for 2005									
2										
3		September	October	November	December	January	February	March	April	May
4	Books	$ 185.00				$ 235.00				
5	Supplies	$ 100.00	$ 75.00	$ 35.00	$ 20.00	$ 125.00	$ 75.00	$ 45.00	$ 35.00	$ 15.00
6	Computer Stuff	$ 575.00	$ 45.00		$ 275.00	$ 50.00			$ 75.00	$ 55.00
7	Gas	$ 35.00	$ 25.00	$ 25.00	$ 45.00	$ 35.00	$ 25.00	$ 30.00	$ 25.00	$ 55.00
8	Repairs		$ 225.00	$ 75.00	$ 50.00	$ 125.00	$ 55.00			$ 35.00
9	Parking	$ 225.00				$ 225.00				
10	Extras	$ 100.00	$ 100.00	$ 100.00	$ 100.00	$ 100.00	$ 100.00	$ 100.00	$ 100.00	$ 100.00
11	Totals	$ 1,220.00	$ 470.00	$ 235.00	$ 490.00	$ 895.00	$ 255.00	$ 175.00	$ 235.00	$ 260.00

Exercise 15

◆ **Named Ranges**

On the Job

At times it may be easier to reference a cell or range of cells with a descriptive name. For example, a range name can make the formulas in your worksheet easier to understand, and the formatting and printing easier to accomplish.

As the owner of Restoration Architecture, you're naturally very busy. So when you learned about range names and how they can make certain tasks easier to understand and complete, you were eager to add them to your worksheets as soon as possible. In this exercise, you'll modify a recent bid analysis worksheet so you can try out range names.

Terms

Range name An identification label assigned to a group of cells.

Name box The text box located to the left of the Formula bar.

Notes

Named Ranges

- A **range name** is a descriptive name assigned to two or more cells for identification.

- After naming a range, you can use the range name anyplace the range address might otherwise be entered—within a formula, defining the print range, selecting a range to format, and so on.

  ✓ *As you learned in Exercise 14, you don't have to name ranges to use your row and column labels in formulas. See Exercise 14 for more information.*

- Range names cannot be repeated within a workbook, even if they are located on different worksheets.

- Range names can be referenced across worksheets.

- A range name may use up to 255 characters, although short descriptive names are easier to read and remember.

- Some rules for naming ranges are:
  - Spaces are not allowed. Use the underscore character to simulate a space.
  - Do not use range names that could be interpreted as a cell address or a number, such as Q2 or Y2004.
  - A range name may include letters, numbers, underscores (_), backslashes (\), periods (.), and question marks (?).
  - You cannot begin a range name with a number.
  - Avoid using your column and row labels as range names, because they could create errors if you should accidentally turn on the natural language feature in the same workbook.

  ✓ *For example, suppose you had a worksheet with column labels Jan, Feb, Mar and so on, and you created a range in the January column and named it Jan.*

✓ *Then suppose you forgot about that and turned on natural language formulas, typed the formula =SUM(Jan) at the end of the January column, and copied the formula to the Feb and Mar columns*

✓ *If you hadn't created the range name Jan, then Excel would have created the formulas =SUM(Feb) and =SUM(Mar) as expected. But because you did, Excel treats the range name as an absolute reference and displays the formula =SUM(Jan) in both the February and March columns, resulting in errors.*

Name box

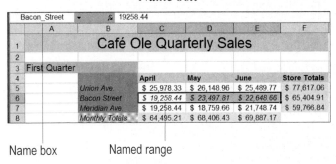

Name box   Named range

Define Name dialog box

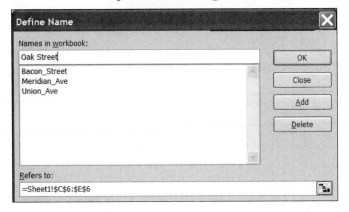

■ Use the Name, Define command or the **name box** to the left of the formula bar to assign a name to a selected range.

■ If you have a lot of named ranges in a workbook, you might want to have Excel insert a list of all your named ranges with their corresponding cell references into the worksheet.

Procedures

Name Range with Menu

1. Select range to name.
2. Click **Insert** .... Alt + I
3. Click **Name** .... N
4. Click **Define** .... D

   ✓ *Note that the selected range appears in Refers to text box and the nearest column or row label appears in Names in workbook text box.*

5. Type name in **Names in workbook** text box ...... Alt + W
6. Click **Add** button

   Add .... Alt + A
7. Click **OK** .... Enter

Name Range with Name Box

1. Select range on worksheet to name.
2. Click in name box.
3. Type name.
4. Press **Enter** .... Enter

Modify Named Range

1. Click **Insert** .... Alt + I
2. Click **Name** .... N
3. Click **Define** .... D

   ✓ *Active cell reference appears in Refers to text box.*

   To delete name:

   a. Click name in list .... Tab, ↑↓
   b. Click **Delete** .... Alt + D

   To change name:

   a. Click name in list .... Tab, ↑↓
   b. Double-click in **Names in workbook** .... Alt + W
   c. Type new name for range.
   d. Click **Add** button

   Add .... Alt + A

e. Click old name in list .... Tab, ↑↓
f. Click **Delete** button

   Delete ...... Alt + D

To change range defined by a name:

a. Click name in list .... Tab, ↑↓
b. Drag through reference in **Refers to** text box .. Alt + R
c. Use collapse button to select cells in worksheet.
   OR
   Type new cell reference.
4. Click **OK** .... Enter

Select Cells in a Named Range

Using Name Box:

1. Click drop-down arrow in name box.
2. Click desired named range.

Using Go To:

1. Press **F5**............................ F5
2. Click name in
   Go to text box .... Alt+G, ↕
3. Click **OK**........................... Enter

Insert List of Named Ranges in Worksheet

1. Click in upper-left cell of range to receive list.
2. Click **Insert** .... Alt+I
3. Click **Name** .... N
4. Click **Paste**........................ P
5. Select range.
6. Click **Paste List**
   button [Paste List] ...... Alt+L

✓ List includes range name with corresponding sheet name and cell references.

Set Named Range as Print Area

✓ This procedure allows you to designate the area you want to print on a regular basis by simply referring to its range name.

1. Click **File**..................... Alt+F
2. Click **Page Setup** .... U
3. Click **Sheet** tab .... Ctrl+Tab
4. Click **Print area** .... Alt+A
   text box.
5. Type name of range.
6. Click **Print** button
   [Print...] .... Alt+P

✓ Choose print options as needed.

7. Click **OK**........................... Enter

Print Named Range

✓ This procedure allows you to select a range quickly and print it, without changing the regular print area.

1. Follow steps to select named range.
2. Click **File** .... Alt+F
3. Click **Print** .... P
4. Click **OK**.......................... Enter

Exercise Directions

1. Start Excel, if necessary.
2. Open 🖮**BidAnalysis**, created in Exercise 13, or open 💿**15BidAnalysis**.
3. Save the file as **BidAnalysis 2**.
4. Assign the range name **Homes** to cell D6.
5. Use the new range name to create a formula in cell C10 that calculates the base bid (the bid per unit times the number of units or homes to be restored).
6. Copy this formula to C11:C20.
7. Use the Format Painter to copy the format from cell B17 to cell C17.
8. To make printing easier later on, assign the following range names:

   ✓ To make selection easier, drag from the bottom right-hand corner of the range to the upper left-hand corner where the picture is located.

   a. Assign the range name **Bid_Results** to the range A1:G22.
   b. Assign the range name **Bid_Analysis** to the range A27:G45.

9. Using the Name box, practice selecting the range Bid_Results.
10. Using Go To, select the range Bid_Analysis.
11. Insert a list of named ranges in cell A47. See Illustration A.
12. Adjust column widths as needed.
13. Spell check the workbook.
14. Print the workbook. Your results should look similar to Illustration B.
15. Close the workbook, saving all changes.

Illustration A

	A	B	C	
43	Restoration Architecture	$ 89,445.00	$ 983,895.00	$ 6
44	Engineers Estimate	$ 91,500.00	$ 1,006,500.00	$ 6
45	Difference (+/-)	-2.25%	-2.25%	-5
46				
47	Bid_Analysis	='Bid Sheet'!$A$27:$G$45		
48	Bid_Results	='Bid Sheet'!$A$1:$G$22		
49	Homes	='Bid Sheet'!$D$6		
50				

Illustration B

	A	B	C	D	E	F	G
	C10	▼	*fx*	=B10*Homes			
4							
5		\multicolumn{6}{l}{Bid Results - Canal Street Neighborhood Homes Restoration Project}					
6		No. of homes to be restored:		11			
7	Restoration Architecture						
8				Additional Bids on Project			
9		Unit Bid	Base Bid	Alt #1	Alt #2	Alt #3	Base Bid + Alt
10	BJW, Ltd.	$ 97,854.00	$ 1,076,394.00	$ 6,981.00	$ 9,726.00	$ 12,758.00	$ 1,105,859.00
11	Craftsman, Inc.	$ 89,475.00	$ 984,225.00	$ 7,051.00	$ 8,974.00	$ 12,332.00	$ 1,012,582.00
12	Meguro Construction	$ 92,441.00	$ 1,016,851.00	$ 6,200.00	$ 9,795.00	$ 9,785.00	$ 1,042,631.00
13	Mendoza Inc.	$ 88,459.00	$ 973,049.00	$ 7,500.00	$ 8,945.00	$ 10,235.00	$ 999,729.00
14	New Mark Designs	$ 99,487.00	$ 1,094,357.00	$ 5,985.00	$ 9,760.00	$ 9,989.00	$ 1,120,091.00
15	Ravuru Renovations	$ 92,335.00	$ 1,015,685.00	$ 6,193.00	$ 8,554.00	$ 11,995.00	$ 1,042,427.00
16	Renovation Ventures	$ 91,415.00	$ 1,005,565.00	$ 6,300.00	$ 10,000.00	$ 10,335.00	$ 1,032,200.00
17	Restoration Architecture	$ 89,445.00	$ 983,895.00	$ 6,115.00	$ 9,784.00	$ 11,578.00	$ 1,011,372.00
18	TOH Construction	$ 91,225.00	$ 1,003,475.00	$ 6,451.00	$ 10,800.00	$ 10,100.00	$ 1,030,826.00
19	Williams Brothers Renovators, Ltd.	$ 96,485.00	$ 1,061,335.00	$ 5,531.00	$ 9,875.00	$ 10,600.00	$ 1,087,341.00
20	Woo Home Designs	$ 93,415.00	$ 1,027,565.00	$ 6,751.00	$ 10,633.00	$ 10,049.00	$ 1,054,998.00

On Your Own

1. Open **OXL13**, created in the On Your Own section of Exercise 13, or open **15CDMANIA**.
2. Save the file as **OXL15**.
3. Delete the data in the range B23:G27.
4. Name the range B4:B8 **JanTotal**.
5. Repeat step 4 for the Feb, Mar, Apr, May, and June data ranges.
   ✓ For example, select the range C4:C8 and name it FebTotal.
6. Using these new range names, reenter the formulas in cells B23:G25.
   ✓ For example, in cell B23, enter =AVERAGE(JanTotal). In cell B24, enter MIN(JanTotal), and in cell B25, enter MAX(JanTotal).
7. Name the range B4:E8 **Qtr1**. Name the range B13:E17 **Qtr2**.
8. Use these two range names to reenter the formula in cell B27, using the COUNTIF function.
9. Redefine the Qtr1 range to be A3:D8. Redefine the Qtr2 range to be A12:D17.
10. Print just the Qtr1 range, then print just the Qtr2 range.
11. Widen columns as needed.
12. Spell check the worksheet.
13. Print the worksheet.
14. Close the workbook, saving all changes.

Exercise 16

Skills Covered:

◆ **Understand IF Functions** ◆ **Nested IF Functions**
◆ **=SUMIF() Statements** ◆ **=COUNTIF() Statements**

On the Job

IF functions allow you to test for particular conditions and then perform specific actions based on the whether those conditions exist or not. For example, with an IF function, you could calculate the bonuses for a group of salespeople on the premise that bonuses are only paid if a sale is over $1,000. With the SUMIF function, you could total up the sales in your Atlanta office, even if those sales figures are scattered through a long list of sales figures. And with the COUNTIF function, you could count the number of sales that resulted in a bonus being paid.

You're the manager of a Whole Grains Bread store in Olympia, Washington, and you've been fiddling with a new worksheet for tracking retail bread sales. You've just learned about various IF functions, and, along with some other new functions you've discovered, you know you can refine the worksheet so that it's simple for your employees to use. With the sales analysis the worksheet will provide, you can refine the retail end of your business to maximize your profits.

Terms

Function A preprogrammed Excel formula for a complex calculation.

Condition A statement in an IF function that if true yields one result and if false yields another result.

Nesting Using a function as an argument within another function.

Argument A variable used in a function. An argument can be a number, text, formula, or a cell reference. A comma separates each argument in a function.

Criteria Similar to a condition. In the case of a SUMIF or COUNIF function, the criteria tells Excel which cells to count or sum. You list the criteria, such as >2000, and Excel counts or sums only the cells with values greater than 2000.

Notes

Understand IF Functions

- With an IF **function**, you can tell Excel to perform one of two different calculations based on whether your data matches a certain **condition**.

  ✓ *For example, you can use an IF function to have Excel calculate a 10% bonus if total sales are over $500,000 and just a 3% bonus if they are not.*

- The format for an IF statement is:
  =IF(*condition,x,y*)
  - The *condition* is a True/False statement.
  - If the condition is true, the result is *x*.
  - If the condition is false, the result is *y*.

- To calculate the bonus described here, you would type =IF(B2>500000,B2*.10,B2*.03)

✓ This function says, "If total sales (cell B2) are greater than $500,000, then take total sales times 10% to calculate the bonus. Otherwise, take total sales times 3%."

✓ Notice that in the IF function, the value, $500,000, is entered without the dollar sign or the comma.

■ You can have words appear in a cell instead of the result of a calculation.

✓ For example, you might type **=IF(B2>500000,"We made it!","Good try.")** to display the words **We made it!** if total sales are over $500,000, or the words **Good try.** if they are not.

✓ Notice here that the words you want to use are surrounded by quotation marks " ".

■ IF statements may use the conditional operators below to state the condition:

=	Equals	<>	Not equal to
>	Greater than	>=	Greater than or equal to
<	Less than	<=	Less than or equal to
&	Used for joining text		

■ For help in entering an IF function, Excel provides a ScreenTip that lists the IF function arguments in order.

■ You can also type =IF(and click the Insert Function button to display the Function Arguments dialog box, which provides a text box for each argument, making it easier to enter them correctly.

Function Arguments dialog box

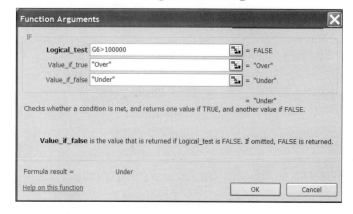

Nested IF Functions

■ You can **nest** an IF function (or any other function) as one of the **arguments** in another function.

■ For example, the formula:
=IF(C3>92,"A",IF(C3>83,"B",IF(C3>73,"C",
IF(C3>65,"D","F"))))

✓ If the average score is greater than 92, then the student gets an A; if the score is less than or equal to 92 but greater than 83, the student gets a B; if the score is less than or equal to 83 but greater than 73, the student gets a C; and so on.

=SUMIF() Statements

■ A SUMIF statement is a logical function that uses a condition to add certain data.

■ If the condition is true, then data in a corresponding cell is added to the total; if it is false, then the corresponding data is skipped.

■ The format for a SUMIF statement is =SUMIF(*range*, **criteria**, *sum_range*)

● The *range* is the range of cells you want to test.

● The *condition* is a True/False statement that defines which cells should be added to the total.

● If the condition is true, the corresponding cell in *sum_range* is added to the total.

● If the condition is false, the corresponding cell in *sum_range* is skipped (not added to the total).

✓ The condition is written using the same symbols (such as >,<>, etc.) as listed in the IF section. However, here, you must enclose the condition in quotation marks "".

■ For example, if you had a worksheet listing sales for several different products, you could total the sales for widgets only by using this formula: =SUMIF(D2:D55,"Widget",G2:G55)

● Assume here that column D contains the name of the product being sold and column G contains the total amount for that sale.

● If column D contains the word "Widget" then the amount for that sale (located in column G) is added to the running total.

✓ Because Widget is a text label, in the formula you must enclose it in quotation marks (" ").

■ You can leave the last argument off if you want to sum the same range that you're testing. For example: =SUMIF(G2:G10,"<=500")

✓ This formula calculates the total of all values in the range G2 to G10 that are less than or equal to 500.

=COUNTIF() Statements

- A COUNTIF statement is a logical function that uses a condition to count the number of items in a range.

- If the result of the condition is true, then the item is added to a running count; if it is false, then the item is skipped.

- The format for a COUNTIF statement is =COUNTIF(*range*, *criteria*).

  - The *range* is the range of cells you want to test.

  - The *condition* is a True/False statement that defines which cells should be counted.

    ✓ *The condition is written using the same symbols listed in the IF section. Again, enclose the condition in quotation marks " ".*

- For example, if you count the number of individual Widget sales, you could use this formula: =COUNTIF(D2:D55,"=Widget")

- Assume here that column D contains the name of the product being sold.

- If column D contains the word "Widget" then that sale is added to the running total.

  ✓ *Because Widget is a text label, you must enclose it in quotation marks (" ").*

- You can combine functions to create complex calculations: =SUMIF(D3:D13,"PASS",C3:C13) /COUNTIF(D3:D13,"PASS")

  - This formula computes the average score of all the students who passed the course.

  - Assume that column D contains the words "Pass" or "Fail" based on the student's final score. The final score is located in column C.

  - The formula sums the scores of all the students who passed and divides that by the number of students who passed, calculating an average score.

Procedures

Enter IF Function

1. Click desired cell.
2. Press **Equal** .... 🔲
3. Type **IF**.

   ✓ *You can click the Insert Functions button* 𝑓x *at this point to display the Function Arguments dialog box, which may make entering the IF function easier, or you can simply type the rest of the function by following these steps.*

4. Press **Left Parenthesis** ...... 🔲
5. Type condition.
6. Press **Comma** .... 🔲
7. Type argument if condition is true.
8. Press **Comma** .... 🔲
9. Type argument if condition is false.
10. Press **Right** Parenthesis..... 🔲

11. Press **Enter** .... Enter

    ✓ *IF statements may be used in combination with OR, AND, and NOT statements to evaluate complex conditions. For example, =IF(OR(B3>C3,B3<1000), D4*1.05,D4*1.03), which says "If B3 is greater than C3 or less than 1000, take D4 times 105%, otherwise, take D4 times 103%"*

Enter SUMIF Function

1. Click desired cell.
2. Press **Equal**........................ 🔲
3. Type **SUMIF**.
4. Press **Left Parenthesis**....... 🔲
5. Type range to test.

   ✓ *You can select the range instead of typing it.*

6. Press **Comma**.................... 🔲
7. Type condition in quotation marks.
8. Press **Comma**.................... 🔲

9. Type range to sum if condition is true.

   ✓ *You can select the range instead of typing it.*

   ✓ *Skip steps 8-9 if the range you're testing is the same as the range you want to sum.*

10. Press **Right Parenthesis**.... 🔲
11. Press **Enter**..................... Enter

Enter COUNTIF Function

1. Click desired cell.
2. Press **Equal** .... 🔲
3. Type **COUNTIF**.
4. Press **Left Parenthesis** ...... 🔲
5. Type range to count.

   ✓ *You can select the range instead of typing it.*

6. Press **Comma** .... 🔲
7. Type condition to test.
8. Press **Right Parenthesis**.... 🔲
9. Press **Enter**.................... Enter

Exercise Directions

1. Start Excel, if necessary.
2. Open 🖸 **16DailyBreadSales**.
3. Save the file as **DailyBreadSales**.
4. In cell N2, use the IF function to enter a formula that displays the value 2.00 if today is a Monday and 2.55 if it is not.
   - ✓ You discount white and wheat bread on Mondays.
   - ✓ To determine if it is Monday, use the WEEKDAY function as the first argument in your IF function, like this:

     =IF(WEEKDAY(argument),then do this, else do this).
   - ✓ As you can see, the WEEKDAY function uses only a single argument, in parentheses, and that argument is the address of the cell that contains the date you want to look at, which in this case is cell J6.
   - ✓ So using the WEEKDAY function fulfills your first argument for the IF function. Based on result of this condition, tell the IF function to return the value 2, then it is Monday or 2.55 if it is not.
5. Enter a similar formula in cell N3, charging 2.00 for wheat bread if it's Monday and 2.60 if it is not.
   - ✓ The date entered in cell J6 is a Monday. So if you enter the formulas correctly in cells N2 and N3, the value 2.00 will display.
6. In cell D42, use the COUNT function to count the number of coupon sales. See Illustration A.
   - ✓ The COUNT function counts nonblank cells in the range you specify, so use it to count the nonblank cells in the Coupon column.
7. In cell D43, use the COUNTBLANK function to count the number of noncoupon sales (the number of blank cells in the Coupon column).
8. In cell D45, use the COUNTIF function to count the number of sales with a credit card.
   - ✓ Count the number of cells with an "x" in the Credit column.
   - ✓ For COUNTIF, the first argument is the range of cells which in this case is the range of cells in the Credit column.
   - ✓ The second argument is the value to look for in order to include the cell in the total count. In this case, you want to tell Excel to look for an x. Since the argument is text, it must be in quotes, like this "x".

9. In cell D46, use the COUNTIF function to enter a similar formula that counts the number of cash sales.
10. In cell D48, use the COUNT function to count the number of sales in the Total Sale column.
11. In cell E42, use the SUMIF function to calculate the revenue from coupon sales.
    - ✓ If a cell in the Coupon column contains a value greater than zero, add the corresponding value in the Total Sale column.
    - ✓ The SUMIF function requires three arguments. The first argument is the range of cells to compare, which in this case is the range of cells in the Coupon column.
    - ✓ The second argument is the value to look for. In this case, you want to look for values greater than zero, which is expressed as >0. However, the criteria must be in quotations, so if you don't use the Insert Function dialog box to create the formula, be sure to type ">0" as the argument.
    - ✓ The last argument is the range of cells to total, which in this case is the range of cells in the Total Sales column.
12. In cell E43, use the SUMIF function to calculate the revenue from noncoupon sales.
    - ✓ You could type just =P37-E42, but for the purposes of this exercise, use SUMIF function. If a cell in the Coupon column is blank "", then add the corresponding value in the Total Sale column.
    - ✓ The first and last arguments are the same as those used in the SUMIF function you entered in cell E42.
    - ✓ The middle argument is the criteria. In this case, you want to total all cells that are blank. To indicate that, simply type "".
13. In cell E45, use the SUMIF function to calculate the revenue from credit card sales.
    - ✓ If a cell in the Credit column contains an "x" then add the corresponding value in the Total Sale column.
    - ✓ The first argument in this SUMIF function is the range of cells in the Credit column; the last argument is the range of cells in the Total Sale column.
    - ✓ The middle argument (the criteria) is the value, x. Since it is text, you must enter the argument with quotations, like this "x".

14. Create a similar formula in cell E46 to total the revenue from cash sales.

15. Use the SUM function in cell E48 to total the sales revenue from the Total Sales column.

   ✓ You could also use the formula =P37 to simply display the total revenue displayed in that cell.

16. Widen columns as needed.

17. Spell check the worksheet.

18. Print the worksheet.

19. Close the workbook, saving all changes.

Illustration A

	A	B	C	D	E	F
40						
41	Recap					
42		Coupon Sales		11	$ 146.72	
43		Sales w/o Coupon		13	$ 290.09	
44						
45		Credit Sales		14	$ 164.58	
46		Cash Sales		10	$ 272.23	
47						
48		Total Sales		24	$ 436.81	
49						

On Your Own

1. Open **OXL14**, the school expenses workbook you created in the On Your Own section of Exercise 14, or open ⊙ **16COLEXP**.

2. Save the workbook as **OXL16**.

3. Below the expense data, add a row labeled **Income**, and input monthly income figures.

   ✓ Your income should be only slightly above your monthly expenses.

4. Enter a formula that calculates your total income for the school year.

5. Enter a formula for calculating the net income (total income minus total expenses) for each month and for the school year.

6. Use an IF function to determine if you will have enough money left in the budget at the end of the year to purchase a new color printer for your computer. The printer costs $279. If you have enough, the formula should display **Yes!**. If you do not have enough, the formula should display **Maybe next year**.

7. Widen columns as needed.

8. Spell check the workbook.

9. Print the workbook.

10. Close the workbook, saving all changes.

Exercise 17

Skills Covered:

◆ **Chart Basics** ◆ **Select Chart Data** ◆ **Chart Elements**
◆ **Create Charts** ◆ **Change Chart Types** ◆ **Select a Chart**
◆ **Resize, Copy, Move, or Delete a Chart**

On the Job

A chart presents Excel data in a graphical format—making the relationship between data items easier to understand. To present your data in the best format, you must select the proper chart type. For example, if you wanted to highlight your department's recent reduction in overtime, you might use a column or bar chart. Whereas, to compare your division's sales with other divisions, you might use a pie chart instead.

The modifications you made to your daily bread sales worksheet is working out very well. Now, as Manager of a Whole Grains Bread store, you're ready to take it to the next level: charts. Being able to visually compare the sales of the various items in your retail store will help you to make the modifications you need to make to maximize profits, so in this exercise, you'll add two charts.

Terms

Chart A graphic that allows you to compare and contrast data in a visual format.

Embedded chart A chart placed as an object within a worksheet.

Chart sheet A chart that occupies its own worksheet.

Plot To position data points on a graph.

Data series For most charts, a data series is the information in a worksheet column. If you select multiple columns of data for a chart, you'll create multiple data series. Each data series is then represented by its own color bar, line, or column.

Legend A key that identifies each of the data series in a chart.

X-axis The horizontal scale of a chart on which categories are plotted.

Y-axis The vertical scale of a chart on which the value of each category is plotted.

Categories For most charts, a category is information in a worksheet row. If you select multiple rows of data for a chart, you'll create multiple categories, and these categories will be listed along the x-axis.

Notes

Chart Basics

- **Charts** provide a way of presenting and comparing data in a graphic format.

- You can create **embedded charts** or **chart sheets**.

- When you create an embedded chart, the chart exists as an object in the worksheet alongside the data.

  ✓ *All illustrations in this exercise use embedded charts.*

- When you create a chart sheet, the chart exists on a separate sheet in the workbook.

- All charts are linked to the data they **plot**. When you change data in the plotted area of the worksheet, the chart changes automatically.

Select Chart Data

- To create a chart, you first select the data to plot. Here are some guidelines for selecting your chart data:

  - The selection should not contain blank columns or rows.

    ✓ *If the data is not in a single range, just press Ctrl and select each range separately, making sure not to select blank rows or columns that may separate the ranges.*

Adjacent and nonadjacent selections

	B	C	D	E
3	**Profit and Loss Statement**			Adjacent
4	**Spring Quarter, 1997**			selection
5				
6	**Income**	**January**	**February**	**March**
7	**Wholesale**	$ 125,650	$122,645	$156,210
8	**Retail Sales**	$ 135,120	$125,645	$145,887
9	**Special Sales**	$ 10,255	$ 21,541	$ 15,647
10			Non-adjacent	
11	**Totals by Month**	$ 271,025	selection	317,744
12				
13	**Expenses**	**January**	**February**	**March**
14	**Disk Production**	$ 15,642	$ 14,687	$ 18,741
15	**Packaging**	$ 2,564	$ 2,407	$ 3,071
16	**Promotions**	$ 4,525	$ 4,248	$ 5,420
17				
18	**Totals by Month**	$ 22,731	$ 21,342	$ 27,232

  - You can select multiple ranges to plot on a single chart.

- You can hide columns or rows you do not wish to plot.

- The selection should include the labels for the data when possible.

- A blank cell in the upper-left corner of a selection tells Excel that the data below and to the right of the blank cell contains labels for the values to plot.

- The selection determines the orientation of the data series (in columns or rows). However, you may change the orientation as desired.

Chart Elements

- The parts of a column chart are labeled in the illustration below.

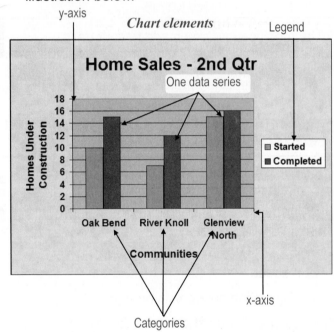

Chart elements

- As you move your mouse over each part of a chart, the name of the chart element displays.

- Typically each chart includes the following parts:

  - **Data series**
    If you include more than one kind of data for each item (such as homes started and homes completed in each community), then you'll create multiple **data series** for each item. In this example, each community was listed on its own row, with data in a Started and a Completed column. On the chart, each series is represented on the chart by a different color bar, column, line, etc.

- **Series labels**

  Labels identifying the charted values. These labels appear in the chart **legend**, which identifies each data series in the chart.

- **Category labels**

  Labels identifying each category shown on the horizontal or **x-axis**. In the sample, each neighborhood community is a different category.

■ For charts which use axes (all except pie charts):

- The **y-axis** is the vertical scale, except on 3-D charts. The scale values are based on the values being charted.

- The x-axis is the horizontal scale and typically represents the **categories** and the various data series.

- The x-axis title describes the x-axis (horizontal) data. (*Communities* in the illustration here.)

- The y-axis title describes the y-axis (vertical) data. (*Homes Under Construction* in the illustration here.)

Create Charts

■ You create charts with the Chart Wizard, which uses tabbed dialog boxes to step you through the entire process.

■ As you make selections, the Chart Wizard shows you exactly how the chart will look.

  ✓ *Previewing your chart enables you to select the chart type and other elements best suited to your data.*

■ Each chart type contains chart subtypes, which are variations on the selected chart type.

■ Excel also offers several customized chart types for specialized data.

Change Chart Types

■ After creating a chart, you can easily change its chart type to something else.

■ There are many chart types from which you can choose:

- **Column charts** compare individual or sets of values. The height of each bar is proportional to its corresponding value in the worksheet.

  ✓ *All of the chart types listed here are available in a 3-D format.*

- **Bar charts** are basically column charts turned on their sides. Like column charts, bar charts compare the values of various items.

- **Line charts** connect points of data and show changes over time effectively. Line charts are especially useful to plot trends.

- **Area charts** are like "filled in" line charts; you use them to track changes over time.

- **Pie charts** are circular graphs used to show the relationship of each value in a data range to the entire set of data. The size of each wedge represents the percentage each value contributes to the total.

  ✓ *Only one numerical data range may be used in a pie chart. For example, if you have sales data for 2003 and 2004 for tricycles, offroad bikes, and helmets, you can only chart one year. If you select all the data, it will be lumped into one big pie, with each element (2003 and 2004 tricycles, 2003 and 2004 offroad bikes, etc.) representing a slice.*

  ✓ *Pie charts may be formatted to indicate the percentage each piece of the pie represents of the whole.*

■ A chart can be copied and then edited to produce a different chart that uses the same worksheet data.

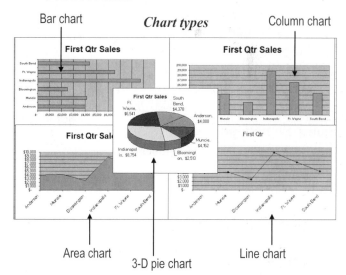

Bar chart · *Chart types* · Column chart

Area chart · 3-D pie chart · Line chart

Select a Chart

■ To resize, copy, or move a chart, you must first select it by clicking anywhere on the chart.

■ A selected chart displays sizing handles. In addition, the Chart toolbar usually appears.

Resize, Copy, Move, or Delete a Chart

- You can resize, copy, or move an embedded chart as needed.

- You can't resize a chart on a chart sheet; however, you can copy or move the chart around on the sheet.

- You can move a chart on a chart sheet to another sheet, creating an embedded object. You can reverse the process when needed to change an embedded chart into a chart sheet.

- If you copy a chart, you can change the copied chart type to present data in a different way.

Procedures

Select Adjacent Data

1. Click on blank cell in upper left-hand corner of data range.
2. Drag downward and right, until you have selected entire data range, including label cells.

Select Nonadjacent Data

1. Click and drag over cells in first range you want to select.
2. Press **Ctrl** and drag over another range of cells. .... `Ctrl`
3. Repeat for additional ranges.

Create Chart with Chart Wizard

1. Select data to chart.
2. Click **Chart Wizard** button 📊.
   OR
   a. Click **Insert** .... `Alt`+`I`
   b. Click **Chart** .... `H`
3. Follow steps to create standard or custom chart type.
4. Click the **Finish** button
   [Finish] .... `Alt`+`F`

Select Embedded Chart

1. Click once on chart to select it.
2. To deselect chart, click anywhere in worksheet.

Select Chart Sheet

1. Click chart sheet's tab.
2. To deselect chart sheet, click different worksheet tab.

Change Chart's Type

1. Select chart or chart sheet.
2. Click **Chart** .... `Alt`+`C`
3. Click **Chart Type** .... `Y`
4. Select standard or custom chart type.

To select standard chart type:

a. Select chart type in **Chart type** list box .... `Alt`+`C`
b. Select sub-type for selected chart in **Chart sub-type** list box .... `Alt`+`T`
c. If desired, click and hold **Press and Hold to View Sample**
   [Press and Hold to View Sample]
   to display preview.

To select custom chart type:

a. Click **Custom Types** tab .... `Ctrl`+`Tab`
b. Select **User-defined** .... `Alt`+`U`
   OR
   Select **Built-in** .... `Alt`+`B`
c. Select desired custom chart in **Chart type** list .... `Alt`+`C`

5. To set current chart type as default, click **Set as default chart** button
   [Set as default chart] .... `Alt`+`E`
6. Click **OK** .... `Enter`

Resize Embedded Chart

1. Select chart you want to resize.
2. Move mouse pointer to handle.

   ✓ Mouse pointer becomes ⬊ when positioned correctly.

   ✓ To size object proportionally, press Shift and point to corner handle.

3. Click handle and drag it outwards to make chart bigger, or inwards to make it smaller.

   ✓ To align edges of chart to worksheet gridlines, press Alt key as you drag.

4. Release mouse button and chart is resized.

Move Chart

1. Select chart you want to move.
2. Click chart and drag it to its new location.

   ✓ As you drag, outline of chart follows mouse pointer.

3. Release mouse button and chart is moved.

Switch from Embedded Chart to Chart Sheet or Vice-Versa

1. Right-click the chart.
2. Select **Location** .... `Alt`+`L`
3. Select **As new sheet** .. `Alt`+`S`
   OR
   As object in .... `Alt`+`O`
4. Click **OK** .... `Enter`

Copy Chart

1. Select chart you want to copy.
2. Click **Copy** button .
3. Click elsewhere in worksheet.
4. Click **Paste** button 📋.

   ✓ You can change chart type of copied chart to view its data in a different way.

Delete Embedded Chart

1. Select chart you want to delete.
2. Press **Delete** .... `Del`

Delete Chart Sheet

1. Click **Edit** .... `Alt`+`E`
2. Click **Delete Sheet** .... `L`
3. Click **OK** .... `Enter`
   OR
1. Right-click sheet tab.
2. Select **Delete** .... `E`

Exercise Directions

1. Start Excel, if necessary.

2. Open ⌨ **DailyBreadSales** or open 💿 **17DailyBreadSales**.

3. Save it as **DailyBreadSales 2**.

4. Select the ranges A12:L12 and A37:L37.

5. Use the Chart Wizard to create your first chart. Make the following selections:

   a. Select the Pie with 3-D visual effect chart type.

   b. Display the data series in rows.

   c. Enter the chart title **Daily Sales by Percentage**.

   d. Do not display the legend.

   e. Display data labels that include the Category name and the Percentage. Include the leader lines.

   f. Save the chart on a new worksheet called **Daily Percentages**. (See Illustration A.)

6. To create a second chart that displays the data in a different format, copy the first chart.

   a. Paste the copied chart to cell A53 of the Retail worksheet.

   b. Change the copied chart from an embedded chart to a chart sheet.

   c. Name the new sheet **Daily Sales**.

7. Change the chart type of the copied chart to Clustered column. (See Illustration B.)

8. Spell check the workbook.

9. Print the workbook.

10. Close the workbook, saving all changes.

Illustration A

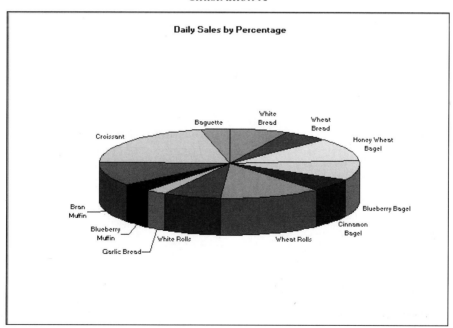

Illustration B

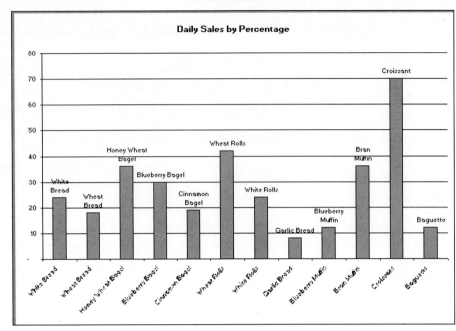

On Your Own

1. Start Excel, if necessary.

2. Open **OXL15**, created in the On Your Own section of Exercise 15, or open **17CDMANIA**.

3. Save the workbook as **OXL17**.

4. Create two charts, stored on chart sheets, using the quarter 1 and quarter 2 totals, respectively.

   ✓ *Be sure to use two different chart types when creating the two charts.*

5. Add sheet titles, chart titles, legends, data labels, and other options as desired to each chart.

   ✓ *Some charts just won't look great until you format them, which you'll learn to do in the next exercise. So resize the charts as best you can to achieve a margin of respectability, and then apply your formatting next exercise to create exactly the effect you want.*

6. Change the Quarter 1 chart to an embedded chart on Sheet 2. Resize and move the chart as needed to fully display its data.

7. Copy the Quarter 1 chart to another location on Sheet 2. Change the chart type of the copied chart.

8. Create a third chart that displays the average sales for January through June. Save the chart as an embedded object on Sheet 3.

9. Add sheet titles, chart titles, legends, data labels, and other options as desired. Resize and move the chart as needed.

10. Spell check the workbook.

11. Print the workbook.

12. Close the workbook, saving all changes.

Exercise 18

Skills Covered:

◆ **Use Chart Toolbar** ◆ **Resize, Move, or Delete a Chart Object**
◆ **Change Chart Text** ◆ **Enhance Chart Background**
◆ **Format Category and Value Axes**

On the Job

There are many ways in which you can enhance your chart: you can format the chart text, add color or pattern to the chart background, and format the value and category axes so that the numbers are easier to read.

The charts you created to analyze daily bread sales in the retail portion of your Whole Grains Bread store are almost completed. Before printing, you want to format them to make them more professional looking and easier to understand.

Terms

Object An item that is treated separately from the main document. In the case of a chart, each chart element is an object that can be manipulated independently.

Chart area The total area occupied by a chart.

Plot area The area defined by the x and y axes.

Tick marks Lines of measurement along the value and category axes.

Notes

Use Chart Toolbar

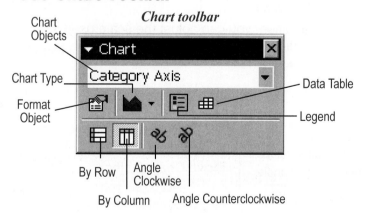

Chart toolbar

- Chart Objects list allows you to select any part of a chart so you can delete or format it.

- Format Object displays format options for the selected chart object.

- Chart Type allows you to change the chart type associated with the selected chart.

- Legend hides or displays the chart legend.

- Data Table hides or displays data used in the chart.

- By Row creates a data series for each row of data.

- By Column creates a data series for each column of data.

- Angle Clockwise angles text downward.

- Angle Counterclockwise angles text upward.

■ Normally, when you select a chart or one of its parts, the Chart toolbar appears.

  ✓ *If needed, you can access the Chart toolbar from the View menu.*

■ The Chart toolbar provides the following tools:

Resize, Move, or Delete a Chart Object

- Before you can resize, move, or delete an **object**, you must select it first.

- By resizing, moving, or deleting the parts of your chart, you may make it more attractive and easier to read.

- If you resize an object that contains text, the font size of the text changes correspondingly.

- When you delete an object from a chart, the remaining parts of the chart are enlarged to fill the gap.

- You can change the value represented by a column or bar by resizing it.

Change Chart Text

- You can edit chart text or change its formatting. For example, you can change the size, font, and attributes of text.

Enhance Chart Background

- A chart actually has two backgrounds: the larger **chart area** and the smaller **plot area**, as shown in the figure to the right.

- You can format the chart area, the plot area, or both.

- To format either chart background, you can:
  - Add a border around the background area.
  - Apply a color to the background.
  - Apply a fill effect, such as gradient (a blend of two colors), texture (such as marble), pattern (such as diagonal stripes), or picture (a graphic file).
  - Add a shadow effect behind the border (chart area only).
  - Round the corners (chart area only).

Chart backgrounds

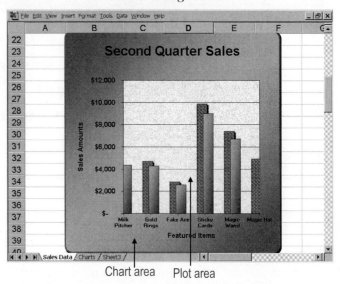

Chart area   Plot area

Format Category and Value Axes

- The category axis, or x-axis, represents the horizontal axis for most charts. Categories and data series are plotted along the category axis.

- The value axis, or y-axis, represents the vertical axis for most charts. The values of various categories or data series are plotted along the value axis.

- You can change the font, size, color, attributes, alignment, and placement of text or numbers along both the category and value axes.

- You can also change the appearance of the **tick marks**.

- In addition, you can adjust the scale used along the value axis.

Procedures

Select Chart Object

- Click the object you wish to select.

OR

- Select the object's name from the Chart Objects list on the Chart toolbar.

Resize Chart Object

1. Select object you want to resize.
2. Move mouse pointer over handle.

   ✓ *Mouse pointer becomes* 🔲 *when positioned correctly.*

   ✓ *To size object proportionally, press Shift and point to corner handle.*

3. Click handle and drag it outwards to make object bigger, or inwards to make it smaller.

4. Release mouse button and object is resized.

Move Chart Object

1. Select object you want to move.
2. Click object and drag it to its new location.

   ✓ *As you drag, outline of object follows mouse pointer.*

3. Release mouse button and object is moved.

Delete Chart Object

1. Select object you want to delete.
2. Press **Delete** .... Del

   ✓ *You can select the plot area, but you can't delete it.*

Change Chart Text

1. Click chart object that contains text you wish to change.
2. Edit the text using normal text editing techniques.
3. Click anywhere outside of chart text when finished.

   ✓ *You can apply any formatting you want to the selected text.*

Enhance Chart Background

1. Select either chart or plot area.
2. Click **Format Chart Area/Format Plot Area** button 📋.
3. On the Patterns tab under Border, select **Automatic** to apply normal border style .... Alt+A
   OR
   a. Select **Custom**.
   b. Select border **Style**... Alt+S
   c. Select border **Color** .... Alt+C
   d. Select border thickness, or **Weight** .... Alt+W

   To fill area with color:
   - On the Patterns tab under Area, select **Automatic** to apply normal background color (usually white).......... Alt+U
   OR
   - Select desired color from color palette.
   OR
   a. Click **Fill Effects** button

      [Fill Effects...]
      Alt+I
   b. On Gradient tab, choose color option you want:
      - Select **One color** .... Alt+O

- Choose color you want to blend from **Color 1** drop-down list ... Alt+1
- Adjust transition from **Dark** to **Light** .... Alt+K
   OR
- Select **Two colors** .... Alt+T
- Choose two colors you want to blend from **Color 1** and **Color 2** drop-down list boxes .. Alt+1, Alt+2
   OR
- Select **Preset** .... Alt+S
- Choose **Preset colors** option you want .. Alt+E
   c. Select one of the **Shading styles**.
   d. Select one of the **Variants** .... Alt+A

To fill area with texture:
a. Click **Texture** tab.
b. Select texture you want.

To fill area with pattern:
a. Click **Pattern** tab.
b. Select **Foreground** color .. Alt+F
c. Select **Background** color.. Alt+B
d. Click **Pattern** .... Alt+T

To fill area with a picture:
a. Click **Picture** tab.
b. Click **Select Picture** .... Alt+L
c. Select desired drive and folder from **Look in** drop-down list .... Alt+I
d. Double-click graphic file.

4. Click **OK** .... Enter
5. Click **OK** .... Enter

Format Category Axis

1. Select category axis.
2. Click **Format Axis** button 📋.
3. If desired, on Patterns tab, select setting:

- Select **Automatic** to apply normal line style ..... Alt+A
   OR
   a. Select **Custom**.
   b. Select border **Style** .. Alt+S
   c. Select border **Color** .... Alt+C
   d. Select border thickness, or **Weight** .... Alt+W
      OR
      Select **None** to remove the axis lines.
4. If desired, change **Major tick mark type** (change its location) .... Alt+M
5. If desired, change **Minor tick mark type** (change its location) .... Alt+R
6. If desired, change location of **Tick mark labels** .... Alt+T
7. Click **Scale** tab.
   a. To change point at which y-axis intersects category axis, enter category number in **Value (Y) axis crosses at category number** text box .... Alt+C
   b. To change frequency of category labels, enter number in **Number of categories between tick-mark labels** text box. (Enter a 2 to display every other label, etc.)...... Alt+L
   c. To change frequency of tick marks along category axis, enter number in **Number of categories between tick marks** text box .... Alt+K
   d. If you do not want first category to be placed right against y-axis, select **Value (Y) axis crosses between categories** .... Alt+B
   e. If desired, select **Categories in reverse order** .... Alt+R
   f. To place y-axis on the right, select **Value (Y) axis crosses at maximum category** .... Alt+M

8. Click **Font** tab and make desired changes to font, size, and other attributes of data labels.

9. Click **Alignment** tab and angle label text:
   - Drag **Text** marker to set degree of rotation.

   OR
   a. Enter positive number in **Degrees** text box to angle text from lower left to upper right, or negative number to angle text from upper left to lower right .... `Alt`+`D`
   b. Select amount of space you want between data labels and x-axis by adjusting **Offset** value........... `Alt`+`O`

10. Click **OK**.......................... `Enter`

Format Value Axis

1. Select value axis.

2. Click **Format Axis** button .

3. If desired, on Patterns tab, select setting:
   - Select **Automatic** to apply normal line style..... `Alt`+`A`

   OR
   a. Select **Custom**.

b. Select border **Style**... `Alt`+`S`
c. Select border **Color**........... `Alt`+`C`
d. Select border thickness, or **Weight** .... `Alt`+`W`
   OR
   Select **None** to remove the axis lines.

4. If desired, change **Major tick mark type** (location).... `Alt`+`M`

5. If desired, change **Minor tick mark type** (location).... `Alt`+`R`

6. If desired, change location of **Tick mark labels**......... `Alt`+`T`

7. Click **Scale** tab.
   a. Set **Minimum** and **Maximum** values used on y-axis .... `Alt`+`N`, `Alt`+`X`
   b. Adjust placement of major and minor tick marks along y-axis by changing values in **Major unit** and **Minor unit** text boxes... `Alt`+`A`, `Alt`+`I`
   c. To change point at which x-axis intersects value axis, enter value in **Category (X) axis crosses at** text box.................. `Alt`+`C`

d. If desired, adjust **Display units** value .... `Alt`+`U`
e. To display values as powers of 10, select **Logarithmic scale** option............ `Alt`+`L`
f. To display **Values in reverse order**, select that option.............. `Alt`+`R`
g. To move category axis to top of plot area, select **Category (X) axis crosses at maximum value**...................... `Alt`+`M`

8. Click **Font** tab and make desired changes to font, size, and other attributes of value labels.

9. Click **Number** tab and select format you wish for your value labels.

10. Click **Alignment** tab and angle label text:
    - Drag **Text** marker to set degree of rotation.

11. Click **OK**........................... `Enter`

Exercise Directions

1. Start Excel, if necessary.

2. Open ⌨ **DailyBreadSales 2** or open 💿 **18DailyBreadSales 2**.

3. Save it as **DailyBreadSales 3**.

4. Change to the Daily Sales chart sheet and make the following modifications:
   a. Remove the data labels.
   b. Change the chart title to **Daily Sales**.
   c. Apply a two color gradient to the Chart Area, using dark red and sea green in a horizontal shading style moving from red at the bottom to green at the top.
   d. Apply a light yellow text color to all text and numbers in the Chart Area.
   e. Apply the Stationery texture to Series 1.
   f. Format the Chart Title with Arial, 20 point light yellow font.

   g. Apply an Ivory fill color to the Value Axis, Major Gridlines, and the Category Axis. (See Illustration A.)

5. Change to the Daily Percentages chart sheet and make the following modifications:
   a. Add the picture 💿 **bread.jpg** to the background of the Chart Area.
   b. Apply Arial, 26-point bold font to the Chart Title.
   c. Apply Arial Black, 16-point font to the Series 1 Data Labels.
   d. Resize the Plot Area to make the pie chart bigger, as shown in Illustration B.

6. Spell check the workbook.

7. Print the workbook.

8. Close the workbook, saving all changes.

Illustration A

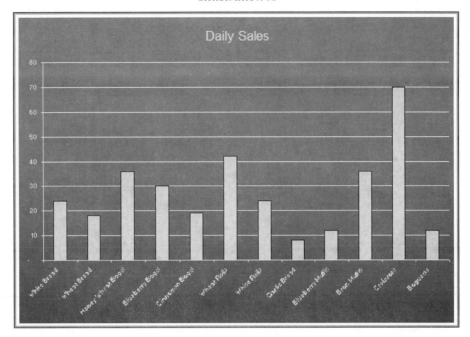

Illustration B

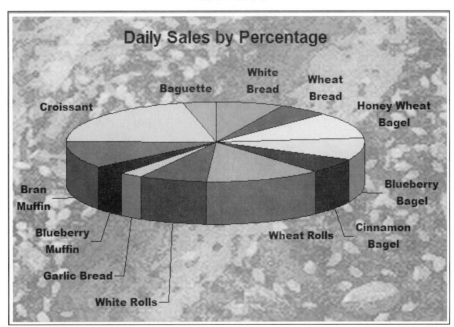

On Your Own

1. Open **OXL17**, the workbook you created in the On Your Own section of Exercise 17, or open ⊙ **18CDMANIA**.

2. Save the file as **CDMANIA**.

3. Rename Sheet 2 **Quarter 1 Sales Charts**.

4. Apply formatting to the two charts on the Quarter 1 Sales Charts sheet.

   ✓ *Be sure to make different selections for the two charts, so that they are unique in appearance.*

   a. Select a small font size for the labels and a larger font size for the title.

   b. Apply formatting to the chart background, and a different format to the plot area.

   c. Adjust the scale used on the y-axis.

   ✓ *For example, you could set the minimum to 50,000 and the major unit to 100,000.*

5. Rename Sheet 3 **Average Sales Chart**.

6. Apply formatting as desired to the chart on the Average Sales Chart sheet.

7. Spell check the workbook.

8. Print the workbook.

9. Close the workbook, saving all changes.

Illustration C

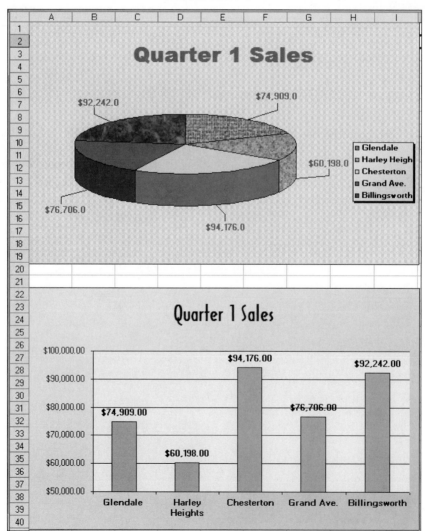

284

Exercise 19

◆ Critical Thinking

The CEO of Restoration Architecture has asked you, the CFO, to add the projected revenue figures to the 3rd Quarter Revenue report you prepared and to use them to perform some analysis on how well the company performed during the third quarter.

Exercise Directions

1. Start Excel, if necessary.

2. Open 🖎 **19RHSales 2**.

3. Save the file as **RHSales 2**.

4. Use the ROUND function to round the calculation results in cells B19:D19 to the nearest dollar.

5. Select the range A1:D19 and name it **Revenues**.

6. Select the range, A1:G19 and name it Revenues_and_Projections.

7. Use the IF function in cell G10 to display the text "**Over**" if the value in cell E10 is greater than the value in cell F10. Display the text "**Under**" if it is not.

   ✓ *Be sure to put quotation marks around the text arguments.*

8. Copy the formula to G11:G16.

9. In cell G18, use the COUNTIF function to count the number of jobs whose quarterly revenues fell under projected revenue.

10. In cell G19, enter a formula to calculate the revenue shortfall for only those jobs that were under projected revenues.

    a. You'll need two SUMIF functions in one formula to perform this calculation. Use the first SUMIF function to total the projected revenues for those jobs that display the word "Under" in the Over Projection? Column.

    b. Subtract from this total the value calculated by the second SUMIF function, which totals the values in the Qtr 3 Totals column, for only those jobs that display the word "Under" in the Over Projection? column. (See Illustration A.)

11. Create a chart, and place it on its own chart sheet named **Revenues Chart**.

    a. Use the range A9:D16.

    b. Choose the chart type Clustered column.

    c. Display data series by columns.

    d. Add the chart title **3rd Qtr Revenues**.

12. Format the chart:

    a. Add the Oak texture to the Chart Area.

    b. Apply Arial, 22 point, bold to the Chart Title.

    c. Apply Arial, 10 point, bold to the Value Axis.

    d. Apply Arial, 10 point, bold to the Category Axis.

    e. Insert the image 🖎 **restoration architecture logo 2.jpg**, to the Plot Area.

    f. Change the fill color of the Series: July to tan.

    g. Change the fill color of the Series: August to dark red.

    h. Change the fill color of the Series:September to coral. (See Illustration B.)

13. Spell check the workbook.

14. Print the workbook.

15. Close the file, saving all changes.

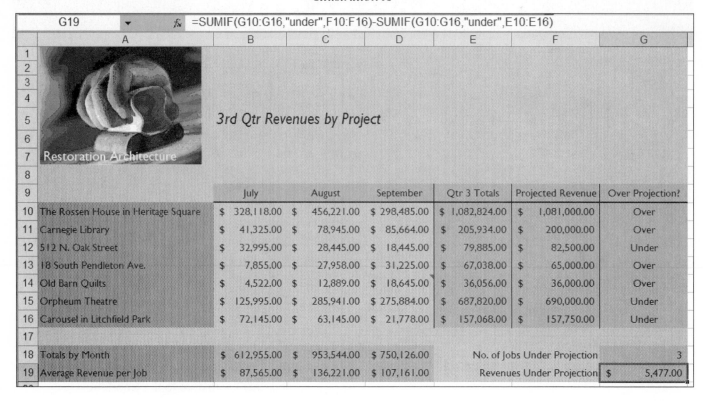

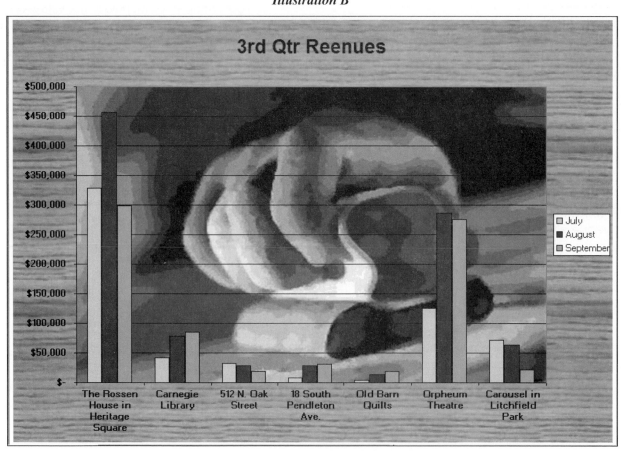

Exercise 20

◆ **Print a Workbook** ◆ **Print Multiple Copies** ◆ **Modify Page Setup**
◆ **Insert Headers and Footers**

On the Job

Change the page setup of your worksheet and use the available print options to control the printed output of a report. For example, if you need to fit the worksheet on one page, you can change the margins, change the print orientation, change the paper size, and change the **scaling**. Add headers and footers to your report to repeat the same information at the top or bottom of each printed page.

You are an Adventure Coordinator for Voyager Travel Adventures, and you have prepared a cost estimate for the Tell City Thrill Seekers Club for their upcoming trip that combines whitewater rafting, backcountry hiking, rock climbing, and all-terrain skating. Now you need to print the estimate, but you want to change the setup so it will print the way you want.

Terms

Scaling Reduce or enlarge information to fit on a specified number of pages.

Print options Selections that control what, where, how, and how many copies of the output to print.

Page Setup A dialog box that includes options to control the appearance of printed output.

Header Repeated information that appears in the top margin of a page.

Footer Repeated information that appears in the bottom margin of a page.

Notes

Print a Workbook

- The Print dialog box allows you to choose from a number of **print options**.

- As you learned in earlier lessons, normally only the active worksheet is printed when you choose File, Print or click the Print toolbar button.

- If you select multiple worksheets and then click the Print button, the selected sheets will print—not just the current worksheet.

- To print a selected range from a worksheet, or to print an entire workbook, you'll need to display the Print dialog box and select the appropriate option.

- If you select a range *and* choose Selection in the Print dialog box, that range will be the only data printed.

- You don't need to select each worksheet in a workbook if you intend to print them all. Just choose the Entire workbook option in the Print dialog box.

- If you preview a worksheet first and you know which pages you want to print, you can print selected pages by entering the first and last page numbers of the range to print in the From and To boxes of the Print dialog box.

Print dialog box

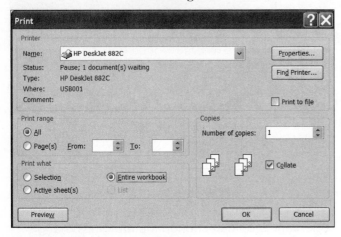

Print Multiple Copies

- You can print multiple copies of your data by increasing the value in the Number of copies box.

- If you print multiple copies of a multipage document, select Collate so that each copy is printed in order: page 1, 2, 3, and so on.

Modify Page Setup

- Access the **Page Setup** dialog box from the Page Setup or Print Preview commands on the File menu to control printed output.

- The following page tabs display in the Page Setup dialog box: Page, Margins, Header/Footer, and Sheet.

  ✓ *You'll learn about the Sheet tab in Exercise 21.*

Page Tab

Page tab of Page Setup dialog box

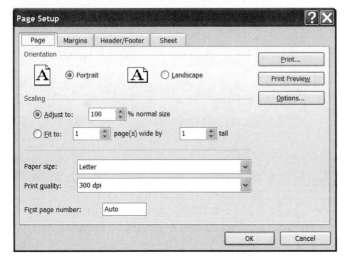

Orientation
- Print the worksheet in Portrait (vertical) or Landscape (horizontal) orientation.

Scaling
- Reduce or enlarge information through the Adjust to % normal size option. Use the Fit to pages option to compress worksheet data to fill a specific number of pages.

Paper size
- Change the paper size when printing on a paper size other than 8½" x 11".

Print quality
- Reduce the print quality to print draft output.

First page number
- Change the starting page number for the current worksheet.

Margins Tab

Margins tab of Page Setup dialog box

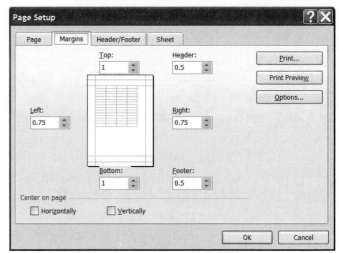

- Increase or decrease the Top, Bottom, Left, or Right margins to control the distance between your data and the edge of the paper.

- Increase or decrease the Header or Footer margins to specify the distance between the top or bottom of the page and the header/footer.

- Print the worksheet centered horizontally and/or vertically on the page.

Insert Headers and Footers

Header/Footer tab of Page Setup dialog box

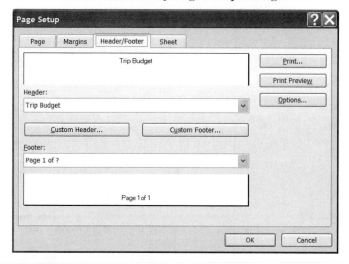

■ When you want to repeat the same information at the top of each printed page, create a **header**.

■ When you want to repeat the same information at the bottom of each printed page, create a **footer**.

- Header and footer information is not displayed in the worksheet window, but it does appear when you print a worksheet.

- The header and footer also appear when you preview a worksheet.

■ You can select a predesigned header or footer from those listed on the Header/Footer tab of the Page Setup dialog box, or create customized ones.

■ A customized header and footer are separated into three sections: left (text is left aligned), center (text is center aligned), and right (text is right aligned).

■ When creating a custom header/footer, simply type the text you want to use into the appropriate section of the dialog box: left, center, or right.

■ Text may be entered on multiple lines as needed.

■ You can also click buttons to insert print codes for the current date, current time (both reset at time of printing), page number, file path, file name, or sheet name.

■ You can also insert a graphic (such as a company logo) into a custom header/footer.

- If you add graphics or additional lines of text, be sure to adjust the header/footer and top/bottom margins on the Margins tab to allow enough space for these elements to print.

- Keep in mind that any graphic you use must be small in order to look proportional to the header/footer text.

- Header/footer graphics do not appear in the regular worksheet window, so you will not see them displayed until you either preview the worksheet or print it.

✓ *Some of the worksheets you've used in the Exercises have included graphics which were inserted into the worksheet and not the header/footer area, using the Insert, Picture command.*

■ The font, font style, and font size of the custom header/footer may also be changed.

✓ *To change the font, style, or size of text in a pre-designed header or footer, just click the Custom Header or Custom Footer button after selecting the header/footer you want, and apply your font changes.*

Custom Header dialog box

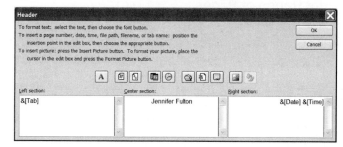

Procedures

Print Entire Workbook

1. Click **F**ile .... `Alt`+`F`
2. Click **P**rint .... `P`
   OR
   Press .... `Ctrl`+`P`
3. Click **E**ntire
   workbook .... `Alt`+`E`
4. Click **OK** .... `Enter`

Print Selected Range

1. Select range to print
2. Click **F**ile .... `Alt`+`F`
3. Click **P**rint .... `P`
   OR
   Press .... `Ctrl`+`P`
4. Click **Selectio**n .... `Alt`+`N`
5. Click **OK** .... `Enter`

Print Multiple Copies

1. Click **F**ile .... `Alt`+`F`
2. Click **P**rint .... `P`
   OR
   Press .... `Ctrl`+`P`
3. Select **Number of**
   copies .... `Alt`+`C`, `↑`
4. Print each copy in its own set
   by choosing **C**ollate .... `Alt`+`O`
5. Click **OK** .... `Enter`

Print Range of Pages

1. Click **F**ile .... `Alt`+`F`
2. Click **P**rint .... `P`
   OR
   Press .... `Ctrl`+`P`
3. Type first page to print in range
   in **F**rom box .... `Alt`+`F`, #
4. Type last page to print in range
   in **T**o box .... `Alt`+`T`, #
5. Click **OK** .... `Enter`

Access Page Setup

1. Click **F**ile .... `Alt`+`F`
2. Click **Page Set**u**p** .... `U`
3. Select options.
4. Click **OK** .... `Enter`

Create Header or Footer

1. Click **F**ile .... `Alt`+`F`
2. Click **Page Setup** .... `U`
3. Click **Header/Footer**
   tab .... `Ctrl`+`Tab`

   To select built-in header
   or footer:
   a. Click **He**a**der**
      drop-down arrow .... `Alt`+`A`
      OR
      Click **F**ooter
      drop-down arrow ..... `Alt`+`F`
   b. Click desired type
      in list .... `↓` `↑`, `Enter`

   To create custom header
   or footer:
   a. Click
      Custom Header ..... `Alt`+`C`
      OR
      Click
      Custom Footer ...... `Alt`+`U`
   b. Click appropriate section.
      • **L**eft section ...... `Alt`+`L`
      • **C**enter section . `Alt`+`C`
      • **R**ight section ... `Alt`+`R`
   c. Type text to appear in
      header or footer.
      ✓ *Press Enter to insert text*
      on another line.
      OR
      Click appropriate button
      to insert print code.
      • **Page**
        Number ...... `Alt`+`T`

- **Total**
  Pages .... `Alt`+`U`
- **Date** .... `Alt`+`D`
- **Time** .... `Alt`+`M`
- **Path and**
  File name .. `Alt`+`P`
- **File name** .. `Alt`+`E`
- **Sheet**
  Name .... `Alt`+`A`
- **Picture** ...... `Alt`+`I`

d. Choose **OK**.

To change font of custom
header or footer text:
a. Select header or footer text.
b. Click **Font**
   button **A** .... `Tab`, `Enter`
   ✓ *Press Tab key until Font*
   button is selected, then
   Enter.
   OR
   Press .... `Alt`+`F`
c. Choose from available font,
   font style, and font size
   options.
d. Click **OK** .... `Enter`

To change format of picture:
a. Select &[Picture] print code.
b. Click **Picture Format**
   button .... `Tab`, `Enter`
   ✓ *Press Tab key until Picture*
   Format button is selected,
   then Enter.
   OR
   Press .... `Alt`+`O`
c. Choose format options.
d. Click **OK** .... `Enter`
4. Click **OK** .... `Enter`

Exercise Directions

1. Start Excel, if necessary.

2. Open 📇**TripBudget** or open 💿**20TripBudget 2**.

3. Save the file as **TripBudget 2**.

4. Spell check the workbook.

5. Create a header and footer.

   a. Select Page 1 of ? from the Header list.

   b. To create the footer, click Custom Footer.

   c. Click inside the left hand section, then click the Date button to insert today's date. (See Illustration A.)

   d. Press Enter and click the Sheet Name button.

   e. Click inside the center section and type your name.

   f. Click inside the right section, and click the Picture button. Select the file 💿**voyager travel logo.gif**.

   g. Click the Format Picture button, and on the Size tab, set the Scale Height and Width to 25%.

6. Change the Bottom margin to 1.2".

7. Print the entire workbook, using the option in the Print dialog box.

   ✓ *Notice that the worksheets print on two pages, and that the data is wider than it is long. In such a case, you may want to use Landscape orientation.*

8. Access Page Setup, and on the Page tab, change to Landscape orientation.

9. Preview just Trip Budget worksheet.

   ✓ *This is better, but perhaps you can fit everything on one page.*

10. Access Page Setup again, and on the Page tab, select the Fit to 1 page(s) wide by 1 tall option.

11. Print the result. (See Illustration B.)

12. Close the workbook, saving all changes.

Illustration A

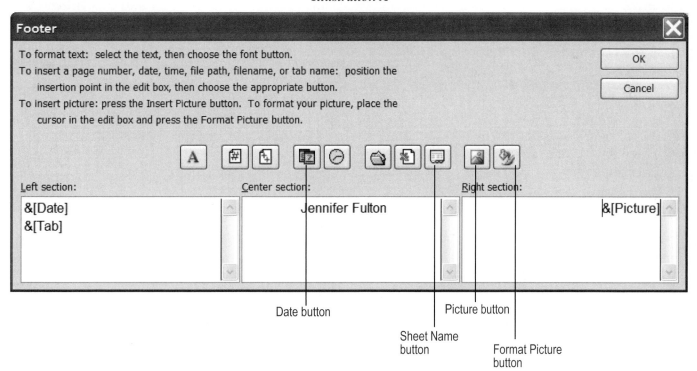

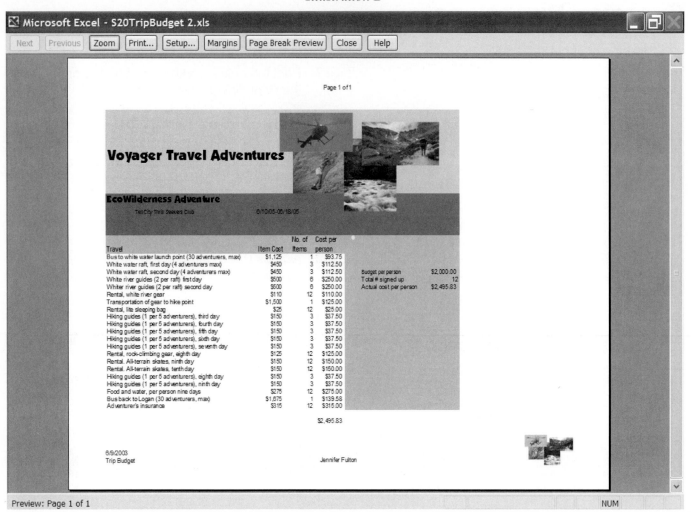

On Your Own

1. Open the file **OXL16** that you created in the On Your Own section of Exercise 16, or open 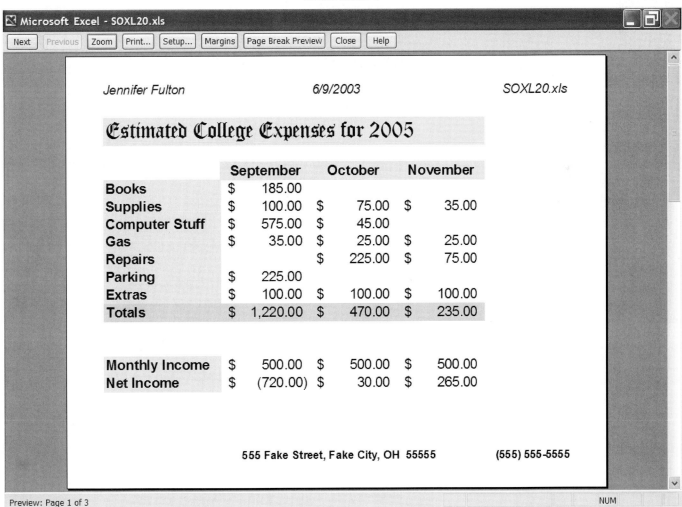**20COLEXP**.

2. Save the file as **OXL20**.

3. Set the worksheet to print in Landscape mode.

4. Adjust the scaling so that the data is printed at 200% its normal size.

5. Create a custom header that includes your name, the current date, and the file name.

6. Format the header text using a font style and size you like.

7. Create a custom footer that lists your address and phone number.

8. Center the worksheet vertically on the page.

9. Widen columns as needed.

10. Spell check the worksheet.

11. Preview the worksheet. The result should look similar to Illustration C.

12. Print two copies of the worksheet.

13. Close the workbook, saving all changes.

Illustration C

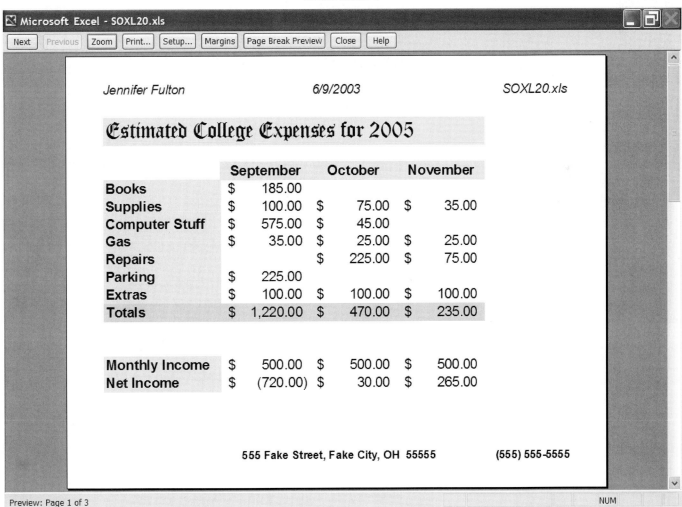

	September	October	November
Books	$ 185.00		
Supplies	$ 100.00	$ 75.00	$ 35.00
Computer Stuff	$ 575.00	$ 45.00	
Gas	$ 35.00	$ 25.00	$ 25.00
Repairs		$ 225.00	$ 75.00
Parking	$ 225.00		
Extras	$ 100.00	$ 100.00	$ 100.00
Totals	$ 1,220.00	$ 470.00	$ 235.00
Monthly Income	$ 500.00	$ 500.00	$ 500.00
Net Income	$ (720.00)	$ 30.00	$ 265.00

Microsoft Excel - SOXL20.xls

Next | Previous | Zoom | Print... | Setup... | Margins | Page Break Preview | Close | Help

Jennifer Fulton   6/9/2003   SOXL20.xls

𝕰𝖘𝖙𝖎𝖒𝖆𝖙𝖊𝖉 𝕮𝖔𝖑𝖑𝖊𝖌𝖊 𝕰𝖝𝖕𝖊𝖓𝖘𝖊𝖘 𝖋𝖔𝖗 2005

555 Fake Street, Fake City, OH 55555   (555) 555-5555

Preview: Page 1 of 3   NUM

Exercise 21

Skills Covered:

◆ **Insert Page Breaks** ◆ **Page Break Preview** ◆ **Set Print Area**
◆ **Repeat Row and Column Labels** ◆ **Other Sheet Tab Options**

On the Job

If you are not satisfied with the page layout defaults set in Excel, you can change them manually. For example, if a worksheet doesn't fit on one page, then Excel sets page breaks automatically for you. These page breaks tell Excel where to start a new page when printing. If you don't like where the automatic page breaks occur, you can manually set your own page breaks before printing. If you need to print only part of a worksheet for a specific report, you can temporarily change the print area. When your printout includes multiple pages, you can reprint the row and column labels for your data on every page, making it easier for you and others to locate data. Other sheet tab options may speed up the printing process or display data in a manner that makes it easier to read.

As the new Franchise Director at HealthNow MedCenter, you've spent a lot of time creating reports that describe your company's fiscal strength. The balance sheet is ready for printing, but you want to modify the print settings first so that it will print exactly as you want.

Terms

Page break A code inserted into a document that forces what follows to begin on a new page; a page break is represented on your screen as a dashed line in the worksheet.

Page Break Preview A view that allows you to move and delete page breaks and redefine the print area.

Print area The specified range of cells to be printed.

Print titles Row and column labels that are reprinted on each page of a worksheet printout.

Gridlines Light gray lines that mark the cell borders.

Notes

Insert Page Breaks

- When worksheet data will not fit on one page, Excel inserts automatic **page breaks** based on the paper size, margins, and scaling options.

- Automatic page breaks appear as dashed blue lines on the worksheet.

  ✓ *Page breaks appear on the worksheet in Normal view after you use Print Preview; they also appear in Page Break Preview.*

- If you prefer, you can override automatic page breaks and set manual page breaks before printing.

- While automatic page breaks (those created by Excel, based on your page setup options) appear as dashed lines, manual page breaks (those you create by either moving the automatic page breaks, or inserting new ones) display on the worksheet as solid blue lines.

Page Break Preview

■ **Page Break Preview** is a special view that displays both automatic and manual page breaks, and allows you to adjust them.

■ When you display a worksheet in Page Break Preview, lines appear, subdividing the worksheet into sections.

- Each section represents a different print page.

- Each section is marked in the center with a large page number displayed in light gray.

- By adjusting the position of these lines, you can change how the worksheet is sectioned off for printing. In other words, you can tell Excel which data to print on each page.

■ In Page Break Preview, when you drag a dashed line (automatic page break) to move it, it changes to a solid line (manual page break).

■ In Page Break Preview, drag a dashed line off the worksheet to remove a page break and reset the page breaks.

■ You can also edit worksheet data and resize the **print area** from Page Break Preview.

■ If you adjust a page break to include a few more columns or rows on a page, Excel automatically adjusts the scale (font size) to make that data fit on the page.

■ You can also use Page Break Preview to adjust how embedded charts print.

✓ *Embedded charts and other objects appear on top of the page breaks, so sometimes it can be difficult to see that a chart spans two pages.*

Set Print Area

■ To print a selected area of data and not all the data on a worksheet, adjust the print area.

■ You can set the print area using Page Break Preview, the Print Area command on the File menu, or with a text box on the Sheet tab of the Page Setup dialog box.

■ In Normal view, the print area appears on the worksheet with a dashed border.

■ In the Page Break Preview, the print area appears in full color, while data outside the area to be printed appears on a gray background.

■ You can define a unique print area for each worksheet in your workbook.

■ To print the entire worksheet again, you must either clear the print area setting, or reset the print area to include all the data.

Repeat Row and Column Labels

■ Using the Sheet tab of the Page Setup dialog box, you can select to reprint the **print titles** on each page of a worksheet printout.

■ Without the row and column labels printed on each page, it might be difficult to decipher your data.

Other Sheet Tab Options

■ The Sheet tab of the Page Setup dialog box provides an option for printing **gridlines** with your data.

■ You can also print your worksheet in black and white (even if it includes color fills or graphics), in draft mode (faster printing, lower quality), with your comments, and with errors displayed.

■ For large worksheets, you can specify the print order (the order in which data is selected to be printed on subsequent pages).

Sheet tab of Page Setup dialog box

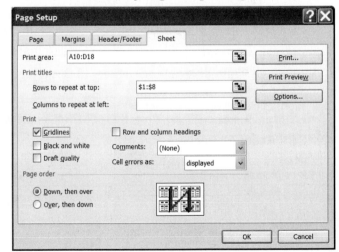

Procedures

Page Break Preview

1. Click **View** .... `Alt`+`V`
2. Click **Page Break Preview** .. `P`

OR

1. Click **Print Preview** button .
2. Click **Page Break Preview** .. `V`

   ✓ *If the Welcome to Page Break Preview dialog box displays, click OK.*

To return to Normal view:

1. Click **View** .... `Alt`+`V`
2. Click **Normal** .... `N`

OR

1. Click **Print Preview** button .
2. Click **Normal View** .... `V`

   ✓ *When you are already in Page Break Preview, the Normal View Button appears on the Print Preview toolbar.*

To move automatic or manual page break:

1. Switch to Page Break Preview.
2. Drag dashed or solid line to its new location.
   ✓ *The automatic page break dashed line changes to a solid line.*
   ✓ *When a manual page break is moved outside of the print area, the automatic page break is restored.*

To remove all page breaks:

1. Switch to Page Break Preview.
2. Right-click cell on worksheet.
   ✓ *Shortcut menu appears.*
3. Click **Reset All Page Breaks** .... `A`
   ✓ *Automatic page breaks are restored.*

To adjust print area:

1. Switch to Page Break Preview.
2. Drag dark outline (outside border of the colored print area) to resize it.

To restore print area:

1. Switch to Page Break Preview.
2. Right-click cell on worksheet.
   ✓ *Shortcut menu appears.*
3. Click **Reset Print Area** .. `Alt`+`R`

Set Manual Page Breaks

✓ *Automatic page breaks that follow a manual page break will adjust automatically.*

To insert horizontal page break:

1. Click at beginning of row where new page should begin.
2. Click **Insert** .... `Alt`+`I`
3. Click **Page Break** .... `B`

To insert vertical page break:

1. Click at beginning of column where new page should begin.
2. Click **Insert** .... `Alt`+`I`
3. Click **Page Break** .... `B`

To insert both horizontal and vertical page breaks:

1. Click cell where new page should begin.
2. Click **Insert** .... `Alt`+`I`
3. Click **Page Break** .... `B`

Remove page break in Page Break Preview:

1. Click on page break.
2. Drag page break off worksheet.

OR

1. Click below or to the right of the page break.
2. Click **Insert** .... `Alt`+`I`
3. Click **Remove Page Break** . `B`

Set Print Area with File Menu

1. Select the worksheet area you wish to print.
2. Click **File** .... `Alt`+`F`
3. Click **Print Area** .... `T`
4. Click **Set Print Area** .... `S`

Clear Print Area with File Menu

1. Click **File** .... `Alt`+`F`
2. Click **Print Area** .... `T`
3. Click **Clear Print Area** .... `C`

Repeat Row and Column Labels

1. Click **File** .... `Alt`+`F`
2. Click **Page Setup** .... `U`
3. Click **Sheet** tab .... `Ctrl`+`Tab`
4. Click **Rows to repeat at top** .... `Alt`+`R`
5. Type the row numbers you wish to repeat at the top of each page.
   ✓ *For example, to repeat the first seven rows, type 1:7.*
   ✓ *You can also click the Collapse button and select the rows you wish to repeat.*
6. Click **Columns to repeat at left** .... `Alt`+`C`
7. Type the column letters you want to repeat to the left of each page.
   ✓ *For example, to repeat the first three columns on the left, type A:C.*
   ✓ *You can also click the Collapse button and select the columns you wish to repeat.*
8. Click **OK** .... `Enter`

Print Gridlines

1. Click **File** .... `Alt`+`F`
2. Click **Page Setup** .... `U`
3. Click **Sheet** tab .... `Ctrl`+`Tab`
4. Click **Gridlines** .... `Alt`+`G`
5. Click **OK** .... `Enter`

Select Other Sheet Tab Options

1. Click **File** .... `Alt`+`F`
2. Click **Page Setup** .... `U`
3. Click **Sheet** tab .... `Ctrl`+`Tab`
4. Select options.
5. Click **OK** .... `Enter`

Exercise Directions

1. Start Excel, if necessary.

2. Open ⊙ **21Balance Sheet 2**.

3. Save the file as **Balance Sheet 2**.

4. Click Print Preview.

   ✓ *Currently, the worksheet is set to print on four pages, but the chart is split up and impossible to interpret.*

5. Click Close to return to Normal view.

   ✓ *Dashed lines appear, marking the automatic page breaks.*

6. Use the Page tab of Page Setup to change to landscape orientation.

7. Click Print Preview to preview the worksheet again.

   ✓ *It's better, but some of the worksheet data has spilled over onto the chart page, and the worksheet and chart are so wide, they spill onto pages three and four*

8. Close Print Preview and return to Normal view.

9. Choose View, Page Break Preview. Click OK if prompted.

10. Drag the automatic page break located below row 36 *down*, to include row 37 of the worksheet data on page one.

11. Drag the automatic page break located on the right, off the sheet to remove it.

12. Click Print Preview to preview how the worksheet looks now. See Illustrations A and B.

13. Return to Normal view, spell check, and then print the worksheet.

14. Select the ranges A1:E18 and A39:K70, then choose File, Print Area, Set Print Area.

15. Preview the worksheet.

16. In Page Setup, change to Portrait orientation. Adjust the scaling to 1 page wide by 2 tall.

    ✓ *Because you selected two different ranges for the print area, they print on separate pages.*

17. Print the worksheet again.

18. Close the workbook, saving all changes.

Illustration A

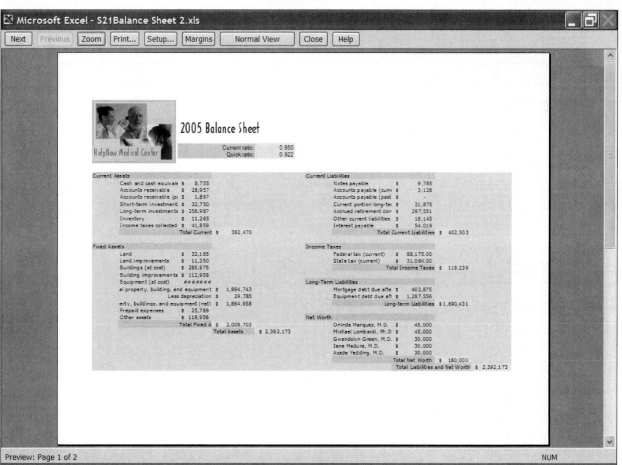

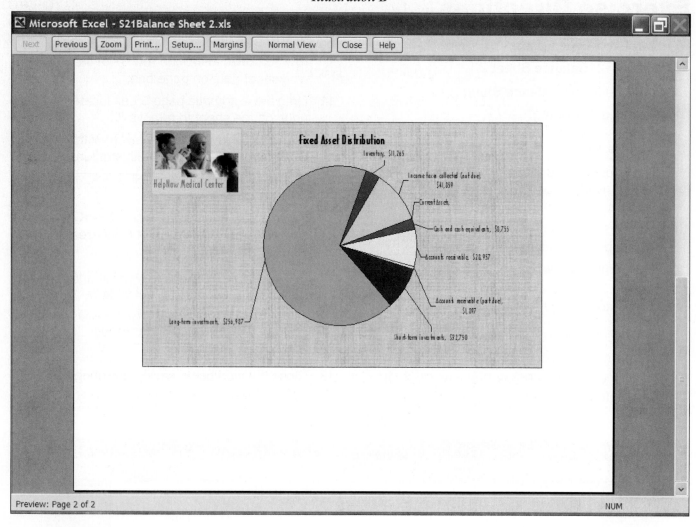

On Your Own

1. Open the **OXL18** file you used in the On Your Own section of Exercise 18, or open ◎**21CDMANIA**.

2. Save the file as **OXL21**.

3. Change to Sheet 1 if needed, then display Page Break Preview.

4. Drag the print area border so that the Summary will not be printed.

5. Remove the automatic page break on the right, so the worksheet will print on one page.

6. Spell check, adjust column widths as needed, then print the worksheet.

7. Insert a page break between the Quarter 1 and Quarter 2 data.

8. Use Page Setup to print the row and column labels on each page of the printout.

9. Print the worksheet.

10. Print the worksheet again, this time with gridlines and in black and white.

11. Return to Normal view.

12. Close the workbook, saving all changes.

Exercise 22

◆ Copy and Paste Special ◆ Transpose Data

On the Job

You can control how to paste data after you copy it to the Clipboard. For example, you may copy cells that contain formulas to the Clipboard but only want to paste the results. Use the time-saving Copy and Paste Special commands for this type of editing.

As the CFO of Restoration Architecture, you need to create a separate revenue analysis report using the data in the 3rd Quarter Revenue report that you prepared last week. In this exercise, you'll use Paste Special to get the job done quickly.

Terms

Paste Special An editing feature used to control how data is inserted from the Clipboard to the current file.

Paste options The attributes of the data to be pasted.

Operation options The mathematical functions that can be applied to copied data.

Skip blanks An option that avoids replacing values in the paste area with blank cells from the copy area.

Transpose An option that pastes a column of data to a row or a row of data to a column in the current file.

Notes

Copy and Paste Special

- The **Paste Special** feature gives you control over how to insert data into a file from the Clipboard.

- The Paste Special dialog box contains the following options:

  - **Paste options** specify the attributes of the selection to be pasted.

    - All: pastes the contents and the formatting of the copied cells.
    - Formulas: pastes only the formulas as shown in the Formula bar.
    - Values: pastes only the values as shown in the cells.
    - Formats: pastes only the formats of the copied cells.

  ✓ *Copying formatting from one cell to another is a very common practice because it makes the process of formatting a worksheet so much easier. Because it's so popular, the Paste Special Formats command has its own toolbar button called the Format Painter, which you used in Exercise 9.*

  - Comments: pastes only the comments attached to the copied cells.
  - Validation: pastes data validation rules for the copied cells.
  - All except borders: pastes the contents and formatting of the copied cells, except for borders.
  - Column widths: pastes the column widths of the selected cells.

- ◆ Formulas and number formats: pastes formulas (not results) and the number formats, but no additional formatting, such as color fills.
- ◆ Values and number formats: pastes the results of formulas (and not the formulas themselves), along with number formats. Additional formatting, such as text colors, is not copied.
- **Operation options** specifies the mathematical operation to use when data from the copy area is combined with data in the paste area.

   ✓ You'll learn more about this option in Exercise 23.

- **Skip blanks** in the copy area so they do not overwrite data in the paste area.

- **Transpose** pastes a column of data in the copy area to a row or a row of data in the copy area to a column.

   ✓ You'll learn about the Paste Link option in Exercise 25.

Paste Special dialog box

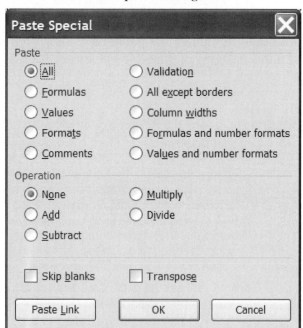

- ■ As you learned in Exercise 9, you can perform some of the Paste Special commands using the down arrow on the Paste button, such as pasting a formula result rather than the formula itself.

- ■ You can also change the formatting that's copied after a paste operation using the Paste Options button that appears on the worksheet next to the copied data.

   ✓ By using the Paste button menu and the Paste Options button, you can perform many Paste Special functions without having to display the Paste Special dialog box. However, certain Paste Special functions, such as pasting validation rules only, skipping blanks, or performing a mathematical operation on data may only be done using the options in the Paste Special dialog box.

Transpose Data

- ■ You can copy data in a column and then paste it into a row, or copy data in a row and then paste it into a column.

- ■ If you're transposing a group of cells containing formulas, Excel will adjust the cell references in the formulas so that they point to the correct transposed cells.

   ✓ You can transpose data with formulas and paste the formula values only by selecting those options in the Paste Special dialog box.

Row labels are transposed and pasted into the column

	A	B	C	D
1	1st Qtr	2nd Qtr	3rd Qtr	4th Qtr
2				
3				
4	1st Qtr			
5	2nd Qtr			
6	3rd Qtr			
7	4th Qtr			

Procedures

Paste Special Using Paste Special Dialog Box	Paste Special Using Paste Menu	Transpose Data

Paste Special Using Paste Special Dialog Box

1. Select range to copy.
2. Click **Edit** .... Alt +E
3. Click **Copy** C
4. Click upper-left corner of range to receive data.
   a. Click **Edit** .... Alt +E
   b. Click **Paste Special** .... S
   OR
   a. Click down arrow on **Paste** button .
   b. Click **Paste Special** .... S
5. Select appropriate option from Paste Special dialog box.
6. Click **OK** .... Enter

Paste Special Using Paste Menu

1. Select range to copy.
2. Click **Edit** .... Alt +E
3. Click **Copy** C
4. Click upper-left corner of range to receive data.
5. Click down arrow on **Paste** button .
6. Select Paste option.
   ✓ The options that appear will vary, based on the contents of the data to be copied.
   ✓ After copying, if you need to adjust the pasted formatting, click the Paste Options button on the worksheet and select the option you want.

Transpose Data

1. Select range to copy.
2. Click **Edit** .... Alt +E
3. Click **Copy** C
4. Click upper-left corner of range to receive data.
5. Click down arrow on **Paste** button .
6. Click **Transpose** .... T
   ✓ The data is transposed. Formulas are adjusted so that cell references point to the correct cells.
   ✓ To transpose data with formulas and to paste only values, use the Paste Values and Transpose options in the Paste Special dialog box.

Exercise Directions

1. Start Excel, if necessary.
2. Open a new workbook.
3. Save the file as **RevAnalysis**.
4. Open ⌨RHSales 2 or 💿 22RHSales 2.
5. On the Revenues sheet in the **RHSales 2** or **22RHSales 2** workbook, select the range A1:G8 and click Copy.
   ✓ Because of the location of the graphic, you might find it easier to select this range by clicking cell G8 and dragging up to cell A1.
6. Click cell A1 on Sheet 1 of the **RevAnalysis** workbook, then click Paste.
   ✓ The data is copied, but the column widths are not right. To fix that, you'll use Paste Special to copy the column widths as well.
7. Click the arrow on the Paste Options button and select Keep Source Column Widths.
8. Change cell B5 to **3rd Qtr Revenue Analysis**.
9. On the Revenues sheet in the **RHSales 2** or **22RHSales 2** workbook, select the ranges A9:A16 and E9:F16, and click Copy.
   ✓ Tip: Select the first range, then press Control and select the second range.
10. Click cell A9 on Sheet 1 of the **RevAnalysis** workbook, then select Edit, Paste Special.
11. Select Values and number formats and Transpose, and click OK.
12. Use Paste Special again to paste the cell formats in this same range.
    ✓ Be sure to use the Transpose option when pasting the formats.
13. Adjust the column widths to fit the data.
14. Copy the cell formats from G1:G9 to H1:H9.
15. Type Amount **Above or Below Projected Revenue** in cell A12. (See Illustration A.)
    a. Copy the format from cell A11 to A12.
    b. Adjust the column width as needed.
16. In cell B12, enter a formula that takes the Quarter 3 total minus projected revenue.
    a. Copy the format from cell B11 to B12.
    b. Copy the formula and format in cell B12 to C12:H12.
17. Spell check the worksheet.
18. Print the worksheet.
19. Close both workbooks, saving all changes.

Illustration A

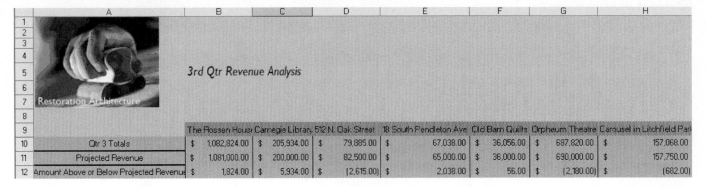

	A	B	C	D	E	F	G	H
1								
2								
3								
4		*3rd Qtr Revenue Analysis*						
5								
6								
7	Restoration Architecture							
8								
9		The Rossen House	Carnegie Library	512 N. Oak Street	18 South Pendleton Ave	Old Barn Quilts	Orpheum Theatre	Carousel in Litchfield Park
10	Qtr 3 Totals	$ 1,082,824.00	$ 205,934.00	$ 79,885.00	$ 67,038.00	$ 36,056.00	$ 687,820.00	$ 157,068.00
11	Projected Revenue	$ 1,081,000.00	$ 200,000.00	$ 82,500.00	$ 65,000.00	$ 36,000.00	$ 690,000.00	$ 157,750.00
12	Amount Above or Below Projected Revenue	$ 1,824.00	$ 5,934.00	$ (2,615.00)	$ 2,038.00	$ 56.00	$ (2,180.00)	$ (682.00)

On Your Own

1. Open the file **OXL20**, created in the On Your Own section of Exercise 20, or open 22COLEXP.

2. Save the file as **OXL22**.

3. In a cell below the data already entered in the worksheet, type the title: **Expense Analysis**.

4. Use Format Painter to copy the format from the worksheet title to the cells occupied by this title.

5. Label a column: **Months**; then label the column to the right of the Months column: **Totals**; and then label the column to the right of the Totals column: **% of Total**.

6. Use Format Painter to copy the format from your column labels above to this group of cells.

7. Select the range of cells at the top of the worksheet containing the labels for the months, and transpose it into the Months column you created in step 5.

   ✓ *Do not copy the formats—copy just the values.*

8. Select the range of cells in the worksheet data displaying the results of the formulas totaling the expenses for each month, and transpose the values into the Totals column you created in step 5.

   ✓ *Paste the values and the number formats, but not the formulas themselves.*

9. At the bottom of the new Totals columns, enter a formula to calculate the total annual expenses. Format the results with Currency Style.

10. In the % of Total column, enter formulas to calculate each month's percent of the total annual expenses (use an absolute reference to the total annual expenses). Apply the Percent Style format with two decimals to the results.

11. Adjust column width and apply formatting to improve the appearance of the worksheet.

12. Spell check the worksheet.

13. Print the worksheet.

14. Close the workbook, saving all changes.

Exercise 23

◆ Combine Data With Copy and Paste Special

On the Job

Use the Copy and Paste Special commands when you need to copy and combine data. For example, you may have individual worksheets containing the items sold each month and a summary sheet showing the total inventory. Use the Paste Special command, Subtract operation to reduce the inventory on the summary sheet by the number of items sold each month.

Your monthly inventory is complete at the Voyager Travel Adventures retail store in Logan, Colorado, and it's time to compute the monthly sales and sales revenue. Unfortunately, the inventory tracker is located in one workbook, and the monthly sales revenue recap is in another. No problem for you, however, since you just learned how to use the Paste Special function to subtract the monthly sales figures from the ending inventory so you can compute the number of each item sold during the month.

Terms

Copied cells Data copied to the Clipboard.

Destination cells The new location to receive the pasted data.

Notes

Combine Data With Copy and Paste Special

- Using the Paste Special Operation commands, you can combine data when you paste it on top of existing data.

- Excel uses the mathematical operation (addition, subtraction, and so on) that you select to combine the data in the **copied cells** with the data in the **destination cells**.

- Operations options include:
  - None: replaces destination cells with copied cells. This is the default setting.
  - Add: adds numeric data in copied cells to values in destination cells.
  - Subtract: subtracts numeric data in copied cells from values in destination cells.
  - Multiply: multiplies numeric data in copied cells by values in destination cells.

- Divide: divides numeric data in copied cells by values in destination cells.

Paste Special dialog box

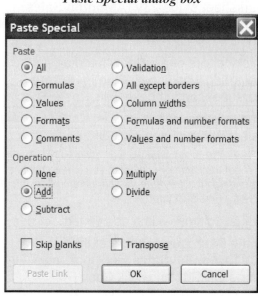

Procedures

Combine Data with Paste Special

1. Select range of cells to copy.
2. Click **Edit** .... Alt + E
3. Click **Copy** C
4. Select upper-left cell of destination area.
5. Click **Edit** .... Alt + E
6. Click **Paste Special** .... S
7. Select **Operation** option:
   - **None** .... O
   - **Add** .... D
   - **Subtract** .... S
   - **Multiply** .... M
   - **Divide** I
8. Select additional Paste Special options as desired.
9. Click **OK** .... Enter

Exercise Directions

1. Start Excel, if necessary.
2. Open 🖥 **23Inventory 3**.
3. Save the file as **Inventory 3**.
4. Open 🖥 **23VTAMonthlySales**.
5. On the Snowboarding and Heliskiing worksheet of the **23VTAMonthlySales** workbook, select the range G9:G27, and click Copy.
6. Click cell H9 of the Snowboarding and Heliskiing worksheet of the **Inventory 3** workbook, and choose Edit, Paste Special.
7. Under Paste, select Values. Under Operation, select Subtract and click OK.
   - ✓ *By subtracting what you've sold through the month from the inventory on hand, you can compute the ending inventory (the number of each item you have left). See Illustration A.*
8. Adjust column widths as needed.
9. In the Backcountry sheet of the **23VTAMonthlySales** workbook, select the range G9:G61 and click Copy.

10. Switch to the Backcountry sheet of the **Inventory 3** workbook. Click cell H9 and choose Edit, Paste Special.
11. Under Paste, select Values. Under Operation, choose Subtract, then click OK.
12. Again, adjust column widths as needed.
13. Once more, change back to the **23VTAMonthlyAnalysis** workbook, and click the tab for the Camping worksheet.
14. Select the range G9:G62 and click Copy.
15. Change to the Camping sheet of the **Inventory 3** workbook, click cell H9, and select Edit, Paste Special.
16. Under Paste, select Values. Under Operation, select Subtract and click OK.
17. Adjust column widths as needed.
18. Close the **23VTAMonthlySales** workbook.
19. Spell check the **Inventory 3** workbook.
20. Print the workbook.
21. Close the workbook, saving all changes.

Illustration A

	A	B	C	D	E	F	G	H	I
7									
8	Item #	Description	Sale Price	Starting Inventory		Additions		Ending Inventory	Monthly Revenue
9	GL101	Heliskiing powder gloves	$ 180.00	175	200			63	$ 56,160.00
10	GL102	Ski gloves	$ 85.00	52	150	200		169	$ 19,805.00
11	SB101	Snowboard, honeycomb	$ 600.00	325	30			198	$ 94,200.00
12	SB102	Snowboard, pact	$ 585.00	118		200		8	$ 181,350.00
13	SB103	Snowboard, freeride, carbon	$ 525.00	114		350		378	$ 45,150.00
14	SB104	Snowboard, freeride, regular	$ 435.00	75	125			110	$ 39,150.00
15	SB105	Snowboard, crossbow	$ 410.00	18	100			56	$ 25,420.00
16	SB106	Snowboard, backcountry, split V	$ 695.00	774	325			582	$ 359,315.00
17	SB107	Snowboard, backcountry, split B	$ 890.00	585	500			490	$ 529,550.00
18	SB108	Snowboard, split trail	$ 735.00	1,125				336	$ 579,915.00
19	SB109	Snowboard, freestyle	$ 545.00	231				28	$ 110,635.00
20	SB110	Backcountry avalanche kit	$ 380.00	328				12	$ 120,080.00
21	SH105	Backcountry snowshoes	$ 160.00	118	50			83	$ 13,600.00
22	SH107	All-terrain cross country skate	$ 570.00	125	220			-	$ 196,650.00
23	SH107	Snowboard boot	$ 250.00	145	50			33	$ 40,500.00
24	SH108	Snow ski boot, alpine	$ 600.00	78	50			45	$ 49,800.00
25	SH109	Snow ski boot, alpine, women	$ 560.00	116				25	$ 50,960.00
26	SH110	Snow ski boot	$ 450.00	41		150		21	$ 76,500.00
27	SH111	Snow ski boot, women	$ 425.00	32		75		-	$ 45,475.00
28									

Sheet tabs: **Snowboarding and Heliskiing** / Backcountry / Camping

On Your Own

1. Open the file **OXL22**, created in the previous On Your Own section, or open **23COLEXP**.

2. Save the file as **OXL23**.

3. Create a semester summary by copying the worksheet title and row labels from the monthly expenses section at the top of the sheet to Sheet 2.

4. For column labels, type **Semester 1** and **Semester 2**.

5. Copy the expenses for September to the Semester 1 column of Sheet 2.

6. Using Paste Special, add the expenses for October, November, and December to the Semester 1 column.

7. Copy the expenses for January to the Semester 2 column of Sheet 2.

8. Using Paste Special, add the expenses for February, March, April, and May to the Semester 2 column.

9. Create formulas that total the expenses for Semesters 1 and 2.

10. Format the Semester Expenses worksheet as you like.

11. Widen columns as needed.

12. Spell check the worksheet.

13. Print the worksheet.

14. Close the workbook, saving all changes.

Exercise 24

Skills Covered:

◆ Freeze Labels While Scrolling ◆ Split a Worksheet into Panes

On the Job

When working with a large worksheet, you can freeze row and/or column labels to keep them in view and split the worksheet window into two or four panes. Freezing labels enables you to quickly identify a piece of data embedded within a large worksheet, while splitting a window into panes enables you to view multiple parts of a worksheet at the same time—in order to compare or copy data, for example.

It's your job at the Whole Grain Breads' home office to complete the payroll for this week. The worksheet you use is getting quite large, and you've decide to utilize the Freeze Panes and Split commands to help you view its information as you work.

Terms

Freeze A method to keep labels in view when scrolling through a worksheet.

Panes Window sections that allow you to see different parts of the worksheet at one time.

Notes

Freeze Labels While Scrolling

- When you need to keep labels in view at the top or left edge of the worksheet as you scroll through it, you can **freeze** them in place.

- Position the insertion point in the column to the right or the row below the data to be frozen, and then select the Freeze Panes command from the Windows menu.

- Thin lines indicate the borders of the frozen area. Within these borders, you can scroll using the arrow keys, and the frozen row/column labels will remain in view.

- To remove the freeze, use the Unfreeze Panes command.

Employee names and IDs remain in view as you scroll the worksheet horizontally

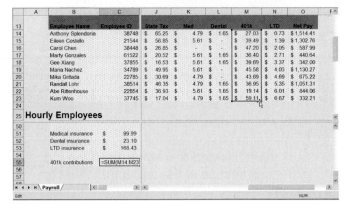

306

Split a Worksheet into Panes

- When you need to view different parts of a large worksheet at the same time, split the worksheet horizontally or vertically into **panes** using the Window menu.

  - When you position the insertion point in a cell in Row 1 and use the Split command, the vertical panes scroll together when scrolling up and down, and independently when scrolling left to right.

- When you position the insertion point in a cell in Column A and use the Split command, the horizontal panes scroll together when scrolling left to right, and independently when scrolling up and down.

- With the mouse, drag the horizontal or vertical split box to split the window into panes.

- When you need to cancel the split, use the Remove Split command from the Window menu.

Window split into four panes

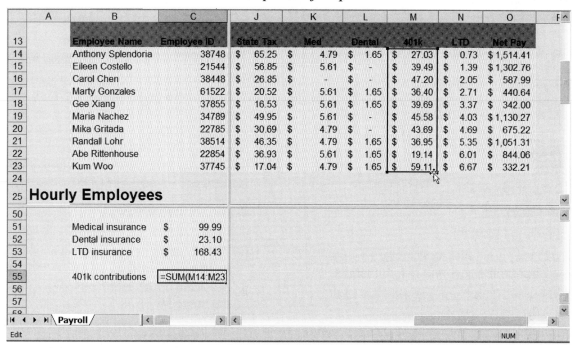

Procedures

Freeze Labels

1. Select the row below horizontal labels to freeze.

   OR

   Select column to the right of vertical labels to freeze.

   OR

   Select cell located in row below horizontal labels and column to right of vertical labels to freeze both row and column labels.

2. Click **W**indow .... Alt + W

3. Click **F**reeze Panes .... F

   ✓ *Use this feature if window is not split into panes.*

Unfreeze Labels

1. Click **W**indow .... Alt + W

2. Click **Un**f**reeze Panes** .... F

Split Worksheet into Panes with Menu

   ✓ *This feature provides simultaneous pane scrolling.*

1. Select row below desired horizontal split.

   OR

   Select column to right of desired vertical split.

   OR

   Select a cell located below and to right of desired horizontal and vertical split.

2. Click **W**indow .... Alt + W

3. Click **S**plit .... S

Split Worksheet into Panes with Split Boxes

✓ *This feature provides simultaneous pane scrolling.*

1. Point to horizontal split box ▶️ on scroll bar.

OR

Point to vertical split box 🔼 on scroll bar.

2. Click and drag mouse split pointer ╫ along horizontal scroll bar until split bar is positioned.

OR

Click and drag mouse split pointer ╪ along vertical scroll bar until split bar is positioned.

Remove Split

• Double-click split bar.

OR

1. Click **Window**..............`Alt`+`W`

2. Click **Remove Split**.............`S`

Adjust Panes

1. Place mouse over split bar until cursor changes to up and down pointing or right and left pointing arrows ╪ .

2. Click and drag the bar to a new position.

Move Between Panes

• Click in desired pane.

OR

• Press **F6 key**......................`F6` until active cell is positioned in desired pane.

Freeze Panes in Split Window

✓ *This procedure is used to lock top or left pane when scrolling.*

1. Click **Window**..............`Alt`+`W`

2. Click **Freeze Panes** ....`F`

Unfreeze Panes in Split Window

1. Click **Window**..............`Alt`+`W`

2. Click **Unfreeze Panes**.........`F`

Exercise Directions

1. Start Excel, if necessary.

2. Open 💿 **24Payroll 2**.

3. Save the file as **Payroll 2**.

4. Click cell D14, and choose Window, Freeze Panes to freeze the row and column labels.

5. Scroll to the right until you can see the Med column.

   ✓ *Note how the row and column labels are frozen so that you can still read the employee names and IDs and the payroll labels.*

6. Change Mike Gritada's Medical payment to **$5.61**.

7. Unfreeze the labels by choosing Window, Unfreeze Panes.

8. Click cell D45, and split the window into four panes by choosing Window, Split.

9. Click cell D38 in the upper-right pane, then use the arrow keys to scroll up to row 14.

   ✓ *Notice that the two upper panes remain in synch, while the two lower panes are frozen.*

10. With the cell pointer in the upper right-hand pane, scroll to the right until you can see the range M14:M23.

    ✓ *If you can't see the entire range M14:M23, adjust the size of the top panes by dragging the horizontal split bar down.*

11. In cell C55, enter a formula:

    a. Start by typing =**SUM(**

    b. Drag over the range M14:M23 to select it.

    c. Type a comma so you can insert another range to sum.

    d. Scroll the upper right-hand pane so you can see the range N27:N38.

       ✓ *If you need to adjust the size of the panes in order to be able to view the range, drag the vertical split bar up or down as needed.*

    e. Drag over the range N27:N38 to select it.

    f. Type **)** and press Enter to complete the formula. See Illustration A

12. Remove the panes by choosing Window, Remove Split.

13. Adjust column widths if needed.

14. Spell check the worksheet.

15. Print the worksheet.

16. Close the workbook, saving all changes.

Illustration A

	A	B	C	J	K	L	M	N	O	P
26		Employee Name	Employee ID	SS Tax	State Tax	Med	Dental	401k	LTD	Net F
27		Thomas Cortese	21875	$ 42.23	$ 16.24	$ -	$ -	$ 25.49	$ 7.33	$ 35
28		Javier Cortez	21154	$ 29.02	$ 11.16	$ 5.61	$ 1.65	$ 29.25	$ 7.99	$ 22
29		Rocio Cortez	23418	$ 39.57	$ 15.22	$ 5.61	$ 1.65	$ 26.15	$ 8.65	$ 31
30		Allen Gaines	23455	$ 33.93	$ 13.05	$ 4.79	$ -	$ 19.45	$ 9.31	$ 27
31		Freda Gage	27855	$ 37.44	$ 14.40	$ 5.61	$ 1.65	$ 28.98	$ 9.97	$ 29
32		Vickie Helms	31851	$ 36.86	$ 14.18	$ 4.79	$ 1.65	$ 40.54	$ 10.63	$ 27
33		Isiah Herron	33252	$ 57.01	$ 21.93	$ -	$ -	$ 58.03	$ 11.29	$ 45
34		Thomas Kaminski	37881	$ 45.63	$ 17.55	$ 5.61	$ 1.65	$ 49.59	$ 11.95	$ 34
35		Jalaine Kane	21154	$ 46.80	$ 18.00	$ 4.79	$ 1.65	$ 34.32	$ 12.61	$ 37
36		Sami Kafrawy	39581	$ 32.76	$ 12.60	$ 5.61	$ 1.65	$ 28.43	$ 13.27	$ 25
37		Akihiko Nakamura	34585	$ 22.82	$ 8.78	$ 5.61	$ 1.65	$ 42.22	$ 13.93	$ 14
38		Chris Nakao	29958	$ 59.56	$ 22.91	$ 4.79	$ -	$ 31.56	$ 14.59	$ 49
55		401k contributions	23,N27:N38)							
56										
57										
58										
59										
60										
61										
62										

Payroll

Edit   NUM

On Your Own

1. Start Excel, if necessary.

   ✓ *Pretend you are a teacher and that you need to create a worksheet to track your students test scores and grades.*

2. Save the workbook as **OXL24**.

3. In row 2, type a title for the worksheet.

4. Enter students' names in column A, beginning in row 5. Enter at least 25 names.

5. In row 4, beginning in column B, enter the labels for the tests and quizzes you need to track.

   ✓ *For example, type Test 1, Test 2, Quiz 1, Test 3, Quiz 2, and so on. Enter labels for a total of at least 12 tests and quizzes.*

6. Split the screen to the right of the student names and below the column labels.

7. Use the split windows to help you enter scores for all the tests and quizzes.

   a. Enter scores as whole numbers, such as 78.

   b. If you want to speed up your data entry, enter a range of scores and then copy those scores to another part of the worksheet.

8. Apply formatting to the worksheet.

9. Adjust column widths as needed.

10. Spell check the worksheet.

11. Print the worksheet.

12. Close the workbook, saving all changes.

Exercise 25

Skills Covered:

◆ **Drag-and-Drop Data Between Workbooks**
◆ **Link Workbooks**

On the Job

Arrange open files on the screen so you can see the worksheets as you work on them. For example, you may want to copy or move information across worksheets using the drag-and-drop procedure. You may want to consolidate information from several workbooks into a single summary workbook using the link feature. With the source and destination workbooks open on the screen, you can see the linked information update as source data changes.

You're an employee at Whole Grains Bread, and it's time to prepare your tax returns. Luckily, the company accountant has been showing you how she uses Excel to make tax preparation easier. You've entered most of the data, and all that's left are a few extra worksheets to see much you can reduce your taxes further. To complete the worksheets, you'll use linking to pull data from the IncomeTax workbook into the special TaxWS workbook you've created.

Terms

Drag-and-drop To use the mouse to copy or move information from one location to another on a worksheet, across worksheets, or across workbooks.

Link A reference in a cell in a dependent workbook to data contained in a cell in a source workbook.

Source The workbook that contains the data being referenced.

Dependent The workbook that references the data in the source.

External references References to cells in other workbooks.

Notes

Drag-and-Drop Data Between Workbooks

- If you arrange open workbooks on the screen, you can use the **drag-and-drop** procedure to copy or move data across workbooks.

- To copy data, press the Ctrl key while dragging the border of the selected range from the source to the destination workbook.

- To move data, drag the border of the selected range from the source to the destination workbook.

Link Workbooks

- When you need to consolidate information from one or more workbooks into a summary workbook, create a **link**.

- The **source** workbook provides the data.

- The **dependent** workbook contains the link to the **external references** in the source workbook.

- The default setting for linking is to update workbook links automatically. This means that, as data in the source workbook is changed, the linked data in the destination workbook is updated as well.

■ If the dependent workbook is not open when data in the source workbook is changed, then the data in the dependent workbook will be changed later, when that workbook is opened.

✓ *If you open a dependent workbook without opening a source workbook first, you'll be asked if you want to update your dependent workbook. You can choose to update at that time, or not to update at all.*

■ You can link a file in one of three ways:

● Copy data from the source workbook and paste it into the dependent workbook using the Paste Special, Paste Link command to create an external reference that links the workbooks.

● Type the external reference as a formula using the following format:

=drive:\path\[file.xls]sheetname!reference

Example:

=c:\excel\mydocuments\[report.xls]\sheet1!H5

✓ *You may omit the path if the source and dependent files are saved in the same folder.*

● While editing or creating a formula in the dependent workbook, you can include an external reference by selecting a cell(s) in the source workbook.

■ When a cell in an external reference includes a formula, only the formula result displays in the dependent workbook.

■ If possible, save linked workbooks in the same directory (folder). You should save source workbooks first, then save the dependent workbook.

The source workbook contains the data being referenced in the dependent workbook

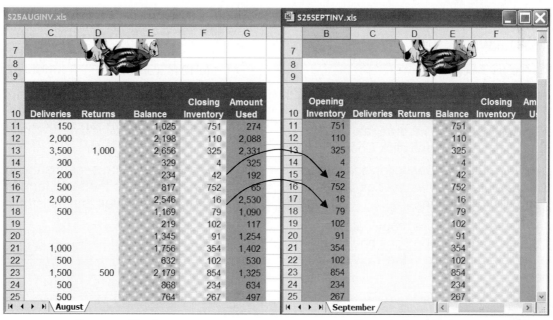

Source workbook   Dependent workbook

Procedures

Use Drag-and-Drop Data Between Workbooks

● Select range.

To copy data:

a. Press **Ctrl** while dragging border of selected range to new location in current worksheet, new worksheet, or new workbook.

b. Release mouse, then **Ctrl** key.

To move data:

● Drag border of selected range to new location in current worksheet, new worksheet, or new workbook.

Link Workbooks Using Paste Link

1. Open source and dependent workbooks.
2. Arrange workbooks on screen.
3. Select cells to reference in source workbook.
4. Click **Edit** .... Alt +E
5. Click **Copy** C

6. Select cells in dependent workbook to receive cell references.

7. Click **Edit** .... `Alt`+`E`

8. Click **Paste Special** .... `S`

9. Click **Paste Link** button

   `Paste Link` .... `Alt`+`L`

   ✓ *You can also click the arrow on the Paste button and select Paste Link from the list.*

✓ *To link to a cell while creating a formula, simply click the cell.*

✓ *For example, you could type =SUM(into a cell, then drag over cells located in another workbook, type) to complete the formula, and press Enter. Links to the cells you drug over are created automatically.*

Exercise Directions

1. Start Excel, if necessary.

2. Open 🖭 **25IncomeTax**.

3. Save the file as **IncomeTax**.

4. Open 🖭 **25TaxWS**.

5. Save the file as **TaxWS**.

6. Arrange the two open workbook windows, using the Horizontal option.

7. On the 1040 sheet of the **IncomeTax** workbook, click cell F26 and click Copy.

8. Click cell C6 on the IRA Deduction sheet of the **TaxWS** workbook, click the arrow on the Paste button, and click Paste Link.

9. Following these same steps, copy data from cells in the **IncomeTax** workbook and link them to the following cells in the **TaxWS** workbook:

Copy data from		Link data to	
Worksheet	Cell	Worksheet	Cell
1040	F10	IRA Deduction	C11
Income	B8	IRA Deduction	D12
Income	B17	IRA Deduction	E12
1040	F26	Student Loan	F4

10. Click cell C7 of the IRA Deduction sheet in the **TaxWS** workbook, and type **=SUM(**.

    a. Change to the IncomeTax workbook, and click cell E27.

    b. Type **,** and drag over cells E31:E37 on the 1040 sheet.

    c. Type **)** to complete the formula and press Enter.

11. Follow these same steps to create another sum:

    a. Click cell F5 on the Student Loan worksheet in the **TaxWs** workbook.

    b. Type **=SUM(** and drag over cells E27:E28 on the 1040 worksheet in the **IncomeTax** workbook.

    c. Type **,** and drag over cells E31:E37 on the 1040 worksheet of the **IncomeTax** workbook.

    d. Type **)** and press Enter.

12. Now that the tax worksheets are complete, link their values back to the 1040 form in the **IncomeTax** workbook (see Illustrations A, B, and C):

Copy data from		Link data to	
Worksheet	Cell	Worksheet	Cell
IRA Deduction	D15	1040	E28
Student Loan	F11	1040	E29

13. After looking it up in the tax tables, you discover that your federal income tax is $11,758. Enter this amount in cell F50 of the 1040 sheet in the 25IncomeTax workbook.

14. Widen columns in both workbooks as needed.

15. Spell check both workbooks.

16. Print both workbooks.

17. Close **TaxWS**, saving all changes.

18. Close **IncomeTax**, saving all changes.

Illustration A

	A	B	C	D	E	F
1	For Tax Filing 4/15/03					
2	Form 1040					
3	Line	Description	Amount			
4	6a	Yourself	1			
5	6b	Spouse	1			
6	6c	Dependents				
7		Therese (222-22-2222)	1			
8		Jorge (333-33-3333)	1			
9	6d	Total exemptions				4
10	7	Wages, salaries, tips, etc.				$ 88,740.00
11	8a	Taxable interest				$ 115.23
12	8b	Tax exempt interest				
13	9	Dividends				$ 78.56
14	10	Taxable refunds from state or local taxes				
15	11	Alimony				
16	12	Business income or (loss)				
17	13	Capital gain or (loss)				$ 3,875.00
18	14	Other gains or losses				
19	15a	Total IRA distributions	$ 31,598.00	15b	Taxable amount	$ -
20	16a	Total pensions and annuities		16b	Taxable amount	
21	17	Rental real estate				
22	18	Farm income or loss				
23	19	Unemployment compensation				
24	20a	Social Security benefits		20b	Taxable amount	
25	21	Other income				
26	22	Total income				$ 92,808.79
27	23	Educator expenses				
28	24	IRA deduction			$ 1,200.00	
29	25	Student loan interest			$ 778.56	
30	26	Tuition and fees deduction			$ 4,450.00	
31	27	Archer MSA deduction				
32	28	Moving expenses				
33	29	One-half of self-employment tax				
34	30	Self-employed health insurance deduction				
35	31	Self-employed SEP, SIMPLE, and qualified plans				
36	32	Penalty on early withdrawal of savings				
37	33	Alimony paid				

Illustration B

76	68	Other payments				
77	69	Total payments				$ 9,761.40
78	70	This is the amount you OVERPAID				$ -
79	71a	Amount to be refunded to you				$ -
80	72	Amount to be applied to 2003 tax				
81	73	The amount you OWE				$ 114.60
82	74	Estimated tax penalty				

Illustration C

	A	B	C	D	E	F
38	34	Total adjustments				$ 6,428.56
39	35	**Adjusted gross income**				$ 86,380.23
40	36	Amount from line 35				$ 86,380.23
41	37a	Check if You are 65 or older				
42		You are blind				
43		Spouse is 65 or older				
44		Spouse is blind				-
45	37b	Married filing separately and spouse itemizes				
46	38	Deduction (married jointly)				$ 7,850.00
47	39	Subtract line 38 from line 36				$ 78,530.23
48	40	Multiply $3,000 by tot. exemptions...				$ 12,000.00
49	41	Taxable income				$ 66,530.23
50	42	**Tax**				$ 11,758.00
51	43	Alternative minimum tax				
52	44	**Add lines 42 and 43**				$ 11,758.00
53	45	Foreign tax credit				
54	46	Credit for child and dependent care expenses			$ 682.00	
55	47	Credit for elderly or disabled				
56	48	Education credits				
57	49	Retirement savings credit				
58	50	Child tax credit			$ 1,200.00	
59	51	Adoption credit				
60	52	Credits from form 8396 or 8859				
61	53	Other credits from form 3800 or 8801				
62	54	Total credits				$ 1,882.00
63	55	Subtract line 54 from line 44				$ 9,876.00
64	56	Self-employment tax				
65	57	Social security tax and medicare tax on tip income				
66	58	Tax on IRAs				
67	59	Advanced EIC payments				
68	60	Household employment taxes				
69	61	**Total tax**				$ 9,876.00
70	62	Federal income tax withheld			$ 9,761.40	
71	63	2002 estimated tax payments				
72	64	Earned income credit				
73	65	Excess social security tax and tier 1 RRTA tax withheld				
74	66	Additional child tax credit				
75	67	Amount paid with extension to file				

On Your Own

1. Open the file **OXL23**, created in the On Your Own of Exercise 23, or open ⊙ **25COLEXP**.

2. Save the file as **OXL25**. This will be your source document.

3. Create a new workbook and save it as **OXL25-2**. This will be your dependent document.

4. Set up the **OXL25-2** worksheet to show the semester totals for expenses:

   a. Enter a title in row 1.

   b. Enter four column labels for 2005 and 2006, semesters 1 and 2.

5. Tile the two files on the screen.

6. Use the Paste Link command to copy the 2005 semester totals from the **OXL25** source workbook to the appropriate cells below the column labels in the **OXL25-2** dependent workbook.

7. Enter estimated expenses for 2006.

8. Format as desired, widen columns, spell check, and print the new worksheet.

9. Close the workbooks, saving all changes.

Exercise 26

On the Job

Write a 3-D formula to reference values in the same cells, across multiple worksheets. For example, you may want to total data from several worksheets into a summary worksheet. When you need to look at more than one of the worksheets in a workbook, create a duplicate workbook window.

As Sales Director at Whole Grains Bread, you designed a workbook to track three months' worth of sales at each of your various locations. It's almost complete, but you need to add some 3-D formulas to summarize the monthly totals into a final set of totals for the quarter.

Terms

3-D formula An equation that references values across worksheets.

3-D reference A reference to a value from any sheet or range of sheets used in a 3-D formula.

Duplicate workbook window An option that allows you to view an exact copy of the active workbook.

Notes

3-D Formulas

- Create a **3-D formula** when you want to summarize data from several worksheets into a single worksheet.

- A 3-D formula contains references to the same cell or range of cells on several worksheets in the same workbook. These cell references are called **3-D references**.

- You can refer to the same cell/range on consecutive (Sheet 1, Sheet 2, Sheet 3) or non-consecutive (Sheet 1 and Sheet 4) worksheets.

  =Sheet1!G24+Sheet4!G24

  ✓ *This formula adds the values in the same cell (cell G24) of the non-consecutive worksheets Sheet1 and Sheet 4.*

  =SUM(Sheet1:Sheet3!G24)

  ✓ *This formula adds the values in the same cell (G24) in the consecutive worksheets Sheet 1, Sheet2, and Sheet3.*

- As you create or edit a formula, you can select the cells of a 3-D reference in the worksheets or type them into the formula.

- When typing a 3-D formula, use an exclamation point to separate the sheet name(s) from the cell reference(s).

  April!G41+September!G41

- Use a colon (:) between sheet names to indicate a range of worksheets.

  April:June!B23:D45

  Sheet2:Sheet3!C21

- Quotation marks surround a sheet name that contains a space.

  "NW Region"D14+"SW Region"D14

  "Tax 2001":"Tax 2003"G23

- Combine a 3-D reference with a function to create a formula that references data on different worksheets.

  =SUM(Exp2000:Exp2002!C14:C22)

G10	▼	*fx* =SUM(May:July!G10)

S26CHIPCOSTS.xls:4

	E	F	G	H
9	LABOR	SHIPPING	NET PROFIT	
10	$ 6,799,914	$ 2,147,341	$ 5,547,298	
11	$ 4,442,097	$ 1,402,767	$ 3,623,816	
12	$ 9,659,206	$ 3,050,276	$ 7,879,879	
13	$ 2,439,142	$ 770,255	$ 1,989,826	
14	$ 2,198,153	$ 694,153	$ 1,793,230	
15				
16	$ 25,538,512	$ 8,064,793	$ 20,834,049	
17				

◄ ◄ ► ►◄ \ **May** / June / July / Qtr 2 /

S26CHIPCOSTS.xls:2

	E	F	G	H
9	LABOR	SHIPPING	NET PROFIT	
10	$ 5,960,221	$ 1,882,175	$ 4,862,285	
11	$ 4,171,813	$ 1,317,415	$ 3,403,321	
12	$ 7,278,890	$ 2,298,597	$ 5,938,042	
13	$ 2,984,889	$ 942,597	$ 2,435,041	
14	$ 2,464,137	$ 778,149	$ 2,010,217	
15				
16	$ 22,859,950	$ 7,218,932	$ 18,648,907	
17				

◄ ◄ ► ►◄ \ May \ **June** / July / Qtr 2 /

S26CHIPCOSTS.xls:3

	E	F	G	H
9	LABOR	SHIPPING	NET PROFIT	
10	$ 7,393,323	$ 2,334,733	$ 6,031,395	
11	$ 6,254,008	$ 1,974,950	$ 5,101,954	
12	$ 10,999,386	$ 3,473,490	$ 8,973,183	
13	$ 4,691,386	$ 1,481,490	$ 3,827,183	
14	$ 3,600,810	$ 1,137,098	$ 2,937,503	
15				
16	$ 32,938,911	$ 10,401,762	$ 26,871,217	
17				

◄ ◄ ► ►◄ \ May / June \ **July** / Qtr 2 /

S26CHIPCOSTS.xls:1

	E	F	G	H
9	LABOR	SHIPPING	NET PROFIT	
10	$ 20,153,457	$ 6,364,250	$ 16,440,978	
11	$ 14,867,917	$ 4,695,132	$ 12,129,090	
12	$ 27,937,482	$ 8,822,363	$ 22,791,104	
13	$ 10,115,417	$ 3,194,342	$ 8,252,051	
14	$ 8,263,100	$ 2,609,400	$ 6,740,950	
15				
16	$ 81,337,374	$ 25,685,486	$ 66,354,173	
17				

◄ ◄ ► ►◄ \ May / June / July \ **Qtr 2** / ◄

Total of cell G10 from three worksheets

Duplicate Workbook Window

- To view more than one worksheet of the active workbook at the same time on the screen, use the New Window command from the Window menu to make a **duplicate workbook window**.

  ✓ *When the new workbook window appears, it is maximized; to see both windows you must arrange them on-screen.*

  - Use the Arrange command from the Window menu to view the duplicate windows on the screen at the same time.

- In each window, click the sheet tab of the sheet you want to view.

- The number of duplicate windows that can be opened is determined by the amount of your system memory and the size of your monitor.

- You can add or edit data in the original or the duplicate window. All edits will be reflected in the other workbook automatically.

- If you close a duplicate window, the workbook remains open.

Procedures

Create 3-D Formula

To type 3-D reference in formula:

1. Position insertion point in formula where cell reference should be typed.

2. Type **=** and any function you wish to use in the formula, such as SUM.

3. Type sheet name.

   ✓ *Remember to type single or double quotation marks surrounding sheet names that contains spaces.*

To type 3-D reference for range of worksheets in formula:

a. Type **colon** (:)................ :

b. Type last sheet name in range.

4. Type **exclamation point** (!) .. !

5. Type cell reference or range.

   ✓ *Some examples are:*
   Sheet2:Sheet6!C4:C10
   'Quarter1'!C4:C10

6. Press **Enter** .... Enter

To insert 3-D reference in formula:

1. Position insertion point in formula where cell referenced should be typed.

2. Click sheet tab containing cell(s) to reference.

   ✓ *The name of sheet will appear in Formula bar.*

3. Select cell(s) to reference.

   ✓ *The complete 3-D reference appears in Formula bar when you selected the cell(s).*

To enter 3-D reference for range of worksheets:

1. Press **Shift** and click last sheet tab in range to reference.

2. Type or insert remainder of formula.

3. Press **Enter** .... Enter

   ✓ *The formula is completed and Excel returns to starting worksheet.*

Open Duplicate Workbook Window

1. Open window to duplicate.

2. Click **Window** .... Alt + W

3. Click **New Window** .... N

4. Click **Window** .... Alt + W

5. Click **Arrange** .... A

6. Select the arrangement you prefer:

   Tiled .... T

   Horizontal .... O

   Vertical V

   Cascade C

7. Select **Windows of active workbook** .... Alt + W

8. Press **Enter** .... Enter

Exercise Directions

1. Start Excel, if necessary.

2. Open 🖸 **26BreadSales 2**.

3. Save the file as **BreadSales 2**.

4. Type the formula **=SUM(July:September!C13)** into cell C13 of the Qtr 3 worksheet.

5. Enter the 3-D formula in cell C14:

   a. Type **=SUM(**

   b. Click cell C14 of the July worksheet.

   c. Press Shift, and click the tab of the September worksheet.

   d. Press Enter to complete the formula.

6. Copy the formula from cell C14 to the range C15:C28. See Illustration A.

7. Copy the formulas in column C to the range D13:F28.

8. Adjust column widths to fit the data.

9. Duplicate the workbook window, and arrange them horizontally.

10. Display the July worksheet in the top window, and the Qtr 3 worksheet in the bottom window.

11. Use Edit, Paste Special to link the values in the range C30:F30 on the July worksheet to the range K13:N13 on the Qtr 3 sheet.

12. In the top window, change to the August worksheet, and link the values in the range C30:F30 to the range K14:N14 in the Qtr 3 sheet.

13. In the top window, change to the September worksheet, and link the values in the range C30:F30 to the range K15:N15 in the Qtr 3 sheet.

14. Close the duplicate window.

15. Widen columns as needed.

16. Spell check the workbook.

17. Print the workbook.

18. Close the workbook, saving all changes.

| | C13 | ▼ | *fx* | =SUM(July:September!C13) | | | | | | | | | |

Spreadsheet screen — Illustration A

	A	B	C	D	E	F	G
11	Qtr 3 Sales Report - Totals by City						
12			Sales	Coupons	Ingredients	Labor	Net Profit
13		Bend, OR	$ 237,455	$ 60,140	$ 20,283	$ 26,120	$ 130,912
14		Eugene, OR	$ 236,054	$ 35,645	$ 20,052	$ 28,250	$ 152,107
15		Larkspur 1, CA	$ 364,269	$ 74,621	$ 30,241	$ 47,016	$ 212,391
16		Larkspur 2, CA	$ 481,331	$ 56,482	$ 36,697	$ 54,684	$ 333,468
17		Olympia, WA	$ 211,711	$ 28,229	$ 16,704	$ 23,288	$ 143,490
18		Portland 1, OR	$ 545,181	$ 57,782	$ 32,713	$ 64,354	$ 390,333
19		Portland 2, OR	$ 507,306	$ 45,442	$ 38,438	$ 55,804	$ 367,622
20		Redmond, WA	$ 567,829	$ 75,870	$ 45,776	$ 61,556	$ 384,627
21		Salem, OR	$ 315,100	$ 61,487	$ 25,262	$ 31,290	$ 197,060
22		San Bernardino, C	$ 311,757	$ 33,029	$ 23,443	$ 36,163	$ 219,122
23		San Diego, CA	$ 261,931	$ 24,820	$ 21,186	$ 32,971	$ 182,953
24		San Francisco, CA	$ 510,187	$ 42,005	$ 40,890	$ 52,229	$ 375,063
25		Seattle 1, WA	$ 710,534	$ 68,782	$ 52,082	$ 78,159	$ 511,511
26		Seattle 2, WA	$ 547,547	$ 44,406	$ 43,201	$ 62,414	$ 397,526
27		Spokane, WA	$ 292,819	$ 28,935	$ 24,150	$ 35,032	$ 204,701
28		Three Sisters, OR	$ 220,859	$ 15,662	$ 23,222	$ 25,415	$ 156,561
30		Totals	$ 6,321,869	$ 753,338	$ 494,342	$ 714,743	$ 4,359,446

Qtr 3 Sales Report - Totals by Month

	Sales	Coupons	Ingredients	Labor	Net Profit
July	$ 1,992,312	$ 235,922	$ 157,193	$ 219,154	$ 1,380,042
August	$ 2,166,278	$ 268,770	$ 177,930	$ 241,334	$ 1,478,244
September	$ 2,163,280	$ 248,646	$ 159,218	$ 254,255	$ 1,501,160
Totals	$ 6,321,869	$ 753,338	$ 494,342	$ 714,743	$ 4,359,446

Sheet tabs: July / August / September / **Qtr 3**

On Your Own

1. Open the file **OXL24**, created in the On Your Own of Exercise 24, or open ⊙ **26GRADES**.

2. Save the file as **OXL26**.

3. Remove the window split bars.

4. Rename Sheet 1 **Sem 1**. Rename Sheet 2 **Grades**.

5. Insert a copy of the Sem 1 sheet between the two sheets, and rename it **Sem 2**.

6. Enter new scores on the Sem 2 sheet.

   ✓ *You do not have to change every score.*

7. Copy the worksheet title and the students' names from one of the semester sheets to the Grades worksheet.

8. On the Grades sheet, enter the column labels **Tests**, **Quizzes**, and **Final Grade**.

9. In the Tests column, for the first student, enter a 3-D formula that averages the test scores for both semesters. Copy this formula down the column.

10. Use a 3-D formula to average the quiz scores for both semesters.

11. Compute the final grades however you like.

    ✓ *For example, you could average the test and quiz scores together, rounded to zero decimal places.*

12. Widen columns as needed to display data.

13. Apply formatting as desired.

14. Spell check the worksheet.

15. Print the worksheet.

16. Close the workbook, saving all changes.

Exercise 27

You are the Accounting Manager at Whole Grains Bread, and you've been working on this quarter's profit and loss statement (income statement). Preparing the statement hasn't been easy, but you're just about done. You need to create some 3-D formulas, link to some data stored in two other workbooks, and then print the result.

Exercise Directions

1. Start Excel, if necessary.
2. Open ☼ **27WGBP&L**.
3. Save the file as **WGBP&L**.
4. Open ☼ **27BreadSales 2**.
5. Arrange the two workbooks on-screen in a tiled fashion.
6. Copy cell K17 on the Qtr 3 sheet of the **27BreadSales 2** workbook, and paste link it to cell F11 of the **WGBP&L** workbook. (See Illustrations A and B.)
7. Copy cell L17 on the Qtr 3 sheet of the **27BreadSales 2** workbook, and paste link it to cell E26 of the **WGBP&L** workbook.
8. Close the **27BreadSales 2** workbook and open ☼ **27WGBInventory**.
9. Save the file as **WGBInventory**. Maximize the workbook window.
10. Copy the range N13:N28 on the Opening sheet of the **WGBInventory** workbook, and link it to the range C13:C28 of the Qtr 3 sheet. (See Illustration C.)
11. Copy the range N13:N28 of the Ending sheet and link it to the range F13:F28 of the Qtr 3 sheet.
12. In cell D13 of the Qtr 3 sheet, create a 3-D formula that sums the values in N13 of the July Purchases, August Purchases, and September Purchases sheets.

13. Copy this 3-D formula down the range D14:D28 on the Qtr 3 sheet.
14. Select C30:D30 on the Qtr 3 sheet and click Copy.
    a. Click cell E14 in the **WGBP&L** workbook.
    b. Use Paste Special to transpose the data and paste the values only.
    c. Copy cell F30 on the Qtr 3 sheet and paste its value in cell E17 of the P&L sheet.
15. Widen the columns in both workbooks as needed.
16. Spell check the workbooks.
17. Print the **WGBInventory** workbook:
    a. For each sheet, change to landscape orientation.
    b. Add a custom footer with your name in the center and the page number on the right.
    c. Reduce the scaling to fit each sheet on its own page.
    d. Preview and then print the entire workbook.
18. Print the P&L worksheet:
    a. Reduce the scaling to fit the sheet on one page.
    b. Add a custom header that includes the date on the left, and the text **Prepared by** followed by your name on the right.
    c. Preview and then print two copies of the worksheet.
19. Close both files, saving all changes.

Illustration A

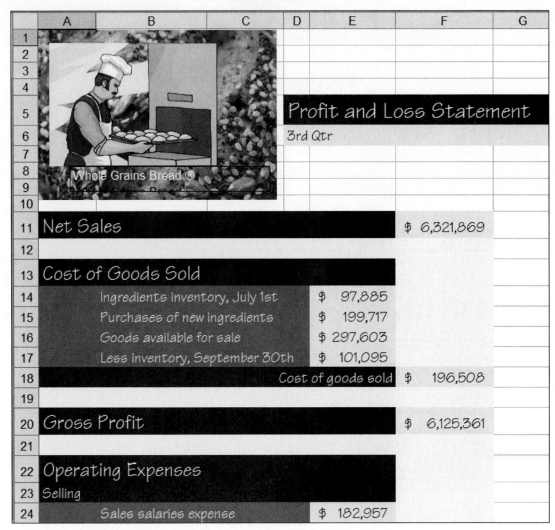

	A	B	C	D	E	F	G
1							
2							
3							
4							
5				Profit and Loss Statement			
6				3rd Qtr			
7							
8		Whole Grains Bread ®					
9							
10							
11	Net Sales					$ 6,321,869	
12							
13	Cost of Goods Sold						
14		Ingredients inventory, July 1st			$ 97,885		
15		Purchases of new ingredients			$ 199,717		
16		Goods available for sale			$ 297,603		
17		Less inventory, September 30th			$ 101,095		
18				Cost of goods sold	$ 196,508		
19							
20	Gross Profit					$ 6,125,361	
21							
22	Operating Expenses						
23	Selling						
24		Sales salaries expense			$ 182,957		

Illustration B

	A	B	C	D	E	F
25		Advertising expense			$ 210,987	
26		Sales promotions and coupons			$ 753,338	
27		Sales tax			$ 379,312	
28		Sales equipment purchases				
29		Sales equipment depreciation			$ 2,185	$ 1,528,779
30	Bakery					
31		Bakery salaries expense			$ 389,441	
32		Bakery equipment purchases			$ 72,187	
33		Bakery equipment depreciation			$ 51,237	$ 512,865
34	General and Administrative					
35		Office salaries expense			$ 142,345	
36		Office equipment purchases			$ 24,189	
37		Office equipment depreciation			$ 4,103	
38		Repairs expense			$ 136,897	
39		Utilities expense			$ 1,688	
40		Insurance expense			$ 2,033	
41		Interest expense			$ 9,713	$ 320,967
42				Total operating expenses		$ 2,362,612
43						
44		Earnings before income tax				$ 3,762,750
45		Income tax			$1,851,468	
46	Net Income					$ 1,911,282
47						
48	Common stock shares outstanding					$ 3,178,977
49	Earnings per share of common stock					$ 0.60

Illustration C

		Opening Inventory		Purchases		Goods for Sale		Ending Inventory	
10									
11	**Inventory Report - 3rd Qtr**								
12		Opening Inventory		Purchases		Goods for Sale		Ending Inventory	
13	Bend, OR	$	7,582	$	15,374	$	22,956	$	6,684
14	Eugene, OR	$	6,503	$	13,108	$	19,612	$	5,625
15	Larkspur 1, CA	$	5,237	$	11,573	$	16,811	$	7,203
16	Larkspur 2, CA	$	4,672	$	11,023	$	15,695	$	5,691
17	Olympia, WA	$	6,092	$	12,981	$	19,072	$	5,668
18	Portland 1, OR	$	5,135	$	14,453	$	19,588	$	6,677
19	Portland 2, OR	$	7,105	$	18,409	$	25,514	$	7,098
20	Redmond, WA	$	5,994	$	9,409	$	15,403	$	4,901
21	Salem, OR	$	6,421	$	15,601	$	22,022	$	7,647
22	San Bernardino, CA	$	6,509	$	13,494	$	20,003	$	6,951
23	San Diego, CA	$	4,626	$	10,569	$	15,195	$	5,220
24	San Francisco, CA	$	7,717	$	9,610	$	17,328	$	4,363
25	Seattle 1, WA	$	6,845	$	9,335	$	16,180	$	4,498
26	Seattle 2, WA	$	5,823	$	10,151	$	15,974	$	4,700
27	Spokane, WA	$	5,435	$	16,159	$	21,594	$	12,924
28	Three Sisters, OR	$	6,189	$	8,467	$	14,655	$	5,246
29									
30	Totals	$	97,885	$	199,717	$	297,603	$	101,095
31									
32									

Opening / July Purchases / August Purchases / September Purchases / Ending \ **Qtr 3** /

Access 2003

Lesson 1

Getting Started with Access 2003
Exercises 1-6

Lesson 2

Working with Tables and Datasheets
Exercises 7-11

Lesson 3

Simplifying Data Entry with Lookups and Forms
Exercises 12-17

Lesson 4

Find Information in a Database
Exercises 18-23

Lesson 5 (on CD ⊚)

Display Information with Reports
Exercises 24-28

Directory of Data Files on CD

Exercise #	File Name	Page #
1	AC01	334
2	AC02	341
3	None	346
4	None	350
5	AC05	356
6	None	357
7	AC07	363
8	AC08, AC08-A.txt, AC08-B.xls	368
9	AC09	373
10	AC10	377
11	AC11, AC11-A.xls	379
12	AC12	384
13	AC13	390
14	AC14	395
15	AC15	400
16	AC16	406
17	AC17	408
18	AC18	412
19	AC19	415
20	AC20	419
21	AC21	425
22	AC22	429
23	AC23	430

Database Basics

Skills Covered:

◆ **What is Access?** ◆ **What is a Database?**
◆ **What is a Database Management System?**
◆ **How is an Access Database Organized?**
◆ **How are Access Tables Related?**

Notes

What is Access?

- Microsoft Office Access is the best-selling personal computer database management system. The notes below describe what a database management system is in more detail.

- You can share data created in Access with other Microsoft Office applications, especially Word and Excel.

What is a Database?

- A **database** is an organized collection of information about a subject.

- Examples of databases include an address book, the telephone book, a CD tower full of music CDs, or a filing cabinet full of documents relating to clients.

- A name, address, and phone listing in an address book is an example of a common manual database. To update an address of a friend in Denver, you would search for the name, erase or cross out the existing address, and write in the new address.

Examples of manual database records

Name: Jim Ferrara Address: 84 Winthrop Rd. City: Denver State: CO Zip: 80209 Telephone: 303-555-5576 Notes: Note new address and phone number.	Part Number: 001759 Part Description: Socket wrench Cost: $3.50 List Price: $14.99 Date Received: 2/23/04
Address Book Entry	Inventory Card

- While updating one or two address in a manual database may not take a lot of effort, searching for all friends in one city or sorting all clients who have done business with you in the last month would take considerable effort.

- An **Access database** is a computer-based equivalent of a manual database. Access makes it easy to organize and update information electronically.

What is a Database Management System?

- A **database management system** such as Access includes both the database information and the tools to use the database. These tools allow you to input, edit, and verify your data.

- With Access, you can sort, find, analyze, and report on information in your database. For example, in a sales management database you could find all clients who bought a mountain bike in the last year and create mailing labels in order to send them an announcement of a new bike trails book.

How is an Access Database Organized?

- Unlike other database software programs, Access maintains all its objects in one database file. This file uses the MDB extension.

The Database Window Organizes Objects

- When you open a database file, you see the **database window**, which displays seven buttons under the Objects button.

- Each button changes the database window to display a list of the database **objects** for each object type. (See the next column and next page for a description of each object type.) For example, click on the Forms button to see a list of all forms.

Access database window

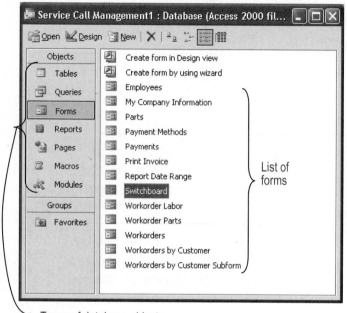

Types of database objects

Tables Store Information

- All Access database information is stored in tables. Each table contains information about a particular topic. For example, a sales inventory database may have separate tables for clients, products, and sales.

- Each row of an Access table is a **record**. A record is a set of details about a specific item. For example, a record for a client may contain the client's name, address, and phone number. A record about a product could include the part number, serial number, and price.

- Each column of an Access table is a **field**. Fields provide the categories for the details describing each record. In the client example above, there would be separate fields for name, address, and phone number.

- Each column is headed by a **field name**.

- The specific field data within a record is the **field contents**.

Tables store information in rows and columns

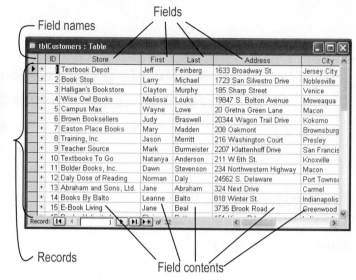

- Good database design may require you to break what you originally thought may be one field into multiple fields. For example, the table shown above might be improved by splitting the Contact Name field into Contact First Name and Contact Last Name fields if that information might ever be used as separate units, such as in addressing correspondence.

- You can decide what to make into fields by thinking about how you will sort or look up the information. Many client lists, for example, sort by last name and then by first name.

Database Objects Help You Search, Analyze, and Present Data

- Database objects are the elements that make up a database. Although each Access database has numerous objects, there are seven major object types that are visible as soon as you open a database.

  - **Table**
    You store database information in one or more tables. You view, edit, and input information in tables in Datasheet view, which has rows and columns, just like an Excel spreadsheet.

- **Form**

  A form is a window for viewing the data in one or more tables. Forms make it easy to view, input, and edit data because forms typically show all the information for one record on a single page.

A form displays information for a single record

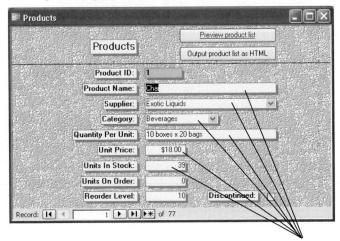

Fields

- **Query**

  A query allows you to see or work with a portion of a table by limiting the number of fields and by selecting specific records. For example, a bank may choose to see just the name, phone, and amount for all clients in Texas whose accounts are over $10,000.

Design queries to sort and analyze data

Table selected for query

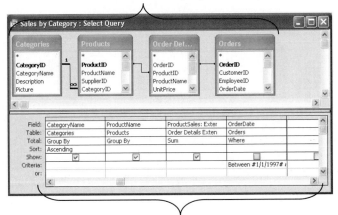

Fields and criteria selected for query

Query results show a portion of table data

Only selected fields appear in query result

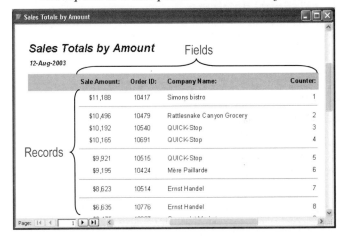

- **Report**

  A report is formatted information from a table or query that you can send to a printer. Reports can include a detailed list of records, calculated values and totals from the records, mailing labels, or a chart summarizing the data.

Use reports to create printed summaries of data

Sales Totals by Amount				
12-Aug-2003			Fields	
Sale Amount:	Order ID:	Company Name:		Counter:
$11,188	10417	Simons bistro		1
$10,496	10479	Rattlesnake Canyon Grocery		2
$10,192	10540	QUICK-Stop		3
$10,165	10691	QUICK-Stop		4
$9,921	10515	QUICK-Stop		5
$9,195	10424	Mère Paillarde		6
$8,623	10514	Ernst Handel		7
$6,635	10776	Ernst Handel		8

Records

- **Macro**

  Macros allow you to automate some processes within Access. Macros are beyond the scope of this book.

- **Module**

  Modules help automate Access tasks. Modules give you more flexibility for each automated process than macros do. Modules are also not included in this book.

- **Page**

  This feature allows you to create Web-based forms that allow users to read data from your database via the Internet. Some pages also allow user input.

Pages let users work with database data on the Web

Input or edit information
using a form on the Web

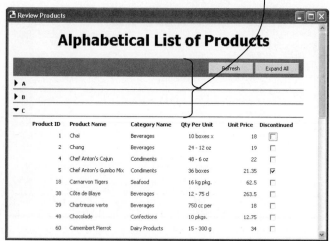

How are Access Tables Related?

- Database tables that share common fields are **related**. Most Access databases have multiple tables that are related to each other, which means you can use Access to create a **relational database**.

- A relational database breaks the "big picture" into smaller, more manageable pieces. For example, if you were gathering information about a new product line, each type of information—product, suppliers, customers—would be stored in its own, related table rather than in one large, all-inclusive table.

- You relate one table to another through a common field. For example, the Products table will have a ProductID field that also appears in the Customers table.

- This capability to store data in smaller, related tables gives a relational database great efficiency, speed, and flexibility in locating and reporting information.

Database tables have relationships between them

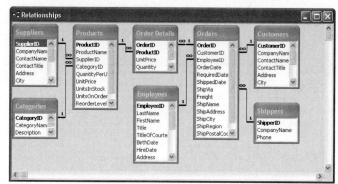

Exercise 1

◆ **Start Access and Open a Database**
◆ **Create a Backup of a Database** ◆ **Navigate in a Database**
◆ **Move through a Datasheet** ◆ **Move through a Form**
◆ **Sort Records**

On the Job

Your first goal in working with a database is to start Access and open a database. You must then be able to identify and move around each of the various objects in the database. A quick sort of the data lets you find data quickly and perform a simple analysis of the information.

You have just been hired as a database specialist for Whole Grains Bread, a California-based bakery chain. One of your responsibilities is going to be maintaining some existing databases. You will start by reviewing the data in a database that stores employee information and sorting this data in several ways.

Terms

Database file The file that contains all objects of your database.

Database window The on-screen container that has a separate button for each object type (tables, queries, forms, reports, pages, and others).

Switchboard An Access form with command buttons or other controls that lead to other switchboard forms, input forms, and reports.

Datasheet view The view of a table that shows you the data in each record. Like a spreadsheet, the datasheet shows rows (records) and columns (fields).

Sort To organize data alphabetically or in numerical order.

Ascending To sort from the smallest to the largest (from A to Z and from 1 to 9).

Descending To sort from the largest to the smallest (from Z to A and from 9 to 1).

Notes

Start Access and Open a Database

- As with other Microsoft Office programs, you can start Access using the Start button or an icon on the desktop.

- When you start the program, Access displays the Getting Started task pane at the right, from which you can open an existing database or start a new one.

Access's Getting Started task pane provides shortcuts for opening and creating database files

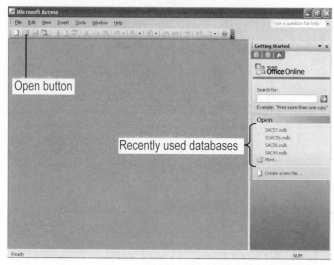

- The most recent databases you have opened appear in the *Open* section in the lower half of the Getting Started task pane. You can quickly reopen one of them by clicking its name.

- If the database you want to open does not appear on that list, click More to use the Open dialog box to locate the file you want.

- You can also display the Open dialog box by clicking the Open button on the toolbar.

- If you need help with the Open dialog box, see Exercise 9 in Lesson 2 of the Word section in this book.

- After the **database file** opens, you see the **database window**.

The database window is a central point from which you can open tables, queries, forms, and so on

✓ Notice that the title bar of the database window reports that the database is in Access 2000 format. By default, all files created in Access 2003 (and also 2002) are in Access 2000 format, for compatibility with the earlier Access version. You will learn more about file formats in upcoming exercises.

- Some databases, such as those created with the Database Wizard, display a **Switchboard** window when you open them. You can close the Switchboard window by clicking its Close button.

- After closing the Switchboard, you might need to maximize the minimized database window. Double-click it to do so.

Close the Switchboard window if it appears when you open a database, and restore the Database window

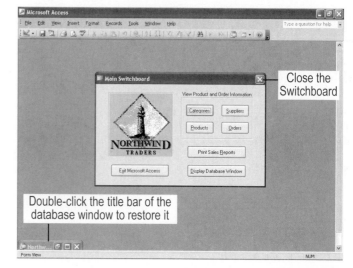

- You can start Access and open a database file at the same time by double-clicking the database file you want to open from Windows Explorer or My Computer.

- You can also use the Open Office Document command on the Start menu in Windows to select a database to open and start Access at the same time.

Create a Backup of a Database

- In previous versions of Access, there was no way to make a copy of a whole database from within Access; users had to do it by copying the file from My Computer or Windows Explorer.

- In Access 2003, a backup feature within Access enables users to copy and save a whole database under a different name. (It starts with the original file name and appends the current date to the name.) You will use this feature extensively in this book to make copies of the data files needed for the exercises.

- After making a backup copy of the database, you must open the copy in order to work with it; otherwise, you will continue working with the original.

Navigate in a Database

Open Objects with the Database Window

- Use the database window to select the type of object you want to work with in Access. Click one of the Objects buttons in the Objects bar to view the available objects of that type, which are displayed in the right portion of the window.

To open an object from the database window, double-click it

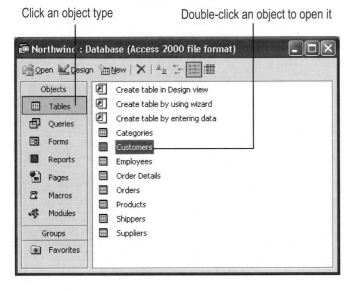

Click an object type — Double-click an object to open it

- Double-click an object to open it and begin work. For example, if you want to open a table called *Customers*, click the Tables button, and then double-click the icon for customers. You can also click on the object icon and click the Open button.

Move through a Datasheet

- When you open a table, data displays in a row and column format similar to a spreadsheet. Each column heading displays the caption or field name for the field, and each row contains all the information for a single record.

- This row and column display is called **Datasheet view**. This view enables you to see more than one record at a time on the screen.

Datasheet view displays data in rows and columns

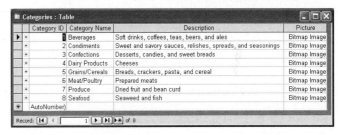

- To move through the datasheet, you can use the navigation buttons at the bottom of the window.

- The navigation buttons also show the current record and the total number of records. You can type a record number in the specific record box and press Enter to move to that record.

Datasheet navigation buttons

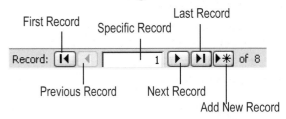

- When you move into a field, you are in one of two modes: *field edit mode* or *navigation mode*. The insertion point displays in the field in edit mode; the entire field entry is highlighted when you are in navigation mode. To switch back and forth between the two modes, press F2.

- Press Tab to go from one column to the next column. In the last column, press Tab to go to the first column in the next record.

- You can use the arrow keys to move around the datasheet, and you can also use a number of shortcut keys to move to specific points in the datasheet.

Move through a Form

- You can navigate through records on a form using the same navigation buttons that appear in Datasheet view of a table or form.

- If you are in navigation mode, you can also use shortcut keys such as Ctrl+Home and Ctrl+End to move to the first or last record on a form.

Sort Records

- Sorting rearranges records in order by one or more fields. Most types of fields can be sorted.

- You can **sort** in **ascending** order (A to Z or 1 to 9) or **descending** order (Z to A or 9 to 1).

- Before sorting, you must first move the insertion point to the field you want to sort. For example, if you want to sort a table of clients by last name in ascending order, move to the Last Name field, then click the Sort Ascending button.

- Some reasons to sort might be to:
  - See groups of data (for example, all clients who live in New York or all of yesterday's sales).
  - See information organized from smallest or largest values.
  - Group all records that have blanks in a field.
  - Look for duplicate records.

- You can sort in Datasheet or Form view. It is easier to see the sort results in Datasheet view.

- You can sort a table by any field.

You can sort a table by any field

Sort buttons

Ascending sort has been done in this column

Procedures

Start Access

1. Click **Start** button .
2. Click **All Programs**.
3. Point to **Microsoft Office**.
4. Click **Microsoft Office Access 2003**.

Open an Existing Database File when You Start Access

✓ *This feature does not work in Windows 2000.*

1. Click **Start** button 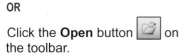.
2. Click **Open Office Document**.
3. Click the desired file.

✓ *You can change to another folder, if needed, to locate file you wish to open.*

✓ *To change folders, select a new folder from Look in drop-down list.*

4. Click **Open**.

Open a Recently Used Database File

• Click the **file name** in the Open section of the Getting Started task pane.

OR

1. Click **File** .... 🄵
2. Click the **file name** at the bottom of the File menu.

Open a Database File

1. Click **More files** on the task pane.
   OR
   Click the **Open** button 📂 on the toolbar.
2. Click the file you want to open.
3. Click **Open** .... 🄾

Copy a Database

1. Open the database file (see preceding steps).
2. Click **File** .... 🄵
3. Click **Back Up Database**. .... Alt + 🄺

4. Type name for the backup copy.

✓ *You can change to another folder, if needed, to save the copy in a different location.*

✓ *To change folders or drives select the desired drive or folder from the Save in drop-down list.*

5. Click **Save** .... Alt + 🅂

Open the Database Copy

1. Click the **Open** button 📂 on the toolbar.
2. Click the copy to be opened.
3. Click **Open** .... 🄾

Navigate in a Database

Open objects with the database window:

1. Click an **Objects** button.
2. Double-click the object you want to open.

OR

1. Click on object icon to select it.
2. Click **Open** in datasheet window. .... Alt + 🄾

Move through a datasheet:

• **Tab** into a field .... Tab
• Press **Ctrl+End** to move to last field and last row .... Ctrl + End
• Press **Ctrl+Home** to move to first field and first row .... Ctrl + Home
• Press **End** to move to last field in row .... End
• Press **Home** to move to first field in row .... Home

In Navigation mode, to move to:

• **Last field, last record of table** .... Ctrl + End
• **First field, first record of table** .... Ctrl + Home

• **Last field, current record** .... End
• **First field, current record** .... Home
• **Last record, current field** .... Ctrl + ↓
• **First record, current field** .... Ctrl + ↑
• **Next field (or if in last field to first field of next record)**.... Tab
• **Previous field** .... Shift + Tab

Sort Records

1. Open datasheet or form.
2. Click in column to be sorted in Datasheet view or one field in Form view.
3. Click **Records** .... Alt + 🅁
   a. Click **Sort**...................... 🅂
   b. Select **Sort Ascending** or **Sort Descending**.. 🄰 or 🄲
   OR
   Click **Sort Ascending** button 🔼 or **Sort Descending** button 🔽

Close a Table

1. Click **File** .... 🄵
2. Click **Close** .... 🄲

✓ *Text changes are saved automatically.*

3. If you are prompted to save design changes, click **Yes** to save changes or **No** to cancel changes.

Close Access

1. Click **File** .... 🄵
2. Click **Exit**............................. 🅇
   OR
   Click the **Close** button ⊠ on the Access window.

Exercise Directions

1. Start Access, if necessary.
2. Open ⊘ **AC01**.
   - ✓ *If you see a macro warning, click Enable Macros. To disable this warning in the future, choose Tools>Macro>Security and set the security to Low. However, check with your instructor before doing this, as it can leave Access vulnerable to security exploits.*
3. Save a copy of the database and name the copy **AC01-A**.
4. Open the **AC01-A** file. (The previous file closes automatically.)
5. In the database window, click **Tables** on the Objects list.
6. Open the **tblEmployees** table.
7. Scroll vertically to review some of the names.
8. Scroll horizontally to review the number of fields in the table.
9. Use the navigation buttons to find the record for **Kathie O'Meara**.
10. Move to the Last Name field and sort the client names in ascending order. After the sort, your table should look like the one shown in Illustration A.
    - ✓ *Choose Records, Sort, Sort Ascending or click the Sort Ascending button.*
11. Now sort the table in ascending order by ID.
12. Close the table without saving any changes.
13. Click the Forms button on the Database window.
14. Open the form **frmEmployees**.
15. Go to the record for **Michael Johnson**.
16. Now go back to the first record. Scroll through the records and count how many of the people are full-time.
17. Sort the records in ascending order by Store.
    - ✓ *Move to the City field, then choose Records, Sort, Sort Ascending or click the Sort Ascending button.*
18. Scroll through the records. Note that this sort groups the clients by city, starting with **Corte Madera** and ending with **Tiburon**.
19. Close the form.
20. Exit the database.
    - ✓ *Click the Close button ⊠ or File, Exit.*

On Your Own

1. Start Access and open the **AC01-A** database that you created in the Exercise. Or, if you did not do the Exercise, open ⊘ **AC01**.
2. Open the **tblEmployees** table.
3. Use keystroke shortcuts to go to the following locations in the table:
   - The current field of the last record.
   - The last field of the current record.
   - The previous field.
   - The first field of the first record.
4. Find the record for **Ellen Mills**. What is her address?

   _____

5. Sort the table in ascending order by ZIP. How many clients live in the **94965** ZIP Code?

   _____

6. Close the table without saving any changes.

Illustration A

ID	Prefix	First Name	Last Name	Address	City	State	ZIP	Phone	
14	Mrs.	Jane	Abrahamson	324 Next Drive	Corte Madera	CA	94925	(415) 555-2828	mailto:ja
3	Ms.	Leanne	Balto	818 Winter St.	Larkspur	CA	94977	(415) 555-2111	mailto:lb
17	Ms.	Elaine	Betts	151 Kings Rd.	Larkspur	CA	94939	(415) 555-3983	mailto:eb
22	Mr.	Korak	Bhimani	425 Circle K. Road	Larkspur	CA	94939	(415) 555-0929	mailto:kb
15	Mr.	Chip	Blair	983 Dude Ranch	Sausalito	CA	94965	(415) 555-1222	mailto:cl
25	Mr.	Tyrone	Braxton	866 Silver Creek	Larkspur	CA	94977	(415) 555-8928	mailto:tb
27	Ms.	Jane	Coffin	3735 Brook Canyon Road	San Rafael	CA	94901	(415) 555-8917	mailto:jc
23	Mr.	Juan	Gomez	1344 Syracuse St.	Larkspur	CA	94922	(415) 555-4943	mailto:jg
12	Mr.	Michael	Johnson	108 Steele St.	San Rafael	CA	94901	(415) 555-1111	mailto:m
9	Mr.	Jamal	Joyner	1 Park Avenue	Larkspur	CA	94977	(415) 555-5192	mailto:jjc
19	Mr.	Chris	Katz	1800 Ridgewood Road	Corte Madera	CA	94925	(415) 555-9100	mailto:ck
24	Mrs.	Judy	Lenardsen	2010 Wall St.	Larkspur	CA	94977	(415) 555-1732	mailto:jle
6	Mr.	Jesus	Martinez	491 Cherokee St.	Larkspur	CA	94977	(415) 555-3333	mailto:jm
11	Ms.	Maria	Martinez	491 Cherokee St.	Larkspur	CA	94977	(415) 555-3333	mailto:...
20	Ms.	Ellen	Mills	1110 Vine	Larkspur	CA	94939	(415) 555-1283	mailto:er
21	Mr.	Allan	Mitra	778 Meadow View Drive	Mill Valley	CA	94941	(415) 555-8472	mailto:ar
10	Ms.	Michele	Mitterand	PO Box 1556	Mill Valley	CA	94941	(415) 555-8917	mailto:m
16	Mrs.	Minny	Moore	888 Market St.	Larkspur	CA	94977	(415) 555-6633	mailto:m
26	Mr.	John	Mozeliak	110 N. Sadle Dr.	San Rafael	CA	94901	(415) 555-1788	mailto:jm
5	Mr.	Al	Nehru	1551 James	Fairfax	CA	94930	(415) 555-3010	mailto:ar
4	Ms.	Kathie	O'Meara	154 Newton	Fairfax	CA	94930	(415) 555-4987	mailto:kc
8	Mr.	John	Smythe	15 Cosby Lane	Corte Madera	CA	94925	(415) 555-9174	mailto:jc

tblEmployees : Table

Record: 1 of 25

Exercise 2

Skills Covered:

◆ **Enter Records** ◆ **Edit Records** ◆ **Select Records**
◆ **Delete Records** ◆ **Print Datasheets and Forms** ◆ **Print Preview**

On the Job

Your main task as a user of a database is to enter and edit data stored in the database. You must be able to enter new records, typically in a form or a datasheet. You will also edit records already stored in the database and correct entries as you enter them. Printing a table or form provides you with a hard copy of the database, which can be used, for example, by a manager for reviewing and on-paper editing.

Part of your job with Whole Grain Breads is to update the employee database when contact information changes or when new people are hired. You will do this by entering records using both a form and a datasheet. You will make changes to existing records and correct information as you enter it. You will then print the updated database to create a hard copy of the information.

Terms

Table A collection of database fields designed to be used together.

Datasheet A grid showing the data in a table, with the field names as column headings and the records in rows beneath them.

Form A window showing the data in a table with one record's fields appearing at a time in individually labeled boxes.

Preview To produce a screen view of what a printed page will look like.

Notes

Enter Records

- When you enter records, they are stored in a **table**. Of all the types of objects in Access, tables are the only object type that can hold records. Most of the other types of objects are simply ways of looking at the data from one or more tables.

- To enter records in a **datasheet** or in a **form**, type the information you want in a field, and press Tab or Enter to go to the next field.

Enter Records in a Datasheet

- To enter records in a datasheet, type the data below each field name as you would in an Excel worksheet.

- Type the information you want for the record, and press Tab or Enter to go to the next field.

- When you enter data in the last field for a record, press Tab or Enter to go to the first field of the next record. If you are at the last record of the table, this will automatically create a new record.

- Unlike other Microsoft Office applications where you have to choose the Save command, Access automatically saves a record when you go to another record.

Special Data Entry Field Types

- Depending on the way the database is set up, some fields may not be simple text boxes; instead they may be drop-down lists or checkboxes.

- A checkbox appears in a logical (yes/no) field. Mark the checkbox by clicking it to choose Yes, or leave it cleared to choose No.

- A field with a drop-down list will have a down-pointing arrow to its left when selected. Click that arrow to open a menu, and then click your selection from the menu.

- A field that is set up for hyperlinks accepts either Web addresses (http://) or e-mail addresses. If you enter an e-mail address, you must precede the address with mailto. For example, mailto:fwempen@wholegrainsbread.com

Special types of data entry fields require more than just simple typing

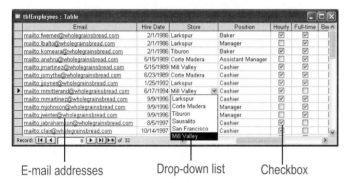

E-mail addresses   Drop-down list   Checkbox

Copy Data

- Use the Copy and Paste commands to enter repetitive data. Select the data you want to copy, and then use the Copy command. Then move the insertion point to the location you want the data to appear. Use the Paste command to insert the copied data.

- To copy, you can choose the Copy command from the Edit menu, press Ctrl+C, or click the Copy button.

- To paste, you can choose the Paste command from the Edit menu, press Ctrl+V, or click the Paste button.

- The Clipboard task pane enables you to store and paste multiple selections. It might appear automatically when you copy twice in a row without pasting.

- If the Clipboard task pane does not automatically appear, choose View, Task Pane and then choose Clipboard from the drop-down list at the top of the task pane.

- To paste a copied selection other than your most recently copied one, you can click it on the Clipboard task pane to paste it.

Select Clipboard from the available task panes

You can select which copied clip to paste from the Clipboard task pane

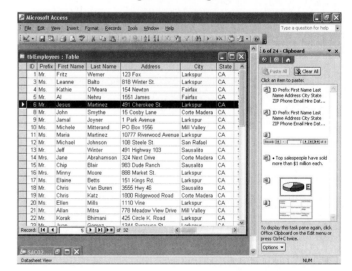

Move Data

- Moving data works the same way as copying it (see above, except you use the Cut command instead of the Copy command).

- To issue the Cut command, choose it from the Edit menu, press Ctrl+X, or click the Cut button.

Copy an Entire Record

- You cannot paste an entire record with the normal Paste command.

- To copy an entire record in Datasheet view, select the record by clicking its record number. Then copy it, select the destination location, and choose Edit, Paste Append. Existing information will be overwritten with the new information.

- The Paste Append command does not have a keyboard shortcut or toolbar button equivalent.

Select a record, copy it; and then use
Paste Append to paste a copy of it elsewhere

ID	Prefix	First Name	Last Name	Address	City	State	ZIP
1	Mr.	Fritz	Werner	123 Fox	Larkspur	CA	94939
3	Ms.	Leanne	Balto	818 Winter St.	Larkspur	CA	94977
4	Ms.	Kathie	O'Meara	154 Newton	Fairfax	CA	94930
5	Mr.	Al	Nehru	1551 James	Fairfax	CA	94930
6	Mr.	Jesus	Martinez	491 Cherokee St.	Larkspur	CA	94977
8	Mr.	John	Smythe	15 Cosby Lane	Corte Madera	CA	94925
9	Mr.	Jamal	Joyner	1 Park Avenue	Larkspur	CA	94977
10	Ms.	Michele	Mitterand	PO Box 1556	Mill Valley	CA	94941
11	Ms.	Maria	Martinez	10777 Riverwood Avenue	Larkspur	CA	94977
12	Mr.	Michael	Johnson	108 Steele St.	San Rafael	CA	94901
13	Mr.	Jeff	Winter	491 Highway 103	Sausalito	CA	94965
14	Mrs.	Jane	Abrahamson	324 Next Drive	Corte Madera	CA	94925

Record: 5 of 32

Click to select entire row

Enter Records in a Form

- You enter records in Form view the same way you do in Datasheet view. Type in a field and press Tab or Enter to go to the next field.

- When you are on the last field of the form and you press Tab or Enter, Access automatically saves the current record and the insertion point moves to the first field of the next record.

- If you are displaying a current record and want to add a new record, choose the New Record command from the Insert menu or click the New Record button ▶✳ on the toolbar or navigation bar.

Edit Records

- You may want to correct field information after you enter it. You can delete and add text in the same way you would in Word or Excel.

- Click to position the insertion point. Press Backspace to remove text before the insertion point or press Delete to remove text after the insertion point.

- You can also drag the mouse pointer to select text and then press Delete to remove the text.

- Select text and type new text to replace the selected text. You can double-click on a word to select a word, then type to replace it.

- If you move the mouse pointer to the beginning of a field, the pointer changes to a white plus sign. Click to select the entire content of that field.

- While you are making changes to a record, a pencil icon appears on the record selector button (to the left of the record). The pencil indicates that any changes are not currently saved.

- If you want to undo your changes, press Esc once to undo the change to the current field and press Esc again to undo all changes to the current record.

- Changes are automatically saved to the record when you go to another record or close the table or form.

Edit Hyperlink Fields

- A hyperlink field such as an e-mail address activates an e-mail or Web application when clicked on; therefore you cannot edit it normally.

- One way to edit it is to delete it and retype it. To delete it, select it and press Delete.

- To edit it, right-click it and point to Hyperlink, then click Edit Hyperlink. A box appears in which you can edit the address.

Edit a hyperlink in the Edit Hyperlink box

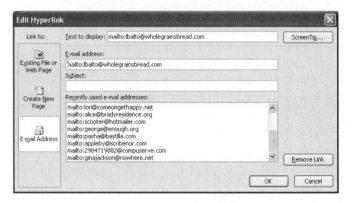

Select Records

- To select a single record, click its record selector button to its left.

- To select multiple contiguous (adjacent) records, select the first one and then hold down Shift as you click the record selector of the last one.

Delete Records

- You can delete the current record or one or more contiguous records.

- When you delete one or more records, Access will ask you to confirm the deletion. After you select *Yes*, you cannot reverse the deletion.

- Access shows the total number of records at the bottom of the window.

- If you have an AutoNumber field in the table, when you delete a record, Access will *not* reuse the numbers of the deleted records. AutoNumber fields are discussed in Exercise 5.

Print Datasheets and Forms

- Print all the records of the current screen in Datasheet or Form view by clicking the Print button ⏣.

- If you want to set print options, open the Print dialog box by choosing Print from the File menu.

Print dialog box

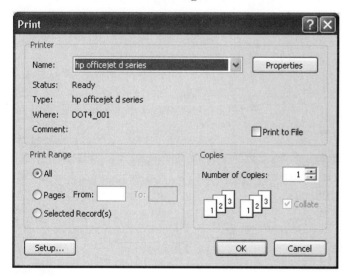

- The Name drop-down arrow in the Print dialog box allows you to choose a different printer.

- To print selected records, click the record selector to the left of one or more records in Datasheet or Form view. Then click File, Print and choose to print Selected Record(s) in the Print dialog box.

- If desired, type more than 1 in the Number of Copies box and then check Collate if you want to print the document in a complete set, or leave Collate unchecked if you want to print multiple copies of page 1, then page 2, and so on.

Print Preview

- Click the Print Preview button 🔍 on the toolbar to see a screen **preview** of what your printing will look like.

- While in Print Preview, click the magnifying glass to see more details or to return to full-page view.

- The Navigation buttons at the bottom of the screen in Print Preview allow you to see the first, previous, specific, next, or last page.

- Print Preview shows what the data will look like when printed

Zoom   Leave Print Preview

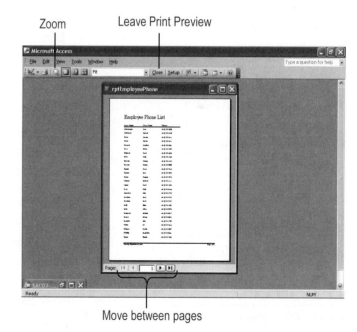

Move between pages

Procedures

Enter Records

To enter records in a datasheet:

1. Click in the first blank cell in the first field (the first column and first row).

2. Type data for field.

3. To correct an error, press **Backspace** .... `Backspace` and type again.

4. Press **Tab** to go to next field .... `Tab`

5. Repeat steps 2–4 for each field in record.

6. Click in first cell in the next row to begin new record.

339

To enter data quickly using shortcut keys:

- Copy value from the same field in the previous record .. `Ctrl` + `'`
- Enter current date .... `Ctrl` + `;`
- Enter current time .... `Ctrl` + `Shift` + `:`

To enter an e-mail address:

1. Click in the cell for an e-mail field.
   - ✓ *Field has to be formatted for hyperlinks.*
2. Type **mailto:** and then the e-mail address.

To enter a yes/no value:

- Click the checkbox to select **Yes**.
- Leave the checkbox empty to select **No**.

To select from a drop-down list of values:

1. Click the cell containing the drop-down list.
2. Click the down arrow button `▼`.
3. Click desired list item.

To enter records in a form:

1. Type data in first field.
2. Press **Tab**............................ `Tab`
3. Repeat steps 1 and 2 until complete.

Copy Data

To copy data from a cell:

1. Select data to copy.
2. Click **Copy** button `📋`.
   OR
   a. Click **Edit** .... `Alt` + `E`
   b. Click **Copy** .... `C`
3. Move insertion point to where you want copied data to go.
4. Click **Paste** button `📋`.
   OR
   a. Click **Edit** .... `Alt` + `E`
   b. Click **Paste** .... `P`

To copy and paste entire record:

1. Click on record selector button to left of record.
2. Click **Copy** button `📋`.
   OR
   a. Click **Edit**................ `Alt` + `E`
   b. Click **Copy** .... `C`
3. Click **Edit** .... `Alt` + `E`
4. Move insertion point to where you want copied data to go.
5. Click **Paste Append** .... `N`

Edit Record Content

Edit a text field:

1. Click in the field you want to edit.
2. Position the insertion point:
   - Click where you want it.
   OR
   - Use arrow keys .... `↑↓←→`
3. Remove unwanted text using these keys:
   - **Backspace**............ `Backspace` to delete to left.
   - **Delete**.......................... `Del` to delete to right.
4. Type replacement text.

Replace text in a field:

1. Select entire field.
2. Click at beginning of field, when mouse pointer shows black arrow.
3. Retype field content.

Edit an e-mail hyperlink:

1. Right-click the field you want to edit.
2. Point to **Hyperlink.** .... `H`
3. Click **Edit Hyperlink**............ `H`
4. Click in the **E-mail address** box.............................. `Alt` + `E`
5. Position the insertion point:
   - Click where you want it.
   OR
   - Use arrow keys............ `↑↓←→`
6. Remove unwanted text using these keys:

- **Backspace** .... `Backspace` to delete to left.
- **Delete** .... `Del` to delete to right.
7. Type replacement text.
8. Click **OK**.

Select Multiple Contiguous Records

1. Click on record selector button to left of first record.
2. Hold down **Shift** key.......... `Shift`
3. Click on the last record selector in group.

Delete a Record

1. Select the record(s) you want to delete.
2. Click **Delete Record** button `✗`.
   OR
   a. Click **Edit** .... `Alt` + `E`
   b. Click **Delete Record** ...... `R`
   OR
   - Press **Ctrl + minus sign** .... `Ctrl` + `-`
   OR
   - Press **Delete** .... `Del`
3. Click **Yes** .... `Enter`

Print Datasheets and Forms

1. Open datasheet or form to print.
2. If desired, click on record selector button on left of datasheet or form to select record(s) to print.
3. Click **File** .... `Alt` + `F`
4. Click **Print** .... `P`
5. Click **Print Range** option to select:
   - **All** .... `Alt` + `A`
   - **Pages** .... `Alt` + `G`
   - **Selected Record(s)** . `Alt` + `R`
6. Select **Properties** .... `Alt` + `P` to make any changes to printer setup.

7. Choose desired option tab and select options:
   - **Paper**
   - **Graphics**
   - **Fonts**
   - **Device Options**

   ✓ *The tabs may be different depending on your printer.*

8. Click **OK**............................ Enter

9. Type number in **Number of Copies** text box .... Alt + C if you want multiple copies.

10. Click **OK**........................... Enter

Print Preview

1. Click **File** .... Alt + F

2. Click **Print Preview**............ V

OR

- Click **Print Preview** button 🔍.

3. Click magnifying glass to see more or less detail (zoom in or zoom out).

4. Click navigation buttons to see the first, previous, specific, next, or last page.

Exercise Directions

1. Start Access, if necessary.

2. Open 💿 **AC02** and save a backup copy of it as **AC02-A**.

3. Open **AC02-A**.

4. Open the **tblEmployees** table.

5. Move to the blank record at the end.

6. Make sure the insertion point is in the Prefix field, and then enter the three new records shown in Illustration A.

   ✓ *Press Tab or Enter to move from one field to the next.*

   ✓ *When entering the e-mail addresses, precede each e-mail address with mailto: as in the existing ones.*

7. Change **Maria Martinez's** address to **10777 Riverwood Road.**

8. Add three more records shown in Illustration B. Use shortcut keys to enter the repeated information in the City, State, and ZIP fields.

9. Copy the entire record for **Leanne Balto** and paste it in the row for the next new record at the bottom of the table.

10. Make these changes to the new record:
    First name: **Steven**
    E-mail address:
    <u>sbalto@wholegrainsbread.com</u>
    Hire Date: (today's date)
    Position: **Baker**
    Hourly: **Yes**
    Full-time: **No**
    Benefits: **No**

    ✓ *Remember that you cannot edit e-mail addresses directly; you might right-click and choose Hyperlink, Edit Hyperlink.*

11. Preview the datasheet and print one copy.

12. Close the datasheet.

    ✓ *Click Close button ⊠ or File, Close.*

13. Open the **frmEmployees** form.

14. Insert a new record and enter the following information:
    Mr. Yancey Bleavins
    2938 Arthur Court
    San Francisco, CA 94106
    (415) 555-1235
    ybleavins@wholegrainsbread.com
    Hire Date: (today's date)
    Store: San Francisco
    Position: Baker
    Hourly: Yes
    Full-time: Yes
    Benefits: Yes

15. Change the ZIP for **Tyrone Braxton** to **94939** and change the phone number to **(414) 555-8888.**

16. Delete the record for **Jane Coffin**.

17. Change **Jane Abrahamson's** record to show that she is full-time with benefits.

18. Print only the last six records in the datasheet.

    ✓ *Select the records and then use the File, Print command. Choose Selection as the range to print.*

19. Close the datasheet.

20. Exit the database.

Illustration A

tblEmployees : Table

ID	Prefix	First Name	Last Name	Address	City	State	ZIP	Phone
28	Mr.	Paul	Gallup	4125 Kessler Ave.	Evergreen	CA	80174	(415) 555-7321
29	Mr.	Mark	Wasser	89 Guilford Lane	Avon	CA	80178	(415) 555-3434
30	Mr.	Toby	Nguyen	229 Kenlock Dr.	Macon	CA	82743	(415) 555-6643
ber)								

Record: 29 of 29

Illustration B

tblEmployees : Table

ID	Prefix	First Name	Last Name	Address	City	State	ZIP	Phone
31	Mr.	Everett	Phillips	214 Ridge St.	Evergreen	CA	80174	(415) 555-8782
32	Ms.	Laurie	Hastings	7789 Adams St.	Evergreen	CA	80175	(415) 555-4935
33	Ms.	Gloria	Sebastia	32 Florida Ct.	Evergreen	CA	80175	(415) 555-0029
ber)								

Record: 32 of 32

On Your Own

1. Start Access and open the ☉**OAC02** database. Save a backup copy of it as **OAC02-A**.

2. Open the **tblClients** table.

3. Enter records for 5 of your friends and family members into the table. Use their real addresses and phone numbers—or make up the address and phone information as you go.

4. Change the address information of the records you entered to fit with the Colorado city, state, ZIP, and phone number information already in the table. For example, use the cities of Denver, Thornton, Westminster, Golden, Blackhawk, etc., use CO for the state abbreviation, use phone numbers with either the 303 or 720 area code, and use some of the ZIP Codes already in the table.

5. Sort the table in ascending order by ZIP Code.

6. Delete the two records that do not have a ZIP Code.

7. Preview and print the table, then close it. If prompted to save the changes to the table layout, choose No.

8. Open the **frmClients** form.

9. Scroll through the new records you added, then add 5 more records for your friends and family members. Make up Colorado city, state, ZIP, and phone number information similar to what you used in the **tblClients** table.

   ✓ You can press Tab to move from field to field.

10. Close the form, and open the **tblClients** table.

11. Select the new records you added.

12. Preview and print the selected records.

13. Close the form.

14. Close the database and exit Access.

Exercise 3

Skills Covered:

◆ **Plan a Database** ◆ **Create a New Database File**
◆ **Create a Table in Datasheet View**
◆ **Change Field Names in Datasheet View** ◆ **Save a Table Design**

On the Job

As well as learning to work with existing databases, you must also learn to plan and create a new database of your own. In planning the database, you need to consider how the database will be used by asking: What information will it store? How will you use the database to analyze the information? After planning the database, you can easily create the new database file and the tables that store the data.

Now that you have become familiar with the Whole Grain Breads current database, you've decided to create a new database that will contain information about the products that each store sells.

Terms

Primary key The field that uniquely identifies each record in a table.

Blank database A database file that does not yet contain any objects (that is, tables, queries, reports, and so on).

Template A predefined group of settings for creating a new database, including what tables will be included, what fields will be used, and so on.

Notes

Plan a Database

- Before you create a database, you must decide which fields you want to include—and if you need a single table or more than one. Consider what information the database will store and how the information will be used.

- To begin, make a list of the fields you want to store in your database, such as last name, first name, address, phone, and so on.

- If you have a lot of categories in mind, break down the field list into specific categories such as Customers, Vendors, Inventory, and so on. Each category will form a separate table in your database.

- If you envision repeated information in a table, plan to split it into separate tables. For example, you might want to store employee contact information in a separate table and employee vacation usage data in another table so that you don't repeat information you already have in the contact table (address, phone, e-mail account, and so on).

- Think about the ways you will want to search or sort the data, and plan the fields to support them.

- For example, if you want to sort by last name, make sure you have separate fields for First Name and Last Name. The same goes for City, State, and ZIP Code. It would be hard, for example, to create mailing labels if client addresses are in one field.

- Each table should have a field in which each record will be unique, such as an ID Number field. This field will be the table's **primary key**.

- Plan the relationships between your tables. Make sure that tables to be related have a common field. For example, the ID field in an Employees table might link to the Employee ID field in the Vacations table.

    ✓ *Relationships between tables are covered more thoroughly in Lesson 2, Exercise 10.*

- When you've finished identifying fields and tables, you are ready to create your new database file and create the tables within it.

Create a New Database File

- The database file contains all Access objects, including tables, forms, queries, pages, and reports. Each database file is stored with an .mdb extension.

- You must create a database file, or open an existing one, before you can enter any data or create any objects (such as tables or queries).

- When you start Access, the New File task pane provides shortcuts for starting a new database or opening an existing one.

- You can reopen the task pane at any time by clicking the New button ⬜ on the toolbar.

Start a new database from the task pane

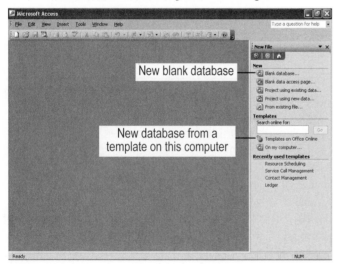

- To start a new database, you can choose to create a **blank database** or create a database based on a **template**.

    ✓ *You can also choose to start a new data access page for a Web page or a new project, but these are not covered in this course.*

    ✓ *You can create a new database by copying an existing one. Use the* From existing file *link in the task pane, or use the Back Up Database feature you learned about in Exercise 1.*

Create a New Blank Database

- To create a blank database, use the Blank database link in the New File task pane.

- The File New Database dialog box appears, and you enter a file name and click Create.

Enter a name for the database file you are creating

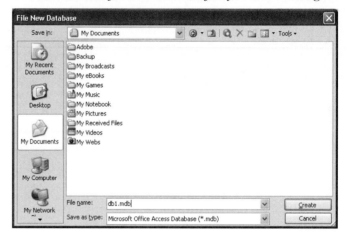

Create a Table in Datasheet View

- There are three ways to create a table: using Table Design view, using a wizard, and by entering data in a new datasheet.

- In this exercise, you will learn about the latter method. Other methods are covered in upcoming exercises.

- To create a new table with a datasheet, click the *Create table by entering data* shortcut from the database window. A new, blank datasheet appears with placeholder field names (Field1, Field2, etc.) in the column heads.

A new table from Datasheet view

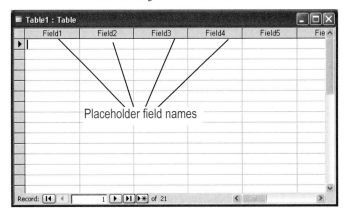

Placeholder field names

Change Field Names in Datasheet View

- A new table in Datasheet view provides placeholder names for each field at the top of each column.
- To change a field name, double-click the existing name and then type a new one.

Save a Table Design

- When you close a table after making design changes to it, Access asks whether you want to save your changes.
- This refers to the structural changes to the table, such as the field names, not to any data you have entered. Data is saved automatically.

- The first time you save changes to a table, Access prompts for a table name.

Name the new table

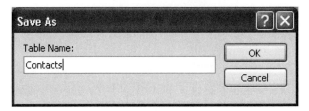

- If there is no primary key field defined for the table, Access asks whether you want to create one.

Define the primary key

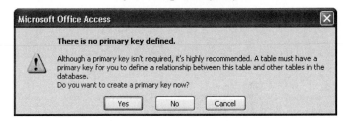

- If you choose *Yes,* it creates a new field called *ID* in the table and sets it as the primary key.
- If you choose *No,* it saves your table without a primary key.
  - ✓ *You cannot choose an existing field to be the primary key field from Datasheet view. In Exercise 5 you will learn about Table Design view.*

Procedures

Display the Task Pane

1. Click **File**.................... Alt+F
2. Click **New**............................ N

Create a New Blank Database

1. In New File task pane, click **Blank database**.
2. Type file name.
3. Choose folder in **Save in** drop-down list.
   OR
   Click folder on the Places bar.
4. Click **Create**.................... Enter

Create Table in Datasheet View

From database window:

- Double-click **Create table by entering data**.
  OR

  a. Click **Insert**............ Alt+I
  b. Click **Table** .... T
  c. Choose **Datasheet View**.
  d. Click **OK** .... Enter

Change Field Names in Datasheet View

1. Double-click field name in column header.
2. Type new field name in column header.
3. Press **Enter** .... Enter
   OR
1. Click in column to change.
2. Click **Format** .... Alt+O
3. Click **Rename Column** .... N

4. Type new field name in column header.
5. Press **Enter**.................... Enter

Save a Table Design

1. Close the table X.
   - ✓ *If this is the first time you've saved the table, continue with the following.*
2. Click **Yes**............................ Y
3. Type table name.
4. Click **OK**.......................... Enter
5. Click **No** .... N
   - ✓ *To bypass creation of primary key.*
   OR
   Click **Yes** to create primary key .... Y

Exercise Directions

1. Start Access and select Blank database from the task pane.

2. Replace the default file name, *db1*, with **AC03** and press **Enter**.

3. Double-click on **Create table by entering data** in the database window.

4. In the Datasheet view for the new table, change the field names as shown in Illustration A.

   ✓ *The field names for this table do not use spaces. Although you can use spaces in file names, spaces can sometimes result in database errors for certain advanced operations.*

   ✓ *Double-click on Field1 and type the new name.*

5. Add the records shown in Illustration A.

   ✓ *Press Tab after each entry to move to the next column.*

   ✓ *You will learn how to adjust column widths in Exercise 9.*

6. Save the table as **tblProducts** and have Access create a primary key.

7. Close the table.

8. Exit the database.

Illustration A

tblProducts : Table

ID	ProductID	ProductName	Description	RetailPrice	DailyQuantity
1	L001	Multigrain loaf	Multigrain bread, loaf	$3.00	100
2	L002	Wheat loaf	Whole wheat bread, loaf	$3.00	100
3	R001	Multigrain rolls	Multigrain rolls, dozen	$4.00	50
4	R002	Wheat rolls	Whole wheat rolls, dozen	$4.00	50
5	L003	French loaf	French bread, loaf	$3.00	50
6	L004	Sourdough loaf	Sourdough bread, loaf	$3.00	50
7	M001	Multigrain mini	Multigrain mini-loaf	$1.75	100
8	M002	Wheat mini	Wheat mini-loaf	$1.75	100
9	M003	French mini	French mini-baguette	$1.75	100
10	M004	Sourdough mini	Sourdough mini-loaf	$1.75	100
(AutoNumber)					

Record: I◄ ◄ [1] ► ►I ►* of 10

On Your Own

1. Start Access and create a new database.

2. Save the database file as **OAC03**.

3. Create a table for storing a telephone list or roster. You can use friends, relatives, associates, club or organization members, or the members of a sports team.

4. Include fields for first name, last name, and telephone number.

5. Save the table with the name **Roster**.

6. Let Access create the Primary Key field.

7. Enter at least five records in the table.

8. Close your database and exit Access.

Exercise 4

Skills Covered:

◆ **Create a Database with Database Wizards**
◆ **Start Database Wizards** ◆ **Use Database Wizards**
◆ **Use Switchboards**

On the Job

Microsoft Access comes with several databases designed for typical purposes. You simply choose the desired wizard—which you can customize to more closely match your needs—and enter data. If you create a database using one of the database wizards, you can save a significant amount of time compared to designing a database from scratch. Access switchboards provide a convenient way to automate your database and make its features and data more *access*ible.

Before you spend a lot of time creating the database objects for Whole Grains Bread, you want to check out the templates that come with Access to see whether one of them might provide a suitable head start for your work. You will create a new database using the Database Wizard to see whether it meets your needs.

Terms

Template A predefined group of settings for creating a new database, including what tables will be included, what fields will be used, and so on.

Database Wizard A step-by-step process for creating a new database using a template.

Switchboard An Access form with command buttons or other controls that lead to other switchboard forms, input forms, and reports.

Notes

Create a Database with Database Wizards

■ Access offers ten **templates** that help you create a database that may match what you need in a database.

  ✓ *You can also download additional templates from the Microsoft Web site if you have Internet access. Just click the* Templates on Office Online *hyperlink on the New File task pane.*

■ In Access, templates are accessed through **Database Wizards**, so the terms *template* and *database wizard* are roughly synonymous in Access. This is not always the case in other Microsoft Office programs, however.

■ These templates provide a basic set of tables, queries, forms, and reports, plus a Switchboard to help beginners navigate among them.

■ You cannot pick and choose among the tables and other objects that Access creates when you use a database wizard. However, you can delete any unwanted objects, or make changes to them, after the database wizard is finished creating the objects.

■ Using a template is helpful primarily if you want to create a database similar to one of the templates. If your database is fairly specific in purpose, whether simple or complex, it is probably easier to build from scratch.

Start Database Wizards

- You can start a database wizard from within Access by clicking *On my computer* in the Templates section of the New File task pane to display the Templates dialog box.

- The Templates dialog box has two tabs: General and Databases. The General tab contains a template for a blank database, a data access page for the Web, and general database projects (not covered in this textbook).

- Click the Databases tab to see icons for the database templates that Access offers. Then double-click the one you want, or click it and then click OK.

  ✓ *A preview pane exists in the Templates dialog box, but it only shows a simple graphic representation of the database. If you need more help choosing the right database template, open it up and examine its features.*

Choose the template you want

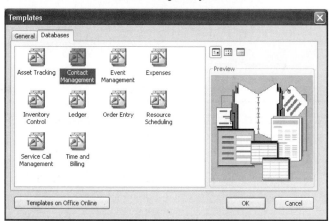

- After you choose a template, a File New Database dialog box appears, just like when you create a new blank database. Enter a name for the new database file in it and click Create. The database wizard then starts.

Use Database Wizards

- The database wizard leads you through a series of dialog boxes that:
  - Show you the tables that appear in the new database and allow you to select optional fields for each table.

    ✓ *The basic list of fields for a particular table is fixed. The field names that appear in italics and that do not have a check mark next to them by default are optional. You can select any or all of these optional fields to include in the table.*

Select optional table fields

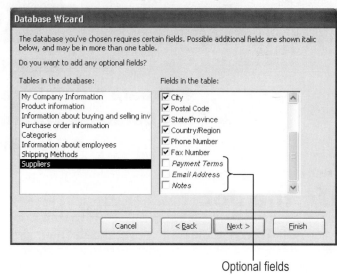

Optional fields

  - Provide choices for form and report formatting.
  - Enable you to enter a title for the database (different from the file name).
  - Enable you to specify a graphic to use as a logo on reports.

- The database wizard does not create any data; you will enter the data yourself, as you learned to do in Exercise 2.

- You can customize the tables and other database objects (queries, forms, and reports) after Access creates them for you.

Use Switchboards

- Databases created with a database wizard automatically include a **switchboard** that allows you to navigate to forms and reports created for the database.

- The switchboard is actually a group of linked forms with buttons for opening certain forms, reports, or queries.

- The main switchboard form opens automatically each time you open that database.

- The database window starts minimized when the main switchboard appears; double-click it (in the bottom-left corner of the Access window) to restore it. You can minimize or close the main switchboard, if desired, to get it out of your way.

A main switchboard

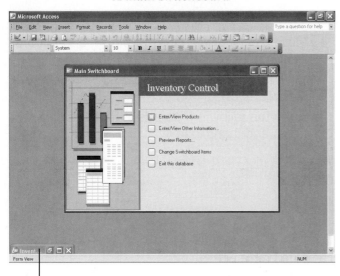

Double-click to restore
database window

Modifying the Switchboard

- You can prevent the main switchboard from opening at startup by choosing Tools, Startup, and choosing None as the Display Form/Page entry.

- You can change the content of a switchboard form, or choose a different form as the default, by clicking Change Switchboard Items on the main switchboard. Such editing is beyond the scope of this book, but you can try it on your own or with the assistance of an instructor.

Procedures

Create a Database with a Template

From the New File Task Pane:

1. Choose **On my computer**.
2. Click the **Databases** tab.
3. Click the template.
4. Click **OK**..........................`Enter`
5. Type file name.
6. Choose folder in **Save in** drop-down list.
   OR
   Click folder on left side of dialog box.
7. Click **Create**....................`Enter`
8. Click **Next**. ....`Enter`
9. If desired, click on each table in database and click on check box in front of italicized entries to add optional fields.
10. Click **Next** ....`Enter`
11. Click style for screen displays.
12. Click **Next** ....`Enter`

13. Click style for printed reports.
14. Click **Next**........................`Enter`
15. Type a title for database.
    ✓ *This name appears on the title bar. It need not be the same as the file name.*
16. If you want a logo on every report, click **Yes, I'd like to include a picture** and click **Picture** button to choose picture.
17. Click **Next**........................`Enter`
18. Click **Finish**.....................`Enter`
    ✓ *Some templates prompt you to enter your company's contact information after the database wizard runs; do so if prompted.*

Use Switchboard

1. Click on button to open form, report, or another switchboard.
2. If another switchboard appears, click on **Return to Main Switchboard** to return.

Close Switchboard

- Click **Close** button on the Switchboard window.

Restore Database Window

- Double-click the database window's **title bar.**
  ✓ *The database window's title bar is in the bottom-left corner of the Access window.*

Prevent Switchboard from Opening Automatically

1. Click **Tools**.................`Alt`+`T`
2. Click **Startup**.....................`U`
3. Click down arrow next to **Display Form/Page**.
4. Choose **(none).**
   ✓ *(none) is at the top of the list; scroll up to find it.*
5. Click **OK**............................`Enter`

Exercise Directions

1. Start a new database using the Inventory Control template.
   - ✓ Click the On my computer *link in the New File task pane, and choose Inventory Control from the Databases tab.*
2. Name the database **AC04**. The database wizard starts.
3. Accepting all defaults for the tables except the following:
   - In the Information About Employees table, add the Email Name field.
   - In the Suppliers table, add the Payment Terms and Email Address fields.
4. Pick your own styles for screen displays (forms) and reports.
5. Title the database **Inventory** and click Finish.
6. Access prompts you for company information. Click OK and enter the following information for the company:
   Company: **Whole Grains Bread**
   Address.: **320 Magnolia Ave.**
   City: **Larkspur**
   State: **CA**
   ZIP: **94939**
   Phone Number: **(415) 555-3200**
   Fax: **(415) 555-3211**
7. Click the Close button ☒ to exit the form.

8. Minimize the Switchboard window, and restore the Database window.
9. Click the Tables object type, and then double-click Categories.
10. Enter the following records in the Categories table, and then close it:
    Loaf
    Mini-loaf
    Roll
    Muffin
    Pastry
    Jams and Spreads
    Other
    - ✓ *Allow Access to automatically assign the ID numbers.*
11. Restore the Switchboard window and click Enter/View Products.
12. Enter the following item:
    Product Name: **Whole grain loaf**
    Description: **2-pound whole grain bread loaf**
    Category: **Loaf**
13. Close the form.
14. Close the switchboard window.
15. Turn off the automatic display of the switchboard at startup.
    - ✓ *Choose Tools, Startup and set Display Form/Page to None.*
16. Exit Access.

On Your Own

1. Start Access and create a database using the Contact Management Wizard.
2. Save the database as **OAC04**. You can use this database to store information about members of a club or organization, or to store customer data.
3. Using the Contacts form, enter at least five people into the **Contacts** table. You can make up the information for each person or use real information. Fill out only Page 1 for each person.
4. Open the **Contact Types** table and create two contact types: Business and Personal.
5. Open the **Contacts** form again, and on Page 2 for each person, select a value in the Contact Type field (Business or Personal).

6. For one of the contacts, double-click the Contact Type field. A form appears in which you can add a new entry for that field. Create a new type of contact called School, and assign that new type to the contact.
7. Close all open forms and tables except the Switchboard. Reopen it from the Forms list if needed.
8. Make some changes to the switchboard using the Switchboard Manager. To access it, click Change Switchboard Items on the Main Switchboard.
9. Close the database and exit Access.

Exercise 5

◆ **Open a Database File** ◆ **Create a Table with the Table Wizard**
◆ **Start a New Table in Table Design View**
◆ **Work in Table Design View** ◆ **Select a Field for the Primary Key**
◆ **Open a Database Exclusively** ◆ **Set a Database Password**

On the Job

You will probably want more than one table in your database. Good database design means having tables for different types of information as you learned in Exercise 3. For example, client information should be in one table (or tables) and employee information should be in another (or others). In this exercise, you will open the database file you created in Exercise 3 and add a few new tables to it. You will also learn how to set a password to protect your database from being modified by others.

You have decided to stick with creating your database from scratch rather than using the database wizard version from Exercise 4. You now need to create a new table to keep track of the customers, as well as a table that describes the various types of customers. This will be important later, as corporate customers receive different pricing for their purchases than individuals.

Terms

Table Design view A view in which you can add, edit, and delete fields from the table, change field types and descriptions, set a primary key, and more.

Data type The type of data that a particular field is designed to hold. Common types include *Text, Number, Date,* and *Memo.*

Field description An optional brief comment or explanation of a field. The field description appears in the status bar at the bottom of the window when its field is selected.

Field properties Characteristics of a field that determine how long an entry can be, how the entry will be formatted, whether there should be a default entry, and what can be entered (for example, numbers only or valid dates only).

Notes

Open a Database File

- To get to any tables or other objects within a database, you need to open the database first.

- Depending on when you last opened the database, you can choose from a list of recently used files on the Getting Started task pane or at the bottom of the File menu.

- If you have not used the database recently, you may need to use the Open dialog box (File, Open) or the More link in the task pane.

Create a Table with the Table Wizard

- The Table Wizard is a handy utility for creating new tables. You can choose fields from many different sample tables that Access provides.

- To create a table using the Table Wizard, you can double-click *Create table by using wizard* in the list of tables of the database window.
- Another way to start the Table Wizard is to display the list of tables in the Database window, click New ⬚ New , and then click Table Wizard in the New table dialog box that appears.
- The Table Wizard walks you step-by-step through all the decisions you must make.

Two ways to start the Table Wizard

Click here and then choose Table Wizard

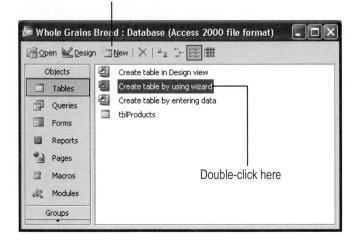

Choosing Table Fields

- The first decision to make is what fields to include. The Table Wizard lets you choose any field from any table in any of the database templates. There are over a hundred tables to choose from.
- The sample tables are broken into two categories: *Business* and *Personal*. Choose one of the two options to switch the sample table listing.
- When you select a sample table, a list of all its fields appears. You can select a field by clicking the ⬚ > button, or select all the fields in that table at once by clicking the ⬚ >> button.
- You can choose fields from as many of the sample tables as you like before moving on.
- You can rename a chosen field by clicking the Rename Field button. This keeps the field's properties but enables you to call it something else.

The Table Wizard helps you choose fields

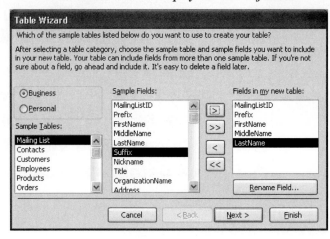

Completing the Table Wizard

- The Table Wizard also prompts you for a table name and lets you specify whether Access should create a primary key field.
- If you choose to create your own primary key field, the Table Wizard displays a list of the fields you have chosen, so you can specify which one should be the primary key.
  - ✓ You won't see this screen (below) if you let Access create a primary key field.

Select the primary key field

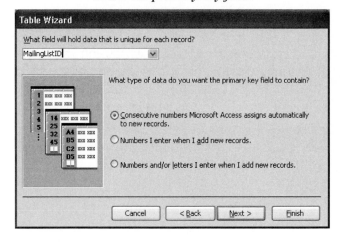

- The Wizard also prompts you for a data type for your primary key field. You can make it an AutoNumber field, a Numeric field, or a Text field.
  - ✓ Data types are explained in the table starting on the next page.
- The Table Wizard also asks about relationships to other tables in your database. The default is for the table to have no relationships.
  - ✓ You will learn about relationships in Exercise 10.

Start a New Table in Table Design View

- You can also create a new table in **Table Design view**. The Table Design view method is more complex, but also more powerful and flexible.

- To start a new table using Design view, you can double-click *Create table in Design view* in the tables list of the Database window.

- Another way is to click the New button 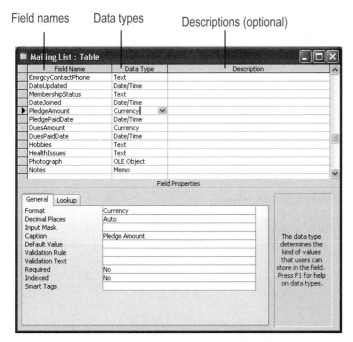 in the Database window, choose Design View from the New Table dialog box, and click OK.

Work in Table Design View

- Table Design view contains a list of the fields in the table, including name, **data type**, and **field description**.

- Wizards that create tables (Database wizard, Table wizard) can assign data types automatically, but you will often need to set or change them manually, too.

- When a field is selected, its **field properties** appear in the lower half of the Table Design view window. Field properties specify advanced options for the field, such as maximum entry length and default value.

  ✓ *Field properties will be covered in Exercise 7.*

Table Design view

Field names   Data types   Descriptions (optional)

Field Names

- Type or edit a name in the Field Name column. Although you may use up to 64 characters, you should keep the name short.

  ✓ *As previously discussed, even though you can include underscores or spaces in the field name, you should avoid doing so. This will help avoid problems with formulas, programming, or converting your database to a different format.*

Field Descriptions

- The field description is optional. You can enter anything you want here, but most people use it to provide comments or hints about the intended use and/or limitations of the field.

- The text you type in the description will appear on the status bar (bottom of the screen) when the user is in this field in Datasheet view or on a form.

Data Types

- The Data type column tells you what kind of information your field can store. Click the drop-down arrow in this cell to choose from the list of data types. You can also type the first letter of the data type to make this choice, if you prefer to use the keyboard:

Data Type	Description
Text	Includes any characters up to a maximum of 255 characters (determined by field size). If the data includes a mix of numbers and any amount of letters, choose Text. Examples include name and address fields. ✓ *The default data type is Text.*
Memo	Use this data type when Text is not large enough. Like Text, this data type can also have letters and numbers but can be much larger— up to 65,536 characters. Don't use Memo unless you need that extra length, however, because you can't perform certain actions (indexing, for example) on a memo field.
Number	Includes various forms of numerical data that can be used in calculations.
Date/Time	Date and time entries in formats showing date, time, or both.

Data Type	Description
Currency	Use for currency values with up to four digits after the decimal place. This data type is more accurate for large numbers than the Number data type, but generally takes up more space.
AutoNumber	Usually this is used to create an identification number for each record. The value for each record increases by one.
Yes/No	Only two possible values can be in this field. Options include Yes/No, True/False, or On/Off. The default style shows a check box with a ✔ for *Yes* or blank ☐ for *No*.
OLE Object	This data type allows you to place another file type into your record. Within the field, you can insert a picture (a company logo, for example), a Word document (employee resume), or an Excel spreadsheet (client summary chart).
Hyperlink	This allows you to insert a Web address such as *www.prenhall.com*, which will launch when you click it in Datasheet view or on a form. You could also type a path and file name to a file on your hard drive (C:\docs\myres.doc) or a network drive.
Lookup Wizard	Creates a lookup column, which creates a list of values from which to choose when entering data.

Select a Field for the Primary Key

- As explained in Exercise 3, a table can have a primary key field that contains unique data for each record. The primary key field helps avoid duplicate records in a table.

- Each table can have only one primary key field.

- For the primary key field, choose a field that will be unique for each record. FirstName and LastName would not be good choices for the primary key because different records could have the same value.

- For an employee database, the primary key could be the Social Security Number, for example. You could also create an Employee ID field specifically to be the primary key field.

- When you create a table without choosing a primary key field, Access asks whether you want a primary key field to be created automatically. If you do so, the new field receives the name "ID."

- From Table Design view, you can choose an existing field to be your primary key by selecting it and then clicking the Primary Key button 🔑 on the toolbar.

Open a Database Exclusively

- To set a database password, you have to open the database in exclusive mode (no one else can be in the database).

- Open Exclusive is most often used to ensure that only one user at a time is trying to change the design of database objects.

- In the Open dialog box, choose the down arrow on the Open button and select Open Exclusive.

Use Open Exclusive rather than the normal Open operation when you want to set a password

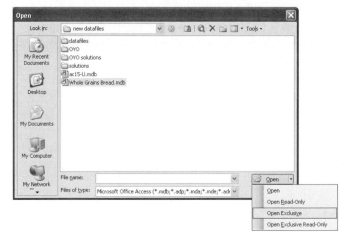

Set Database Password

- When you set a password, you must type the password again to verify accuracy. The password does not show when you type; asterisks display instead. Note that passwords are case-sensitive.

Enter the password to use, and then reenter it to confirm

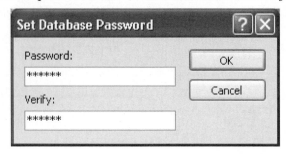

Remove Database Password

- You have to type the password again when you want to remove the password.
- If you forget your password, you will not be able to open the database.

Procedures

Open a Recently Used Database File

From the Getting Started task pane:

- Click the file name.

From the menu bar:

1. Click **F**ile.....................`Alt`+`F`
2. Click the file name.

Open a Database File

1. Click **Open** button `[icon]`.
   OR
   a. Click **F**ile................`Alt`+`F`
   b. Click **O**pen....................`O`
   OR
   - Click **More** on the task pane.
2. Select file to open.
3. Click **Open**.................`Alt`+`O`

Create a Table with Table Wizard

From the Database window:

1. Click **Tables**.
2. Double-click **Create table by using wizard**.
3. Click **Bu**siness...................`S`
   OR
   Click **P**ersonal.................`P`
4. Click a sample table.
5. Click a field you want.
6. Click `>` to add the field ...`[>]`

   ✓ Click `>>` to choose all fields from the sample table at once.

   Click `<` or `<<` to remove fields from your list.

7. Repeat steps 5–6 as needed.
8. Repeat steps 4–6 to choose more fields from another table.

9. (Optional) Rename a field:
   a. Click a **field** on the Fields in my new table list.
   b. Click **R**ename Field.......`R`
   c. Type the new name.
   d. Click **OK** ....`Enter`
10. Click **N**ext............................`N`
11. Type the table name.
12. Choose one:
    - Click **Y**es, **set a primary key for me** ....`Alt`+`Y`
    - Click **N**o, **I'll set the primary key** ....`Alt`+`N`
13. Click **N**ext............................`N`

    ✓ If you chose Yes in step 12, skip to step 18 now.

14. Click the down arrow next to **What field will hold data that is unique for each record?**.............`Alt`+`W`
15. Click the primary key field you want.
16. Choose the data type for the primary key field:
    - **C**onsecutive numbers **Microsoft Access assigns automatically to new records**.................`Alt`+`C`
    - **Numbers I enter when I add new records**...`Alt`+`A`
    - **Numbers and/or letters I enter when I add new records** ....`Alt`+`L`
17. Click **N**ext............................`N`
18. (Optional) Set relationships to other existing tables.

    ✓ Relationships are covered in Exercise 10. You can skip them for now.

19. Click **N**ext. ....`N`
20. Click **F**inish........................`F`

Create Table in Table Design View

From the Database window:

1. Click **Tables**.
2. Double-click **Create table in Design view**.

Create a Field in Table Design View

1. Click in the **Field Name column** of an empty row.
2. Type field name.
3. Press **Tab**......................`Tab`
4. Click the **down arrow** in the Data Type column `[v]`.
5. Click the field type.
6. Press **Tab**......................`Tab`
7. (Optional) Type field description.

Select a Field for the Primary Key

1. Click in the field to use.
2. Click **Primary Key** button `[icon]` on toolbar.

   ✓ Click Primary Key button again to remove primary key.

   ✓ Click in another field and click Primary Key button to change primary key.

Open a Database Exclusively

1. Click **F**ile ....`Alt`+`F`
2. Click **O**pen ....`O`
3. Move to database file.
4. Click on **Open** drop-down arrow.
5. Click **Open Exclusi**ve ....`V`

Set Database Password

1. Open database exclusively.
2. Click **T**ools .... `Alt`+`T`
3. Click **Security** .... `T`
4. Click **Set Database Password** .... `D`
5. Type password.
6. Press **Tab** ....`Tab`
7. Type password again.
8. Click **OK** ....`Enter`

Remove Database Password

1. Click **T**ools .... `Alt`+`T`
2. Click **Security** .... `T`
3. Click **Unset Database Password** .... `D`
4. Type password.
5. Click **OK** ....`Enter`

Exercise Directions

1. Start Access, if necessary.

2. Open 💿 **AC05**.

   ✓ *From this point on, directions to copy the database will not be given. However, you should check with your instructor to see if you should continue to make copies of the database.*

3. Start a new table using the Table Wizard.

4. Choose the **Customers** sample table, and transfer all of its fields to the Fields in My New Table list.

5. Remove the CompanyOrDepartment and Country/Region fields from your Fields in My New Table list.

6. Rename the PostalCode field to **ZIP**.

7. Name the table **tblCustomers**.

8. Choose to set your own primary key field, and set it to the CustomerID field.

9. Specify that the primary key field should contain numbers and/or that you will enter yourself.

   ✓ *Do not create any relationships at this point for the new table.*

10. Create a new table using Table Design view with the following information:

Field Name	Data Type
CustTypeID	AutoNumber
Type	Text

11. Make CustTypeID the primary key.

12. Close the table, saving it as **tblCustomerTypes**.

13. Open the **tblCustomerTypes** table in Datasheet view and enter two types: **Individual** and **Corporate**.

14. Close the database and reopen it with Open Exclusive.

15. Create a password for the database.

    ✓ *Start with Tools, Security.*

16. Close and reopen the file by typing the password.

17. Remove the password.

18. Close the database.

On Your Own

1. Open 💿 **OAC05**, which contains a simple database with the beginnings of a sports team roster.

   ✓ *Check with your instructor to see if you should make a copy of the database.*

2. Create a new table with the Table Wizard that will hold data about the equipment that the organization owns.

   ✓ *You might want to pull fields from several different sample tables.*

3. Create another new table, this time using Table Design view, to hold data about various categories of membership in the organization.

4. Password-protect the database using the word *password* as the password, and then close it and reopen it.

5. Remove the password.

6. Close the database and exit Access.

Exercise 6

◆ Critical Thinking

The Michigan Avenue Athletic Club has just completed a survey of members to determine their interest in a new Water Aerobics program. You are in charge of collecting this information in a database, which will later be used to send postcards to people who participated letting them know the start date of the new program. Design a database that will hold the information from the form.

Exercise Directions

1. Create a blank new Access database named **AC06**.

2. Create a new table using the fields in Part I of Illustration A.
   - ✓ Do not use spaces in the field names.
   - ✓ Separate the member's first name and last name into separate fields: FirstName and LastName.
   - ✓ The field containing the membership number should be a Number field; all the other fields should be Text.
   - ✓ For the Membership Number, use the field name MemNum.
   - ✓ Make the MemNum field the primary key.

3. Save the table design; name it **tblMembers**.

4. Create another table using the fields shown in Part II of Illustration A.
   - ✓ Abbreviate the question names and use appropriate field types for each field. For example, you could use the following abbreviations and types:

Field Name on Form	Field Name in Table	Field Type
How many water-based fitness classes have you taken in the past 12 months?	NumClasses	Number
On a scale of 1 to 10, with 10 being the most interested, how interested are you in taking a water aerobics class?	InterestLevel	Number

Field Name on Form	Field Name in Table	Field Type
What day of the week would be the most convenient for you?	PreferredDay	Text
Do you prefer mornings, afternoons, or evenings?	PreferredTime	Text
Would you need a baby sitter to be available?	Sitter	Yes/No
Would you like to receive a postcard letting you know the date and time of the water aerobics class when it is determined?	Postcard	Yes/No
Comments	Comments	Memo

5. Add a MemberID field with the Number type at the top of the field list, and make it the Primary Key.
   - ✓ You will use this field to join the two tables in a later exercise.

6. Save the table design; name it **tblWASurvey**.

7. Enter the data from the completed customer form shown in Illustration A into the tables.

8. Close the Access database.

357

Water Aerobics Survey

Part I: About You

Membership Number: __2003__

Name: ___Sandy Keller___

Address: ___207 Lakeside Drive___

City: ___Chicago___ State: __IL__ ZIP: __60601__

Part II: Your Interest in Water Aerobics

How many water-based fitness classes have you taken in the past 12 months? __2__

On a scale of 1 to 10, with 10 being the most interested, how interested are you in taking a water aerobics class? __8__

What day of the week would be the most convenient for you? __Monday__

Do you prefer mornings, afternoons, or evenings? __evening__

Would you need a baby sitter to be available? ☐ Yes ☒ No

Would you like to receive a postcard letting you know the date and time of the water aerobics class when it is determined? ☒ Yes ☐ No

Comments:

I would like class to be at least 60 minutes in length.

Exercise 7

- ◆ **Open a Table for Editing in Table Design View**
- ◆ **Rename a Field** ◆ **Add a Field** ◆ **Delete a Field**
- ◆ **Reorder Fields** ◆ **Change Field Properties**

On the Job

After you design a table and begin to add data, you may discover that you don't have a place to put some of the information or that the data you have for a field doesn't fit. In this case, you will have to edit the design of the table. You may also want to set some field properties that help speed up data entry or help ensure that you enter the data correctly.

Now that you have begun working with the tables you created in Lesson 1, you realize that they could stand some improvement. You need to add more fields, rename some existing fields, and make changes to field type and field properties,

Terms

Field properties Characteristics of a field that determine how long an entry can be, how the entry will be formatted, whether there should be a default entry, and what can be entered (for example, numbers only or valid dates only).

Input Mask A field template to validate how each character is entered into the field, such as parentheses and dashes in a phone number.

Validation Rule A rule that defines what data may be entered into a certain field. It can specify a number of characters and/or a range of values.

Index A predefined sort on a particular field. Having a field indexed means that database searches and sorts based on that field will be faster.

Notes

Open a Table for Editing in Table Design View

- To edit an existing table's design, select it from the list of tables in the Database window and then click Design ![Design button].
- You can also right-click an existing table and choose Design View.

- While viewing an existing table in Datasheet view, you can also click the Design button ![button] on the toolbar to switch to Design view.
  - ✓ *The Design button on the toolbar is also a drop-down list. You can switch among Design view, Datasheet view, PivotTable view, and PivotChart view.*

Table Design view

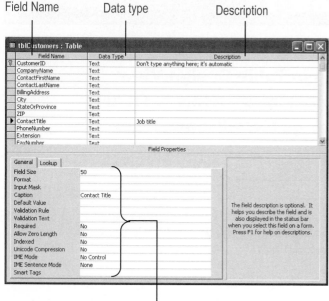

Field Name   Data type   Description

Field properties for current field

- You can edit the name, data type, and field description just as you did when you created the table initially (see Exercise 5). Even if you created the table some other way, such as with the Table Wizard, you can still edit it in Table Design view.

- When a field is selected, its **field properties** appear in the Field Properties half of the Table Design window. Field properties specify advanced options for the field, such as maximum entry length and default value.

Rename a Field

- To rename a field, move to the *Field Name* box and edit or replace the name there.

- Any forms, reports, or queries based on this table will need to be changed or recreated; the name change does not automatically transfer to related objects.

Add a Field

- You can add new fields to your table in Design view. Move to a blank row and type the field name you want. Select a data type and enter a description for the field if you like.

- To insert a new field between two existing ones, or at the top of the list, select the field above which the new one should appear and click the Insert Rows button ![icon] on the toolbar (or choose Insert, Rows).

Delete a Field

- If you make a mistake creating new fields, you can remove a field from Table Design view.

- Removing a field deletes all data that was entered in that field from the table.

- To delete a field, select it and press the Delete key, or click the Delete Rows button ![icon] on the toolbar.

- You can also delete a row (that is, a field) by choosing Edit, Delete Rows from the menu bar. When you do so, a confirmation box appears; click *Yes* to confirm.

Reorder Fields

- The order in which fields appear in Table Design view does not directly affect objects based on the table, like queries and reports.

- However, when you build reports, queries, forms, and so on with a table, you work with a *field list,* and the order shown on that list is the order shown in Table Design view.

- To move a field on the list, select it by clicking the field selector (the gray square to the left of the field name) to select the entire row. Then drag it up or down on the list.

Select a field and then drag it up or down

	Field Name	Data Type	
🔑	CustomerID	Text	Don't typ
	CompanyName	Text	
	ContactFirstName	Text	
▶	ContactLastName	Text	
	BillingAddress	Text	
	City	Text	
	StateOrProvince	Text	
	ZIP	Text	
	ContactTitle	Text	Job title
	PhoneNumber	Text	
	Extension	Text	

Change Field Properties

- In most cases you do not have to change the field properties at the bottom of the Table Design view window; you can accept the defaults.

- To see an explanation of each field property, click in the property and see the description on the right side of the screen or press F1 to see more detailed help.

Set Field Size

■ The field size for Text data types determines the maximum number of characters you can type.

■ Choose a Field Size option on the drop-down list for Number data types to determine how large the number can be and if you can have decimal places. For numbers 0 to 255 with no decimal places, choose Byte. For the largest numbers without decimal places, choose Long Integer, and for the largest numbers with decimal places, choose Double.

Field size options for Number fields

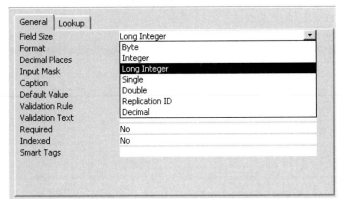

Choose a Format

■ Especially for number and date/time data types, choose an option on the Format drop-down list to choose how you want the values displayed. Each drop-down choice shows an example of what the value will look like.

Format options for date/time data types

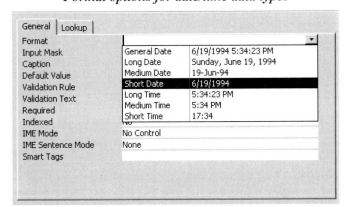

■ You can also type codes in the Format box. (See Help for an explanation for codes.) For example, type m/d/yyyy for a date type to display 1/1/2004.

Enter a Caption

■ A caption is an alternative name for the field. For example, if you have a field called FNAME, you might assign a caption of First Name.

■ Captions appear on forms and reports instead of the field name, helping make those objects more understandable.

Enter a Default Value

■ You can type a Default Value you want to appear in new records.

■ The Default Value is used for the most common value for records but the user can always type over any value in the field.

■ An example would be 0 for a sales field or CO for the state field in a table where addresses, for example, are typically located in Colorado.

Use an Input Mask

■ The **Input Mask** is a field template to validate how each character is entered into the field.

■ For example, you can show parentheses for a telephone field or dashes for a social security number field. Some of the fields you worked with in the first few exercises used input masks for data like phone numbers and ZIP Codes.

Use Data Validation

■ The **Validation Rule** property allows you to verify data as the user enters it into the table.

■ Examples include <Date() (less than today's date), Between 0 and 100, "CO", "TX", or Is Null (blank).

■ You can use the Expression Builder by clicking the Build button 🔲 to the right of the field property box.

✓ *The Expression Builder is a dialog box from which you can choose various fields or objects and math operators. It is a very powerful tool, but not covered in any detail in this book; you might want to experiment with it on your own.*

■ The Validation Text appears in a dialog box when a Validation Rule is broken.

Require an Entry

■ Required means that a user has to fill in this field before going to another record.

■ You might want to set a field to Required if that field is an essential part of the record, such as Invoice # or Customer ID.

Index a Field

- An **index** is a precreated sort on a certain field. Having an index makes searches and sorts on this field go quicker.

- Do not set all fields to Indexed; instead, set this value only for the field (or two) on which you think you will search or sort most often.

Switch between Views

- To switch to Datasheet view from Table Design view, click the View button ⊞ ▾ on the Standard toolbar. It is the left-most button on the toolbar.

- When in Datasheet view, the button's face changes (✍ ▾), and clicking it switches you to Table Design view.

- This button also has a drop-down list, so you can choose other views from it.

- You can also choose a view from the View menu if you prefer.

Procedures

Open a Table for Editing

In Database view:

1. Click **Tables**.
2. Click the table to edit.
3. Click **Design** button
    .... Alt + D

Rename a Field

1. Double-click the field's name.
2. Type a new name.

Insert a Field

1. Select the field above which the new field should appear.
2. Click **Insert Rows** button ⬚.
   OR
   a. Click **Insert** .... Alt + I
   b. Click **Rows**. .... R
3. Click in the **Name column** of the new row.
4. Type field name.
5. Press **Tab** .... Tab

6. Click the down arrow ▾ in the Data Type field.
7. Click the field type.
8. Press **Tab** .... Tab
9. (Optional) Type field description.

Delete a Field

1. Select the field.
2. Click **Delete Rows** button ⬚.
   OR
   a. Click **Edit** .... Alt + E
   b. Click **Delete Rows** .... R

Move a Field

1. Select the field.
2. Drag it up or down on the list.

Change Field Data Type

1. Click in the field's Data Type column.
2. Click the down arrow ▾.
3. Click the new field type.

Set Field Properties

1. Select a field.
2. Click the property you want to change.
3. Type a value, or select from the drop-down list.
   ✓ For example, to enter a caption, click in the caption field and enter the caption you wish to display.
4. Repeat steps 2–3 as needed to set properties in other fields.

Switch Between Views

1. Click **View** .... Alt + V
2. Click **Datasheet View** .... S
   OR
   Click **Design View** .... D
   ✓ You can also use the View button, the left-most button on the Standard toolbar, to switch views.

Exercise Directions

1. Start Access, if necessary.

2. Open ⊙ **AC07**.

3. Open the **tblProducts** table in Design view.

4. Delete the ID field.

5. Make the ProductID field the primary key, and change its caption to **Product ID** (with a space between the words.

6. Add an InputDate field at the bottom of the field list, with a Date/Time data type and Short Date format.

7. Add a Discontinued field with a Yes/No data type and **Discontinued?** as the caption.

8. Add a VendorWebPage field with a Hyperlink data type, and use **Vendor Online** as the caption.

9. Add a Notes field with a Memo data type.

10. Create captions for all field names that contain more than one word and do not already have a caption. For example, type **Product Name** as the caption for the ProductName field.

11. Save the table's design.
    - ✓ Click the Save button.

12. Look at the table in Datasheet view.
    - ✓ Click first toolbar button.

13. Return to Design view.
    - ✓ Click again on the first toolbar button.

14. Make the ProductID field required and set its Field Size to 10.

15. Move the InputDate field between ProductID and Product Name, and make it required.

16. Set the ProductName field to be indexed (duplicates OK).

17. Save the table's design. Ignore any warnings you see.

18. Switch to Datasheet view again, and enter today's date in the Input Date field for all records. (You can type it once and then use copy and paste.)

19. Close the **tblProducts** table, saving any changes.

20. Open the **tblCustomers** table in Design view.

21. Create a 9-digit ZIP code input mask for the ZIP field.

22. Create a phone number input mask for the PhoneNumber field.

23. Close the **tblCustomers** table, saving the changes to it.

24. Close the database.

On Your Own

1. Open the database **OAC05** that you worked with in the On Your Own section of Exercise 5, or open ⊙ **OAC07**.

2. In Design view, edit the **Roster** table to add two new fields. Make one of the fields a different data type. For example, you can add a Position field or a birthday field. If you add a birthday field, you can also add a Yes/No field to indicate whether or not you should send a card.

3. Enter captions for any fields that have multi-word names. For example, add a caption like First Name for the FirstName field.

4. Save the changes to the table.

5. Switch to Datasheet view, and add information in the newly added fields for each record.

6. Close the table.

7. Close the database and exit Access.

Exercise 8

Skills Covered:

◆ **How Data is Stored in a Plain Text File**
◆ **Import Data** ◆ **Export Data**

On the Job

Many times data will come to you from outside sources—and this is good, because it saves you the trouble of reentering it manually. Access accepts data from several types of sources, including other database applications and plain text files. You can also export your data from Access to other file formats, for use in other applications.

Your manager at Whole Grains Bread has given you a disk containing some additional customer data that should be merged into the database you have been creating. Some of the data is in Excel format, and some is in a plain text file.

In addition, one of the IT (Information Technology) specialists is currently in the process of developing a centralized inventory database in a database application on a Macintosh computer and would like for you to export your tblProducts table in tab-delimited format so he can incorporate its records into his database.

Terms

Plain text A file that contains no formatting or structural codes—only text.

Delimiter The character that separates one field from another in a plain text file. Common delimiters are tabs or commas.

Notes

How Data is Stored in a Plain Text File

- You can import and export text between Access and plain text files.

- A **plain text** file can contain database data, as long as there is a way of telling where one field ends and the next one begins for each row (each record).

- Each record is typically indicated by a hard return (Enter).

- There are two ways of indicating where a field ends—with a **delimiter** character or with fixed width.

- A delimited file uses a certain character, such as tab or comma, as a delimiter character to mark the separation between one field and another.

A tab-delimited text file—the arrows are the tabs

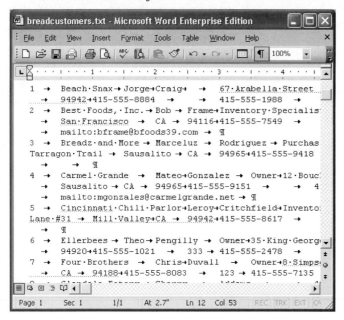

■ A fixed-width file uses a fixed number of characters for each field. If an entry in a field is smaller than the fixed number of characters, extra spaces are added at the end to fill it out.

A fixed-width text file—the dots are the spaces

Import Data

■ Data may be imported from any of a wide variety of sources, including text files, Excel, Word, or other database programs such as FoxPro or dBASE. The procedure for doing so is roughly the same for all types.

Import Data from a Text File

■ To import data into Access from a text file, use the Get External Data, Import command on the File menu.

■ A Wizard walks you through the process. After specifying a text file as the source, you are guided through a process of selecting how the fields are delimited and which table should receive the imported data.

Importing data from a tab-delimited text file using the Import Text Wizard

■ You can import into an existing table, but only if there are exactly the same fields in the incoming data as in the table, and only if the incoming data does not violate any rules set up for any of those fields.

✓ *If you cannot import into an existing table for some reason (type mismatches or rule violations, for example), you can import into a new table and then manually copy the data from one table to another in Access.*

■ Data imported into an existing table is appended to the end of the table. You can re-sort it after the import if desired, as you learned in Lesson 1.

Import Data from Excel

■ Importing from Excel is very simple since the data is already pre-delimited into columns. Use the File, Get External Data, Import command, and select the Excel file to import.

■ The Import Spreadsheet Wizard guides you through the process.

- As with text files you can import it into an existing table or a new table. Importing into an existing table works only if the fields have the same names and if the data fits.

  ✓ *You cannot directly import from a Word table, but you can import the Word data into Excel, save it as an Excel file, and then open it in Access.*

Export Data

- You can export data from any table into a variety of data formats.

- If you need to share data with an application that is not on Access's list of supported export formats, use Text Only, either delimited or fixed width. Almost all database programs accept input in that format.

- If you need to share data with a different platform, such as Macintosh or Unix, Text Only is also a good choice for that.

- Choose File, Export to start exporting some data. The file format you choose for the exported data determines what happens next.

Export to a Text File

- If you choose .txt as the format for the exported data, the Export Text Wizard runs to guide you through the process.

- Just like when importing, you specify whether you want delimited or fixed width.

Use the Export Text Wizard to export to a plain text format

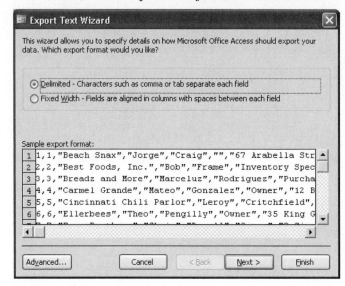

Export to an Excel File

- If you choose Excel as the file format for your Export, the Export Spreadsheet Wizard guides you through the process.

- It is a simpler process than for exporting text because you do not need to specify a delimiting method.

Procedures

Import Data from a Delimited Text File

1. Click **File**..................... Alt + F
2. Click **Get External Data** ..... G
3. Click **Import**....................... I
4. Click the down arrow ▾ in the **Files of type** box.
5. Click **Text Files**.

   ✓ *The list of files changes to show only files of that type.*

6. Click the file from which to import.
7. Click **Import**............... Alt + M
8. Click **Delimited**.................. D
9. Click **Next** .... N

10. Click the character used as the delimiter.
11. If the first row contains field names, click **First Row Contains Field Names** .... R
12. Click **Next**............................ N
13. See one of the following sections:
    - Import Data into a New Table
    - Import Data into an Existing Table

Import Data from a Fixed Width Text File

1. Click **File**..................... Alt + F
2. Click **Get External Data** ...... G
3. Click **Import**........................ I

4. Click the down arrow ▾ in the **Files of type** box.
5. Click **Text Files**.

   ✓ *The list of files changes to show only files of that type.*

6. Click the file from which to import.
7. Click **Import** .... Alt + M
8. Click **Fixed Width** .... W
9. Click **Next**............................ N
10. Do any of the following if needed to adjust the field breaks:
    - Drag a break line to move it.
    - Click to create a new break line.

- Double-click a break line to delete it.

11. Click **Next** .... N

12. See one of the following sections:
    - Import Data into a New Table
    - Import Data into an Existing Table.

Import Data from an Excel File

1. Click **File** .... Alt + F

2. Click **Get External Data** ...... G

3. Click **Import** I

4. Click the down arrow [▼] in the **Files of type** box.

5. Click **Microsoft Excel**.

   ✓ *The list of files changes to show only files of that type.*

6. Click the file from which to import.

7. Click **Import** .... Alt + M

8. If prompted to select a worksheet or named range:
   a. Click the worksheet.
   b. Click **Next** .... N

   ✓ *You might not encounter step 8, depending on the file.*

9. If the first row contains field names, click **First Row Contains Column Headings** .... R

10. Click **Next** .... N

11. See one of the following sections:
    - Import Data into a New Table
    - Import Data into an Existing Table.

Import Data into a New Table

From the Import Text Wizard:

1. Click **In a New Table** .... W

2. Click **Next** .... N

3. (Optional) Modify any of the fields to be imported:
   a. Click a field to select it.
   b. Do any of the following as needed:

- Click **Do not Import field (Skip)** to omit it from the import.. Alt + S

- Type a different name in the **Field Name** box .... Alt + M

- Click the down arrow [▼] in the **Field Type** box and click a different type .... Alt + T

- Click the down arrow [▼] in the **Indexed** box and click Yes or No. .... Alt + I

   c. Repeat steps a and b for each field.

4. Click **Next** .... N

5. Select a primary key method for the table:

   - Click **Let Access add primary key** to create a new field for this purpose .... A

   - Click **Choose my own primary key**, and then click the down arrow [▼] and select a field, to use an existing field .. C

   - Click **No primary key** to not use a primary key in this table. .... O

6. Click **Next** .... N

7. Type a name for the new table.

8. Click **Finish** .... Alt + F

Import Data into an Existing Table

From the Import Text Wizard:

1. Click **In an Existing Table** .. X

2. Click the down arrow [▼] and select an existing table.

3. Click **Next** .... N

4. Click **Finish** .... Alt + F

Export Data to a Text File

1. Open the table in datasheet view that you want to export.

2. Click **File** .... Alt + F

3. Click **Export** .... E

4. Click the down arrow [▼] in the **Save as type** box.

5. Click **Text Files**.

6. Click in the **File name** box .... Alt + N

7. Type a name for the exported file.

8. Click **Export All** .... Alt + X

9. Do one of the following:
   For delimited export:
   a. Click **Delimited** .... D
   b. Click **Next** .... N
   c. Click the desired delimiter character.
   d. (Optional) Click **Include Field Names on First Row** .... Alt + I
   e. Click **Next** .... N

   For fixed-width export:
   a. Click **Fixed Width** .... W
   b. Click **Next** .... N
   c. (Optional) Do any of the following to adjust the field positioning:
      - Drag a break line to move it.
      - Click to create a new break line.
      - Double-click a break line to delete it.
   d. Click **Next** .... N

10. Click **Finish** .... Alt + F

Export Data to Excel

1. Open the table in datasheet view that you want to export.

2. Click **File** .... Alt + F

3. Click **Export** .... E

4. Click the down arrow [▼] in the **Save as type** box.

5. Click **Microsoft Excel 97-2003**.

6. Click in the **File name** box .... Alt + N

7. Type a name for the exported file.

8. Click **Export All** .... Alt + X

Exercise Directions

1. Start Access, if necessary.

2. Open ⊘ **AC08**.

3. Import the data from the file ⊘ **AC08-A.txt** into the **tblCustomers** table.

   ✓ *It is a tab-delimited file, and the first row contains field names.*

4. Import the data from the file ⊘ **AC08-B.xls** into the **tblCustomers** table.

   ✓ *The first row contains column headings.*

5. Display **tblCustomers** in Datasheet view.

   ✓ *Notice that it sorts as if the numbers in the ID field were text; 1 is followed by 10, and so on. This is because the field type is set to Text.*

6. Switch to Design view, and change the field type for the **CustomerID** field to Number.

7. Save the changes to the table design, and switch back to Datasheet view.

   ✓ *Notice that now the records are correctly sorted by ID number.*

8. Export **tblCustomers** to an Excel file called **AC08-C.xls**.

   ✓ *Use Microsoft Excel 97-2003 format.*

9. Export **tblCustomers** to a fixed-width text file called **AC08-D.txt**.

10. Close the database.

On Your Own

1. Open ⊘ **OAC08**.

2. Import the data from the Word document ⊘ **OAC08-A.doc** into the **Roster** table.

   ✓ *Access does not directly import Word files, so you must use an intermediary format that both programs recognize, such as Excel. Use the Clipboard to copy the data from Word to Excel, and then save in Excel format.*

   ✓ *Do not worry about the data being imported not having an ID number; Access will add it automatically because that field is set to AutoNumber as the field type.*

3. Import the file ⊘ **OAC08-B.xls** as a new table called **Venues**, and let Access add a primary key.

4. Export the **Roster** table to a new dBASE 5 file named **OAC08-C.dbf**.

   ✓ *Two additional files will be created automatically due to the nature of the dBASE file format: one with an .inf extension and one with an .mdx extension.*

5. Close the database and exit Access.

Exercise 9

Skills Covered:

◆ **Switch among Open Objects** ◆ **Insert a Column** ◆ **Delete a Column**
◆ **Move a Column** ◆ **Hide and Unhide Columns** ◆ **Change Datasheet**
Column Width ◆ **Remove Gridlines** ◆ **Freeze Columns**

On the Job

If you plan to work with your data in Datasheet view a lot, you might want to adjust the layout so you can see your data more clearly as you work. You can make changes that affect the underlying table, such as inserting and deleting columns (fields). You can also make cosmetic changes that affect only Datasheet view, such as removing gridlines, hiding certain columns, freezing certain columns so they remain visible when you scroll, and adjusting the width of a column.

At Whole Grains Bread, customers can sign up for the company's quarterly newsletter, including coupons and recipes. You would like to add a field to your tblCustomers table to indicate whether each customer has signed up. You would also like to add a Prefix column for each record (for Mr., Mrs., and so on) and make some on-screen formatting changes to the table so you can enter and view records in it more easily.

Terms

Column header The gray box containing the column (field) name.

Hide To remove an object, such as a column, from view on the screen without deleting it.

Gridlines Lines that outline each row and column on-screen.

Freeze To fix the position of certain columns so that when you scroll to the right, those columns remain on-screen while other columns move.

Notes

Switch among Open Objects

■ The bottom of the Window menu shows you a list of all objects such as tables and forms that are currently open. Click or type the number on the menu to move to the object.

■ You can also see each object or document that is open on the Windows taskbar. Click on the document button on the taskbar to go to the object.

✓ *You can press F11 to go to the database window, no matter which window is currently displayed.*

■ Newer versions of Windows such as XP and Windows Server 2003 are set up to group all the windows for a particular application into a single button on the taskbar; if that's the case on your PC, you can click the single button for Access on the taskbar to see a menu of the open Access windows.

✓ *If you don't like the windows to be grouped on the taskbar, right-click the taskbar and choose Properties and then deselect the Group Similar Taskbar Buttons checkbox.*

Switch between open windows within Access with the taskbar or Window menu

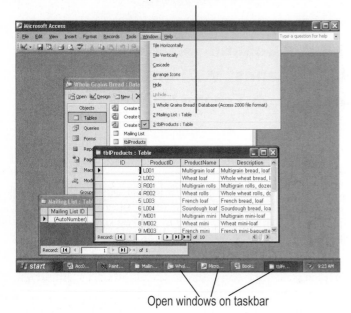

Open windows on menu

Open windows on taskbar

Insert a Column

- When you add a column in Datasheet view you are adding a field to the underlying table.

- To insert a column, open the Insert menu and choose Column. The field name will be a placeholder name (Field#); you can change the name as you learned in Exercise 3.

- When you insert a column, it appears to the left of the column that was selected before you issued the insertion command.

A new field inserted between two existing fields

	Customer ID	Company Name	Field1	Prefix	Contact First Name	Cont
▶	1	Beach Snax		Mr.	Jorge	Craig
	2	Best Foods, Inc.		Mr.	Bob	Fram
	3	Breadz and More		Ms.	Marceluz	Rodri
	4	Carmel Grande		Mr.	Mateo	Gonz
	5	Cincinnati Chili Parlor		Mr.	Leroy	Critch
	6	Ellerbees		Mr.	Theo	Peng
	7	Four Brothers		Mr.	Chris	Duval
	8	Glendale Eatery		Ms.	Sherry	Adda
	9	Gotta Eat, Inc.		Ms.	Amy	Burro
	10	High-Tech Café		Ms.	Midori	Waka
	11	Klein Deli		Ms.	Allison	Klein
	12	Malibu Grill		Ms.	Sally	Lowe
	13	Natural Foods Unlimited		Ms.	Juliana	Smith
	14	Nosh Emporium		Ms.	Abby	McNa
	15	The Breakfast Table		Ms.	Lashonda	Brow

Record: 1 of 36

- If you want to add a description, change the data type, or change any properties, you must go to Design view.

- If you have already entered data into the table, you will need to go back and fill in the value for the new field for each record.

- Adding, deleting, and moving a column from a table does not change any forms, reports, or queries that you've created based on that table. You must modify these objects separately. For this reason, it is advantageous to finalize the lists of fields you plan to use in a table before you create forms, reports, or queries based upon it.

Delete a Column

- Deleting a column on the datasheet removes the field from the underlying table, including any data that was stored in it.

  ✓ *To hide a field temporarily without deleting it, see Hide and Unhide Columns later in this exercise.*

- After deleting a field, you cannot get the data back that the field contained, so be careful when deleting fields.

Move a Column

- After you select the column header, you can use the drag-and-drop method to move a column in Datasheet view.

- Click the **column header** to select it. The entire column becomes highlighted. Then drag the column name left or right to move the column.

- A black vertical line shows where the column is going. When you release the mouse button, the column drops into the new location.

Move a column by dragging its header

	Customer ID	Company Name	Field1	Prefix	Contact First Name	Cont
▶	1	Beach Snax		Mr.	Jorge	Craig
	2	Best Foods, Inc.		Mr.	Bob	Fram
	3	Breadz and More		Ms.	Marceluz	Rodri
	4	Carmel Grande		Mr.	Mateo	Gonz
	5	Cincinnati Chili Parlor		Mr.	Leroy	Critch
	6	Ellerbees		Mr.	Theo	Peng
	7	Four Brothers		Mr.	Chris	Duval
	8	Glendale Eatery		Ms.	Sherry	Adda
	9	Gotta Eat, Inc.		Ms.	Amy	Burro
	10	High-Tech Café		Ms.	Midori	Waka
	11	Klein Deli		Ms.	Allison	Klein
	12	Malibu Grill		Ms.	Sally	Lowe
	13	Natural Foods Unlimited		Ms.	Juliana	Smith
	14	Nosh Emporium		Ms.	Abby	McNa
	15	The Breakfast Table		Ms.	Lashonda	Brow

Record: 1 of 36

Hide and Unhide Columns

■ If you don't want to view or print certain columns in Datasheet view, you can **hide** them. Simply select the column(s) and choose the Hide Columns command from the Format menu. To redisplay the columns, choose the Unhide Columns command from the Format menu and check all the columns you want displayed.

Change Datasheet Column Width

■ If the field entry is too wide to see in Datasheet view, you can change the width to display more of the column.

■ The column width does not affect the field size in table design; it is only for your convenience when viewing the datasheet.

■ You can change column width for automatic fit to the widest entry by double-clicking the double-headed arrow mouse pointer between two column headers.

■ Or, change the column width manually by dragging the right border of the column header to the desired width.

Drag column dividers or double-click to autosize

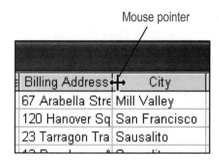

Mouse pointer

■ You can also change column width by choosing the Column width command from the Format menu and typing the width or clicking the Best Fit button.

Remove Gridlines

■ If you don't want the **gridlines** between rows and columns to appear on-screen and when you print the datasheet, you can choose to remove the gridlines.

■ In the Datasheet Formatting dialog box, you can also change the color of the gridlines and background as well as the effect of shown gridlines.

Datasheet Formatting dialog box

Freeze Columns

■ If there are too many columns, you may not be able to see all fields at once in Datasheet view.

■ If certain columns are important to view at all times, you can **freeze** them so that they remain on the screen as you scroll to the left or right.

■ To freeze the selected column(s), choose Format, Freeze Columns.

■ A divider line appears between the frozen columns and the unfrozen ones.

Three columns have been frozen at the left

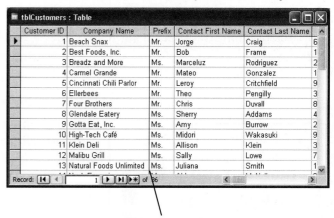

Columns to the left of this line are frozen

- You can unfreeze columns by choosing the Unfreeze All Columns command from the Format menu.
- If you freeze a certain number of contiguous columns starting with the leftmost column, they will simply appear fixed as you scroll from side to side.
- If you freeze individual columns that are not already at the leftmost edge of the table, they will be moved to the left edge when you freeze them.

Procedures

Switch Among Open Objects

1. Click **Window** .... `Alt`+`W`
2. Click number of desired object.
   OR
   Click desired object in Windows taskbar.
   OR
   Press **F11** to go to the database window. .... `F11`

OR

- Press **Alt+Tab**............. `Alt`+`Tab`

Insert a Column

1. Display Datasheet view.
2. Click in column to right of location for new column.
3. Click **Insert** .... `Alt`+`I`
4. Click **Column**...................... `C`

OR

1. Right-click column header.
2. Click **Insert Column** .... `C`

Delete a Column

1. Click on column header you want to delete.
2. Click **Edit** .... `Alt`+`E`
3. Click **Delete Column** .... `M`
4. Click **Yes**..................... `Y`

OR

1. Right-click column header.
2. Click **Delete Column**........... `M`
3. Click **Yes** .... `Y`

Move a Column

1. Click on column header you want to move.
2. Click and drag the selected column to new position.

Hide and Unhide Columns

Hide columns:

1. Click in column you would like to hide.
2. Click **Format**................ `Alt`+`O`
3. Click **Hide Columns**............ `H`

Unhide columns:

1. Click **Format**................ `Alt`+`O`
2. Click **Unhide Columns** ......`U`
3. Check column(s) to unhide.
4. Click **Close** .... `Enter`

Change Datasheet Column Width

Menu:

1. Click in field for column.
2. Click **Format**................ `Alt`+`O`
3. Click **Column Width**........... `C`
4. Click **Best Fit**.............. `Alt`+`B`
   OR
   Type column width.
5. Click **OK** .... `Enter`

Mouse:

- Double-click on right edge of field name cell.

OR

- Drag double-headed mouse pointer on right edge of field name cell.

Remove Gridlines

In Datasheet view:

1. Click **Format** .... `Alt`+`O`
2. Click **Datasheet** .... `E`
3. Deselect Gridlines Shown for:
   - **Horizontal**...................... `H`
   - **Vertical** .... `V`
4. Click **OK** .... `Enter`

Freeze/Unfreeze Columns

1. Select one or more columns.
2. Click **Format** .... `Alt`+`O`
3. Click **Freeze Columns**........ `Z`
   OR
   - Click **Unfreeze All Columns** .... `A`

Exercise Directions

1. Start Access, if necessary.

2. Open 💿 **AC09**.

3. Open the **tblCustomers** table.

4. Switch back to the database window without closing the datasheet.

5. Switch back to the datasheet again.

6. Insert a **Prefix** column to the left of the Contact First Name column, and type appropriate prefixes for each record.

   ✓ Use Mr. for all male names, and use an assortment of Mrs., Miss, and Ms. For the female names.

7. Hide the Customer ID column.

8. Increase or decrease the width of each column so that it is large enough to see all data within it but small enough that it does not waste space on-screen.

   ✓ Double-click the column heading borders.

9. Freeze the first two columns.

10. Scroll all the way to the right, so the last field is visible on-screen (Notes).

11. Insert a new field to the left of the Notes field, and name it **Newsletter**.

    ✓ Select the Notes field, then choose Insert, Column. Then double-click the column header and type the new field name.

12. Change the field type to Yes/No for the Newsletter field.

    ✓ Hint: you will need to go into Table Design view.

13. Return to Datasheet view, and place a check mark in the Newsletter column for the first five records.

14. Unfreeze all columns.

    ✓ Format, Unfreeze All Columns.

15. Move the Newsletter field to the right of the Notes field.

16. Turn off the vertical gridline display. (Leave the horizontal gridlines showing.)

17. Unhide the Customer ID column.

18. Close the datasheet, saving your changes to it.

19. Close the database.

On Your Own

1. Open the database 💿 **OAC09**.

2. Open the **Roster** table in Datasheet view.

3. Delete the Send a Card? column.

4. Insert a Position column, and enter baseball positions for each person.

   ✓ Valid baseball positions are Pitcher, Catcher, First Base, Second Base, Third Base, Shortstop, Right Field, Center Field, Left Center Field, and Left Field.

5. Make a printout that contains just the First Name, Last Name, and Position fields, and that does not contain any gridlines.

   ✓ To do so, hide all the fields except the ones you want, hide the gridlines for the table, and then print the datasheet. Don't forget to unhide the fields and turn the gridlines on again when you're finished.

6. Move the Position column between Last Name and Telephone.

7. Resize each column so it is exactly as wide as it needs to be to display the widest entry in it.

8. Close the table, saving your changes.

9. Close the database and exit Access.

Exercise 10

Skills Covered:

♦ Relate Tables ♦ Enforce Referential Integrity ♦ Print Relationships
♦ Close Relationships Window ♦ Show Related Records

On the Job

When you create relationships between tables, you associate a field in one table with an equivalent field in another. Then the two tables can be used in queries, forms, and reports together, even if there is not a one-to-one relationship between entries. For example, a Customers table can be linked to an Orders table by the customer ID number, so that you can pull up a customer's contact information on a form when entering a new order.

You have added some new tables in the Whole Grains Bread database for order tracking, but they are not currently related to any of the existing tables. You will need to create the appropriate relationships between the tables so that they can be used together in queries, forms, and reports.

Terms

Foreign key A field in the child table that is related to the primary key in the parent table.

Parent table The main table of a relationship. When creating a relationship, this is the "one" side of the relationship and contains the primary key.

Child table The second table of a relationship. When creating a relationship, this is generally the "many" side of the relationship. One record from the parent table (such as clients) can be related to one or more records of the child table (such as sales).

Referential Integrity A property of a relationship between two tables. When Referential Integrity is on, the child table cannot contain a foreign key value that does not have a corresponding value in the primary key of the parent table.

Orphan A value in the foreign key that does not have a corresponding primary key in the parent table.

Cascade Update When the primary key field is updated in a relationship, the corresponding foreign key value(s) in the child table's related records automatically updates.

Cascade Delete When a record in a parent table is deleted, Access deletes all the related records from the child table where the value from the primary key matches the value in the foreign key.

Subdatasheet A child table related to the main (parent) table.

Master field The related field from the main (parent) table of the relationship.

Child field Related field from the child table of the relationship.

374

Notes

Relate Tables

- To create a relationship between two tables, the same field (or equivalents) must appear in both tables. It is desirable, but not required, to use the same field name in both tables.

- In most cases the field is unique in one table (usually the primary key) but not unique in the other. This results in a one-to-many relationship.

- The related field in the second table is called the **foreign key**. The foreign key field must have the same data type as the related primary key, unless the primary key is an AutoNumber type. In that case, the foreign key field must be a Number type.

- The table containing the primary key field being linked is in the **parent table**, and that field is the "one" side of the relationship, indicated by a "1" in the Relationships window.

- The table containing the foreign key field is the **child table**, and that field is the "many" side of the relationship, indicated by an infinity sign (∞) in the Relationships window.

- You set relationships in the Relationships window. In the Relationships window, primary key fields are indicated in bold.

- In the Relationships window, drag a primary key to the related foreign key to open the Edit Relationships dialog box. You can also double-click on the space between two tables in the Relationships window to open the Edit Relationships dialog box.

Relationships window and Edit Relationships dialog box

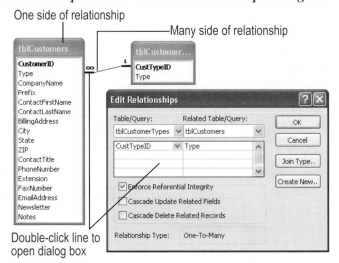

One side of relationship

Many side of relationship

Double-click line to open dialog box

Enforce Referential Integrity

- On the Edit Relationships dialog box, you can choose to Enforce **Referential Integrity** so that you won't have an **orphan** in the child table. For example, you won't be able to enter an order for a customer that does not exist.

- If you select Enforce Referential Integrity, you can choose two additional options: Cascade Update Related Fields and Cascade Delete Related Records.

- **Cascade Update** Related Fields means that when you change the value in the primary key of the parent table, the related foreign key field in all related records of the child table will automatically change as well. If you don't check this box, Access will give an error message when you try to change the primary key.

- **Cascade Delete** Related Records means that when you delete the record in the parent table, all related records in the child table will be deleted as well. If you don't check this box, Access will give an error message when you try to delete the record in the parent table.

- When referential integrity is enabled, the parent table shows a "1" next to the primary key and the child table most often shows an infinity symbol next to the foreign key.

- If the two related fields are primary keys, you'll see a "1" on both fields.

Print Relationships

- To print the Relationships window contents, open the File menu and choose Print Relationships. Access creates a report that contains a replica of the window contents. Print it using the Print button on the toolbar or the File, Print command.

Close Relationships Window

- After setting table relationships, click File, Close or click the window's Close button to close the Relationships window.

Show Related Records

- You can view the parent table and the child table in Datasheet view. After you create a relationship between tables, return to the Datasheet view of the parent table and click on the plus sign (+) on the left edge of a record to see the related rows from the child table.

Subdatasheet for current record

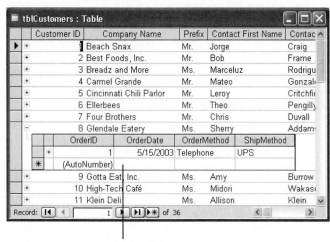

Subdatasheet

✓ If you have more than one child table, you can change the **subdatasheet** attached to the datasheet. Choose Insert, Subdatasheet and in the dialog box choose the child table and, if necessary, identify the **master fields** and **child fields**.

Insert Subdatasheet dialog box

Procedures

Relate Tables

1. Click the **Relationships** button on the Standard toolbar.

   OR

   a. Click **Tools** .... Alt + T

   b. Click **Relationships** .... R

   ✓ *Relationships Window opens. The Show Table dialog box may open automatically. Use step 2 if it does not.*

2. Click the **Show Table** button.

   OR

   a. Click **Relationships** .... Alt + R

   b. Click **Show Table** .... T

3. Click table you want to include.

4. Click **Add** .... Alt + A

5. Repeat steps 3–4 for all tables that are part of relationships.

6. Click **Close** .... Alt + C

7. Drag from primary key of one table to foreign key of another table.

   ✓ *Edit Relationships dialog box opens. See next procedure to enforce referential integrity.*

8. Click **Create** .... Enter

Enforce Referential Integrity

1. If necessary, open Edit Relationships dialog box again and do steps a–c:

   a. Click **Enforce Referential Integrity** .... Alt + E

   b. Click **Cascade Update Related Fields** ...... Alt + U

   c. Click **Cascade Delete Related Records** ... Alt + D

2. Click **OK** .... Enter

Print Relationships

1. Click **File** .... Alt + F

2. Click **Print Relationships** ... R

3. Click **Print** button .

   OR

   a. Click **File** .... Alt + F

   b. Click **Print** .... P

   c. Click **OK** .... Enter

   ✓ *After printing the relationships, a report remains on-screen.*

4. Click the **Close** button X to close the report.

5. Click **No** to not save changes............................. N

Close Relationships Window

- Click the **Close** button ⊠.

OR

1. Click **File**..................... Alt + F
2. Click **Close** C

Show Related Records

1. Click **Tables** object button on database window.
2. Click name of table.
3. Click **Open** .... Alt + O
4. Click **+** before record to show subdatasheet for selected record.
5. Click **–** before record to hide subdatasheet.

Set Subdatasheet

1. Open main table in Datasheet view.
2. Click **Insert** .... Alt + I
3. Click **Subdatasheet**........... S
4. Choose child table.
5. If necessary, choose an option from **Link Child Fields** drop-down list.............. Alt + C
6. Click **OK**.......................... Enter

Exercise Directions

1. Start Access, if necessary.
2. Open 💿 **AC10**.
   - ✓ *Do not open any tables, queries, or forms. You cannot create a relationship to a table already in use.*
3. Open the Relationships window, and add all the tables *except* **tblCustomerTypes** to the Relationships window display.
   - ✓ *Choose Tools, Relationships or click the Relationships button on the toolbar.*
4. Create the relationships shown in Illustration A.
5. Close the Relationships window.
6. Reopen the Relationships window, and edit the relationship between the CustomerID fields so that Cascade Delete is turned off (deselected).
7. Print the Relationships window content, and then close the Relationships window. Close the report without saving it.
8. Open the **tblCustomers** table in Datasheet view.
9. Click on the + before Customer ID to see the subdatasheet for Best Foods, Inc.
   - ✓ *This subdatasheet is for the tblOrders table.*
10. Click on the – to close the subdatasheet for Best Foods, Inc.
11. Open the subdatasheet for Glendale Eatery.
12. Enter the following order:

    OrderDate: **(today's date)**
    OrderMethod: **Telephone**
    ShipMethod: **UPS**
    - ✓ *Do not enter the OrderID; it is an AutoNumber field. Simply Tab past it.*
13. Press Tab from the ShipMethod box to end the entry. A new plus sign appears next to the OrderID field.
14. Click the plus sign next to OrderID to open the **tblOrderDetails** subdatasheet.
15. Minimize the **tblCustomers** window, and open the tblProducts table. Look up the product ID number for Wheat Rolls.
16. Close the **tblProducts** table, and restore the **tblCustomers** table window. Then enter the product ID for Wheat Rolls in the **tblOrderDetails** subdatasheet. Enter a quantity of 20.
17. Close all subdatasheets and all open tables.
18. Open the **tblOrderDetails** table and verify that a record has been entered into it; then close it.
19. Close the database and exit Access.

Field	Field	Referential Integrity?	Cascade update?	Cascade delete?
OrderID in tblOrders	OrderID in tblOrderDetails	Yes	Yes	No
ProductID in tblProducts	ProductID in tblOrderDetails	Yes	Yes	No
CustomerID in tblCustomers	CustomerID in tblOrders	Yes	Yes	Yes

On Your Own

1. Open ◎ **OAC10**.

2. Open the **Equipment** table in Design view and change the field type for the Owner field to Number. Close the table.

   ✓ *This is necessary because you will be relating those fields to the Roster via the primary key field, which has a type of AutoNumber.*

3. Open the **Roster** table in Design view and add a Category field to the bottom of the field list. Use a Number field type. Then close the table, saving changes to it.

4. Open the Relationships window and add the **Roster**, **Equipment**, and **Categories** tables to the layout.

5. Create a relationship between the CategoryID field in the **Categories** table and the Category field in the **Roster** table. Do not enforce referential integrity.

6. Create a relationship between the ID field in the **Roster** table and the Owner field in the **Equipment** table. Use referential integrity and cascade update and delete. Close the Relationships window.

7. Open the **Roster** table, and enter two new pieces of equipment using subdatasheets.

8. Close the Access database, saving all changes, and exit Access.

Exercise 11

Because of your experience with databases at Whole Grain Breads, you have been hired to create a database for HelpNow MedCenter. This company wants a database that will contain contact information for each of its employees and keep track of the number of hours that each employee works per week. You have already started the database, but now you need to improve it.

Exercise Directions

1. Open ✪ **AC11**.

2. Import the data from the file ✪ **AC11-A.xls** into a new table, and call it **tblEmployees**. Include the column headings. Make the EmployeeID field the primary key. Accept all other defaults when importing.

3. In Table Design view (**tblEmployees** table), apply an input mask for phone numbers to the HomePhone, CellPhone, and Pager fields.

4. For all fields that have more than one word in their names (like MailingAddress, for example), create captions that are either one word or have spaces between the words.

5. Set up an input mask for ZIP codes for the ZIP field.

6. Make the following field size changes:

   EmployeeID: 10
   Prefix: 5
   FirstName: 50
   LastName: 50
   Suffix: 5
   MailingAddress: 100
   City: 50
   State: 2
   ZIP: 10
   HomePhone: 20
   CellPhone: 20
   Pager: 20
   Position: 100

7. Save your changes to the table, and then switch to Datasheet view.

   ✓ *If you see a message about some data possibly being lost, click Yes to continue. It does not apply in this case.*

8. Resize all the column widths in the datasheet so that all the data fits but there is no wasted blank space.

9. In the datasheet, move the Position field between Suffix and Address.

10. Add the position **Registered Nurse** for employee E004 (Joyce Probasco).

11. Hide all the gridlines, sort the datasheet by position, and print a copy of the datasheet. Then redisplay the gridlines.

12. Close the **tblEmployees** table, saving changes.

13. Create a relationship between the **tblEmployees** and **tblTimecards** tables by connecting the EmployeeID field to the Employee field. Enforce referential integrity with cascade update and cascade delete.

14. Using the subdatasheets from the **tblEmployee** table in datasheet view, enter 40 hours of regular work and 10 hours of overtime for each of the Registered Nurses. See Illustration A. Use the current week's Monday date as the date.

15. Export the data from the **tblTimecards** table to a plain-text comma-delimited file named **AC11-B.txt**.

16. Close the Access database and exit Access.

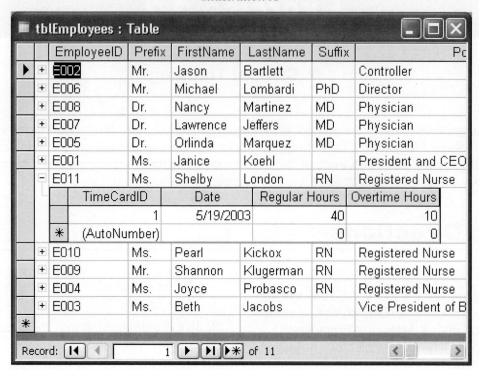

Exercise 12

◆ **Create a Lookup for a Field** ◆ **Create a Value List with the Lookup Wizard** ◆ **Lookup Field Values from another Table**

On the Job

Some fields store data that can contain only a limited range of valid values, such as Marital Status or Gender. To simplify data entry and prevent entry errors, you can create a lookup for a field that presents the user entering records with a drop-down list of options from which to choose.

The Michigan Avenue Athletic Club's owner has asked you to help his assistant improve a database that she has been creating for tracking the club's members and its class offerings. The database already contains all the tables and relationships, but the assistant is finding it awkward to enter the data into it. You will help her by creating some lookups for some of the fields.

Terms

Lookup Field A list of values from which to choose when entering information into a field.

Notes

Create a Lookup for a Field

- If you have several values that can appear in a field, consider using a **lookup field**.

- A lookup field appears as a drop-down list during data entry, and you can choose from the list rather than typing an entry. This minimizes data entry errors and ensures consistent formatting (such as capitalization).

- When you enter data for a record, an arrow appears within the lookup field indicating that you can choose from a list of options.

A lookup field during data entry

- You can use the Lookup Wizard to create a lookup field with values you enter.

- You can also use the Lookup Wizard to create a lookup field that looks up values from another table.

- To create a lookup for a field, go to Table Design view and change the field's type to Lookup Wizard. The Lookup Wizard will automatically run.

Create a Value List with the Lookup Wizard

- The Lookup Wizard provides a list in which you can type the values you want to appear on the list.

- This method works well when the values on the list will seldom or never change. If the values change frequently, use the table lookup method instead.

✓ *When creating your list, try to enter the values in a useful order. An alphabetical list of states, for example, is easier to use than one that doesn't have a recognizable order. A list of prospect levels might be ordered by the frequency with which they are used.*

Lookup Field Values from Another Table

- If your list often varies, you can create a separate table for the list instead and then create a lookup field that looks into that table.

- Before creating the lookup, you must first create the additional table. Then run the Lookup Wizard and select the table to be used.

- Creating a lookup also creates a relationship between the tables, which will be reflected in the Relationships window. The relationship it creates does not enforce referential integrity but you can edit it to do so later.

- The Lookup Wizard first helps you choose the lookup table or query.

Select the table from which to look up values

- It then prompts you to choose which fields from the table or query to include.

  ✓ *If the table you choose for the lookup has a primary key field, it's a good idea to choose it along with the field that you actually want to appear in the lookup list. You can then hide the primary key field. The users will choose from the "friendly" field, such as the text names, but the entry in the table will be the unique primary key value for that choice.*

Select the fields to include

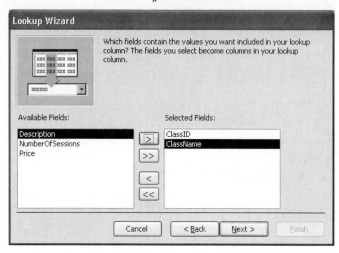

- You next choose how wide to make each chosen field. By default the primary key field is hidden.

Select the column widths for the lookup field(s)

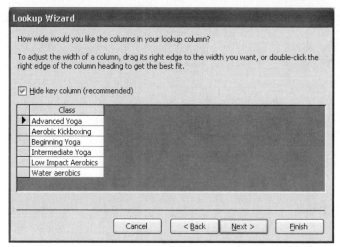

- On the last step of the wizard, you can change the field name. Keep the field name the same if you are changing an existing field and if you've already created a query, form, or report based on this table.

  ✓ *If you have text values in a field that you are converting to a lookup field, and the new lookup will contain the numeric ID numbers from the corresponding table rather than the values, creating the lookup will delete all the nonnumeric previous entries in that field, and you will need to reenter them. For this reason, it's best to set up any lookups you want to use before you do much data entry.*

Procedures

Create a Lookup List for a Field

1. Open the table in Table Design view.
2. Click in the **Data Type** column for the field.
3. Click the **down arrow** `▼`.
4. Click **Lookup Wizard**.
5. Click **I will type in the values that I want** .... `Alt`+`T`
6. Click **Next** .... `Alt`+`N`
7. Press **Tab** .... `Tab`
8. Type a value for the list.
9. Press **Tab** .... `Tab`
10. Repeat steps 8–9 as needed.
11. Click **Next** .... `Alt`+`N`
12. Click **Finish** .... `Enter`

Use a Table as a Lookup

1. Create a **table** to be used as a lookup.
   OR
   Decide on an **existing table** to use as a lookup.
2. Open the **table** containing the field in which you want to use the lookup in Table Design view.
3. Click in the **Data Type** column for the field to receive the lookup.
4. Click the **down arrow** `▼`.
5. Click **Lookup Wizard**.
6. Click **I want the look up column to lookup the values in a table or query** ...... `Alt`+`L`
7. Click **Next** .... `Alt`+`N`
8. Click the table to use.
9. Click **Next** .... `Alt`+`N`
10. Click a **field** to include.
11. Click `>` button .... `>`
12. Repeat steps 10–11 as needed.
13. Click **Next** .... `Alt`+`N`
14. Adjust column width if desired.
15. Click **Next** .... `Alt`+`N`
16. Click **Finish** .... `Enter`

Use a Lookup Field in Data Entry

1. Click the **down arrow** `▼`.
2. Click the **value** you want.

Exercise Directions

1. Open ⊙ **AC12**.

2. Open the **tblClassOfferings** table in Design view.

3. Create a lookup for the Class field that looks up the classes in the **tblClasses** table.

   ✓ *Use the ClassID and ClassName fields. Sort by ClassName. Hide the key field (ClassID). Accept the default label.*

4. Create a lookup for the Instructors field that looks up the instructors in the **tblInstructors** table.

   ✓ *Use the InstructorID and LastName fields. Sort by LastName. Hide the key field (InstructorID). Accept the default label.*

5. Create a lookup for the Location field that provides the following values from which to choose:

Aerobics room
Basement studio
Central gymnasium
Upstairs studio

6. Close the table, saving your changes.

7. Open the **tblClassOfferings** table in Datasheet view, and edit the data in the following ways:

   - For record 1, choose **Landis** as the instructor and Aerobics room as the location.

   - For record 2, choose **Stevens** as the instructor and Upstairs studio as the location.

   - Enter a new record:
     Class: **Advanced Yoga**
     Start: *today's date*
     Days: **MW**
     Start Time: **8:00 AM**
     Duration: **1 hour**
     Instructor: **Landis**
     Location: **Basement studio**
     Size Limit: **20**

8. Close the table.

9. Open **tblClassEnrollment** in Design view.

10. Create a lookup for the MemberID field that looks up the class offerings in the **tblMembers** table.

    ✓ *Use the MemberID, FirstName, and LastName fields. Sort by LastName. Hide the key field (MemberID). Accept the default label.*

11. Close **tblClassEnrollment**, saving your changes.

12. Open **tblClassEnrollment** and enroll Amy Burrow in class 1.

    ✓ *Why did we not create a lookup for the ClassID field in the tblClassEnrollment table? Because it would be better to base that lookup on a query, and we haven't yet learned to create queries in this course. Instead we will manually create a relationship there, in step 14.*

13. Close the **tblClassEnrollment** datasheet, and open the Relationships window.

14. Add all the tables in the database to the Relationships window, and drag the table windows to make the relationship lines easier to see.

15. Create a relationship between the ClassOfferingID fields in the **tblClassOfferings** and **tblClassEnrollment** tables.

16. Edit the relationships between all tables so that they all use Enforce Referential Integrity with Cascade Update and Cascade Delete. Illustration A shows the finished result.

17. Close the Relationships window, saving your changes.

18. Close the database and exit Access.

Illustration A

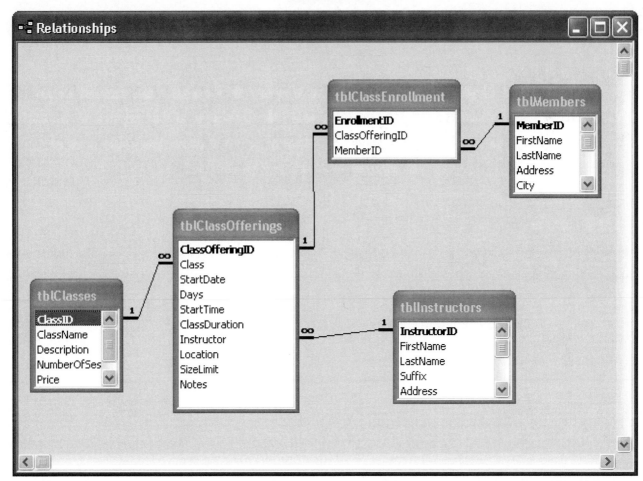

On Your Own

1. Open ⊙ **OAC12**.

2. In the Relationships window, delete the relationship between the **Roster** and **Categories** table. To do this, select a relationship line and press the Delete key.

3. In the **Roster** table, set up a lookup for the Category field that looks up the values in the **Categories** table.

4. For the Position field, create a lookup that takes its values from a list of valid baseball positions.

   ✓ *Valid positions are Pitcher, Catcher, Shortstop, 1st Base, 2nd Base, 3rd Base, Right Field, Center Field, Left Center Field, and Left Field.*

   ✓ *The lookups you create will reestablish the relationships.*

5. In Datasheet view, select categories for each of the existing players in the table.

6. Enter a new record into the table, using information you make up.

7. Close the database and exit Access.

Exercise 13

Skills Covered:

◆ **Compare Datasheet and Form View** ◆ **Create an AutoForm**
◆ **Create a Form with the Form Wizard** ◆ **Create a Form from Scratch**
◆ **Enter Form Design View** ◆ **Work with Form Design View**
◆ **AutoFormat a Form**

On the Job

If your table contains many fields, entering records in Datasheet view can become cumbersome. Many people find it easier to create a data entry form that displays all the fields on-screen at once, one record at a time.

As you add more information to the Michigan Avenue Athletic Club database, you're finding that you're spending too much time scrolling through the records in Datasheet view. You've decided to create some forms to help navigate the information.

Terms

Form view The view that generally shows many fields for one record on one screen.

Form Design view The view in which you can edit the controls on a form.

Form selector A box at the upper left of Form Design view, where the two rulers intersect. Clicking this box selects the form as a whole.

Control An item such as a text box, label, or line on a form or report.

AutoFormat A feature that applies a formatting template to a form, including background and fonts.

Notes

Compare Datasheet and Form View

- In Datasheet view, each row is a record and each column is a field.
- If there are many fields, you must scroll to the left/right to move among them.

Datasheet view

		ID	First	Last	Address	City	State	ZIP	
►	+	1	Leroy	Critchfield	97 Calla Lane #31	Chicago	IL	60601-	3·
	+	2	Juliana	Smith	144 Tournament Lane	Chicago	IL	60603-	3·
	+	3	John	Kemmerly	86 March Road	Chicago	IL	60604-	3·
	+	4	Abdul	Norcutt	97 Rose Lane	Chicago	IL	60605-	3·
	+	5	Mabellina	Jackson	3988 West 14th Street	Chicago	IL	60604-	3·
	+	6	Hermione	Hernandez	23 Tarragon Trail	Chicago	IL	60601-	3·
	+	7	Margaret	Faderman	7758 Wood Street	Chicago	IL	60605-	3·
	+	8	Maurice	Simpson	6988 West 22nd Street	Chicago	IL	60605-	3·
	+	9	Anna	Roecher	4885 Tamarind Drive	Chicago	IL	60605-	3·
	+	10	Melinda	Goldstein	68772 McKeown Road	Chicago	IL	60605-	3·
	+	11	Robert	Kroeker	120 Forte Square	Chicago	IL	60605-	3·

Record: ◄◄ ◄ 1 ► ►► ►* of 36

■ **Form view**, on the other hand, displays one record at a time, and shows all the fields at once (in most cases).

Form view

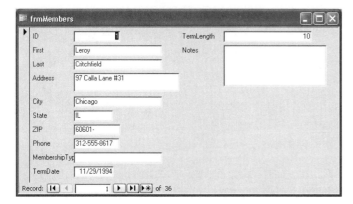

■ Think of a form as a window to the table. When you add data to a form, it automatically fills in the underlying table(s).

Create an AutoForm

■ There are several ways to create a new form. The easiest is to use AutoForm, which creates a simple form containing all the fields in a particular table or query.

■ An AutoForm is very basic and might not be formatted exactly the way you want. However, you can edit it in **Form Design view** after you create it.

■ You have a choice of several types of AutoForms. The most common type is Columnar, which arranges the field names in columns. The form shown on the preceding page is a columnar AutoForm.

■ Other types resemble datasheets, or enable you to drag-and-drop fields into a PivotTable or PivotChart.

■ To create an AutoForm, display the Forms tab on the database window, click the New button, and choose the type of AutoForm you want and the table or query on which the form should be based.

Create a Form with the Form Wizard

■ The Form Wizard offers a good compromise between the simplicity of an AutoForm and the time needed to create a form from scratch.

■ It asks questions in a series of dialog boxes, walking you step-by-step through the process of selecting tables/queries, fields, and formatting.

■ To start a form with the Form Wizard, display the Forms tab in the database window and double-click *Create form by using wizard.*

The Form Wizard

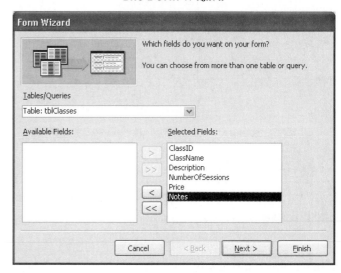

Create a Form from Scratch

■ You can also create a new form from scratch in Form Design view. This creates a blank form, onto which you can place fields and other controls.

■ To start a form in Design view, double-click *Create form in Design view* from the Forms tab of the database window.

Form selector　　　　　　　*A blank form*

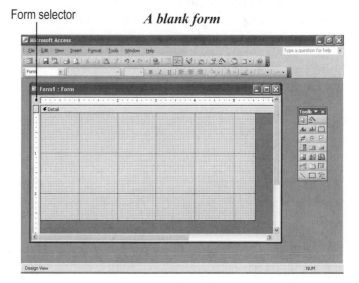

- If you start a new form using the above method, no table or query is associated with it. You can edit the form properties to attach one by right-clicking the **form selector** (the box in the top-left corner, where the rulers intersect) and choosing Properties, and then choosing a table or query from the Record Source list on the Data tab.

Edit a form's properties to change the table or query on which it is based

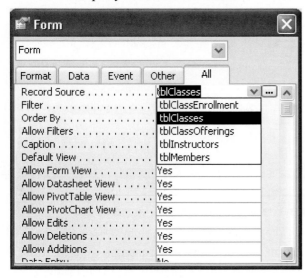

- The attached table/query will become important in Exercise 14, when you learn how to add fields to a form from the Field List.
- If you would prefer to specify a table or query when creating a new form, use the New button in the database window. The New Form dialog box enables you to choose a table or query before creating the form.

Using the New Form dialog box enables you to select a table or query for your new blank form

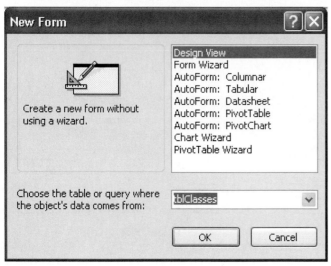

Enter Form Design View

- If you start a form using AutoForm or the Form Wizard, you might want to edit the form in Design view.
- You can switch between Form view and Form Design view by making a choice on the View menu or by clicking the View button on the toolbar.
- You can open a saved form in Design view by selecting it in the database window and clicking the Design button.

Work with Form Design View

- Each item on a form (or report) is called a **control**. Controls include text boxes where you type in the information for a field, labels to describe the field and the form, lines, and many other items.
- While you are in Form Design view, click on a control to select it. Selection boxes surround the control.

Form Design view

Selected Control

- You will learn more about controls and Form Design view in upcoming exercises.

AutoFormat a Form

- When you create a form with the Form Wizard, it asks you to choose a design to apply. The design includes a background, font choices, and color choices.

388

■ You can choose a different design at any time, or apply a design to a form that was not created with the Form Wizard at all.

■ To choose a different format, choose Format, **AutoFormat** or click the AutoFormat button on the toolbar.

■ Then select a format from the AutoFormat dialog box that appears.

Select an AutoFormat

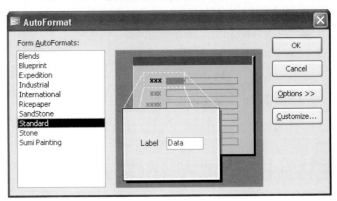

Procedures

Create a Columnar AutoForm

1. Open table in Datasheet view.
2. Click **AutoForm** button [icon].

Create Any Type of AutoForm

From the Database window:

1. Click **Forms**.
2. Click **New**.................... Alt + N
3. Click **AutoForm: Columnar**.
   OR
   Click **AutoForm: Tabular**.
   OR
   Click **AutoForm: Datasheet**.
   OR
   Click **AutoForm: PivotTable**.
   OR
   Click **AutoForm: PivotChart**.
4. Click **down arrow** next to Choose the table or query where the object's data comes from.
5. Click the **table** or **query** to use.
6. Click **OK**.......................... Enter

Create a Form with the Form Wizard

From the Database window:

1. Click **Forms**.
2. Double-click **Create form by using wizard**.
3. Click **down arrow** next to Tables/Queries.
4. Click **table** or **query**.
5. Click **Available Fields** to include.

6. Click **right arrow button**
   [>].
7. Repeat steps 5–6 as needed.
8. Return to step 4 to select fields from other tables/queries if needed.
9. Click **Next**.................... Alt + N
10. Click a layout:
    - **Columnar** .... Alt + C
    - **Tabular** .... Alt + T
    - **Datasheet** .... Alt + D
    - **Justified** .... Alt + J
    - **PivotTable** .... Alt + I
    - **PivotChart**............. Alt + V

    ✓ *Columnar is the most common type and the one that produces a traditional type of form.*
11. Click **Next**.................... Alt + N
12. Click a format style.
13. Click **Next**.................... Alt + N
14. Type a title.
15. Click **Finish** .... Enter

Create a New Form from Scratch

From the Database window:

1. Click **Forms**.
2. Double-click **Create form in Design view**.
   ✓ *The above steps do not attach a table or query to the form.*

OR

From the database window:

1. Click **Forms**.
2. Click **New**.................... Alt + N
3. Click **Design View**.
4. Click **down arrow** [▼].
5. Click the **table** or **query** name.
6. Click **OK**.

Attach a Table or Query to a Form

✓ *You can also use the following procedure to change which table or query is attached.*

1. In Design view, right-click **form selector**.
   ✓ *The form selector is the box at the top left, at the intersection of the vertical and horizontal rulers.*
2. Click **Properties** .... P
3. Click the **Data** tab.
4. Click **down arrow** [▼] next to Record Source.
5. Click **table** or **query** to use.

Switch from Form View to Form Design View

1. Click **View** .... Alt + V
2. Click **Design View** .... D
   OR
   Click **Design View** button .

Switch from Form Design View to Form View

1. Click **View** .... Alt + V
2. Click **Form View** .... F

   OR

   Click **Form View** button 📇▼.

AutoFormat a Form

From Form Design view:

1. Click **Format** .... Alt + O
2. Click **AutoFormat** .... F
3. Click the desired format.
4. Click **OK** .... Enter

Exercise Directions

1. Start Access, if necessary.
2. Open 💿 **AC13**.
3. Create a columnar AutoForm based on the **tblClasses** table.
4. Save the new form as **frmClasses** and close it.
5. Create a form based on the **tblMembers** table using the Form Wizard. Use the following settings:
   - Use all the fields.
   - Use a Columnar layout.
   - Choose the Industrial design.
   - Name the form **frmMembers**.

6. Change the form's AutoFormat to the Expedition style.
7. Close the form, saving your changes.
8. Start a new, blank form without specifying a table.
9. Attach the **tblInstructors** table to the form using the form's Properties box.
   - ✓ Hint: Right-click the form selector in Design view, and select Properties.
10. Save the form as **frmInstructors** and close it.
11. Close the form and database.

On Your Own

1. Open 💿 **OAC13**.
2. Create a form for the **Roster** table using the Form Wizard. Include all fields.
3. Save the form with the name **Roster**.
4. Display the form in Design view.
5. Apply an AutoFormat to it.
6. Switch to Form view, and enter a new record into the table using the form.
7. Close the form, saving your changes.
   - ✓ When you enter Form view through Form Design view, the design changes you have made to the form are not immediately saved. They are not saved until you close the form, whether from Form view or Form Design. That's why you're prompted to save your changes when you close the Form view in step 7.

8. Create a new form for the Equipment table using AutoForm:Tabular. Name it **Equipment**.
9. Close the database and exit Access.
   - ✓ In these On Your Own exercises, you are creating some forms and tables with the same names. Although this is not such a great idea from a database design perspective because of the potential for confusion, many people do create databases that way in real life. These exercises give you the opportunity to try it out and see whether you find it confusing or convenient.

Exercise 14

Skills Covered:

◆ **Add a New Field to a Form** ◆ **Select Controls on a Form**
◆ **Delete a Control from a Form** ◆ **Move Controls** ◆ **Reset Tab Order**
◆ **Change Control Formatting** ◆ **Resize Fields and Other Controls**
◆ **Align Controls** ◆ **Form Backgrounds**

On the Job

Regardless of how you created your form, you might like to make some changes to it. The AutoForm and Form Wizard methods create nice basic forms, but sometimes field labels are truncated or there is not enough space between fields. In addition, you might want to add more fields to the form that you originally omitted, or change the text formatting.

In the Michigan Avenue Athletic Club database, you have decided to add another field to your tblMembers table, and you want it to appear on the frmMembers form as well. You would also like to apply some additional formatting on the form to make it more attractive.

Terms

Field List A floating box in Form Design view containing the names of all the fields in the associated table or query.

Control A field, label, option group, box, or other object on a form.

Selection handles Black squares around the border of a control that indicate it is selected.

Tab order The order in which the insertion point moves from field to field on a form.

Notes

Add a New Field to a Form

- To add a new field, drag it from the **Field List**. If the Field List does not appear, click the Field List button on the toolbar.

   ✓ Don't worry if you don't get the positioning exactly right; you can move the field and/or its associated label at any time.

Adding fields to the form

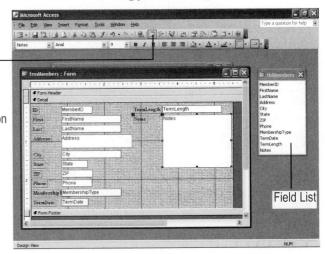

Field List button

391

Select Controls on a Form

- To select a field or other **control**, click on it. **Selection handles** appear around it.

- When you select a field, its associated text label is also selected, so that moving the field also moves the label. It works in reverse, too: clicking a text label also selects the associated field.

A selected field and label

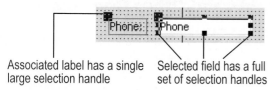

Associated label has a single large selection handle

Selected field has a full set of selection handles

- To select multiple controls, click on the first control, hold the Shift key down, and click on additional controls. You can also "lasso" controls by dragging a box around them.

Delete a Control from a Form

- To delete a field or other control, select it and press the Delete key.

- When selecting a field for deletion, click on the field itself, not its associated text label. If you select the label before pressing Delete, only the label will be deleted, and the field itself will remain.

Move Controls

- To move a field, select it, and then position the mouse pointer anywhere over it *except* over a selection handle, so the pointer becomes an open hand. Then drag to a new location.

Drag a field and its label as a pair with the open-handed mouse pointer

Mouse pointer

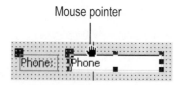

- The field and its associated label move as a pair when you drag with the open-hand mouse pointer.

- If you want to move the field or the label separately from one another, click on the one you want to move and then drag it by the large selection handle in the top-left corner. The mouse pointer appears as a pointing finger in this case.

Drag a field or label separately by dragging by the selection handle in the upper-left corner

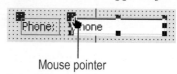

Mouse pointer

Reset Tab Order

- If you add or move controls, you may want to reset the order in which each field appears when you or another database form user presses Tab to navigate in the form.

- You might also want to set an alternate **tab order** so that users don't have to tab past a seldom-used field such as Suffix or Middle Initial during data entry.

- Choose the Tab Order command from the View menu.

- In the Tab Order dialog box, drag the fields into the order you want them.

- Click the Auto Order button to set the order from left to right and top to bottom based on the fields' current positions on the form.

Set tab order

Tab Order	? ☒

Section
- ○ Form Header
- ● Detail
- ○ Form Footer

Click to select a row, or click and drag to select multiple rows. Drag selected row(s) to move them to desired tab order.

Custom Order:
- MemberID
- FirstName
- LastName
- Address
- City
- State
- ZIP
- Phone
- MembershipType
- TermDate

OK	Cancel	Auto Order

Change Control Formatting

- While a control on a form is selected, you can click on the Formatting toolbar to do any of the following:
  - Change the item's font type or font size.
  - Change whether the text is bold, italic, or underlined.
  - Choose left-aligned, centered, or right-aligned.

- Choose the color of the background, text, and border.
- Choose the style and width of the line or of the border surrounding the box.

■ All of the above formatting features work just as they do in other Microsoft Office programs that you might already be familiar with.

■ When you select multiple objects, you can use the Formatting toolbar to change more than one at a time.

■ If you make an error while formatting, choose the Undo command immediately after a change.

■ To copy all enhancements, select a control with the enhancements you want to copy, click the Format Painter button 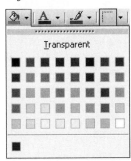 and then click the object to change.

■ If you want to change multiple objects with Format Painter, double-click the Format Painter button and click on each control you want to change. Click the Format Painter button again to turn it off.

Resize Fields and Other Controls

■ To resize a control, drag any selection handle except the one in the upper-left corner.

■ To resize several controls at once, select them all and then resize one; the others will resize, too.

■ If you need to resize a text box so that text is not truncated, double-click a selection handle to automatically expand or contract the size so that the text exactly fits.

■ To make a group of controls the same size, select them all, choose Format, Size, and then select To Widest, To Narrowest, To Tallest, or To Shortest.

Align Controls

■ One of the challenges in creating a form from scratch is to get all the fields precisely aligned with one another.

■ To align several fields, place the first one where you want it, and then choose Format, Align. You can choose alignment options such as Left, Right, Top, Bottom, or To Grid.

✓ The dots on the background in Form Design view form the grid referred to in the To Grid option.

Form Backgrounds

■ You can change the color of any part of a form by clicking on the background in Design view, and then clicking the drop-down arrow of the Fill/Back Color button on the Formatting toolbar and choosing a color from the palette.

Make a choice from the Fill/Back Color palette

■ You can add a logo or other graphic as a background for the form. You do this through the Property sheet of the form.

■ Double-click on any object to open its Property sheet. For the form, use the Form selector above the vertical ruler and to the left of the horizontal ruler.

Property sheet

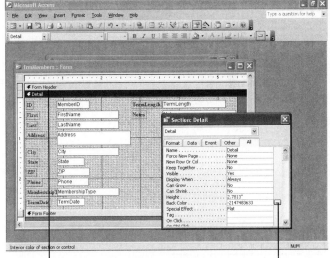

Double-click on the Section Selector to open the Property Sheet for the Detail section

Build button

■ The Build button appears on the toolbar and as an ellipses button 🔲 at the end of some properties when you select them, such as the Picture property. This button opens a dialog box that allows you to make a choice from a list.

■ If you want the picture repeated throughout the form, change Picture Tiling to Yes.

Procedures

✓ *All the following procedures take place in Form Design view.*

Display the Field List

1. Click **View** .... `Alt`+`V`
2. Click **Field List** .... `L`
   OR
   Click the **Field List**
   button `▣`.

Add a Field

- Drag field from field list to form.

Select Fields or Other Controls

- Click on a **control** to select it.
OR
1. Click on first control.
2. Hold down **Shift** and click on additional controls to select them.
OR
1. Position **mouse pointer** outside first control.
2. Drag a box around all controls to select.

Delete a Field or Other Control

1. Select **control** to delete.
   ✓ *If deleting both a field and its label, click on the field itself, rather than the label.*
   ✓ *If deleting only a field label, select the label.*
2. Press **Delete key** .... `Del`

Move a Field or Other Control

Move a field and label as a pair, or move other type of control:

1. Click on **field** you want to move.
2. When the mouse pointer is a hand 🖐, drag control and attached label and drop in new location.

Move a field or label separately:

1. Click on **field** or **label** you want to move.
2. Point **mouse pointer** to upper-left selection handle.
3. When mouse pointer is a pointing hand 👆, drag and drop to new location.

Reset Tab Order

1. Click **View** .... `Alt`+`V`
2. Click **Tab Order** .... `B`
3. Click **Auto Order** .... `A`
   OR
   Drag fields into order you want.
4. Click **OK** .... `Enter`

Change Control Formatting

1. Select **control** you want to format.
2. Click desired button from Formatting toolbar.
   OR
1. Click **Format** .... `Alt`+`O`
2. Click desired change from Format menu.

Resize Controls

1. Click on **control** you want to size.
2. Point to **selection handle** so mouse pointer becomes an arrow ⬉ ↔ ↕
3. Drag to resize.
OR
1. Change first item to proper size.
2. Select first item and other items to size.
3. Click **Format** .... `Alt`+`O`
4. Click **Size** .... `S`
5. Click **To Widest** .... `W`

Align Controls

1. Move first item to proper location.
2. Select first item and other items to align.
3. Click **Format** .... `Alt`+`O`
4. Click **Align** .... `A`
5. Click desired alignment option.

Change Form Background Color

1. Click the **form background**.
2. Click down arrow on **Fill/Back Color** button `🪣▾`.
3. Click the desired **color**.

Use a Background Image

1. Click the **Form Selector**.
2. Click **View** .... `Alt`+`V`
3. Click **Properties** .... `P`
4. Click **Format** tab.
5. Scroll down to **Picture** field and select it.
6. Click **Build** button `…` next to Picture field.
7. Choose a file that contains the picture you want.
8. Click **Open** .... `Enter`
9. Click the **Close** button `✕`.

Remove a Background Image

1. Click the **Form Selector**.
2. Click **View** .... `Alt`+`V`
3. Click **Properties** .... `P`
4. Click **Format** tab.
5. Delete the entry in the **Picture** field.
6. Click the **Close** button `✕`.

Exercise Directions

1. Start Access, if necessary.

2. Open ⊘**AC14**.

3. Open the **tblMembers** table in Table Design view, and add a new field to the left of the TermDate field called **PoolPrivileges**.

4. Set the field type to Yes/No and set its caption to **Pool?**.

5. Close the table, saving changes. Then Open the **frmMembers** form in Form Design view.

6. Change the label for the MembershipType field on the form so that it reads **Type**.

7. Add the PoolPrivileges field to any blank spot on the form.

8. Drag the PoolPrivileges field's checkbox (separately from its label) to the right of the label, so that the label is to the left of the box.

9. Position both the checkbox and the label (together as a group) to the right of the Membership Type field. See Illustration A.

10. Use the Align command to ensure that the MembershipType and PoolPrivileges fields are top-aligned with one another.

11. Edit the labels for the TermDate and TermLength fields so that there are spaces between the words.

12. Reset the tab order so that the PoolPrivileges field falls between MembershipType and TermDate.

13. Resize the Notes box so that it is twice as tall as it originally was.

14. Select all the field labels, italicize them (as a group), and make them dark green.

15. Set the background color for the Detail area of the form to pale yellow.

16. Remove the background image from the form so that the yellow background shows.

17. Preview the form in Form view; it should look like Illustration B. Then return to Form Design view and save your changes.

18. Close the form and database.

Illustration A

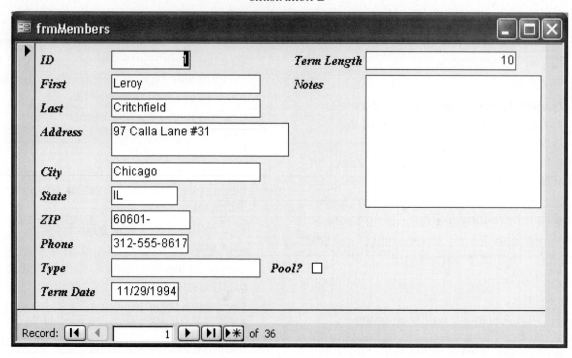

On Your Own

1. Open ⊙ **OAC14**.

2. Delete the **Equipment** form.

3. Create a new, blank form in Form Design view with the **Equipment** table associated with it.

4. Manually add and arrange the fields from the Field List.

   ✓ You can enlarge the form size by dragging its bottom-right corner of the grid area outward.

5. Format the fields in whatever way you think is attractive. This can include:
   - Aligning fields with one another
   - Changing font, text size, and color
   - Rearranging fields
   - Increasing or decreasing field or label size
   - Changing the background color or adding a background picture

6. Check the tab order, and reset it if needed.

7. Save the new form as **Equipment**.

8. Close the database and exit Access.

Exercise 15

Skills Covered:

◆ **Use Form View Toolbox** ◆ **Add Labels** ◆ **Add Lookups to Forms**
◆ **Add an Option Group** ◆ **Add a List Box or Combo Box**

On the Job

You might want to dress up your basic form with some extra text labels, or place special controls on the form that make data entry easier for the user. Some of these extras include option groups, list boxes, and combo boxes. They're similar in function to the lookups you created in Exercise 12, but work only within the form on which they are created.

As Michigan Avenue Athletic Club employees use the frmMembers form you have created, you notice that they are making some data entry errors. You think that perhaps creating option groups or combo boxes for some fields will help improve data entry accuracy. You would also like to add a note to clarify the purpose of the Notes field.

Terms

Toolbox A floating toolbar in Form Design view that provides buttons for adding various types of controls to the form.

Option group A set of buttons or check boxes on a form that present a finite set of acceptable values from a lookup.

List box A box on a form that lists a finite set of acceptable values for a field from a lookup.

Combo box Like a list box, except the user can also enter new values if the existing values in the lookup are not appropriate.

Label A frame containing descriptive text on a form. A label is different from a text box in that a text box can be bound to a field in a table, while a label exists only on the form.

Text box A box on a form that contains text and that can be bound to a field in a table. Fields on a form appear as text boxes, for example.

Notes

Use Form View Toolbox

- The **Toolbox** appears in Form Design view. It can be used to add items (controls) to a form.
- If the toolbox does not appear, click the Toolbox button 🛠 on the toolbar.
- The toolbox contains a Wizard button near the top. It is an on/off switch; by default it is on.

The Toolbox

Wizard button

- When the Wizard feature is on, a wizard walks you through the process of creating certain types of controls (such as **option groups** and **list/combo boxes**).

- When the Wizard button feature is off, all types of controls can be manually placed on the form without using a wizard.

- Using the wizards makes learning about the different kinds of controls easier.

Add Labels

- A **label** is a descriptive bit of text that you add to a form that is not associated with a field in a table. The label exists only on the form.

- To add a label, click the Label button *Aa* on the Toolbox and then drag on the form to create the label's frame. Then type your text.

- The button to the right of the Label button is the **Text Box** button `ab|`. You can use it to create unbound text boxes that will later be associated (manually) with fields. Beginners will not do this very often.

Add Lookups to Forms

- Access offers various types of lookups you can add on a form. These are like the lookups you can set for fields in Table Design view (see Exercise 11), except you create them from the form.

- You do not need to create lookups on the form for fields that have already been set up with the Lookup Wizard in Table Design view; these appear with lookups by default when placed on a form.

- The default setting for a field with a lookup is Combo Box when placed on a form, but you can change that setting. To do so, go to the Lookup tab for that field's properties in Table Design view and set the Display Control setting to Text, List Box, or Combo Box.

Add an Option Group

- An option group is a group of mutually exclusive buttons representing various lookup choices. You can make them appear as square buttons, as round dots, or as check boxes.

An option group

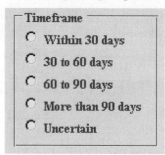

- The Option Group Wizard makes it easy to create an option group on a form. Click the Option Group button in the Toolbox and then click or drag on the form where you want it to appear. Then step through the wizard to complete the option group.

The Option Group Wizard at work

- A limitation of an option group is that you cannot specify that it take its values from a table or query; you must manually type in the values to appear in the group.

- If you need the values to come from a table or query, use a list box or combo box instead.

Add a List Box or Combo Box

- List boxes and combo boxes work the same way, except a combo box enables users to enter additional values, while a list box restricts them to the choices you provide.

- Both a list box and a combo box can either take their values from a list you provide or from a table or query, just like a lookup (from Exercise 12).

  ✓ *Make sure you have completed Exercise 12 before working on this exercise, so you will understand the concepts behind lookups.*

- A combo box, by default, appears as a single-line text box with an associated drop-down list. Users can type in the text box normally, or select from the list.

- If there are more entries for a list box than will fit in the allotted space on the form, Access automatically adds a scroll bar to the list box.

A combo box (left) and a list box (right)

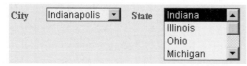

- To create a list box or combo box, click the List Box button 🔳 or Combo Box button 🔳 on the Toolbox and then follow the Wizard's prompts.

- Just like with the Lookup Wizard, you can specify a table or query, or you can type the values you want.

Adding Other Types of Controls

- The Toolbox has other buttons as well, for other kinds of controls you can place on a form.

- To find out what type of control a button inserts, point to it and review the ScreenTip that appears.

- Some of the more common additional controls include Image, Page Break, Tab Control, Line, and Rectangle. These can be used to dress up the form or to organize a complex form into manageable sections.

Procedures

Display the Toolbox

From Form Design view:

- Click on **Toolbox** button 🔧.

OR

1. Click **View** .... Alt + V
2. Click **Toolbox** X

Add a Label

1. Click **Label** button Aa.
2. Drag diagonally on form.
3. Enter text.
4. Resize box as necessary.

Create an Option Group

1. With the Control Wizard on, click **Option Group** button.
2. Click on form.
3. Type **label names**, pressing Tab after each.
4. Click **Next** .... Alt + N
5. Do one of the following:
   a. Click **down arrow** ▾.
   b. Click choice of **default label**.
   OR
   - Click **No, I don't want a default**.

6. Click **Next** .... Alt + N
7. Accept the default values.
   OR
   Enter values to correspond to each label.
8. Click **Next** .... Alt + N
9. Click **down arrow** ▾.
10. Click the **field** to store the value in.
11. Click **Next** .... Alt + N
12. Click the **button type** to use.
13. Click the **button style** to use.
14. Click **Next** .... Alt + N
15. Type a caption.
16. Click **Finish** .... Enter

Create a List Box or Combo Box using Values from a Table or Query

1. Click **List Box** button 🔳.
   OR
   Click **Combo Box** button 🔳.
2. Click and drag to insert.
3. Select how you want to get its values.
4. Click **Next** .... Alt + N

5. Click the table to use.
   OR
   a. Click **Queries** .... Alt + Q
   b. Click the query to use.
6. Click **Next** .... Alt + N
7. Click the field from which to take data.
8. Click **>** >.
   ✓ Usually you will want only one field. However, in some cases you might want two or more, such as First Name and Last Name.
9. Click **Next** .... Alt + N
10. Select a sort order for the list.
11. Click **Next** .... Alt + N
12. Drag edge of sample list to adjust width.
13. Click **Next** .... Alt + N
14. Click **down arrow** ▾.
15. Click field to store value in.
16. Click **Next** .... Alt + N
17. Type a label for the list or combo box.
18. Click **Finish** .... Enter

Create a List Box or Combo Box by Typing Values

1. Click **List Box** button [⊞].

   OR

   Click **Combo Box** button [⊟].
2. Click and drag to insert.
3. Click **I will type in the values that I want** .... [Alt]+[T]
4. Click **Next** .... [Alt]+[N]
5. Type the number of columns you want.

   ✓ *One column is sufficient in most cases.*

6. Press **Tab**. .... [Tab]
7. Type a list entry.
8. Repeat steps 5-6 as needed.
9. Drag edge of list to adjust width.
10. Click **Next** .... [Alt]+[N]
11. Click **down arrow** [▼].
12. Click field to store value in.
13. Click **Next** .... [Alt]+[N]
14. Type a label for the list or combo box.
15. Click **Finish** .... [Enter]

Exercise Directions

1. Start Access, if necessary.
2. Open ⌨**AC15**.
3. Open **frmMembers** in Form Design view.
4. Move the Notes field down, and add a label above it with the following text:

   Enter any information gathered during conversation with member, such as employment, family, or favorite activities.

5. Format the text in the new label as 8-point italic.
6. Switch to Form view to check your work. It should resemble Illustration A. Then switch back to Form Design view.
7. Delete the City field from the form, and create a combo box in its place called **City** that takes its values from the following list:

   Chicago
   Naperville
   Aurora
   Gary
   Arlington Heights

8. Set the combo box to store its value in the City field, and name the combo box **City**.
9. Delete the State field from the form, and create a list box called **State** in its place that takes its values from the **tblStates** table and stores its value in the State field.
10. Use Format Painter to copy the label formatting from existing fields and field labels to the new ones.
11. Resize/reposition fields as needed. You might want to move some fields into the second column or make the form longer (drag the Form Footer bar down) to make room for the new State list box, as in Illustration B.
12. Close the database.

Illustration A

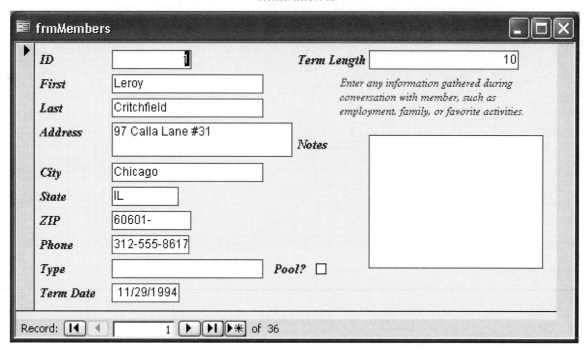

Illustration B

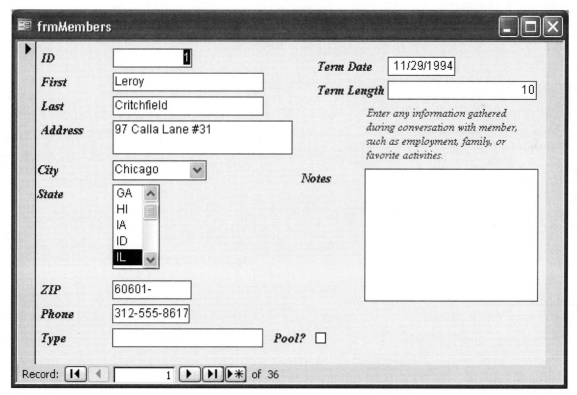

On Your Own

1. Open ⊛ **OAC15**.

2. Display the **Equipment** table in a datasheet. Which fields do you think would benefit from a combo box, list box, or option group?

3. Create a new table based on one of the fields you identified in step 2, and include values in that table for all the current field entries.

   ✓ *For example, if you decided to create a combo box for Item Type, your new table might include* Ball, Bat, Glove, Miscellaneous, *and* Safety.

4. Open the **Equipment** form in Form Design and create a combo box based on the table you just created that replaces the existing field on the form.

5. Create other combo boxes, list boxes, or option groups for any other fields that you identified in step 2.

   ✓ *For example, you might change use a List Box for item condition, and limit the entries to the values* Excellent, Good, Fair, *or* Poor.

   ✓ *Make sure that anything you add gets the same formatting applied to it as the other controls of its same type already on the form.*

6. Close the database and exit Access.

Exercise 16

Skills Covered:

◆ **Work with Headers and Footers** ◆ **Display Header and Footer Areas**
◆ **Add Page Numbers or Date and Time** ◆ **Page Setup**

On the Job

Form headers and footers help users to identify a form's purpose and to give the form a professional, attractive appearance both on-screen and in printouts. If you think you might want to print your records in Form format at some point, the Page Setup features in Access will be helpful in setting margins and page orientation.

You would like to add a title to the form you have been working on, and you think the form header might be a good place to add it. You would also like to print a copy of the membership list using the form and would like to adjust the margins and page layout before you print.

Terms

Page header Same as form header except it applies to individual printed pages instead of to the form as a whole.

Form header An area at the top of the form, above the Detail area, in which you can enter titles, explanatory text, graphics, or anything else that applies to the form as a whole.

Form footer Same as form header, except it appears below the Detail area.

Page footer Same as form footer except it applies to individual printed pages.

Margin The space on all sides of a page where no printing appears.

Orientation The direction the printing appears on the page, either across the width of the page (portrait) or the length of the page (landscape).

Notes

Work with Headers and Footers

- Headers and footers on a form provide a place to enter objects that relate to the entire form or entire page, rather than to an individual record.

- On-screen, headers and footers appear at the top and bottom of a form (or page, on a multipage form), providing information. For example, you might enter a form title in the Form Header area.

- When you print in Form view, the headers and footers appear on the printout.

- There are two kinds of headers: page header and form header.

- Whatever you enter in the **page header** appears in each page of a multipage form or printout. You might place a page numbering code here, for example, to print a page number at the top of each page.

- Whatever you enter on the **form header** appears only once, at the top of the on-screen form or at the beginning of the printout.

- The **form footer** displays in Form view and on the last page of a printout. The form's footer is a good place for controls that you always want to see if the detail section requires scrolling.

- Footers work the same way; you can have a **page footer** and a form footer that appear on the bottom of each page and at the bottom of the last page, respectively.

Display Header and Footer Areas

- By default, only the Detail area appears in Form Design view. To display form headers/footers or page headers/footers, choose them from the View menu.

- You can drag the bars for each section up or down to increase or decrease the section's size.

- Refer to the vertical and horizontal rulers on-screen to help gauge the size of the header or footer when printed. However, the actual size that appears on-screen will depend on the monitor size and resolution.

Form with all headers and footers displayed

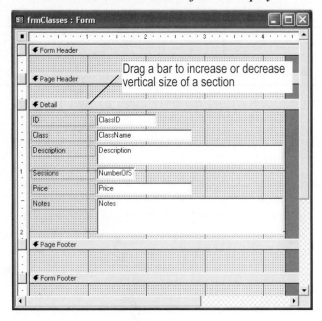

- The page header and footer prints at the top and bottom of the page but does not display in Form view.

- After displaying the header or footer area, use the Toolbox tools to place objects into it, such as text labels.

Add Page Numbers or Date and Time

- You can also add controls that will show page numbers and the date in the header or footer section of a form.

- To do so, click on the section in which you want the item, and then use the Page Numbers or Date and Time command on the Insert menu.

- These commands place codes in text frames on the form.

- Page Numbers codes can be inserted only in a page header or footer and do not display anything on-screen.

- Date and Time codes can be inserted only in a form header or footer and *do* display in the on-screen form.

Page Setup

- Page Setup enables you to change the way your datasheet or form appears on the page. You can set Page Setup settings from either Form Design or Datasheet views.

  ✓ *Page Setup settings are saved with a form, but not with a datasheet. The settings go back to the defaults when you close a table after changing page setup. If you want to save settings with a datasheet, create a datasheet-style form.*

- The Page Setup dialog box contains tabs for Margins and Page for both Datasheet and Form view, and an additional tab, Columns, in Form view.

- To open the Page Setup dialog box, choose File, Page Setup.

Margins Tab

- Use the **Margins** tab of the Page Setup dialog box to change the margins.

  ✓ *Before you print, use File, Print Preview to check what the page settings will look like.*

- The Print Data Only option specifies that the field names not be printed, only the data within the fields will be printed.

Set print margins

Page Tab

■ Use the Page tab of the Page Setup dialog box to change the print **orientation** to landscape or portrait.

Set page orientation and size

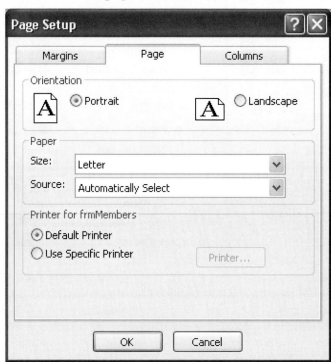

■ You can also specify a paper size and source, and choose to use a specific printer for the print job. This can be useful if you have multiple printers with different capabilities.

Columns Tab

■ Here you can set the spacing between rows and the number and width of columns in which to print.

Set number and width of columns

✓ *The width of the detail section plus the left and right margins must be equal to or less than the width of the page for the form to print correctly. If you get two pages for each form when you expect one, try reducing the margins or decreasing the form width in Form Design view.*

Procedures

Display or Hide Headers or Footers

From Form Design view:

1. Click **View**.................... Alt + V
2. Click desired option to select or delete:
   - **Page Header/Footer**...... A
   - **Form Header/Footer** ..... H

Insert Page Numbering

From Form Design view:

1. Click **Insert**................. Alt + I
2. Click **Page Numbers** .... U
3. Select page number format:
   - **Page N** .... N
   - **Page N of M** .... M
4. Select location:
   - **Top of Page**................. T
   - **Bottom of Page**........... B

5. Select **Alignment**:
   - **Left**
   - **Center**
   - **Right**
   - **Inside**
   - **Outside**
6. Click **OK**.......................... Enter

   ✓ *Control is inserted on document.*

7. If desired, drag control to different location.

Insert Date and Time

From Form Design view:

1. Click **Insert** .... `Alt`+`I`
2. Click **Date and Time**.......... `T`
3. Select options.
4. Click **OK**........................ `Enter`
5. If desired, drag control to different location.

Page Setup

Change page orientation:

1. Click **File**.................... `Alt`+`F`
2. Click **Page Setup**.............. `U`
3. On **Page** tab, select orientation:
   - **Portrait**.................. `Alt`+`R`
   - **Landscape**............ `Alt`+`L`
4. Click **OK**........................ `Enter`

Change margins:

1. Click **File**.................... `Alt`+`F`
2. Click **Page Setup** .... `U`
3. On **Margins** tab, enter margins:
   - **Top**........................ `Alt`+`T`
   - **Bottom**.................. `Alt`+`B`
   - **Left**...................... `Alt`+`F`
   - **Right**.................... `Alt`+`G`
4. Type margin in inches.
5. Click **OK** .... `Enter`

Change columns settings:

1. Click **File** .... `Alt`+`F`
2. Click **Page Setup**.............. `U`
3. On **Columns** tab, enter settings for:
   Grid Settings:
   - **Number of Columns**.............. `Alt`+`C`
   - **Row Spacing**........ `Alt`+`W`
   Column Size:
   - **Width** .... `Alt`+`I`
   - **Height**................. `Alt`+`E`
   Column Layout:
   - **Down, then Across** .... `Alt`+`O`
   - **Across, then Down**............ `Alt`+`N`
4. Click **OK** .... `Enter`

Exercise Directions

1. Start Access, if necessary.
2. Open ⊚ **AC16**.
3. Open **frmMembers** in Design view.
4. Enlarge the Form Header area to about 3/4" in height.
5. Change the form header's background color to match that of the Detail area.
   - ✓ *Tip: Display the Properties box for the Detail area and copy the number representing the background color; paste it into the corresponding field in the Properties box for the Form Header.*
6. Create a **Members** label in the center of the form header area (using the Label tool in the Toolbox), and format it as Arial 28-point bold. See Illustration A.
7. Display the page header/footer, and place a page number code in the footer. Make the page number right-aligned.
8. Save your work.

9. Use Print Preview to see how the printout will look; then return to Form Design view for the form.
   - ✓ *Click the Print Preview button on the toolbar. When you are finished, click the Design View button to return.*
10. Insert a date code only (no time) in day, date, year format in the form header.
11. Move the date code to the form footer.
    - ✓ *By default the form footer has no area; drag the Form Footer bar downward to create some space for it.*
12. Change the form footer's background color to match that of the Detail area.
13. Change the page margins to .5" on all sides.
14. Change the page layout to Landscape.
15. Change the number of columns to 2.
16. Preview your printout in Print Preview.
    - ✓ *Access reports a problem. Why?*
17. Change the paper size to Legal.
18. Preview the printout again.
19. Close the database, saving all changes.

Illustration A

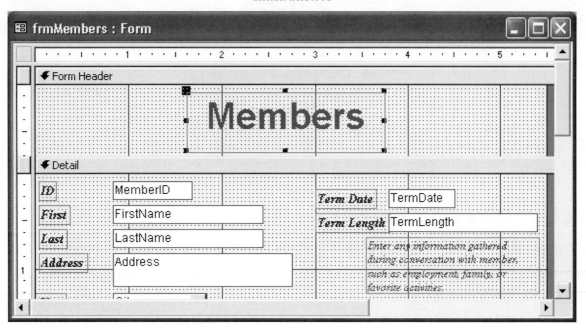

On Your Own

1. Open ☉ **OAC16**.

2. Add a title to the **Equipment** form in the Form Header area. Use any font, size, and color you like.

3. Place page numbering in the page footer area. Then turn off the page footer with the View menu. What happens?

4. Delete the Owner field from the form, and in its place create a list box that selects the owner from the **Roster** table. Sort the list by last name. Format the new field's label to match the others.

5. Experiment with various settings to find settings that allow you to at least five full records on a single page. Use Print Preview to check your work.

   ✓ *Use different sizes of paper, different orientations, and different numbers of columns. You can adjust the form size too if that will help.*

6. When you find the right combination of settings, print your work.

7. Close the database and exit Access.

Exercise 17

◆ Critical Thinking

As you learn more about Access, you have new ideas for improving the database for the HelpNow MedCenter that you worked on in Exercise 11. Now that you know about lookups and forms, you would like to use some of those elements to enhance the database.

Exercise Directions

1. Open ⊘**AC17**.
2. Create a new form using AutoForm:Columnar based on the **tblTimeCards** table.
3. Save the form as **frmTimeCards** and close it.
4. Create a new form using the Form Wizard based on the **tblEmployees** table.
   - Use all the fields.
   - Use a columnar layout.
   - Choose the Expedition style.
   - Name the new form **frmEmployees**.
5. In Form Design view, add the title **Employees** to the form header area. Center the label and format it as 18-point.
6. Switch to Form view to review the changes. Use Window, Size to Fit Form if necessary to view the entire form.
7. Close the form, saving your changes.
8. Create a new table called **tblPositions** with a single field called **Positions**. Make that field the primary key.
9. In Datasheet view, create these entries in the new table:
   - **Physician**
   - **Registered Nurse**
   - **Licensed Practical Nurse**
   - **Medical Records Assistant**
   - **Controller**
   - **Director**
   - **President and CEO**
   - **Vice President of Business Development**

10. Close the table.
11. Use the newly created table as a lookup for the Position field in the **tblEmployees** table (in Table Design view). Then close **tblEmployees**, saving changes.
12. Open **frmEmployees** in Design view, and delete the Position field.
13. Add it back to the form from the Field List, so that the new lookup takes effect there.
14. Change the label for the BasePayHourly field to **Base Pay.**
15. Resize the text box for the BasePayHourly field so it is the same length on the form as the other fields in its same column.
16. Edit the labels for the FirstName and LastName fields so that there are spaces between the words.
17. Format and reposition any other fields as needed on the form to make them consistent and readable.
18. Save and close the **frmEmployees** form, and open the **frmTimeCards** form in Form Design view.
19. Apply the Expedition AutoFormat to the form.
20. Add the title **Time Cards** to the form header and format it attractively.
21. Add a page number code to the page footer.
22. Replace the Employee field with a list box that takes its values from the FirstName and LastName fields from the **tblEmployees** table.

23. Rearrange the other fields on the form, and make the form larger overall, if necessary, to accommodate the larger size of the new list box. Illustration A shows an example, previewed in Form view.

24. Switch to Form view to inspect your work; then save the form and close it.

25. Save your work and exit Access.

Illustration A

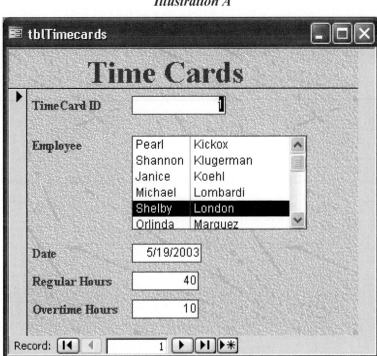

Exercise 18

Skills Covered:

◆ **Find and Replace Data** ◆ **Find Data**
◆ **Replace Data** ◆ **Search Using Wildcards**

On the Job

One of the primary purposes of a database is to store data so you can look it up later. You use the Find procedures to locate data and Find and Replace to locate data and change it to something else. You can search on an exact match or use wildcards that help you find information if you don't know the exact spelling.

You have received some updated information for some of your customers of the Michigan Avenue Athletic Club and need to enter the changes into your tblMembers table. Since you find it easier to work with a form than with raw data in a datasheet, you will make these changes to tblMembers from the frmMembers form.

Terms

Find To locate text within a record that matches characters you type.

Replace To substitute new text after finding a string of text.

Wildcard A character (? or *) that signifies one or more unspecified characters when finding text.

Notes

Find and Replace Data

■ You can **find** and **replace** data in Datasheet view and in Form view.

■ Move to the field where you want to search for data (unless you want to search all fields). Then open the Find and Replace dialog box to begin your search.

Find Data

■ The Find and Replace dialog box contains options for how you want to search for data. The options include:

- *Find What*
  Type the word or phrase you want to look for. You can include **wildcards**. You can also pick from your last six searches.

- *Look In*
  This defaults to the current field. You can choose this field for the entire table or form from the drop-down list.

Find and Replace dialog box, Find tab

- *Match*
  Using the text in the Find What text box, find an exact match using the entire field, any part of the field, or the start of the field.

- *Search*
  You can choose to search the entire list or in a particular direction through the records.

- *Match Case*
  Check this box if you want the capitalization of the Find What entry to match the case of the value in the field exactly. For example, "Broadway" will not match with "broadway."

- *Search Fields As Formatted*
  Find exact matches for date and number formats. When checked, 2/21/99 will not match February 21, 1999. When unchecked, these two dates will match.

■ Click Find Next to find the next record that matches (in the direction indicated by the Search box).

Replace Data

■ When you have some text that needs to be replaced with other text, use the Replace tab of the Find and Replace dialog box. For example, if area code 303 changes to 720, you can replace each occurrence of 303 with 720.

Find and Replace dialog box, Replace tab

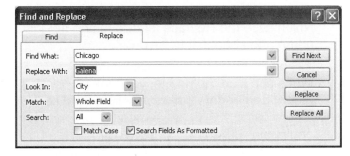

■ In the Replace With text box, you type the text that will replace Find What text.

■ Click the Find Next button to find a match.

■ If the text is found, choose Replace to replace the text in the current record or Replace All to replace all occurrences in all records.

■ Notice in the figure that Start of Field is chosen for the Match setting. This is appropriate since we are looking for area code changes only, not changing the phone numbers that happen to have "303" in the rest of the number.

■ Unless you are sure you won't create errors in your database, you should choose Replace rather than Replace All. You can undo only the last replace.

Search Using Wildcards

■ You can use wildcards in the Find What text box if you don't know the exact spelling, but do know some of the characters.

■ The most common wildcard is the asterisk (*). The asterisk can replace any number of characters. For example, Sm*th will find Smyth, Smith, and Smooth.

■ You can use more than one asterisk. Sm*th* will find Smith, Smooth, Smothers, and Smythe.

■ To speed up filling in the Find or Replace dialog boxes, you don't need to change the Match choice from the default Whole Field option. Type *Broadway* to find a record when Broadway is anywhere within the field.

■ The question mark (?) wildcard is a substitute for an unknown single character. ?oss will find Boss and Hoss, but not Floss.

Procedures

Find and Replace Data

Find data:

1. Click field to match, in Form or Datasheet view.
   OR
   In Datasheet view, click field selector or any field in column.

2. Press **Ctrl + F** .... Ctrl + F
   OR
   Click the **Find** button 🔍.
   OR

a. Click **Edit** .... Alt + E
b. Click **Find** .... F

3. Type data to find in **Find What** text box.

4. Click **Look In** list box to select current field, form, or table.

5. Click **Match** list box to select desired option:
   - **Any Part of Field**
   - **Whole Field**
   - **Start of Field**

6. Click **Match Case** .... Alt + C
   to restrict search to the case that you typed in Find What box.

7. Click **Search Fields As Formatted** .... Alt + O
   to match dates and numbers as they are displayed in the field.

8. Click **Search** list box to select desired option:
   - **Up**
   - **Down**
   - **All**

9. Click **Find Next**...........![Alt]+![F]

10. Click **Close** button ![X] when finished.

Replace data:

1. Click field to match.

   OR

   In Datasheet view, click field selector or any field in column.

2. Press **Ctrl+H**...............![Ctrl]+![H]

   OR

   a. Click the **Find** button ![binoculars].

   b. Click the **Replace** tab.

   OR

   a. Click **Edit** ....![Alt]+![E]

   b. Click **Replace** ....![E]

3. Type data to replace in **Find What** text box.

4. Type replacement data in **Replace With** text box.

5. Click **Look In** list box to select current field, form, or table.

6. Click **Match** list box to select desired option:
   - **Any Part of Field**
   - **Whole Field**
   - **Start of Field**

7. Click **Match Case**.........![Alt]+![C] to restrict search.

8. Click **Search Fields As Formatted**...................![Alt]+![O] to match dates and numbers as they are displayed in the field.

9. Click **Search** list box to select desired option:
   - **Up**
   - **Down**
   - **All**

10. To replace text in current field:
    - Click **Replace** ....![Alt]+![R]

11. To replace text in all matching fields at once:
    - Click **Replace All**...![Alt]+![A]

12. To view next matching field:
    - Click **Find Next**......![Alt]+![F]

13. Click **Close** button ![X] when finished.

Search Using Wildcards

In **Find What** text box on Find or Replace tab:
- Type text and * to replace multiple characters.
- Type text and ? to replace one character.

Exercise Directions

1. Start Access, if necessary.

2. Open 💿 **AC18**.

3. Open **frmMembers** in Form view.

4. Chris Duvall, Allan Barnett, and Todd Greenburg have all recently signed up for swimming pool privileges. Locate their records with the Find command, and place a checkmark in the Pool checkbox for each record.

5. Jacob Hill has just become a lifetime member. Find his record with the Find command, and change his Term Length to 0. Then type **Lifetime** in the Notes field.

6. Molly Crowley sent you an announcement that she is married and changed her last name to Nixon. Use the Replace feature to find her last name and change it to Nixon.

7. Allison Kline (or Klein?) calls for information. While she's on the phone, you look up her record and update her information. Find her record using a wildcard search for last names beginning with **Kl**.

   ✓ Use Kl* to find her record, since you are not sure about the spelling of the name.

8. Close the database.

On Your Own

1. Open 💿 **OAC18** and open the **Roster** form in Form view. Perform all of the following steps from the form or datasheet.

   ✓ Try each step first from the form, and if it can't be done there, accomplish it with the datasheet.

2. Find Melissa Louks' entry and change her phone number to **555-7899**.

3. Use wildcards to look up the street address of the person whose house number is 1911.

4. Use Replace All to find and replace the word "Macn" with "Macon" in the City field.

5. Close the database and exit Access.

Exercise 19

On the Job

When you have unorganized lists, the data is sometimes difficult to digest or use. If you sort records by the field(s) such as last name, you can look up the information quickly. If you are interested in the most or least active customers or largest orders you can quickly view this information through sorting. You learned about basic sorts back in Exercise 1; in this exercise you will learn about more complex sorting options.

Not everyone at the Michigan Avenue Athletic Club has a computer at his or her desk. However, it is very important for employees to be able to look up information quickly about a member, so you will print the tblMembers table for employees to refer to. Some employees need a printout sorted by Last Name and First Name; while others need one sorted by Term Date.

Terms

Multiple sort To use more than one field to sort. If there are duplicates for the first field, the second field is used to organize the records for each set of duplicated values in the first field.

Sort To arrange records alphabetically or numerically according to a specific field.

Ascending From A to Z or 1 to 9.

Descending From Z to A or 9 to 1.

Notes

Multiple Sorts

- With a **multiple sort** you can **sort** by more than one column. For example, you could sort by State and then by City. All the records containing CA as the State, for example, would be grouped together, and then all the records with San Diego as the City would be grouped within the CA grouping.

- You can sort on multiple columns through Datasheet view but not Form view.

- You can sort fields with Text, Number, Currency, Date/Time, and Yes/No data types.

- You cannot sort fields that have Memo, Hyperlink, or OLE Object data types.

- You can sort in **ascending** order (A to Z or 1 to 9) or **descending** order (Z to A or 9 to 1).

  ✓ *You can also use filters and queries to sort records (see later exercises in this lesson).*

Change Column Order

- When you sort by multiple columns, columns are sorted from left to right. You cannot specify a different sort priority.

- However, you can temporarily rearrange the columns before you sort so that the column by which you want to sort first appears to the left of the other columns that should be subordinate in the sort.

- If the fields you want to use for the sort are not adjacent, you can rearrange them before sorting, just as you did in Exercise 7.

- If you do not want the rearrangement to be permanent, do not save your changes when you close the datasheet.

413

Remove a Sort

- If you save a table or form after sorting, the sort order becomes a property of the table or form. You can change this property by sorting on a different field.

- To undo any sort, choose Records, Remove Filter/Sort.

- If there is no primary key, records within a table (and its corresponding forms) are placed in input order when you remove the sort.

- If there is a primary key, records are ordered by the primary key when you remove the sort.

Procedures

Change Column Order

1. Click on column header.
2. Drag column to desired position in table.

Multiple Column Sort

1. Drag across field names to select columns.
2. Click **Sort Ascending** button ![A Z↓] or **Sort Descending** button ![Z A↓].

   OR

   a. Click **Records** .... ![Alt]+![R]
   b. Click **Sort** .... ![S]
   c. Select **Sort Ascending** or **Sort Descending** .. ![A] or ![D]

Remove Sort

1. Click **Records** .... ![Alt]+![R]
2. Click **Remove Filter/Sort** ... ![R]

Exercise Directions

1. Start Access, if necessary.

2. Open 💿 **AC19**.

3. Open **tblMembers** in Datasheet view.

4. Hide the following columns: ID, Membership Type, Pool, Term Length, and Notes.

   ✓ *You learned to hide columns in Exercise 9. Select the column and then choose Format, Hide Columns.*

5. Autosize the widths of each column so that their contents exactly fits.

   ✓ *You learned to resize columns in Exercise 9. Double-click between column headers to autosize them.*

6. Change the column label for the TermDate column so that there is a space between the words.

   ✓ *You learned this in Exercise 3. Right-click it and choose Rename Column.*

7. Sort the list by Last Name, then First Name. To do this:

   • Move the Last Name column to the left of the First Name column.

   • Select the Last Name and First Name columns.

   • Click the Sort Ascending button.

   ✓ *In this data, there aren't any people with the same last name as another, so sorting only by last name would have given the same effect. However, as your database grows, you will probably have duplicate last names and need this multi-field sort capability.*

8. Print the datasheet.

9. Close the datasheet, saving your changes to it; then reopen it. Notice that your sort, field arrangements, and hidden fields are all just as you left them.

10. Remove the sort, and move the Last Name column back to its previous position.

11. Sort the list by Term Date and then by Last Name.

12. Without undoing the sort, put the fields back in the original left-to-right order (First, Last, Address, City, State, ZIP, Phone, Term Date).

13. Print the datasheet.

14. Remove the sort.

15. Unhide all the hidden columns.

16. Close the datasheet, saving your changes.

17. Close the database.

On Your Own

1. Open 💿 **OAC19**.

2. Open the **Roster** table in Datasheet view.

3. Create a printout of the roster sorted by ZIP code and then by last name. The printout must contain at least the names, addresses, phone numbers, and positions, and must fit on a single sheet of paper.

   ✓ *Need some help? Here's how to do it:*

   • Hide all the fields except those containing names, addresses (including city, state, and ZIP), phone numbers, and positions.

   • Sort the list in Ascending order by ZIP code and then by Last Name. (You'll need to move the ZIP column.)

   • After sorting, move the ZIP column back to its normal position.

   • Preview the printout, and then close Print Preview.

   • Return to the datasheet and make any adjustments needed for a better printout. You might change the page layout to Landscape, for example, and/or adjust column widths.

   • Print the datasheet.

4. Close the datasheet, saving your changes to it.

5. Reopen the datasheet and remove the sort.

6. Unhide all the hidden columns.

7. Close the database, saving changes, and exit Access.

Exercise 20

◆ **Filter a Record Subset** ◆ **Filter By Selection**
◆ **Filter Excluding Selection** ◆ **Filter For Entry** ◆ **Filter By Form**

On the Job

Sometimes you will want to look at all records that match certain criteria. Although you could sort a list, it may be easier to isolate (filter) only the records you want to see. Then when you use the navigation buttons or keys to move through records, you see only relevant records.

There is a new promotion going on at the Michigan Avenue Athletic Club. Members who have not yet signed up for swimming pool privileges are being given the opportunity to do so at a 50% discount for the first year. Your boss would like you to print a list of people who do not yet have pool privileges and their phone numbers. In addition, you want to generate another list for a special mailing to people who are either Lifetime members or who have been members since 1997 or before.

Terms

Filter To display only certain records.

Filter By Selection To filter based on the data in current field.

Filter By Form To show a form that allows you to enter criteria for the filter.

Notes

Table Datasheet toolbar

Filter By Selection

Apply (or Remove) Filter/Sort

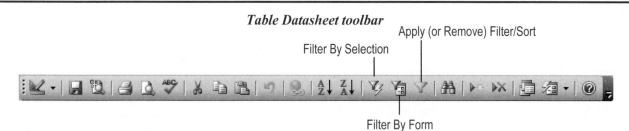

Filter By Form

Filter a Record Subset

- When you **filter** records, you see a subset of the records in the datasheet or form.

- The number of records that match the filter displays to the right of the navigation buttons at the bottom of the datasheet or form.

- You can filter using toolbar buttons (see above), by right-clicking a field and choosing a filter from the shortcut menu that appears, or by choosing a filter from Records, Filter. Not all filter types are available using all filtering methods.

- Here are types of filters available:
  - **Filter By Selection**: choose only records that match the current field. Available from the toolbar, shortcut menu, and Records menu.

- Filter Excluding Selection: choose all records that don't match the current field. Available only from the shortcut menu and the Records menu.

- Filter For: choose records containing a field that matches what you type. Available only from the shortcut menu. This is a short version of Filter By Form that works with only a single field at a time.

- **Filter By Form:** choose records where one or more field entries match what you type. Available only from the toolbar and Records menu.

- Advanced Filter/Sort: create more complicated filters in conjunction with sorting. Available only from the Records menu and not covered in this book.

  ✓ *If you are interested in learning about Advanced Filter/Sort, see the book* Learning Microsoft Access 2003.

Filter By Selection

- The Filter By Selection option is the easiest way to filter your records.

- When you click in a field and then choose Filter By Selection, Access shows all records that match the value that is in the field.

- You can also select a portion of a field and then choose Filter By Selection. If the selection is at the beginning (or end) of the field, Access will show all records that have the same text at the beginning (or end) of the field.

- If you select text in the middle of the selection before Filter By Selection, Access shows all records that have the selected text anywhere in the field.

- You can do Filter By Selection more than once to limit your records further. Such a multilevel filter might be more easily accomplished with Filter By Form, however.

Filter Excluding Selection

- When you want to find all records that do not match the current field, choose Filter Excluding Selection.

Filter For Entry

- If you want to type in the text that will become the filter, choose Filter For, then enter the text. You can use wildcards in specifying the criteria. (See Exercise 18 for information on using wildcards.)

Filter By Form

- Filter By Form gives you options to filter on multiple fields and to use wildcards in the filter criteria.

Filter by Form

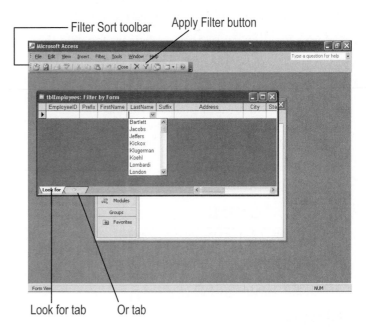

- The Filter By Form opens a form that allows you to do the following in each field in either Datasheet or Form view:

  - Click the drop-down arrow to the right of the field and choose from the entries in the field.

  - Type the value you want.

  - Type the value with a wildcard asterisk (*) for any number of characters or question mark (?) for one character.

  - Type > (greater than), < (less than), >= (greater than or equal to), or <= (less than or equal to) and then a number.

    ✓ *When using greater than or less than, put quotation marks around criteria that should be interpreted alphabetically (such as A being before B in the alphabet), or hash marks (#) around criteria that should be interpreted numerically.*

- Type **Between firstvalue and secondvalue**. For example, Between 1/1/99 and 3/31/99.
  - Type **IS NULL** to find empty fields, or **IS NOT NULL** to find non-empty ones.

- If you have entries in multiple fields on the Look for tab, Access finds all records that match for all entries. For example, if Smith is in Last Name and Denver is in City, records that have both Smith and Denver show.
  - ✓ *When you use Filter By Form on a Memo type field, the only choices are Null or Not Null. If you want to filter by form on such a field more precisely you just change its field type to Text.*

- If you have an entry on the Look for tab and then an entry on the Or tab(s), Access finds all records that match any of the entries. For example, if Smith is on the Look for tab and Denver is the Or tab, Access will find all the Smiths whether or not they live in Denver and all people who live in Denver whether or not their name is Smith.

- After you enter in your criteria in the Filter By Form window, you can:
  - Choose the Save to Query button 💾 to create a query from these criteria. The Load from Query button 🗁 brings in criteria from a query. (Queries are covered in later exercises.)
    - ✓ *Filters are saved automatically with the table or form if you close the object with the filter applied; the Save to Query feature merely saves them as separate entities. To get rid of a filter so that it is not saved with the table or form, clear the filter grid and then choose Apply Filter.*
  - Click Close [Close] to return to the form or datasheet without filtering data.
  - Click Clear Grid [X] to remove all entries and start over.
  - Click Apply Filter [▽] to filter the data. When data is currently being filtered, this becomes the Remove Filter button; click it again to remove the filter.

Procedures

Apply or Remove a Filter

Apply filter:

1. Create a filter (see following procedures).
2. Click **Apply Filter** button [▽].
   OR
   a. Click **R**ecords........ [Alt]+[R]
   b. Click **Apply Filter/Sort** .. [Y]

Remove filter:

- Click **Remove Filter** button [▽].
OR
1. Click **R**ecords............. [Alt]+[R]
2. Click **R**emove Filter/Sort ... [R]

Filter By Selection

✓ *Filters and displays records that match selected item.*

1. View desired form or datasheet.
2. Select desired item in field location.
3. Click **Filter By Selection** button .
   OR
   a. Click **R**ecords .... [Alt]+[R]
   b. Click **F**ilter..................... [F]
   c. Click **Filter By Selection**.................. [S]
   OR
   a. Right-click field.
   b. Click **Filter By Selection**.................. [S]

✓ *Records that match selected item will appear.*

Filter Excluding Selection

1. Select field data you want to exclude.
2. Right-click field.
   OR
   Click **R**ecords............. [Alt]+[R]
3. Select **Filter Excluding Selection** .... [X]

✓ *Records that do not contain selected data will appear.*

Filter For Entry

1. Right-click field in datasheet or form.
2. Select **Filter For:** .... [F]
3. Type filter value, using wildcards if desired.
4. Press **Enter** .... [Enter]

✓ *Records that match will appear.*

Filter By Form

✓ *Filters and displays records that meet specified criteria.*

1. View desired form or datasheet.
2. Click **Filter By Form** button [🔽].
   OR
   a. Click **Records** .... Alt+R

b. Click **Filter**..................... F
c. Click **Filter By Form** ...... F

3. Type entries in the appropriate fields, using wildcards if desired.
   OR
   a. Click on desired field list box arrow.
   b. Select desired entry.

4. Click **Apply Filter** button [▽].
   OR
   a. Click **Records** .... Alt+R
   b. Click **Apply Filter/Sort** .. Y
      ✓ *Result of filter will appear.*

Exercise Directions

1. Start Access, if necessary.
2. Open ✪ **AC20**.
3. Open **tblMembers**.
4. Use Filter By Selection to display only the customers who do not have the Pool? check box marked.
   ✓ *When you click the check box to select a field, be careful you do not change the check box state for that record. You might need to click it a second time to restore its original state.*
5. Without removing the first filter, use Filter By Form to further filter the list to show only customers who don't have the Pool check box marked *and* for whom you have a phone number.
   ✓ *Type IS NOT NULL in the Phone field in the filter form.*

6. Hide all fields except First Name, Last Name, and Phone.
7. Print the datasheet.
8. Remove the filter to show all clients.
9. Hide the Phone field, and unhide the Address, City, State, and ZIP fields.
10. Using Filter By Form, display only records where the Term Date is before (less than) 01/01/97.
    ✓ *Use <01/01/97. If Access puts quotation marks around the date, replace them with hash signs #, like this: <#01/01/97#.*
11. Print the datasheet.
12. Save this filter as a query named **qryPre1997**.
13. Unhide all fields and remove all filters.
14. Close the database.

On Your Own

1. Open ✪ **OAC20**.
2. Open the **Roster** table in Datasheet view.
3. Use any filtering method to create separate roster datasheet printouts for players living in each town.
4. Remove all filters.
5. Display the **Roster** form, and filter to *exclude* players from Macon.

6. Without removing the existing filter, add another criterion: show only players with Active in the Category field.
7. Print the filtered roster from form view.
8. Remove all filters.
9. Close the database, saving all changes, and exit Access.

Exercise 21

Skills Covered:

◆ **Compare Queries to Sorts/Filters** ◆ **Ways to Start a New Query**
◆ **Create a Query with a Wizard** ◆ **Create a Query in Query Design
View** ◆ **Choose Fields for a Query** ◆ **Sort Records in a Query**
◆ **Criteria in Query** ◆ **Display the Query Datasheet** ◆ **Save a Query**

On the Job

When sorting and filtering isn't enough, you're ready to move up to queries. With a query, you can create a very powerful sort/filter specification and save it to be reused over and over again.

You need to create some permanent lists for mailings to members of the Michigan Avenue Athletic Club and for providing reports to the Club owners on a regular basis. You will create queries that satisfy these needs.

Terms

Query A defined set of operations to be performed on a table (or on the results from another query).

Select query A query that sorts and filters a table or other query to extract certain fields and records based on criteria you specify. This is by far the most common type of query.

Query Design view A window that allows you to choose the fields in a query, to sort, and to set criteria.

Query design grid The lower half of the Query Design view that shows the field name, table name, sort order, show box, and criteria rows for selecting records. In earlier versions of Access, this was called the QBE grid.

Show box The check box on the query design grid that allows you to display or hide a column that may be used in criteria or sorting.

Notes

Compare Queries to Sorts/Filters

- **Queries** are like advanced sort/filters except you can save a query and store it in the database window.

- Queries also make possible some specialized operations like performing calculations on field values and placing the result in a new column in a datasheet.

- Like sorting/filtering, queries let you sort and define criteria to select the records you want to see.

- Unlike sorting/filtering, a query enables you to choose a subset of fields to display. You need not hide the columns you don't want; they simply don't appear in the query results.

- You can also use certain fields in the query as filters without including those fields in the query output.

- Queries, like tables, can be used as a starting point for reports or forms.

420

■ There are several kinds of queries, but the most common type is a **select query**. The main purpose of a select query is to extract fields and records from a larger table and present the results in a specific sort order.

Ways to Start a New Query

■ As with most other database objects in Access, you can start a new query using a wizard or using **Query Design view**.

■ To create a new query in Query Design view, the fastest method is to double-click *Create query in Design view* from the Database window.

■ If you want to create a new select query using a wizard, the fastest way is to double-click *Create query by using wizard* from the Database window.

■ If you want some other type of specialized query, you must use the New button in the database window (with Queries selected at the left). This displays the full list of the various query wizards.

New Query dialog box

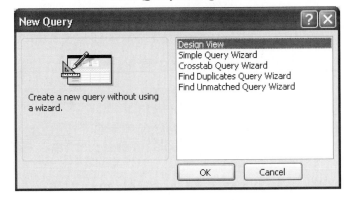

■ Choosing the Simple Query Wizard from the New Query dialog box is the same as double-clicking the *Create query using wizard* shortcut in the Database window.

■ Another way to open the New Query dialog box is to display the table on which you want to base the query and then open the drop-down list for the New Object button and choose Query.

Select Query from the New Object button

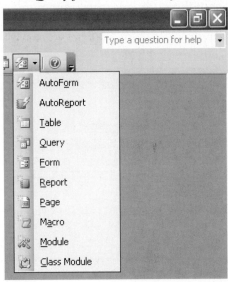

Create a Query with a Wizard

■ The Simple Query Wizard walks you step-by-step through the process of selecting fields to include in a query. It lets you create a version of a table (or other query) that contains a subset of fields.

■ For example, you might want to see only the name and address fields for a contact list rather than all data about each person.

Simple Query Wizard

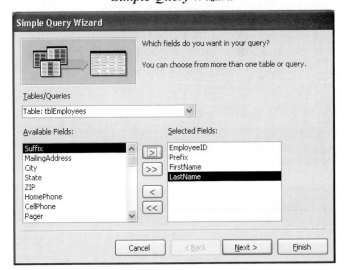

■ If your selections include numeric fields, the Simple Query Wizard also allows you to specify whether you want a summary or detail query. A detail query displays all records individually; a summary query summarizes based on a particular field value.

- If you choose a summary query, you can choose to present the sum, average, minimum value, or maximum value of any numeric fields.

Set summary options for a summary query

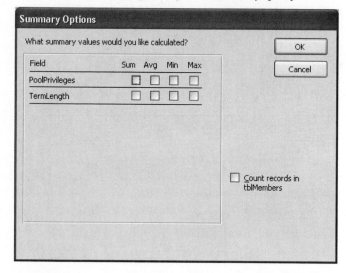

- Query results appear in a Datasheet view, similar to a table.

  ✓ *The Simple Query Wizard cannot filter records and cannot sort them in a particular order, so you will probably need to use Query Design view to get the exact query results you need.*

Create a Query in Query Design View

- You can start a new query from Query Design view, or you can modify any existing query there.
- When you start a new query in Query Design view, the Show Table dialog box automatically appears. Choose the tables you want for the query.

Choose the tables/queries

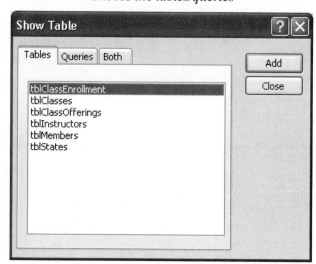

- If you choose more than one table, the tables must have a relationship between them.

  ✓ *A query is a great way to create a single object containing fields from multiple related tables. For example, suppose you want to create a form that includes fields from both a Customers and an Orders table. You could create a relationship between the tables, then create a query that includes the fields from both, and then create a form based on that query (see Exercise 10).*

- Query Design view consists of two sections. At the top are field lists for the tables/queries to work with. At the bottom is the **query design grid**, where you place the individual fields (one per column) and define how they should be acted upon.

Query Design view

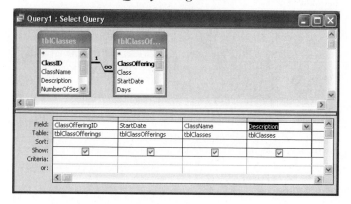

Choose Fields for a Query

- The order you choose fields in the Query design determines the column order for the resulting datasheet.
- You can choose a field in any of the following ways:
  - Double-click on the field in the Field List to place the field to the right of the previous field.
  - Drag the field from the Field List to a field in the query design grid to insert this field where you want it in the grid.
  - Click on the drop-down arrow or type in the Field cell to choose a field from the list of fields.
- You may need to use fields for sorting or criteria but not want to see the fields in Datasheet view. If you don't want to see the fields in Datasheet view, uncheck the **show box**.

Sort Records in a Query

- Underneath the fields you want to sort, do one of the following in the Sort box to choose a sort order:
  - Double-click in the Sort box to cycle through Ascending, Descending, or no sort (blank).
  - Click on the drop-down arrow and choose Ascending or Descending.
  - Type **a** for Ascending or **d** for Descending.

- The position of the sort fields from left to right determines the sort order. The left-most field with a sort specified is the primary sort; the remaining fields with sorts specified are subsorts and are sorted in order from left to right.

Criteria in a Query

- The same rules for filters apply to queries for criteria as well as sorting. Here is a review:
  - You can type the complete value in the criteria row or use wildcards. For example, you can type **Denver** or **Den*** to choose Denver.
  - You can also type the following symbols or text in the criteria row:

Use:	For and example:
<	Less than. <30
<=	Less than or equal to. <=#1/1/99#
>	Greater than. >100
>=	Greater than or equal to. >=Date()
<>	Not equal to. <>"Denver"
Like	Match a pattern of characters. Like "Den*"
And	Match 2 or more conditions. >5 And <10
Or	Match any of the conditions. "CO" Or "CA"
Between … And	Match values in a range. Between #1/1/98# and #1/15/98#
In	Select from a list of values. In ("NM","NY","NJ")
Is Null	If there are no values in the field.
Is Not Null	If the field has any values.

- All entries in one criteria row mean that every condition must match to find the record.

- Entries in the Criteria and Or rows mean that a record must match one of the conditions to be included in the result to find a record.

Display the Query Datasheet

- There are two ways to see the results of a query. One is to preview the results in Datasheet view, by switching to Datasheet view. The other is to run the query with the Run button ⚠.

- For a select query, there is no real difference between these two methods. However, when you get into action queries that actually perform operations on the data rather than just displaying it, the difference becomes important.

- Query results appear in Datasheet view and resemble a table.

Save a Query

- When you close a query window, if you have made design changes to it, you are prompted to save your work.

- You can also save a query from Design view before you are ready to close it.

- The first time you save a query, you will be prompted for a name. Although the name can be a maximum of 64 characters including spaces, you should keep the name short and use no spaces.

- Many people use the convention of preceding the query name with *qry* to identify the object type.

Procedures

Start the Simple Query Wizard

From the Database window:
1. Click **Queries**.
2. Double-click **Create query by using wizard**.

From a datasheet:
1. Open table or query that will be the source for new query.
2. Click down arrow on **New Object** button .
   - ✓ *The image on the New Object button changes depending on your last selection.*
3. Click **Query** .... $\boxed{Q}$
4. Click **Simple Query Wizard**.
5. Click **OK** .... $\boxed{Enter}$

Complete the Simple Query Wizard

1. Start the Simple Query Wizard using one of the methods just described.
2. Click **Tables/Queries** down arrow $\boxed{\blacktriangledown}$.
3. Click table or query to use.
4. Click a field to include in the query.
5. Click **Add Field** button $\boxed{>}$.
6. Repeat steps 4–5 to add more fields from same table or query.
7. Return to step 2 to select fields from other tables/queries if desired.
8. Click **Next** .... $\boxed{Alt}+\boxed{N}$
   - ✓ *If you included any Numeric fields, you are prompted to choose between Detail and Summary.*
9. If prompted, do one of the following:
   To create a detail query (i.e. a normal query):
   - Click **Next** .... $\boxed{Alt}+\boxed{N}$
   Or, to create a summary query:
   a. Click **Summary** ...... $\boxed{Alt}+\boxed{S}$
   b. Click **Summary Options** .... $\boxed{Alt}+\boxed{O}$
   c. Click check box(es) for fields to summarize.

d. (Optional) Click **Count records in** *tablename* check box.
e. Click **OK** .... $\boxed{Enter}$
10. Click **Next** .... $\boxed{Alt}+\boxed{N}$
11. Type query name.
12. Click **Finish** .... $\boxed{Alt}+\boxed{F}$

Start a Query in Design View

From the Database window:
1. Click **Queries**.
2. Double-click **Create query in Design view**.

From a datasheet:
1. Open table or query that will be the source for new query.
2. Click down arrow on **New Object** button .
   - ✓ *The image on the New Object button changes depending on your last selection.*
3. Click **Query** .... $\boxed{Q}$
4. Click **Design View**.
5. Click **OK** .... $\boxed{Enter}$

Select Tables/Queries to Use

1. With Select Query Window displayed, click **Show Table** button (if the Show Table dialog box does not automatically appear).
2. Click table to use.
3. Click **Add** .... $\boxed{Alt}+\boxed{A}$
   - ✓ *To select a query instead, click the Queries tab. The Both tab shows both tables and queries at once.*
4. Repeat steps 2–3 to add more tables or queries.
5. Click **Close** .... $\boxed{Alt}+\boxed{C}$

Add Fields to a Query

- Double-click a field in the field list.

OR

- Drag a field into the query design grid.

Sort by a Field

1. Click in the **Sort** row for a field in the query design grid.
2. Click the **down arrow** $\boxed{\blacktriangledown}$.

3. Choose **Ascending** or **Descending**.
   - ✓ *To remove a sort, choose (not sorted).*

Enter Filter Criteria

1. Click in the **Criteria** row for a field in the query design grid.
2. Enter criteria.
3. Repeat steps 1–2 for additional fields.
   - ✓ *To enter either-or criteria, enter each criterion on a separate Or row in the grid.*

Preview Query Results

1. Click **View** .... $\boxed{Alt}+\boxed{V}$
2. Click **Datasheet View** .... $\boxed{S}$
   OR
   Click the **Datasheet View** button .

Return to Query Design View

1. Click **View** .... $\boxed{Alt}+\boxed{V}$
2. Click **Design View** .... $\boxed{D}$
   OR
   Click the **Design View** button .

Save a Query

1. Click **Save** button $\boxed{\blacksquare}$.
   OR
   a. Click **File** .... $\boxed{Alt}+\boxed{F}$
   b. Click **Save** .... $\boxed{S}$
2. Type query name if saving query for first time.
3. Click **OK** .... $\boxed{Enter}$

Save and Close a Query

1. Click **Close** button $\boxed{X}$ on query window.
2. Click **Yes** .... $\boxed{Alt}+\boxed{Y}$ or $\boxed{Enter}$
3. Type query name.
4. Click **OK** .... $\boxed{Enter}$

Run a Query

From Query Design view:
- Click the **Run** button .

From the database window:
1. Click **Queries**.
2. Double-click the query name.

Exercise Directions

1. Start Access, if necessary.

2. Open ⊙ **AC21**, and open **tblMembers**.

3. Using the New Object button, create a new query with the Simple Query Wizard that:

   a. Includes FirstName, LastName, and Phone fields only.

   b. Is named **qryMemberPhoneList**.

4. Close all open datasheets, and open the **qryMemberPhoneList** query in Query Design view.

5. Add a criterion so that only records in which Phone is not empty appear.

6. Set up the query to be sorted alphabetically by last name.

7. Save your work on the query, view it in Datasheet view, and then close it.

8. Start a new query in Query Design view, and add the **tblMembers** table.

9. Add the FirstName and LastName fields to the query design grid, and sort in Ascending order by LastName.

10. Add the **tblClassEnrollment**, **tblClassOfferings**, and **tblClasses** tables to the query.

    ✓ Click the Show Table button to open the Show Table dialog box.

11. Add the following fields to the query design grid:

    a. From **tblClasses**: ClassName

    b. From **tblClassOfferings**: StartDate and StartTime

12. Save the query as **qryMemberClasses** and switch to Datasheet view to check it out; then close it.

    ✓ There will be only one record shown because not much data has been entered yet; this is normal. For most databases it is a good idea not to enter a lot of data until after you get your basic structures set up.

13. Start a new query in Query Design view.

14. Add the **tblMembers** table.

15. Add all fields necessary for mailing (FirstName, LastName, Address, City, State, and ZIP) to the query design grid.

16. Sort in Descending order by ZIP.

17. Use criteria to include only records where the City is Chicago or Aurora.

    ✓ You will need to use the Or line.

18. Add a criterion so that only records in which the PoolPrivileges field is No are included

    ✓ You will need to add the Pool field to the grid, but then you must clear the Show check box for it so that the Pool field does not display in the query results.

19. Preview the query results in datasheet view.

20. Save the query as **qryPoolMailing1** and close it.

21. View **qryPoolMailing1** from the database window.

22. Close the database and exit Access.

On Your Own

1. Open ⊙ **OAC21**.

2. Using the Simple Query Wizard, create a query that would be useful for creating mailing address labels for a team mailing. Include only the fields you need for mailing labels. Name it **Labels**.

3. Edit the query in Design view so that the records are sorted by ZIP Code and so that only Active players are included.

    ✓ One way to do this would be to add the Categories table, add the MembershipCategory field to the query, filter by it containing "Active", and turn off its display in the query results.

4. Save the query and close it.

5. Create a new query that displays the first and last names and the positions of only people who play a "base" position (that is, First Base, Second Base, or Third Base) or who pitch, catch, or play shortstop.

    ✓ One way to do this would be to enter "*base" as the criterion. Then on the Or row, enter "pitcher." On subsequent Or rows, enter "catcher" and "shortstop".

6. Save the new query as **Infielders.**

7. Close the database and exit Access.

Exercise 22

Skills Covered:

◆ **Open a Query for Editing** ◆ **Select a Field** ◆ **Delete a Field**
◆ **Move a Field** ◆ **Use All Fields of a Table for a Query**
◆ **Rename a Query** ◆ **Save a Query with a Different name**

On the Job

After you have built simple queries, you may need to change your initial query design. You can change query design by adding, deleting, or moving fields. You can also quickly add all fields from a table to your query. After changing the design, you may want to rename the query and print a query datasheet.

The staff member for whom you created the qryPoolMailing1 query in Exercise 21 has requested some changes to that query. You will make these changes. You will also create a couple of new queries that show the instructors and what classes they are teaching.

Terms

Field selector The gray bar above a field in the query grid; click it to select that field, in preparation for moving or deleting it.

Property sheet A dialog box that shows properties for all aspects of an object. Each query has a property sheet, as does each individual object (such as a field or label).

Notes

Open a Query for Editing

- If you want to edit a query after you've saved it, choose the query name on the Queries window of the Database window and click the Design button.

- You can add more fields to the query by dragging them into the grid, as you learned in Exercise 21.

Select a Field

- To delete or move a field, you must first select it in the grid.

- To select a field in the grid, click the **field selector**. When the mouse pointer is over the field selector, the pointer appears as a down-pointing black arrow.

Mouse pointer over field selector

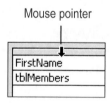

Delete a Field

- To delete a field, select it and press the Delete key.

Move a Field

- To move a field, select it and then point to the field selector. The mouse pointer changes to a white arrow. Drag to the new position. (A vertical line will indicate the new position.)

Field selected and ready to move

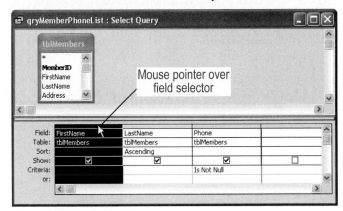

Query with the asterisk dragged into the grid

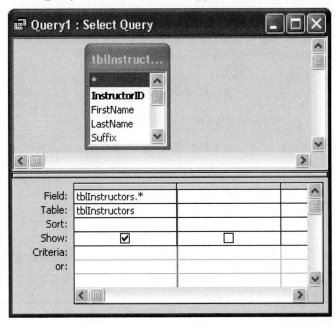

- You can also move a field in the query results datasheet. Then, when you close the datasheet and save your changes, the column order will be saved, too, and will override the order specified in Query Design view.

- Making design changes to a query in Datasheet view is useful when you have added the fields to the query using one of the methods that inserts a single entry that represents all fields (as in the following section).

Use All Fields of a Table for a Query

- You saw in Exercise 21 how to place individual fields in a query. You can include all fields from a particular table by placing each one individually in the query grid.

- There are also three shortcut methods for including all fields in a query.

- One method is to double-click the title bar of the field list, so that all fields are selected, and then drag them as a group to the grid.

- Another method is to select and drag the asterisk from the top of the field list into the grid. It represents all fields as a group.

  ✓ *If you want to sort or enter criteria, you will need individual fields to appear in the grid. If you have included all fields using the asterisk method, add the needed fields to the grid individually, too, and enter your sorting or filtering criteria. Then deselect the show box for the individual field, so it won't appear in the query twice.*

- The third method is to set the query properties to include all fields.

- After you create the query, double-click in the gray area behind Field List. The **property sheet** appears for the query. Change the Output All Fields property to Yes.

Property sheet for the query

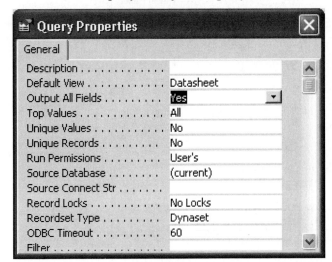

427

Rename a Query

- You may want to change the name of a query because of a typo or you may want to include the *qry* naming convention.

- To rename a query, right-click it in the Database window and choose Rename.

  ✓ *If you change the name of a query, any reports or forms you already created based on this query will not run. To avoid recreating all your forms and reports, you can modify the properties of the existing ones to point to the new query. To do so, display the property sheet for the report or form and change the Record Source property to the new query name.*

Save a Query with a Different Name

- After making changes to a query, you might want to save it with a different name to preserve the original version.

- To do so, with the query displayed in Datasheet or Design view, use the File, Save As command.

Procedures

Open a Query for Editing
From the Database window:
1. Click **Queries**.
2. Click the query.
3. Click **Design** button

    .... Alt + D

Select a Field in the Grid
- Click the field selector.

  ✓ *The entire column is highlighted.*

Delete a Field from the Grid
1. Select the field.
2. Press **Delete** .... Del

Move a Field in the Grid
1. Select the field.
2. Position mouse pointer over field selector.
3. Drag to new location.

Place All Fields in Query Grid
1. Double-click title bar of field list.
2. Drag selection to query grid (lower pane).

Place a Single Field Representing All Fields in Query Grid
- Double-click asterisk at top of table field list.
  OR
- Drag asterisk to query grid.

  ✓ *Any fields that appear individually in the query will now appear twice unless you turn off their Show check boxes.*

Edit Query Properties to Include All Fields
1. Right-click the empty gray area behind field lists or grid.
2. Click **Properties** .... P
3. Click in the **Output All Fields** box.
4. Click **down arrow** .
5. Click **Yes**.
6. Click **Close** button ☒.

   ✓ *Any fields that appear individually in the query will now appear twice unless you turn off their Show check boxes.*

Rename a Query
1. View Database window.
2. Click **Queries** button.
3. Right-click query to rename.
4. Click **Rename** .... M
5. Type new name.
6. Press **Enter** .... Enter

Save a Query with a Different Name
From Query Design view:
1. Click **File** .... Alt + F
2. Click **Save As** .... A
3. Type new name.
4. Click **OK** .... Enter

Exercise Directions

1. Start Access, if necessary.

2. Open 💿 **AC22**.

3. Open **qryPoolMailing1AC22** in Design view.

4. Transpose the order of the FirstName and LastName columns.

5. Sort by LastName in Ascending order.

6. Add the Notes field to the query, to the right of the other fields.

7. Remove the criteria from the City field.

8. Save the query as **qryPoolMailing2AC22** and switch to Datasheet view to see its result. Then close it.

9. Create a new query in Design view that includes all the fields from the **tblInstructorsAC22** table (using the asterisk).

10. Sort the list alphabetically by last name.

   ✓ *To do this, you will need to add the LastName field individually to the query, set up the filter, and deselect the Show check box for the field.*

11. Add the **tblClassOfferingsAC22** and **tblClassesAC22** tables to the query.

12. Add the Description field from the **tblClasses** table to the query grid.

13. Add the StartDate field from the **tblClassOfferings** table to the query grid.

14. Save the query as **qryInstructorTeaching** and view it in Datasheet view.

15. Reopen **qryInstructorTeachingAC22** in Design view, and save it as **qryInstructorTeachingShortAC22**.

16. Remove the entry representing all fields from the query grid (the one with the asterisk).

17. Add FirstName and LastName from the **tblInstructorsAC22** table to the beginning (left end) of the query grid.

18. Save the query and display it in Datasheet view.

19. Close the datasheet, saving your changes.

20. Exit the database.

On Your Own

1. Open 💿 **OAC22**.

2. Create a new query that shows the first and last name of each equipment owner from the **Roster** table and all the fields from the **Equipment** table *except* EquipmentID and Owner.

3. Sort the query by the ItemType field in Ascending order.

4. Save it as **WhoOwnsWhat**.

5. Create a new query based on the Venues table. Do not add any fields to the grid, but make the query use all fields from that table.

   ✓ *Hint: Remember the Output All Fields setting in the Properties box for the query?*

6. Sort the new query by the City field.

   ✓ *Hint: Add City to the query grid, and sort by it, but then do not display it in the query results.*

7. Save the new query as **VenuesByCity** and display it in Datasheet view.

8. In Datasheet view, hide the ID column.

9. Close the database, saving all changes, and exit Access.

Exercise 23

◆ Critical Thinking

The HelpNow MedCenter has been using the database you created for them, but several members of the staff have expressed wishes for sorted and filtered data. Some of these are one-time requests; others are requests for data that will be needed repeatedly. You know that queries can answer these needs, so you will create several queries that will take care of them.

Exercise Directions

1. Open ⊚ **AC23**.

2. Dr. Jeffers has a new cell phone number: 316-555-1112. Find his record in the **tblEmployees** table and enter it.

3. Sort the **tblEmployees** table in ascending order by Position and print it. Then restore it to its normal sort order.

4. Create a query called **qryPhoneList** that generates a phone list of employees, sorted by last name. Put the last name first. Include only the first and last names and all three of the phone number fields (home, cell, and pager).

5. Make a copy of **qryPhoneList**, and name the copy **qryDoctorPhoneList**.

6. Edit **qryDoctorPhoneList** so that only people with Physician as their Position appear in the list, but do not show the Position field in the results.

7. Make a copy of **qryDoctorPhoneList**, and name the copy **qryMedPhoneList**.

8. Edit **qryMedPhoneList** so that it also includes all nurses, as well as Physicians, and turn on the display of the Positions field.

   ✓ You can either set up separate Or criteria for the two nurse positions (Registered Nurse and Licensed Practical Nurse) or you can set up an Or criteria that the Position field must contain the word "nurse".

9. Create a new query called **qryHoursWorked** that uses the **tblEmployees** and **tblTimeCards** tables.

10. In this new query, use the FirstName and LastName fields from **tblEmployees** and the WeekStartDate, HoursWorkedBase, and HoursWorkedOvertime fields from the **tblTimeCards** table.

11. Display and print each query; then close the database and exit Access.

PowerPoint 2003

Lesson 1

Getting Started with PowerPoint 2003
Exercises 1-7

Lesson 2

Editing and Formatting a Presentation
Exercises 8-16

Lesson 3

Setting Up a Slide Show
Exercises 17-24

Directory of Data Files on CD

Exercise #	File Name	Page #
1	None	438
2	PPT02	444
3	PPT03	448
4	PPT04	453
5	PPT05	457
6	PPT06.doc, 06WORKSH.xls	461
7	None	464
8	PPT08	470
9	PPT09	475
10	PPT10	481
11	PPT11	487
12	None	490
13	PPT13	494
14	PPT14, 14Sales.xls	500
15	PPT15	505
16	None	507
17	PPT17	514
18	PPT18	517
19	PPT19	521
20	PPT20	525
21	PPT21	528
22	PPT22	531
23	PPT23	535
24	PPT24	536

Exercise 1

Skills Covered:

◆ **About PowerPoint** ◆ **Start PowerPoint**
◆ **The Blank Presentation Option** ◆ **Apply a Slide Layout**
◆ **The PowerPoint Screen** ◆ **Use Shortcut Menus**
◆ **Use Slide Design Templates** ◆ **Use Placeholders**
◆ **Add Slides to a Presentation** ◆ **Save a Presentation**
◆ **Add Summary Information** ◆ **Save File as a Web Page**
◆ **Close a Presentation/Exit PowerPoint**

On the Job

Use a presentation to supplement a speech or lecture. You can show an audience the main topics you will discuss as you illustrate items with charts or tables. For example, you might present a talk to prospective customers about services your company performs or products you sell.

You are in charge of creating a slide presentation for HelpNow MedCenter. HelpNow MedCenter has created a new laser eye surgery unit and wants you to create a presentation explaining their services to local doctors' offices. As a bonus, you will save the presentation for the Web because you know the company uses the Internet to promote services directly to patients.

Terms

Presentation A set of slides or handouts that contain information you want to convey to an audience.

Clip art Predrawn artwork, photos, animations, and sounds clips that you can insert into your files.

Design template A preformatted slide design that contains colors and graphics to make your presentation consistent and attractive.

Slide layout Predetermined sets of placeholders for various types of slide content.

Placeholder Designated areas in PowerPoint layouts that can be used to easily insert text, graphics, or multimedia objects.

HTML Hypertext Markup Language is the file format used for files accessed on the World Wide Web.

Notes

About PowerPoint

- PowerPoint is a presentation graphics program that lets you create slide shows that can be shown on a computer screen with a projector, or as a Web page or Web broadcast.

- A **presentation** can include handouts, outlines, and speaker notes.

- PowerPoint slides may contain text and various objects, such as charts and **clip art**.

- You can import data from other Microsoft Office programs to a PowerPoint slide.

Start PowerPoint

- When you start PowerPoint, the screen appears with a slide, ready for you to work.

The PowerPoint Screen

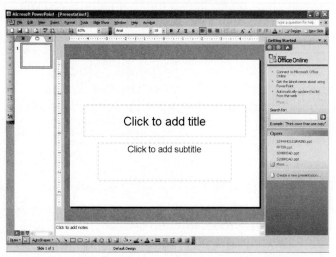

- PowerPoint offers a variety of designs and **design templates** on which to base a new presentation. There is also a blank template so you can create your own design.

The Blank Presentation Option

- A blank presentation doesn't have any graphics or backgrounds applied to it, but it does contain a single slide with the Title Slide layout applied. You can change the layout, create additional slides, apply colors, background patterns, and other formatting. You can then insert text, charts, drawings, clip art, and various multimedia effects to build your presentation content.

- The different kinds of slide layouts offer placeholders for entering content and text.

- After you create the presentation, you can add design elements, such as backgrounds, font styles, and color, if you want.

- If you do not have time to create your own design—or if you're new to creating presentations—you can use one of PowerPoint's predesigned design templates to enhance the appearance of your slides quickly and consistently.

New Presentation task pane

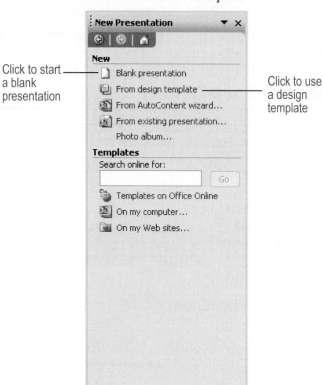

Click to start a blank presentation

Click to use a design template

Apply a Slide Layout

- When you start a new presentation or add a slide to a presentation, it will appear with a default **slide layout**. You can use that layout, or select a new layout from the Slide Layout task pane.

- The Slide Layout task pane supplies 27 different slide layouts you can use to build your own unique presentation.

- Slide layout arranges the standard objects of a presentation—titles, charts, and clip art, for example—on the slide to make it attractive.

- The placeholders and options for slide layouts help you create the text and content for each slide of a presentation.

The PowerPoint Screen

The PowerPoint Screen

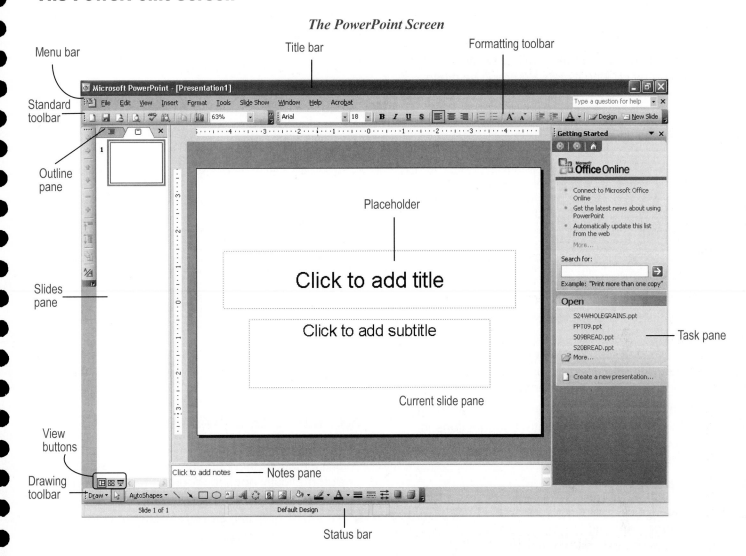

- PowerPoint supplies the default title "Presentation" and a number (for example, "Presentation1") in the title bar of each presentation you create. This title should be changed when you save the presentation with a new and descriptive name.

- A menu bar displays below the title bar.

- Toolbars are located under the menu bar. The Standard toolbar contains some buttons you'll see in other applications, such as Open, Save, and Print, as well as buttons unique to PowerPoint.

- The Formatting toolbar, which also contains some familiar buttons, lets you change font styles and sizes, among other things.

- By default the Standard and Formatting toolbars are displayed on one line, but you can set them to display on two lines.

- The Formatting toolbar also includes buttons for common tasks, such as adding a design or a new slide; clicking these buttons activates the task pane.

- The Drawing toolbar contains line, color, shape, and other drawing tools to use in your presentation.

- View buttons can be used to quickly switch among the three views: Normal (where you enter content on slides or in an outline format), Slide Sorter (the view used to rearrange and organize slides), and Slide Show (the presentation mode).

- The status bar displays information about the presentation, such as the slide number and template name.

- Normal view contains four panes: Slides, Current slide, Notes panes, and Outline, which you can access by clicking its tab. You can use these panes to enter information, arrange objects on the slide, and navigate among different slides.

Use Shortcut Menus

- Right-clicking elements in PowerPoint—such as **placeholders**, slides, text, and graphics—displays a shortcut menu that lets you quickly perform tasks and procedures related to the item you've clicked on.

Use Slide Design Templates

- The Template option lets you create slides with a preplanned layout. There are two types of templates—design templates and content templates.

- Design templates contain various colorful backgrounds, graphics, and text colors and styles to apply to a presentation.

- Content templates contain sets of slides with design elements and content suggestions for specific types of presentations, such as a company handbook or financial overview.

Use Placeholders

- PowerPoint displays placeholders to define the arrangement and location of text and other objects you can add to a slide.

- There are three types of text placeholders: title, subtitle, and text (bulleted lists of content). Each of these contains preset formatting for text font and size.

- When you click on a placeholder, PowerPoint selects the box, displays sizing handles for sizing, and a cursor for typing.

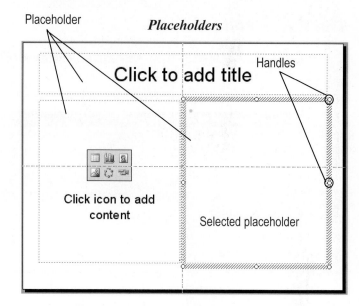

Placeholders

- Graphic placeholders included in Content layouts provide a place for charts, clip art, tables, and other objects you can add to the presentation.

- If you are new to creating presentations, placeholders can help you create a professional-looking slide set.

Add Slides to a Presentation

- When you add a second slide to your presentation, the Title and Text slide layout is automatically applied. You can replace it with another layout from the Slide Layout task pane.

- The new slide is inserted immediately after the slide currently displayed or selected.

Title and Text slide layout

Click to add title

• Click to add text

Save a Presentation

- If you want to have a file available for future use, you must save it on a removable disk or on an internal fixed drive.
- Save a PowerPoint presentation using the same procedures you use to save a Word document or Excel spreadsheet.
- PowerPoint automatically adds a .ppt extension to a saved presentation and changes the presentation's name in the title bar.

Add Summary Information

- As in Word, you can also add summary information—title, author, keywords, and so on—about the presentation and view statistics in the Properties dialog box (File, Properties).

Save File as a Web Page

- You can save a presentation in **HTML** (Hypertext Markup Language) format for publishing on the World Wide Web.
- When you save a presentation in HTML, you can open it in a browser, such as Internet Explorer.

Close a Presentation/Exit PowerPoint

- PowerPoint prompts you to save a presentation that has not been saved or has been modified before letting you close the presentation or exit the program.
- Follow the same procedures for closing a presentation file and exiting PowerPoint as in Word and Excel applications.
- Close a document when you are finished working on it.

Procedures

Start PowerPoint
1. Click **Start**
   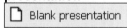 .... Ctrl + Esc
2. Click **All Programs** .... P
3. Click **Microsoft Office**.
4. Click **Microsoft Office 2003 PowerPoint**.

Open a New Presentation
1. Start PowerPoint.
2. In the New Presentation task pane, click **Blank presentation**

   [ ] Blank presentation .

   ✓ *If the New Presentation task pane isn't displayed, click View, Task Pane.*
3. In the task pane, click the Slide Layout you want to use.

Use Template Option
1. Start PowerPoint.
2. In the New Presentation task pane, click **From design template**

3. Click the design template you want to use.

Use Right-clicks
1. Place your mouse cursor over a PowerPoint item.
2. Right-click the mouse.
3. Click a command.

Use Placeholders
1. Click once in text placeholder.
2. Enter text.
OR
1. Click on a content placeholder.
2. Insert a specific type of content, such as clip art.

Insert New Slide (*Ctrl+M*)
1. Click **Insert** .... Alt + I
2. Click **New Slide** .... N
   OR

   Click **New Slide** button .
   OR
   Press **Ctrl+M**.
3. From Slide Layout task pane, select layout.

Add Summary Information about Presentation
1. Click **File** .... Alt + F
2. Click **Properties** I
3. Add desired information.
4. Click **OK** .... Enter

Save Presentation (*Ctrl+S*)
1. Click **File** .... Alt + F
2. Click **Save** .... S
   OR

   Click **Save** button [🖫] .
3. Click **Save in** drop-down arrow .... Alt + I
4. Select **drive** and **folder**.
5. Double-click **File name** text box .... Alt + N
6. Type **file name**.
7. Click **Save** .... Alt + S

Save as Web Page
1. Click **File** .... Alt + F
2. Click **Save as Web Page** .... G
3. In **File name** text box, type file name............. Alt + N
4. Click **Save** .... S

Close Presentation
1. Click **File** .... Alt + F
2. Click **Close** C

Exit PowerPoint
1. Click **File** .... Alt + F
2. Click **Exit** X

Exercise Directions

1. Start PowerPoint, if necessary.

2. Create a new blank presentation.

3. Save the file as **01LASER**.

4. Accept the default Title Slide layout for the first slide.

5. Type the title and subtitle as shown in Illustration A.

6. Insert a new slide and accept the Title and Text layout for the second slide.

7. Type the title and bulleted list as shown in Illustration B.

8. Fill in the summary information for the file as follows:

Title:	**HelpNow MedCenter**
Subject:	**Laser Eye Surgery**
Author:	**Your name**
Manager:	**Your supervisor or teacher's name**
Company:	**Communications Solutions, Inc.**
Category:	**Promotion**
Keywords:	**Laser, Eye, Surgery**

9. Save the file, but don't close it.

10. Save the presentation as a Web page using the same name.

11. Close the file and exit PowerPoint, saving all changes.

Illustration A

HelpNow MedCenter

Laser Eye Surgery Unit

Illustration B

Laser Eye Surgery Unit

- Opens March 22
- Headed by Dr. Martin Talbot from the Eastern Eye Surgery Clinic
- Safe, fast, and reliable surgery
- Covered by most insurance carriers
- The key to clearer vision

On Your Own

1. Start PowerPoint and use a design template to create a presentation about yourself.

2. Select the default title slide layout and type a title for the presentation. For example, you might type **My Life**, or **All About Me**. Enter your name as the subtitle.

3. Insert a second slide using the Bulleted list layout.

4. Type a title on the second slide, and then type at least three items describing what the presentation will be about. For example, the first item might be **The Early Years**, the second item might be **A Budding Athlete**, and so on.

5. Insert a third slide using the Title, Text, and Content layout.

6. Type a title on the third slide based on the first bulleted item that you entered on the second slide.

7. Type at least three bulleted items related to the topic.

8. Insert a fourth slide using the Title, Text, and Content layout.

9. Type a title on the fourth slide based on the second bulleted item that you entered on the second slide.

10. Type at least three bulleted items related to the topic.

11. Save the presentation with the name **OPP01**.

12. Close the presentation and exit PowerPoint.

Exercise 2

Skills Covered:

◆ **Open an Existing Presentation**   ◆ **Slide Views**
◆ **Move from Slide to Slide**   ◆ **Spell Check**   ◆ **Print a Presentation**
◆ **Change a Slide's Layout or Design Template**

On the Job

Check the spelling and otherwise refine the design of your presentation to make the best impression possible. For example, you may show a presentation to a prospective client who might purchase your product. A well-designed presentation can be the turning point in such a sale.

You want to make some changes to the slide presentation for HelpNow MedCenter to make sure that your client will like it. Any presentation you plan to show a client should have no spelling errors. Also, you should review the design and organization of the presentation to make sure it is suitable for the client's tastes and requirements. Often, printing the presentation to hard copy gives you a better idea of how it will look to the customer.

Terms

Views PowerPoint offers several different ways you can view the presentation as you work on it: Normal view, which includes the Slide, Note, and Outline panes, Slide Sorter, and Slide Show views. Each view has its own advantages and features.

Automatic spell checking A feature that checks spelling as you enter text. A wavy red line in the text indicates a possible spelling error.

Notes

Standard toolbar

Open

Print

Spelling

Open an Existing Presentation

■ Open an existing presentation to modify, add, or delete material, print, or run the presentation as a slide show.

Slide Views

■ In PowerPoint, you can create and view a presentation in three different **views** plus two tabs that display additional panes within Normal view.

440

Normal view

Outline tab

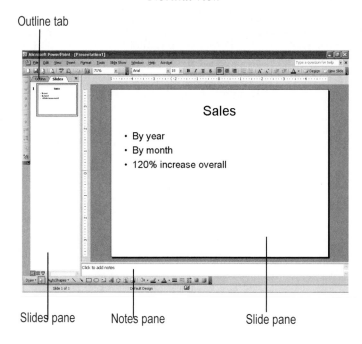

Slides pane   Notes pane   Slide pane

Outline pane

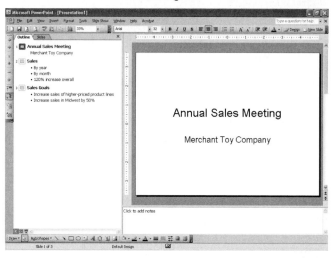

- Normal view (default) provides two panes, or views, of the slide and its contents—Slide pane and Notes. It also includes two tabs—Slides and Outline.
  - The Slide pane displays the contents as it will look on the slide.
  - The Notes pane lets you add text for personal reference—or as handouts to an audience.
  - The Slides tab lets you organize slides and easily see a thumbnail of each slide.
  - The Outline tab lets you view all slide content in outline format.
- Slides pane in Normal view displays the slides in the presentation so that you can quickly switch to the slide you want to view by clicking on it.
- The Outline pane in Normal view displays the outline of the presentation (slightly reducing the size of the Slide pane as it does so). Each high level bullet point in the outline represents a slide.

- Slide Sorter view displays the entire presentation in large thumbnails so you can easily identify slides to add, delete, and rearrange them in the presentation. This view is also suitable for easily adding and previewing animations, transitions, and sound effects to an entire presentation.
- Slide Show view displays one slide at a time, displaying a slide as it would be displayed in a slide show. This view is used to run an on-screen slide show.

Move from Slide to Slide

- Most presentations include multiple slides.
- You will need to move from slide to slide in Normal view to enter text and modify the presentation.
- PowerPoint offers a variety of ways to select and display slides including selecting them in the Slide pane, using the scroll bar in Normal view, and using the navigation arrows at the bottom of the scroll bar.

Move from slide to slide using the navigation arrows

Next slide ——— Previous slide

Spell Check

- PowerPoint provides two methods of spell checking in your presentations: automatic and manual.

- **Automatic spell checking** works while you're typing.

- Automatic spell checking displays a wavy red line under words PowerPoint doesn't recognize.

- PowerPoint activates the automatic spell checker by default.

  ✓ *You can use manual spell checking at any time.*

- The use of the spell checker is similar to that in other Microsoft Office applications.

- A professional presentation must have no spelling errors.

Print a Presentation

- Printing PowerPoint slides is similar to printing pages in other Microsoft Office programs, with a few exceptions.

- A presentation can be printed in various formats, including as speaker's notes, handouts, slides, or as an outline. You choose the settings in the Print dialog box.

Print dialog box

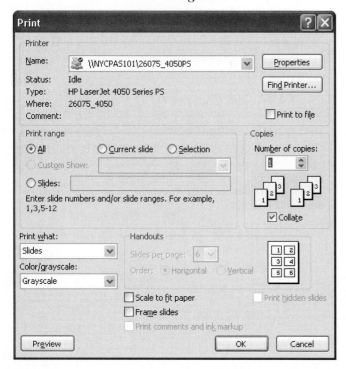

Print Options

Option	Description
Properties	Click to change printer conditions, such as paper size, orientation, and graphics.
Print to file	Creates a printer file (.PRN) that can be printed on another computer that doesn't have the PowerPoint program.
Print range	Defines whether to print all slides, the current slide only, or a range of slides in the presentation.
Copies	Defines the number of copies to print.
Collate	When printing multiple copies, prints the slides in their order in the presentation.
Print what	Choose to print slides, handouts, notes, or an outline.
Handouts	Select the number of slides to print per page.
Order	Select horizontal or vertical order of the slides on the handout page.
Color/gray-scale	Select to print colors, shades of gray, or pure black and white.
Scale to fit paper	Changes the size of the slide to fit the selected paper size.
Frame slides	Adds a frame border around the slides when printed.
Print Comments	Check the option to include inserted comments.
Print hidden slides	Prints any hidden slides in the presentation.

- Sometimes printing a slide set helps you to see any flaws to the design and to proofread content.

- You specify page setup before you print the contents of the presentation. Select Page Setup from the File menu.

- Page setup lets you define the page size and orientation.

Page Setup dialog box

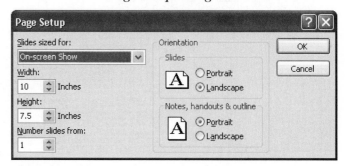

Change a Slide's Layout or Design Template

- You may need to change a slide's layout or a presentation's template as you work.
- Change a slide's layout to add additional text or elements, such as a graph or chart.
- Change the template to modify background, text color, or design elements.
- Try to choose a template design that suits the subject matter.

- You can view a color presentation in black and white or grayscale while you are working on it, for example, if you wanted to see how a printed version of the presentation would look when printed on a non-color printer.
- When viewing a presentation in grayscale or black and white, PowerPoint automatically displays a Grayscale View toolbar that allows you modify the settings for shadings used in each view.

Black and White view

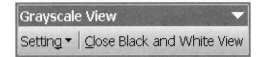

Procedures

Open Existing Presentation

1. Start PowerPoint.
2. Click **File** .... Alt + F
3. Click **Open** .... O
4. Click on file to open.
5. Click **Open** button .... O

OR

1. Click the **Open** button 📂 on the Standard toolbar.
2. Browse to locate and open the file.

OR

- Click to open a file from the New Presentation task pane.

Slide Views

- To change views, click appropriate button on View bar or click appropriate tab.

OR

1. Click **View** .... Alt + V
2. Click one of the following:
   - **Normal** .... N
   - **Slide Sorter** .... D
   - **Slide Show** .... W

OR

- Press **F5** F5
  for Slide Show view.

Move from Slide to Slide

1. Press **Page Down** to display next slide.
2. Press **Page Up** to display previous slide.

OR

1. Click **Next Slide** button ⬇ on vertical slide scroll bar.
2. Click **Previous Slide** button ⬆ on vertical slide scroll bar.

OR

- Click on a slide on the Slides or Outline pane.

OR

- Double-click on a slide in Slide Sorter view.

Disable or Activate Automatic Spell Checker Features

1. Click **Tools** .... Alt + T
2. Click **Options** .... O
3. Click **Spelling and Style** tab .... Ctrl + Tab
4. To disable the automatic underlining of suspect words, select **Hide all spelling errors** check box .... S
5. To activate automatic correction of misspellings as you type, check **Check spelling as you type** .... P
6. Click **OK** .... Enter

Manually Spell Check Presentation (*F7*)

1. Click **Tools** .... Alt + T
2. Click **Spelling** .... S

OR

Click **Spelling** button ✓.

Change Page Setup

1. Click **File** .... Alt + F
2. Click **Page Setup** .... U
3. Indicate page specifications.
4. Click **OK** .... Enter

Change Slide Layouts

1. Click **Format** .... Alt + O
2. Click **Slide Layout** L
3. Click layout you want to apply.
4. Click the **Close** button ✕ on Slide Layout task pane.

Change Design Templates

1. Click **Format** .... Alt + O
2. Click **Slide Design** .... D
3. Select template design from Slide Design pane.
   - ✓ *Clicking the arrow on the design preview gives the option of applying the design to all slides or selected slides.*
4. Click the **Close** button ✕ on Slide Design pane.

View Slide in Black and White

1. Click **View** .... `Alt`+`V`
2. Click **Color/Grayscale** .... `C`
3. Click **Pure Black and White** ... `U`
4. To change view back to color, repeat steps 1 and 2 and then click **Color**.

Print Presentation (*Ctrl+P*)

1. Click **File** .... `Alt`+`F`
2. Click **Print** .... `P`
3. Choose desired print options.
4. Click **OK** .... `Enter`

OR

- Click **Print** button .
  - ✓ *Your presentation will print based on the default or last options you selected in the Print dialog box.*

Exercise Directions

1. Start PowerPoint, if necessary.
2. Open 📁**01LASER** or 💿**PPT02**.
3. Save the file as **02LASER**.
4. Move to slide 1 and insert a new slide using the Title and Text layout.
5. Enter the text as shown in Illustration A.
6. Switch to Outline pane. In the Notes pane, enter the following text:
   Discuss issues for astigmatism
7. Switch to Slides pane.
8. Move to slide 3 and insert another slide using the Title and 2-Column Text layout.
9. Enter the text shown in Illustration B.
10. Change to Slide Sorter view.
11. Check the presentation for spelling errors.
12. Apply the design template Edge.
13. Print a handout with three slides per page.
14. Close the file and exit PowerPoint, saving all changes.

On Your Own

1. Open the **OPP01** presentation you created in the On Your Own section of Exercise 1, or open 💿**02MYLIFE**.
2. Save the file as **OPP02**.
3. Check the spelling in the presentation.
4. Scroll through the second, third, and fourth slides.
5. Change to Slide Sorter view.
6. Display the Outline pane.
7. Change to Normal view.
8. Display the slide in black in white.
9. Display the title slide.
10. Change back to color.
11. Change the design template.
12. Display slide four.
13. Change the slide layout to Title and Text.
14. Print the entire presentation.
15. Save the presentation, close it, and exit PowerPoint.

Illustration A

Laser Eye Surgery Facts

- LASIK is most common refractive surgery
- Relative lack of pain
- Almost immediate results (within 24 hours)
- Both nearsighted and farsighted can benefit

Illustration B

Laser Surgery Pros and Cons

- Virtually painless
- Fast procedure
- Immediate improvement

- Not everybody is candidate
- Cost
- Some risk of corneal damage

Exercise 3

Skills Covered:

◆ **Work with Content Layouts** ◆ **Insert Objects without a Content Layout** ◆ **Insert a Text Box** ◆ **Use Undo and Redo**

On the Job

Add objects to your slides to make them more interesting to the audience. You might, for example, add clip art to a slide presentation to break up the text or emphasize certain points.

The client has supplied your company with information for use in a chart and other slides. They also asked that you add clip art to the presentation to make it more interesting for their prospective clients. In this exercise, you will enhance your presentation with clip art and **WordArt**.

Terms

WordArt A feature used to transform text into a picture object.

Object An item other than text, such as a table, chart, clip art, WordArt, or worksheet.

Embed Inserting an object created in another application into your PowerPoint presentation. Embedded objects are easy to edit and update.

Notes

Work with Content Layouts

- The Slide Layout task pane contains placeholders for **objects**, such as clip art, WordArt, and charts, in addition to placeholders for text. These are referred to as *content placeholders*.

- In PowerPoint, the Slide Layout task pane provides previews of various layouts that use text placeholders, or a combination of text and content placeholders.

- A content placeholder helps you add objects by displaying an icon box in the placeholder; you insert an object by simply clicking on the corresponding object icon.

- You can also insert objects manually into new and preexisting slides using menus and toolbar buttons.

- **Embed** a content object, such as an Excel worksheet, so you can edit it easily within PowerPoint.

- Objects add interest to a presentation.

Icon box for adding an object

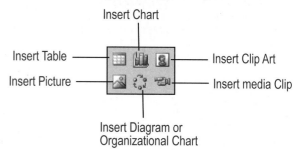

Insert Chart

Insert Table ——— ——— Insert Clip Art

Insert Picture ——— ——— Insert media Clip

Insert Diagram or Organizational Chart

Insert Objects without a Content Layout

- You can insert objects without using a content layout placeholder using the Insert menu.

- Inserting an object through the Insert menu allows you to insert an object from an existing file, or to create a new file.

- More object types are available to insert with this method than with the content placeholder method.

Insert a Text Box

- You can insert a text box using the Drawing menu. A text box is not a placeholder and not part of a slide layout.

- Text you enter in a text box will not be reflected in your presentation outline.

Use Undo and Redo

- PowerPoint contains an Undo feature, as in other Microsoft Office applications, which reverses the most recent action.

- With Undo, you can often reverse one or multiple actions you have performed in PowerPoint.

- You can redo actions after you undo, if you change your mind.

Procedures

Insert Object into Placeholder

1. Add new slide layout that contains a content placeholder.
2. Click the appropriate object icon.
3. In the resulting dialog box, choose the appropriate options.
4. Click **OK**............................ Enter

Insert Clip Art

1. Add new slide layout that contains a content placeholder.
2. Click **Insert Clip Art** icon ⑧ in the placeholder·
3. In Select Picture dialog box, click desired art.
   OR
   a. Type a keyword in the Search text box.
   b. Click **Go**.
4. Select desired clip art.
5. Click **OK**.

Insert WordArt

1. Click **Insert** .... Alt + I
2. Click **Picture** .... P
3. Click **WordArt** .... W
   ✓ You can add WordArt to a new or existing slide.
4. Click the WordArt style you'd like to apply.
5. Click **OK**.
6. Type text.
7. Click **OK** .... Enter
8. Select options from WordArt toolbar.

Insert Object using No Placeholder

1. Open a new or existing slide.
2. Click **Insert**.................. Alt + I
3. Click one of the following:
   - **Picture** .... P
   - **Diagram** .... G
   - **Te**x**t box** X
   - **Mo**v**ies and Sounds**...... V
   - **Chart** .... H
   - **Ta**b**le** .... B
   - **O**bject .... O

4. Choose from the submenu or dialog box that appears depending on the object you selected.

Insert a Text Box

   ✓ Drawing toolbar must be displayed for the first method.

1. Click **Text Box** button ⊞ on the Drawing toolbar.
   Or
   a. Click **Insert** .... Alt + I
   b. Click **Te**x**t box**............... X
2. Click and drag the text tool on the slide.
3. Type the text.

Undo (Ctrl+Z)

1. Click **Edit** .... Alt + E
2. Click **Undo** .... U
   OR
   Click the **Undo** button ↺ ▾ on the Standard toolbar.

Undo Multiple Actions

1. Click **Undo** button's down arrow ▾.
2. Click the recent actions you want to undo.

Exercise Directions

1. Start PowerPoint, if necessary.
2. Open ⌨️**02LASER** or 💿**PPT03**.
3. Save the file as **03LASER**.
4. Move to slide 4 and insert a new slide.
5. Select Title, Text, and Content slide layout.
6. Enter the text as shown in Illustration A.
7. Insert a relevant clip art in the content placeholder. Select a clip and then double-click it to insert into the document.
   - ✓ *Use the keyword "eye" to search for appropriate clip art.*
8. Insert a new slide at the end of the presentation.
9. Double-click the Title Only slide layout.
10. Type the title shown in Illustration B.
11. Insert a text box and type the text as shown in Illustration B.
    - ✓ *See procedures for inserting text boxes.*
12. Insert a relevant clip art. Resize or move the text and art as necessary.
    - ✓ *To resize the clip art click on the clip to select it and then drag one of the sizing handles. To move a clip, click on the clip to select it. Holding down the mouse button, drag the clip to a new location.*
13. Insert a new slide after slide 5 using any Slide Layout.
14. Undo the new slide insert.
15. Move to the end of the presentation and insert a new slide.
16. Select the Title Only slide layout.
17. Enter the title text as shown in Illustration C.
18. Click Insert, Picture, and WordArt.
19. Choose a WordArt style and click OK.
20. For the WordArt, type **Laser Eye Surgery**.
21. From WordArt's toolbar, choose any design or text formatting you want and close the WordArt by clicking OK. You can resize or reformat the WordArt.
22. Spell check the presentation.
23. Print the slides as handouts, with four slides to the page.
24. Close the file, saving all changes.

Illustration A

The Cost of Laser Surgery

- Typically as low as $499 per eye
- Lower cost than two sets of contact lenses
- Covered by most insurance

Illustration B

Clear Vision in a Day

In most cases vision clears immediately, or within 24 hours of surgery. The patient should avoid strenuous exercise for a week after surgery, and avoid rubbing or irritating eyes for 48 hours. Except for taking these sensible precautions, the patient should be back to his or her normal activities in a day and feel no discomfort or side effects from laser eye surgery.

Illustration C

Your Vision Solution

Laser Eye Surgery

On Your Own

1. Open the **OPP02** presentation you created in Exercise 2, or open ◉ **OPP03**.

2. Save the file as **OPP03**.

3. Insert a clip art picture on to slide 3. Try to select a picture that is somehow related to the text on the slide.

4. Insert a clip art object on slide 4.

5. Undo the insertion.

6. Insert a different clip art object on slide 4.

7. Print the presentation as handouts with two slides on a page.

8. Save and close the presentation.

Exercise 4

Skills Covered:
◆ Move, Copy, Duplicate, and Delete Slides
◆ Slide Sorter View

On the Job

As you work on a presentation, you can move slides around, copy slides, and even delete slides you don't want in the presentation to make it more compact or descriptive. You might also, for example, create a presentation for one group of people in your company and then customize the presentation for another group by copying and changing some slides.

After reviewing your presentation, you decided to change the presentation's organization and make some additional changes before showing it to the client. In this exercise, you will duplicate slides and add new slides to your presentation.

Terms

Duplicate To create a copy of a slide that includes all text, content objects, and formatting of the original. A duplicate slide is inserted after the original slide in the presentation.

Slide Sorter view A method of viewing and organizing multiple slides in the presentation at one time.

Notes

Move, Copy, Duplicate, and Delete Slides

- A presentation typically contains multiple slides, any of which you can move, copy, **duplicate**, or delete.

- To move a slide, click the slide icon on the Outline tab, or click the slide in the Slides tab in Normal view or in Slide Sorter view and drag it to the new position.

- You can also move and copy slides from one presentation to another.

- Duplicating creates a copy of a slide so you can make use of custom formatting and other features of the original slide to create a new slide.

- If you move, copy, duplicate, or delete a slide, you can use the Undo command to reverse the action.

- Save a presentation before you edit a slide so you can revert to the previous version if you make a mistake or lose data.

451

Move slides

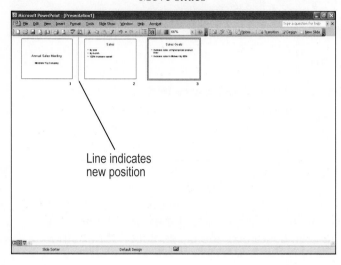

Line indicates
new position

Slide Sorter View

- **Slide Sorter view** enables you to organize your presentation as a whole.
- Slide Sorter view displays slides as miniatures so you can arrange them as you work or as the final step to completing the presentation.
    - ✓ *Note that Slide Sorter view displays a Slide Sorter toolbar in place of the Formatting toolbar to help you work with multiple slides.*
- You cannot edit slide content in Slide Sorter view.
- To edit slide content, double-click a slide to display it in Normal view.

Procedures

Copy Slide (*Ctrl+C*) and Paste Slide (*Ctrl+V*)

1. In the Slides or Outline pane of Normal view or in Slide Sorter view, select slide to copy.
2. Click **Copy** button .
    OR
    a. Click **E**dit .... Alt + E
    b. Click **C**opy C
    ✓ *If you want to copy a slide from one presentation to another, display the other presentation.*
3. In the Slides or Outline pane of Normal view or in Slide Sorter view, select slide after which the copied slide will be pasted.
4. Click **Paste** button.
    OR
    a. Click **E**dit .... Alt + E
    b. Click **P**aste .... P

Duplicate Slide

1. In the Slides or Outline pane of Normal view or in Slide Sorter view, select slide.
2. Click **I**nsert .... Alt + I
3. Click **D**uplicate Slide .... D

Delete Slide

1. In the Slides or Outline pane of Normal view or in Slide Sorter view, select slide.
2. Press **Delete** key .... Del
    OR
    a. Click **E**dit............... Alt + E
    b. Click **D**elete Slide .... D
OR
1. Right-click slide in the Slides or Outline pane of Normal view or in Slide Sorter view.
2. Click **D**elete Slide .... D

Move Slide

1. In the Slides or Outline pane of Normal view or in Slide Sorter view, select the slide thumbnail.
2. Drag the slide thumbnail button to new position.
3. Release mouse button.

Change to Slide Sorter View

- Click **Slide Sorter View** button.
    OR
1. Click **V**iew .... Alt + V
2. Click **Sli**de Sorter .... D

Exercise Directions

1. Open 🖳**03LASER** or 💿**PPT04**.
2. Save the file as **04LASER**.
3. Select slide 2 and copy it.
4. Paste the slide so it becomes slide 3.
5. Change the contents of slide 3 as shown in Illustration A.
6. If necessary, switch to the Slides pane in Normal view.
7. Duplicate slide 5.
8. Switch to Slide Sorter view.
9. Delete slide 5.
10. Move slide 4 to the second slide position.
11. Edit slide 8 to change the title to **Your Affordable Vision Alternative.**
12. Add a new slide after slide 8 and choose the Title, Text, and Content slide layout.
13. Add the text as shown in Illustration B.
14. Insert appropriate clip art.
15. Spell check the presentation.
16. Close the file, saving all changes.

Illustration A

Is Laser Eye Surgery for You?

- You want a safe form of refractive surgery
- You want to avoid pain
- You expect almost immediate results
- You are nearsighted or farsighted

State of the Art Facility

- Modern equipment
- High patient safety standards
- Private recovery areas
- Amenities for patient comfort

On Your Own

1. Open the **OPP03** presentation you created in Exercise 3, or open ⊙**OPP04**.

2. Save the file as **OPP04**.

3. Insert a new slide after slide 2 using the Title and 2-Column Text layout.

4. Give the slide a title related to the third topic on slide 2.

5. Type at least two items in each column.

6. Change to Slide Sorter view.

7. Move the new two-column slide to the end of the presentation.

8. Make of copy of the fourth slide and paste it at the end of the presentation.

9. Undo the paste.

10. Save the presentation.

11. Close the presentation and exit PowerPoint.

Exercise 5

Skills Covered:
◆ Outline Pane   ◆ Summary Slide

On the Job

Use the Outline pane in Normal view to help you organize a presentation. For example, you can add new slides and move slides around in the Outline pane so you can better organize the presentation content.

You will continue working on the sample slide presentations for your client, HelpNow MedCenter. In this exercise, you will check each slide for organization, spelling, and other details in the Outline pane, so that you can easily rearrange text and make modifications to the presentation.

Terms

Outline pane Selecting the Outline pane in Normal view lets you see the outline of a slide presentation in text form organized by outline levels.

Collapse Hiding all except main, or selected, headings in an outline.

Expand Showing all levels of an outline.

Outline A technique of arranging major topics and their subordinate topics to organize a presentation.

Notes

Outline Pane

- The **Outline pane** displays a presentation so that you can see an overview and organize content more easily.

- You can create a presentation in Normal view with the Outline pane displayed.

- Use the Outline pane to check the text content of a presentation for consistency and the overall flow of information.

- You can print a customized Outline view by **collapsing** or **expanding** certain headings or showing all formatting, for example.

- The Outlining toolbar makes it easy to rearrange content throughout the entire presentation; the toolbar tools are available only when the Outline pane is selected.

- The Outlining toolbar also helps you view the **outline** in different ways, for easier organization.

Outline pane

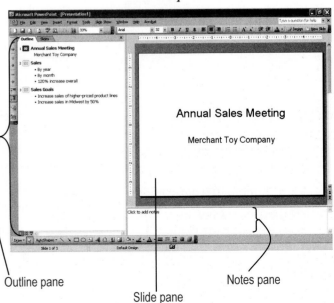

Outline pane

Slide pane

Notes pane

Outlining toolbar

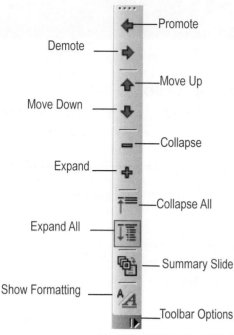

- Promote
- Demote
- Move Up
- Move Down
- Collapse
- Expand
- Collapse All
- Expand All
- Summary Slide
- Show Formatting
- Toolbar Options

- Promote/Demote buttons change a heading level in the outline structure and apply styles, such as bulleted text, to selected text.

- Move Up/Move Down buttons let you move text up or down in the outline.
- Expand button displays the title, subtitle, and all bullet levels of the text in the selected slides.
- Collapse button hides the text levels in the selected slides and displays only the title text.
- Expand All button displays all levels of text for all slides in the presentation.
- Collapse All button displays only the title text for all slides in the presentation.
- Summary Slide button creates a new slide consisting of the titles of selected slides in Outline view.
- Show Formatting button displays text formatted as it will look on the slide.

Summary Slide

- Create a Summary Slide made up of the titles of each slide in your presentation.
- A Summary Slide can be used as an agenda or overview.

Procedures

Display Outlining Toolbar

1. Click **View** .... `Alt`+`V`
2. Click **Toolbars** .... `T`
3. Click **Outlining**.
   ✓ *The Outlining toolbar does not appear by default when the Outline tab is displayed.*

Move Text in Outline View

1. Select the text to move.
2. Click **Move Up** 🔼 or **Move Down** 🔽 buttons.
3. Click **Demote** ➡️ or **Promote** ⬅️ buttons to change the outline level of the text.

OR

1. Select the text to move.
2. Drag the text to new location.
3. Release mouse button.

Select Slides in Outline View

1. Click the slide's number or Slide icon [5] 🔲 .
2. To select additional slides, press Shift and then click Slide icon for each slide.

Display Titles in Outline View

- Click the **Collapse All** button 📑 .

Insert Summary Slide

1. Select all slides in presentation .... `Ctrl`+`A`
2. Click **Summary Slide** button 🗂️ on the Slide Sorter toolbar or Outlining toolbar.

Print an Outline *(Ctrl + P)*

   ✓ *Collapse or expand slide titles and text as you want them to appear on printout.*

1. Click **File** .... `Alt`+`F`
2. Click **Print** .... `P`
3. Click Outline View in **Print what** drop-down list..... `Alt`+`W`
4. Click **Outline View**.
5. Click **OK** .... `Enter`

Exercise Directions

1. Open 🖮**04LASER** or 💿**PPT05**.

2. Save the file as **05LASER**.

3. If necessary, click the Outline pane.

4. Move slide 4 to the third slide position.

5. Move slide 2 so it appears after slide 4.

   ✓ *Hint: Collapse the slides before you move slide 2.*

6. Move the following bullets on slide 9:
   - Amenities to the first bullet position on the slide.
   - High patient safety standards to the second bullet position.
   - Modern equipment to the last bullet position on the slide. See Illustration A.

7. Collapse all.

8. Select all slides and add a summary slide at the beginning of the presentation.

9. On the summary slide, as shown in Illustration B:
   - Delete the HelpNow MedCenter bullet.
   - Move the Laser Surgery Pros and Cons bullet to the second position on the Summary Slide.

10. Expand all in the outline.

11. Spell check the presentation.

12. Print the outline.

13. Close the file, saving all changes.

Illustration A

State of the Art Facility

- Amenities for patient comfort
- High patient safety standards
- Private recovery areas
- Modern equipment

Summary Slide

- Is Laser Eye Surgery For You?
- Laser Surgery Pros and Cons
- Laser Eye Surgery Facts
- Laser Eye Surgery Unit
- The Cost of Laser Surgery
- Clear Vision In a Day
- Your Affordable Vision Alternative
- State of the Art Facility

On Your Own

1. Open the file ⊙ **OPP05**.

2. Save the new presentation as **OPP05**.

3. In the Outline pane, enter text for at least four slides. Make the presentation about an organization or club to which you belong, about the place where you work, about a class you are taking, or about school in general.

4. Change to Slide Sorter view.

5. Create a Summary slide from the headings on the slides in the presentation.

6. Move the Summary slide to the end of the presentation.

7. Change back to Normal view and the Outline pane.

8. Use the Outlining toolbar to rearrange slides and promote/demote text.

9. Print the collapsed outline and then print the expanded outline.

10. Apply a design template to the presentation

11. Check the spelling.

12. Save the presentation.

13. Close the presentation and exit PowerPoint.

Exercise 6

Skills Covered:

◆ **Import/Export an Outline**

◆ **Link an Excel Worksheet**

On the Job

Use data created in other programs for slide material to save time. You might have written a paper that, when collapsed in Word's outline feature, creates the perfect outline for a presentation. Or, perhaps you created an Excel worksheet that you can link to a presentation that gives your audience the most up-to-date material.

Your client, Voyager Travel Adventures, has supplied you with files that they want you to use in the presentation you're creating for them. Using the client's files from Word and Excel means the data is accurate and up-to-date and the organization is already arranged as the client wants. You'll also add some design elements to spice up the presentation.

Terms

Import To bring a copy of text or data created in another program into PowerPoint.

File formats Each program saves a file as a specific type, or format. Many programs can convert file types so files can be used by several different programs.

Export To send a copy of text or data from one program, such as PowerPoint, to another program.

Link To connect two files so that when an original file is updated, the linked file reflects the changes.

Source The file from which you are copying or moving information.

Destination The file to which you are copying or moving information.

Notes

Import/Export an Outline

- You can use text created in other programs, such as Word, in your PowerPoint presentation.

- You might want to **import** text so that you don't have to retype the text or because you prefer organizing the contents of the presentation in Word.

- Import a DOC, RTF, TXT, or HTM format, as well as other formats from Excel, WordPerfect, and other programs.

  ✓ *You may need to install a file converter to load certain types of files.*

- PowerPoint recognizes many **file formats**. When you open a file created in another format, PowerPoint automatically converts it to a PowerPoint outline.

  ✓ *Some files you open may not be suitable for a PowerPoint outline. When you choose the Outline Files type when importing an outline, PowerPoint lists only those formats that do work as outlines.*

- Word formats an outline exported from PowerPoint with headings and bullets that are indented.

- You might **export** an outline to Word so that you can use the text in another document, such as a report or letter.

Link an Excel Worksheet

- You can **link** an Excel worksheet to a PowerPoint presentation to keep your information up-to-date and accurate.

- A linked object is one that's created in a **source** file and inserted into a **destination** file.

- A linked object does not become a part of the destination file.

- The link connects the files so that when the source is modified, the destination automatically updates the information.

- You can link to any program that supports linked and embedded objects.

- PowerPoint lets you create a new object to link or select an existing file to link to your PowerPoint presentation.

Link an Excel worksheet

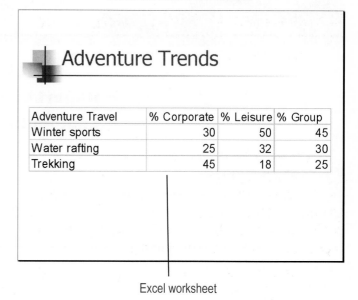

Adventure Travel	% Corporate	% Leisure	% Group
Winter sports	30	50	45
Water rafting	25	32	30
Trekking	45	18	25

Excel worksheet

- An inserted worksheet may display empty cells, but you can resize the worksheet to hide unnecessary cells and better fit the slide.

- When you click in an inserted Excel worksheet, the Excel toolbar appears for you to use.

Procedures

Import Outline from Word
(Ctrl+O)

1. Click **File** .... `Alt`+`F`
2. Click **Open** .... `O`
3. In **Files of type**, click **All Outlines**.
4. In **Look in** list, select the folder where the Word file is stored.
5. Select file to import.
6. Click **Open** .... `O`

Export Outline to Word

1. Click **File** .... `Alt`+`F`
2. Click **Send To** .... `D`
3. Click **Microsoft Office Word** .... `W`
4. Click **Outline only** .... `O`
5. Click **OK** .... `Enter`

Insert New Excel Worksheet

1. Click **Insert** .... `Alt`+`I`
2. Click **Object** .... `O`
3. In Insert Object dialog box, select **Create new** .... `Alt`+`N`
4. In **Object type** list box, select **Microsoft Office Excel Worksheet**.
5. Click **OK** .... `Enter`
6. Enter data in worksheet.
7. Click outside of worksheet to return to presentation and display data.

Insert Existing Object File

1. Click **Insert** .... `Alt`+`I`
2. Click **Object** .... `O`
3. In Insert Object dialog box, click **Create from file** .... `Alt`+`F`
4. Click **Browse** .... `B`
5. Select file.
6. Click **OK** .... `Enter`

7. Select **Link** check box .... `L`
8. Click **OK** .... `Enter`

Crop Excel Worksheet

1. Double-click worksheet.
2. Click any of the eight handles on border of object.
3. Drag double-headed arrow to resize object box.

Size Worksheet

1. Select worksheet by clicking it once.
2. Drag corner handle to resize.

Move Worksheet

1. Click worksheet to display four-headed arrow.
2. Drag object box to new position.

Exercise Directions

1. Open **PPT06.doc** as an outline in PowerPoint.

   ✓ *You will need to select All Outlines from the Files of type drop-down list in the Open dialog box.*

2. Save the file as **06TRAVELS**.

3. Apply the Blends design template to the presentation.

4. Go to slide 1 and add the bulleted text shown in Illustration A.

5. Go to slide 2 and insert a clip art. Resize and move the clip art to fit the slide content.

6. Insert a new slide after slide 3. Choose the Title Only text layout slide.

7. Add the title: **Adventure Trends**.

8. Insert a new Microsoft Excel Worksheet and add the data as shown in Illustration B.

   ✓ *Set the view to 100% to make working in the worksheet easier. The toolbar changes, which allows you to format the table as needed.*

9. Crop and resize the worksheet so it looks similar to the one in Illustration B.

10. Move slide 4 to the slide 3 position.

11. Add a new slide to the end of the presentation. Use the Title Only layout.

12. Add the title: **Services**.

13. Insert an existing worksheet and link it. Use the worksheet **06WORKSH.xls**.

14. Crop, size, and move the worksheet if necessary, as shown in Illustration C.

15. Spell check the presentation.

    ✓ *PowerPoint spell check will not catch spelling errors in the embedded Excel worksheet.*

16. Print the presentation as slides.

17. Close the file and exit PowerPoint, saving all changes.

Illustration A

Adventure Travel Packages

- White water rafting
- Backcountry trekking
- Heliskiing
- Snowboarding
- Rock climbing
- ...and more

Adventure Trends

Adventure Travel	% Corporate	% Leisure	% Group
Winter sports	30	50	45
Water rafting	25	32	30
Trekking	45	18	25

Illustration C

Services

Service	Fee	Comments
Custom Group Package	$250.00 per package	Includes consultation, itinerary, travel arrangements
Travel Guide Services	$1000 per week	One travel guide; guide travel expenses not included
Outdoor Gear Rental, Rafting	$25 per person	Includes jacket and headgear for one day
Nature Picnic Catering	$15 per person	Includes a healthy and delicious meal

On Your Own

1. Start PowerPoint and create a presentation outline from the ☉ **OPP06.doc** Word document file.

2. Save the presentation as **OPP06**.

3. Use the outline to create a presentation telling people why they should donate money to a particular charity. You can select any charity you want. Personalize the outline text by replacing the sample text in the outline.

4. Apply a design template to the presentation.

5. Change slide layouts as necessary to set up the slides for titles and bulleted lists. Include space for clip art and an Excel worksheet.

6. Insert clip art where necessary.

7. Save the presentation.

8. Start Excel and create a new workbook, or open ☉ **OPP06XL.xls**.

9. Save the worksheet as **OPP06XL**.

10. Enter or edit the data to set up a worksheet to insert in your presentation. For example, list the income and expenses for the charity, or how much money comes from fundraising.

11. Save the worksheet, close it, and close Excel.

12. Insert the **OPP06XL.xls** worksheet on a slide in the **OPP06** presentation.

13. If necessary, move, crop, or resize the worksheet on the slide so it looks good.

14. Print the slides.

15. Save the presentation and exit PowerPoint.

Exercise 7

When presenting an advertising campaign to a client, you want to offer two or three different designs so that the client can compare layouts and then make a choice. In this exercise, you will create another sample presentation for your client Voyager Travel Adventures.

Exercise Directions

1. Start PowerPoint, if necessary.
2. Create a new presentation using the Watermark design template.
3. Save the file as **07VOYAGER** .
4. Use the Title Slide layout as your first slide.
5. In the Outline pane of Normal view, enter the text as shown in Illustration A.
6. Move to slide 1. Add a clip art or WordArt to one corner of the slide that serves as a logo for Voyager Travel Adventures. You might use a mountain range or travel-oriented clip art.
7. Resize and move as necessary. The logo should be small.
8. Create three more slides adding text to each slide and clip art, if you want.
9. Switch to Slide Sorter view.
10. Move slide 2 after slide 4.
11. Switch back to Normal view.
12. Edit slide 6 by inserting an Excel spreadsheet using the following data:

	1 week	2 weeks	3 weeks
Water Sports	$750	$1075	$2000
Snow Sports	$800	$1250	$2500
Trekking and Climbing	$750	$1000	$1800

13. Resize the worksheet so it fits on the slide and is easy to read.
14. If necessary, switch to the Outline pane in Normal view.
15. Collapse all and print the outline.
16. Select all slides and create a summary slide.
17. Move the summary slides to the end of the presentation and insert a logo on the first summary slide.
18. Spell check the presentation.
19. Expand all and print the outline.
20. Switch to Normal view and print handouts with 3 slides per page in pure black and white.
21. Save the file.
22. Close the file and exit PowerPoint, saving all changes.

Illustration A

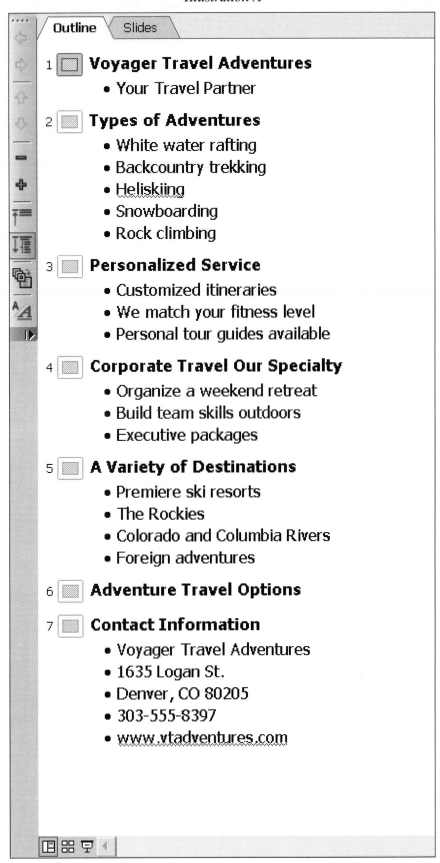

465

Exercise 8

◆ **Select Text** ◆ **Align Text** ◆ **Change the Appearance of Text**
◆ **Change Case** ◆ **Change Slide Color Scheme**
◆ **Change Slide Background**

On the Job

You can change the appearance of text to make it fit the space on the slide better or to add emphasis and interest. Change color schemes or text styles to give a presentation more interest or excitement. For example, a presentation about a sale would use bright colors and informal font styles, whereas a presentation about a financial institution would use more subdued colors and formal fonts.

You work for Regency General, Inc. as a Web site designer. Whole Grains Bread, a company that sells fresh baked bread at various locations around the Western United States, wants you to help them with a Web site to which they can refer prospective customers. One of Whole Grains Bread employees created a PowerPoint presentation. The owner wants you to improve upon the design of the presentation.

Terms

Justified Text is spaced so that both left and right edges of text are even.

Format To change the text appearance by applying a new font face, size, alignment, color, or style.

Color scheme A set of compatible colors in a slide used for background, type, lines, and objects.

Notes

Select Text

- You select text so that you can modify it in some way, like making it larger or bold.

- You can select and edit text in Normal view.

- You can use the mouse pointer either as an I-beam or 4-way arrow to select text in PowerPoint's Outline pane. Drag the I-beam across the text you want to select. Point the 4-way arrow at a line of text to select one or more lines.

- With text in placeholders you must first click on the placeholder to select it, and then double-click to select a line of text.

Align Text

- Align text to the left, center, or right in a placeholder to add interest and to enhance the design.

- You can also use **justified** text alignment, although too much justified text can be difficult to read.

- You can align any one paragraph of text in a text placeholder without changing the other paragraphs of text. In a title placeholder, however, aligning one paragraph realigns all of the paragraphs.

- Align text in the slide pane in Normal view to see the effects on the slide.

Formatting toolbar

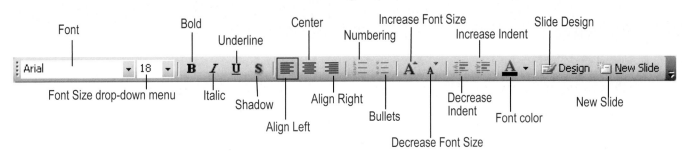

Change the Appearance of Text

■ You can **format** the appearance of text to emphasize it or to make your presentation more readable, interesting, or unique.

■ Text appearance attributes include font family, size, color, style, and special effects.

■ You can change text attributes using techniques similar to those that you used in Word and Excel.

■ As in Word, when changing the appearance of a single word, you do not need to select the word first. You can simply click in the word and apply a new text attribute.

■ Use the Formatting toolbar to change one text attribute at a time.

  ✓ *If you cannot see all of the above buttons, drag the Formatting toolbar below the Standard toolbar to display all of its tools.*

■ Use the Font dialog box to change multiple attributes at one time.

Font dialog box

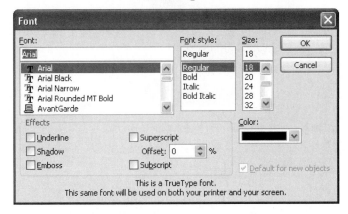

■ You can modify text appearance in Normal view.

  ✓ *Formatting doesn't change the appearance of the outline in the Outline pane even though you can format the text of the slide by selecting and formatting outline text.*

■ When changing a font, you can change a selection on one slide or you can replace one font with another throughout the entire presentation.

■ Be aware that too many text attributes can make a presentation appear "busy" instead of adding to its power to communicate.

Change Case

■ You can change the case of existing text to make it consistent or to correct a typing error.

■ As in Word, you can change the case of text to one of the following:

  • Sentence case: Initial capital letter and lowercase for the rest of the text in the sentence.

  • lowercase: All selected text is lowercase.

  • UPPERCASE: All selected text is uppercase.

  • Title Case: Each word is capitalized.

  • tOGGLE cASE: Reverses the case of the selected text.

Change Slide Color Scheme

■ PowerPoint's design templates each come with a set of predesigned **color schemes** from which you can choose.

■ Each color scheme consists of eight colors that are applied to the slide background, text, lines, shadows, title text, fills, and accents.

■ Click Design on the Formatting toolbar to access the Slide Design task pane. Click Color Schemes to view the different color schemes.

Color Schemes in task pane

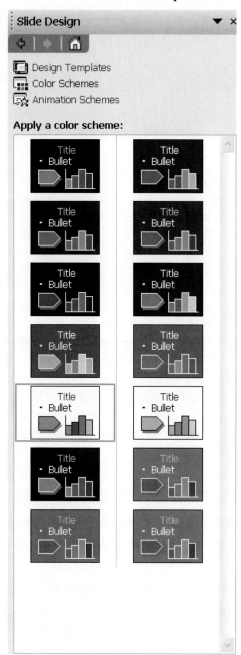

- You can apply a different color scheme to an entire presentation or to just one slide. You might, for example, change the colors on one slide to emphasize that portion of the presentation.

- You can customize a color scheme by changing the colors of individual items, such as the background, title text, or shadows.

Edit Color Scheme Custom tab

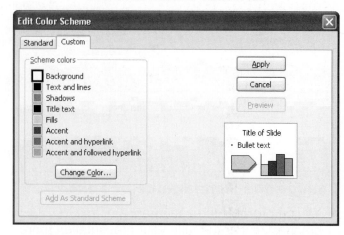

- Avoid using too many different colors, which can make a presentation hard to read.

Change Slide Background

- You can change the color of a slide background, enhance it with a color gradient or pattern, or replace it with a texture effect or picture.

- Change background colors in the Colors dialog box.

Colors dialog box

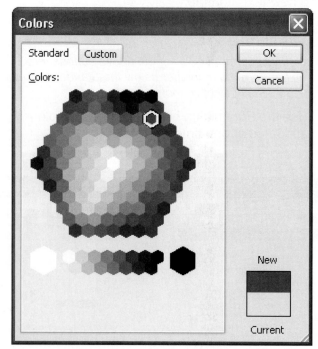

- Although you can combine a background color with a pattern or color gradient, you cannot combine a picture or texture with any other effect.

- You can change the background for a single slide, selected slides, or all slides in a presentation.

Procedures

Select Text

- Double-click to select word.
- Point mouse arrow ⟍ at text in Outline pane and click to select it.

    ✓ *When you select an upper-level title all subtitles and bullets beneath it are selected as well.*

- Click the I-beam at the beginning of the text and drag the mouse to the end of the text to select it.
- Click anywhere on a text placeholder to select the text box.

Align Text *(Ctrl+L, Ctrl+E, Ctrl+R)*

1. Select text or placeholder, or click mouse anywhere in paragraph you want to align.
2. Click **Left Align** ≣, **Center** ≣, or **Right Align** ≣ button.

OR

1. Click **F**ormat .... `Alt`+`O`
2. Click **A**lignment .... `A`
3. Click appropriate alignment:
    - **Align L**eft .... `L`
    - **C**enter .... `C`
    - **Align R**ight .... `R`
    - **J**ustify .... `J`

Change Appearance of Text

1. Select text or click mouse within text to be changed.
2. Click appropriate button on Formatting toolbar.

OR

1. Click **F**ormat .... `Alt`+`O`
2. Click one of the following:
    - **F**ont .... `F`
    - **B**ullets and Numbering .... `B`
    - Line **S**pacing .... `S`
    - **R**eplace Fonts .... `R`
3. Make desired changes in the dialog box that appears.
4. Click **OK** .... `Enter`

Change Case (Shift+F3)

1. Select text.
2. Click **F**ormat .... `Alt`+`O`
3. Click Change Cas**e** .... `E`
4. Click one of the following:
    - **S**entence case. .... `S`
    - **l**owercase .... `L`
    - **U**PPERCASE .... `U`
    - **T**itle Case .... `T`
    - t**OGGLE** c**ASE** .... `G`
5. Click **OK** .... `Enter`

Change Slide's Color Scheme

1. Click **F**ormat .... `Alt`+`O`
2. Click Slide **D**esign .... `D`

OR

    Click the **Design** button .

3. Click **Color Schemes** in the task pane.
4. Click one of the color scheme drop-down arrows to display the pop-up menu.
5. Click one of the following:
    - **Apply to A**ll Slides to apply the scheme to all slides.
    - **Apply to S**elected Slides to apply scheme to selected slides.

    ✓ *You can click the Show L**arge Previews option to view the color schemes in a larger preview.*

Change Color within Color Scheme

1. Click **F**ormat .... `Alt`+`O`
2. Click Slide **D**esign .... `D`
3. Click on Color Schemes.
4. Click **Edit Color Schemes** in the task pane.
5. Click the **Custom** tab .... `Ctrl`+`Tab`
6. In the **Scheme colors** list, select an element .... `S`

7. Click **Change Color** button `Change Color...` .... `O`
8. Click **Standard** tab ...... `Ctrl`+`Tab` for standard colors.

OR

    Click **Custom** tab .... `Ctrl`+`Tab` to add custom color.

9. Click **OK** .... `Enter`
10. Click one of the following:
    - **Preview** button `Preview` .... `Alt`+`P` to view scheme on slide.
    - **Apply** button `Apply` .... `Alt`+`A` to apply scheme to selected slides.

Change Slide Background

1. Click **F**ormat .... `Alt`+`O`
2. Click Bac**k**ground .... `K`
3. Click fill color drop-down box and choose one of the following:
    - **Automatic** to choose assigned scheme color.
    - **Color box** to choose color within scheme.
    - **M**ore Colors to choose custom color .... `M`
    - **F**ill Effects to choose gradient, texture, picture, or pattern .... `F`
4. Select **Omit background graphics from master** check box to remove any lines, boxes, or other graphics inserted on the slide master but retain color on all slides .... `Alt`+`G`
5. Click one of the following:
    - **Preview** button `Preview` .... `Alt`+`P`
    - **Apply** button `Apply` .... `Alt`+`A`
    - **Apply to All** button `Apply to All` .... `Alt`+`T`

Exercise Directions

1. Start PowerPoint, if necessary.

2. Open ⊙ **PPT08**.

3. Save the file as **08BREAD**.

4. In slide 1, select the title **Whole Grains Bread** and enlarge its font size to 80 points.

5. Select the subtitle text that begins **Fresh Baked**… and change it to Times New Roman, italic, 42 points.

6. In slide 2, change the title to **The Freshest Ingredients** and left align it. Change the title to uppercase.

7. In slide 3, left align the title. Change the title to uppercase.

8. Change the remaining slide titles in the presentation to uppercase and left aligned.

9. In slide 4, select the title that begins **Cafe**… and change that text to Algerian, centered, and enlarge the text size to 45 points. Move the Bulleted list object so it doesn't overlap the title object.

10. Replace all occurrences of the Arial font with Times New Roman (Format, Replace Fonts).

11. In slide 7, select row 1 of the table and change the font to Arial, 22-point bold.

12. Select the items (**Bread, Croissants, etc.**) in the table and change the text to Arial, 22-point bold. Select the rest of the table and right-align the text.

13. Select the text **Prices are per item** and change it to Arial, 15-point left aligned. See the example in Illustration A.

14. Change the design template to the Network template.

    ✓ Note that when you apply a design template, individual settings you've made to text format will be overwritten by settings in the template.

15. Change the slide color scheme to the first color scheme. Change the background color in the scheme to a dark blue and look at each slide.

16. Change the color scheme to another scheme and change the background color in that scheme to a lighter color. Apply the change to all of the slides in the presentation.

17. Omit Master Graphics from the first slide.

18. Spell check the presentation.

19. Print the slides.

20. Close the file and exit PowerPoint, saving all changes.

Illustration A

QUANTITY PRICING AVAILABLE

Prices are per item

Item	Dozen	Two Dozen
Bread	$2.99	$1.99
Croissants	$1.75	$1.25
Bagels	$0.60	$0.45
Baguettes	$2.00	$1.75

On Your Own

1. Open **OPP06**, the presentation you used in the On Your Own section of Exercise 6, or open ⊙**OPP08**.

2. Save the file as **OPP08**.

3. Change the case of the titles on all of the slides.

4. Change the font of the subtitle on the Title slide.

5. Change the color scheme for all slides.

6. Change the background for the first slide and the last slide.

7. Save the changes, close the presentation, and exit PowerPoint.

Exercise 9

◆ **Copy Text Formatting** ◆ **Move and Copy Text**
◆ **Increase/Decrease Paragraph Spacing**
◆ **Move, Size, Copy, and Delete Placeholders and Other Objects**

On the Job

Modify text formatting and size placeholders to make more room on a slide for text or objects. For instance, you might need to add an extra bullet to the list, add a chart to a slide, or move text from one slide to another.

Your client asked that you revise the presentation to make it a bit less crowded and change some of the formatting. In this exercise, you'll enhance and edit the presentation for Whole Grains Bread.

Terms

Format Painter A tool that lets you copy text formatting from one text selection and apply it to any other text in the presentation.

Paragraph spacing The amount of space between two blocks of text, such as two bullet points.

Placeholder border A gray shaded area around the edge of a placeholder, used to move a placeholder. You can also click on a placeholder to select the text or apply font changes.

Sizing handles Any of eight small black boxes located on a placeholder's border, used to resize the placeholder.

Notes

Copy Text Formatting

- Just as in Word, you can quickly copy and apply text formatting in PowerPoint by using the **Format Painter**.
- You can copy text and object formatting and apply it to one or multiple text blocks or objects.

Move and Copy Text

- As you review a slide or presentation, you may rearrange the text to make it easier to follow.
- Just as in Word, you can move text in PowerPoint using drag-and-drop or cut-and-paste methods.

- Use the drag-and-drop method to move text to a nearby location. When you move text, a vertical line moves with the mouse to help you position the text.
- Use the cut-and-paste method to move text between two locations that are set far apart.
- You can also use the drag-and-drop feature to move text on a slide or between slides in a presentation from the Outline pane. You can move text to a new location on a slide in the Slide pane.
- You can cut and paste text to a new location on the same slide, a different slide, or a different presentation using either the Slides or the Outline pane.
- You can also copy and paste text between slides and between presentations.

Increase/Decrease Paragraph Spacing

- Adjust **paragraph spacing** between bullets or other paragraphs to make text easier to read or to balance the space better.
- You can adjust the space between paragraphs gradually by using the Increase 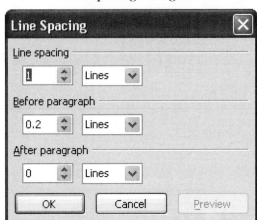 and Decrease Paragraph Spacing buttons.
- To set paragraph spacing to a specific amount, use the Line Spacing dialog box.

Line Spacing dialog box

Move, Size, Copy, and Delete Placeholders and Other Objects

- You can move or size any text or object placeholder or any other object, such as a clip art image, to make room for slide contents.
- You can also delete or copy any placeholder or other object.
- To move, size, copy, or delete an object, you need to select it first so that its **placeholder border** and **sizing handles** appear.

Placeholder border and handles

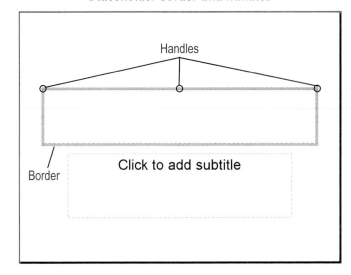

- Then drag the border or sizing handles to complete the task.
- When you click on a placeholder and drag it, the border changes from cross-hatching to dots.

Procedures

Copy Text Formatting to One Item

1. Select text containing format you want to copy.
2. Click **Format Painter** button 🖌️ on the Standard toolbar.
3. Select text that you want to change.

Copy Text Formatting to Multiple Items

1. Select text containing format you want to copy.
2. Double-click **Format Painter** button 🖌️ on the Standard toolbar.
3. Select text that you want to change.
4. When you're done formatting, press **Esc** or click the **Format Painter** button 🖌️ to deactivate Format Painter.

Drag-and-Drop Text

1. Position mouse to left of text in Outline pane so pointer changes to four-headed arrow ✛.
2. Click once to highlight a bullet item and its subitems.
3. Drag mouse pointer to its new position.
4. Release mouse button.
   - ✓ *When moving text, make sure horizontal line representing text is in appropriate position before you release mouse button.*

Cut or Copy and Paste Text

1. Select text to be moved or copied.
2. Click **Cut** button ✂️ to move text. .... Ctrl + X

   OR

   Click **Copy** button 📄 to copy text. .... Ctrl + V
3. Position mouse where you want to insert text.
4. Click **Paste** button 📋.

Add Increase/Decrease Paragraph Spacing Buttons to Toolbar

1. Display Formatting toolbar.
2. Click **Toolbar Options** button ▾.
3. Click **Add or Remove Buttons, Formatting** .... A
4. Click the **Increase Paragraph Spacing** 📑 and **Decrease Paragraph Spacing** 📑 buttons.
5. Click outside of menu to close it.

Increase/Decrease Paragraph Spacing

1. Select paragraphs you want to adjust.
2. Click **Increase** 📑 or **Decrease** 📑 **Paragraph Spacing** button until space is as you want it.

Move Placeholder or Other Object

1. Click in placeholder or graphic to select it.
2. Position mouse on border so pointer changes to four-headed arrow ✛.
3. Drag object to new position.

Size Placeholder or Other Object

1. Click in placeholder or graphic to select it.
2. Position mouse on sizing handle so pointer changes to two-headed arrow ↘.
3. Drag handle in or out until placeholder is desired size.

Copy Placeholder *(Ctrl+C, Ctrl+V)*

1. Click in object placeholder to select it.

   OR

   Select text placeholder and click placeholder border.
2. Click **Edit** .... Alt + E
3. Click **Copy** C
4. Move to slide, presentation, or position in which you want the copied material to appear.
5. Click **Edit** .... Alt + E
6. Click **Paste** .... P

Delete Placeholder

1. Click in object placeholder to select it.

   OR

   Select text placeholder and click placeholder border.
2. Press **Delete** key. .... Del
   - ✓ *The placeholder "Click to add" text returns when you delete the placeholder's contents.*

Exercise Directions

1. Start PowerPoint, if necessary.

2. Open 💿 **PPT09**.

3. Save the file as **09BREAD**.

4. In Normal view, go to slide 2. Change the text in the title **THE FRESHEST INGREDIENTS** to Times New Roman, 44 point.

5. Copy that formatting to all titles in the remaining slides of the presentation, except for the title on slide 4.

   ✓ Note that some titles may resize slightly to fit in the allotted space. Also some titles may have to be repositioned to fit on the slide once the font is enlarged.

   ✓ Note that if you want formatting to be consistent on most slides in a presentation you can use the Slide Master feature rather than copying. Slide masters are covered in Exercise 10.

6. In slide 3, delete the third and fourth bullets: **Bagels** and **Muffins**.

7. Add an appropriate clip art image.

8. Move and size the clip art to fit in the lower-right corner, as shown in Illustration A.

9. In slide 4, change the bullet to read: **Gourmet soups, sandwiches, and salads at reasonable prices**.

10. Add a second bullet point: **Franchises available**. Move the first bullet to the end of the bulleted list.

11. Change the text format of all of the bullets on slide 4 to Times New Roman, 24 point. Add a clip art to the right corner of the slide, as shown in Illustration B.

    ✓ Resizing a placeholder can result in changing the font size.

    ✓ If you don't have the Algerian font on your computer, the title may not display correctly. If so, select a different font.

12. Change the slide layout in slide 6 to Title and 2-Column Text and add the text shown in Illustration C.

13. Move the **Fresh-picked fruits** bullet to the first bulleted list. Move or resize the bullet placeholders to balance them on the page.

14. In slide 7, move the Title placeholder (**Quantity Pricing Available***)* down about 1/4". Move the table down about 1/4" as well.

15. Spell check the presentation.

16. Print the slides in Slide view.

17. Close the file and exit PowerPoint, saving all changes.

A VARIETY OF BAKED GOODS

- Breads and baguettes
- Croissants
- Rolls
- Pastries

CAFÉ BRANCHES AROUND THE WEST

- Franchises available
- Gourmet soups, sandwiches, and salads at reasonable prices

Illustration C

On Your Own

1. Open **OPP08**, the presentation you used in Exercise 8, or open ⊙ **OPP09**.

2. Save the file as **OPP09**.

3. Copy the formatting from the subtitle on the Title slide to the bulleted text on all other slides.

4. Move the bulleted items on slide 2 to rearrange them.

5. Increase the paragraph spacing on slides 2 and 3 to improve the appearance of bulleted items.

6. Decrease the size of a clip art object on a slide and position it so it looks good.

7. Save the presentation, close it, and exit PowerPoint.

Exercise 10

◆ **Use Slide and Title Masters** ◆ **Slide Master View**
◆ **Insert Slide Numbers, Date and Time, and Footer Text**
◆ **Format Bullets**

On the Job

Use a slide or title master to make each slide in the presentation consistent. You might, for example, want to add the same art or logo to each slide and to change the format of the bullets so they match throughout the presentation.

You have created a second presentation to show your client Whole Grains Bread because you know it is always best to give a client at least two ideas from which to choose. You still need to go over the second presentation to make it more interesting and professional.

Terms

Slide master A template slide that contains colors, text, placeholders, and other items that appear on all slides in the same position. If you make a change to the slide master, all slides in the set change, too.

Title master A template slide that contains text or design elements for the title slide only.

Footer An area at the bottom of a slide in which you can enter a date, slide number, or other information. Any text you enter in the footer appears on all slides in the presentation.

Notes

Use Slide and Title Master

- Each design template has its own **slide master**.
- A slide master contains text characteristics, background and other colors, and placeholders.
- If you want to make a change to all the slides in a presentation (except for the title slide), change the slide master. You might, for example, want to add a logo or slogan to each slide.
- Changes that affect all slides might include adding a picture, adjusting a placeholder, or changing fonts.

- To add text or objects to a slide master, insert a text box or an object box.
    - ✓ Note that text entered in a text box will not appear in the presentation outline.
- If you want to use different default elements for all slides with the title slide layout in a presentation, use the **title master**.
- A title master contains characteristics and elements for only the title slide layout.

Slide Master View

■ You edit the slide master in Slide Master view.

Slide Master view

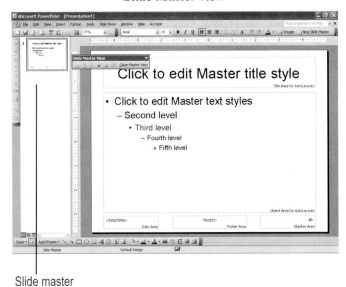

Slide master

■ Changes you make in Slide Master view apply to all slides within the presentation, except title slides.

■ You can make changes to the title or master slide at any time during the creation of a presentation.

■ Formatting changes that you make to individual slides after you finalize the slide master will override slide master settings.

■ You can also customize individual slides to omit slide master background graphics.

Insert Slide Numbers, Date and Time, and Footer Text

■ Include a slide number in the **footer** of a slide to identify the slide's position in the presentation.

■ Add the date and time to a slide footer so you can tell when it was created or updated.

■ You can use a slide footer to identify a presentation's topic, author, client, or other information.

Header and Footer dialog box

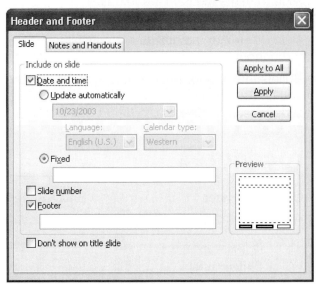

■ You can include slide numbers, dates, times, and other footer text on one slide or every slide in a presentation.

■ Placeholders for slide numbers, the date and time, and footer text appear on the slide and title masters.

■ If you want to change the location of an element in the footer, you must do so on the slide master.

Format Bullets

■ You can change the color, size, and/or character of any bullet.

Bullets and Numbering dialog box

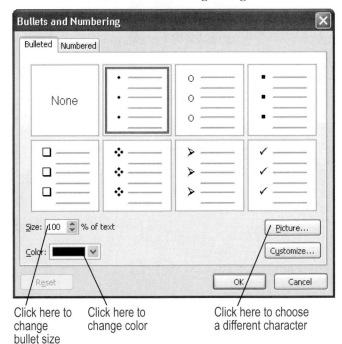

Click here to change bullet size

Click here to change color

Click here to choose a different character

- Change the characteristics of a bullet on one slide to make the item stand out.
- Change the characteristics of bullets in a slide master so the bullets are consistent throughout the presentation.
- Bullets that you format on individual slides after you finalize the slide master will override the slide master settings.

- As in Word or Excel, you can turn a bullet off if you prefer text without bullets.
- Too many bullet types in a slide put emphasis on design instead of on the content, so use your discretion.

Procedures

View Slide Master

1. Click **View** .... `Alt`+`V`
2. Click **Master** .... `M`
3. Click **Slide Master** .... `S`

   OR

   Press Shift and click the **Slide Master View** button `⊞`.

   ✓ *The Normal View button changes to the Slide Master View button when Shift is pressed.*
4. In the Slides pane, click on either the slide master or title master to make changes.

View Footers

1. Click **View** .... `Alt`+`V`
2. Click **Header and Footer** ... `H`

Enter Date and Time

1. Click **View** .... `Alt`+`V`
2. Click **Header and Footer** ... `H`
3. Select **Date and time** check box .... `D`
4. Click one of the following:
   - **Update automatically** .... `Alt`+`U`

     Select date/time format.
   - **Fixed** .... `Alt`+`X`

     Enter date and/or time.
5. Click one of the following:
   - **Apply** button [Apply] to apply change to one slide .... `Alt`+`A`
   - **Apply to All** button [Apply to All] to apply change to all slides .. `Alt`+`Y`

Enter Slide Number

1. Click **View** .... `Alt`+`V`
2. Click **Header and Footer** .... `H`
3. Select **Slide number** check box .... `Alt`+`N`
4. Click one of the following:
   - **Apply** button [Apply] to apply change to one slide .... `Alt`+`A`
   - **Apply to All** button [Apply to All] to apply change to all slides ... `Alt`+`Y`

Enter Footer Text

1. Click **View** .... `Alt`+`V`
2. Click **Header and Footer** .... `H`
3. Click **Footer** check box .... `F`
4. Enter text in **Footer** text box.
5. Click one of the following:
   - **Apply** button [Apply] to apply change to one slide .... `Alt`+`A`
   - **Apply to All** button [Apply to All] to apply change to all slides ... `Alt`+`Y`

Format Bullets

1. Select bulleted text.
2. Click **Format** .... `Alt`+`O`
3. Click **Bullets and Numbering** .... `B`
4. Click **Bulleted** tab ...... `Ctrl`+`Tab`
5. Click bullet example or choose your own **Picture** to use art or **Customize** to change the bullet character.
6. Click **Color** .... `Alt`+`C` to change bullet color. (You may need to repeat steps 1–4 if the dialog box closed.)
7. Click **OK** .... `Enter`

Omit Master Graphics on Individuals Slides

1. Display the slide on which you want to omit the graphics.
2. Click **Format** .... `Alt`+`O`
3. Click **Background** .... `K`
4. Click the **Omit background graphics from master** .... `G` check box.

Exercise Directions

1. Start PowerPoint, if necessary.

2. Open the file ☉ **PPT10**.

3. Save the file as **10BREAD**.

4. Go to title Slide Master view and display the title master.

5. Follow the steps to create a logo for Whole Grains Bread using an appropriate clip art image with a text box over it, and place it in the upper-right hand corner of the slide, as shown in Illustration A.

   a. Insert appropriate clip art.

   b. Resize and move the clip art to the upper-right corner as shown in the illustration.

   c. Insert a text box and enter the text **WGB**.

   d. You may want to change the color or typeface of the text so it stands out (Format, Font, Color or Font).

6. Follow these directions to copy the logo (hold the Shift key as you select the clip art and the logo text) and paste it to the bulleted list slide master.

   a. Copy the logo in Slide Master view.

   b. Click the slide master in the Slides pane.

   c. Paste the logo in the lower-right corner.

   ✓ If text and other graphics interfere with the logo, you can resize the placeholder of the bulleted text to make room for the logo.

7. Display the title master. Change the color scheme on the title master. Add a striped background (Format, Background).

8. Switch back to Normal view.

9. Go to the end of the slide presentation and add a slide. Choose the Title Slide layout. Enter the text as shown in Illustration B.

10. Add a new slide using the Title and 2-Column Text slide layout. Add text as shown in Illustration C.

11. Move to slide 1. Insert an automatically updating date, left aligned, and the text **The West's Best Bread**, center aligned. Do not apply the footer to all slides.

12. Move to slide 7 and omit the master graphics from it.

13. Move to slide 3 and change the color of the bullets.

14. Move the clip art where it overlaps the logo on the bottom of the slide, and place it as shown in Illustration D.

15. Increase the paragraph spacing between the bullets in slide 5.

16. On slide 5, change the numbers into a different character, size, and color to make them stand out more. Illustration E offers one example.

17. Spell check the presentation.

18. Save the file.

19. Print handouts of the slide presentation with 4 slides per page.

20. Close the file and exit PowerPoint, saving all changes.

On Your Own

1. Open **OPP09**, the presentation you used in Exercise 9, or open ☉ **OPP10**.

2. Save the file as **OPP10**.

3. Add the date, time, and slide number in the footer of all slides except the title slide.

4. Change the slide master to include the name of the organization in the upper-right corner of all slides.

5. Select a different style for the bullets on the slide master.

6. On one slide in the presentation, use a different bullet style in a different color.

7. Save the presentation, close it, and exit PowerPoint.

Illustration A

Illustration B

Illustration C

Illustration D

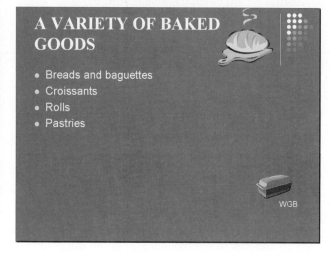

Illustration E

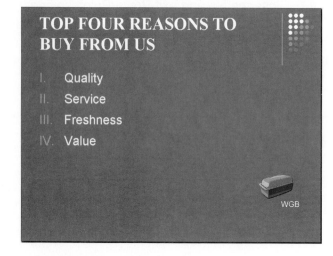

Skills Covered:

◆ **Use Rulers and Guides** ◆ **Floating Toolbars** ◆ **Draw Graphic Objects**
◆ **AutoShapes** ◆ **Group and Ungroup Objects** ◆ **Layer Objects**

On the Job

Use PowerPoint's many drawing tools to help enhance a presentation. You might use rulers and guides to line up text or drawing objects, for example. You might draw logos, illustrations, or other objects to add to your slides.

The owner of Whole Grains Bread is thinking about putting the presentation that you are designing on the Web. In this exercise, you will add design elements to the second presentation you created for them. You'll also add some buttons that make the presentation more suitable to the Web.

Terms

Guides Nonprinting vertical and horizontal lines you can use to align objects on a slide.

Floating toolbar Any toolbar that you can move with the mouse around on the screen for easier access and viewing.

Dock To affix a floating toolbar to the edge of the PowerPoint screen.

AutoShapes A set of tools that makes drawing common geometric shapes fast and easy.

Group To join multiple objects into a single object so that they are easier to move and manipulate.

Notes

Use Rulers and Guides

Rulers in Normal view

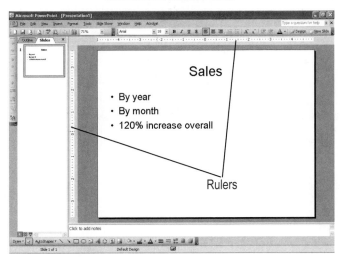

- PowerPoint provides a vertical and horizontal ruler that you can show or hide at any time.
- Use the rulers to adjust indents or add tabs to text.
- You can also use rulers to align objects on the slide.
- The ruler's origins (0 measurement on the ruler) change depending on whether you're using text or an object.
- The origin appears on the edge of the ruler when you're working with text and in the center point of the ruler when you're working with an object.
- As you move the mouse pointer, an indicator moves on each ruler showing your horizontal and vertical locations.

- **Guides** are alignment tools that help you line up objects and text.

Guides in Normal view

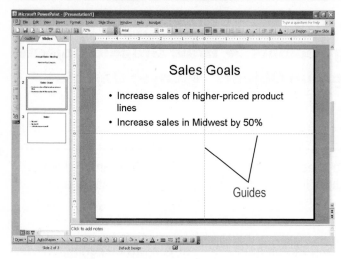

- PowerPoint supplies one vertical and one horizontal guide that you can move and copy.
- Use rulers and guides to make your work look more exact and professional.

Floating Toolbars

- A **floating toolbar** is one that is not attached to the edge of the program window. Certain toolbars float by default, such as the WordArt and Tables and Borders toolbars. The Standard and Formatting toolbars do not float by default, but they can be dragged from their position and float anywhere in the program window.

- A move handle on a floating menu's submenu enables you to create a floating toolbar from the submenu.
- You can resize a floating toolbar and move it anywhere on the screen.

Floating toolbars

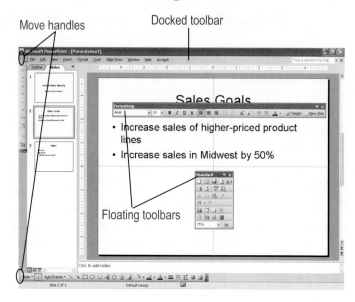

- Use a floating toolbar to see all available buttons on it or to move it closer to a section on which you're working.
- You can **dock** a floating toolbar on the left, top, or bottom of the program window. The Standard and Formatting toolbars are typically docked by default.

Draw Graphic Objects

Drawing toolbar

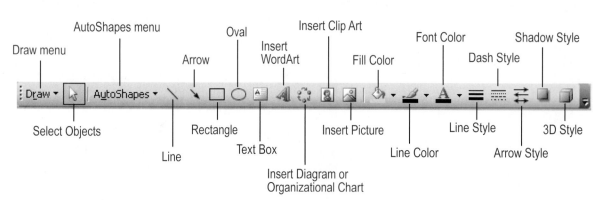

- Use the Drawing toolbar to create objects such as lines, rectangles, and ovals.

- Drawings are objects that you can move, size, copy, and delete, just like any other object in PowerPoint.

- You can draw on a slide master, or on a slide in Notes Page view, but whatever you draw on a notes page will not be reflected on slides in any other view.

- Using the Drawing toolbar, you can also fill the shapes and draw lines with colors. You can change line styles and colors, arrow styles, and fill colors.

- The Drawing toolbar displays with all views except Slide Sorter.

AutoShapes

- Use **AutoShapes** to draw arrows, stars, circles, and other shapes into a slide quickly and easily.

- AutoShapes are objects, so they can be copied, resized, and moved just like placeholders and other objects.

- You can use the tools on the Drawing toolbar to enhance and modify AutoShapes.

  - Use Lines to create curves, arrows, and freeform lines.

  - Use Connectors to connect objects on a slide.

  - Basic Shapes include circles, rectangles, triangles, parentheses, brackets, and so on.

  - Block Arrows are decorative arrows of all kinds.

  - Use Flowchart to create organizational chart shapes.

  - Stars and Banners include ribbon and star shapes.

  - Use Callouts to create special text boxes that can be used to create labels in slides. There are several styles, including cartoon bubbles.

- Use Action buttons to create navigation buttons such as Next, Back, and Help. You use Action Buttons to give users control over the presentation.

Group and Ungroup Objects

- You can **group** the objects within a drawing to make them into one composition that will keep the position of each object. Grouped objects are also easier to copy or move.

- When you group objects, you only need to click once to select the entire group of objects.

- You can ungroup objects when you want to edit or delete an individual object in the group.

- When ungrouped all the individual objects are still selected. Click anywhere outside of the objects to deselect them.

Ungrouped and grouped objects

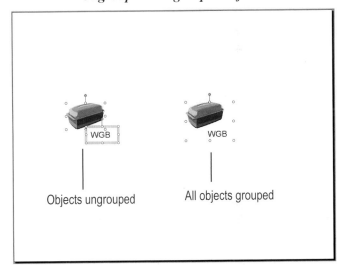

Objects ungrouped   All objects grouped

Layer Objects

- You can layer objects one on top of another to create depth or add perspective in a drawing.

- After drawing an object, you can move it to the front or to the back of a layered stack.

- You can also move objects forward or backward in a layer one object at a time.

Procedures

Display Rulers and Guides

1. Click **View**.................. `Alt`+`V`
2. Click **Ruler**....................... `R`
3. Click **View**.................. `Alt`+`V`
4. Click **Grid and Guides**...... `I`
5. Click **Display drawing guides on screen**...................... `I`
6. Click **OK**........................ `Enter`

Copy Guide

• Hold **Ctrl** key and drag existing guide.

Delete Guide

• Drag guide off screen.

Floating Toolbars

To create floating toolbar:

1. Drag toolbar's handle away from program window's edge.
   ✓ *Some toolbars float by default but can be docked.*
   OR
   Drag move handle away from submenu to create floating toolbar.
2. Move floating toolbar by dragging its title bar.
3. Size floating toolbar by dragging its border .

To dock floating toolbar:

• Move toolbar to edge of program window.

Draw Graphic Objects

1. Click **Line** , **Arrow** , **Oval** , or **Rectangle** tool on Drawing toolbar.
   ✓ *Press Shift key as you draw rectangle or oval to create a straight line, a perfect square, or circle.*
2. Position crosshair ╋ on slide and drag to create object.
3. Click **Select** tool .
4. Select object by clicking it.
5. Click one of the following buttons on Drawing toolbar to apply to selected object:

   • **Fill Color** to display colors and fill effects.
   • **Line Color** to display colors and fill effects.
   • **Line Style** to display various line widths.
   • **Dash Style** to display available dash types.
   • **Arrow Style** to display various arrow shapes.

Draw AutoShapes

1. Click **AutoShapes** menu...... `Alt`+`U` on Drawing toolbar.
2. Click one of the following:

   • **Lines**........................... `L`
   • **Connectors**.................. `N`
   • **Basic Shapes**.............. `B`
   • **Block Arrows**............... `A`
   • **Flowchart**.................... `F`
   • **Stars and Banners**........ `S`
   • **Callouts**...................... `C`
   • **Action Buttons**............. `I`
   • **More AutoShapes**......... `M`

3. Select shape you want from submenu.
4. Click or drag mouse on slide to create shape.

Group Objects

1. Click first object.
2. Hold down **Shift** key while clicking other objects to be grouped.
3. Click **Draw**.................. `Alt`+`R`
4. Click **Group**........................ `G`

Ungroup Objects

1. Select object.
2. Click **Draw**.................. `Alt`+`R`
3. Click **Ungroup** .... `U`
   OR
   a. Right-click object.
   b. Click **Grouping**............. `G`
   c. Click **Ungroup** .... `U`

Layer Objects

1. Select object.
2. Click **Draw**.................. `Alt`+`R`
3. Click **Order**.......................... `R`
   OR
   a. Right-click object.
   b. Click **Order** .... `R`
4. Click one of the following:
   • **Bring to Front**.............. `U`
   • **Send to Back** .... `K`
   • **Bring Forward** .... `F`
   • **Send Backward** .... `B`

Exercise Directions

1. Start PowerPoint, if necessary.

2. Open 💿 **PPT11**.

3. Save the file as **11BREAD**.

4. Display the Slide Master view and click on the title master. Add two horizontal lines of different weight (one thicker than the other) near the bottom of the slide, above the footer area, similar to those in Illustration A.

   ✓ *Press and hold the Shift key while drawing the line to make it absolutely straight. Release the mouse button before you release the Shift key.*

5. Apply colors to the lines that match the slide color scheme by selecting the line and clicking the Line Color button.

6. Create a new Whole Grains Bread logo in the title master to replace the existing one. You can use AutoShapes, lines, WordArt, and other drawing tools. Apply a color fill to part of the logo, such as gray or yellow. An example appears in Illustration B.

7. Change to Normal view.

8. Switch to slide 5. Omit master graphics from the slide.

9. Draw three AutoShape stars as in Illustration C, and apply a different fill color to each. Make sure the colors match the slide's color scheme.

10. Overlap the stars as shown in Illustration C. Move the last star you drew to the back and the first star to the front. Group the stars and position them as shown in Illustration C.

11. Add a text box below the stars with the text shown in Illustration C. Format the text to Times New Roman, 24 points, bold, and italic.

12. Display the rulers.

13. Move to slide 3. Remove the bullets from the bulleted text.

14. Widen the placeholder so it reaches the right side of the slide and, using the ruler, set tabs so that the second line of text is 1", the third line another 1" and the fourth line another 1".

    ✓ *Note: You may have to adjust the indent markers.*

    ✓ *Refer to the Word section for information about setting tabs.*

15. Move the clip art near the title to the bottom-left corner of the slide. Resize the clip art if necessary.

16. Go to slide 9. Insert any Action button from AutoShapes. In the Action Settings dialog box, select the First Slide hyperlink. Select any sound option you want. Position the button as shown in Illustration D.

17. Go to slide 7 and omit the background graphic from the Slide Master.

18. Run the presentation to make sure the effects work.

    ✓ *To run the presentation, click View, Slide Show.*

19. Spell check the presentation.

20. Print the presentation.

21. Save and close the file.

Illustration A

Illustration B

Illustration C

TOP FOUR REASONS TO BUY FROM US

I. Quality

II. Service

III. Freshness

IV. Value

Award Winning!

Illustration D

Catering

- Restaurant service
- Custom catering for large parties
- Do-it-yourself party platters

- Full line of bread products
- Homemade soups
- Gourmet sandwiches

WGB

On Your Own

1. Open **OPP10**, the presentation you used in Exercise 10, or open ⊙**OPP11**.

2. Save the file as **OPP11**.

3. Display the slide rulers.

4. Insert an AutoShape on the title slide. For example, insert a lightning bolt, a star, or any other object.

5. Use the Drawing tools to draw a simple picture on a different slide. For example, draw a bunch of balloons, a cat, or a flower.

6. Group the drawn objects and move them to a different location on the slide.

7. Save the presentation, close it, and exit PowerPoint.

Exercise 12

On the Job

Customize a template to create your own unique presentations. Your custom template, for example, might contain the same color scheme and graphic images that you use in your other company materials, such as a newsletter, letterhead, and brochure.

You work for Murray Hill Marketing, LLC. Michigan Avenue Athletic Club is a client of your company. The company runs a fitness center in Chicago. The owner of Michigan Avenue Athletic Club wants you to create a custom template in PowerPoint that you can use for several presentations as part of a special public relations campaign for the company.

Terms

Template A foundation on which to build a presentation; a template may contain colors, graphics, fonts, and type styles.

Notes

Customize a Template

- You can customize a **template** to suit your presentation topic better. Or, you can create a template from a presentation you have already created. Any text, graphics, or other contents of the existing presentation will be saved with the template.

- Customize a template to change color schemes, background graphics, font formatting, and so on.

- Use the slide master to add modifications to all slides in a template.

- After you create the look you want, save the template so you can base other presentations on it.

Save and Apply a Custom Template

- You can save any presentation as a custom template.

- After you save a custom template, you can use it as a basis for other presentations.

- Modifying a content template can make creating custom presentations quick and easy.

Procedures

Create Custom Template

1. Open existing presentation.
   OR
   Open new blank design template or content template presentation.
2. Modify slide master, fonts, contents, color schemes, and other design elements.
3. Click **File** .... `Alt`+`F`
4. Click **Save As** .... `A`
5. Click **Save as type** ..... `Alt`+`T`
6. Select **Design Template**.
7. Save template in default folder:
8. Name the template.
9. Click **Save** .... `Alt`+`S`

Add Custom Template to AutoContent Wizard *(Ctrl+N)*

1. Click **File**.................... `Alt`+`F`
2. Click **New** .... `N`
3. In the task pane, click **From AutoContent wizard**.
4. Click **Next** .... `Alt`+`N`
5. Click **General** button ... `Alt`+`G`
   - ✓ *You cannot add content template to All category.*
6. Click **Add**.................... `Alt`+`D`
7. Name your custom template.
8. Click **OK** .... `Enter`
9. Click **Finish** .... `Alt`+`F`

Apply Custom Template

1. Click **File** .... `Alt`+`F`
2. Click **New** .... `N`
3. In the task pane, click **On my computer** in the **Templates** section.
4. Click the **General** tab.
5. Select the custom template on which to base new presentation.
6. Click **OK** .... `Enter`

Exercise Directions

1. Start PowerPoint, if necessary, and open a blank presentation.
2. Add a slide color scheme. You can customize the colors, if you want. Apply the color scheme to all slides.
3. Go to the Slide Master view. Replace all Arial or Times New Roman fonts with Goudy Old Style or any other serif font.
4. On the slide master, add some graphic lines, shapes, clip art, and/or other design effects to make the slide interesting. See Illustration A for an example.
5. Create a logo for Michigan Avenue Athletic Club. You can use clip art images or create a drawing. Place the logo on the slide master.
6. Save the file as a template: **12Michigan.pot**.
7. Close the file.
8. Start a new presentation using the custom template.
9. Save the file as **12Michigan.ppt**.
10. Enter text in the title slide as shown in Illustration B.
11. Add a bulleted list slide and enter the text as shown in Illustration C.
    - ✓ *You may have to resize the placeholder.*
12. Spell check the presentation.
13. Print the presentation.
14. Save and close the file.

Illustration A

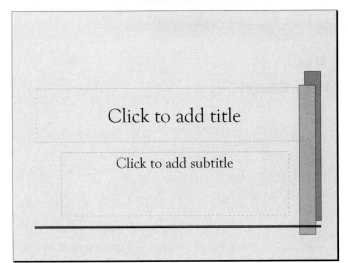

Illustration B

Illustration C

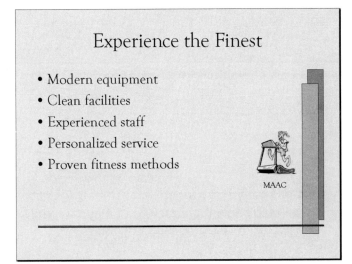

On Your Own

1. Create a new presentation based on a blank template.

2. On the master slide apply colors, select fonts, select bullets, and insert graphics as desired to customize the template.

3. Save the presentation as a template with the name **OPP12.pot**.

4. Create a new presentation based on the **OPP12.pot** template.

5. Save the presentation as **OPP12-2.ppt**.

6. Create a presentation about a friend, family member, or pet. Include at least three slides.

7. Save the presentation, close it, and exit PowerPoint.

Exercise 13

Skills Covered:

◆ Insert Organization Chart Slide

On the Job

Add an organization chart to your presentation to illustrate the structure of your organization. For example, show the relationship between store managers and their staff or between the vice presidents of the company and their assistants and managers.

Recently there have been changes in employee status at Restoration Architecture—several people were promoted and others left the company. The owners of Restoration Architecture have asked you to create an organization chart showing the current company structure.

Terms

Organization chart An illustration of the top-down structure (the *hierarchy*) of positions within an organization, usually starting with the chief executive.

Notes

Insert Organization Chart Slide

- An **organization chart** can illustrate a company's or organization's structure.

Organization chart

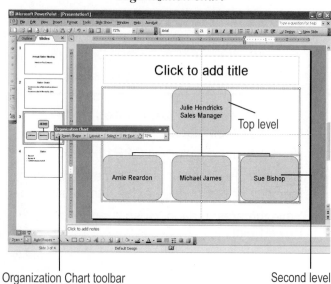

Organization Chart toolbar   Second level

- It can also show the structure of a department, project, exercise, process, procedure, or family tree.

- You can create an organization chart by using any layout that includes a content placeholder and clicking the Insert Diagram or Organization Chart icon. You can also insert one without a placeholder by using the Insert menu.

- You can choose to insert any diagram type, including the Organization Chart, a Pyramid Diagram, Target Diagram, and others.

- When you insert an organization chart, four boxes appear. You can add, delete, and type in the boxes as desired.

- PowerPoint includes an Organization Chart toolbar that has menus for adding boxes, changing the layout of the chart, and selecting parts of the chart.

- An organization chart can be moved, copied, and deleted just like any other object.

Procedures

Create Organization Chart

1. Apply a layout that contains a content placeholder.
2. Click the **Insert Diagram or Organization Chart** icon 🔄.
3. Click the **Organization Chart** icon 🖧 and then click **OK**.
4. Click in any box and begin typing to enter text.
5. Press **Enter** to add another line of text in box.

Select Box

- Click the border of a box.
    - ✓ *If you want to format text in a box be sure when you click the border of a box that 8 sizing handles appear around the edges. If you want to edit text in a box click in it so that a gray shaded area appears around it.*

Add New Boxes to Organization Chart

1. Select box to which you want to attach new box.
2. To add box, click the arrow on **Insert Shape** .... `Alt`+`N` and then press up or down to select a shape type.
    - **Subordinate**................... `S`
    - **Coworker** .... `C`
    - **Assistant**........................ `A`
3. Repeat step 2 until chart is complete.

Type in a Box

- Click within the box and enter text.

Select Multiple Boxes

1. From Organization Chart toolbar, click **Select** ..... `Alt`+`C`
2. Choose one of the following:
    - **Level** .... `L`
    - **Branch** .... `B`
    - **All Assistants** .... `A`
    - **All Connecting Lines** .... `C`

OR

- Hold down **Shift** key and click on multiple boxes.

Delete Box

1. Select box.
2. Press **Delete** key .... `Del`

OR

1. Right-click the box.
2. Click **Delete**......................... `D`

Format Fonts

1. From Organization chart, select box that contains text you want to format.
2. Click **Format** .... `Alt`+`O`
3. Click **Font**........................... `F`
    - ✓ *You can also select a box and use the tools on the Formatting toolbar to apply formats one by one.*
4. Click **OK** .... `Enter`

Change Chart Layout

1. From Organization Chart toolbar, click **Layout** .... `Alt`+`L`
2. Click one of the following:
    - **Standard**........................ `S`
    - **Both Hanging**................. `B`
    - **Left Hanging** .... `L`
    - **Right Hanging**............... `R`
    - **AutoLayout** .... `A`

Change Alignment

1. From Organization chart, select the box containing text you want to align.
2. Click **Format** .... `Alt`+`O`
3. Click **Alignment**................. `A`
4. Click one of the following:
    - **Align Left**...................... `L`
    - **Center**........................... `C`
    - **Align Right** .... `R`
    - **Justify**........................... `J`

Change Box Color

1. From Organization chart, double-click box.
2. Click **Colors and Lines** tab.
3. Click **Color**................. `Alt`+`C`
4. Select color.
5. Click **OK**........................... `Enter`

OR

1. Select the box to be formatted.
2. Click the drop-down arrow of the **Fill** button 🖌▼ on the Tables and Borders or the Draw toolbar.
3. Select a color from the display.

OR

- Click **More Fill Colors**... `M`
    - ✓ *This option displays a color palette from which you can select a suitable color.*
- Click **Fill Effects** .... `F`
    - ✓ *This option displays a dialog box from which you can choose:*
    - **Gradient**
    - **Texture**
    - **Pattern**
    - **Picture**
    - ✓ *The row of colors under Automatic lets you apply a color that is consistent with the color scheme of the design template you are using for the presentation.*
    - ✓ *Other colors may appear if you have selected fill colors on other slides.*

Change Box Border

1. From Organization chart, double-click box.
2. Click **Colors and Lines** tab.
3. Click one of the following:
    - **Line Color** .... `O`
    - **Style** .... `S`
    - **Weight**........................... `W`
    - **Dashed**.......................... `D`
4. Click **OK** .... `Enter`

Exercise Directions

1. Start PowerPoint, if necessary.

2. Open 💿 **PPT13**.

3. Save the file as **13ARCHITECTS**.

4. Add a slide after slide 2 and choose a Content slide layout that includes a title.

5. Add the title **Company Structure**.

6. Add an organization chart. Increase the zoom to make it easier to see.

7. Use the toolbar buttons to add a co-worker, subordinates, and assistants as shown in Illustration A and enter the text in each box as shown.

   ✓ *Hint: Colin Smith is a subordinate of Mary Frank.*

8. Scale the chart to better fit the slide. Move the chart as necessary to fit the chart on the slide. Click Fit Text on the Organization Chart toolbar to adjust the text in the boxes.

9. Select the boxes and change the color to any color that matches the color scheme.

   ✓ *Hint: You should make all assistants one color, all associates another color, and so on, to differentiate between levels.*

10. Click outside of the chart to deselect the organization chart.

11. Add a slide after slide 4, using a Content slide layout that includes a title.

12. Enter the title **Architects** on the slide.

13. Add an organization chart. Enter text and boxes as shown in Illustration B.

    ✓ *Hint: Use the both hanging layout.*

14. Change the color of the boxes to similar colors you used on the previous chart.

15. Scale and move the chart to center it on the slide.

16. Spell check the presentation.

17. Print the presentation.

18. Close the file and exit PowerPoint, saving all changes.

On Your Own

1. Open **OPP04**, the presentation you created about yourself, or open 💿 **OPP13**.

2. Save the file as **OPP13**.

3. Insert a new slide using the Title and Diagram or Organization Chart slide layout.

4. Create a family tree organization chart on the new slide.

5. Format the chart any way you want.

6. Place the slide in the order in which it belongs in the presentation. It should make sense in the flow of the presentation.

7. Format the slides using fonts, colors, and drawing objects, if you want.

8. Save the presentation, close it, and exit PowerPoint.

Illustration A

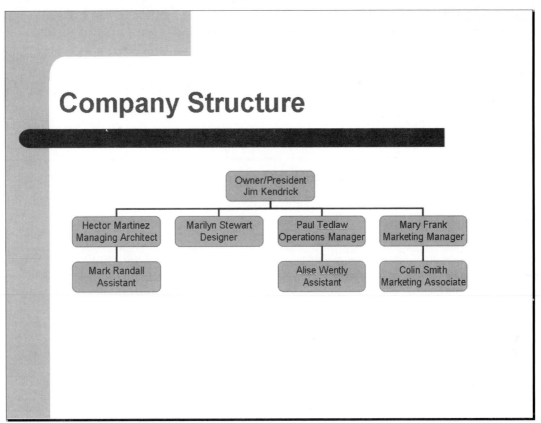

Illustration B

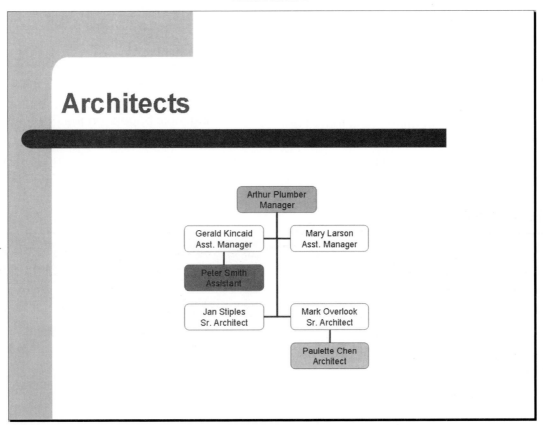

Exercise 14

◆ Create a Chart ◆ Create a Table

On the Job

Add charts or tables to a presentation to illustrate data in an easy-to-read format. Sales figures represented in a chart, for example, are easier to understand than if they're simply listed or just read aloud to the audience.

The owner of Restoration Architecture has given you some data that you can add to the presentation in the form of charts, tables, and worksheets. In this exercise, you will continue work on the Restoration Architecture project.

Terms

Chart A graphic illustration of numbers, percentages, or other data.

Datasheet A worksheet for the graph and charting program. A datasheet contains columns and rows in which you can enter text.

Data label Text that identifies your data.

Table A structure for organizing data in rows and columns.

Notes

Create a Chart

■ You can add a **chart** to your presentation to illustrate data in an easy-to-understand format or to compare and contrast sets of data.

■ You can create a new chart and data in PowerPoint using Microsoft Graph, a charting program that comes with PowerPoint.

■ As you learned in Exercise 6, you can also insert an existing chart as an object from Excel to use in a slide.

■ You can insert a chart into a content slide layout or add it without a placeholder using the Insert Chart button on the Standard toolbar.

■ When you insert a new chart, a Chart toolbar is added to the Standard toolbar and several charting tools appear on the Formatting toolbar.

■ A sample chart and a **datasheet** window containing sample data also appear. You can type in replacement data or import data from an existing Excel file.

Datasheet window

PPT13Architecturesol - Datasheet		A	B	C	D	E
		1st Qtr	2nd Qtr	3rd Qtr	4th Qtr	
1	East	20.4	27.4	90	20.4	
2	West	30.6	38.6	34.6	31.6	
3	North	45.9	46.9	45	43.9	
4						

Create a Chart on a Slide

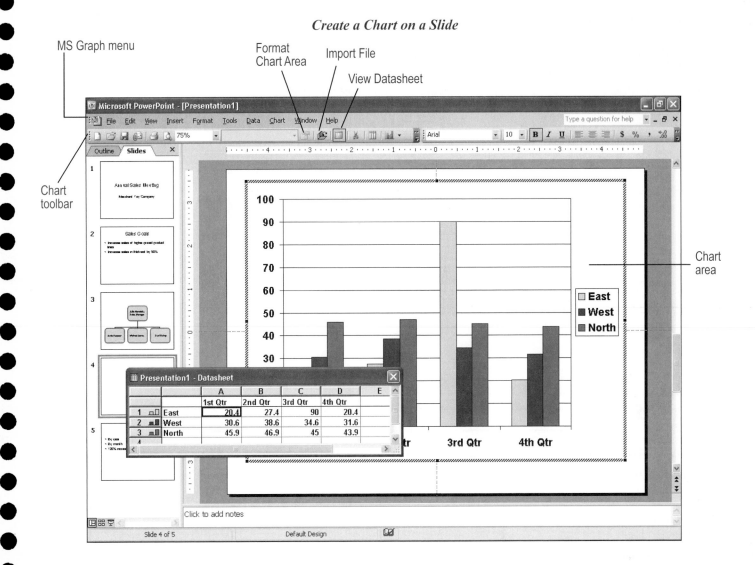

- The default chart type is 3-D Column. You can, however, choose from several chart formats, including bar, line, pie, area, scatter, doughnut, radar, surface, bubble, and stock.

- You can move, copy, size, and delete a chart just like any other slide object.

- You can show or hide gridlines, or measurement guides, within a chart to help you read the chart information.

- You can include a title, **data labels**, and a legend with your chart. A legend identifies the data in a chart by listing each type of data with a color key to its corresponding chart element.

Create a Table

- Use a **table** to organize information into rows and columns.

- You can create a new table using the placeholder in a Title and Content layout, or insert a table without a placeholder by using the Insert Table button on the Standard toolbar.

Insert Table dialog box

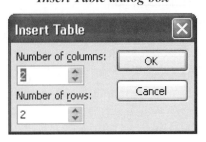

- When you insert a table, you may need to adjust row or column width or resize and move the table.

- When you insert a new table or click an existing table, the Tables and Borders toolbar appears with tools you can use to edit the table.

- After creating a table, you can format the text, resize the cells, insert and delete columns and rows, and change borders on the table.

- You can format the font, color, and size of table text just as you would regular slide text.

Tables and Borders toolbar

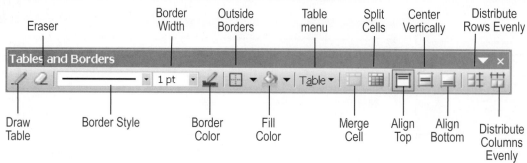

Procedures

Create New Chart

1. Click **Insert** .... Alt+I
2. Click **New Slide** .... N
3. Select any layout with a chart object included.
4. Double-click chart placeholder or click a chart icon.

OR

- Click **Insert Chart** button .

Insert a Chart on a Slide without a Chart Placeholders in the Layout

1. Enter data for chart in datasheet.
2. Click outside chart and datasheet to close datasheet and update chart on slide.
3. Return to chart for edits by double-clicking chart.

Import Chart from Excel

1. Double-click chart placeholder on Chart slide.

1. Click **Import File** button .
2. In the **Look in** drop-down list, locate the folder where the Excel chart is stored.
3. Select Excel file to insert.
4. Click **Open** .... Alt+O
5. Select sheet you want to use from list.
6. Click **OK** .... Enter
7. Click outside chart and datasheet to close datasheet and update chart.
8. Return to datasheet for edits by double-clicking chart.

View Datasheet

- Double-click chart.

Close Datasheet

1. Click datasheet.
2. Click the **Close** button X.

Change Chart Type

1. Double-click chart to display the datasheet.
2. Click down arrow on **Chart Type** button .
3. Select chart type from drop-down palette.

OR

1. Click **Chart** .... Alt+C
2. Click **Chart Type** .... Y
3. Select chart type and subtype.
4. Click **OK** .... Enter

Show/Hide Gridlines and Show/Hide Legend

1. Double-click chart.
2. Click **Category Axis Gridlines** button .
   OR
   Click **Value Axis Gridlines** button .
   OR
   Click **Legend** button .

Insert Table

1. Click **Insert Table** button 🔲 and drag down and to the right to select number of cells to include in table.
   OR
   a. Click **Insert** .... `Alt`+`I`
   b. Click **New Slide** .... `N`
   c. Select any layout with a table object included.
   d. Double-click table placeholder or icon in the slide.
   e. Enter **Number of columns** .. `Alt`+`C`, *number*
   f. Enter **Number of rows** .... `Alt`+`R`, *number*
   g. Click **OK** .... `Enter`
2. Click in a cell to enter text.
3. Press **Tab** key to move insertion point from cell to cell.
4. Click outside of table to return to slide.
5. Return to table for edits by clicking table.

Format Table

1. Click **Table and Borders** button 🔳 if necessary to display Tables and Borders toolbar.
   OR
   Right-click the Standard toolbar and click Table and Borders.
2. Use Table and Borders toolbar to format table.
3. To format a border:
   a. Click from following buttons and make selection:
      - **Border Style**
        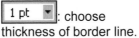 : choose solid, dashed, or dotted lines for table border.
      - **Border Width**
        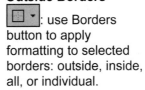 : choose thickness of border line.
      - **Border Color** 🖌 : choose color for borders.
      - **Outside Borders**
        ▦ ▾ : use Borders button to apply formatting to selected borders: outside, inside, all, or individual.
   b. Click the border to apply formatting, or draw lines to add new cells in the selected border settings.

4. Select cell(s) and then click any of the following buttons.
   - **Fill Color** 🖌 ▾ : fill table with color. Select a color or fill effect.
   - **Merge Cells** ▦ : joins two or more cells.
   - **Split Cell** ▦ : divides cell in half.
   - **Align Top** ▤ : aligns table text to top of cell.
   - **Center Vertically** ▤ : aligns table text to vertical center of cell.
   - **Align Bottom** ▤ : aligns table text to bottom of cell.

Change Column Width/Row Height of Table

1. Position mouse over border line.
2. Mouse pointer changes to double-headed arrow ↔ .
3. Click and drag border to move it.

Exercise Directions

1. Start PowerPoint, if necessary.

2. Open 📠**13ARCHITECTS** or 💿 **PPT14**.

3. Save the file as **14ARCHITECTS**.

4. Add a new slide at the end of the presentation using the Title and Content layout. Enter the slide title **Client Breakdown**.

5. Insert a chart and replace the data from the datasheet with the data as shown in Illustration A.

6. Close the datasheet and adjust the chart position or resize the chart so you can view all of the data.

7. Change the chart type to a 3-D Bar Chart.

8. Add value axis gridlines if they are not showing.

9. Add a new slide at the end of the presentation using the Title only layout. Enter the slide title **Sales by Quarter**.

10. Insert a chart using the Chart button and import Sheet 1 of the file 💿 **14Sales.xls** to the datasheet.

11. Close the datasheet and adjust the chart on the slide as shown in Illustration B.

    ✓ *Hint: You can resize the chart separately from the chart area placeholder. You can also move the legend.*

12. Add a new slide at the end of the presentation using the Title and Content layout. Add the slide title **Planning Services Price List**.

13. Insert a 5 x 5 table and enter the text as shown in Illustration C. Do not press Enter after typing the chart information.

14. Format the text in the first row and the first column of the table as Arial Narrow, 18 points, and centered. Format the rest of the table text to 18 points and centered.

15. Resize the table to fit on the slide without overlapping other elements and adjust the row and column widths to fit the text.

    ✓ *To resize the table, click on the table to select it and drag the sizing handles.*

16. Spell check the presentation.

17. Print the slides as handouts with four per page.

18. Close the file and exit PowerPoint, saving all changes.

Illustration A

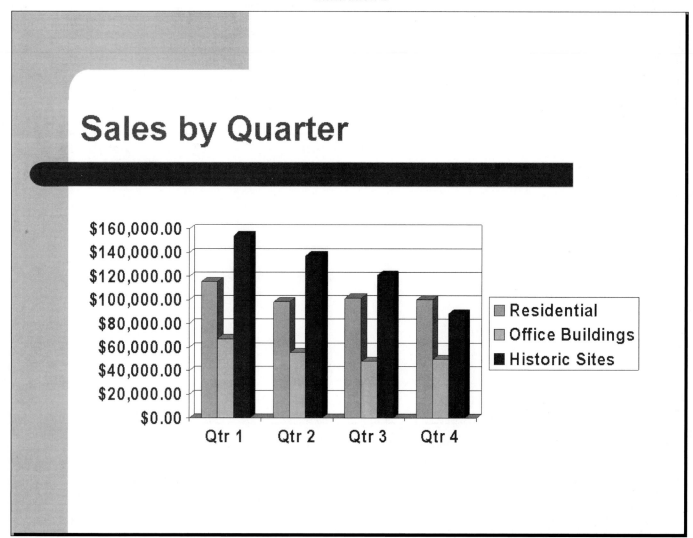

		A	B	C	D	
		2000	2001	2002	2004	
1	Residential	25	45	40	53	
2	Office Buildings	48	38	34	15	
3	Historic Sites	27	17	26	32	
4						

Illustration B

Illustration C

Planning Services Price List

Service	Zone 1	Zone 2	Zone 3	Zone 4
Permits	$100	$250	$150	n/a
Site Study	$1,500	$2,250	$3,000	$1,500
Planning	$50/hour	$60/hour	$75/hour	$50/hour
Design	$100/hour	$125/hour	$250/hour	$150/hour

On Your Own

1. Open **OPP11**, the charity presentation you last worked with in Exercise 11, or open ⊙**OPP14**.

2. Save the file as **OPP14**.

3. Insert a chart slide illustrating where income for the organization came from last year. For example, it might come from donations, fundraising, grants, membership dues, and so on.

4. Insert another chart slide and import the Breakdown of Expenses pie chart from the ⊙**14CHART.xls** Excel workbook file.

5. Format the chart so it is easy to read and looks good on the slide and add a slide title.

6. Insert another slide showing a table listing the officers of the organization and move, resize, or format the table to be easy to read.

7. Save the presentation, close the presentation, and exit PowerPoint.

Exercise 15

◆ **Embed a PowerPoint Slide in a Word Document**
◆ **Export PowerPoint Slides and Notes to a Word Document**
◆ **Export PowerPoint Text to a Word Document**

On the Job

Share information between two applications to save yourself work and to provide consistency between documents. You might, for example, create a presentation in PowerPoint that contains information you can use in a report you're preparing in Word. Rather than type the information over again, export the text to Word.

The owner of Restoration Architecture wants to create a report in Word for the partners of her company. Since she's not familiar with PowerPoint, you are going to help by creating several sample documents using various data and slides from the PowerPoint presentation. After she picks the one she wants, you can then explain to her how to complete her report.

Terms

Embed To insert a copy of an object from one application into another so that object in the second program is not affected by changes to the original object. Compare *Link*.

Object Any text, table, picture, slide, spreadsheet, or data treated as a unit for formatting, copying, or moving.

Link To insert a copy of an object from one application into another so that the copied object is automatically updated when it is changed in the original file.

Export To send a copy of an object from one application to another application. The object may be embedded in the other application or it may be linked to the original.

Notes

Embed a PowerPoint Slide in a Word Document

- You can use simple copy and paste operations to **embed** a slide in a Word document to illustrate a report or enhance the document.

- The slide appears in Word in full color, with graphics and text.

- You can size and move the slide after it's copied to the Word document.

- Embedded **objects** are similar to **linked** objects except that the embedded object does not change when the original file changes.

Export PowerPoint Slides and Notes to a Word Document

- You can send PowerPoint slides and notes to a Word document to include in a report or other document.

- When you use the Send To command to export slides, miniatures of your slides appear in the Word document. You also can print blank lines with the slides for notes or comments.

- You can choose to link to the PowerPoint source document. Then, when you make a change to the presentation, the linked document in Word updates automatically.

Export PowerPoint Text to a Word Document

- You can **export** PowerPoint text to a Word document to save yourself from retyping the text.
- You can choose to export only the text to the document, not graphics.

Procedures

Embed PowerPoint Slide in Word

1. Open presentation in PowerPoint.
2. Go to Slide Sorter view.
3. Select slide to copy.
4. Click **Copy** button 🗐 .... `Ctrl`+`C`
5. Switch to Word document and position cursor.
6. Click **Paste** button 🗐 .... `Ctrl`+`V`

    OR

    a. Click **Paste Special** .... `S`
    b. Click **Paste link** .... `L`
    c. Click **OK** .... `Enter`

Export PowerPoint Slides and Notes to Word

1. Open presentation in PowerPoint.
2. Click **File** .... `Alt`+`F`
3. Click **Send To** .... `D`
4. Click **Microsoft Office Word** .... `W`
5. Select one of the following options for Page layout in Word.

    ✓ The images beside each option in the Send To Microsoft Word dialog box indicate the Page layout.

- **Notes next to slides** ..... `N`

    ✓ The presentation is inserted into a new Word document in a three-column table. The slide number appears in the left column, the slide in the center column, and any notes in the right column.

- **Blank lines next to slides** .... `A`

    ✓ The presentation is inserted into a new Word document in a three-column table. The right column contains blank lines for notes or comments.

- **Notes below slides** ...... `B`

    ✓ The presentation is inserted into a new Word document with one slide per Word page. The slide is preceded by its number in the upper left and any notes are displayed below the slide image.

- **Blank lines below slides** .... `K`

    ✓ The presentation is inserted into a new Word document with one slide per Word page with blank lines under each slide for notes or comments.

- **Outline only** .... `O`

    ✓ Only the text of the presentation is inserted into a new Word document.

6. For all options except Outline only, select either:
    - **Paste** .... `Alt`+`P`
    - **Paste link** .... `Alt`+`I`
7. Click **OK** .... `Enter`
8. Save the Word document.

Export PowerPoint Outline to Word

1. Open presentation in PowerPoint.
2. Click **File** .... `Alt`+`F`
3. Click **Save As** .... `A`
4. Click **Save as type** .... `Alt`+`T`
5. Select **Outline/RTF (*.rtf)**.
6. Click **Save** .... `Alt`+`S`
7. Switch to Word.
8. Click **File** .... `Alt`+`F`
9. Click **Open** .... `O`
10. Click **Files of type** ..... `Alt`+`T`
11. Select **Rich Text Format (*.rtf)**.
12. Select the file.
13. Click **Open** .... `Alt`+`O`

    OR

1. Open presentation in PowerPoint.
2. Click **File** .... `Alt`+`F`
3. Click **Send To** .... `D`
4. Click **Microsoft Office Word** .... `W`
5. Select **Outline only** .... `O`
6. Click **OK** .... `Enter`

Exercise Directions

1. Start PowerPoint, if necessary.

2. Open ⌨14ARCHITECTS or 💿PPT15.

3. Save it as 15ARCHITECTURE.

4. In Slide Sorter view, copy slide 7 and paste it into a new Word document. Press Enter in the Word document to leave space at the top of the page. Enter the text you see in Illustration A to show how the slide and text look together in a document.

5. Select the slide and center it.

   ✓ Hint: You can use View, Print Layout in Word or check the results in Print Preview if you're not sure of the position of the slide.

6. Save the document in Word as 15ARCHITECTURE.doc. Print the document and close it.

7. In PowerPoint, using the same presentation, export the file to a new Word document using the Send To command. Show the slides next to notes.

8. Save the document as 15ARCHITECTURE-2.doc. Print the document and close it.

9. In PowerPoint, using the same presentation, save the file as an Outline/RTF file named 15ARCHITECTURE-3.rtf. Switch to Word and open that file into a new Word document.

   ✓ Note: Only the text is saved in Outline/RTF format. The tables, charts, and organization charts do not save to the Word document.

10. Save the file as 15ARCHITECTURE-4.doc. Print the document and close it. Exit Word.

11. Close the file and exit PowerPoint, saving all changes.

12. Open the .RTF file in Word to view it, then close the file and exit Word.

On Your Own

1. Open OPP14, the presentation you were working with in Exercise 14, or open 💿OPP15.

2. Save the file as OPP15.

3. Start Word, create a new document, and type a letter to the president of your organization explaining the presentation you have created, or open the document 💿PPT15LETTER.

4. Save the Word document as OPP15LETTER-2.doc.

5. Select the slide with the title **Income** in the OPP15 presentation, and paste it at the end of the OPP15LETTER-2.doc document.

   ✓ If you are working off a presentation that you created and don't have an **Income** slide, select another slide.

6. Export the entire presentation to a new Word document, including blank lines for notes.

7. Save the document as OPP15LETTER-3.doc.

8. Save all open Word documents, close them, and exit Word.

9. Save the PowerPoint presentation, close it, and exit PowerPoint.

Restoration Architecture Sales for 2004

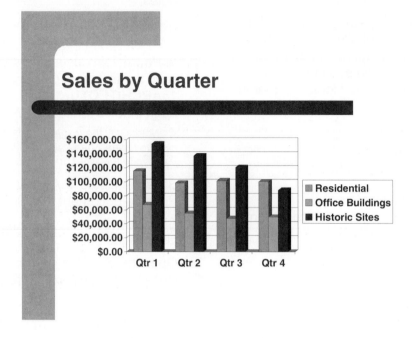

Exercise 16

Although the owner of Restoration Architecture is pleased with your work so far, she would like another presentation design to choose from. She's also given you some additional information to use for this presentation. In this exercise, you will create one more presentation for Restoration Architecture.

Exercise Directions

1. Start PowerPoint, if necessary.
2. Create a new blank presentation.
3. Save the file as **16ARCHITECTURE**.
4. Using the slide master, create a new presentation background for Restoration Architecture. Apply a color scheme, clip art, AutoShapes, or other design elements to make it attractive. Make sure that you insert at least one clip art graphic and that you apply a custom color scheme or background colors.

   ✓ *Hint: The background for the illustration is changed in the Background dialog box accessed by choosing Format, Background; instead of picking a color, try Fill Effects in the Background fill drop-down list.*

5. Create a logo for Restoration Architecture and place it on the slide master. Combine a clip art image or an AutoShape with a text box to create the logo to fit in the corner of the slide as shown in Illustration A.
6. On the title slide, enter the text as shown in Illustration A. Select the title text and enlarge it to 48 points and left align the title text.
7. Left align the subtitle text.
8. Show the rulers and use tabs to indent the second line of the subtitle text as shown.
9. Add a slide based on the Title and Table slide layout. Enter the text as shown in Illustration B.
10. Resize the cells to fit the text as shown in Illustration B. Center the text in the heading row both horizontally and vertically. Resize the table on the slide if necessary.

11. Omit the Master background graphics from this slide.
12. Add a Title and Text slide and enter the text as shown in Illustration C.
13. Change the bullet characters to any desired shape. Increase the paragraph spacing in the bullet text.

    ✓ *Hint: Use Wingdings characters for the larger bullets.*

14. Add a fourth slide and use the Title Only slide layout. Add the title **Site Study Services**.
15. Insert a bar chart using the following data:

	Survey	Soils Testing	Drainage Survey
Small Property	2500	2000	2750
Medium Property	6000	2000	3800
Large Property	10000	2000	5000

16. Adjust the position of the chart on the slide to fit the space without overlapping other slide items.
17. Change the chart type, as shown in Illustration D.
18. Send the PowerPoint presentation to Word with blank lines below the slides for notes to be added.
19. Spell check the presentation.
20. Save the file as **16PPTRESTORATION.doc** and print it.
21. Close the file and exit PowerPoint.

Restoration Architecture

Design for Life

Design that Lasts

Restoration

Architecture

Design Specialists

Style	Sample Project	Cost
Victorian	22 Hastings St.	$132,333
Italianate	4 Bellevue Ave.	$101,993
Georgian	123 Elm St.	$114,432

Illustration C

Illustration D

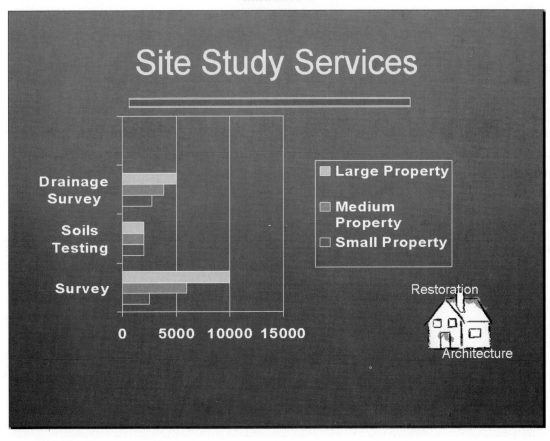

Exercise 17

Skills Covered:

◆ **Check Slides for Style and Consistency** ◆ **Show a Presentation**
◆ **Add Transitions** ◆ **Add Sound** ◆ **Advance Slide** ◆ **Hide Slides**

On the Job

When you show your presentation, you can add certain elements to make it more interesting. You might want to show a presentation automatically, in which case you can use timings to give the audience the right amount of time to read each slide. Transitions and sound can be set to play as each slide changes into the next.

The Vice President of HelpNow MedCenter informed you that she will present the laser surgery unit slide show to a large audience. She wants automatic timings, although she also wants the capability to advance the slides manually. Additionally, she wants transitions and sounds. In this exercise, you will prepare the custom presentation you created earlier for viewing.

Terms

Kiosk A booth or counter that can hold a computer that displays continuously running presentations, usually found in visitors' centers, trade shows, or conventions.

Transitions The visual effect used when one slide moves off of the screen and another moves onto the screen.

Sound clip Recorded audio clips that you can play automatically as a slide changes from one to the next or by clicking a sound button on the slide.

Advance Slide timing A setting that controls the amount of time a slide displays on the screen.

Notes

Check Slides for Style and Consistency

- You can set up PowerPoint to check your slides as you create them for style and consistency, such as the number of font types and the minimum font sizes.
- PowerPoint displays a light bulb to warn you of discrepancies. Click the light bulb to read suggestions.
- You can change the style items that PowerPoint checks or turn the Check style feature off.

Show a Presentation

- You can show a presentation on your computer screen, project it on a larger screen, or show it at a **kiosk**.
- You can navigate through a slide show automatically or manually when you click the mouse.
- You can also run a show continuously.
- Each slide displayed in the Slide Show view fills the entire computer screen.
- PowerPoint displays a black screen with the words *End of slide show* at the end of the presentation.

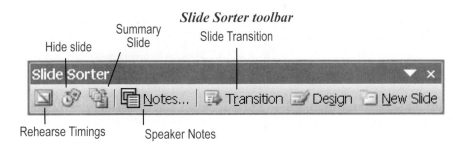

Slide Sorter toolbar

Hide slide
Summary Slide
Slide Transition
Rehearse Timings
Speaker Notes

Add Transitions

- PowerPoint provides **transitions** that you can use to make the slide show more interesting.

- You can apply transitions in any view. However, Slide Sorter view is the easiest because it provides several transition tools on its toolbar and you can apply transitions to several slides at once.

- Apply an animation effect to one slide by selecting the effect. Apply to all slides by clicking the Apply to All Slides button on the Slide Transition task pane.

- To access all of the transition options at once, open the Slide Transition task pane.

- You can preview transitions before you apply them and you can control the speed of each transition from the Slide Transition task pane.

- Slides with transitions are marked by a Slide Transition icon in Slide Sorter view. You can click the icon to preview the transition.

Slide with transition

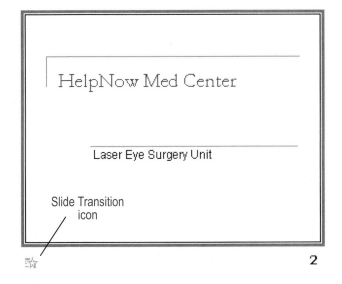

HelpNow Med Center

Laser Eye Surgery Unit

Slide Transition icon

2

- If you use too many different transitions, viewers may find it distracting.

Add Sound

- Use a **sound clip** in your presentations to add interest and emphasis.

- You can add any sound file to a slide. Sound files often have a .wav or .mid extension. You can insert a sound from Microsoft's Clip Gallery or from any file on your computer. You can even record your own sounds.

- Sound files play when you move from one slide to another, or when you click the sound button on the slide in Slide Show mode.

- You can also play CD tracks or recorded narration in a slide show. See Exercise 19 for information.

Advance Slide

- If you do not want to advance slides manually by mouse clicks in a presentation, you can have PowerPoint advance each slide automatically.

- **Advance Slide timing** defines the amount of time a slide is on the screen before PowerPoint automatically advances to the next slide.

- You can set Advance Slide timing in the Slide Transition task pane for individual slides or for all slides in a presentation. Set advance slide timing in seconds or minutes and seconds.

- Even if you set advance timings for your slides, you can also choose to advance a slide manually.

- PowerPoint provides a play feature you can use to set and check Advance Slide timings.

- The Advance Slide timing for each slide is indicated in Slide Sorter view by a number below each slide.

Slide with advance slide timing

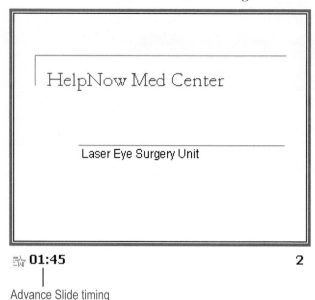

🖳 **01:45**   **2**

Advance Slide timing

Hide Slides

- You can hide slides in your presentation so they do not show when you run the slide show. For example, you might hide some slides to shorten the presentation, or hide slides that don't apply to a specific audience.

- Hidden slides remain in the file and can be displayed again at any time.
- PowerPoint places an indicator under a hidden slide in Slide Sorter view.

Hidden slide

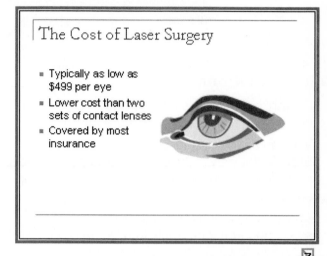

Hidden slide indicator

Procedures

Set Options for Style and Consistency

1. Click **Tools**................. `Alt`+`T`
2. Click **Options**...................... `O`
3. Click **Spelling and Style** tab .... `Ctrl`+`Tab`
4. Click **Check style** .... `C`
5. Click **Style Options** button

   Style Options... .... `Alt`+`T`
6. Make necessary changes in Style Options dialog box.
7. Click **OK**.......................... `Enter`
8. Click **OK** again .... `Enter`

   ✓ *If you have turned off the Office Assistant feature at this point you will see a message asking if you wish to enable it.*

Start Slide Show *(F5)*

1. Click **Slide Show** button .

   OR

   a. Click **Slide Show** .... `D`
   b. Click **View Show**............ `V`

   OR

   a. Click **View** .... `V`
   b. Click **Slide Show** .... `W`

2. Press `Page Down` to advance to next slide. Press `Page Up` to go to previous slide.

   OR

   Click mouse to advance slide show.

3. Click the last slide to end the show.

   OR

   Click **Esc** to end slide show .... `Esc`

   OR

   Right-click and select **End Show**.......................... `E`

Add Transitions

1. Display slide to add transition effect in Normal view.

   OR

   Select one or multiple slides to affect in Slide Sorter.

2. Click **Slide Show** .... `Alt`+`D`
3. Click **Slide Transition** .... `T`
4. Select a transition in the **Apply to selected slides** list.

5. Click modify transition speed:
   - **Slow**
   - **Medium**
   - **Fast**
6. Click Apply to All Slides if you want the transition to apply to more than the selected slide.

Add Transition Effect from Slide Sorter Toolbar

1. Switch to Slide Sorter view.
2. Select slide or slides to affect.
3. Click **Transition** button ⊞ Transition .
4. Select options from Slide Transition task pane.

Add Sound

1. Select slide or slides to affect.
2. Click **Sli̲de Show**.........Alt+D
3. Click **Slide T̲ransition**.........T
4. Select a sound in the **Modify transition Sound** drop-down list.
5. Click **Loop until next sound** for continuous sound.
6. Click Apply to All Slides if you want the sound to apply to more than the selected slide.

Insert Sound Objects

1. Display slide in Normal view.
2. Click **I̲nsert**.................Alt+I
3. Click **Mo̲vies and Sound**....V
4. Click one of the following:
   - **Sound from Clip Organizer** ....S
   - **Soun̲d from File**...........N
5. Select sound.
6. Click **OK** ....Enter
7. Choose **Automatically** or **When Clicked** when you are prompted.
8. Position the sound button on the slide.

Add Advance Slide Timings

1. Switch to Slide Sorter view.
2. Select a slide to apply timing to or select multiple slides by pressing the **Ctrl** or **Shift** key as you click the slides.
3. Click **Sli̲de Show** ....Alt+D
4. Click **Slide T̲ransition** ....T
5. In **Advance slide**, click **Automatically after.**
6. Enter time in spin box.
7. Click **On mouse click** to add manual advance as option.
8. Click Apply to All Slides if you want the timing to apply to all slides.

Check Timings

1. In Slide Sorter view, click **Rehearse Timings** button .
2. Walk through the presentation, reading slide contents and any comments you intend to make in the presentation.
3. Advance from slide to slide as you intend to during an actual presentation.
4. When you're done, press **Esc**...........................Esc
5. PowerPoint asks if you wish to save these timings. Select **Yes** to save them.

Hide Slide

1. Switch to Slide Sorter view.
2. Select slide to hide.
3. Click **Hide Slide** button ▨ .
4. Click **Hide Slide** button ▨ a second time to redisplay hidden slide.

Remove Slide Transition.

1. Click the slide.
2. Display the Slide Transition task pane.
3. Click **No Transition** in the **Apply to selected slides** list.

Exercise Directions

1. Start PowerPoint, if necessary.
2. Open ⊙ **PPT17**.
3. Save the file as **17SURGERY**.
4. Check the presentation for any spelling errors or style inconsistencies.
5. Show the presentation as a slide show.
6. Switch to Slide Sorter view.
7. Apply the Random Transition effect to all slides using a fast speed. Show the presentation.
8. Apply the Comb Vertical transition to the second slide.
9. Rehearse the show to set transition timings. As you rehearse, read each slide. Allow 10 seconds of time after you finish reading before moving to the next slide.
10. After rehearsal, in slide 2, set the timing to 2 minutes. On slides 5, 6, and 7, set the timing to 3 minutes.
11. Hide slides 3 and 4.
12. Run the presentation.
13. Add transition sounds to the slides. You can add one sound to all slides or use different sounds for multiple slides.
    ✓ *Your computer may not be equipped to play sound.*
14. Spell check the slide presentation.
15. Print the presentation.
16. Show the slide presentation.
17. Close the file and exit PowerPoint, saving all changes.

On Your Own

1. Open **OPP15**, the presentation for the charity that you last used in Exercise 15, or open ⊙ **OPP17**.
2. Save the file as **OPP17**.
3. Run the slide show.
4. Set the slide show to run automatically with an interval of 5 seconds.
5. Add a dissolve transition effect to all slides at a medium speed.
6. Add the sound of applause to the title slide and the final slide.
7. Run the slide show again.
8. Save the presentation, close it, and close PowerPoint.

Exercise **18**

Skills Covered:

◆ **Animate Text and Objects** ◆ **Preset Animation**
◆ **Custom Animation**

On the Job

Animate text and objects to add interest and emphasis to certain slides and items in the presentation. Animate a bulleted list of topics that build in importance, for example, with timed pauses to catch the audience's attention.

The President of HelpNow MedCenter liked your presentation but she wants more movement and some sound added for emphasis. She also asks that you prepare a second presentation with sound and movement, so she has a choice. In this exercise, you will add animation to the custom presentation you created.

Terms

Animate To apply movement to text or an object. For example, text might fly onto the screen from the left or drop in from above.

Preset animation Several types of movements included in PowerPoint that you can apply quickly and easily.

Notes

Animate Text and Objects

- You can **animate** text on slides to add interest to your presentation or to emphasize special points.

- You can make animated text appear one letter or one paragraph at a time, for example. Or, you can animate text to use effects such as flying in or bouncing in.

- You can use PowerPoint's **preset animations** or design your own custom animations.

- You can preview animations and adjust timing before you show the presentation.

- Apply an animation effect to one slide by selecting the effect. Apply to all slides by clicking the Apply to All Slides button in the Animation Schemes task pane.

- Use the Animation Schemes task pane to apply preset animation effects quickly and preview those effects.

Preset Animation

- PowerPoint supplies Subtle, Moderate, and Exciting animation schemes you can apply to your slides.

- Use preset animations on bulleted lists, titles, subtitles, and other text.

- You can apply preset animations from Normal or Slide Sorter view using the Animation Schemes task pane.

- You can click AutoPreview to preview an animation when you select it from the Animation Scheme list box.

Custom Animation

- Use the Custom Animation task pane to set animation effects, direction, property, and speed for text in a slide.

- You can apply custom animations to tables, charts, and organization charts. You can also apply custom animations to lines, shapes, clip art, and AutoShapes.

- You can choose the order in which objects and text appear on a slide.

Custom animation order

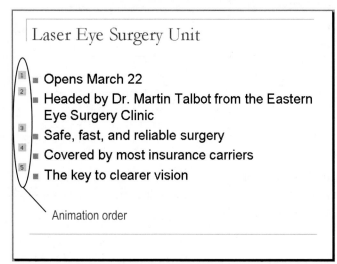

Animation order

- You can also apply various properties to the animations. For example, you can choose the amount of spin or the direction of a checkerboard effect.

- You can set the speed of the animation.

- You can set details for each effect applied to bullet text, for example.

Set details for single animations

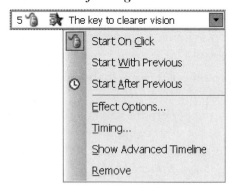

- You can set effect options, such as direction or size. Most effects also include sound enhancements.

Set effect details

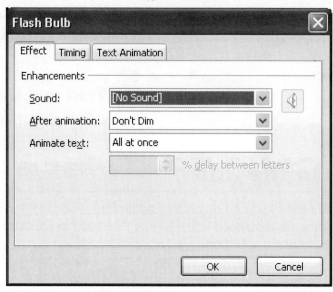

- You can set timing details, such as speed, delay, or repeat, for each effect.

Set timing details

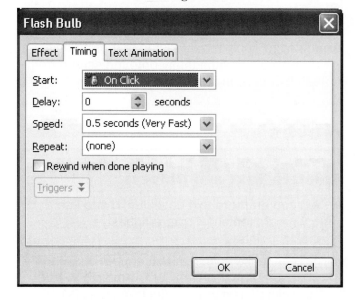

- Depending on the type of object you are animating, you may have a third tab in the Effect Options dialog box; for example if you are animating text you will have a Text Animation tab and if you are animating a chart there will be a Chart Animation tab. Use these tabs to define how multiple items are grouped in the animation.

- You can set the order of the effects using the Re-Order buttons on the Custom Animation task pane.

Procedures

Display Animations Schemes Task Pane

1. Click **Slide Show**.................🄳
2. Click **Animation Schemes**..🄲

Preset Animation

1. In Normal or Slide Sorter view, display slide.
2. Click in text or object to be animated.
3. Click desired animation effect in Animation Schemes task pane.

Preview Animations

- Click Animation Preview button ⭐.

OR

1. Select slide containing animation you want to preview.
2. Open Animation Schemes task pane.
3. Click **Play**.

Custom Animation

1. In Normal view, display slide.
2. Click the item to be animated.
3. Click **Slide Show** ....🄰🄻🄽+🄳
4. Click **Custom Animation**....🄼
5. Click **Add Effect** button ⭐ Add Effect ▼.
6. Choose appropriate command:
   - **E̲ntrance**......................🄴
   - **Emphasis** ....🄼
   - **E̲xit**..............................🄧
   - **Motion P̲aths**.................🄿
7. Choose effect you want to apply.
8. Click **Start** drop-down arrow. Choose appropriate option:
   - **On Click**
   - **With Previous**
   - **After Previous**
9. Click the property drop-down arrow and choose appropriate option.
   - ✓ *The property will change depending on which effect you have selected.*
10. Click **Speed**. Choose appropriate option:
    - **Very Slow**
    - **Slow**
    - **Medium**
    - **Fast**
    - **Very Fast**
11. Click **Close** button 🄧 to close the task pane.

Set Effect Details

1. Open the Custom Animation task pane.
2. Click the effect in the Effects list.
3. Click the drop-down arrow.
4. Click **Effect Options**...........🄴
5. Click the appropriate tab:
   - **Effect**
   - **Timing**
   - **Text Animation**
   - ✓ *If the object you are animating is not text, the Text Animation tab will not display.*
6. Set the details.
7. Click **OK**..........................🄴🄽🄵🄴🄰

Turn Animation Off

1. Select text or object from which to remove animation.
2. Open Animation Schemes or Custom Animations task pane.
3. Click **No Animation** in the **Apply to selected slides** list box.

Exercise Directions

1. Start PowerPoint, if necessary.
2. Open 🖥️**17SURGERY** or 💿 **PPT18**.
3. Save the file as **18SURGERY**.
4. Switch to Slide Sorter view.
5. Remove all transition effects from all slides; keep the timings.
6. Switch to Normal view.
7. In the first slide, select the title text and apply the preset animation Big title (an Exciting animation).
8. Remove Hide Slide from slides 3 and 4.
9. Select slide 3 and apply the Faded zoom animation.
10. Select slide 4 and apply Faded zoom.
11. Switch to slide 5.
12. Apply the following custom animation:
    - Display the title first, using any entrance effect.
    - Display the bulleted text with a Fly In entrance effect.

13. Switch to slide 7 and apply any custom Emphasis effect to the clip art object. Repeat the effect 3 times.

    ✓ Hint: Use the Timing tab to set the details of the effect.

14. Switch to slide 8 and apply any custom exit effect to the textbox.
15. Switch to Slide Sorter view.
16. Play the effects on each slide and make any adjustments you think necessary.

    ✓ Illustration A shows that you see transitions and animations indicated by icons in this view.

17. Spell check the presentation.
18. Print the presentation.
19. Close the file, saving all changes.

On Your Own

1. Open **OPP17**, the presentation you used in the On Your Own section of Exercise 17, or open 💿 **OPP18**.
2. Save the files as **OPP18**.
3. Display the Custom Animation task pane.
4. Apply a custom animation to the AutoShape on the title slide. (If you do not have an AutoShape on the title slide, use one on a different slide or create one.)

5. Animate the slide text for all slides with bullet lists.
6. Use Custom Animation to animate one of the charts in the presentation.
7. Run the presentation.
8. Save the presentation, close it, and exit PowerPoint.

Exercise 19

◆ **Annotations** ◆ **Pause and Resume Show**
◆ **Add Music** ◆ **Add a Movie**

On the Job

Use annotations during a slide show to highlight certain information or key points. For example, you can underline points to emphasize or check off topics as you discuss them. For a really dynamic presentation, you can add music or movie clips. Adding a limited amount of multimedia to a presentation can make it more interesting and entertaining.

The President of HelpNow MedCenter is pleased with the content of the presentation, but she wants you to add some pizzazz to it. She is planning on showing the presentation to a new group of investors and wants to really impress them.

Terms

Annotation feature A method of writing or marking on a slide during a presentation.

Notes

Annotations

- You can add annotations, such as writing or drawing, to a slide during a slide show.
- When you use the **annotation feature**, the mouse becomes a pen.
- You may want to annotate to modify a chart or data in a table based on viewer input, for instance, as you present a slide show.
- Annotations do not change the slide; they only appear during the presentation.
- PowerPoint suspends automatic timings while you use the annotations feature.
- You can choose different colors to use for the pen and different pen styles, such as ballpoint or highlighter.
- When you close the slide show you will be offered the option of saving your annotations, or discarding them.

A slide with pen annotation added

Is Laser Eye Surgery For You?

- You want a safe form of refractive surgery
- You want to avoid pain
- You expect almost immediate results *1day*
- You are nearsighted or farsighted

Pause and Resume Show

- You can pause a slide show when you want to elaborate on a point or hold a discussion. When you are done, you can resume the show.

Add Music

- You can add music clips to your presentation to make it more interesting or to emphasize a slide.

- Your computer must have speakers and a sound card to play music during the presentation.

- You might want music to play in the background as the viewer reads the slide or as you talk.

- Insert a music clip as a slide object in Normal view.

- A music clip is indicated by a sound button 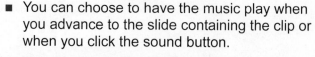.

- You can choose to have the music play when you advance to the slide containing the clip or when you click the sound button.

- You can insert a music file, CD track, or music from Microsoft's Clip Gallery.

- Microsoft's Windows\Media folder often includes sounds, music, and other clips for you to use with a presentation. You can also find additional sound files on the Internet.

Add a Movie

- You can insert movie clips or videos into a presentation.

- Insert a movie clip in Normal view.

- Movies files typically end with an .avi, .mpe, or .mpg extension.

Procedures

Add Annotations

1. Show the presentation.
2. Click the **Pen** button ![pen icon] on the shortcut menu that appears in the lower-left corner of the screen.
3. Select a pen style.
   OR
   a. Right-click on screen.
   b. Click **Pointer Options** ... Ⓞ
   c. Click a Pen style
      - **Ballpoint Pen** .... Ⓑ
      - **Felt Tip Pen** .... Ⓕ
      - **Highlighter** .... Ⓗ
   OR
   - Press **Ctrl+P** .... Ctrl + Ⓟ
4. Hold down the mouse button and drag to write annotations.

Erase Annotations

- Press **E** on keyboard .... Ⓔ
OR
1. Right-click the slide or click the **Pen** button ![pen icon] on the shortcut menu.
2. Click **Eraser** .... Ⓡ
3. Move your mouse cursor over ink you wish to erase.
OR
1. Right-click the slide or click the Annotation button on the shortcut menu.
2. Click **Pointer Options** .... Ⓞ
3. Click **Erase All Ink on Slide** .... Ⓔ

Change Ink Color

1. Right-click on screen.
2. Click **Pointer Options** .... Ⓞ
3. Click **Ink Color** .... Ⓒ
4. Click on a color in the drop down palette.

Pause Show

1. Right-click the screen.
2. Click **Pause** .... Ⓢ
OR
1. Click **Navigation** button ![navigation icon] on shortcut menu.
2. Click **Pause** .... Ⓢ

Resume Show

1. Right-click the screen.
2. Click **Resume** .... Ⓢ

Turn Off Annotation Feature

1. During slide show, right-click any slide.
2. Click **Pointer Options** .... Ⓞ
3. Click **Arrow** .... Ⓐ
OR
- Press **Esc** .... Esc

Add Sound

✓ *Insert sounds and movies in Normal view.*

1. Select slide with which to associate music.
2. Click **Insert** .... Alt + I
3. Click **Movies and Sounds** .. V
4. Click one of the following:
   - **Sound from Clip Organizer** .... S
   - **Sound from File** .... N
   - **Play CD Audio Track** C

5. Select a sound and click on it in Clip Organizer.
   OR
   Click **OK** if sound from file or CD .... Enter
6. Click **Automatically** to play music automatically when slide advances .... A
   OR
   Click **When Clicked** to have music play when you click Sound button C

Add Movie

1. Open slide presentation.
2. Select slide with which to associate video clip.
3. Click **Insert** .... Alt + I
4. Click **Movies and Sounds** .. V
5. Click one of the following:
   - **Movie from Clip Organizer** .... M
   - **Movie from File** .... F
6. Choose file to add.
7. Click **OK** .... Enter

Exercise Directions

1. Start PowerPoint, if necessary.
2. Open 📻18SURGERY or 💿PPT19.
3. Save the file as **19SURGERY**.
4. Run the slide show. On the second slide, activate the annotation feature and circle **Laser Eye Surgery Unit** with the pen.
5. On the fifth slide change the color of the pen and draw an arrow to point to **Opens March 22**. Erase the annotation you just created.
6. On slide 6, circle the word **Cost** in the bullet list.
7. Move to slide 7 and pause the show.

8. Resume the show and end it, saving the annotations.
9. In Slide view, insert a Title Only slide at the end of the presentation.
10. Insert the title **HelpNow MedCenter's Future**.
11. Insert a sound or movie clip. If you choose a sound have it play automatically in the slide show.
12. Size the sound or movie clip as you would size any type of object.
13. Show the presentation.
14. Close the file, saving all changes.

On Your Own

1. Open **OPP18**, the presentation you used in the On Your Own section of Exercise 18, or open 💿**OPP19**.
2. Save the file as **OPP19**.
3. Add a music clip or a video clip to one or more of the slides.
4. Run the slide show. Stop the show to annotate one of the slides. For example, circle important text.

5. Run the presentation.
6. When exiting the presentation, save the annotations
7. Exit the presentation saving any annotations.
8. Save the presentation, close it, and exit PowerPoint.

Exercise 20

Skills Covered:

◆ **Create Notes Pages and Handouts**
◆ **Notes Master and Handout Master** ◆ **Package for CD**
◆ **Take Speaker Notes During a Presentation**
◆ **Send Speaker Notes to Word**

On the Job

PowerPoint provides ways for you to maximize the impact of your presentations. You can distribute handouts with a presentation, for example. Or, you can also pack up your presentation on a CD (or floppy disk) to display it on another computer. You can even show a presentation to different people on different computers during an online meeting.

The CEO of Whole Grains Bread wants you to create notes pages and handouts of a presentation for his audience. He also needs the presentation saved to a CD so he can show it on a computer that doesn't have PowerPoint. Finally, the CEO has asked you to show him how to take notes during an online presentation so he can create a report from the notes after the presentation.

Terms

Notes Comments added to the presentation that can be for the speaker's eyes only.

Handouts Printed copies of the presentation for the audience to refer to during and after the slide show.

Package for CD A feature that lets you save the presentation to a CD-ROM disc and then show it on a computer that doesn't have PowerPoint installed.

Notes

Create Notes Pages and Handouts

■ **Notes** help you remember key points you want to make about each slide in a presentation.

■ You can enter speaker's notes for a slide in the Notes pane in Normal view, or in a placeholder below the slide in Notes Page view.

  ✓ *You can also enter speaker notes while you're showing a presentation.*

■ You can then print your presentation in Notes Page format for reference while giving a presentation or to hand out to the audience.

■ You can also print and hand out notes pages with a blank notes area, so that audience members can take their own notes in the empty placeholders.

■ You can give the audience **handouts** of the presentation for future reference.

■ Printed handouts do not show notes.

Notes Master and Handout Master

■ You can add text, pictures, and other information to a notes or handout master.

Notes Master view

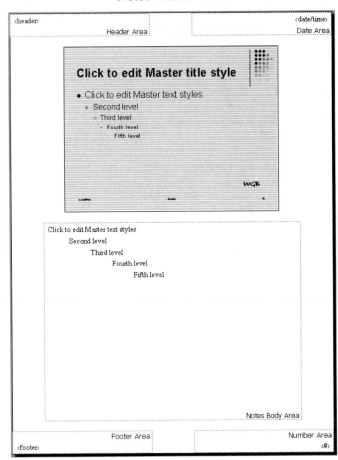

■ Anything added to a master appears in all notes or handouts you print.

■ Either master can include your company logo, the date, and your phone number, for instance.

■ You can enter a header or footer, page numbers, and dates in a master as well.

Package for CD

■ Use the **Package for CD** feature when you want to run a slide show on another computer.

■ If the computer you plan to run the packed show on doesn't have PowerPoint, you can include the Viewer in the Pack and Go file.

■ The Viewer is a program that lets you run a PowerPoint slide show without the use of PowerPoint.

■ The Package for CD feature automatically includes any linked files by default.

■ You can unpack the slide show on any PC.

Package for CD dialog box

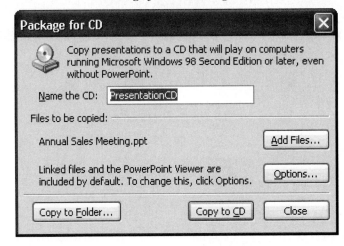

Take Speaker Notes During a Presentation

■ You can use the Speaker Notes feature to take notes during a slide show.

Speaker Notes dialog box in a presentation

■ During an online meeting, anyone can take notes and everyone can view those notes while online.

■ After the slide show, you can view the notes and comments in the Notes pane of Normal view, or the Notes Page view.

Send Speakers Notes to Word

- You can send Notes to Word and choose to have them placed either next to or below slides.
- If you only want the notes but not slides, you can delete the slides from the Word document.

- By sending Notes to a Word document you can use them as the basis for a report or memo about your presentation.
- Use the Send to Microsoft Office Word dialog box to choose where to place the notes you send.

Procedures

Create Notes Pages

- Enter notes in Notes pane in Normal view.

OR

1. Click **View** .... Alt+V
2. Click **Notes Page** .... P
3. Click in notes placeholder and enter notes.

Print Notes Pages *(Ctrl+P)*

1. Click **File** .... Alt+F
2. Click **Print** .... P
3. Click **Notes Pages** in **Print what** drop-down list .... Alt+W
4. Click **OK** .... Enter

Create Handouts *(Ctrl+P)*

1. Click **File** .... Alt+F
2. Click **Print** .... P
3. In the **Print what** drop-down list, click **Handouts** ..... Alt+W
4. In **Slides per page** drop-down list, choose 1, 2, 3, 4, 6, or 9 .... Alt+R
5. Choose slide order:
   - **Horizontal** .... Alt+Z
   - **Vertical** .... Alt+V
6. Click **OK** .... Enter

Edit Notes or Handout Master

1. Click **View** .... Alt+V
2. Click **Master** .... M
3. Click **Notes master** .... N

   OR

   Click **Handout master** .... D
4. Enter any text or graphic you want to display on all notes or handouts.
5. Click **Close Master View** button
   Close Master View .... Alt+C

Package for CD

1. Open presentation.
2. Click **File** .... Alt+F
3. Click **Package for CD** .... K
4. Enter a title in the **Name the CD** field ...... Alt+N
5. Click **Options** if you want to change what items the PowerPoint Viewer includes on the CD and click **OK** ... Alt+O
6. Click **Copy to CD** .... Alt+C
7. When asked if you want to copy the files to another CD, click **No** .... N
8. Click **Close**.

Unpack and Run Presentation

1. Insert CD in computer.
2. Open My Computer in Windows Explorer, locate the CD drive, and double-click.
3. To accept the terms of use of PowerPoint Viewer, click **Accept** .... A.
4. The show runs. To end the show press **Esc**
   - ✓ *Note: You can use all the tools available from the shortcut menu to write on slides with ink or navigate through the show.*

Add Speaker Notes

1. Show presentation in Slide Show view.
2. Right-click screen.
3. Click **Screen** C
4. Click **Speaker Notes** .... K
5. Enter notes in dialog box.

Send Notes to Word

1. Click **File** .... Alt+F
2. Click **Send To** .... D
3. Click **Microsoft Office Word** .... W
4. Click **Notes next to slides** .... N

   OR

   Click **Notes below slides** .. B
5. Click **OK** .... Enter

Exercise Directions

1. Start PowerPoint, if necessary.

2. Open 📠**11BREAD** or 💿**PPT20**.

3. Save the file as **20BREAD**.

4. Switch to Normal view and select the first slide. Add the following notes in the Notes pane:

   Mention research and development of future products.

5. View notes pages. Print the notes page for slide one.

6. Print as handouts with 4 per page.

7. Go to the Notes Master view and add a header and date. Use your name as the header and the month and year as the date. Print all slides as notes pages.

8. Go to the slide master and copy the logo text box.

9. Switch to the handout master and paste the logo text box and move it to the top middle of the page. Add the following footer: **Whole Grains Bread**.

   ✓ *You may have to reduce the size of the handout master to see the logo. It may appear off the page.*

10. Print the handout for the slide show.

11. Run the presentation. During the presentation, open the Speaker Notes for Slide 2 and enter the following notes:

    Suggestions:

    Gourmet muffins

    Scones

12. Export the speakers notes to appear next to slides in Word and print the Word document.

13. Save the document as **20WHOLEGRAINS.doc**.

14. Close the Word document and the file. Return to PowerPoint.

15. Save the file.

16. Pack the presentation to a CD.

    ✓ *Hint: Embed the fonts. Include the Viewer only if you plan to show the presentation on a computer that does not have PowerPoint installed.*

    ✓ *If you don't have access to a CD burner, skip this step.*

17. Close PowerPoint.

18. If you've packed the presentation, unpack it and run it to make sure it works.

On Your Own

1. Open **OPP19**, the presentation you used in Exercise 19, or open 💿**OPP20**.

2. Save the file as **OPP20**.

3. Type notes for at least three slides.

4. Open the handout master.

5. Add your name, the date, and the page number to the handouts master.

6. Insert a clip art image on the handout master.

7. Set formatting options as desired.

8. Insert a different clip art image on the notes master.

9. Set formatting options as desired.

10. Print handouts for the presentation using 6 slides per page.

11. Save the presentation, close it, and exit PowerPoint.

Exercise 21

Skills Covered:

◆ Set Up a Presentation   ◆ Set Up Show Dialog Box Options

On the Job

Set up a slide show so you can use it in different situations. For example, if you run a slide show at a kiosk, you will want the show to run continuously so no one has to monitor it. At the same time, you don't want anyone to alter the show or add to it while it's running. You can control this by setting up the show.

The owner of the Michigan Avenue Athletic Club wants you to set up two presentations—one he can use on a kiosk and a second he can use at a computer at a health and fitness trade show.

Terms

Custom Show A show in which you specify the slides and the order in which the slides appear during presentation.

Narration A voice recording that describes or enhances the message in each slide.

Notes

Set Up a Presentation

- You can set up PowerPoint to show a presentation on a computer, either accompanied by a speaker, or running on its own continuously in a kiosk or trade show booth.

Set Up Show dialog box

Set Up Show Dialog Box Options

Option	Description
Presented by a speaker	Shows the presentation full screen.
Browsed by an individual	Shows the presentation in a window on the screen with menus and commands an individual can use to control and change slide show.
Browsed at a kiosk	Shows the presentation full screen; automatically sets the show to loop continuously; viewer can advance slides and use action buttons/hyperlinks but cannot change slide show.
Loop continuously until 'Esc'	Runs a presentation over and over continuously.
Show without narration	Displays the slide show with no voice.
Show without animation	Displays the show with no animation.
Pen color	Enables you to choose a pen color for annotation.

Option	Description
Show scrollbar	Shows scrollbar on-screen with presentation; available only when Browsed by an individual is selected.
Show slides	Choose All or enter numbers of specific slides to show.
Custom show	Choose specific slides or presentations.
Advance slides	Choose Manually or Using timings if present.
Multiple monitors	Default is primary monitor; choose if second monitor is attached.

- You may want to show the presentation at a trade show or convention or at your place of business.
- You can choose to set up a presentation so that the viewer can manipulate the screen or set it up so the viewer cannot manipulate or change the slide show.
- You can run a presentation in a continuous loop.
- PowerPoint lets you run a presentation with or without **narration** and animation.
- If you run a slide show that is unattended you should include timings and voice narration.

Procedures

Set Up and Run Presentation

1. Open presentation.
2. Click **Sli̲de Show** ....`Alt`+`D`
3. Click **S̲et Up Show** ....`S`
4. Choose one of the following show types:
   - **P̲resented by a speaker** ....`Alt`+`P`
   - **B̲rowsed by an individual** ....`Alt`+`B`
   - **Browsed at a k̲iosk** ....`Alt`+`K`
5. Choose other options.
6. Click **OK** ....`Enter`

Set Up Custom Slide Show

1. Click **Sli̲de Show** ....`D`
2. Click **Custom Sho̲ws** ....`W`
3. Click **N̲ew** ....`N`
4. Click slide to add to presentation.
5. Click **A̲dd** ....`Alt`+`A`
6. Repeat steps 4 and 5 to add additional slides.
7. Name the show.
8. Click **OK** ....`Enter`
9. Click **C̲lose** ....`Alt`+`C`

Exercise Directions

1. Start PowerPoint, if necessary.
2. Open ⊙ **PPT21**.
3. Save the file as **21SLIDESHOW**.
4. Set the slide show up to be browsed by an individual, with all slides and using timings.
5. Loop the show continuously.
6. View the show.
7. Change the setup so it doesn't show the animation.
8. View the show.
9. Save the changes.
10. Save the file as **21KIOSK**.
11. Set the show up to run on a kiosk and show the animation.
12. Change timings in the show to use 10 second timing to advance slides.
13. View the show.
14. Close the file and exit PowerPoint, saving all changes.

On Your Own

1. Open **OPP20**, the presentation you used in Exercise 20, or open ⊙ **OPP21**.
2. Save the file as **OPP21**.
3. Set up the slide show to be presented by a speaker and to loop continuously.
4. Run the slide show. (Press Esc to stop it.)
5. Save the file as **OPP21-2**.
6. Set up the slide show to be browsed at a kiosk without animation.
7. Run the slide show.
8. Save the presentation, close it, and exit PowerPoint.

Exercise 22

◆ **Save a Presentation as a Web Site**

◆ **Publish a Presentation**

◆ **Make Your Web Presentation More Efficient**

On the Job

Publish a presentation to the Web so that a larger audience can view it. You might, for example, already have a Web site established for customers to view your products or services. Add a presentation to the site to interest more customers and provide an additional information resource.

The owner of Voyager Travel Adventures wants to use one of the presentations you created as a Web site. You will need to check the presentation for consistency and add a few things to it before you save it as a Web page and publish it.

Terms

Web site A collection of Web pages; a site usually contains information with a common focus.

HTML (Hypertext Markup Language) A formatting language used to create documents on the Internet.

Browser A program, such as Internet Explorer, used to view Web pages and sites.

Web page One document on the Web, usually containing information related to one topic.

Publish To set options to make the presentation more suitable for viewing on the Web.

Notes

Save a Presentation as a Web Site

- Save a presentation as a **Web site** so you can publish it to the World Wide Web.

- PowerPoint lets you save a presentation in **HTML** format so it can be opened in a Web **browser**, such as Internet Explorer.

- When you save as a **Web page**, PowerPoint stores all HTML files in a folder named for the saved file. PowerPoint also saves the original file so you can open the presentation any time you want.

- You can save a PowerPoint slide as a Web page or save multiple PowerPoint slides as a Web site.

Publish a Presentation

- You **publish** a presentation to prepare it for the Web.

- Publishing lets you choose options for how people will view the pages.

Web Options dialog box

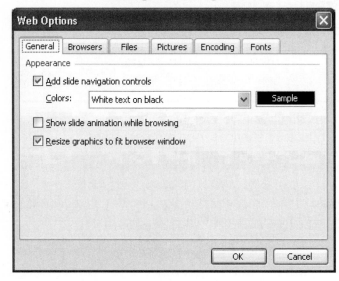

- Choose browser support when you publish a presentation. Browser support determines which browsers can view the Web page.

- Change colors and resize graphics when you publish to the Web so the text and objects look their best on the page.

- Organize files and locations in the Web site for efficiency.

Files tab of the Web Options dialog box

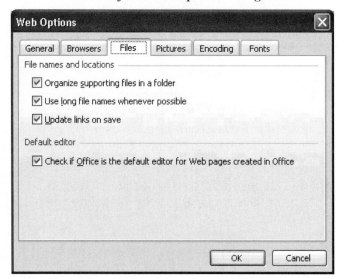

Make Your Web Presentation More Efficient

- An efficient Web site makes it easy for people to display topics quickly. If your site is easy to navigate, people will spend more time looking at your site.

- Add Action buttons for easier navigation.

- Use small graphics and pictures to reduce downloading time.

- Use one major heading on each page to let viewers know where they are.

- Don't squeeze too much text on one slide or one page.

- Save as a Web archive if you wish to e-mail a Web presentation; this format saves a presentation as a single file rather than a set of files.

- Use lists or tables when possible, because they are easier and faster to read than paragraphs of text.

- Use the GIF image format for cartoons, line drawings, or pictures with few colors.

- Use JPEG format for scanned photographs or images with several colors.

- Use PNG format for buttons, bullets, and small images.

Procedures

Preview Presentation in Web Page View

1. Open a presentation.
2. Click **File**...................`Alt`+`F`
3. Click **We**b **Page Preview** ....`B`
4. Close browser to return to PowerPoint.

Save Presentation as Web Page

1. Open or create presentation.
2. Click **File**...................`Alt`+`F`
3. Click **Save as Web Page**.....`G`
4. Click **Save in** and select a folder in which to save the Web page.............`Alt`+`I`
5. Accept or change suggested **File** **name** ....`Alt`+`N`

   ✓ *See your system's administrator for information on saving your Web page to a Web server.*

6. Click **Change Title** button

   `Change Title...` ....`Alt`+`C`

   to display the Set Page Title dialog box and change the page title:

   a. Type the **Page title** ....`Alt`+`P`
   b. Click **OK** ....`Enter`

7. Click **Save** button

   `Save` ....`Alt`+`S`

Publish Web Page

1. Open or create presentation.
2. Click **File** ....`Alt`+`F`
3. Click **Save as Web Page** ....`G`
4. Click **Save in** and select a folder in which to publish the Web page ....`Alt`+`I`

5. Accept or change suggested **File** **name** ....`Alt`+`N`
6. Click **Publish** button

   `Publish` ....`Alt`+`P`

7. Click desired options.
8. Click **Web Options** button `Web Options...` `Alt`+`W`
9. Click desired options.
10. Click **Browsers** tab.....`Ctrl`+`Tab`
11. Click desired options.
12. Click **Files** tab.............`Ctrl`+`Tab`
13. Click desired options.
14. Click **Pictures** tab.......`Ctrl`+`Tab`
15. Click desired options.
16. Click **OK**.........................`Enter`
17. Click **Publish** button

    `Publish` ....`Alt`+`P`

Exercise Directions

1. Start PowerPoint, if necessary.
2. Open 🖩**07VOYAGER** or 💿**PPT22**.
3. Save the file as **22VOYAGER**.
4. Switch to Normal view and add the following Action buttons to the presentation (AutoShapes, Action Buttons). You can place the buttons anywhere on the slide.

   Slide 1: Add the End button
   Slide 12: Add the Home button

   ✓ *See Exercise 11 for review of Action buttons.*
   ✓ *Hint: Leave the hyperlinks with default settings by clicking OK in the Action Settings dialog box.*

5. Save the presentation.

6. Save the presentation as a Web page and publish the complete presentation. Do not display speaker notes. Set browser support for Microsoft Internet Explorer 4 or later.
7. Change the following Web option when you publish the presentation:

   Show slide animation while browsing.

8. View the Web pages using your browser.
9. Close Internet Explorer.
10. Close the file and exit PowerPoint, saving all changes.

    ✓ *Some formatting may change when you save in HTML.*

On Your Own

1. Open **OPP21**, the presentation you used in Exercise 21, or open 💿**OPP22**.
2. Save the file as **OPP22**.
3. Save the presentation as a Web page, changing the name to **OPP22-2**.

4. View the presentation in your Web browser.
5. Close the browser.
6. Save the presentation, close it, and exit PowerPoint.

Exercise 23

◆ **Export to Overhead Transparencies** ◆ **Export to 35mm Slides**
◆ **Find Clip Art on the Internet** ◆ **Use the Research Feature to Find Online Materials** ◆ **Presentation Conferencing**

On the Job

Export a presentation to another format, such as slides or overheads, so you can show it on a projection system. For instance, export to overheads so you can show your presentation to a larger audience than you could on a computer screen.

Voyager Travel Adventures has asked you to prepare a presentation to send to an imaging company for slides and transparencies. Also, they've asked you to assist them in holding an online meeting with the President of Voyager Travel Adventures and co-workers to review the presentation and discuss possible modifications.

Terms

Transparencies Clear sheets of plastic on which you print a slide so it can be shown on an overhead projector, which displays the slide on a large screen.

Imaging company A company that specializes in printing 35mm slides, transparencies, and other computerized images to various media.

Real time An event that is taking place live, as opposed to a later time.

Whiteboard An electronic tool, similar to a blackboard, on which you can enter text.

Notes

Export to Overhead Transparencies

- PowerPoint lets you set up a presentation so you can create **transparencies** to show on an overhead projector.

- You can load transparency sheets into many printers and simply print your slides on them.

- For best results, let a professional **imaging company** print the transparencies for you.

- Check with the imaging company for the correct file format, although the PPT file format generally works well.

Export to Overhead in Page Setup dialog box

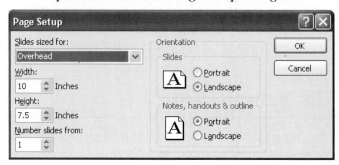

Export to 35mm Slides

■ You can save a presentation in a format appropriate for creating 35mm slides.

■ You should send your presentation to a professional imaging company to have the slides made.

■ Avoid a blue and red color scheme because it can be hard to read or visually distracting.

Find Clip Art on the Internet

■ In addition to the clip art that is included with Microsoft Office 2003, you can also buy clip art collections from other resources or download clip art from the Internet.

Use the Research Feature to Find Online Materials

■ PowerPoint's new Research tool allows you to search Internet research sites and reference books by keyword.

■ Reference sites include eLibrary, Encarta Encyclopedia, and several business and financial sites.

■ Reference books include the Encarta Dictionary and a Thesaurus.

■ A Translation feature allows you to look up the meaning of foreign words.

The Research task pane

Presentation Conferencing

■ You can share your presentation with others online via NetMeeting, Microsoft's **real** (actual) **time** conferencing program.

■ Your computer must be networked or attached to the Internet to use NetMeeting.

■ You can start a spontaneous meeting as long as coworkers are running NetMeeting and are online. You can schedule the meeting beforehand using e-mail or the telephone.

■ During a meeting, you can show and edit a presentation.

■ The person who initiates and controls an online meeting is called the host. The host can show the presentation to others without allowing them to edit the presentation.

■ The host controls the online meeting by clicking the appropriate button on the Online Meeting toolbar, which appears when you connect with NetMeeting.

■ The host can also allow coworkers to edit the presentation, if desired, by turning on the collaboration feature.

■ Only one person can control/edit the presentation at a time. The initials of that person are displayed next to the mouse pointer.

■ While others edit the presentation, the host cannot use the cursor.

■ Only the host of an online meeting needs to have the file and application installed.

■ The host can start the Chat feature to allow participants to discuss the presentation with coworkers.

■ The host can start the **whiteboard** feature to allow participants to make notes and record comments.

■ Several people can simultaneously send messages or files in Chat or add notes to the whiteboard if the collaboration feature is turned off.

■ The first time you use the online conferencing feature, you must enter some basic information.

Procedures

Set Up Presentation for Overhead Transparencies

1. Open presentation.
2. Click **File** .... `Alt`+`F`
3. Click **Page Set<u>u</u>p** .... `U`
4. Click **Slides sized for** .... `Alt`+`S`
5. Scroll down the list and click **Overhead**.
   OR
   a. Press the down arrow to reach **Overhead**.
   b. Press **Enter**.
6. Click **OK** .... `Enter`
7. Save presentation.

Export to 35mm Slides

1. Open presentation.
2. Click **File** .... `Alt`+`F`
3. Click **Page Set<u>u</u>p** .... `U`
4. Click **Slides sized for** .... `Alt`+`S`
5. Click **35mm slides**.
   ✓ *Image size changes to 11.25 x 7.5. Leave it at this size.*
6. Click **OK** .... `Enter`
7. Save presentation.

Start Online Meeting

1. Click **Tools** .... `Alt`+`T`
2. Click **O<u>n</u>line Collaboration** .... `N`
3. Click **<u>M</u>eet Now** .... `M`
   ✓ *If you've never used NetMeeting, the NetMeeting dialog box appears.*
   a. Enter your personal and server information for NetMeeting.
      ✓ *For help with this information, see documentation on NetMeeting.*
   b. Click **OK** .... `Enter`
4. Click **<u>T</u>ype name or select from list** .... `Alt`+`T`
5. Enter names of desired participants or select them from list.
6. Click **Call**.
7. Computer dials number.
8. When the receiving computer answers and displays NetMeeting, you can begin the meeting.

Search Using Research Feature

1. Click on **Tools** .... `T`
2. Click on **Research** .... `R`
3. In the **Search for** box, enter a keyword.
4. In the drop-down **Search for** list click on a source to search.
5. Click the **Start Searching** arrow.

Exercise Directions

1. Start PowerPoint, if necessary.
2. Open 📻**22VOYAGER** or 💿**PPT23**.
3. Save the file as **23VOYAGER**.
4. Use the Research feature and search the Thesaurus: English (US) with the keyword **adventure**.
5. On slide 1 click on the subtitle object to open it for editing.
6. Click after the word Travel and add the word **Exploration** into the subheading, so that it reads **Your Travel Exploration Partner**.
7. Click Clip art on Office Online on the Clip Art task pane.
   - ✓ *If you do not have an Internet connection, locate a file from another clip collection.*
8. Type **travel** in the Search text box and click the Search button.
9. Scroll the page to locate an appropriate clip.
10. Download the file to your computer.
11. View slide 2 of the presentation.
12. Insert the clip on the slide.

13. Size and position the clip art in the bottom-right corner.
14. Change the page setup of the presentation to overhead transparencies.
15. Print the presentation as slides.
16. Change the page setup to 35mm slides.
17. Print the presentation as slides and compare the size and shape of the slides to the first set you printed.
18. Schedule an online meeting with others in your network.
    - ✓ *If your computer is not networked or NetMeeting is not installed to your computer, you may skip this part of the exercise.*
19. Start the online meeting and run your presentation.
    - ✓ *You run a presentation the same way, whether you're online or not.*
20. End the meeting by clicking the End Meeting button on the Online Meeting toolbar.
21. Close the file and exit PowerPoint, saving all changes.

On Your Own

1. Open 💿**OPP23**.
2. Save the file as **OPP23**.
3. Change the page setup of the presentation to overhead transparencies.
4. Print the presentation as slides.
5. Change the page setup to 35mm slides.

6. Print the presentation as slides and compare the size and shape of the slides to the first set you printed.
7. If you're attached to a network, hold an online meeting and run the presentation during the meeting.
8. Save the presentation, close it, and exit PowerPoint.

Exercise 24

◆ **Critical Thinking**

When you show a presentation, you want to make sure the audience gets the most out of the information you present. By setting transitions, adding sound, and otherwise setting up a presentation, you can present the slide show in the best possible way for your audience to understand and enjoy.

Exercise Directions

1. Start PowerPoint, if necessary.
2. Open ⊙ **PPT24**.
3. Save the file as **24WHOLEGRAINS**.
4. Apply transitions, sounds, and timing to all slides. View the presentation.
5. Hide slide 3.
6. Animate the bullets on slide 2 with preset animations.
7. Animate the text and objects on slide 4 with custom animations. You can choose to use sounds, if desired. View the presentation.
8. Save the timings.
9. Add a slide at the end of the presentation using the Title Only layout. Add the title **Thank You!**
10. Add a music or video clip to the last slide.
11. On the notes master, replace the current header text with the following header:

    Whole Grains Bread
    Eileen Costello, CFO

12. In Notes Page view, add notes to the final slide as shown in Illustration A.

13. Add notes to slide 4 as shown in Illustration B.
14. Print the notes pages as handouts, 4 per page.
15. Unhide slide 3 and show the presentation. During the presentation, open the Speaker's Notes for slide 3 and enter these notes:

    Look into gourmet scones as a new product line.

16. Export the slides with notes to Word.
17. Save the Word file as **24WHOLEGRAINS.doc** and print it.
18. Close the file and exit Word.
19. Finish showing the presentation and then set up the slide show to run on a kiosk. View the slide show.
20. Save the presentation as a Web page (**24WHOLEGRAINS.html**). Publish the presentation using all slides, no speaker notes, and open it to a Web browser.
21. Run the presentation and then close the browser.
22. Close the file and exit PowerPoint, saving all changes.

Illustration A

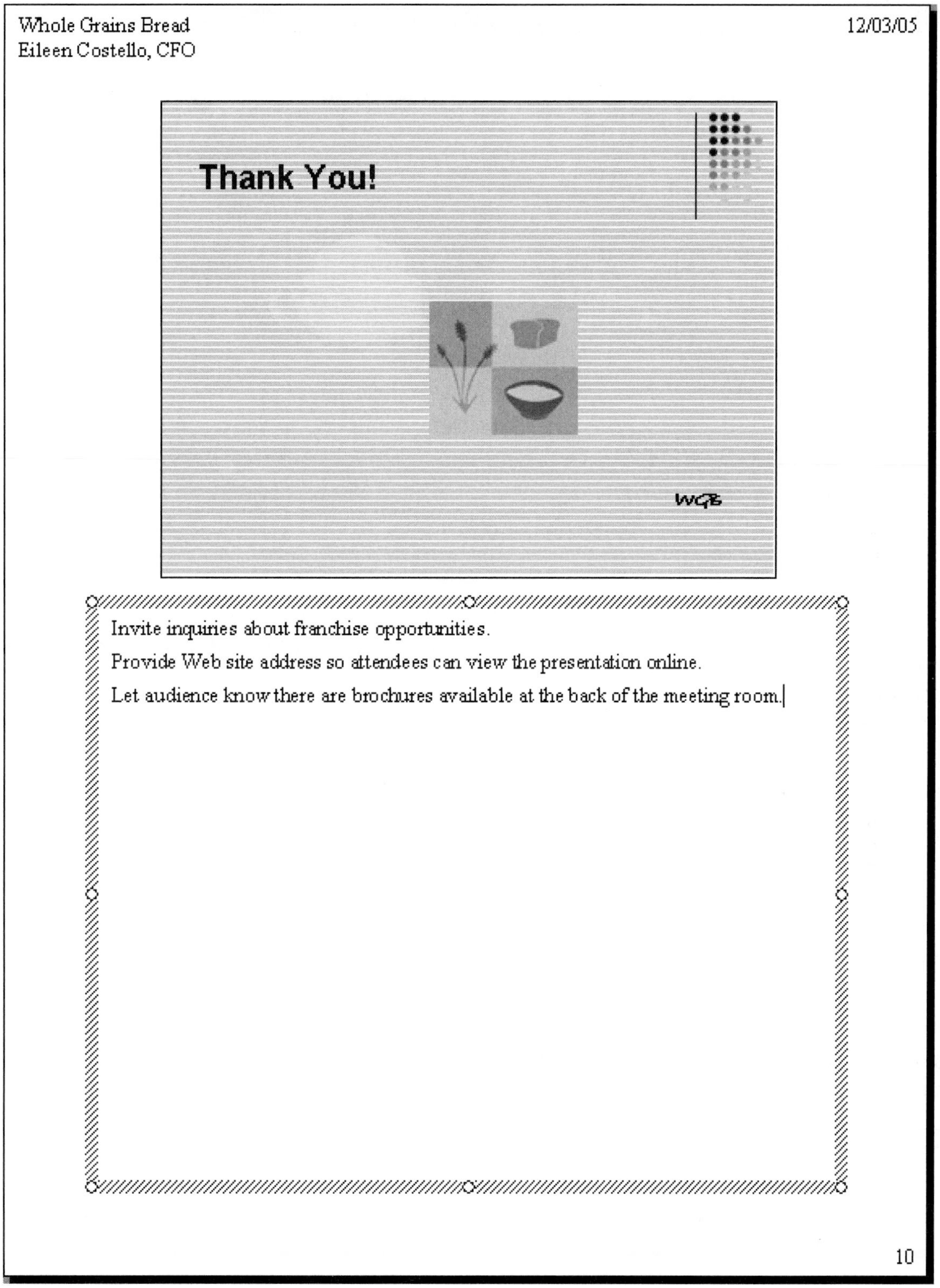

Whole Grains Bread
Eileen Costello, CFO

12/03/05

Thank You!

WGB

Invite inquiries about franchise opportunities.

Provide Web site address so attendees can view the presentation online.

Let audience know there are brochures available at the back of the meeting room.

10

Whole Grains Bread
Eileen Costello, CFO

12/03/05

CAFÉ BRANCHES AROUND THE WEST

- Franchises available
- Gourmet soups, sandwiches, and salads at reasonable prices

WGB

Visit our Web site to view sample menus.

Do you have ideas about additional menu items you'd like to see us offer?

4

Index

Index

Index

Notes

Notes

Notes

Notes

Notes

Notes

Notes

Notes

Notes

Notes